THE POLITICS OF METHOD IN
THE HUMAN SCIENCES

THE POLITICS OF METHOD IN

THE HUMAN SCIENCES

Positivism and Its Epistemological Others

GEORGE STEINMETZ, EDITOR

Duke University Press   Durham/London 2005

Portions of Webb Keane's essay originally appeared in "Self-Interpretation, Agency, and the Objects of Anthropology: Reflections on a Genealogy," *Comparative Studies in Society and History* 45, 2 (2003). Reprinted with the permission of Cambridge University Press.

Michael Dutton's essay originally appeared in *Nepantla* 3, 3 (2002). Copyright Duke University Press.

Portions of William Sewell's essay originally appeared in "Whatever Happened to the 'Social' in Social History," in *Schools of Thought: Twenty-Five Years of Interpretive Social Science*, edited by Joan W. Scott and Deborah Keates. Copyright Princeton University Press, 2001.

CONTENTS

ACKNOWLEDGMENTS

Earlier versions of some of the papers in this volume were presented at sessions of the Social Science History Association and American Sociological Association. The Wilder House at the University of Chicago, under the direction of Bill Sewell and Lisa Wedeen, sponsored a miniconference in 2001 at which drafts of many of the papers in this volume were discussed. Beth Buggenhagen helped organize that conference, and Moishe Postone served as discussant. I especially wish to thank my editor Raphael Allen, who attended the 2001 Chicago conference and who has been instrumental in shaping this book and guiding it through its various stages of development. Webb Keane and Dan Breslau helped with the book's title. Thanks to Rick Smoke for technical support. Andy Clarno helped with the bibliography. Claire Decoteau did a tremendous job refining the manuscript at the copyediting stage.

Above all, I want to thank Julia Hell. More than anyone else, she deserves credit for helping to deprogram me each time I have been hit by scientistic broadsides or urged more subtly to respect the entrenched epistemic dogmas of sociology.

Positivism and Its Others in the Social Sciences

GEORGE STEINMETZ

This collection explores the vicissitudes of positivism and its epistemological others in the contemporary human sciences. The volume's
overarching goal is to provide a mapping of the contemporary human
sciences from the standpoint of their explicit and especially their *implicit* epistemologies, asking about the differences and similarities among
and within these disciplines' epistemological cultures. Taken together, the
essays provide a portrait of epistemology and methodology (writ large) in
the contemporary social sciences.[1] Given the contemporary conjuncture
of epistemological crises and conflicts in the human sciences and the
proliferation of nonpositivist alternatives, the present is an ideal moment
for taking stock of the underlying assumptions of the human sciences.
Only by making the epistemological stakes and disputes explicit will it
become possible to heed the call to "open the social sciences" (Wallerstein
et al. 1996).

This book also offers the rudiments of a comparative historical narrative of these disciplinary developments since the beginning of the twentieth century, with an emphasis on the period beginning with World War
II. Recent writing has pointed not just to the present-day conjuncture of
epistemological uncertainty but also to the middle decades of the twentieth century as critical moments in the transformation of the social sciences' deep culture. The varying epistemological effects and textures of
these midcentury and contemporary changes, and the connections between the two periods, have yet to be interpreted.[2]

While providing an opportunity to compare disciplinary developments,
this volume is also concerned with the interconnections among disciplines, their mutually imbricated developments. Many of the essays ex-

plore patterns of imitation and repulsion, the introjection and rejection of theories and practices from outside disciplines, the dynamics of self-definition and redrawing of disciplinary boundaries via constructions of disciplinary Others. Thus, while economics suffered from a sort of "physics envy" (Mirowski 1989), sociology suffered from a parallel "economics envy" (Somers, this volume). The political science subfield of *political theory* defined itself against its own "bad others"—positivism and sociology—during the 1950s (Hauptmann, this volume), while mainstream political science defined itself initially against classical political theory and increasingly in terms of rational choice and game theoretic models imported from economics. Psychoanalysis has worked the fraught boundary between the human sciences and their biomedical outside (Elliott, this volume). Many social historians have shifted from an admiring emulation of sociology during the 1960s and 1970s to theoretical approaches drawn from cultural anthropology, linguistics, and literary criticism (Sewell, this volume). In addition to these sociological and historical questions about the relations among the disciplines, this volume asks whether this overall configuration of disciplines makes sense. Is there an inherent social-onto-logical logic to this peculiar array of disciplines? Or, as some would argue, is our inherited disciplinary landscape merely the historical residue of colonialism and imperialism, long forgotten intellectual fashions, or the ephemeral priorities of states and corporations?

The other overarching aim of this book is to survey the landscape of alternatives to positivism in the human sciences; the entire second half is given over to this task. An earlier working title for this volume included the phrase "genealogies of positivism and postpositivism." From a certain perspective, postpositivism is little more than a description of the historical supersession of logical positivism and empiricism in the history of philosophy (H. Putnam 1990b). Yet, as some commentators and contributors to this collection observe, the term postpositivism is sometimes overly self-congratulatory and teleological. Indeed, the adjective postpositivist might be described as itself positivist, insofar as it suggests an image of scientific history as following a linear course in which positivism eventually becomes historically obsolete. The sheer fact that positivism was already declared anachronistic in the 1900s and 1930s (Lenin 1908/1927; Parsons 1937/1949) and again in the 1960s and 1970s (Adorno 1969/1976; Gouldner 1970; Giddens 1975, 1–22) cautions us against any finalist illusions in this realm. Many of the contributors to this volume track positivism's uncanny persistence in the human sciences up to the present moment. As Mirowski (this volume) reminds us, revised versions of positivism are alive and well even in the philosophy of science. Harding (this volume), a founder of standpoint epistemology, cautions against a wholesale rejection of the positivist philosophical legacy. Hence my recourse to the more neutral language of "nonpositivism."

These considerations also steer us away from attempting to canonize any particular nonpositivist theory of knowledge. The word postpositivism indicates a greater degree of unanimity among the alternatives than actually exists in the world, or in this volume. Indeed, some antipositivists endorse a pluralization of knowledge cultures (as suggested by Bourdieu's "Vive la Crise!", 1988–89) rather than reconsolidation around a new orthodoxy. The only epistemological stance shared by all of the contributors to the present volume seems to be a desire to move beyond existing forms of social science positivism. The theoretical and methodological positions represented and performed here are diverse, encompassing standpoint theory, narrative analysis, critical realism, the ethnography and historical sociology of scientific fields and actor networks, critical or postmodern psychoanalytic theory, neo- and post-Marxism, poststructuralism, and a rejection of the fact/value dichotomy. The differences among the contributors' epistemic programs are in some respects as great as their shared distance from philosophical positivism.[3] The presentation here of partially incompatible alternatives differentiates this collection from previous volumes on postpositivism, which have tended to focus on one or another philosophical program (e.g., Archer et al. 1998; Lopez and Potter 2001; Pickering 1992; Law and Hassard 1999). This pragmatic approach makes sense if we accept the hypothesis that a revised positivism is alive and well in many of the social sciences.[4]

A Kaleidoscope of Disciplines and Their Epistemological Cultures

Nature is organized by simple universal laws of physics to which all other laws and principles can eventually be reduced.—Edward O. Wilson, *Consilience: The Unity of Knowledge*
Social science cannot ignore philosophical assumptions, since they will help to govern the focus of its attention.—Roger Trigg, *Understanding Social Science*

One of the guiding threads in this volume concerns the surprising longevity of positivism—especially in latent, unexamined, or unconscious forms —in the human sciences. Despite repeated attempts by social theorists and researchers to drive a stake through the heart of the vampire, the disciplines continue to experience a positivistic haunting. There is also a great deal of variation across the disciplines and historical epochs in the forms of positivism and in the waxing and waning of positivist dominance (Knorr-Cetina 1991). A central goal of this collection is thus to allow the reader to explore the intimacies between positivism and the disciplines in different times and places and to facilitate other sorts of comparisons, including contrasts that track the migration and indigenization of concepts across social scientific space.

The essays in the first part of this book examine some of the main disciplines in the human sciences. The historical emphasis here is on the twentieth century, especially the period beginning with World War II; the geographical focus is on the United States due to that country's dominant position in the production and politics of social science knowledge.[5] The exceptions to this U.S. focus are mainly in the second part of the book, which is focused on *alternatives to positivism*. Some of these resources, not surprisingly, are generated outside the U.S. core, just as logical positivism originated not in the United States but in Europe. The division between more historical accounts of disciplines in part 1 and nonpositivist alternatives in part 2 does not mean that the first avoids discussion of earlier nonpositivist alternatives. For example, Keane analyzes the entire field of cultural anthropology as resistant to positivism throughout the twentieth century, while Mirowski discusses the philosophy of science of John Dewey. For the most part, however, the first part emphasizes not only historical accounts of the U.S. social sciences but also careers of positivist dominance in these disciplines.

Disciplinary Histories

Anthropology has shown the strongest divergence from modern epistemological versions of positivism. *History* is a discipline that has been deeply influenced by two versions of positivism, one oriented toward the search for general laws and the other emphasizing what historians call a positivist approach to source material. But the discipline of history is also widely described as having moved into a state of epistemic and methodological pluralism in more recent years. *Psychoanalysis* contained both scientistic-positivist and radically antipositivist potentials from the outset, as Anthony Elliott argues here. Recent theoretical developments in psychoanalysis have drawn out the nonpositivist elements, but the seemingly inexorable medicalization of psychological treatment and the ever increasing control of psychic health care by the pharmaceutical industry lends power to the scientistic tendencies. Diagnosing *economics* with respect to issues of epistemology turns out to be an extremely complex problem.

Economics is described by the contributors to this volume variously as dominated by epistemological positivism and empiricism, by a "depth realist"[6] (or "theoretically realist") epistemology, or by an antiempiricist idealism; alternatively, economists are said to combine realist and idealist approaches willfully and eclectically. By contrast, most writers seem to agree that U.S. *sociology* was captured by scientistic positivism during the postwar decades, even if different explanations have been offered for this disciplinary transformation. There is less agreement about the contemporary epistemological structure of the sociological field: some anticipate a breakup of positivist dominance; others see a shift in the *form* of positivism but not its prevalence. Most analysts of *political science* agree that positivism has been hegemonic throughout the postwar period, outside the political theory subfield, but the prevailing version of positivism has shifted over time. This collection also considers *area studies*, a set of interdisciplinary fields that occupied a central place in postwar U.S. research universities and that was connected in multifarious ways to the social sciences. The funding structures and policy aims of postwar area studies favored positivist approaches, as did the infrastructure of language training and the insistence on learning portable comparative lessons. At the same time, the inclusion of the language- and culture-oriented humanities in the overall mix of area studies introduced a potential for epistemic dissonance, as did the intrinsic focus of each speciality on a single sociocultural area (e.g., South Asia or Latin America). The final field examined here is the *philosophy of science* itself. As in many of the human sciences, the zenith of positivist dominance in the philosophy of science was during the two decades after 1945, even if most of its component building blocks were created much earlier. The philosophy of science is more than a metareflection on the sciences; it was also shaped by those sciences and by the broader sociopolitical environment.

Anthropology as an exception
The situation in cultural anthropology since the 1960s is often described in terms of a fragmentation into myriad different nonpositivist and "antiscience" positions.[7] In his contribution to this volume, Webb Keane does not reject this diagnosis of the present but questions whether this is best understood only as a post-1960s phenomenon. Keane argues that there has been a less visible but pervasive adherence among American cultural anthropologists to a version of nonpositivism since the days of Boas. He identifies a widely shared commitment to a quasi-Romantic syndrome that he calls the "epistemology of intimacy," a position centered on the

assumption of the incomparable singularity of cultures and the method-ological necessity for self-interpretation as well as interpretation of the observed other. This epistemology also adheres to a belief that human agency is generally capable of defying "structural" constraints. U.S. cul-tural anthropology's common culture or philosophical center of gravity during the twentieth century stood in direct tension with the generalizing epistemology of positivism.

As George Stocking has argued, Boas himself was torn between a gener-alizing "scientific" approach to anthropology and a particularizing, histor-icizing stance that insisted that "in ethnology all is individuality" (Boas 1887b, 589). In addition to his natural science orientation, Boas was deeply influenced by neo-Kantian idealism and Wilhelm Dilthey's neo-Herderian hermeneutic historicism (Stocking 2001b, 37), arguing for a historical approach to geography and anthropology that aimed at "thorough *under-standing*" (Boas 1887a, 138, emphasis added).[8] Boas was an adamant cul-tural relativist who held that "our ideas and conceptions are true only as far as our civilization goes" (1887b, 589). He insisted that the meaning of a given sign or cultural artifact varied according to context and actors' interpretations. And while he distinguished between physical science and cosmography, Boas applied the label "science" to both approaches. He also bequeathed the four-field arrangement to anthropology, which reserved a place for physical anthropology and archaeology alongside the cultural and linguistic branches. Boas was by no means a lone wolf; he and his students and allies controlled the American Anthropological Association. He suffered a "momentary setback" during and after World War I, when he was "censured and removed from office" in the Association for his antiwar activism, "pressured into resigning from the National Research Council" (created in 1916), and marginalized from the Galton Society, which was created in 1918 (Stocking 1968, 273, 289; Stocking 2001b, 314; Patterson 2002, 55–57). By the 1920s, however, the views of Boas and his students regained their leading position. Sociocultural anthropology dominated the discipline in quantitative terms as well as prestige: by 1932, more than 50 percent of the PhDs being awarded in the small field were on ethnological topics (Stocking 2001b, 289, 314–317; Patterson 2002, 64). Most of the leading departments in this period were dominated by Boa-sians.[9] Many new anthropology departments were created during the postwar decades (often by hiving themselves off from sociology depart-ments), and they were typically founded by cultural anthropologists (Pat-terson 2002, 107). Those influenced by Boas radicalized some of the non-positivist aspects of his approach, intensifying his bias toward studying individual cases and interpreting them as complex wholes, rejecting the "scientific" quest for general laws, and emphasizing an approach that today might be thought of as a genealogical "history of the present": studying the contingent historical shaping of the contemporary sociocultural totality (Stocking 2001b, 42). Boas himself became increasingly skeptical about "the possibility of establishing valid categories for the comparison of cultural phenomena" and about "the possibility of establishing significant 'laws' in the cultural realm" (40). By the end of the 1920s, the object of anthropology for the Americans "became the construction or reconstruction of the uniqueness of individual cultures in relation to their histories" (Cohn 1981, 232). British-trained Bronislaw Malinowski agreed with Boas that the "goal, of which the Ethnographer should never lose sight," was to "grasp the native's point of view, his relation to life, to realize *his* vision of *his* world" (1922/1984, 25).

In the mid-1930s, however, " 'science' began to assert itself more strongly against 'history' " in anthropology, as in the other social science disciplines (Stocking 2001b, 45). During and after World War II anthropology saw a significant increase in funding opportunities from state and private sources, mainly oriented toward "big science" projects. Evolutionary theory made a comeback under various rubrics, including modernization theory. A collection of papers "from an international stock-taking symposium sponsored in 1952 by the Wenner-Gren Foundation and attended by eighty leading anthropologists" (318; see Kroeber 1953) had a largely positivist-scientistic tenor. The cultural ecologists, represented by such figures as Leslie White, Elman Service, and the young Marshall Sahlins, were pitted against what came to be called the symbolic anthropologists, whose most influential defenders were Clifford Geertz, Victor Turner, and David Schneider, in a "Manichean struggle" pitting the "emic" against the "etic" (Ortner 1984, 134). By the late 1960s, generalizing (though not quantitative) approaches appeared to be dominant in anthropology.[10] The crisis in the United States and the world at the end of the 1960s led to a resurgence of the post-Boasian cultural anthropologists, now mobilizing behind calls to "reinvent anthropology." The collection *Reinventing Anthropology* (Hymes 1972) "foreshadowed disciplinary developments of the next quarter century" (Stocking 2001b, 278). Among their concerns, the dissidents in anthropology at the time "shared in the then widespread disillusion with the 'positivistic scientism' of the anthropology and many other social science disciplines during the postwar period" (63).

The main disagreement among historians of twentieth-century U.S. anthropology, it seems to me, concerns the relative prominence and significance of positivistic approaches during the 1945–1980 period. Hollinger (1996, 144 n. 32) agrees with Keane that even in this period anthropology largely resisted efforts to encompass it within the natural science model, in contrast to sociology and political science. What is clear is that it became impossible to speak of any postwar positivist predominance in anthropology by the 1970s at the latest. As Keane points out, anthropologists today almost instinctively reject any conception of doing science as a "depersonalizing gaze that separates subject from object" (Jean Comaroff and Comaroff 1992, 8; see also Clifford and Marcus 1986; Trouillot 1991). Among all of the social sciences, anthropology has continued to produce some of the most explicit critiques of comparison (see Povinelli 2001; Stoler 2001). Even if anthropology has lost its original object as modernity has "wiped out the empirical trace of the savage-object" (Trouillot 1991, 35), the field's inherited Boasian epistemological predilections predispose it to absorb postpositivist theories of singularity and incommensurability (Derrida 1995; Nancy 2000). The traditionally dominant methodical approach—intensive long-term fieldwork by an individual researcher—militates against the comparative design that is required by generalizing models of science, positivist or nonpositivist. The discipline's more recent moves in the direction of practice theory (Bourdieu 1977, 1990; Ortner 1984), multisited ethnography (Marcus 1995), discourse analysis (Clifford and Marcus 1986), and historical anthropology (Cohn 1987b; Axel 2002; Stoler 2002) have diverged in different ways from the natural science model.

Is it, then, correct to say that anthropology was "positivist in a positivist age" (Trouillot 1991, 29) during the twentieth century, and that it is nonpositivist in a nonpositivist age? The middle decades of the century, which saw a partial bending of anthropology in the direction of positivism, certainly were the heyday not only of government funding for appropriately configured social sciences, but also of logical positivism in the philosophy of science. The 1920s and 1930s, when the Boasians had their greatest triumph, were also less strictly positivist in the neighboring disciplines of sociology and political science (see Parsons 1937/1949; Steinmetz and Hauptmann, both this volume). Whether the current era is truly postpositivist is also open to interrogation. This question can be answered for the social sciences at large only through continuing discussion and observation. We should keep in mind the ongoing production of exceptions to the supposed rule of nonpositivism. Keane mentions the Human Relations Area Files, which started in 1949 with the ambition of collecting and coding comparable ethnographic data on all human cultures to facilitate generalizing comparisons. This project still exists and continues to advocate a positivist-style approach to comparative cultural anthropology (Ember 1988, 2001). Yet these are not very popular topics for current anthropological dissertation research.[11]

Anthropology has also seen an ongoing internal backlash against Keane's "epistemology of intimacy," and major departments have split partly along these lines. Disputes over evolutionary genetics and what is now called sociobiology, from Boas to Sahlins (1976) and on to the recent controversies around Napoleon Chagnon's work on the Yanomami, revolve around core issues in the positivism/antipositivism debate: value-free science versus the interpenetration of facts and values; biological reductionism versus the ontological irreducibility of the social-cultural; the validity and ethics of the subject-object distinction, and so on.[12] The discipline's culturalist mainstream has been attacked by anthropological materialists who would limit study to *observable* behaviors (Wolf 1980). It thus seems advisable to consider anthropology as a field that is "structured in dominance" but by no means univocal, even if a neo-Boasian non-positivist worldview prevails in a Bourdieuian sense. This configuration represents something of an extreme in the epistemological space of all of the human sciences.

The history of history

Positivism has been somewhat stronger in history than in anthropology. The U.S. history profession was long dominated by an empiricist epistemology, labeled "objectivism" by Peter Novick (1988), even if historians never wholeheartedly embraced the idea of positive laws of social behavior (Kloppenberg 1989).[13] As Kloppenberg (1022) notes, there were already "some historians intoxicated by the idea of becoming scientists" in the immediate postwar period. Furthermore, many New Left historians during the 1960s and 1970s were "anything but radical in their sometimes un-selfconscious and sometimes defiant commitment to a naïve objectivist epistemology" (1023; see also Megill 1991). Positivist philosophers of science devoted a great deal of energy in this period to proposing ways that singular historical processes and events could be subsumed under (a series of) covering laws (Mandelbaum 1938; Hempel 1948/1965, 1974; Nagel 1961/1979, ch. 15). Their interventions did not lack influence among historians.

In his contribution to this volume, Bill Sewell focuses on the 1960s and 1970s and on the subfield of social history, which he helped to create and then to transform. Sewell points out that social history's political project of bringing to light the voices and invisible histories of the subaltern classes led somewhat ironically to a reinforcement of a positivist or empiricist ethos.[14] Social history in this period was motivated by the laudable desire to study "new categories of people," especially ordinary people who had not left written records, and to ask "new questions about them" (Sewell, this volume). Along with these new substantive foci came a borrowing of methods from the social sciences as well as the epistemological approach typical in sociology and political science at the time. Sewell calls attention to the "new social history's uncritical objectivism, its presumptive preference for quantitative data, its default economic determinism, [and] its blindness to questions of meaning" (Sewell, this volume). Yet he lauds its "sense of the social," which was more "robust" than that of the subsequent cultural history.

With the consolidation of the "epistemological left" in academic historiography during the 1980s (Novick 1991, 703), however, this mixture of leftist populism and positivist epistemology began to seem strained and internally contradictory. The linguistic and cultural turns in history threw overboard most of the new social history and its social science methods and worldview, as well as the older commitment (see, e.g., Joan Scott 1988b; Megill 1989). Although social history had briefly become "hegemonic in the field," defining the very "terms of historiographical debate," cultural history now replaced it as the new orthodoxy (Sewell, this volume).[15] Novick paints a more pluralized picture of the post-1980s field, quoting a scriptural passage: "In those days there was no king in Israel; every man did that which was right in his own eyes." What Novick would define as objectivism lives on in several historiographic subfields. But it has become just one position among many.[16]

Even social history was never uniformly positivist, as Geoff Eley (this volume) reminds us. Eley associates social history with the goals of *explanation* and "grasping society as a whole." His main example of a social historian, E. P. Thompson, was connected to the cultural Marxism of the less economistic British New Left rather than positivistic social science. Thompson's (and Eley's) British social history thus differs in certain key respects from the U.S. version discussed by Sewell. Among other things, as Eley points out, Thompson was centrally concerned with cultural traditions and their complexities; Sewell notes that Thompson was "almost allergic" to quantification. With respect to the epistemological issues emphasized here, this means that Thompson's approach embraced an interpretivism that positivists usually reject because it is difficult to reconcile with deductivist covering laws.[17] Even if Thompson believed that "the development of capitalism was determining in the final analysis," his was clearly not a deductivist or positivist covering law version of Marxism.[18] This was evident both in the historical contingencies opened up by his emphasis on ideological constructions and transformations and in his rich description of the real alternatives to capitalism that were "championed by working-class communities" (Sewell, this volume; Sewell 1990; Thompson 1966).

Eley also alludes, however, to an image of historians becoming social scientists by "collecting, counting, and measuring data," which suggests that he too sees the earlier social history as epistemologically double-edged. Both Eley and Sewell thus reject the scientistic tendencies of the older social history while calling attention to that tradition's politically progressive and partially antipositivist potentials.

Eley's image of historians as accountants also recalls an alternate definition of positivism that one often encounters among historians and in the humanities. Ultimately, this is a methodological statement, but one that connotes an empiricist and antitheoretical unwillingness to depart from the narrowest reading of the sources, whether literary or archival (see Smail 2000).[19] Significantly, this version of positivism does not support any specific explanatory strategy but tends instead to eschew the goal of explanation altogether. This indicates an important difference from the dominant social science understanding of positivism. Indeed, there are similarities between the humanistic and historiographic version of positivism and anthropologists' hesitations about comparison and commensuration. Philosophical positivism, by contrast, requires the commensuration of events as a precondition for identifying "constant conjunctions." What is often called positivism in the humanities is opposed even to the level of theoretical abstraction required to commensurate events, and thus actually has partly nonpositivist entailments.[20] Traditional empiricist historiography thus shares some common ground with cultural anthropology.

The disciplines of anthropology and history thus represent two distinct disciplinary trajectories that have arrived at a similarly nonpositivist present-day condition, even if they differ in many other respects. This is especially remarkable in light of the fact that both disciplines were offered the opportunity to reconfigure themselves along the lines of the imagined natural sciences during the middle decades of the twentieth century. Positivism has been much more powerful and durable in the other fields explored here, even if it has undergone certain transformations and appeared in differing guises according to discipline and historical context.

Psychology and psychoanalysis

The associations between positivism and psychology were especially strong during the second half of the twentieth century, as indexed by the prevalence of behaviorism in that field (see Buckley 1989; L. Smith and Woodward 1996; L. Smith 1986). The subfield of social psychology has generally been just as hostile to nonpositivism.[21] Even to locate a frontier between positivism and nonpositivism in the fields concerned with the psychic, then, we are best advised to move beyond psychology into *psychoanalysis*.[22] Given its emphasis on the complex and unpredictable subterranean workings of the unconscious, one might expect psychoanalysis to have been less susceptible to the positivist temptation. Psychoanalysis is a prime example of a human science organized around depth-realist theoretical objects such as repression, the unconscious, fetish, and fantasy.[23] It is also an ideal arena for studying battles over social epistemology. Positivists—most prominently, Karl Popper—have been more interested in eliminating psychoanalysis than in assuming control of it or reconstructing it along the lines of the natural sciences. Psychoanalysis has been attacked from the start on empiricist methodological and epistemological grounds (Freud 1924/1961), and these criticisms have never really subsided.[24] Andrew Collier, in his contribution to this volume, points explicitly to psychoanalysis as one of the areas in which critical realism can offset some of the effects that "inadequate philosophical premises" have had on them.

As Anthony Elliott argues here, the institutions and sciences of the psychic—psychoanalysis, psychiatry, and psychology—have been attracted (especially in the United States) to a reduction of the psychic to a medicalizing "neuromechanical logic." They have promoted and attended to rationality as against fantasy, engaging in the "psychologization of desire." Elliott presents Freud himself as resisting or disavowing some of his own radically nonpositivist discoveries, above all, the irreducible dynamics of fantasy and unconscious sexuality and imagination. Freud was ostensibly committed to a naturalistic understanding of his own project, but Elliott argues that he also reached nonpositivist conclusions despite his original inclinations. Freud denied the possibility of using experimentation to test psychoanalysis or to measure concepts like libido, for example, and he resisted the idea of general laws of psychic development or uniform rules for treatment.[25] Freud's vigorous defense of lay analysis, as Russell Jacoby notes, was based on his prescient anticipation that "monopolization by medical doctors would degrade psychoanalysis into a specialty" (1983, 145; see Freud 1926/1959). Movements of psychoanalytic renewal from Lacan to Marcuse, and from feminist psychoanalysis (J. Mitchell and Rose 1982) to the contemporary Slovenian school (Žižek 1989), have repeatedly drawn sustenance from these sources in Freud. Focusing on Freud's unfinished 1895 paper "Project for a Scientific Psychology" (1895/1966), Elliott shows how both the biologistic and antipositivist potentials of psychoanalysis were present from the start. U.S. psychoanalysis aligned itself early on with the medical profession, which exposed it to the persistent pressures of a biologizing scientism. Clarence Oberndorf, one of the founders of American Freudianism, observed caustically that psychoanalysis, "once incorporated into medical schools . . . came to attract those who 'find security in conformity and propriety'" (1953, 127, 209–210). The flip side of this medicalization was "theoretical banalization" (Jacoby 1983, 23), meaning above all the marginalization of the unconscious and the erotic in favor of concepts located closer to the conscious or surface level, as in ego psychology.[26] This was part of a more general effort to provide a "strictly scientistic defense of psychoanalysis" (Whitebook 1999; see also Hale 1995, 2001).

No other field has had to confront such an onslaught of corrosive resistances. The broadest of these pressures are the general surrounding social conditions, which are conducive to an empiricist understanding of subjectivity. Elliott refers here to the "modernist tension between imagination and rationality" and "between imagination and specialized knowledge." Also important are the many ways capitalist modernity makes the sovereign, rational individual into the self-evident basic unit of social existence. A third factor is the presence of well-articulated theoretical approaches like behaviorism and brain chemistry around which scientistic-positivist resistance can be organized. Finally, there is the state, oriented especially in the past three decades toward cutting spending on mental health, and the pharmaceutical industry, perpetually oriented toward maximizing profits. These last two forces combine to replace the supposedly more expensive and less easily measured practices of psychoanalysis with pharmacological approaches to the management of symptoms (Roudinesco 2001). Although this displacement has been especially relentless in the recent past, it was already well under way in the middle of the twentieth century (Oberndorf 1953, 236–237). Criticisms of psychoanalytic practice by radicals like R. D. Laing, Michel Foucault (1980), and Deleuze and Guattari (1972/1983) ironically joined forces in this respect with the antipsychoanalytic campaigns of the health industry (Hale 1995).

Economics: a bifurcated discipline?
The field of economics has been paradigmatically committed to an atomizing ontology and a *deductivist* epistemology of lawlike generalizations,

according to Dan Breslau and Tony Lawson (both this volume). One of the sociointellectual conditions of possibility for consolidating this methodological approach was the construction of a delimited social object called "the economy" in the twentieth century (Mitchell, this volume). Tim Mitchell's essay here focuses on the pre–World War II period, Phil Mirowski's on the early and middle decades of the twentieth century, and Lawson and Breslau both emphasize the recent past and present state of the discipline.

Mitchell argues that social scientists invented the supposedly discrete spheres called the economy, the political system, the social system, and culture in the middle part of the twentieth century. He reminds us that Schumpeter thought that quantitative measures were especially adequate to the economic sciences due to the quantitative nature of the objects studied. The distinction between the national economy and external perturbances to the economy allowed economists to make generalizing statements, "if-then" statements, and predictions. Mitchell thus provides us with a succinct historical account of the processes by which positivism was able to become more plausible for economists. He also points out at the end of the essay that even mainstream economists in recent years have acknowledged the increasing proportion of economic activity that is *not* quantitatively measurable in any obvious way. The essay thus elegantly points to a sort of shearing pressure or contradiction between an established form of knowledge and its object. The question that remains open is whether these ongoing changes will actually unsettle entrenched forms of economics, and how. Breslau and Lawson address this more directly.

Positivism in economics has *not* tended to take the biologistic forms typical of Americanized psychoanalysis; nor has it eschewed all discussion of theoretical mechanisms, in contrast to psychological behaviorism. Mainstream economics does resemble psychological behaviorism, however, in its lack of interest in theorizing seriously about human rationality (Mirowski 1991, 2002) and its equation of science with the search for universal laws: the assumption of "regularity determinism" (Bhaskar 1975/1997, 69–71).[27] As Mirowski (1991) argues, the emergence of early game theory, including that of Von Neumann and Morgenstern (1944/1964), was related to the changing images of the natural world during the 1930s, including critiques of determinism and causality. Game theory could be described as nonpositivistic due to its open and apparently interactive imaging of the social, and to the possibility of multiple solutions to games, in contrast to more mechanical versions of regularity determinism. Yet Mirowski also shows that game theory's relationship to strategic military practices closed off certain epistemological possibilities. Actual applications of game theory in economics and strategic modeling emphasized static or nonrepeated games and singular solutions for games; subjectivity was construed as a rational black box. This realigned the approach with regularity determinism. As Lawson (this volume) and others (Yonay 1998; Weintraub 2002) argue, economic practice has been constituted above all by an a priori commitment to mathematicization, which militates against construing social processes as yielding a "myriad of incommensurate solution-concepts" (Mirowski 1991, 247); this is rooted in a deeper commitment to measurement and quantification (Porter 2001).[28]

Mirowski's contribution to the present volume situates the triumph of neoclassical economics in the years after 1940. This period also saw the ascendancy of a formulation I call methodological positivism in sociology, of logical positivism in the philosophy of science, and of behaviorism in psychology and political science. Of course, many of the raw materials for these postwar disciplinary formations originated in the interwar period or even earlier. Logical positivism traced its antecedents to the British empiricists, for example, and sociological positivism harkened back to Comte. But the period between World War II and the mid-1960s comes together as a rather coherent era for the social sciences, characterized by a relatively homogeneous regime of social science and an epistemological predilection for positivism.

When we turn to the present state of economics, however, it becomes more difficult to summarize in epistemological terms. Dan Breslau argues here that contemporary research by elite economists tends to be methodologically polymorphous, drawing at will on empirical-realist and aggressively antirealist forms of discourse. Lawson's analysis of mainstream economists supports this diagnosis, showing that economists alternate between depth-realist and antirealist/actualist (e.g., Friedman 1953b; Lucas 1986) formulations. Economists' more explicit and self-conscious methodological formulations may be more consistent than this, however. Breslau finds that the discipline is stratified between a dominant group of antirealist theoreticians and an empirically realist group of dominated econometricians and empirical researchers. He faults the "postautistic economics" movement (see below) for falling back into a naïve empiricism and for implicitly embracing its own dominated position. Yet, he concludes that a more adequate version of economics would attend to both empirical events and underlying causal structures (perhaps to structures of the sort identified by Breslau's own sociology of science, such as disciplinary or intellectual "fields"). The strategies associated with mainstream economics as well as its "postautistic" challengers can thus be criticized for embracing either an antirealist and actualist theoreticism or its mirror image, an empiricist realism. Both strategies fail to move decisively beyond positivism. By the same token, both of the main postpositivist alternatives in economics, the analysis of rhetoric (Donald McCloskey 1985; Deirdre McCloskey 1994) and critical realism (Ehrbar 2002; Fleetwood 1999; Lawson 1997), can be faulted for reinscribing an inherited distinction between words and things that Breslau, like Latour (1999) and (post-)Wittgensteinian linguistics more generally, finds problematic. This division between words/rhetoric and things/realism is itself, Breslau suggests, a "product of the division of labor of knowing" in economics. Finally, Burawoy (this volume) reminds us that economics, like the communist parties of old, generates "rare but distinguished dissidents," but that these exceptions do not call into question the general organizational pattern.

Sociology: postpositivism eternally deferred?
U.S. sociology has been dominated by a positivist scientism throughout most of the postwar period, as Smelser (1986) argued, reaching something of an apotheosis during the decade of prosperity, social security, and unbridled optimism about science, the 1960s. U.S. positivism has encompassed a belief in the possibility of lawlike generalizations that are independent of time, space, and cultural meaning, the emulation of a misunderstood model of the natural sciences, and the deployment of philosophically misleading concepts such as middle-range theory, nomothetic (as opposed to idiographic) science, and falsification as a judgmental strategy (see Steinmetz and Chae 2002, and my own essay in this volume). Qualitative sociologists have often adopted a version of the Humean "constant conjunctions" model that is ironically more strictly positivist than the approaches adopted by most quantitative sociologists (e.g., Skocpol 1979; 1984, 378; compare Lieberson 1991). Mainstream sociology has also been characterized by a radically ahistorical sense of temporality and a disavowal of the narrative structures underpinning its ostensibly achronological, statistical approaches (Abbott 1992a, this volume). Abbott assails a reigning understanding of temporality that construes social processes as having a determinant endpoint and that therefore fit neatly into the inherited constant conjunctions model of explanation (see below). My essay offers a historical sociology of postwar U.S. sociology that reconstructs the macrosocial conditions that led sociologists to find it increasingly *plausible* to describe the social world in a positivist-scientistic manner. These constructed social "facts" were then used by positivistic camps in their "trials of

strength" (Latour 1987, 78) with less positivistically inclined groups in the field. The goal was to transform the positivists' methodological, ontological, and epistemological preferences into seemingly obvious features of any sociology claiming to be a science. But none of this was a foregone conclusion: prewar U.S. sociology was far from unifed in epistemologic terms. Some of its leading figures explicitly opposed positivism and the natural science method. The question for sociology today concerns the likely effects of the fading of the macrosocial conditions that made positivism seem more immediately plausible than the alternatives, conditions I summarize under the heading of Fordism. The current reemergence of explicit epistemological dissent in sociology poses the question of whether the long period of positivist preeminence is finally coming to an end. Will the combination of post-Fordist social conditions and internal epistemic challenges succeed in dislodging positivist domination of the discipline, or will factors *internal* to sociology prolong positivism's life "unnaturally"? My essay sketches some of the possible implications of the transition to post-Fordism for sociologists' spontaneous social epistemologies and concludes that the grip of positivism on sociologists' imaginations may be weakening.

Margaret Somers's essay, on the other hand, provides a sobering counternarrative. Somers explores the recent penetration of sociology and some of the other social sciences by a reductively economistic understanding of the social encapsulated in the idea of "social capital." Somers's explanation of the growing popularity of this construction brings together intrascientific and environing social processes. With respect to the former, she points out that sociology has always looked to economics as a more successful social science. Sociologists were therefore thrilled when some economists began to adopt the ideas of social capital and the social embeddedness of markets. The idea of social capital was then reimported back into sociology (and political science) with the economists' stamp of approval, where it proceeded to displace genuinely relational concepts of the social. The proliferation of the idea of social capital, Somers argues, is actually at odds with taking the social seriously. Its use reinforces a central tenet of the postwar positivist settlement in sociology, which eschewed robust or depth-realist constructions of the social (Frisby and Sayer 1986). Somers argues further that the idea of social capital is theoretically incoherent, insofar as the social should be construed as a third term between the economy and the state (Arendt 1958). The social cannot be construed as a form of capital, because capital, at least in modern economic theory, is defined subjectively and atomistically, whereas the social has (at least partly) a transindividual character.

The permeation of sociology by the discourse of social capital may be an example of the successful resistance to pressures from the environing macrosocietal context that are undercutting positivism's instinctive plausibility. Positivism in sociology is finding new scientific allies to recruit in this effort. Additional concepts that were previously identified with nonpositivist sociology are being reappropriated by varying positivisms. The struggle over the ownership of the concept of "mechanism" is also suggestive of this dynamic. In the hands of critical realists, the idea of mechanism is distinctly unmechanistic and nonreductionist (see Bhaskar 1975/1997, 1979; Elster 1998; Mirowski 1988), but in other renderings of mechanism this is not the case (see Hedstrøm and Swedberg 1998). In short, sociological positivism may be able to successfully resist extrascientific developments urging the field to adopt more adequate epistemologies.

Political science and political theory
Both of the essays on political science in this volume agree that positivism has been all-powerful in the discipline throughout the postwar period. This began with the so-called behavioralist revolution in the 1950s, which explicitly adopted the language of empiricism and positivism and modeled the discipline "after the methodological assumptions of the natural sciences" (Easton 1965, 8; Gunnell 1975, 1–31; 1993, ch. 10; 1995, 924). Harold Laswell and Abraham Kaplan, in their 1950 manifesto for the behavioralist approach, insisted on "a thoroughgoing *empiricist* philosophy of science" and on "relating scientific ideas to materials ultimately accessible to direct observation" (xi–xii).[29] According to David Easton, another leading proponent of this movement, behavioralism emphasized "discoverable uniformities in political behavior, quantification, and value-freedom," all mainstays of the positivist tradition (1965, 17). Charles Lindblom argued years later that this movement "carried many political scientists toward a more *scientific* practice of their discipline" (1997, 231, my emphasis). Positive theory, introduced by William Riker, explicitly emulated the physical sciences (1962, 3–4). According to a recent overview, "The discipline has tended to accept implicitly a rather simple and, crucially, an uncontested set of positivist assumptions which have fundamentally stifled debate over both what the world is like and how we might explain it" (S. Smith 1996, 11). A content analysis by Schwarz-Shea and Yanow (2002, 457) of fourteen research methods texts used in political science found "a textual consensus on positivism as *the* mode of scientific research" in the discipline.[30] During the 1960s, rational choice theory began to replace behavioralism as the most powerful theoretical method

in the discipline, and it currently reigns supreme.[31] As I argue below, many versions of rational choice theory are also epistemologically positivist.

Unlike sociology, political science has preserved a specific subfield in which positivism has held little attraction: political theory.[32] In this arena, normative analysis is the rule, rather than a forbidden activity, as Mihic, Engelmann, and Wingrove detail here. Members of the theory subfield have long defined their topic as politically engaged commentary and interpretation anchored in a canonical set of texts, as Emily Hauptmann (this volume) points out. Furthermore, they have portrayed their subfield in explicitly anti-positivist terms, especially in the 1950s and 1960s. Those in political theory cannot be said to be doing "the work of theorizing" for those located in subfields like comparative politics, international relations, or political behavior, however, because these fields deal with questions of "is" rather than "ought." In these other parts of the discipline, theory tends to mean "formal" or "positive" theory.

The essay by Mihic, Engelmann, and Wingrove argues that political science's postwar settlement—the division between a distinct subfield of political theory and the rest of the discipline—has had marked effects on the overall epistemological power structure and unconscious of the field. This division serves to reinforce positivist hegemony in the discipline as a whole, despite, or because of, the explicitly normative and antipositivist orientation of the political theory subfield. The authors begin from the premise that facts and values are not amenable to radical separation but should instead be seen as mutually constitutive.[33] Yet the very division between theory and the rest of the discipline strengthens this untenable dichotomy. More specifically, the discipline's institutional division contributes to the doctrines of *value neutrality*, "the presumption that normative commitments and/or assumptions can and should be set aside, or 'bracketed,' in the process of scientific analysis," and its mirror image, *fact neutrality*, "which presumes that data are ancillary to the main preoccupations of the analyst." This institutionalized separation allows most of political science to continue to propose universal lawlike statements with little concern for the imbrication of facts and values, and also permits political theory to proceed in pristine isolation from the real (recalling mainstream economics, as analyzed by both Lawson and Breslau in this volume).

Critics have argued variously that a political science organized first around behavioralism and later centered on positive theory (Riker 1962) and then rational choice theory both *undercuts* and tacitly *endorses* liberal democracy. In a sustained critique of a behavioralism he characterized as positivistic, Leo Strauss (1962) argued that there was an "unavowed commitment built into the new political science" to a version of "liberal democracy" that was not discussed openly or impartially "with full consideration of all relevant pros and cons." By looking for "laws of political behavior to be discovered by means of data," Strauss continued, behaviorism put a premium on "the study of things which occur frequently now in democratic societies; neither those in their grave nor those behind the Curtains can respond to questionnaires or to interviews. Democracy is the tacit presupposition of the data; it does not have to become a theme; it can easily be forgotten. . . . [But] the laws of human behavior [that it discovers] are in fact laws of the behavior of human beings more or less molded by democracy; man is tacitly identified with democratic man" (326).

Rational choice theorists who did address the question of real alternatives to liberal democratic capitalism of the sort Strauss had in mind (e.g., some sort of socialism, as opposed to technical adjustments to the existing system) focused mainly on distributions of material resources and assets and on economistic cost-benefit calculations (compare Przeworski 1985), downplaying the specifically *political* considerations, arguments about the formation of preferences or values that Strauss, among others (e.g., Sahlins and the cultural anthropologists discussed here by Keane), saw as crucial and irreducible to economics or sociology. Rational choice theory, even of the Marxist variety, can thus be seen as tacitly reinforcing the existing *metapolitical* rules of the game even when it discusses transitions to noncapitalist *rules* (Roemer 1982). Rational choice theory can also be criticized for undermining those selfsame rules, of course, by emphasizing the economic irrationality of voting (as stated most famously by Mancur Olson 1965), the inefficiency of democratic decision making (Luke 1999, 347; Green and Shapiro 1994), and "the incoherence of the idea of popular sovereignty" (Mihic, Engelmann, and Wingrove, this volume).

Area studies
The funding and direction of social research by corporations and, especially after 1940, by the U.S. state played a crucial role in all of these disciplines, but it was more pronounced in some than others, and perhaps nowhere more than in area studies (Robin 2001; Miyoshi and Harootunian 2002; Patterson 2002, 115–132). For the most part, corporate and state funders have favored social research patterned on the natural sciences and focused on the production of general and empirical laws of behavior with practical applications. The emphasis on immediately applicable results has been relaxed in certain periods and places, but not the overarching preference for social science packaged according to positivist protocols.

The area studies fields have not promoted a single version of positivism, however. Instead, they have combined forms of objectivism, such as the position analyzed by Novick (1988) in history, with the search for covering laws. In addition, these two sorts of positivism can be related to different moments in the development of area studies. In his contribution to this volume, Michael Dutton analyzes the specific interdisciplinary field of Asian area studies. Dutton begins with the observation that Asian area studies has been resistant to theory in the name of a "truculent antitheoretical empiricism" (see also Rafael 1994, 101). Asian studies resembles other area fields that emerged in the nineteenth century in emulating a distorted version of the natural sciences and eradicating "unwanted signs of the heterogeneous that cannot be incorporated into the homogeneous world" of social science models (Dutton, this volume).

Dutton's central evidence for area studies' descriptivism concerns the privileged role of *translation* in its procedures and self-understandings. As Dutton points out, area studies' insertion into the positivist mainstream was abetted by its fetishization of acts of translation. Indeed, the basic empiricism of Asian studies flows directly from the "types of methods employed in language training itself." Rather than engaging with "people's way of thinking and feeling" (Dutton, quoting Michel Bréal) in terms of analysis of the disjunctures between surface and depth, area studies remained at the surface level and emphasized descriptive and applied research, often in the service of colonial power and, more recently, in the service of business. Whereas mainstream positivist social science has denigrated area studies as merely idiographic, the emphasis on translation actually suggests that cultures can be compared in a common metric. It is a small step from there to the search for empirical generalizations across time and space.

At the same time, Asian studies, like other area studies fields, "has the potential to send ripples of doubt through the dominant positivist social science 'stories.'" This intrinsic potential for epistemological dissent is lodged in area studies due to the difficulty of excluding from it the humanities and the more humanistic social sciences completely. Even if translation tends to inculcate the belief in ready comparability and generalization, it is rooted in philology, and some of the most dramatically nonpositivist epistemological programs have grown out of an engagement with classically philological themes. Although Oriental studies chose to become an empiricist "content provider" rather than following Freud, Nietzsche, and Marx into a radical interrogation of language, it has the potential for once again becoming "postpositivist" by rejoining earlier lines of inquiry.[34] The nonpositivist promise of area fields also stems from the fact that each of them is concerned with a specific region and hence with unique sociohistorical totalities. The natural science persuasion in the human sciences, by contrast, has long been oriented toward dissolving social wholes into elements and substituting "names of variables for the names of social systems, such as Ghana, the United States, Africa, or Asia" (Przeworski and Teune 1970, 8). Area studies' ability to be "enchanted with difference" stands in sharp contrast to the procedures of nomothetic mainstream social science, for whom radical alterity is mere noise (or grist for "deviant case analysis"). Concerted efforts to remove the area focus from area studies have not been entirely successful, partly because a globally active hegemon often demands detailed empirical knowledge of very specific places, and partly due to refusal within the area studies community itself (D. Cohen 1997).

The philosophy of science

The final discipline examined here is the philosophy of science, whose twentieth-century U.S. history is examined by Philip Mirowski. Mirowski explores the shifting interplay between the philosophy of science and social change, looking specifically at relations among science, state, church, and corporation. He asks about earlier antecedents of the post-1980s acceptance of the social embeddedness of science. Like Dutton's reading of Asian area studies and my own depiction of sociology, Mirowski describes a partly nonpositivist past being overshadowed during the middle decades of the twentieth century by a positivism linked with the state and business. More specifically, he discusses the displacement of the pragmatists by the logical positivists in the U.S. after World War II. The question he asks here is "how it was that science came to be portrayed by philosophers as asocial and autarkic and value-free in the United States in the middle of the twentieth century." Mirowski argues that the dominant views of the society-science relationship in the 1914–1940, 1940–1980, and post-1980 periods can be understood in relation to "the types of environments in which scientific research was being prosecuted" and the types of social theories dominant in these eras. During the first period, John Dewey opposed the prevailing cult of the expert (itself a product of the concentration of scientific research in private corporations) with a dream of science dedicated to and embedded within the wider democratic community. In the second period, the funding and organization of U.S. science was assumed by the military and the state more broadly. The Operations Research (OR) profession that emerged in World War II "was a practical response to the problems . . . of the military planning and organization of science" (Mirowski, this volume). Just as U.S. foreign policy was characterized by a mixture of "absence in principle and presence in practice" (Ulmen 2003, 26; C. Schmitt 2003, 255), the OR framework allowed scientists to construct a "delicate amalgam of engagement and aloofness": they could enjoy "military largesse" while gaining "a fair amount of latitude in evading direct control by the military" (Mirowski, this volume). Operations Research thus provided the template for the concept of the autarkic "scientific community" completely separate from society, a notion codified by Robert Merton and Michael Polanyi and by the other philosopher Mirowski examines here, Hans Reichenbach. According to Mirowski, the pact between OR and philosophers of science also accounts for various features of the new scientific regime, including its preference for mathematical formalisms and the "conflation of mathematical prowess with intellectual virtue"; its "insistence on a generic scientific method based on logic and probability and indifferently portable to any subject or discipline"; its antidemocratic elitism and "contempt for tradition"; its supposed value-freedom; and Reichenbach's (1951, 231) well-known distinction between the "context of discovery" and the "context of justification," which drove a wedge between philosophy and sociology. Various protocols that were worked out during World War II, including the fact that "grant overheads could buy off the principal investigator's academic obligations to his or her home institution," worked "in favor of treating the scientist as though he or she were a member of a community apart from the general run of intellectual life" (Mirowski, this volume). The logical positivist program in the United States thus "owed its good fortune to OR."

Elsewhere, Mirowski (forthcoming) characterizes the science regime of the more recent period, roughly since 1980, in terms of the outsourcing of research activities and the growth of a thicket of legal regulations and conflicts around intellectual property, the death of the idea of the freedom of the individual scientist, and the erosion of authorship. But most philosophers of science, he argues, have registered these drastic changes only indirectly via a partial acceptance of the "social dimensions of science." Biology and economics have replaced physics as the more "progressive" (i.e., profitable) sciences from which to derive epistemological generalizations. The exemplar of the new philosophy of science analyzed by Mirowski, Philip Kitcher, adopts the language of the social sciences most palatable to the new corporate clients—economics—and models all agents as "neoclassical rational choosers" with "preferences" in a self-avowed "methodological individualism."[35] Of course, some philosophers of science, including the ones in this volume (Harding and Collier), reject this recharged positivism. Harding's standpoint theory has long acknowledged the importance of social (especially gender) locations for science; Collier's critical realism embraces what Bhaskar called "epistemic relativism"[36]—that is, a post-Kuhnian certainty that the choice of scientific theories is determined at least in part by "social" factors rather than the correspondence of a theory to its object of analysis.

Combined and Uneven Developments

As disciplines dominated by tenacious positivist or late positivist assumptions, sociology, political science, area studies, and even the philosophy of science provide strong contrast cases with anthropology and (post-1980s) history. But the epistemic cultures and latent underpinnings of these disciplines also differ in specific ways, many of them having to do with differing understandings of "theory." Sociological positivism has encompassed a doctrine of value-neutrality similar to the configuration in political science as described by Mihic, Engelmann, and Wingrove. Indeed, this assumption was codified by Max Weber, whose methodological essays were canonized in postwar U.S. sociology (see especially Weber 1949). Yet there has been no parallel mapping of facts and values onto disciplinary subsections of sociology; rather, there has been less space overall for theory tout court.[37] Partly due to this absence, the discussion of normative theory/values has been less sustained in sociology than in political science. Efforts to reintegrate values and facts within sociology have typically emerged in the framework of broader epistemic and theoretical disturbances in the field as a whole and not in any particular subfield.[38] By the same token, the sort of atheoretical quantitative description of statistical correlations between variables and outcomes that is typical of "journal sociology" (Abbott 1992a, this volume), and that was often the end product of the empirical materials provided by area studies specialists, seems somewhat less widespread in political science.

Other differences can be gleaned from a comparison of economics, history, political science, psychology/psychoanalysis, and sociology. Economics, as Lawson observes, has been primarily deductivist, whereas sociological positivism has more often been inductivist, discovering supposed regularities through the manipulation and massaging of statistical data (Hanushek and Jackson 1977, 1).[39] Explanations in economics and sociology rarely take biologistic forms nowadays (although this may be changing with the increasing availability of funding from the life sciences);

this boundary has been less taboo in psychology. Nor have economics and sociology tended to adopt explicitly *behaviorist* forms of explanation, a version of empiricism that eschews the unobservable theoretical object altogether, even as a causally salient black box. This differentiates both fields from psychology and political science. Rational choice theory has made fewer inroads into sociology than into political science, and almost none at all into history or anthropology. Yet, as Somers argues here, one of rational choice theory's "part objects"—social capital—has had enormous success recently in sociology, operating as a Trojan horse for mainstream economics.

The timing of shifts in epistemological focus also varies from one field to the next. Freud's epistemologically contradictory writings have allowed antipositivist tendencies to resurface periodically in psychoanalysis, challenging the biomedical mainstream. Sociology has been predominantly positivist since 1945, aside from a brief period of epistemological turbulence between the end of the 1960s and the mid-1970s. Philosophical positivism had a relatively brief heyday among some historians during the 1950s and 1960s, even if positivism understood as an atheoretical and empiricist unwillingness to depart from a narrow reading of archival facts has had a much stronger grip on that field. Economics has been much less prone to movements of self-criticism than anthropology and sociology, even if the current context of the "science wars" has allowed some dissent to emerge even there (see especially Hands 2001; Weintraub 2002; Dierdre McCloskey 1994; Mirowski 1989, 2002). Nonpositivist approaches are well entrenched in some of the "interdisciplines" like science and technology studies, cultural studies, and gender and race studies.

Alternatives to Positivism in and beyond the Disciplines

The reader of the essays in part 1 might justifiably be left asking, Quo vadis? Besides examining the differing textures and chronologies of the relationship between positivism and the human sciences, a second goal of this collection is to lay out some of the metatheoretical alternatives. All of the contributions to this volume, including those in the first part, discuss and exemplify nonpositivist approaches of one sort or another. The second part, however, provides more of a *tour d'horizon* of alternatives. As noted, this collection does not propound any specific nonpositivist alternative. There is little agreement even in the most solidly postpositivist sectors of the human sciences about epistemological questions beyond a common rejection of positivism, and this is partly true of the contributors to this book as well. Nonetheless, these essays taken together conjure up a pluralistic postpositivist counterworld.

Positivism and antipositivism in the social sciences have both drawn sustenance from philosophy over the course of the past century. The first two essays in part 2 are by philosophers, and both of them are explicitly programmatic. Sandra Harding traces the development of standpoint epistemology, which emerged as a critique of positivism's "view from nowhere" and its doctrine of the unity of the sciences. Harding also touches on the Frankfurt School as a precursor to standpoint theory.[40] She explores the mutually constituting relationships between standpoint epistemology and the new social movements, especially in the context of the "Network Society" as described by Castells (1996/2000a). Harding also emphasizes some of the continuities between positivism and standpoint theory, reminding us that logical positivism encompassed a commitment to democracy, rationality, objectivity, and fairness.[41] The liberal left politics of early logical positivism are indisputable, even if this seems somewhat puzzling in light of the contemporary association between the epistemological and political lefts. As Carnap recalled, "All of us in the Circle were strongly interested in social and political progress" and "most of us, myself included, were socialists" (1963, 23).

Andrew Collier discusses the critical realist philosophy of science, which positions itself explicitly as an "underlaborer" for the sciences and as an alternative to both positivism and the various antipositivist positions it calls idealism or conventionalism. The *transcendental realist* half of this program develops an ontology of "hidden mechanisms, unexercised powers, and unrealized possibilities," going beyond the "actualist" proscription on disjunctures between the empirical and the real. This ontology "shows that there is a *plurality* of mechanisms conjointly determining events," meaning that constant conjunctions are an extremely rare exception in natural (nonlaboratory) settings, rather than the norm. As a result, prediction is demoted, becoming a rare event rather than some general goal for science. The "rainforestlike profusion of different kinds of reality" that critical realism's ontology takes for granted should be reflected in a "plurality of sciences." The *critical naturalist* half of this program contains a careful explication of the similarities and differences between the social and natural sciences and argues against both positivism and the actor-network approach to science studies (Latour 1999) with respect to their rejection of any differentiation between the two. Without denying that the study of the social can be quasi-scientific, critical naturalism specifies a set of specific differences between the objects of the natural and social sciences. A transcendental retroductive argument that asks "how any human activity in society is possible" allows critical realism to deduce the necessary existence of "two distinct kinds of being": on the one hand, "social institutions that preexist the agent," on the other, "an intentional [though not necessarily transparently rational] agent whose action presupposes and makes use of these institutions" but is not fully explained by them. Combined with other ontological peculiarities of the social, such as the time-, space-, practice-, and concept-dependence of social structures (Bhaskar 1979; Steinmetz 1998), the positivistic thesis of the unity of the sciences, at least in its simpler forms, is revealed as problematic. Ontological divisions in the realm of the human or social also suggest the rationality of different social sciences, or at least distinct theories mapped onto these distinct divisions (see also Burawoy, this volume, for a related critique of the idea of collapsing the social science disciplines).

Tony Lawson's essay presents a critical realist approach to the field of economics. It begins, however, with an analysis of the dominant orientation in economics toward mathematicization and deductivism. Lawson proposes that economists instead begin by developing substantive ontologies that recognize the openness of the social (including specifically economic practices) and thus the implausibility of deductive models. Like Lawson's, Dan Breslau's contribution also could have been placed in either the first or the second part of this book. Breslau presents the results of an ethnography of methodological discourse in contemporary economics. He finds that economists' discourse on method is structured in a way that corresponds to the overall structure of the field: theory dominates substantive inquiry, purity dominates worldliness, and antirealism dominates empirical realism. Elite economists are liberated from the demands of empirical verification and rationalize these privileges by defending an antiempiricist methodology. Dominated economists, by contrast, tend to articulate a moralistic respect for the concrete observable realities of economic life.

Andrew Abbott's essay analyzes the different conceptions of time in sociology and economics, focusing on the ubiquitous idea of "outcome." The fetishization of outcomes flows from an understanding of social science as oriented toward identifying stable concatenations of events. He juxtaposes this approach to a more processual, Bergsonian understanding of time. To establish the existence of these two models of temporality in sociology, Abbott examines the work of Angus Campbell and Paul Lazarsfeld, two leading postwar researchers, finding evidence of a more processual approach in the work of the latter. Abbott insists that social scientists think seriously about the metaphysics of temporality that informs their work, rather than accepting the ontology that is suggested implicitly (or promoted explicitly) by a configuration of research around the explanation of fixed outcomes.

In the concluding essay of part 2, Geoff Eley surveys three salient epistemic/methodological moments in the writing of history during the past four decades, tracking the seismic shift from social to cultural history and beyond. Eley focuses on the politics and the overall "structure of feeling" that informed and emerged from these ways of writing history, following an arcing movement from the *optimism* of the early era of radical social history (exemplified by E. P. Thompson), through to the *disappointment* of the society- and class-based project of social history (exemplified by German historian Tim Mason). The third moment in this narrative, a self-reflexive approach to cultural history, is epitomized for Eley by Carolyn Steedman's *Landscape for a Good Woman* (1987). Eley concludes with a call for a "defiant" historiography, one that connects resistance in the present (specifically, resistance to the new neoliberalism, imperialism, and domestic authoritarianism) to thinking about the past. Like Sewell, Eley calls for a recovery of the more politically engaged spirit of the earlier social history, without abandoning the intervening lessons learned.

In the final essay in this volume, Michael Burawoy begins with three problems raised by the Gulbenkian Commission (Wallerstein et al. 1996). The first traces the connections between colonialism/imperialism and social science (e.g., Asad 1973; Connell 1997) and connects these to a universalistic denial of difference, crystallized by nineteenth-century social evolutionary theory (Stocking 1987) but persisting into the present. The second is a scientistic context-free positivism. Third is the supposedly arbitrary division of the disciplines, which can be overcome by unifying them. As Burawoy suggests, this utopian program of unification neglects the findings of science studies and the sociology of knowledge and the principle of epistemic relativism and proposes that the social sciences "can finally escape the stamp of the society they interpret." Burawoy proposes instead *provincializing* the social sciences in the sense of grounding them in their particular contexts of production and objects of knowledge. This involves asking explicitly normative questions about the *addressees* (internal and external to academic fields) and the *goals* (instrumental vs. reflexive) of disciplinary knowledge. Situating different styles of social science in a table generated by these two dimensions (audiences and goals), Burawoy suggests that the social sciences, such as sociology, are necessarily located at the "intersection of the humanities and natural sciences." Like Mihic et al. (this volume), this suggests that the human sciences need to avoid both value-neutrality and fact-neutrality. Social sciences have to both interrogate and criticize "factish" (Latour 1999) knowledge and avoid becoming fact-neutral in a gesture of Olympian disdain.

The current epistemological conjuncture of possibilities in the human sciences is thus exceedingly varied and complex. The contributions to this volume may help readers make sense of these complexities and sort out their own positions. Would-be nonpositivists embrace a wide array of philosophical positions nowadays. An almost equally wide range of *political* positions is imputed to both nonpositivists and positivists as well, belying the simple heuristic that opposes an "epistemological left" to an "epistemological right."[42] Further complicating the issue is the fact that social scientists designated as working in a positivist way often refuse this description of their work. Raymond Williams once remarked that positivism has become "a swear-word, by which nobody is swearing" (1983, 239). Williams acknowledged, however, that "the real argument is still there." Our next task, then, must be to provide a working definition of this "swear-word" to make sense of the "real argument" that encompasses it.

The Uncanny Persistence of Positivism

If we take in our hand any volume . . . let us ask, *Does it contain any abstract reasoning concerning quantity or number? No. Does it contain any experimental reasoning concerning matter of fact and existence? No.* Commit it then to the flames.—David Hume, *An Enquiry Concerning Human Understanding*

Thus in advancing we have insensibly discovered a new relation betwixt cause and effect. . . . This relation is their constant conjunction.—David Hume, *A Treatise of Human Nature*

Recently Dahrendorf implied that the positivism criticized by the Frankfurt School no longer existed. . . . Nevertheless, one should not lose sight of what continues to survive untouched in positivism. . . . Unified science has triumphantly ousted the schools as archaically qualitative entities.—Theodor Adorno, introduction to *The Positivist Dispute in German Sociology*

The humanists . . . suffer from feelings of inadequacy in a world dominated by statistics and technology . . . the radical and "critical" political theorists, like the ancient prophets, lay about them with anathemas against the behaviorists and positivists. . . . But their anti-professionalism must leave them in doubt whether they are scholars.—Gabriel Almond, "Separate Tables"

There are good reasons nevertheless to take positivism as one of our starting points here. Most important, there is ample evidence that positivism is alive and well in at least some of the human sciences, even if it usually goes under different names nowadays, presenting itself in guises that differ from the versions popular between the 1920s and the 1960s. Thus, for every observer who insists that renewing the positivism debate is beating a dead horse there is another who identifies a resilient "positivist empiricism" (John Comaroff 1981–82, 144). The continuing hold of the positivist imagination can be felt in an emphasis on general, and usually empirical, laws; in doctrines of falsification or prediction; in a spontaneous preference for "parsimonious" explanations (forgetting that the first meaning of parsimonious, in the OED, for example, is "stingy") or for mathematical and statistical models; and in adherence to a caricatured view of the natural sciences as a role model. Each of the disciplinary-specific epistemological protests discussed in part 1 underscores the continuing existence of a robust, if updated (and sometimes camouflaged or unconscious) positivism.

Another reason for organizing a volume partly around positivism and nonpositivist alternatives is that positivism is still an important folk category among social scientists. On the one hand, positivism functions as an epithet among what Peter Novick (1991, 703) calls the "epistemological left." Understanding the differing ways this "bad other" is defined in the various disciplines can be useful in diagnosing and distinguishing their understanding of nonpositivist alternatives. On the other hand, a handful of scientists have somewhat defiantly embraced and defended positivism in recent years, sometimes under new labels such as "consilience" (E. Wilson 1998/1999).[43] Concepts like objectivism and scientism, lacking the august philosophical tradition of positivism, are genuine "swear-words" with no actual defenders. Before we can understand the epistemological reactions for and against positivism by contemporary participants in the human sciences, we need a stronger sense of the actually existing positivisms that have resided in each of the fields.

A final reason for beginning with the category of positivism is explicitly historical, at least if we understand history in terms of what Foucault called the "history of the present." Well into the 1950s positivism was still being explicitly defended by prominent philosophers (see Ayer 1959) and leading social scientists (e.g., Lundberg 1939a, 1955). Logical positivism or logical empiricism may have lost some of its luster by the 1950s, but there were few serious contenders. Positivism still constituted the telos of Bertrand Russell's widely read *History of Western Philosophy*, which was published in 1945. Many influential contributions continued to be made within the tradition, even if they increasingly avoided the language of positivism and empiricism (see Reichenbach 1951; Nagel 1961/1979; Schlipp 1963; Hempel

1948/1965; Stinchcombe 1968). Since the 1960s most social scientists have rejected any explicit association with positivist positions.[44] Hilary Putnam (1990b, 44) wrote at the beginning of the 1980s that Ayer's (1982) still partially positivist "style and spirit no longer speak to the concerns of practicing philosophers." Yet introductory philosophy courses today usually include sections on epistemology and treat precursors to twentieth-century positivism such as Locke, Hume, Comte, and John Stuart Mill. A. J. Ayer's classic collection, *Logical Positivism* (1959), is still in print. As Sandra Harding notes in her contribution to this volume, positivism's core beliefs continue to shape research disciplines as well as "our social institutions." The contemporary philosophy of social sciences has an important neo-positivist wing,[45] even if this is only a subsection of a subfield of a discipline. A recent reassessment concludes that logical positivism "provided the working framework of most philosophers of science from roughly the 1930s to the 1960s" but that more recent projects in the philosophy and social study of science continue to be motivated by positivism's demise (Richardson 1996, 1).

Additional questions concern the forms, definitions, locations, and sources of positivism. Reconstructing the genealogy of twentieth-century positivism is crucial for alerting present-day readers to a core cluster of ideas that resurface periodically under different names and in varying guises. We can then ask why certain disciplines and periods have been more inclined to adopt a positivist self-understanding than others. Why have some social science fields been more eager to accept the resources offered to those who would adopt a natural science approach? What explains the differential timing, the variable ebbing and flowing, of positivist approaches in history, sociology, anthropology, psychoanalysis, economics, political science, and philosophy? Which contemporary epistemological positions can usefully be designated as (neo, or neo-neo) positivist, and how do they resemble and differ from the positivisms of previous eras? Are alternative terms like "objectivism" (R. Bernstein 1983; Novick 1988; Megill 1994; Keane, this volume), "theoretical realism" (Gunnell 1995; Somers 1998), "deductivism" (Lawson, this volume), "instrumentalism" (Gunnell 1995), or "mitigated positivism" (C. Taylor 1985b) better or more precise descriptions of the social scientific practices under discussion?

Before we begin to explore the answers to these questions, or to ask why positivism is perpetually disavowed and unconsciously embraced, it will be useful to provide a working definition. As both Collier and Lawson argue in their contributions to this volume, the version of positivism that is most relevant for discussions of contemporary social science is one derived ultimately from Hume. It has been championed and developed further by John Stuart Mill, Ernst Mach, Karl Pearson, Rudolf Carnap, Moritz Schlick, Carl Hempel, Otto Neurath, Ernest Nagel, and Karl Popper. Positivism in this sense is above all a position within *epistemology*, even if it also entails implicit ontological assumptions, like any other theory of knowledge. Specifically, positivism insists that scientific explanations take the general form "if A then B" or more elaborate (including probabilistic and multivariate) versions of these Humean "constant conjunctions." As Hume wrote, "We may define a cause to be *an object, followed by another, and where all the objects similar to the first are followed by objects similar to the second*" (1748/1975, 76). Such statements presuppose the *invariance* of causal relationships.

Any theory of knowledge must also assume "that the nature of reality is such that it could be the object of knowledge of the required or specified sort" (Lawson, this volume). Causal invariance of the Humean sort is rendered possible by assuming the ontological *closure* of the observed system. Logical positivism in its original form made no claims about causal powers, of course, but was strictly a description of empirical correlations.[46] It was associated with an *empiricist* ontology, even if it made no explicit ontological claims, and was thus also called logical empiricism (Carnap 1928; 1963b, 870). According to empiricists, underlying causal structures or mechanisms either do not exist, or they are imperceptible and inaccessible like Kantian noumena, and are therefore off-limits for scientific statements. Even after Carnap and other logical positivists began at the end of the 1930s to acknowledge that scientific concepts could *not* be reduced "to the given, i.e. sense-data, or to observable properties of physical things" and to admit the possibility of "theoretical concepts" (Carnap 1956; also Carnap 1966, ch. 23), the latter were "regarded as mere devices for deriving the sentences that *really* state the empirical facts, namely the observation sentences" (H. Putnam 2002, 24).

One of the most significant developments in positivism's career during the second half of the twentieth century was the acceptance of theoretical terms as real entities. This allowed another revision that combined the Humean rule of invariance ("regularity determinism") with stronger notions of causation and the acceptance of unobservable, conceptual, or theoretical causal objects. The original empiricism of Hume and the logical positivists was thus severed from the epistemological commitment to constant conjunctions; these might now connect an unobservable cause to an observable event.[47] This version of positivism, which can be called a *depth-realist positivism*,[48] retains the basic positivist commitment to covering laws as well as the ontological premise of all covering laws: system closure. Depth realism thus turns out to be compatible with positivism, as long as the relevant causal mechanisms or explanans are uniform across all instances of a given explanandum. Recall that earlier positivists held that "no fact is explainable without a law, which asserts a causal correlation, no matter whether the law is arrived at inductively as a generalization from instances or is deduced from a set of more general laws or theories" (Lloyd 1986, 48).[49] For Carnap (1966, 4), universal laws took the form (x) (Px * Qx). It was then a simple step to define the property P of x as an unobservable and theoretical term referring to a mechanism. Although the 1929 logical positivist manifesto had emphasized *both* positivism and empiricism (Der Wiener Kreis 1929/1973, 309),[50] the two were able to part ways. By the early 1960s the logical positivists "had more or less collectively developed and agreed" on a revised version of their approach that allowed systematic correspondence rules linking observables and nonobservables (Lloyd 1986, 51; Hempel 1948/1965), even if they could not agree on whether the theoretical postulates referred to "real but as yet undiscovered entities or mechanisms"— which would constitute a form of *positivist realism*, or *depth-realist positivism*—or merely to "useful fictions or instruments for deriving empirically testable statements (instrumentalism)" (Lloyd 1986, 53). What they retained was an updated version of the constant conjunctions model, now renamed (by Hempel) the deductive-nomological model. According to this D-N model, events are explained by being subsumed under a general law that can take both deductive and "inductive-statistical" forms (Hempel 1948/1965, 1966, 1974; S. Smith 1996, 15).

Positivism has therefore been neither monolithic nor immutable. It has continued to evolve from Hume to Comte (who coined the term), via Mach and the logical positivists, and on into the present (R. Miller 1987). Some social scientists continue to understand positivism in classical Humean terms as necessarily combining three features: regularity determinism, empiricism, and empirical testability (the "logic of justification").[51] This is the view that "*science* and *scientific*... are words that relate to only one kind of knowledge, i.e., to knowledge of what is observable" (Van Dyke 1960, quoted in C. Taylor 1985b, 58). To take a more recent example, Hassard (1993, 6) claims: "The crux of positivist inquiry is that we can only have true knowledge of *explicit* phenomena and the relations between them. Scientists should not make hypothetical inferences about the essence of the implicit structure of phenomena; they should instead identify phenomena which are systematically connected to one another by way of invariable and universal laws." This passage combines the doctrines of empiricism (only "explicit phenomena" and not "implicit structures" can be the object of science) and regularity determinism ("invariable and universal laws"). But many contemporary social scientists link "implicit structures" causally to empirical phenomena under universal laws (depth-realist positivism), while others engage in an "actualist positivism," concocting theoretical statements with overtly fictitious concepts.

Depth-realist positivism can be found in a variety of different theoretical and methodological programs. Contemporary statistical approaches in the quantitative social sciences such as structural equation modeling often allow for latent (i.e., unobservable) constructs. These latent constructs are "indicated" by observable "explanatory" and "response" variables, that is, by variables meant to represent causes and effects (Jöreskog and Sörbom 1996).[52] If the relationships between latent and observed constructs are assumed to be constant, we can infer that the approach is premised on system closure. It can then be described as a version of depth-realist positivism.

Turning to substantive social theory, orthodox Marxism also often takes the form of a depth-realist positivism. Traditional Marxism posits some unitary underlying cause—the mode of production, social class, technological change, the organic composition of capital—that explains all instances of an empirical phenomenon (prices, revolutions, forms of state).[53] Depth-realist positivism also characterizes the subset of rational choice approaches that are realist about ontology but positivist about epistemology (see Green and Shapiro 1994, 30; Somers 1998).[54] Of course, many rational choice theorists are not realist at all about human rationality (their central explanans), but describe it as heuristic fiction (Friedmann 1953b). As Lawson (this volume) points out, many modern economic formulations "are couched in terms of categories that, though lying at the level of the actual, are not even real." At the same time, even these deliberately fictional constructs are connected to outcomes via general rules. If "perfect foresight is . . . widely acknowledged as a claim that is quite fictitious," for instance, it is also deployed in economic models as "a potential . . . that is *always* actualized" (my emphasis). The essence of the positivist stance, regularity determinism, is thus preserved in both the depth-realist and the willfully antirealist or idealist forms of rational choice theory (even as the latter rejects empiricism, empirical realism, and depth realism). In short, the ontological status of the concepts linked via a constant conjunction is less relevant for qualifying this approach as positivist than the supposed universality of the causal connection.

The common denominators of all positivist positions are thus *regularity determinism* and *system closure*. In light of this working definition, we can now return to the puzzle of positivism's unexpected and largely un-acknowledged longevity in the social sciences. At the most general level, one might associate epistemological and ontological beliefs with structures and strategies of power, as suggested by theories about genealogies of discourse, ideology and hegemony, and the sociology of knowledge. But if claims to knowledge are also claims to power, what sort of power is this? Who is exercising it, and why? How does the specific arena of methodology and epistemology relate to knowledge more generally? Are external funding agencies able to mold scientists' basic epistemological and ontological beliefs (D. Ross 1991; Ahmad 1991; Fisher 1993)? Are the disciplines organized around a dominant epistemological *mentalité* or set of disciplining practices, a core episteme, as Foucault (1966/1970) claimed with respect to the human sciences? Mitchell (this volume) argues, for instance, that both orthodox economists and their critics agree that there really is such a thing as the economy, whose elements form a dynamic system that is separable from other systems and that could in principle be accurately represented. This suggests that disciplines can be characterized as *hegemonized*. Mihic et al. (this volume) argue the same with respect to political science. Are social scientific fields ever *paradigmatic* in the strong sense proposed by Kuhn (1962/1970, 1977)? If so, does this imply that a specific group—of scientists, class actors—controls the scientific field?

Sociological approaches suggest that the disciplines should be seen as structured *fields* within which actors internalize an epistemological or methodological habitus (Bourdieu 1981, 1984/1988, 2001). The image of a stratified, structured field implies that a multiplicity of positions, including epistemological ones, may well be thinkable and even *desirable* (because actors develop a "taste for necessity"; Bourdieu 1979/1984, 372–396), even if every location is not equally "profitable." Academic distinction or scientific capital might accrue to certain positions—epistemological, methodological, stylistic, and so on—more than others. Bourdieu also suggests that positivism is the "spontaneous epistemology" of the natural sciences, which themselves are always pressing up against the social sciences, urging them to emulate their greater success by adopting their implicit methodology (1981, 282). But a completely homogeneous scientific field is sociologically implausible, as it would not allow social actors to make claims to scientific capital or to exchange recognition of such claims with other actors. The very functioning of a social field (like science) depends on the existence of distinctions; an intellectual *Gleichschaltung* would make competition impossible. If the hierarchy of power in a scientific field requires epistemological differences and is correlated with them, as Bourdieu argues, it may well contain nonpositivist as well as positivist positions. The actor-network approach developed by Latour and Callon also rejects the idea that all scientists necessarily "use the 'paradigm' in the same fashion, or that they mean the same thing when they refer to the underlying assumptions" (Yonay 1998, 23).

For each of these theorists, science is understood as an effect of power, a grid of inequality and domination, or, at the very least, as the product of strategic machinations that are driven by motives other than (or at least in addition to) discovering the truth. It is also possible, however, that positivism has been retained for reasons having little to do with scientists' quest for recognition, domination, distinction, or profits. Social-epistemic positions may represent cognitive responses to the structuring and restructuring of the social world, as suggested by neo-Marxist writers such as Jameson (1984, 1991) and Harvey (1989).[55] The determinative relationship between social structures and scientific knowledge does not entail any implications concerning the latter's cognitive adequacy or accuracy. Indeed, these writers tend to suggest that social knowledge describes social reality in oblique and distortive ways. But its content and form still do relate to social reality.[56] I refer to these positions as *social-epochal* or *macrosociological* accounts of social epistemology.

Some macrosociological accounts argue that positivism is perpetually reinforced and generated anew by the very character of the social arrangements of capitalist modernity (Horkheimer 1995). Others propose more historically specific accounts of positivist influence, linking social science epistemologies to the historical configurations of Fordism and post-Fordism (see Steinmetz 1999, forthcoming a; Steinmetz and Chae 2002). This particular social-epochal interpretation of social science epistemology originates with Marx, especially "The German Ideology." Adorno traced what he saw as the pervasiveness of positivism to the specific historical period of "administered capitalism," writing that "a social science which is both atomistic, and ascends through classification from the atoms to generalities, is the Medusan mirror to a society which is both atomized and organized according to abstract classificatory concepts, namely those of administration." For Adorno, positivism's categories were "latently the practical categories of the bourgeois class." Positivism's "elective affinity" with this class was to be found especially in the static, noncontradictory, repetitive character of modern administered capitalism. Positivism for Adorno represented an internalization of "the constraints exercised on thought by a totally socialized society," a sort of "puritanism of knowledge" (1969/1976, 56–59). Once one understands positivism as something akin to sexual repression it becomes more difficult to reduce that position to a mere veil for class interests. Indeed, Lukács (1968b) implies that bourgeois economists are themselves epistemic victims of the reified illusions of commodity capitalism which directs their attention toward empirical surfaces and away from real underlying structures.

Whatever the explanation for the current epistemological conjuncture in the human sciences—and this introduction cannot claim to legislate an answer for the diverse contributions to the present volume—it is a strange one indeed. A number of writers have referred to a positivist "haunting" of the sciences, depicting positivism's paradoxical power as a zombie-like refusal to stay buried (R. Miller 1987, 8; Elliott, this volume; Collier, this volume). In a slightly different register, positivism can be described as a kind of trauma from which the human sciences are still trying to recover. Like the macrosocial or epochal approach pioneered by Marx, Lukács, and Adorno, the sociopsychoanalytic one cannot be reduced to an account of scientists' strategically rational maneuvering or of the variable profitability of scientific positions.

The absence of any reference to positivism in the main title of this book stems partly from the conviction that positivism is too small a net in which to capture all of the problems addressed in this volume. Both the persistence and the critique of positivism can seem anachronistic in fields and disciplines for which positivism is now a strictly historical topic of analysis.[57] Some contributors to the interdisciplinary field of science studies argue that the entire category of epistemology is misleading and that efforts to distinguish it from ontology are miscast (Latour 1999).[58] Two of the essays here, for example (Lawson's and Breslau's), question whether positivism best describes mainstream economics, even if this discipline is often seen as one of the most recalcitrantly scientistic of the social disciplines.

But even if these intellectual disputes seem familiar from certain vantage points, one message of the essays in the first part of this book is that reinvigorated modes of positivism remain powerful in a wide swath of the social sciences. Indeed, positivism seems to be gaining strength in some sites. Political science, sociology, economics, psychology, and psychoanalysis all remain deeply enmeshed in a world that many in anthropology, history, and philosophy would locate firmly in their historical past. This explains how an era in which positivism is widely disparaged and barely recognizable might nonetheless give rise to a renewed *Positivismusstreit*.[59] The next section examines a series of such intellectual-political upheavals in economics, political science, and sociology. These movements challenge what they describe as entrenched epistemic and methodological orthodoxies in their respective fields.

Social Science Wars: An Intellectual-Political Conjuncture

When a department is organized not around a discipline aimed at advancement of knowledge, but around a field associated with a social movement (as are many "women's studies" departments, or "African-American studies" departments), the criterion changes. It is no longer the criterion of how best to advance knowledge, but is instead the criterion of how best to advance the cause.—James S. Coleman, "The Power of Social Norms"

September 2000 saw the emergence of a movement based among a large number of economics students and faculty in France calling for a "postautistic" economics and attacking the perceived hegemony of rational choice theory and econometrics within their field. Their petition demanded a "reform of the curriculum to incorporate a 'plurality of approaches adapted to the complexity of the object studied' " and decried the fact that "mathematics had become an end in itself, resulting in an 'autistic science with no relation to real life' " (Jacobsen 2001). This movement spread internationally to Britain and other parts of Europe, although the welcome has been noticeably cooler on U.S. soil. Indeed, from a certain angle, postautistic economics looks almost like an intellectual pendant to the broader antiglobalization movement and the widening sociocultural gap between Europe and the United States in many other realms. The neoclassical approaches against which the protest is directed are entrenched most powerfully in the United States and neoliberal NGOs and are understood to be helping to legitimate global inequality from which U.S.-based firms profit most. The field of economics thus sharply raises the question of the role of social movements in scientific conflict and change and points to differences in national and regional contexts (see Michael Burawoy's remarks in this volume).

The postautistic polemic also forces us to ask whether economics is indeed best characterized as *hypertheoretical* and oblivious to the empirical. Dan Breslau's contribution in this volume addresses the relations between the theoretical and the empirical in contemporary economic research via an ethnographic and textual study of the work of practicing economists. Breslau concludes that the most prestigious economists are able to take the intellectual high road of abstract theory and antirealism, but that less powerful economists tend to insist on the *moral* high ground of empirical realism. This difference emerges sharply in economists' programmatic, methodological, and epistemological statements. In their actual research, however, elite economists are promiscuous in their combination of (antirealist) abstract theory and empirically realist data. Tony Lawson's paper supports some of the antiautistic movement's claims, arguing that mathematicization, rather than realism or explanatory capacity, is the common coin of professional economics. At the same time, Lawson, like Breslau, finds that elite economists appeal rhetorically to reality and empirical explanatory power whenever they find it convenient. At a different level, Tim Mitchell stresses the contribution of practical economic discourses to specifically *empiricist* social effects, as opposed to the hypertheoreticist effects that are implied by the language of the antiautistic social movement. By staging an "effect of the real" in the representation of the economy, Mitchell argues, economics helps to produce the simpler, empiricist metaphysics that organizes our lives. The essays thus support the protesters' description of economics only in part, although none of them endorses the opposing position (e.g., Solow 2001) that finds nothing to criticize in contemporary economics.

In the United States, the most vigorous movement against entrenched social science orthodoxies in recent years has arisen in political science, sparked by the anonymous and eponymous "Mr. Perestroika" (see Mihic et al., this volume; also R. Smith 2002). The so-called glasnost-perestroika movement in political science called for the democratization and reform of the political scientists' professional association and flagship journal and criticized the discipline's preference for rational choice and game theory approaches, econometrics, and mathematical and statistical methods. This movement arose in the wake of concerted efforts during the 1990s to solidify the domination of the field by a basically positivist approach that could encompass both qualitative and quantitative methods (see King, Keohane, and Verba 1994). The perestroika movement has not produced a coherent epistemological alternative, however, but has instead forged a motley coalition of strange epistemic bedfellows. The movement has been directed mainly against the hegemony of a particular kind of theory (rational choice) and against a specific methodology centered on statistics and surveys. One of the most influential critiques of rational choice theory in political science, however, recommends a return to an empiricist covering law format (Green and Shapiro 1994, 31). Few of the dissidents have undermined the fundamental doctrines of fact- and value-neutrality that Mihic et al. (this volume) see as the bedrock of positivism in the field. These authors argue that the epistemological mainstreaming of political science cannot be understood without attending to the overall intellectual configuration of the discipline, especially the definition of political theory as a particular subfield solely responsible for the values side of the "facts versus values" dichotomy.

U.S. sociology has also been riven in the recent past by debates around the methodological and sociological narrowness of its main journal, the *American Sociological Review*. An essay in the *Chronicle of Higher Education* in 1999 by the president of the American Sociological Association at that time, Joe Feagin, criticized the *ASR* and ended with a call for the profession to embrace the "self-reflexive tradition that is one of Sociology's recurring virtues" (1999, 86). Many sociologists felt that the Association ignored such calls by granting the editorship of the *ASR* to an "insider" department traditionally associated with more positivist and quantitative methods.[60] Even more unsettling for sociology's still dominant but largely unacknowledged positivism has been the emergence of epistemological challenges from a variety of corners in recent years. One of these is cultural sociology, which in some cases has rejected the scientistic insistence on treating social practices as "thinglike" and accessible to analysis without interpretation of their contextual meaning. Another challenge comes from the new sociology of science (see Shapin 1995 for a review). Given its commitment to the idea that scientific practice and theory choice is driven by more than simple correspondence with data or the truth, and its occasional claim that "there is no transcendent context of rational justification that renders some scientific hypotheses more credible than others" (Luke 1999, 345), recent work in the sociology of science embodies a frontal disagreement with the prevailing positivism. This subfield tends to reject the entire distinction between subject/scientist and object, and thus rejects not just positivism but the various critical realisms as well.[61] Not surprisingly, the sociology of science has become a flashpoint for opponents of Novick's "epistemological left" in the so-called science wars (e.g., Sokal and Bricmont 1998, ch. 5), although some view the Sokal affair as an aberration (e.g., Schabas 2002, 219). Other criticisms of positivism are associated with feminist and other new social movements and with the poststructuralist and postmodernist theories that have sometimes been linked to these movements. Methodological conservatives in sociology have regarded the emerging possibility of epistemological polycentrism as a threat to the field's always tenuous scientific status and have been especially vexed by the penetration of the field by social movements (see the epigraph to this section and Horowitz 1993, ch. 1).

Countering this epistemological blowback, the current president of the American Sociological Association, Michael Burawoy, has intervened with a series of analyses of the connections between sociology and its publics (see Burawoy 2004 and his conclusion to this volume). These articles challenge the effort to (re)erect a firewall between sociology and its constitutive social "outside," which Burawoy sees as fully a part of its "inside." Positivism, according to Burawoy, is above all the "self-misunderstanding" of the "professional" sector of social science knowledge; it is the idea that "knowledge is and has to be autonomously produced" in "an autonomy without embeddedness." A vibrant sociology, according to Burawoy, "depends on reciprocal relations between professional sociology and both the self-reflexive critical branches of the field and the discipline's extra-academic audiences" (this volume).

This is by no means the first wave of epistemological upheaval in sociology's relatively short history. There have been at least three periods in which positivism became an explicit target of critique: around the turn of the twentieth century, in response to the doctrines of Mach, Pearson, Poincaré, and other influential positivists; during the 1930s, when logical positivism was criticized by such writers as Parsons (1937/1949) and Sellars (1939); and again in the 1960s and 1970s, which saw antipositivist movements that were closely tied to other cultural and political rebellions (Adorno et al. 1976; Gouldner 1970; Schwendinger and Schwendinger 1974; Giddens 1975).[62] The recurrence of these disturbances underscores the fact that they have failed to dislodge positivism permanently. In the present period there is more confusion and disagreement than in the past. Yet it is not at all evident that the current challenges will succeed in shifting the discipline's ontological-epistemethodological center of gravity. As Craig Calhoun (1996) has argued with respect to the initially antipositivist historical turn in sociology, the most dissonant and threatening aspects of such movements can be successfully "domesticated." My own paper in this collection examines a subset of these movements and finds that they have indeed been reconciled with sociological positivism to a surprising degree.

The configurations of dispute in economics, political science, and sociology are less alike than they might at first appear. The antiautistic movement in economics is directed in part against the dominance of abstract theory and mathematicized methods. In sociology, by contrast, it is abstract theory that has been especially taboo, due to the empiricist proscription on theoretical (or "unobservable") structures. And in a gesture reminiscent of sociological positivism, political scientist Charles Lindblom (1997, 243) refers to Joseph Schumpeter (!) as "more . . . a debater than . . . a scientist." Of course, theory has not so much been proscribed in political science as set off behind an intellectual *cordon sanitaire*, according to Hauptmann and Mihic et al. And yet, neoclassical economics, rational choice theory, and game theory emphatically claim the right to make abstract assumptions and to posit the existence of theoretical objects, whether realist or antirealist (Somers, this volume).

We might anticipate similar expressions of epistemic discontent in the fields of psychology and psychoanalysis. After all, U.S. psychology was dominated throughout much of the twentieth century by one of the most extreme versions of an empiricist positivism: the behaviorist schools of John Watson and B. F. Skinner. As one recent collection of essays on psychology points out, however, there has been little consensus about the nature of positivism in the field or the character of its influence (Tolman 1992). Another psychologist notes that although there is "still argument over the precise extent to which psychology ever adopted or paid attention to the logical positivists," it is "less disputable . . . that positivist notions already prevalent in the late 19th century came to inform psychological research for much of [the 20th] century" (Stam 1992, 259). Despite the strong impact of positivism on psychology, or perhaps because of it, that field has not seen any explicit movements of epistemological dissatisfaction. In more recent decades, many psychologists have become interested in opening up the behaviorists' "black box" and started to introduce realist concepts and objects such as cognition, narrative, and the self that were declared off-limits by behaviorism.[63] But the furious campaign by pharmaceutical companies for the full-scale medicalization of psychopathology continues to reinforce the spontaneous ideologies of the self that are already generated by a neoliberal capitalism "unfettered" by solidaristic welfare policies and dedicated to the hyperindividualism of the market.[64] Just as social movements do not necessarily arise where grievances are most severe (Zald and McCarthy 1979), movements of intellectual renewal do not always emerge where they would seem to be most urgently needed.

As noted earlier, U.S. psychoanalysis aligned itself with a scientistic and medicalized approach that led it away from the theory's most significant depth-realist constructs, including the unconscious. Dissidents like Norman O. Brown, whose *Life against Death* (1959/1985) was published in the same year as C. Wright Mills's *Sociological Imagination* (1959), attempted to stave off the ongoing scientization of the field. But as Jacoby (1983, 135) argues, such isolated attempts to defend Freud against Freudianism failed to disturb the "theoretical sleep" of psychoanalysis. The 1960s saw a renewal of nonpositivist protests in psychoanalysis from figures like Marcuse (1964; see Zaretsky 2000). This era also saw the consolidation of the antiscientistic French school of psychoanalysis led by Lacan (Roudinesco

1990; Foucault 1994, 204). By the beginning of the 1980s, Jacoby (1983, 136) could sense that "the antipsychoanalytic wind [had] weakened." The intervening period has seen continuing opposition to psychoanalysis in the culture at large and in the fields of the psychic more narrowly, however. The proliferation of psychoanalytic theorizing in the humanities should not be seen as a sign of the theory's weakness, *pace* Jacoby, but neither does it gainsay the theory's institutional weakness.

The fields with perhaps the most corrosive effects on positivism are science studies and the new sociology and historiography of science. The very existence of the Strong Program in science studies represents a sort of historical paradox, of course. On the one hand, science and technology have become increasingly interwoven in all aspects of social life (Castells 1996/2000a; Mirowski 2002), and science's claims to a superordinate position in social, cultural, and philosophical debate have been raised ever more insistently as a result. At the same time, however, the intellectual orientation that Karl Mannheim (1929) called "unmasking" (*enthüllen*), the claim that one can unveil the social determinants of knowledge, has become more widespread. This debunking posture clashes with science's overweening claims to authority to constitute the unsettled and unsettling conjuncture of current debates around (social) scientific epistemology.[65] It is impossible to predict whether science studies will wither under the onslaught of big science; alternatively, the skepticism about science that feeds this field may continue to grow, or the two may remain at loggerheads.

The simultaneous focus on epistemological issues in scientific fields and in some of the antiorthodox social movements distinguishes the present moment from earlier waves of dissatisfaction with social science positivism. Earlier critiques of positivism were usually a subordinate part of wider political programs; one thinks of Lukács's *History and Class Consciousness* (1922/1968a) or Lenin's critique of Mach and the Machists (1908/1927).[66] Parsons may have argued against positivism in the 1930s, but this was by no means his main focus, and he seems to have abandoned the theme after the war. The polemic against Popperian positivism was only one of Adorno's many interests in the 1960s. By contrast, questions of science, epistemology, methodology, and technology have moved in recent years to the center of critical attention.

The Epistemological Unconscious:
Politics of Method in the Human Sciences

The overwhelming majority of philosophers regard as mental only the phenomena of consciousness. . . . What, then, can a philosopher say to a theory which, like psycho-analysis, asserts that on the contrary what is mental is itself *unconscious* . . . ?

The strongest resistances . . . were not of an intellectual kind but arose from emotional sources. This explained their passionate character.—Freud, "Resistances to Psycho-Analysis"

The notion of an "epistemological unconscious" in the human sciences might seem jarring in light of the conventional associations of epistemology with explicit, conscious processes of generating and adjudicating knowledge claims.[67] Yet, as Tony Lawson reminds us, Alfred North Whitehead (1925, 71, quoted in Lawson, this volume; my emphasis) observed in 1925 that in every period "there will be some fundamental assumptions which adherents of all the variant systems within the epoch *unconsciously* presuppose." Pierre Bourdieu (1972/1977, 23, 92), a theorist who avoided explicit psychoanalytic theorizing and criticized certain versions of it, often used the adjective "unconscious" in describing the operation of the habitus, and this certainly extended to his view of the scientific habitus (1990, 55–56; 2001).[68]

We can define the unconscious as a deep structure encompassing processes and forms of knowledge that are not accessible to conscious awareness but that are nonetheless capable of patterning conscious thought and manifest practice. The concept then resonates with many alternative terms used by the authors in this volume to describe epistemic convergence in science: ideology, doxa, hegemony, disciplining, tacit understandings, knowledge postulates, and more. The concept of the unconscious in this context suggests that fundamental intellectual alignments within disciplines are partly generated and reproduced without the explicit agreement of the participants—violating the liberal self-understanding of science. Positivism may also offer more specific attractions. The positivist world of repeated conjunctions of events is, among other things, reassuringly stable. The psychoanalytic concept of the unconscious is necessary for analyzing the desire for knowledge: Freud's "drive for knowledge" (*Wisstrieb*) or "epistemophilia" (Moi 1988/1999). It may also shed light on some of the ways a discipline-specific habitus is inculcated through processes of identification with ideal egos and ego ideals (Žižek 1989), including identification with imagos of heroic figures (and impossible antiheroes) in one's own discipline and beyond.

The idea of a "politics of method" has several implications. As William Baxter (2002, 42–43) writes:

Method is originally from Greek *méthodos*, a compound of *meté* "after" and *hodós* "way, road." Classical Greek *méthodos* originally means "following after, pursuit," hence (in philosophical contexts) "pursuit of knowledge, investigation"; by further extension, it refers to a plan or strategy for carrying out an investigation. . . . But for many nineteenth-century writers . . . *method* or *méthode* has a stronger and more specific sense which is probably to be traced to René Descartes. . . . The fourth of his *Regulae* is . . . "A method is necessary for investigating truth. . . . By method I mean certain and easy rules, *such that those who use them precisely will never suppose anything to be true which is false.*"

Method in this sense is a central site for the reinforcement of positivist hegemony in the social sciences. Tony Lawson argues, for instance, that the axiomatic privileging of mathematics in economics is inculcated in economists during their earliest training, coming *prior* to the substantive epistemology and ontology it supports.[69] Positivist assumptions are typically communicated to sociology graduate students not by reading Comte, Carnap, or Nagel but through practical training, *dressage*, in statistics classes.

Method in the narrower sense is relatively independent of epistemology, as illustrated by the elaboration of forthrightly positivist qualitative methods for sociology or political science (e.g., Esping-Andersen 1990; Mahoney and Rueschemeyer 2002). Epistemological-ontological positions and methodologies are typically "mutually implicating" through patterns of elective affinity (Schwarz-Shea and Yanow 2002, 460). One of the aims of this volume is to chart the differing articulations between methods in this sense—a focus on issues of technique or technology, writing and research, rhetoric, and disciplinary socialization—and broader assumptions about social knowledge and the social world (see also J. Nelson, Megill, and McCloskey 1987).

Another common thread in these essays is the *political* character of epistemology. Fredric Jameson (1981) famously analyzed the *political* unconscious of fictional texts. By the same token, the human sciences and their texts have tacit and explicit political (and antipolitical or depoliticizing) messages. Examples of the former include the separation of values from facts and the assumption of repeated conjunctions. Like the cyclical worldviews discussed by Bourdieu (1972/1977), positivist regularity determinism suggests that the modern world is itself unchanging, or changing only in predictable and predetermined ways. This is not only profoundly tranquilizing but also, for a modernist philosophical position, paradoxically "traditionalist."

All of the contributors to this volume have studied questions of socio-cultural practice and change in different disciplinary, transdisciplinary, historical, and geospatial settings. They have analyzed academic or scientific knowledge and less elite knowledge cultures and discursive communities.[70] Some of the authors approach positivism and antipositivism via close readings of influential texts in their respective disciplines; others engage in ethnographies of the present-day human sciences; a third group focuses on elaborating alternatives to positivism. And because it is impossible to understand contemporary positivism and nonpositivism outside of particular histories and places, many of the essays approach.

One of the questions that immediately arose in organizing this volume was whether to privilege practioners' histories or "self-histories" (Mirowski 2002, 382–383) as opposed to accounts written by outsiders to the various discplines. Discussions of standpoint theory and scientific self-reflexivity have made it clear that outsiders do not necessarily have a *more* objective vision of their object; but neither do they always have a *worse* perspective. *Participants* in particular social practices have better "opportunities for knowledge" (New 1998); for the study of science this includes personal, specialized, and embodied training. There are also practical advantages to locating criticism of the social sciences *within* the specific sciences (see Burawoy, this volume). Students are likely to be exposed to their own discipline's orthodoxies, internal conflicts, and hegemonic imagined histories as part of their professional training. Yet the field's power structure may also subject them to systematic blindness, self-censorship, and pressures to intellectual conformity. There is no obvious progression in the history of science in which fields are first studied by insiders, followed by "maturation" and movement into the "autonomy" of professional history and sociology of those same sciences (*pace* Schabas 2002). Such autonomization may simply generate new forms of intra-disciplinary heteronomy, as science studies generates its own internal orthodoxies.[71] The essays herein are mainly by practitioners of their own fields. This has the additional advantage of refuting the slur that "those who can, do science; those who can't prattle about its methodology" (Samuelson 1992, 240), for all of the contributors to this volume are conducting "scientific" work on topics other than their own disciplines as well. One of the disadvantages of self-histories, however, is that researchers on the various fields remain separated from one another. This volume attempts to overcome this problem.

Although focused on the United States, this volume also provides a starting point for thinking about the differences and relations between social science in the United States and the rest of the world. Whether the interdisciplinary and chronological patterns that emerge here would hold in other national contexts remains an open question. Two relevant points are worth recording, however. On the one hand, a focus on the United States is crucial to the extent that contemporary scientific life worldwide continues to be dominated by U.S. universities and research institutes, for better or worse. It makes sense, then, to turn our attention first to the social scientific metropole before exploring the "reverberations of empire" (Stoler and Cooper 1997, 1). On the other, it would be worth exploring the hypothesis advanced in a different context by Fredric Jameson (1998b) concerning a growing divide between U.S. and European political culture and to direct this toward the problem of social scientific cultures.[72] Anyone familiar with, say, German or French social sciences will immediately be able to think of a series of differences from those fields in the United States. In psychoanalysis, the scientizing and antiscientistic tendencies developed at different moments and in different forms on the two sides of the Atlantic (Zaretsky 2004). Geoff Eley's essay in this volume suggests that British social history followed a political-epistemic trajectory that was quite different from its U.S. counterpart. Michael Burawoy discusses the "global division of social science labor" and the split between "opposition and attachment to" U.S. and "Western" forms of professional knowledge. Dutton's "Asian Area Studies" has a global genealogy and reach.

This collection is meant to stimulate comparisons over time and across disciplines and epistemologies. Because most of the essays develop more than a single argument—historical, descriptive, critical, programmatic— there was more than a single possible way to arrange them in the book. All of the essays engage in historical genealogies and criticize contemporary social scientific practice. All make recommendations for a non- or post-positivist social science. Even where alternatives to positivism are not the explicit topic they are performed or exemplified by these articles. Overall, the arrangement of the volume is a trajectory running from the past through the present and on to different possible futures. Without ignoring the "collapse of the fact/value dichotomy" (H. Putnam 2002), it is possible to say that this book is structured by an overarching movement from "is" (or "was") to "ought."

Notes

For their detailed comments on this introduction I would like to thank Webb Keane, Peggy Somers, four anonymous reviewers, and the indefatigable Raphael Allen.

1   I am using the term epistemology in the general sense of theories of knowledge of the world, not in the historically narrower sense of the sterile "quest for certainty" (Rorty 1979, 61), or for absolute truth based on "internal representations and the correct evaluations of those representations" (Rabinow 1986, 234), under this more capacious definition. Pragmatic postmodernism is (among other things) an epistemological position, as it makes claims about knowledge: knowledge has no stable foundations, but should be useful or edifying, and so on. As I am using the term methodology, it is also very broad, designating research design, case selection, techniques of analysis, and forms of presentation.

2   Research on this period is referred to in the rest of this introduction and in the other essays here. To cite just two recent historical accounts of scientific change focused on the middle of the twentieth century and emphasizing the effects of military funding and research priorities, see Mirowski (2002) and Robin (2001).

3   As Gunnell (1995, 930) points out, however, contemporary realism and antirealism both "abjure the legacy of positivism," even if adherents to the two positions often accuse the other camp of slipping back into positivism.

4   Of course, epistemological pluralism may end up reproducing "the underlying structures that sustain a uniform core" (Mihic et al., this volume), just as multicultural liberalism is delimited by a set of examined and unexamined strictures that determine which practices are thought to lie beyond the pale (see Povinelli 2002; Rasch 2003). Bourdieu (1981, 2001) recognized that the existence of a plurality of positions does not eliminate unequal hierarchies in fields of knowledge, suggesting instead that such pluralism is a condition of existence for any field.

5   Eley and Elliott focus on European texts; Collier's critical realist position is based mainly in Britain; Breslau's post-Mertonian sociology of science draws on European social theorists like Bourdieu and Latour; Dutton's analysis of Asian area studies spand the globe.

6   By depth realist I mean the same thing Gunnell (1995) means by theoretical realism, namely, the willingness to maintain theoretical claims about objects, structures, or mechanisms that cannot be reduced to observables (or even to potential observables; see R. Miller 1987).

7   See Ortner (1994) for a relatively approving summary along these lines and Wolf (1980) for a critique; Cohn (1981, 244) speaks of a "deconstruction" of the field. George Stocking (2001b) refers often to "sociocultural anthropology" to underscore the similarity between the United States, where the adjective "cultural" was used to refer to the dominant sector of the Boasian four-field definition of the discipline, and Britain, where the adjective "social" was used. Stocking's emphasis on common features of British and U.S. anthropology is generated out of a broad contrast with the French and German formations; he also attends to key figures like Radcliffe-Brown, who operated in more than one Anglophone setting. Because the present discussion is focused on U.S. developments, I use the term "cultural anthropology."

8   Although this article was written in English, Boas clearly had in mind the method of *Verstehen*, a term commonly translated as "understanding." Boas's essay is ostensibly about geography, but the term is used in the sense of the German geographical tradition associated with Karl (Carl) Ritter and Friedrich Ratzel. Ratzel was the author of a highly influential two-volume book called *Anthropogeographie* which argued against evolutionist theory and in favor of a diffusionist approach to cultural change. The topic

of his "geography" was what in English was called ethnology (also called *Ethnologie* in German). Boas's later writings on ethnology shift to the more Anglophone usage of the term but continue to argue along the same epistemical lines as the 1887 essay.

9   Alongside Boas himself at Columbia, examples include Alfred Kroeber at Berkeley, who in 1915 was already strongly antibiologistic, arguing that "civilization" (later called "culture") "springs from the organic, but is independent of it," and opposed to geographic-materialist reductionism, insisting that "civilization reacts to civilization, not to geography" (1915, 284–285). Kroeber, like Boas, rejected all forms of social evolutionary theory, which had dominated anthropology during the nineteenth century and which resurfaced repeatedly in the twentieth (in forms like modernization theory), asserting as a premise that "all men are totally civilized" and that "the ranging of the portions of civilization in any sequence [is] always valueless" (286). Other influential Boasians included Robert Lowie (at Berkeley), Melville Herskovits (Northwestern), Edward Sapir (mainly Chicago and Yale), Ruth Benedict (Columbia), and Margaret Mead, who taught at a number of universities and was based at the American Museum of Natural History (Stocking 2001c, 45).

10 I disagree with Stocking's tendency to describe all comparative research as "scientistic" (e.g., Stocking 2001b, 46, 289). This seems to ignore the possibility of nonpositivist versions of comparison (see Steinmetz forthcoming b; Lawson 1999b).

11 This is based on personal communications from Webb Keane and Ann Stoler. The methodological trend toward *multisited ethnography* (Marcus 1995; Appadurai 1990) does not contradict this claim, because comparison here is interested in tracing a single cultural formation that is produced "in several locales" and "across and within multiple sites of activity" in ways that destabilize the distinction between the "local" and the "global" (Marcus 1995, 99, 96). Although "conventional controlled comparison in anthropology is indeed multi-sited . . . it operates on a linear spatial plane . . . comparisons are generated for homogeneously conceived units" (102). I would characterize this as a subtype of "depth-realist comparison" (Steinmetz forthcoming b) because, as Marcus says, there is still a common object of study (a person, community, etc.) across the multiple sites.

12 On Boas's deep antipathy to biological determinism and the overall "debiologization" of anthropology, see Stocking (2001b, 67, 315; 1968). On the recent debate, see Chagnon (1968), Tierney (2000), Geertz (2001), American Anthropological Association (2002), and the reviews in *Current Anthropology* 42, 2 (April 2001), especially Coronil (2001). See also Latour (1999), who focuses on soil scientists in the part of the Amazon inhabited, ironically, by the Yanomami. Latour distinguishes between his own "philosophical" analysis of these scientists and a "sociological" focus on colonialism, race, and gender.

13 In a response to critics, Novick (1991) denied that he was talking about history's *epistemological* stance, but most critics recognized that this was in fact precisely the topic of his book (see the reviews by Hollinger, Megill, and Ross in *American Historical Review* 1991). Novick was awarded the American Historical Association's most distinguished prize, yet, as Dorothy Ross (1991, 706) pointed out, his book "was not awarded the prize of the Social Science History Association." The implication is that at least one section of the historical discipline, the one most strongly associated with quantitative approaches to history, was less approving of Novick's analysis. Such disagreements can be examined in the reviews by Kloppenberg (1989) and Hexter (1991). Kloppenberg accuses Novick of

philosophical vagueness, but this seems to mask a more fundamental disagreement with his insistence on the relative autonomy of theory from empirical history. On the internal divisions among historians, see Abbott (2001a, especially ch. 4).

14 This is perhaps not so paradoxical, of course, if one recalls the leftism of the Russian Machists and Carnap's advocacy of socialism, not to mention the scientistic left's attack on postpositivism (e.g., Sokal and Bricmont 1998).

15 But see Eley (1996). There were many examples of nonsynchronicity, however, such as Baldwin's (1990), a historical study that seems to emulate mainstream sociology even as it was published a good decade after historians' cultural turn.

16 The linguistic turn in history or the new cultural history also occasioned, as Sewell (this volume) notes, a shift away from some of the more populist political themes of social history and a move back to a more elite-centered topic. For evidence that these methodological and political developments are not inextricably and necessarily bound together, however, one need look no further than Sewell's own *Work and Revolution in France* (1980), not to mention the work of Patrick Joyce, Craig Calhoun, Jacques Rancière, Bill Reddy, and others.

17 For a recent attempt to declare interpretation anathema to properly scientific comparative-historical research, see Mahoney and Rueschemeyer (2002).

18 Thompson (1978), of course, confusingly described Althussser's radically antirealist, antiempiricist, and antipositivist philosophy of science and social theory as positivist, muddying the waters considerably on this issue (see P. Anderson 1980).

19 Of course, some historians explicitly engage with the philosophical understanding of positivism; see Lloyd (1986), who discusses positivism in terms identical to those in the next section of this introduction.

20 Needless to say, this version of so-called positivism is superempiricist; see the next section for the distinction between positivism and empiricism.

21 See the special issue of the *Journal of the History of the Behavioral Sciences* 36, 4 (fall 2000).

22 We can pass over nonpsychoanalytic psychiatry here; psychiatry's positivist fixation on reductive and predictive generalization should surprise no one; see Scull (1999) for a review of recent historiography. I also ignore psychoanalysis's antithesis from the 1960s, antipsychiatry; see Will (1984) on that movement's relationship to positivism.

23 Norman O. Brown (1959/1985, 94) insisted that psychoanalysis claims to "break through phenomena to the hidden 'noumenal' reality."

24 The first landmark of positivist criticism of Freud was Popper's rejection in 1919 (see Popper 1983, 174). For a recent overview of the criticisms of psychoanalysis, see Forrester (1997); Grünbaum (1984) provides one of the most thoroughgoing nonpositivist critiques; see Frosh (1999) for a response to Grünbaum. Popper revised classical logical positivism, but his falsification doctrine was empiricist and positivist in its denial of a "vertical" stratification of real structures (the latter means that a causal structure such as the unconscious in Freudian theory may be prevented from being expressed at the level of the actual). Freud's central argument is that unconscious materials are *not* always or continuously expressed the same way at the empirical or symptomatic level. Any simple version of falsificationism is therefore inadequate to the ontological complexity of the world. Popper's theory is indeed *antiempiricist* in its embrace of conceptual causal structures; he insisted that his theory was a form of realism. But this tended to reduce to a form of *depth-realist positivism* due to its retention of the "constant

conjunction" model (see below on the notion of depth-realist positivism, and Popper 1957/1991, 141–142 for an example of his acceptance of a deliberately unrealistic rational choice model of human practice). In 1957 he listed a number of "sociological laws or hypotheses," all of which took the form of constant conjunctions, and later insisted that even in the social sciences, "the basic logical schema of every explanation consists of a (logical) deductive inference whose premises consist of a theory and some initial conditions" (1957/1991, 62–63; 1969/1976a, 100). He also defended experimentation and prediction as goals for the social sciences and opposed the "belief that the description of a social situation should involve the mental . . . states of everybody concerned (1957/1991, 94–95, 120–130, 140).

25   See Rustin (1991, 115–144; 1999) and Collier (1994), who discuss psychoanalysis as a critical realist form of science; Frosh (1999) draws out its distinctively antipositivist epistemology from a different point of view. Freud stressed individual variations in responses to general conditions as much as the general situations they face. As a result, despite modal conditions like the Oedipus conflict, it is impossible to generate general narratives of individual development.

26   In light of Jacoby's (1983, 15, 139) critique of theoretical banalization, it is ironic that he is so intolerant of newer nonpositivist directions in psychoanalytic theorizing. Jacoby fails to notice, or cannot abide the fact, that much of the creative political and theoretical energy he so misses in current medical psychoanalysis (141) has migrated to the humanities.

27   Lawson (this volume) suggests that the term "deductivism" may be a more appropriate description of mainstream economics than positivism, which he equates with empiricism. But he admits that mainstream economics does "appear to resonate" with positivism "in many ways." The terminological disagreement seems less important than Lawson's points about the centrality of mathematicization and regularity determinism in economics.

28   The reasons for economists' unwavering commitment to mathematicization are not developed here, but see Mirowski (1989) for one account of the influence of physics on economics and the resultant prioritization of mathematics. It is also important that many of the objects of economics (money, interest rates) themselves take an ontologically quantitative form, which lends greater credibility to the privileging of mathematical methods. Other sorts of social practice, from sex to speaking and writing a language, do not necessarily present themselves at the level of the "actual" in an already quantified form.

29   As Robin (2001) points out, Laswell propagated a mechanistic version of psychoanalysis during the prewar period, but by 1950, economics had replaced psychoanalysis as his ideal science (see also Gunnell 1993, 226).

30   Although Schwarz-Shea and Yanow (2002) never actually define positivism here, they seem to mean something quite similar to the formation I define in the next section.

31   See Emily Hauptmann's essay in this volume for a discussion of this rise to preeminence and of the question of its status as theory or method.

32   On positivism in the contemporary subfield of international relations, see Ashley (1984, 248–254); S. Smith, Booth, and Zalewski (1996). Positivism in the subfield of comparative politics is exemplified by Mahoney and Rueschemeyer (2002).

33   The most influential modern statement of the fact/value dichotomy is Hume's thesis that the "propositions, *is,* and *is not*" should never be "connected with an *ought,* or

ought not" (*A Treatise of Human Nature,* 1739–1740/1969 bk. 3, pt. 1, sect. 1). The argument *against* the fact/value dichotomy can be traced back to Aristotle. Discussing the classic Aristotelian "three intellectual virtues, *episteme, techne,* and *phronesis"* (the latter translated as "practical wisdom"), Flyvberg notes that "whereas *episteme* is found in the modern words 'epistemology' and 'epistemic,' and *techne* in 'technology' and 'technical,' it is indicative of the degree to which thinking in the social sciences has allowed itself to be colonized by natural and technical science that we today do not even have a word for the one intellectual virtue, *phronesis,* which Aristotle saw not only as the necessary basis for social and political inquiry, but as the most important of the intellectual virtues" (2001, 3; Aristotle, *Nicomachean Ethics,* 1140a, 24–30). Criticism of the fact/value dichotomy was developed further by Marx starting in the *Theses on Feuerbach* and by later Marxists (e.g., Lukács 1968b, 153–157); by the pragmatists Peirce, Dewey, James, and Mead (H. Putnam 2002, 30); by Leo Strauss (1962) and his followers; and by Adorno (1969/1976), Charles Taylor (1979, 1985b), and Roy Bhaskar (1979). For a recent discussion, see H. Putnam (2002); for an account of the necessary normativity of the social sciences, see Freitag (2001).

34   See, for example, Liu (1999). Liu (forthcoming) connects the desire for an unambiguous translatability with imperialism.

35   It is more than ironic in light of this adherence to methodological individualism that Kitcher (2000, S38) passes judgment on sociology, a discipline defined by its rejection of methodological individualism and its insistence on the ontological emergence of the social. For a sustained critique, see Mirowski (1996).

36   On Harding, see Pohlhaus (2002) and Lawson (1999b). Presumably, Mirowski might reject critical realism for retaining a neo-Reichenbachian distinction between what it calls "epistemic relativism" (which it accepts) and "judgmental realism" (which it rejects). The latter is not antisociological across the board, however, but only with respect to its claim that truth is "a value that is presupposed by all our doings as cognitive beings" (Collier 1994, 179). In effect, judgmental realism is a normative program but not one that claims to explain anything about the actually existing sciences. One also needs to ask whether it is not misleading to equate the critical realist critic of science with the hegemonic logical positivist. Critical realism does not want to restrict science to "tutored" legitimate agents or even to replace untutored with tutored ones, but to criticize the social conditions that produce systematically distorted knowledge. Thus, the parallel between its judgmental rationalism and Reichenbach's "context of justification" is only partial, stemming from a common ethical commitment to the idea of truth.

37   Even if most U.S. sociology departments have social theory courses and some have full-time theorists, and even if the American Sociological Association has a subsection devoted to theory, there is almost no systematic training of graduate students for this subfield and there are almost never entry-level jobs in social theory. The rare PhD in sociology with a theory dissertation often ends up working in another field. Existing theorists in U.S. sociology departments generally began their careers as empirical reseachers, or continue to combine theoretical and empirical work, or have been trained in other countries. The exceptions prove the rule.

38   I discuss these intellectual movements in my contribution to this volume; see Calhoun (1996) and the essays in Adams, Clemens, and Orloff (forthcoming) for detailed discussion of one of these challenges and of historical sociology.

39   The authors of this influential introduction to statistical methods single out economics as the only social science in which genuine deductivism is accepted (Hanushek and Jackson 1977, 1).

40   Adorno's criticique of positivism is dicussed below.

41   See Neurath (1931/1973, 356–371) for an early example of an explicit logical positivist Marxism, written long before "rational choice Marxism." On Neurath's views of the "social extraterritoriality of science," see Uebel (2000b).

42   I am grateful to Raphael Allen for helping me with this formulation.

43   See Jonathan Turner (1993) and Gerhard Lenski (1988) for defenses in sociology; for discussion, see J. Bryant (1992) and Despy-Meyer and Devriese (1999, 95–143). E. O. Wilson's (1999) treatise on the "unity of science" directly reprises the logical positivists' earlier slogan (see Carnap 1930–31/1959, 1934).

44   It seems to be precisely this unfashionableness that explains the periodic appearance of soi-disant positivists in sociology (J. Turner 1993), often among those whose positions are not truly positivist in any recognizable sense (e.g., R. Collins 1989; Stinchcombe 2002).

45   Private communication by Daniel Little, November 2003. See Kitcher (1993, 2002).

46   As Carnap (1963b, 870) observed, Schlick originally was a realist but abandoned realism as a result of "discussions in the [Vienna] Circle."

47   See, for instance, Green and Shapiro, who "insist that scientific advance comes only with developing theory—*that is, establishing the existence of covering laws*" (1994, 31, my emphasis). They add that these covering laws have to be "both general and empirical," thus seeming to slip back into a simple Humeanism. Shapiro (1990) gestured in an earlier book toward a "pragmatic realism" that transcended surface empiricism.

48   I call this depth-realist, rather than simply realist, in recognition of the fact that many empiricist positivists were in fact realist about the intransitive existence of the objects of science, contra Marxists like Lenin, who collapsed positivism and empiricism with idealism. But the original logical positivists were quite adamant about their opposition to the "metaphysics" of contemporary "critical realism" (which at the time was associated with Roy Wood Sellars), writing, "*For us, something is 'real' through being incorporated into the total structure of experience*" (i.e., empirical experience; see Der Wiener Kreis 1929/1973, 308; italics in original).

49   Thus, the discussion of induction versus deduction fails to get at the essential issue, which is a view of the (social) world as static and monologic (Adorno et al. 1976, 76).

50   This was true of all the logical positivists, many of whom also called themselves logical *empiricists* (H. Putnam 2002, ch. 1). Bhaskar (1975/1997, 1979, 1986) and Collier (1994, this volume) also distinguish positivism from empiricism. Sandra Harding (1999) points out that although the two positions have been closely interwoven in the course of philosophical history, they have also periodically diverged.

51   Sociologists also often equate positivism with Comte's positivism, which is understandable given his role in the history of the discipline; see C. Bryant (1975) on this conflation; Gouldner (1970) for an example of the elision; and Steinmetz and Chae (2002) for a critique of the latter.

52   Various unrealistic assumptions are also made about the distribution of random qualities or error terms.

53   This is why Althusser referred to Hegelian Marxism as essentialist: it reduced all phe-

nomena to epiphenomena of a common essence. See Althusser (1977), Althusser and Balibar (1968/1979).

54   Gunnell (1995) and Somers (1998) refer to this combination as "theoretical realism," which resonates with the logical positivists' notion of "theoretical terms." I prefer the term depth-realist positivism because positivists often refer to statements of constant conjunctions of empirical events as "theories."

55   This sort of explanation recalls the position Popper (1957/1991, 7) called "historism" (as opposed to "historicism"), one that explains "the differences between the various sociological doctrines and schools, by referring . . . to their connection with the predilections . . . prevailing in a particular historical period."

56   The actor-network approach argues that "facts" may be mobilized as "allies" by scientists engaged in "trials of strength." The argument I am making is that even social facts that are not mobilized by any particular group of scientists (as allies) can influence spontaneous social epistemologies.

57   But see Poovey (2001), who identifies an orientation toward the use of models in literary criticism that one might call positivist (although she does not use that word).

58   Latour (1999) argues that this distinction is an effort to ward off "mob rule," recalling Lakatos's (1970) critique of Kuhn. Some of the contributors to this volume deploy the epistemology-ontology distinction, but their critiques tend to be closer politically to what Latour would consider the "mob" position than that of the rulers (see especially the contributions by Sewell and Eley). Clearly, this is a fluid distinction, but without it we would not be able to track the emergence of phenomena such as the new depth-realist variants of positivism. As H. Putnam (2002) argues with respect to facts and values, distinctions are often less objectionable than dichotomies.

59   We should recall that some of the main participants in the 1960s positivism debate, including Popper, also refused to recognize themselves in that mirror (see the essays in Adorno et al. 1976).

60   Namely, the University of Wisconsin sociology department, which, as Sewell notes in his paper here, has long been the most "powerful and notoriously positivist" department and which is also regularly ranked at the very top of graduate sociology departments in the United States. Even though the journal's recent editor, Charles Camic, hardly represented the positivist mainstream of sociology, little seemed to change with the *ASR* during his stewardship, suggesting that the discipline (rather than the demonized Wisconsin department), was the source of the problem.

61   See Latour (1999), who argues implausibly that "we in science studies may be *the first to have found a way to free the sciences from politics*" (22). He offers a compelling critique of the thesis of the unbridgeable gulf between scientific subject and observed object, a criticism shared by many modern philosophies of science—though certainly not by standpoint theory (Gadamer 1975) or critical realism. Latour argues convincingly that facts are "clearly fabricated" by scientists, nonscientists, and nonhumans (15), but he fails to address the critical realist distinction between the ontological levels of the *real*—of structures that are indeed largely "intransitive" and thus independent of scientists—and the *actual* (events). Bhaskar (1975/1997) would agree that the latter, in scientific settings, are "clearly fabricated" by scientists. Indeed, he argues, the logic of the experiment is that it is a highly artificial construct intended to produce specific effects. Critical realism asks what *intransitive* properties of the world allow humans to fabricate certain facts but not others in the laboratory, a question that Latour's approach cannot

ask. Latour does claim to be moving toward a "more 'realistic realism'" (1999, 14). Science studies is certainly a form of realism, but it is generally an *empirical* realism, and not one that allows for an ontological stratification into the levels of the real and the actual (see the comments of Yonay 1998, 15, who even claims the mantle of positivism, though not a "traditional" version, for his constructionism). As Latour notes, what science studies does best is to pay "close attention to the details of scientific practice" (1999, 24). Latour's attraction to photography (which he introduces by writing somewhat naïvely that "a picture is worth a thousand words") seems to be motivated by photography's empirical-realist power, as he presents photographs as unvarnished records of "the facts" (at least in his 1999 book).

62 A lone voice in the 1950s was C. Wright Mills, whose *Sociological Imagination* (1959) resembled the arguments of the contemporary antiautistic economics movement in opposing both abstracted empiricism *and* grand theory.

63 For an excellent overview of the literature on narrative and the self, see Linde (1993); see also Steinmetz (1992).

64 For an example of Eli Lilly's brazen attack on opposition to medicalization as mere superstition or politics, compare the interview given to *The World* on Public Radio International in "Depressed in Japan," Nov. 19, 2002.

65 Another component of this critical conjuncture, one that is even more nondisciplinary than science studies, is cultural studies. The rise of cultural studies has even started to erode the long-enforced boundary between the humanities and the social sciences, at least in certain places. It is impossible to trace this shift to any single source, but fields like women's studies, minority studies, and the revitalized area studies point in a similar direction epistemologically (although European studies is a partial exception; see Steinmetz 2003a). The role of neo-Marxism in this history also should not be underestimated. Neo-Marxism simply ignored barriers between the humanities and the social sciences (I am thinking of journals like *New Left Review, Das Argument, Cultural Critique, Social Text,* and *Boundary* 2). A final critical component of this conjuncture is Foucault, whose radical antidisciplinarity and antipositivism was crucial in broadcasting a nonpositivist message across the humanities and social sciences. Evidence has been found in Foucault's writings to support almost every conceivable position, of course. One of his most influential books, *The Order of Things,* was concerned with what used to be called intellectual history, or what in another discipline is known as the sociology of knowledge. Foucault's thesis of the existence of a time-bound episteme ordering the various fields of knowledge in a given epoch may have proved objectionable even to Foucault himself in later years, due to its underestimation of the multiaccentuality of discursive formations (Steinmetz 2002), but it gave a fillip to a radicalized post-Kuhnian view of science as ordered by principles that are not readily or consciously available to participants in a given scientific arena. Foucault rejected the distinction between ideology and science that was still being maintained by writers like Althusser, strengthening the project of studying science critically and in its own right.

66 Lenin (1908/1927) discussed the "new positivism," equating it with his main target, idealism. He located the idealism of Mach and Richard Avenarius in a direct lineage with Berkeley and Hume. Lenin's own materialist philosophy of reflection boiled down to an empiricist rather than a depth realism, however. Lenin faults the idealists, for instance, for "not regard[ing] *sensations* as the true copy of this objective reality,

independent of man" (127, my emphasis). By contrast, Lukács's (1968b) approach was an explicit depth realism, organized around dialectical oppositions between essence and appearance, immediacy and mediation, and the capitalist irrationality of the whole as opposed to the limited rationality of its parts. Lukács suggested that scientistic social science provided a correct *phenomenal* description of capitalism, given the latter's calculating and fragmented character, which allowed for the local regularities codified in positivist general laws. As society became more rationalized, it did actually become somewhat more predictable. In response to this the (scientific) subject could then "pounce on opportunities created by the system of laws" and use them according to his "best interests" (130). Each bourgeois science, according to Lukács, was characterized by blindness to a particular area of reality—not because that area was impervious to knowledge but due to social reality's surface-level fragmentation and to the class bias of the bourgeois vision of the world.

67 Kant's analysis of the a priori categories of understanding is a closer approximation to the idea of an epistemological unconscious than positivist ideas of fully conscious knowledge production.

68 Bourdieu avoided a properly psychoanalytic understanding of the term unconscious, however (Steinmetz 2002).

69 See also the autobiographical observations by Sewell (this volume) and Weintraub (2002, ch. 7). Luke (1999) makes a similar argument for the "normalizing effects" of disciplinary practices in political science.

70 See Abbott (1999, 2001a), Breslau (1998), Burawoy (1979), Burawoy and Lukács (1992), Collier (1994), Dutton (1998), Eley (1980/1991, 1996, 2002), A. Elliott (2000), Engelmann (2003), Sandra Harding (1991), Hauptmann (1996), Keane (1997), Lawson (1999b), Mihic (1999), Mirowski (1989, 2002), T. Mitchell (2002), Sewell (1980, 1996), Somers (1996), Wingrove (2000).

71 It is revealing, for instance, that Schabas (2002, 219) is ostensibly concerned with gaining autonomy for a "mature" field of economic history while emphasizing that this would help historians of economics "garner more respect from the economics profession." A truly autonomous discipline would presumably be less concerned with gaining respect from exterior disciplines.

72 This question was recently posed in different terms with respect to the differing European and U.S. orientations to military hegemony (Kagan 2003; Meyerson 2003); see also Fourcade-Gourinchas (2003).

PART ONE

*Positivism and Nonpositivism
in Twentieth-Century Social Science*

Estrangement, Intimacy, and the Objects
of Anthropology

WEBB KEANE

One of the mandates of this volume is to bring to light what George Steinmetz (this volume) has called the epistemological unconscious of the contemporary social sciences. In most cases, this has meant exposing the scientistic or objectivistic assumptions that underwrite the various paradigms that have dominated the respective disciplines. Given this context, it becomes apparent that cultural anthropology has a peculiar position among the other social sciences. Although the discipline presents us with a complex range of methods and a huge diversity of norms for what count as well-formed questions, significant evidence, and satisfactory answers, certain patterns are evident. The one I want to draw out in this chapter is that positivism, however understood (see Steinmetz's introduction to this volume), has *not* dominated the main currents of cultural anthropology in recent generations. To be sure, anthropology is a vast, unwieldy business and includes important work that is nearly indistinguishable from that of, say, certain kinds of statistical demographers, empirically oriented economists, or comparative political scientists. The traditional four-field department that includes biological or physical anthropology, linguistic anthropology, archaeology, and the social or cultural subfields persists, if in somewhat beleaguered form. Moreover, members of the various subfields often find close allies in neighboring disciplines in which classic scientific models are normative. Linguistic anthropologists, for instance, may work closely with cognitive scientists or developmental psychologists, archaeologists with demographers or geneticists, social anthropologists with economists or sociologists, and so forth. The combinations are fluid, the conjunctions sometimes surprising, and, compared to some fields, the lack of tightly regulated or hegemonic disciplinarity rather striking. This fluidity makes both generalization and prediction about the future course of anthropology even more difficult than it might be for other academic fields. Nonetheless, the thrust of this essay is to argue that if we confine ourselves to cultural anthropology, which numerically has always been by far the largest subfield, a discernible pattern is to be found.[1] I argue that cultural anthropology has long manifested a deeply embedded tendency to be resistant to positivism, however loosely defined. And I want to suggest some aspects of the subdiscipline's epistemological unconscious that might explain this.

Again, I must stress that even the subfield of cultural anthropology is not uniformly *anything*, much less "antipositivist" or, as critics sometimes put it, "antiscience." Rather, I want to account for the *relative* dominance of alternative understandings of the kind of knowledge anthropologists might seek and the kinds of objects of knowledge this presumes. To exemplify the problem, consider the enormous impact of the work of Clifford Geertz. From the 1970s at least up through the 1990s, he was by far the most frequently cited anthropologist (see Sewell 1999). Until his recent retirement from the founding professorship in social science at the Institute for Advanced Studies, his intellectual influence was matched by institutional centrality and the structural clout that goes with it. For more than a generation, other cultural anthropologists have had to somehow position themselves with respect to his work. He has been held responsible for cultural anthropology's purported lack of "predictability, replicability, verifiability, and law-generating capacity" (Shankman 1984, quoted in Sewell 1999, 35). My starting point is this: in most of the social sciences, such an accusation would, I take it, represent the voice of the established mainstream. In cultural anthropology, by way of contrast, it is the cry of those who see themselves having to *resist* a dominant style of thought.

It may even turn out, on close examination, that a majority of cultural anthropologists are, in fact, quietly practicing some manner of normal science. But it is significant that positivist models (broadly speaking) have *not* been established as normative for the field. In the light of the normative claims of such models of science for related disciplines, it is this that remains to be explained.

This essay is not about Geertz, about whose work it is hard to imagine there remains anything interesting still unsaid. It could be argued that the concept of culture he championed and the interpretive style he took that concept to require are no longer central to current work in the subdiscipline. At least, they meet strong competition from political economy and a variety of post- or anticulturalist starting points. Rather, I invoke him here to characterize the distinctive place of cultural anthropology among the social sciences. My claim is that Geertz's influence on the field is less a source of its present character than it is a *symptom* of an epistemological unconscious that is shared across a range of sometimes antagonistic approaches to anthropology. That is, to understand the peculiarity of cultural anthropology, we should look at what it is about the field that has made it so receptive to the influence of thinkers such as Geertz.

The state of play is, I propose, expressed by a remark by Jean and John Comaroff, whom no one would ever mistake for "Geertzians." Two influential anthropologists with solid roots in long-term fieldwork, the sobriety of British social anthropology, and the tough-minded realism of the Marxist tradition, they write that ethnography "refuses to put its trust in techniques that give more scientific methods their illusory objectivity: their commitment to standardized, a priori units of analysis, for example, or their reliance on a depersonalizing gaze that separates subject from object" (1992, 8). These words, offered almost in passing, express a fairly widespread perception among cultural anthropologists that certain important arguments are settled. In this view, it is no longer in much dispute that cultural anthropology is not merely at an "immature" stage, en route to something more akin to natural science. Most significant, perhaps, is the assumption that the separation of subject from object can be understood only in negative terms: that to say that a field of knowledge "depersonalizes" is ipso facto to discredit it. Yet, in their own ethnographic and historical work, the Comaroffs, like most of their colleagues, take their empirical materials very seriously and do *not* wholly reject the separation of subject from object. What is at issue, rather, is what kinds of objects and subjects, and what categories of analysis and comparison, are epistemologically appropriate and ethically legitimate for the study of social actions and self-understandings. It involves closely linked questions about purposes and values: How does what we take to be the object of doing anthropology determine what are, or should be, the objects of its knowledge?

The ultimate aim of this essay is to propose that we rethink the problem of "objectification" in the study of culture and society. A productive understanding of objectification should go beyond the commonplace critiques of scientism or ideological reification. It would take seriously the materiality of signifying practices and the ubiquity and necessity of conceptual objectification as a component of human action and interaction. But first I want to step back for a look at the way this point has come to be obscured for us. I begin by revisiting some old arguments about the nature of culture, meaning, and social science that have become a relatively taken-for-granted background shared by opponents in more recent debates about power, identities, and the observer. If, as I suggest, ethnographic knowledge has always been marked by a tension between epistemologies of estrangement and of intimacy, the latter has increasingly claimed the epistemological and moral high ground in much cultural anthropology, especially in the United States. The result is a number of familiar dilemmas about incommensurability, comparison, translation, and the possibilities for understanding. This essay focuses on the themes of antideterminism, meaning, agency, and particularism as they have marked U.S. cultural anthropology in contrast to much of the rest of social science. I want to suggest that there is more underlying unity across at least some of the battle lines than is commonly recognized.[2] But this unity is obscured not least because its roots in certain intuitions about freedom and agency are so deep, long-standing, and yet little examined. Although the current emphasis on intimacy and engagement and the suspicion of objectification are associated with postcolonial critique, practice theory, deconstruction, power/knowledge, and identity politics, I argue that its roots are deeper. To the extent that certain well-trod paths in anthropology converge with other antifoundationalist disciplines in an intellectual world informed more by, say, Nietzsche than by Comte, by the later Wittgenstein than Chomsky, they do so from a distinctive angle.[3]

In the first part of this essay, I sketch out some of the ways the Boasian, Weberian, and Durkheimian understandings of the objects and categories of sociocultural knowledge were transformed by the interpretive and symbolic turns in cultural anthropology in the 1960s and 1970s. I then look at two critiques of the culture concept, by Lila Abu-Lughod and by James Ferguson and Akhil Gupta, that exemplified the situation a generation or so later. Although both critiques are animated by problems of power, knowledge, and agency, they work toward opposite ends of the spectrum of intimacy and estrangement. Yet they share certain assumptions about meaning and determinism not only with each other, but with those whom they attack. These assumptions are shaped by an underlying, often unspoken ethic that stresses the value of human self-determination and opposes it both to reductionism and to mere contingency.

Thus, for example, the participants in one of the most notorious debates in anthropology in the previous generation, between Marshall Sahlins (1985, 1995) and Gananath Obeyesekere (1992) over the proper explanation of Captain Cook's death in Hawaii, remained within at least some of the parameters of interpretive rather than positivistic social science. The facts of what actually happened, after all, were in little dispute. Sahlins's and Obeyesekere's respective *ethical* claims—proper respect for indigenous agency, for instance—were inseparable from their *epistemological* assumptions. What was in question was an interpretation, as each asserted himself to hold the greater insight into how Hawaiians understood the British explorers.

This essay does not pretend to be a history, nor does it claim to be inclusive. Rather, it is an interested reading, which tries to draw out certain themes that run through the effort to place people's self-interpretations at the center of study and the privileging of intimacy over estrangement as a source of legitimate understanding. By retracing the logic of some of the earlier arguments about objectivism and "the particular," I hope to clarify their contribution to the present moment. If the central part of this essay focuses on the so-called symbolic and interpretive turns in the United States, it is because their enormous impact, in light of the dominance of scientism, positivism, and functionalisms elsewhere in the social sciences, is what most needs to be understood. It does, however, begin with the intuition that many of the contemporary debates can take place, their terms of relevance making sense to the participants, only to the extent that they are predicated on certain shared assumptions and even ethical motives evident in those earlier generations.

Anthropology and the Particulars

The antipositivism that I claim characterizes much of cultural anthropology at the beginning of the twenty-first century is, perhaps, stronger than it has ever been before. Yet the general resistance to positivistic models in some form or other has long been evident, if not always regnant. If positivism, for instance, aspires to create a unified field of sciences, anthropologists have long complained about their discipline's fragmentation (e.g., H. Moore 1999; Ortner 1984; Wolf 1980). Indeed, Franz Boas, the founder of U.S. academic anthropology, saw the field's dissolution as imminent sixty years ago (Stocking 1992b, 346; 1992a, 148). In which case, the discipline by now has been "dissolving" as long as it has been "united"—and, some might point out, with greater financial resources, more publications, and ever increasing numbers of participants. If positivism begins with the establishment of careful procedures of study, consider Marshall Sahlins's remarkably offhand discussion of his fieldwork methods of the 1950s, when he still identified himself as a scientific cultural ecologist: "As to anthropological field techniques, there is nothing new to say. I used the standard ones, having in each village a few outstanding, most-used informants. I interviewed, cross-checked, kept a daily journal, observed and took part in ceremonies and social gatherings, used the genealogical method, and did mostly as trained" (1962, 3). That's virtually all he has to say.

Crucial to the idea of positivism is the goal of nomothetic explanation, especially as expressed in abstract statements about general relations of cause and effect.[4] For proponents of nomothetic models of explanation, much of cultural anthropology is vitiated by excessive particularity, excessive concreteness, and favoring interpretation or description over causality. Almost forty years ago, Marvin Harris, who advocated a positivistic science of cultural evolution, complained that "there emerged a view of culture that exaggerated all the quixotic, irrational, and inscrutable ingredients in human life. Delighting in diversity of pattern, anthropologists sought out divergent and incomparable events. . . . By emphasizing inscrutable values, vain prestige, irrational motives, they discredited the economic interpretation of history. Anthropology came increasingly to concern itself with idiographic phenomena, that is, with the study of the unique and the nonrepetitive aspects of history" (1968, 1).

Although the complaint concerns the U.S. scene of an earlier generation, a similar objection has been expressed by scholars of very different perspectives and generations, from contemporary France (Sperber 1996) to England of the 1950s, when the structuralist Edmund Leach (1959/1961, 1) remarked, "Most of my colleagues are giving up the attempt to make comparative generalizations; instead they have begun to write impeccably detailed historical ethnographies of particular peoples." If anthropology can look too particularistic from several quite distinct points of view, it also seems to persist in whatever it is doing that provokes these complaints.

Some, of course, simply take this condition to be a symptom of confusion, incoherence, or worse. But I think we need to take it seriously as an approach to knowledge. There is something about what anthropology has been doing that, for all the shifts of paradigm and the fires of internal critique, continues to produce *both* the particularistic symptom *and* the theorizing complaint. If this is a dialectic, it is recurrently threatened with collapse when either side, what might be called the epistemologies of estrangement and of intimacy, is favored at the expense of the other. Although the U.S. academy has most elaborated the side of intimacy, the basic problems are of more general relevance.

The authority of ethnographic particularity for contemporary anthropologists is famously exemplified by Clifford Geertz, who asserted a generation ago that what anthropologists *do* is ethnography (rather than, say, theory building), which is "microscopic," and that "the important thing about anthropology's findings" (and not just its methods or data) "is their complex specificness, their circumstantiality" (1973d, 21–23; see also Ortner 1995). But the epistemological and ethical claims of concrete particularity were already laid out with remarkable vividness in 1887 by Franz Boas, before he became one of the founding figures of anthropology in the United States.[5] Like the historian, and in contrast to the natural scientist, Boas states, the geographer does not seek general laws, but rather "the thorough understanding of the phenomena" (1887/1940, 641) as singular facts. Not only is this interest in what actually exists for its own sake a legitimate alternative to the formulation of laws, the two are even antithetical: it is precisely *because* he or she takes an interest in them that the historian "is unwilling to consider" peoples and nations "as subject to stringent laws" (642). Boas here makes two distinct points at once. First, he poses as alternatives the taking of the singular as evidence for a law and as worthy of attention for its own sake. Second, these are not merely perspectives but are in conflict, for only when peoples are taken for their own sake can they be seen as agents and thus not subject to laws.[6] Thus, Boas can be read either to emphasize historical contingency or human agency; I suggest it is the latter that has tended to prevail.

But Boas makes two further, mutually implicated claims. In contrast to the physicist, who analytically resolves the phenomenon into its elements, the geographer takes "the whole phenomenon, and not its elements" as the object of study. Yet the geographer's phenomena have no objective unity at all, but form "an incidental conglomerate" (geology, meteorology, and so forth); "Their connection seems to be subjective, originating in the mind of the observer" (Boas 1887/1940, 642). By contrast, the physicist, in comparing elements taken out of context, "loses sight altogether of the spot from which he started" (646). Our interest is a matter of contingency: the motive of cosmography is "love for the country we inhabit" (647), in contrast to the naturalist, who views the whole world disinterestedly. The Grand Canyon is interesting because it exists for me, as part of *my world.* Its weather, color, age, and size, each of which could be analytically distinguished for purposes of comparison to those of other physical entities, form an object only insofar as they are unified within my experience. That is, the very unity of the geographer's object of study is conditional on the situated character of human experience, which is what *motivates* the interest in the object in the first place.

This is a very peculiar kind of knowledge, and, as I suggest below, it encounters serious dilemmas that are both epistemological (what kind of starting point can something as problematic as "experience" possibly offer?) and ethical (whose "country" is this, anyway?). But I propose that in this foundational moment Boas named something peculiar about a kind of knowing that might be sought by a human science that survived the demise of his own school and that predisposed it toward the antifoundationalist thought of the twentieth century.

The High Positivist Moment

Remarkably, positivism failed to achieve an entirely stable hegemony even in the heyday of modernist optimism about the sciences in the 1950s and 1960s.[7] After World War II, anthropology, like much of the Third World it studied, seemed poised for developmental takeoff. In the teleological narrative common to the era, it was about to become a true science. This vision was supported by the field's demographic explosion, expanded sources of funding, new fieldwork realities, and a sense of mission to aid the development of the Third World (Murphy 1976). Such social engineering seemed to require a predictive social science. Thus, Marvin Harris said he aimed "to reassert the methodological priority of the search for the laws of history in the science of man. There is an urgency associated with this rededication . . . [especially given] the role anthropologists have been asked to assume in the planning and carrying out of international development programs" (1968, 3).

Three versions of positivist anthropology became apparent in the 1950s.[8] These might be arranged in terms of their degrees of relative commitment to the development of nomothetic laws and the level of abstraction to which they aspired. At the most empiricist end was George Peter Murdock's (1949) Cross Cultural Survey and Human Relations Area Files, aiming by means of statistical correlations to establish a firm typology of social forms that would permit comparison across all cases. British structural-functionalism, which had emerged out of Durkheimian functionalism, also made relatively modest claims to offering scientific laws (Radcliffe-Brown 1952). The most ambitious effort to create a "science of culture" was that of the cultural evolutionists Julian Steward (1949/1976, 1955) and Leslie White (1949). Despite varying degrees of success, none of these three was able definitively to set the agenda for the field for long. To clarify the terms of their failure, I will briefly sketch a few of the central assumptions that became issues for their critics beginning in the late 1950s.

The evolutionists held the goal of social science to be the discovery of the laws of history, by which they meant evolutionary processes. In Harris's words, "Similar technologies applied to similar environments tend to produce similar arrangements of labor in production and distribution, and . . . these in turn call forth similar kinds of social groupings, which justify and coordinate their activities by means of similar systems of values and beliefs" (1968, 4).

This simple assertion displays many of the terms in which positivism rose and fell. First, materialism: the assumption that the causal arrow points from things to ideas. Second, the hierarchical ordering of the phenomena, with a technological base, a mediating social organization, and finally, the domain of "values and beliefs." Third, reductionism: that is, it follows from the first two premises that a satisfactory explanation will lead one to some more fundamental, truly causal level than that of the socio-cultural phenomena being explained as having been caused.

Culture, Context, and the Ends of Action

From the 1960s onward, an antireductionist reaction increasingly set the agenda in U.S. cultural anthropology. It was several decades before the influence of the early materialists took on high visibility again (notably by way of Eric Wolf [1982, 2001], who spanned the era), with the revival of Marxist approaches to cultural anthropology. Yet, even then, the newly powerful Marxist, political economic, and ecological forms of anthropology did not attempt to return to the large model-building and reductionistic explanations that had characterized the earlier generations. Marx was back in strong form, but he was no longer read as a social evolutionist. Instead, the frame was provided by such figures as Antonio Gramsci (1971b), Pierre Bourdieu (1972/1977), Ernesto Laclau and Chantal Mouffe (1985), Raymond Williams (1977), and others. Too many of the objections raised in the 1960s and 1970s had to be taken seriously, and it was these others who seemed to offer resolutions.

What were the objections that demanded a response? Here I want to trace just a few themes through certain texts, with particular attention to the unlikely convergence among structuralism, Boasian culturalism, symbolic anthropology, and the interpretive turn, which developed Boas's interest in freedom at the expense of contingency.[9] Marshall Sahlins is an exemplary figure with whom to start because he himself, once a student and colleague of White, Service, and Harris, made the transition from a nomothetic model of science, and because he offered a rebuttal of positivism and functionalism that did not require one to abandon an idea of objective knowledge. Moreover, his appropriation of structuralism manifests the sea change undergone by French thought in the U.S. context, as its positivistic potential was muted in favor of the symbolic turn.

The study of linguistic sound systems by Boas (1910) and Edward Sapir (1925/1949a) and Ferdinand de Saussure's structuralism as elaborated by Claude Lévi-Strauss (1962/1968) showed that entities that, in strictly empirical terms, seem to be identical may in fact have quite different functions when analyzed in the context of different sound systems. It follows that no sound can *even be identified* independently of the linguistic system that specifies its relevant features. Taking this as foundational, Sahlins offers a critical difference from his teachers and contemporaries, such as Harris, Service, and White. The difference does *not* concern the nature of the material world, causality, or the hope for objectivity. Rather, it lies in the conditions for establishing identity among observed entities. The argument from language forms a direct challenge to the possibility of specifying social or cultural units across the board. This kind of analysis depends on a concept of context that presumes three things, namely, that languages are best understood as total systems, that they are clearly bounded from one another, and that the units (being only "arbitrarily" connected to the object world) have no functionality apart from that of the overall system of which they are a part.

Much of Sahlins's writing is a defense and elaboration of these points.[10] Now, because it is common for critics to label him a "cultural determinist," he would seem to present an especially hard case for my claim that human self-determination has been a core value in U.S. cultural anthropology. It is not my purpose to rehash the many debates about his work, but simply to point out the extent to which it offers a series of arguments against any purported "external" determinations of cultural form such as biology, ecology, or economics. Even before his full turn to structuralism, he was already arguing (1968/1972) that some societies have opted out of the maximization of material gain in favor of greater leisure time, and therefore cultures are not adaptive according to a single standard of utility or rational choice. Culture is thus in essence excessive (it goes beyond the demands of reproduction) and irrational, or at least, not in itself explicable in terms of means-ends rationality (because it defines the very terms by which things are valued as ends, it is exogenous to rational calculation). It manifests human self-creation at the level of communities. If this point has become difficult to see, it is in part because the very idea of collectivities has been put in question in the contemporary United States.

Sahlins's attack on determinism is linked to a second, logically independent, assertion: that cultures can be understood as ethical or aesthetic unities. Sahlins himself attributes his view of culture as a unified ethos to Alfred Kroeber's (1917) "superorganic," that which is distinctively human by virtue of not having "organic" or biological determinants. It is thus ironic, in view of later attacks on cultural holism in the name of agency, that it is precisely this unity that was supposed to provide humans with their independence from external determination. It is in the nature of moral or aesthetic ends that they impose a unity on the diverse activities to which they provide guidance.[11]

In Sahlins's work, holism helps explain culture's nonutilitarian character. Culture cannot be a thing of "shreds and patches" (Lowie 1920, 441), because those could never provide a context that would give coherence to ultimate ends. The underlying assumption is the relative underdetermination of significance. And this in turn is associated with an ontological distinction between material and conceptual that is already evident, for example, both in Kroeber and in Saussure's doctrine of the arbitrariness of the sign. That interpretation of material reality is mediated conceptually had become a commonplace. But the symbolic does not simply mediate *reference* to the things that exist in the world (a system of categories that tells us this is blue, that green, or this a wink, that a twitch). More than that, it facilitates questions of *ends* and their value. Sahlins's "culture," taken as existential stances toward life, seeks to provide an account of ends. It is meant to show, for instance, that economic maximization is a choice (one rejected by his "original affluent society"; 1968/1972), not a given, something the West is driven toward not by the facts of the matter, but by an underlying vision of humans as "imperfect creature[s] of need and desire" (1988/2000, 453–454).

Culture in Its Own Terms

The symbolic and interpretive turns are perhaps most commonly identified with Victor Turner (1967), Mary Douglas (1966), and Clifford Geertz (1973a, 1973d), and arguments for irreducible cultural specificity are found well beyond them (e.g., Louis Dumont 1966/1970). I draw here on David Schneider because of the polemical sharpness and explicitness with which he articulated some of the more radical criticisms of comparison and displayed the conceptual links among particularism, totality, and cultural value.

Schneider's attack on structural-functionalism involves five logical steps. First is an attack on superficial empiricism and the production of simplistic models. Second, he challenged the idea that societies lend themselves to scientific comparison because they fall into objectively given types. Third, if societies are not natural things, then the categories by which they had heretofore been compared must be ethnocentric. Fourth, if the categories are not universal, then any analysis that uses them is taking its data out of context, and instead (fifth), the appropriate context within which to make sense of cultural categories is "the cultural system." None of these steps logically requires the subsequent one. For instance, the first criticism alone could simply have led to a call for better categories and more complex models. The third could have led him to construct Weberian ideal types for analytic purposes. Instead, Schneider ends up discrediting categories, models, generalities, and comparison altogether.

The reasons for this can be seen by considering the second step, exemplified in the statement "It is too late in the history of the social sciences to think we can go out among societies and, by keeping our eyes open, sort them out into their natural classes" (Schneider 1965, 78). Where neopositivism would jettison the sociocultural level of explanation in the name of sound methods, Schneider sought to preserve the level of explanation by abandoning an inappropriate method. Indeed, he writes as if this were a foregone conclusion. The attack on empiricism as ethnocentric and thus unrealistic (that is, not true to ethnographic particulars) became an attack on sociological comparison.

Instead, Schneider maintained that anthropology's purpose is the study of cultures as "different conceptual schemes of what life is and how it should be lived" (1972, 44). Notice here the implicit role of the normative: cultures are concerned with how life *should* be lived. Such a definition seems to express an underlying commitment to the empirical study of self-determination, insofar as cultures manifest a generic capacity to *decide* how to live. But in this view, the normative is above all *conceptual* in status; indeed, Schneider (1976, 202–203) eventually took a strong position against any cultural determination of action. Formed, like Geertz, in Talcott Parsons's milieu, Schneider presumed a clear distinction between social and cultural systems and insisted that culture was distinct from actual behavior.[12] In the struggle to distinguish social from natural science and to escape functionalism and determinism, the value orientation I have noted was often neglected in favor of concepts. What is important about culture here is that it imposes meaningful (and, by implication, arbitrary) categories on an otherwise meaningless and unorganized world. This is one reason culture came to be identified, for some, with structure and in sharp opposition to agency. Geertz (1973a, 443) quoted W. H. Auden to exemplify his antifunctionalist view of culture: "Poetry makes nothing happen."

With the destruction of the cross-cultural category "kinship," Schneider (1972) produced òne template for postmodern particularisms in anthropology. Cultural categories for Schneider could only be understood in the context of the entire "cultural system." Though he was no structuralist, the logic is close to that of the arbitrary sign. Thus, kinship or gender categories, for instance, cannot be compared across cultures because the apparent biological referents do not reflect their articulation with other components of a given culture. It is at this juncture, in justifying the autonomy, relatively undetermined character, and holism of cultures, that the potentially opposed forces of symbolic anthropology and structuralism made common cause. Schneider and Sahlins differed on much, but they shared an underlying vision that human projects are more than aleatory *only to the extent that* they are identified with a cultural, and thus collective, enterprise. As I suggest below, subsequent critics of the concept of culture attacked its totalizing character, but they commonly did so on the antiempiricist and antideterminist grounds that were established by these earlier arguments. And herein lies one basis for the more radical conclusion that "cultural meanings" are irreducible and therefore potentially incommensurable and untranslatable (see Chakrabarty 2000; Povinelli 2001; Steinmetz forthcoming b).

Metalanguages of Agency

What kind of knowledge ought we to hope for from this? Perhaps the most conventional answer is a richer access to "meanings." One of the founding statements for this approach is Geertz's (1973d) appropriation of Gilbert Ryles's "thick description" for anthropology and his image of the anthropologist reading a cultural text over the native's shoulder (1973a; see also Ricoeur 1971). The debates about this are well-known. But I want to draw out an aspect of these meanings that is sometimes neglected: their implicit relationship to action. The philosopher Charles Taylor, in his contribution to Rabinow and Sullivan's seminal volume *Interpretive Social Science* (1971/1987), gives an especially clear account of what that "text" is doing for the person's capacity to be an agent. I suggest that a critical reading of this account can usefully be brought to bear on subsequent critiques, especially on the assumptions they make about the necessarily malign effects of objectification. If the interpretive turn was attacked from one side for lacking the rigor of natural science, it has increasingly been attacked from another side for objectifying and essentializing culture. But what Taylor's account should make clear, whatever its shortcomings, is that we can understand the object of interpretation to be, not categories and meanings per se, but the very capacity for agency that they mediate. By extension, we can see one opening to other social dimensions of power.

Taylor defines a text as a metalanguage, an expression that captures the same meaning as some original "text analogue."[13] This meaning is not simply semantic or expressive, and Geertz's portrayal of culture as something like a Shakespearian drama read over the native's shoulder turns out to be a poor illustration, as do many efforts in more recent cultural studies to link cultural forms directly to political positions. Rather, Taylor's account of "the meaning of a situation for an agent" (1971/1987, 42) centers on the purposiveness and the self-consciousness (and implicit bracketing of contingency) that distinguish action from mere behavior, and hearkens back to Max Weber's (1968) definition of the proper object of interpretive social science as meaningful action.

What kind of object of knowledge is this? For Taylor, "descriptions [of action] are not all on the same footing" (1985a, 259): "As I type, I am also displacing air, raising the noise level in the house, wearing out typewriter ribbons, increasing the custom of our local typing supplies shop, and so on. But what I'm *doing* is writing a paper."

Some obvious objections: Why, after all, stop with "writing a paper"? What of seeking fame, or a promotion, or to best an opponent, or to make mother proud, or to avoid facing a troubled domestic life? What of expressing a bourgeois worldview or a male subject position? What of a habitus for which the writing of papers is a naturalized mode of action regardless of individual intentions, like, say, a ritual?

Taylor claims that ordinary language serves as a metalanguage (reflexive language about action) that both defines actions for the actor and makes them available for the interpreting outsider. Its role in defining the boundaries of action explains why interpretation is not unbounded. We need to be specific about what this metalanguage does and does not offer us. Taylor is arguing against the objectivist metalanguages of positivist social science. Therefore, the crucial point is to show that actions depend on self-interpretation. In this respect, the outsider's metalanguages of class or gender, unconscious desires, and so forth are not immediately pertinent. The crucial metalanguage is that which guides the actor *himself or herself* with a description of what is going on. But intuitive introspection is not sufficient, for that description must be drawn from a vocabulary of actions shared with others, and it comes into play when one is accounting for one's own actions *to* them. Shared language provides a "public space, or common vantage point" (1985a, 273; compare 1971/1987, 59–61) that persons can share and *know that they share*. The alternative descriptions I have just offered may count as descriptions *of someone else* but they are not likely to function either in the agent's *own* self-accounting or in his or her sense of being with others.

A generation later, however, those who take the question of objectivism as settled may ask different questions of this account. First, who owes an account to whom? The existence of a shared moral domain, Taylor's "public," and the conditions that call for an accounting have become unobvious. If accounting to others is interaction, it is likely to occur between people with unequal capacities and claims on one another, their very status as "insiders" to the same community potentially subject to question. Second, the existence of a moral domain does not guarantee shared descriptions of action. The husband who insists on his conjugal rights confronts the wife who fears domestic rape; the joker's "fun" is the victim's "ethnic slur."[14] Third, as the development of the category "domestic rape" suggests, the contest of interpretations involves a historical dynamic, in which, for example, emergent descriptions will have "looping effects" (Hacking 1995) as they provide actors with new kinds of action. Finally, "culture's" relation to "society" is altered from the sharp distinction maintained by Parsonians if, as Taylor implies, it is not just sharing a culture but *awareness* of sharing it that forms a pragmatic condition for having a community (Urban 2001) or a public (Appadurai 1990/1996a) in the first place.

The actions that most concern Taylor are those that require terminology like "shame" and thus "a certain language of mutual action and communication by which we blame, exhort, admire, esteem each other" (1971/1987, 43). By acting we make ourselves available to evaluations by others. Hence, cultural interpretation is possible because the interpreter, in principle, has available the very same interpretive possibilities that the insider has (46). They cannot, at least in principle, be radically "other" to one another—at least as long as the interpreter situates himself or herself within the moral sphere defining the actor's "public."

At this point, Taylor's account captures some essential strengths and weaknesses of the interpretive turn in its heyday. By showing that the local relevant terms for self-interpretation are necessary conditions for action, he helps fill out the argument for the particular. Local metalanguages demand an epistemology of intimacy. Indeed, they demand more, for it is not just a question of "perspective." For if metalanguages of action mediate people's moral engagement with one another, what of the anthropologist's traditional licence to enter and leave communities with ease, exempt from the give and take of claims making? Certain Native American groups, for instance, have come simply to deny it altogether.

But an epistemology of intimacy, if necessary, is not sufficient. First, to the extent that metalanguages are not merely neutral guides to action but part of the discourse of self-justification, they offer poor purchase for certain kinds of critical insight, help in sorting through the unequal relations among counterclaims, or understanding which of them wins out. And so the lineage I have sketched here has been confronted by, and often grafted to, critical theory, postcolonialism, Marxism, and feminism. Second, intimacy alone does not help us understand in semiotic, pragmatic, or cognitive terms what metalanguages are possible or likely, what forms they may take, and how those forms have consequences. Interpretation too often moved directly to "meaning" without, for example, analyzing how those meanings are objectified and circulate in public. Both of these points suggest that an epistemology of estrangement is crucial.

What does turning text analogues into texts do? As Taylor (1971/1987, 46–47) remarks, once interpretation is internalized, it changes the actor. Consider his example of religious beliefs learned in a colonial missionary school. They are held only by individual subjects, in contrast to the circumstances of "the same" beliefs in the missionary's own society, where, being part of the background domain of "common meanings," they are known by all members of that society to *be* meanings they share (58). They are *still* part of the common meanings of the home society even for atheists who have rejected them (what might today be called "contestation"), in contrast to the missionized subject who accepts them, but in the context of a different set of common meanings. The distinction introduces one critical difference between the domain of actions and the metalanguages that might interpret them. Today's anthropologists might find it not coincidental that this distinction occurs precisely across the nonreciprocal space between colonizer and colonized.

In addition, the beliefs taught in the missionary school are introduced in an explicit form. They are, that is, doctrines to which one could give or withhold one's adherence (Asad 1993). Their epistemic and practical status is quite distinct from, say, Bourdieu's "habitus," Foucault's "discipline," or "iterable" sign forms to which no particular belief can be securely attached (Derrida 1972/1982). To the extent that what Taylor calls common meanings are objectified as cultural metalanguages, they have a status distinct from the domain of unselfconscious practices: the stuff of culture in the Boasian tradition, or of everyday frames for action (Bateson 1955/1972;

Goffman 1974). They are forms that exist apart from actors and face them as texts to be read from outside.

Where is one standing when one stands outside that text? To privilege the agent's own description of the action, especially as it is linked to intentionality, commonly presupposes a sovereign self-consciousness, a figure whose increasingly spectral character for psychological, psychoanalytic, and political thought I need not rehearse here. But explicit descriptions of action raise other questions as well. As Gilbert Ryle (1946) long ago pointed out, to transform "knowing how" into the object of "knowing that" is to change its very nature. Because Taylor's main concern is to argue against efforts to determine interpretation-free objects of social science on the model of natural science, he leaves this question largely unexamined. Nor is the distinction merely epistemological or cognitive (though it is those, too; Chaiklin and Lave 1993). Bourdieu (1972/1977), for instance, argues that "officializing" and "synoptic" metalanguages manifest a distance from practical activity that only the privileged can enjoy. But, lest we conclude that none but the powerful have access to the self-consciousness afforded by metalanguages, we must allow for a much wider range of modes of self-objectification. These may derive from everything from ritual distantiation (Keane 1995) to the alienation of the oppressed (J. C. Scott 1990).[15] And these are insights the epistemology of intimacy cannot offer by itself. The lack of further inquiry into the character of metalanguages and their role in the processes of objectification and the transformations of social self-consciousness has remained a persistent weakness in the interpretive approach as well as for many of its critics.

What I want to stress here is the centrality of agency to the subject implied by certain features of the interpretive turn. Moreover, Taylor's rejection of positivism implies that positivism necessarily eliminates agency for *both* the object of knowledge *and* the knowing subject—and thus, their capacity to forge, out of the contest among competing interpretations, new, more insightful, metalanguages *together.*

The Call for More Particularity

In the previous section, I characterized certain themes at the heart of U.S. cultural anthropology's interpretive turn during the 1960s and 1970s. I suggested that a rejection of comparative categories in favor of particularism and an epistemology of intimacy, and an underlying antideterminism, became part of the taken-for-granted across much of cultural anthropology. But by the end of the next decade, the discipline seemed increasingly riven with hotly contested divisions and sometimes acidic self-critique. There are many reasons for this, including the postindependence transformations of formerly colonial field sites, challenges to the Euro-American dominance of representations, the politics of identities, and legitimation crisis in the academy. In theoretical terms, these forces commonly added vigor to poststructuralist challenges to coherent and totalizing models, a revival of more culturally inflected Marxism and critical theory, and the Foucauldian development of the Nietzschean thesis that the critique of knowledge must go beyond disowning claims to objectivity and reveal its inseparability from the power that produces it.

Nonetheless, I suggest that *some* aspects of these critiques were animated by the same general assumptions and values as their targets'. Indeed, certain debates could transpire only to the extent that the participants agreed on what was most important (thus their greater impact in anthropology than, say, sociology; see Steinmetz essay "Sociology" in this volume). For all their differences, many protagonists in the debates can be understood as competing over whose approach better recognizes human agency and self-determination. To exemplify this I turn to Lila Abu-Lughod's "Writing against Culture" (1991) and Akhil Gupta and James Ferguson's "Beyond 'Culture': Space, Identity, and the Politics of Difference" (1992/1997). Although these essays are over a decade old, they remain exemplary of two prominent, if distinct, directions for contemporary internal critiques of anthropology. Both raise important questions about the identity, coherence, and power relations of the "we" that has been tacitly presupposed by anthropological discourse. Both respond to the changing status of particularism when ethnographic attention shifts to colonialism and globalization. Both are concerned with the politics and ethics of representing "otherness" and take as a touchstone Clifford and Marcus's *Writing Culture* (1986), which is both apotheosis and immanent critique of the textualism of the interpretive turn. In their efforts to provide an alternative to "culture," however, they would push the anthropologist to opposed ends of the anthropological dialectic, Abu-Lughod inward, toward individual subjectivities, Gupta and Ferguson outward, toward global political-economic forces. And yet, I argue, they remain within the parameters developed in the genealogy I am tracing, sharing the high value it places on agency and a tendency to associate agency with self-interpretation.

Lila Abu-Lughod has been an especially eloquent exponent of anthropology's responsibilities to multiple constituencies. Certainly since September 2001, her call to humanize the Muslim world for Euro-Americans remains urgent. My concern here is her assertion that the culture concept is inherently a vehicle of unequal power between knower and known because it does violence to the actualities of lived experience. To be sure, her portrayal is a straw man, for few anthropologists have ever seen people as "robots programmed with 'cultural' rules" (1991, 158), and traditional fieldwork would have been impossible if they really thought there was "a fundamental distinction between self and other" (137). But this is the stuff of polemics, and we might charitably reframe her question: the Boasian geographer can treat the Grand Canyon as a unity because it can be taken as a given that the canyon is in "his or her own" world. But who am "I," and what is "my" world such that "Bedouin culture" is "in" it? The question has become unavoidable (see Appadurai 1986; Asad 1973; Clifford 1988; Coronil 1996; Dirks 1992; Fabian 1983; Ortner 1995; Said 1978; Trouillot 1991).

There have been two common strategies for responding to the problem by restaging anthropology's claims to an epistemology of intimacy. One is to present oneself as a mere reporter of others' stories. Yet, of course, stories are not transparent; indeed, even simple transcription already implies theoretical choices (Ochs 1979), to say nothing of the pragmatics of interaction (C. Briggs 1984) and the politics of choosing among the stories that result (F. Myers 1988; Steinmetz 1992). Speaking in a singular or monologic "voice"—and thus, with a singular social identity relative to a clear and distinct project—is the highly marked outcome of political effort rather than a natural or neutral condition (see Bakhtin 1981; Hanks 1996; Hill and Irvine 1992; Irvine 1996; Lee 1997; Voloshinov 1930/1973b).

The second strategy is to claim some identity with the people being represented. But on what grounds? For clearly, there are innumerable dimensions along which preexisting identification can be asserted, denied, or confused (Alcoff 1991; Bhabha 1994b; Butler 1997; Caton 1999), and the resulting reification itself can be dangerous (Said 1993). Indeed, it is not only outsiders who betray intimacies (Herzfeld 1997). Moreover, as Susan Harding (1991) has observed, strategies that link insight directly to political identification with those one studies also fare poorly in the case of "the repugnant other," in her case, the radical Christian right, with whom one does not sympathize. How one defines the communities within which one has moral commitments cannot be given entirely in advance.

If, as I have suggested, the models of culture that were dominant by the 1970s were motivated in part by the effort to demonstrate a locus of autonomy for human enterprises, they share with Abu-Lughod's "humanism" an underlying antideterminism. To be sure, they seek that autonomy at very distinct planes. For the former, self-determination is collective; for the latter, individual. But both take as their starting place an ethical commitment to an object of study that is not reduced to external determinants, and both seek its confirmation in people's self-interpretations, linked to an ideology of the particular.

Consider Abu-Lughod's (1991, 145) proposal that anthropologists write " 'ethnographies of the particular' as instruments of tactical humanism," stressing specificity and internal complexity over generality and simplicity. She is writing in a long, if unacknowledged, tradition. Anthropologists have claimed to humanize others, however naïvely or paternalistically, at least since Lewis Henry Morgan (1851, ix) opened his study of the Iroquois by declaring his aim was "to encourage a kinder feeling towards the Indian, founded upon a truer knowledge of his civil and domestic institutions." Much, of course, depends on what *counts* toward that goal. Whereas Morgan would humanize the Iroquois by showing them to have *institutions* comparable to those of Europeans, Abu-Lughod would humanize the Arabs by showing them to have similar *subjectivities*. Other matters aside, the latter strategy risks what she herself characterizes as a "public display of family secrets" (159), or, more generally, perhaps, a violation of what Michael Herzfeld (1997) calls "cultural intimacy."

Given the considerable risk of betrayal, what justifies this approach? Only by viewing individuals, Abu-Lughod asserts, can one restore to people their actuality as doers. We must shift away from the metalanguages that they share with one another, which Taylor sees as the very condition for the possibility of agency. Rather, Abu-Lughod seems to imply that what is shared with others functions only as a constraint. Throughout, her focus is on conscious experience, taken as a foundation for intimate knowledge.

There is a paradox here.[16] It arises, in part, from conflating the metalanguages that mediate actions and those an outsider to the action might construct about them. By trying to reject the latter, Abu-Lughod ends up treating the former as transparent, and, in effect, she silently smuggles in her own metalanguages to replace them. Consider her interest in how people go "through their life agonizing over decisions, making mistakes, trying to make ourselves look good, enduring tragedies and personal losses, enjoying others, and finding moments of happiness" (1991, 158). Can we understand why people can anticipate and make sense of what happens now, what happened before, what might happen, what could never happen, what had better not happen simply by appealing to "how life is lived"? Yet even such apparently natural and intuitively obvious concepts are not immediately present to the senses but depend on some mode of self-interpretation, and thus some potential for self-objectification.

Abu-Lughod's (1991, 154–156) specific example of what a humanistic ethnography of the particular would consist of requires both author and reader to accept as transparent certain categories such as piety, immorality, the unthinkable, nostalgia, honor, reputation, authority, and prayer. This is what lends her "humanism" its sense of intimacy and familiarity. For this view of humanism assumes there is nothing problematic about ordinary language, as if we had full mastery of it and as if it did not bring all sorts of things into our lives, including both tacit values and modes of self-deception and domination. To point this out, I think, does not mean that others are not like us. Rather, the point is that even we (whoever that problematic category might be) are not fully transparent to ourselves.[17] By favoring the epistemology of intimacy, Abu-Lughod pushes anthropology toward the concreteness of fieldwork and virtually eliminates, or renders covert, the analytical distance that follows it.[18] Note the irony: whereas the individual in a Boasian life history is supposed to be "typical" of a status, role, or community, Abu-Lughod's particulars offer us individuals who, in the final instance, seem to be typical at the *greatest* level of social generality altogether: of humanity writ large.

The Call for Greater Scope

Akhil Gupta and James Ferguson (1992/1997), although oriented by similar political concerns about power and identity, exemplify the important, indeed, many would argue crucial, effort to push anthropology in the opposite direction, broadening in spatial and temporal terms what counts as the relevant context. Abu-Lughod dispenses with the question of "larger forces" by asserting that "because these 'forces' are only embodied in the actions of individuals living in time and place, ethnographies of the particular capture them best" (1991, 156). In contrast, Gupta and Ferguson follow the lead of earlier writers such as E. E. Evans-Pritchard (1961/1962) and Bernard Cohn (1980), who argued for greater historical awareness in anthropology on the grounds that too close a focus—a perspective restricted only to what one can see in fieldwork—tends to *conceal* the workings of such larger forces.

Because it is easy to read Gupta and Ferguson as part of a turn to political economy, I want to draw attention to the other term in their discussion. "Culture" plays several conflicting roles in their writing. First, it refers to discrete public categories of identity. For example, they quote a man from Birmingham, England, discussing the mix of ethnicities in northern England (1992/1997, 38, from Hebdige 1979). As their use of the tag "young white reggae fan" suggests (his own self-description being "I'm just a broad person"), this man's identity lies in his own hands, an active mode of self-construction. It is largely a matter of allegiances, manifested in choices among coexisting options for expression and consumption. Although this view of culture shares a great deal with the externally imposed reifications Abu-Lughod criticizes, here, by contrast, it implies conscious self-possession, in contrast to the unconscious habits of Boasian culture.[19]

But as a bounded whole, culture *denies* self-creation, involving "supposedly natural connections between peoples and places" (Gupta and Ferguson 1992/1997, 39; see Appadurai 1986, 1988). Yet this naturalization in turn stands opposed to "cultural construction" (Gupta and Ferguson 1992/1997, 36), a mode of self-creation that it suppresses. The latter includes "conceptual processes of place making" by which "space is made meaningful" (39–40). As they note, this emphasis on imagination and meaning has been well established in anthropology since Durkheim and Mauss (1903/1963), and their use of the modifier "cultural" seems to point to how humans impose meaning on an otherwise meaningless world. It poses, and valorizes, what humans create, over against mere givens, non-human determinants. One might recall here Boas's geographer, for whom the unity of the Grand Canyon exists not in nature but by virtue of his or her relationship to it.

Where Gupta and Ferguson see themselves differing from earlier anthropologists is in asking Who has the power to make places of spaces? Who contests this? Now, one might ask cui bono, even of agentless structures. But Gupta and Ferguson seek an agent. At this point, they face a dilemma, for they seem to reproduce an earlier dichotomy between the meaningful and the material, locating agency in the former but subjecting it to power derived from "political-economic determinations that have a logic of their own" (1992/1997, 40). To analyze power, therefore, ultimately requires one to turn away from self-interpretation and toward the entities, forces, and causalities captured by an observer's independent categories of analysis.

If Abu-Lughod pushes anthropology toward particularities at the expense of any capacity to make a comparative claim, Gupta and Ferguson seem, at moments, on the verge of heading in the opposite direction, toward a general political economy whose workings transcend particulars —not just physical localities—to provide an ultimate foundation for explanation. At the far end of that trajectory, perhaps, the concept of power threatens to become less a way of identifying the effects of actions and circumstances than of postulating their autonomous cause. And now we might find ourselves back at Abu-Lughod's side to ask, Can this perspective give an account not only of "who contests" but to what ends, in light of what values and desires, and guided by what imaginable possibilities or presumed constraints? To the extent that such an approach presupposes an opposition between "cultural" processes and "political-economic determinations," it is in danger of reproducing the separation of meaning and values from causality and action, granting, perhaps, too much to *both* sides of the opposition. At that point, the relative freedom of self-interpretation becomes a function of its distance from power.[20]

The Self and the Interpretation in Self-Interpretation

My discussion of Taylor should suggest, first, that to understand even personal experience requires a capacity to shift between epistemologies of intimacy and of estrangement. Second, this very capacity for shifting is *already* inherent to experience, action, and self-understanding. But does not estrangement lead to betrayal or reification, as Abu-Lughod claims? I suggest that, real as these dangers are, they do not inhere in either objectification or metalanguages per se. And clarifying the distinctions among kinds of objectification and their roles in social action may help us reconfigure what kinds of knowledge the human sciences might claim. To ask "What are you doing?" seeks your language of self-description. To answer it requires both close understanding and its externalization. But the question, *even if asked of oneself*, sees actions as a problem in search of a response, a stance that opens out toward estrangement and the possibility of reformulation, of new answers. This becomes apparent when the question provokes reflection on what is otherwise tacit. As E. Valentine Daniel (1996) puts it, anthropological dialogue is like the disruption of habit that can produce objectification. And, one might add, no one ever lives by unreflecting habit alone.

Disruption and objectification are already innate possibilities, because metalanguages of action are not simply for "me," private and conceptual; they are also for "you." They are thus subject to objectification and circulation in semiotic form. As semiotic forms, they circulate publicly and are realized materially. Metalanguages are therefore not simply more or less arbitrary interpretations of a world. Rather, they are *causally* linked to material processes along several dimensions and in multiple directions. Semiotic forms are not arbitrary in the Saussurean sense and do not merely exist in a separate, disembodied world of ideas. If, for example, they purport to resemble their object, they depend on the specific qualities of things. If they are indexical, in Peircean terminology (Peirce 1955), such as knowledge, skills, habits, distinctive possessions, class and regional accents, they are subject to scarcity and causality and thus exist in dynamic articulation with political economy and social institutions (see Bourdieu 1979/1984). This should figure into any analysis of power's authority, without collapsing authority into power (see Keane 1997).

Conversely, objectifications are subject to recontextualization embedded in actions. In contrast to the romantic critique of objectification as, say, inherently alienating or a violation of self-presence (see Miller 1987), whether objectification is negative or not is a function of who I am for you and what epistemic status I accord that moment of objectification. Actions and tacit knowledge, for instance, are neither encompassed by nor ultimate foundations for explicit self-interpretation or even further metalanguages, because all enter into ongoing transformations of one another. This is one reason it is a mistake to align "meaning" with the conceptual in a domain of freedom, over against "materiality" in a domain of determinism. Objectification puts actions and actors at risk by giving them semiotic (thus public) form and changing their epistemic and pragmatic status (see Keane 1995, 1997). But, far from being only a disease of social science, this is the very politics of everyday awareness and interaction.[21]

Local metalanguages, however, cannot in themselves provide a sufficient account of action. Even as guides to self-understanding they cannot simply replace tacit know-how or intuitions of value.[22] They must be understood for what they are: potentially explicit objectifications that mediate but do not fully ground the actions within which they are situated. Narrative, for instance, has long been posed as an alternative to totalizing and distancing formulations. But narratives are not simply waiting for listeners to come along; they are crystallized contextual moments of explicitness, discursive actions that turn other actions, other contexts, into texts recognizable within genres (Bakhtin 1986).[23] Contrary to Abu-Lughod's (1991, 158) assumption, so-called ordinary and distancing discourses do not exist in isolation from one another. As Bakhtin pointed out, the languages of officials, experts, journalists, and so forth saturate so-called everyday speech with varying degrees and kinds of authority.[24] And local metalanguages are not exhaustive; they neither can nor aim to specify everything socially or conceptually relevant about an action or its context but only what is selected by the publicly available terms for the self-awareness of actors.

These remarks about metalanguages of action constrain and contextualize (but do not eliminate) the importance that interpretive and symbolic anthropology accorded "the actors' own" categories. It should become apparent that the capacity to reflect on, criticize, and, especially, show the links among local metalanguages depends on the availability of some further metalevel. To understand the nonexplicit features of action, the habitual or the covert, requires an epistemology of intimacy, but to take them as anything other than obvious, natural, self-contained, and unshakeable—or as private, vulnerable, or even dangerous—requires an epistemology of estrangement. This further level need not derive from something external to a community, because it builds on pervasive capacities for self-reflection inherent in the semiotic mediation of action.

It is when we imagine that agency is naturally located in preexisting individuals, rather than, say, forged among them, that other formations such as families, institutions, societies, and so forth seem most determinist. This parochial perspective is not only theoretically problematic, it is ill-equipped to deal empirically with people who would deny that they themselves are or would want to be humanist or liberal subjects (Keane 1996, 1998, 2002; Mahmood 2001; Miyazaki 2000), even in "the West" insofar as it contains such powerful alternatives as, say, technoscience (Rabinow 1996) and Christian fundamentalism (Crapanzano 2000; Susan Harding 2000). Indeed, the critique of anthropology should not stop at its understanding of so-called others, but should help show how, in any given instance, even we (however defined) are not who we think we are. It should insist on sustaining the project of anthropology as an epistemological critique of received categories, of their "givens," and to accept that this project involves the anthropologist in commonplace strategies of (partial and situated) estrangement and self-estrangement, objectification and self-objectification. If this observation is not entirely new, it does seem to demand relegitimation.

An Ethic and Its Objects

I have suggested that certain core themes in the Boasian vision of geography run through a wide range of subsequent and sometimes antagonistic visions of human science. The impulse toward comparison and theorization has always encountered a deep countervailing insistence on ethnographic particularity, its most sweeping claims always threatened by the pointed exception. At either end of cultural anthropology's historical vagrancies, Boas's geographer joins forces with postmodernism in insisting on the historical situatedness and moral commitments that bind the observer and the observed. I want to close, however, by reasserting the other side of that dialectic: cultural anthropology's engagement with the ambitions of social theory.

The privileging of the particular has come to be intertwined with the concept of self-interpretation. This is not an inherent or necessary relationship but a genealogical one. It is at least conceivable that the terms for self-interpretation will turn out to have universal underpinnings, that the categories of actions and actors are, underneath it all, natural kinds. Or that they are ultimately produced by "external" powers, or remain irreducibly contingent. But the genealogy delineated here has led elsewhere. The insistence that cultural things make comparative metalanguages suspect has become for many anthropologists mere common sense. But the results can verge on the incommunicable. And this can invite, by way of reaction, the return of a potentially imperial common sense: the notion, for instance, that "globalization" means that observers need no longer doubt their categories.

What has given these intertwined themes their persistence, their urgency, and perhaps even their sense of obviousness, I suggest, is in part the underlying ethic of demonstrating some locus of human self-creation not reducible to external determinations. To be sure, few would eliminate determinations altogether, debates over structure and agency, the historical turn, and so forth being efforts to reconcile this project with a sober appreciation of power effects. But the epistemic and even ethical project seems recurrently to circle back to the particularity and treacherously obvious grounds of "experience" (J. W. Scott 1991a). These grounds are where people interact with one another, where decisions are, or seem to be, made, actors identified, responsibilities allocated, actions justified, moral claims asserted, and possible futures imagined. Where the contending versions of cultural anthropology that I have sketched differ is in situating the locus of self-creation and of that which lies "outside" it. It is perhaps the implicit values underwriting their shared interest in agency that will later, after this set of factions has been reconfigured, seem most distinctive about the study of culture at the beginning of the twenty-first century.

But more than its parochialism should make us question this ethic. Seeking to overcome determinism, it tends toward an equally problematic notion of freedom. Pitted against a hypostasized notion of science, it risks reifying a rather specific, humanist model of the subject. Identifying freedom with the domain of ideas, it risks opposing them to a domain of material determinants. And when linked to the epistemology of intimacy, it can encourage disingenuous claims to be eschewing analytic categories. In short, this ethic is in perpetual danger of reproducing the original terms of the opposition.

To this there seem to be three broad avenues of response. First, cultural anthropologists might decide openly to claim the project of demonstrating human self-determination, even if that means, say, insisting on the local genealogy of liberalism as part of their inescapable positionality or in the name of an overriding set of moral and political commitments—to make its normativity explicit (A. Anderson 2000). But to do so requires (at least) a certain disciplinary modesty in the face of potentially irreconcilable ethical stances and reality claims.

Second, cultural anthropologists might reject the terms of the antideterministic project. Indeed, alongside the genealogy traced out here, there has always been a parallel effort along these lines. We can see this today in the growing popularity in many fields of evolutionary and genetic models, some quite sophisticated, others breathtakingly reductive. It may be that a revived economism will produce a similar return to foundations. Nor would it be adequate to counter such models by saying they deny human agency. After all, they could reply that the prevailing visions of agency are psychological or ideological illusions, that we must face up to how things actually are. But even this response cannot tell us why *these* are their objects, why their explanations *matter*, and *for whom*.

But there is a third possibility, that of keeping in sight the problematic ground of the ethnographic particular neither as a privileged foundation for knowledge nor as a locus of self-determination. Rather, this ground characterizes the space of encounter in which people seek or deny one another's recognition. The dialectic between estrangement and intimacy continually passes through, but should not simply rest at, these encounters. On the one hand, our analyses must take us away from them and demand some portable objectifications. On the other hand, to the extent that our most distinctive questions begin with the fact that both we and our interlocutors act, think, hope, remember, foresee, and form judgments amid a world of other people, our engagements should return us to them again. This, at least, would acknowledge that the instigation for social knowledge arises from within sociality.

Notes

I am grateful to Julia Adams, Fernando Coronil, Sandra Harding, Don Herzog, Fred Myers, Anne Norton, Adela Pinch, Lee Schlesinger, Peter Stallybrass, George Steinmetz, Greg Urban, Elizabeth Wingrove, and Yanna Yannakakis, and to participants in panels and workshops at the Social Science History Association, Wilder House, the University of Pennsylvania, and the University of Michigan for their insights, and to the Center for Advanced Study in the Behavioral Sciences (Stanford, California) and the University of Michigan Institute for the Humanities for support. My debt to Marshall Sahlins, who was one of my teachers, and David Schneider, an occasional sparring partner, has made this a difficult exercise in the dialectic of intimacy and estrangement. This essay appeared in a somewhat different version in *Comparative Studies in Society and History.*

1   According to the most recent survey of departments by the American Anthropological Association, in 1998, 49 percent of academically employed anthropologists identified themselves as in the sociocultural subfield, compared to 27 percent archaeology, 15 percent biological or physical, 5 percent applied (a field that overlaps the others), and 2 percent linguistic. I am grateful to Kathleen Terry-Sharp for providing these figures.

2   The preoccupation with cultural meaning and positionality is most obvious in the U.S. academy (the chief targets of Renato Rosaldo's 1989 attack on "objectivism," for instance, were British and French). Writing from the perspective of British social anthropology, Kuper (1999) traces this distinctiveness to the division of social scientific labor mapped out by Parsons, Kluckhohn, and Kroeber in the 1950s, which encouraged anthropology to grant too much to "culture." By repeatedly labeling the result "idealism," however, Kuper tends to reproduce the very materialist-idealist opposition that should be in question. Although the focus in the present essay is on work based in the United States, given the flow of ideas and persons across national boundaries, it is impossible to maintain strict distinctions among national traditions.

3   Not that the battles are over. As recently as 2001, a furious quarrel about the ethics and research methods of the anthropologist Napolean Chagnon in the Amazon a generation before once again put into play categories, such as the charge that Chagnon's critics are antiscience, from that earlier era (see Coronil et al. 2001; Sponsel et al. 2001). In these debates, however, positions have so tended to harden as to make it difficult to imagine alternative visions of objectivity.

4   Strong versions of positivism, such as those of Auguste Comte and the Viennese logical positivists, follow Hume in rejecting inferences about causality as metaphysical in nature (see Hacking 1983). But this anticausalism has not had a significant impact on most anthropologists who aspired to create a natural science of society.

5   For the intellectual background to and appreciation of the significance of this essay, see the articles in Stocking (1996).

6   The academic discipline of history has, of course, been defined by a similar sense of particularity (e.g., Mink 1987), but the terms of relevance have been different, as they have tended to be given in advance by the terms of national identities (Chakrabarty 2000; Cohn 1980). As any U.S. publisher will tell you, books on the Civil War require no theoretical justification, because the topic is interesting to its audience in its own right. By contrast, anthropologists traditionally wrote about places that (as one editor told me) "no one cares anything about."

7   By way of contrast, as George Steinmetz's contribution to this volume ("Sociology") shows, positivism was becoming increasingly dominant even in the closely related field of sociology, to say nothing of economics and political science.

8   Other scientific models were also emerging in the field at this time. For instance, the influence of formal linguistics had a very strong impact on what became cognitive anthropology, usefully summarized in D'Andrade (1995).

9   For reviews of this period, see Knauft (1996), Kuper (1999), Marcus and Fisher (1986), and Ortner (1984). Especially relevant for the issues I discuss here are the contemporaneous developments, too complex to cover here, in the articulation of material forces and consciousness (influenced by Althusser 1971c; Gramsci 1971b; and Williams 1977), sociological phenomenology (influenced by Schutz 1932/1967), symbolic interactionism (Bateson 1955/1972; Goffman 1974; Mead 1934), the ethnography of speaking (Bauman and Sherzer 1974; Hymes 1975), and the work of Foucault (e.g., 1971/1972, 2000).

10   His later turn to history (e.g., Sahlins 1985, 1988/2000) can be seen as an effort to reconcile the autonomy represented at the level of culture with orders of autonomy (e.g., "individual") and contingency (e.g., "event"), viewed as different from but not contradictory to it.

11   There is clearly much more to be said on the subject of holism in anthropology. For one thing, the emergence of the anthropological culture concept was roughly coeval with nineteenth-century formulations of national identity and the Romantic visions of a lost unity to be found behind existing fragments. But more generally, as Martin Jay has observed of the idea of the more encompassing concept of totality, it has "enjoyed a privileged place in the discourse of Western culture . . . resonating with affirmative connotations" (1984, 21).

12   Note that the particularistic argument was not confined to the Americans. For instance, in England, Rodney Needham (1962) drew similar conclusions from his Durkheimian readings of structuralism. See also the strong relativistic position of Peter Winch (1958), who reread Weber (among others) through the lens of the later Ludwig Wittgenstein (1953).

13   I leave aside the questions raised by the relation between "meaning" and "expression"; see Davidson (1974/1984), H. Putnam (1975), Quine (1969).

14   I thank Anne Norton for suggesting these examples.

15   *Pace* James C. Scott, however, metalanguages of oppression are not thereby *privileged* (see T. Mitchell 1990).

16   Indeed, more than one. Identifying cultural anthropology with the quest for intimacy (recall, after all, that the anthropologist might have settled for, say, public institutions) produces a dangerous situation in which it might be epistemologically more secure and ethically safer simply to avoid "others" altogether.

17   Stated as a principle, this may seem a truism, yet scholarly and popular practice too often forget it. There are many not mutually exclusive grounds on which the argument can be made, from deconstruction to ideology critique. For a psychoanalytic approach, see Elliott (this volume).

18   One might respond, as does Johannes Fabian (1983), by privileging fieldwork and denying the value of the effects he identifies with subsequent "writing up." But I am arguing that the analytical distance is not simply an effect of writing, but finds its parallels even in the initial face-to-face interaction.

19   Thus, when Appadurai asserts that culture in the contemporary world has ceased to be

a matter of habitus and has become "an arena for conscious choice, justification, and representation" (1990/1996a, 44), he is emphasizing the liberatory potential of self-awareness. As such, culture can also be property with all the political struggle that entails (Kirsch 2001).

20 Laclau and Mouffe's (1985) critique of the dualisms of ideal-material and freedom-determination that this entails is especially germane here, coming as it does from within the Marxist tradition.

21 Some of the crucial arguments compressed here go back to Voloshinov (1930/1973b) on reflexive speech as a mode of social evaluation, Goffman (1981) on the shifting alignments toward one's own words that characterize everyday interaction, and Schutz (1932/1967) on the processes of typification. Important recent work on metalanguages includes Hanks (1996), Lee (1997), Lucy (1993), Silverstein and Urban (1996); see also the useful review in Ahearn (2001).

22 The most prominent sociological account of tacit know-how is, of course, Bourdieu's habitus, but the basic notion is crucial to both Boasian and Durkheimian approaches to social action and culture (Sapir 1927/1949b; Mauss 1935/1979). For the historical specificity and politics of "instincts" such as contempt, see Herzog (1998).

23 For good examples of how to rethink the historicity of narratives, see S. Amin (1995), Chakrabarty (2000), Stoler and Strassler (2000), Steedly (1993). For the general processes of decontextualization and recontextualization of discourse, see Silverstein and Urban (1996) and Tedlock and Mannheim (1995). For the politics of entextualization, see Shryock (1997).

24 See, for instance, Ivy (1995) on Japanese cultural nostalgia, Rofel (1999) on the impact of official discourses on Chinese workers' subjectivities, Susan Harding (2000) on the Bible's role in the self-consciousness of American fundamentalists, Donham (1999) on transnational narratives in the Ethiopian revolution, Tsing (1993) on parodistic appropriations of state discourses in Indonesia, and Riles (2000) on the transnational circulation of documents. For a close analysis of the struggle between more and less "external" discourses within a single monologue, see Hill (1995). Abu-Lughod (1999) herself has written sensitively about the impact of elite discourses on village television viewers.

The Trick of Words:
Asian Studies, Translation, and the Problems of Knowledge

MICHAEL DUTTON

begin this work with a simple question: Why is it impossible to imagine, much less write, a work like Michel Foucault's *Discipline and Punish* in Asian area studies? The impossibility I am referring to is not of content but of form. It is not just about writing such a text but about having it read as something more than a description, having it read for its theoretical significance more generally. That is to say, it is about the impossibility of writing a work that is principally of a theoretical nature but that is empirically and geographically grounded in Asia rather than in Europe or the United States. Why is it that, when it comes to Asian area studies, whenever "theory" is invoked, it is invariably understood to mean "applied theory" and assumed to be of value only insofar as it helps tell the story of the "real" in a more compelling way?

To some extent, what follows is an attempt to explain historically how Western area studies on Asia came to appreciate theory in this limited and limiting way. At the same time I began to investigate the history and prehistory of this diaphanous field, I began to recognize the possibilities of a very different form of area studies that could have emerged had different sets of pressures pushed it in a slightly different direction. This essay is therefore an attempt to recuperate these now forgotten possibilities and to build on them to produce a different way of seeing, writing, and theorizing Asian area studies.

Tales of Translation

Story One

There is a story told today about an event in ancient China wherein five hundred archers were said to have been dispatched, on the emperor's express orders, to a coastal location near Hangzhou that was about to be reclaimed by imperial engineers. There, in an event that enabled the commencement of this major project, arrows were fired into the sea to ward off the dragon god. These "opening shots" are, in a contemporary Western recollection of the event, said to be "ceremonial," warning the dragon god not to make (violent) waves. Yet the object of this form of ceremony and the engineering project that it celebrated were, in fact, of equal weight, for both were designed to outwit the dragon god and fend off the tempestuous sea so that the land could be reclaimed for the emperor. The techniques differed—the archer used the bow, the engineer, science and technic (in Georges Bataille's 1979 sense)—but their objects were identical. Yet when this account is retold in our time and in our functionalist logic, it becomes a story of scientific discovery, and the archers' tale is relegated to a "ceremonial space" somewhere on the margins of this main scientific account. For me, while the functionalist analysis is a useful corrective to idealism, there is much more to tell, both in the archers' tale and in its retelling as ceremonial.[1]

How much can we trust the unity imposed by this (positivist) narrative strategy? Surely the instrumentalist (re)telling of the archers' tale as a "ceremonial aside" within an overarching story of a developing technical and scientific proficiency should set off a ripple of doubt. After all, the story of scientific curiosity, technical advance, and careful and exact inquiry into currents, winds, and sea patterns, a tale familiar to any contemporary Western reader, now appears stalked by another (more ominous) figure. The shadow of the inexplicable "other" side and "other" logic darkens this figure of ceremony, which threatens to turn the tranquil and familiar waters of "our" comprehensibility into something far more uncertain and incalculable. To "read" sea currents anthropomorphically, as the emperor surely did when he dispatched a team of archers to tame the sea dragon, threatens the exactness of calculation and the economy of science that contemporary positivist accounts of these events promote. It threatens to disrupt the unity of what Bataille (1979, 65) once described as the "homogeneous world"—that is, a world of production, science, technic, and rationality—with the disquieting, inexplicable murmur of "unproductive" excess and transgression that he would come to call "heterogeneity." It is for this reason that, in (re)telling this tale in a story of scientific development, it proves all too tempting to render this hetero- geneous event as "nothing more" than the popping of a champagne cork, the smashing of a bottle on the bow of a boat, or the "ceremonial" firing of arrows into the sea. It is convenient to treat this moment as that cere- monial preface that is always already familiar to us and, one may care to add, that thereby comes to count for very little.

The reproduction of this event as a mere ceremonial aside, a somewhat comical, eccentric interlude before the "main act," or better still, to retell this heterogeneous tale homogeneously by describing it as the "ideological [ceremonial] kernel" around which an otherwise healthy scientific seed was growing, is not only designed to make us feel we have left the troubled and threatening sea for the security of more solid ground, but also to describe the very basis of the Western scientific method. And it is in the work of Bruno Latour and the retelling of another seaside tale that the most compelling evidence of this point can be found.

Story Two

In the final part of Latour's (1987) remarkable account of the development of scientific method, he illustrates his argument about "science in action" by recourse to the narrative technique of allegory. Scientific "action at a distance," in Latour's exemplification, takes place on a faraway island (in the distance), with the visit of a Western boat (action) and the recording techniques, transmissions, and finally incorporation into a Western canon of the captain's notes (science).[2] This parable of science, almost in opposi- tion to its own emphasis on rationality, begins, like most fairy tales, with the dawning of a new day:

> At dawn, 17 July 1787, Lapérouse, captain of *L'Astrolabe*, landed at an unknown part of the East Pacific, on an area of land that was called "Segalien" or "Sakhalin" in the older travel books he had brought with him. Was this land a peninsula or an island? He did not know, that is, no one in Versailles at the court of Louis XVI, no one in London, no one in Amsterdam in the headquarters of the West Indies Company, could look at a map of the Pacific Ocean and decide whether the engraved shape of what was called "Sakhalin" was tied to Asia or was separated by a *strait*. (215)

As Latour points out, it was the task of the comte de Lapérouse to solve the riddle of these lands. With notebook in hand and "natives" before him, the captain began a process of extraction that culminated in revelations being told about this land and the mysteries that surrounded it. Lapérouse's role was not to write down everything his informants told him. His task was to extract from the otherwise "fuzzy, approximate and sometimes ungrounded beliefs of local knowledge" what was deemed to have value as scientific raw material (Latour 1987, 216). Having extracted, Lapérouse then compressed. Lengthy tales of gods and legends were "translated" into more "rational" instrumental accounts. The scientific seed was extracted, the information translated, and the detail compressed into a mere diary entry. The lived knowledge of the indigenous informant that had taken years to acquire was noted down in summary form that would require no more than a few hours to write and much less time than that to read. Lapérouse would then move on to other islands, other accounts, other extractions, other compressions—other translations. The indigenous inhabitants' stories would be told time and time again, but in a translated form they would neither know nor recognize as their own. While they drew maps in the sand for Lapérouse, told him of gods and serpents, and used their version of time to indicate distance—a map was drawn to indicate how far their canoes would take them in one day—this information, when it found its way back to France and into that elaborate dispersed knowledge machine that was the scientific community, would end up taking on a very different form.

There, in this community of scientists, technicians, and planners, all dedicated to making the world manageable, intelligible, and portable, Lapérouse's notes were translated into details that would enhance the "bigger picture" of the world known in the language of Western cartographers as the navigational chart. The islands he had "discovered" and the details he had taken from the indigenous inhabitants now reappeared in a translated form as a mark on a map. It is this map that marks the distances traveled not only by Lapérouse's boat, but also by Western scientific mapping.

From the earliest Christian T-O maps that placed the holy city of Jerusalem at their heart to the later, more elaborate medieval maps that were like logs of pilgrimages undertaken and wondrous religious sites seen, charts of this European past were largely elaborate ideological mapping exercises (Mignolo 1993, 221–222).[3] These intricately coded systems, carrying both ideological and geographic meaning, display a European sensibility very different from the one in which Lapérouse's "discoveries" would finally find their home. Sometime between the fifteenth and seventeenth centuries the tour disappeared and the itinerary was put under erasure. The stories of life, travels, and tours were "flattened out" and vanished. No longer a heterogeneous collection of ideologically invested signs, the map became instead the site of a new clustering of knowledge we would come to call interdisciplinary. It would draw on the fields of geometry, navigation, and observational ethnography and "speak" in the table language of science rather than in a dialect of the pilgrim's tale. Maps became the "proper places in which to *exhibit the products* of knowledge, [and] form tables of *legible* results" (de Certeau 1984, 121). This "colonization" of space by the map and chart was one of the effects of the birth of science (120). With science, rather than religion, now being the guiding ethos, the map was transformed into a very different type of instrumentalist "technology." Ultimately, with new additions and clarifications, it would redraw the world along vectors that would make a return journey from Europe to the islands of Lapérouse not only possible, but far more predictable (Latour 1987, 221). Extraction, translation, mobility, and an ability to combine with and reconfigure other elements of an existing story: this was the very stuff of "science in action."

It is also the stuff that ties Latour's vignette of Lapérouse back to the contemporary account of an ancient Chinese engineering work. Like the extractive science work undertaken by Lapérouse, this contemporary account of ancient Chinese dyke making extracted the ceremonial conditions and translated the valued remainder into something that could be combined with other knowledge. It would, by exclusion, define what was deemed the essential component of indigenous knowledge. Having removed the dross, it would confidently (re)classify the building of dykes as an engineering project. Both this story and that of Lapérouse are tales of extraction, translation, mobility, and an ability to combine with and reconfigure other elements of an existing story. They are, methodologically, discrete domains of science in action, and, as one moves from the natural sciences to the nascent social sciences and from the end of the eighteenth to the middle of the nineteenth century, one discovers that the buried ideological effects of this rigorous, objective, and scientific remapping of the world would take another name: imperialism. To excavate this requires moving to my third and final vignette.

Story Three

At the end of the nineteenth century, in the middle of Paris, the Exposition Universelle opened its gates to the French public and its sights to the public gaze. The world, as Timothy Mitchell (1988, 6) puts it, was thereby enframed. It was rendered, Mussorgsky-like, as a picture at an exhibition, but one that clearly put trade "in the frame." The earlier Crystal Palace exhibition in England offered a stunning example of this. Exhibiting space was granted only on the basis of the value attributed to what one had to sell. It was on this basis, and no other, that nations and space were reordered in a calibrated hierarchy which led to the non-Western world occupying small, marginal corners of the exhibition site: non-Western countries had little of value and therefore little to say in a world ordered around the market and the modern. Indeed, the vast majority of the non-Western exhibits were supplied by European colonizers who treated these lands and their commodities as little short of a joke. Costumes, trinkets, carpets, and hookahs appeared to be the standard array of goods, says C. R. Fay (1951, 88) in his account of the Crystal Palace, and these sat somewhat uncomfortably alongside the West's latest technological inventions. Here was a mapping exercise very different from the one that occupied the mind of Lapérouse, but the logic and method behind it were eerily familiar. Extraction, mobility, and an ability to combine with and reconfigure other elements of an existing story were not only the stuff of science in action, but clearly also a central part of imperialism in action.

Like secularized T-O maps of old, these trade fairs reveal an ideological remapping of the world with the West in the center and its agenda on top. In Paris this would be embodied by Gustave Eiffel's tower, the ultimate sign of Western artistic, engineering, and "natural" brilliance.[4] Mimicking the structure of plant life in a manner that would later find full artistic expression in the photography of Karl Blossfeldt, Eiffel created an engineering masterpiece using load-bearing iron girders connected in a manner reminiscent of the common plant. Yet there was nothing common about Eiffel's tower. Built for the Exposition Universelle and located in the center of the site, it offered an overview of all below and stood as the ultimate sign of Western (and bourgeois) dominance over nature and the world. As if to reinforce this, on the grounds below, and in the shadow of the tower itself, sat another sign of Western dominance: a French-built Egyptian exhibit that reproduced perfectly a winding backstreet scene from Cairo. Such perfect reproduction was confirmation of Western brilliance, not simply because of the architecture of the streetscape but because of the Western technical ability to replicate, in the heart of Paris, the soul of Cairo. Here was a streetscape complete with traditional Egyptian house veneers and the façade of a mosque modeled on the one in Qaitbay. Here was a street scene populated by imported Egyptian donkeys complete

with handlers offering rides, Egyptian dancing girls entertaining the pas-
sersby, and French traders dressed as Arabs selling trinkets from their
bazaar stalls. Even the dirt on the painted buildings was replicated (T.
Mitchell 1988, 1). Old Cairo was transported and in the process transformed. Yet this process of transformation, from lived social form to
sideshow, only confirmed the power of the West to extract, replicate, and
make anything, anywhere, portable and intelligible in its own terms.

It is with this form of mimesis, where the eye is firmly fixed on trans-
porting things into the homogeneous world, that the logic of the trade
exhibition, the diary of Lapérouse, and the contemporary rendition of
traditional Chinese engineering meet. It is in these three stories that one
confronts the relationship between science, translation, and the epistemic
violence of imperialism. The West, it seems, could translate anything.
Through the spread of scientific method, texts, buildings, and even life
itself were opened to the West's gaze. The tower of Gustave Eiffel became
its Babel and the new universal message was that science could conquer all
and would make the world whole and wholly intelligible. A new universal
language was emerging, not out of the rubble of philology or even out of
language proper. Rather, this new universal language was "reason" and its
battering ram, capitalism.[5] Capitalism dreamed of flattening the world in
the way science had once flattened the monastic pilgrimage maps into
navigational charts. Now the desire to trade would flatten difference. Consumption and material desire would point to a new universal language.
Materialism would obliterate the dialects of dissent, be they the sacred, the
opaque, or the heterogeneous. The homogeneous world would be vic-
torious and, like the colonists of old, would redraw the map and paint
each land in its own colors. If the nineteenth century held out this promise, it is in the twenty-first that we are told the promise is being fulfilled. As
globalization spreads, it cuts its way through different cultural and lived
forms and leads to claims not only about shared desires but also about a
shared universal logic of desire. It is in critiquing this logic, a logic now
transformed into a more general "style of thought" and sometimes spoken
in the "objective" language of the contemporary social sciences, that I
want to begin to speak of a dialect of potential dissent offered from within
a new type of Asian area studies. It is my contention that, if reconfigured
into a domain that speaks to, and of, the occluded heterogeneous world of
otherness, Asian area studies has the potential to send ripples of doubt
through the dominant positivist social science "stories."

Bringing the Stories Up to Date

Basing themselves on a (predominantly nineteenth-century) notion of how the "hard" sciences work (Cumings 2002), these social sciences have produced "applied" models that enlist the now familiar methodology outlined above. Indeed, it is through this methodology that they now lay claim to being objective, rigorous, and scientific. This, of course, involves the eradication or dismissal of unwanted signs of the heterogeneous that cannot be incorporated into the homogeneous world of "their" reason. Nowhere was this process more in evidence than in the ongoing, troubled marriage of comparativist social science modeling and the scholarship that supplied these models with much of their raw data on other cultures. As this marriage disintegrates, one begins to notice the social scientific process through which that which cannot easily be incorporated is assimilated, then repressed. Yet, as is clear from the tale of the Chinese dyke builders and their penchant for ceremony, "the mystery that is incorporated, then repressed, is never destroyed. . . . history never effaces what it buries; it always keeps within itself the secret of whatever it encrypts, the secret of its secrets" (Derrida 1995, 21). It is in disinterring this "secret of its secrets" that the heterogeneous possibilities of a new area studies of the sign are revealed and the radical potential of the field made real. But there is much to do before that possibility can be realized.

As a geographically defined area of study rather than a theoretically driven discipline, area studies had long argued that it was interdisciplinary. But, as it looked over its shoulder at the hard social sciences, it was stalked by the fear that it had no discipline at all. The social sciences had for years made this claim about area studies, and the latter's response, in arguing for a more "area-centric knowledge," only reinforced the suspicion that area studies was indeed a field dominated by descriptive "social translators." Lacking the type of theoretical and "scientific" rigor the disciplines claimed to offer, area studies defined itself only in the shadows of other disciplines and reified its unique quality: translation. But it was this one thing that would damn it in the eyes of social scientists.

The most recent and formidable critiques of area studies come from political scientists, and of those the most vocal is Robert H. Bates. In a series of articles that damned area studies for lacking the necessary theoretical rigor to rival the social sciences intellectually, Bates called for a new approach that would merely reinforce the already existing role of area studies as subservient subordinate translator. Social science knowledge would be privileged in this arrangement, for, unlike the translational practices of the empirically based area study, only it was "equipped to handle area knowledge in a rigorous fashion" (Bates 1996, 2). For Bates, at least, the new universal scientific techniques deployed by the rigorous social scientist were all versions of rational choice theory. With this approach, cultural difference becomes but one variable in a game that is constantly reworked to "prove" both the particular argument being proffered and, more important, the universalism of the model being deployed.[6] In fact, all that this model building proved, if proof be needed, was the logocentric nature of the paradigms that dominate the contemporary social science disciplines. The faith of political scientists in both the rationality of political actors and the objectivity of their theoretical models required only empirical verification. It was at this point that the social sciences would require local translators from whom they could gain useful descriptive information that could be reworked into empirical proof of their scientific theories. For the social scientist, the usefulness of the local knowledge supplied by the area studies specialist was therefore also a sign of the theoretical weakness of the field. In many respects, area studies had only itself to blame for this predicament, for it has always, and quite promiscuously, offered itself in this way.

In the subfield of area studies I know best, a line can be traced from the very earliest Jesuit encounters with China through to our day and, despite massive shifts in what and how objects of desire are translated, the model of the area studies scholar as translator remained dominant. Indeed, the one defining characteristic of the sinologist was this ability to translate, both linguistically and culturally. As David Mungello (1985, 135) points out in his examination of some of the earliest European attempts to theorize China and its language, theorists always seemed to have "knowledgeable friends." Gottfried Leibniz had Joachim Bouvet, Athanasius Kircher had Michael Boym, and Christian Mentzal had Philippe Couplet, in much the same way that Julia Kristeva had her sinologist-translator Marcel Garnet. Even when theoretical opportunities do emerge as possibilities for area studies—as happened in recent times when Edward Said rendered the empirical relationship between "Europe and its other" theoretical by describing it as an ontologically and epistemologically charged "style of thought"—they are brought down to earth and employed in area studies as a means to reinforce what could only be described as the "translator's advantage." Paul Cohen (1984), who offered possibly the first detailed response from within Chinese studies to *Orientalism*, employed this work to authorize his "China-centric approach," which was little more than a critique of theory based on an unreconstructed (and unrealizable) form of empiricism. Why is there such truculent antitheoretical empiricism in area studies? The reasons are manifold, but one key reason that has never fully been scrutinized relates to training.

Western area studies' knowledges are language-based, and learning languages has come to operate as a rite of passage into Asian area studies for any scholar. Yet it has also, unconsciously, become much more than that; the narrowly defined applied nature of area studies, which lies at the heart of its truculent empiricism, is based on unconscious appropriations from, and a close kinship to, the types of methods employed in language training itself. This methodological kinship between textual and cultural translation is not fortuitous, I would argue, but emerges from a path taken out of the philological tradition by Oriental studies, a path that would become fully developed by the time it was named Asian area studies. I suggest that the transition from classical philology, of which Oriental studies was a part, into comparative philology, from whence it departed, laid the intellectual ground on which area studies' descriptive and applied translational practices reified an observational method of knowledge acquisition. It is this history that I want to retrace to bring forth a repressed alternative of "doing" that could establish the basis for a very different Asian area studies.

Philology, that "empirical science of the spirit," as Ernest Renan (quoted in Olender 1992, 52) so romantically called it, was a nodal point in a discursive field that not only gave birth to linguistics, but also played a key role in the formation of Oriental and later Asian area studies. Although it is certainly true that Oriental studies was irreducible to philology and philology was much more than Oriental studies, the degree of interpenetration and mutual authorization for works undertaken in these paired fields was nonetheless significant.[7] Oriental studies was crucial to philology insofar as the Oriental languages gave added impetus to the changes in language study, which then moved philology away from its search for a theological origin. The philological tradition was, in turn, pivotal to Oriental studies, because it predisposed the field to a way of seeing that would add a social, political, economic, and cultural dimension to Roman Jakobson's (1992) now famous formulation that anything is translatable. It was this type of formulation that would solidify and stabilize around the methodology of applied language appropriation and translation; for, as is well-known, language is the one and only unifying criteria of this field.[8] This would then be reified by the protocols of academic publishing and the utilitarian demands of missionaries, colonists, governments, and, more recently, business. The applied nature of this field came to set the boundaries for what would become an acceptable form of scholarship. In other words, the applied methods of language acquisition shone a light on more general forms of applied knowledge acquisition.

The repetitive, rote learning techniques employed to acquire language inadvertently reinforced a particular understanding of the relationship between text and interpretation, and this would then solidify into a mimetically recoded and quite classical binary between "real" and "thought" (Niranjana 1992). This slippage would then produce a set of unconscious understandings that dialectically fed back into the general scholarly program of area studies, producing a tautological justification for the realist, empiricist, and applied approach to knowledge acquisition. The self-evident obviousness and pregiven "realness" of the text became metonymically linked to the pregiven obviousness and realness of nation or culture; and it was this form of "applied translational practice" that came to constitute the very basis of area studies knowledge.[9] While there are, of course, stakeholders (government and business, to name but two) demanding this, the particularly trenchant resistance to theory in this field is not reducible to mere outside pressure groups. The point I want to stress is that there was nothing inevitable about the field's developing in this way. Indeed, a focused reading of its history opens a window onto other ways it could have developed and may yet still. Indeed, it is the purpose of this genealogy to highlight just this possibility.

I use the term *genealogy* rather than *history* quite deliberately. What I have written is not history in the traditional sense. Thus, experts in any of the various subfields that operate under the rubric of Asian area studies, be they China, Japan, or Indic studies, may well fail to see their own subfield's history fully and clearly explored in these pages. That is because the tale I wish to tell is not merely an amalgam of all of the constitutive parts of Asian area studies. In other words, the order of appearance of events, or the relative weight or standing of concerns in any of these subfields, is not merely a version of the area studies field in miniature. Area studies, quite to the contrary, selectively developed some concerns and not others, and the order of appearance of what would become important may not have been reflected equally in all fields. Thus, in research on China, the philological urge would remain long after it had faded in other branches of area studies. Similarly, the concerns of colonial governance would fuel an interest in administration and observation that would be much less powerful in research on countries that were not colonized. Rather than plot the development of each subdiscipline and explore the way they contributed to the development of the field as a whole, I have focused on those practices in philology and Oriental studies that would come either to direct the discursive field or to play a pivotal role in the formation of the field. This essay is, therefore, very much a "history of the present," for I am interested in how area studies came to be formed in such a way that its radical potential was neutralized. It is my contention that in employing this genealogical method in a scrutiny of Asian area studies practices and prehistories, the field turned its back on certain possibilities that could have transformed and could yet transform area studies into a more theoretically informed set of intellectual practices. Like the seas that constantly lashed the dykes in Hangzhou, the alternative area studies of which I speak offers the possibility of eroding the shorelines of certainty on which the practices of homogeneous social science incorporation have been built.

By broadening out and theorizing its understanding and appreciation of language study, area studies would come to recognize the theoretically charged nature of any notion of linguistic and cultural difference. Through this recognition, a set of practices could be adopted that not only would help area studies overcome its empiricism, but would also expose the "epistemic violence" of social scientific model building that currently attempts to colonize area studies. A careful examination of the prehistory of area studies not only helps explain why a type of ideologically invested, logocentric, but theoretically informed translational practice gave way to a descriptive applied practice, it also helps situate a recuperative move from within the trope of language study itself. After all, the study of language lies behind many of today's most dissonant scholarly practices.

From Lacanian psychoanalysis to the structural anthropology of Claude Lévi-Strauss, language formed the basis on which a set of new grammars of understanding came into being. Barthesian semiotic studies also drew on linguistic notions of the signification process to formulate a social semiotics that would reveal a "latent" (connotative) meaning behind the explicit (denotative) one.[10] Like area studies, these three discrete grammars of understanding owe their very existence to philology, but what they would take from this now defunct field was a set of practices very different from those adopted by area studies. And while none of these is without its own problems, they at least share the common virtue of appreciating that "language has not only a grammatical logic but also an historical memory" (Mignolo and Schiwy 2003, 8), and this forces them to explore a world that goes beyond the manifest descriptive and empiricist forms that dominate area studies' knowledges. They hint at the possibilities available for an alternative way of doing language study that is theoretically nuanced and culturally embedded and speaks directly to the language core of the area study knowledge form.

Despite an abiding logocentrism, philology also (and from its very earliest moments) employed a set of buried semiotic practices, which enabled language and knowledge to be tied together in a quest for the truth of the cosmos. They would also infect the early days of Oriental studies and lead the young Victor Hugo to proclaim, "In the century of Louis XIV one was a Hellenist: today one is an Orientalist" (quoted in Schwab 1986, 15). This enchantment with difference underpinned the privileged status Oriental studies once occupied in the Western academy and, in a radically different and far less theological way, has reappeared to inform postcolonial discourse as a parallel and possibly rival humanities discourse to area studies' social scientism.

To validate the myriad contentious claims made in these opening remarks requires a detailed examination of philology and a recognition of that field as the precursor to Oriental and Asian studies. Such recognition not only highlights the translational nature of Asian area studies but also helps locate the suggestion that more recent theoretical reflections on translational practices speak directly to issues that should be central considerations in Asian studies. In short, this close examination of the prehistory of Asian area studies raises the specter and possibility of other ways of "doing Asia." To develop this, however, requires a detailed mapping of how the field has become a domain of applied translation, and to tell this tale requires starting, as all good stories do, at the beginning. In this particular case, that beginning is Genesis.

Lead Us Not into Translation

In the first book of the Bible, we are told that Noah's three sons, Shem, Ham, and Japheth, settled on the plains of Shinar and attempted to build a tower to touch the gates of heaven. We are also told of God's response. Where once there was one language and one people, God's wrath led to their being scattered and their tongues confounded. Where once "word" and "thing" were one and humankind basked in the wisdom and unity of the "name giver" Adam (who, despite the Fall, was still the most knowledgeable sage the world had known), after Babel, what John Locke described as "the trick of words" prevailed.[11] Undeterred by God's wrath, later Christian philologists would try to build a new tower and recover this "primitive" transparent language, but they would avoid heresy by building on Scripture.

Read literally, the Bible offered a road to redemption and a clue to the recovery of the original transparent language, itself a path back to the wholeness of humankind. Whether one started from the book of the original scribe, Enoch, or from Babel, a reading practice developed that Jacques Derrida (1974, 75) would later describe as the theological prejudice and Hans Aarsleff (1982) would call Adamicism, a notion, Aarsleff stressed, that went well beyond the question of "resemblance," for it was too infected by the religious to be reduced to this one notion.[12] The point to note is that, by the sixteenth century, "in becoming Bible-conscious, Europe became Babel-conscious" (Bodmer 1944, 444).

The literal reading of the Bible fueled a scholarly quest for origin that informed the endeavors of archaeologists, philologists, linguists, and theologians alike. It led to studies of arcane language forms that centered on the language of the Bible. If truth were to be found in the revealed nature of Scripture, then the language of Scripture must be the earliest.[13] Hence, under the influence of the Church, scholars of the Renaissance sought to recover the original primitive language, as early philologists called it, for this language would unlock the oneness of humankind. This early comparative language study involved the comparison of biblical words, especially verbs or nouns (words of action and naming words), as "signs" that could lead to the (re)discovery of the original primitive language. At the center of this teleologically conceived quest was a belief that inscribed in origin was immanent future. Variants on this theme would eventually lead away from the Semitic languages to those that displayed an arcane and distinctive form. Chinese, because of its pictographic characters and ancient lineage, proved to be of particular interest.

In this regard, the work of the Jesuit Athanasius Kircher was both idiosyncratic and exemplary. Like many before him, Kircher ascribed central importance to overcoming the "word-thing split," and this, in turn, led him to value highly the pictographic, nonphonetic language forms. He saw a link between Chinese characters and Egyptian hieroglyphics and argued that this pointed to a genealogy of the greatest import (Mungello 1985, 134–164). Kircher was not alone in his high valuation of Chinese. John Webb (1669), the first to write in English of the importance of Chinese script, was also the first to posit the idea of Chinese as the "mother tongue" of God. While Origen believed that the non-Semitic world had been left to God's angels, Webb suggested that they had simply avoided the great flood and, therefore, the wrath of God.[14]

Webb's argument highlighted a minor trend in late-seventeenth-century scholarship known as the Noachidian theory of descent. In essence, Noachidian theory put forth the idea that Noah's three sons, Shem,

Ham, and Japheth, had gone forth and spread God's Law throughout the world, including Asia. According to Leibniz, the prominent German astronomer Johannes Kepler drew on this idea to suggest that the origins of Chinese civilization bore a "remarkable similarity to the Noachide theory" (Mungello 1985, 35). This theory was, however, greatly challenged because of the reduced role it attributed to the Jews as the chosen people. Clearly, if China was to be so highly valued, the role of the Jews would, by necessity, diminish. That was, of course, until the discoveries at Kaifang.

"On May 16, 1707," Maurice Olender (1992, 21) tells us, "*Le Journal des Scavans* announced to its readers 'a very important discovery' made in K'ai-feng [Kaifang] in the province of Hunan, China." The Jews of China had been discovered, and their lineage led back to a time before Christ. From these ancient peoples, it was hoped, an authentic, uncorrupted version of the Bible would be found and Providential truth would be restored. The long-simmering controversy over the 1546 decision of the Council of Trent to recognize the Vulgate as the sole authentic biblical text would finally be challenged by this news from the East.

Alas, such hopes would not be realized. By 1723, textual research revealed that the Kaifang version of the Bible was virtually identical to the Amsterdam version (Olender 1992, 22). Nevertheless, this failed to diminish the belief held by some that in the ancient, sacred, and mysterious scripts of the East an answer to the Western "self" could be found that would prove revelatory. As God was slowly replaced by Mammon, this search for an original language that was itself a search for origin was joined by a newer set of influences emanating from mathematics. The slow emergence of the experimental sciences led to speculation about a new kind of language key that would be based on mechanical and mathematical principles (Mungello 1985, 39).

In crucial respects, this new tendency was itself religiously based insofar as it relied on a methodology employed in the religious exegetical tradition, which searched not for an original language but for "a universal matrix for all languages" (Eco 1995, 49). That is to say, it sought the universal formula beneath the surface of language. The mystical cabalistic techniques of textual decoding offered an example of this religious practice, and they would later play a key role in informing the calculus-based language-generating schemas of Raymond Lull and Nicholas of Cusa (Eco 1995, 60, 69). While such techniques began as a mechanism for the revelation of hidden religious truths and, in Lull's case, offered the possibility of conversion to the universal Truth of Christ, they also led, in part, away from the unity of the Church: like other tendencies abroad at this time, they raised the possibility of challenges to the canonical status of Church readings based on Latin translations.

The principal challenge to Latin, however, came not from language research but from Protestantism, which refused to accept the truth of the canonical Latin translations offered by the Catholic Church. Latin's inability to offer an incontestable textual certainty would lead to its decline. Hence, what was once the universal language of "the known world," held together by sacred commitments, was, by the sixteenth century, a language in rapid decline (B. Anderson 1983, 24–25). Increasingly, universality would come not from a shared language of communication but in the form of shared formulas. By 1662, even the Royal Society had abandoned Latin; within thirty years, the French Society did the same. The universal language that had tied Christendom together on the basis of a shared set of linguistic expressions of that religious commitment was no more. In its place there emerged a new linguistic nationalism, on the one hand, and a growing scientific language of universalism, on the other.

Perversely, this decline in Latin led to increased scholarly concern about language, which translated in some quarters into further research on language keys. Through the development of such keys, it was hoped that any linguistic meaning from whatever language group could be immediately translated, thereby obviating the need for a single universal language (B. Anderson 1983, 194). In this respect, the decline of Latin and the rise in interest in language signaled the shift from an old, religiously based form of universality to a new, more abstract form that was being imagined and written in the language of science or pseudoscience. A desire for a new language or a new understanding of language based on logarithmic and algebraic principles was emerging (Bodmer 1944, 443–444). From Francis Bacon to Robert Boyle, this desire found expression in the various schemes to promote a new, "rational" language, one that would mimic the symbolism of science itself. A new way of seeing was therefore slowly emerging out of old exegetical methods.

This shift from the exegetical to the scientific signaled, according to Michel de Certeau, a movement from symbol, where hidden textual meanings were interpreted by authorized commentary, to the "cipher," where analytical techniques offered a "totalizing taxonomy" and "universal instruments" to ensure "comprehensiveness." The cipher, as Certeau (1988, 74) notes, was a model that could come into effect only through a homology between erudition and mathematics. Yet, although symbol and cipher appear to speak to different worlds, they were not entirely oppositional: both grew from the same desire for God's truth and for linguistic "transparency." Science, therefore, could work in the interests of the one true religion. Unity could once again be restored, but this time it would be proven through the universal truths of science. Indeed, as Renan notes, philology would create the "irrefutable scientific basis for Christianity" and establish a "firm and objective link" between Christian truth and scientific truth (quoted in Olender 1992, 77).

Once again, the nonphonetic basis of Chinese proved wondrously portentous. Jesuit linguistic discoveries in China seemed to work in sympathy with scientific innovations in the West to awaken interest in the character-based script of Chinese. At the very time symbolic algebra was forging a new universal community of understandings among scientists built on shared knowledge of symbols and calculi rather than shared linguistic knowledge, China's character-based language was found to offer an example of these same principles at work in language itself. The religious privilege became a scientific one, as Chinese appeared to be an identikit of what Bacon would call "Real Characters." Chinese, however, was not the only non-Western language to be privileged, nor the only one to undergo a partial revolution in the way that privilege was ascribed.

If the search for the Primitive Language venerated antiquity, then the discovery in 1785 of the ancient Indic script of Sanskrit, which was far older than any Semitic language, would, as Schwab (1986) notes, put the final nail in the coffin of a world considered to be only biblical. He argues that this (re)discovery not only upset existent philological theory but, given the early language scholars' insistence on the unity of language and humanity, opened the whole of scholarship to its impact. The problem with this argument is that by the time of Sanskrit's (re)discovery, the old philological argument was a mere shadow of its former self. Even in the religious community the idea of a primitive language had, by this stage, given way to a belief in linguistic diversity before Babel and to the radical idea that linguistic confusion was natural (Eco 1995, 86). Moreover, the view of script itself as sacred had long since been eroded, as interest in primitive languages developed into the studies of mother tongues (85).

Nevertheless, even in accepting these important caveats, one should not dismiss Schwab's thesis in toto, for, as even Umberto Eco admits, these theological arguments faded rather than vanished.[15] Moreover, even in faded forms, these old theological arguments unconsciously reinforced the prestige of this ancient language that was now being openly privileged on a very different basis. "All the human sciences," writes Olender (1992, 7), "from history to mythology, and soon to include 'racial science,' were affected by the discovery of a tongue that was known not only as Indo-European but also Aryan." Sanskrit would seal the fate of those old biblically based attempts to forge a close alliance between philology and theology, for the idea of the Semitic languages as origin was no more. At the same time, however, it opened up new intellectual vistas. In this new world of scholarship, the privilege of Sanskrit would derive less from its senescence than from its relationships with European languages. A substantial part of its newly privileged status came from the central place it occupied in Franz Bopp's new field of comparative philology. The importance of Sanskrit to Bopp and other comparative philologists largely rested on the findings of Sir William Jones (as articulated in his 1786 presidential discourse to the Asiatic Society). He was the first to make the now famous correlation between the internal structure of Sanskrit and European language forms (de Saussure 1959, 2). According to Jones, Sanskrit is very close to European languages for it "bears a stronger affinity, both in the roots of verbs and in the forms of grammar, than could possibly have been produced by accident" (quoted in Pedersen 1931, 18).

Whether one followed Friedrich von Schlegel, who argued that Latin, Greek, and the Germanic and Persian languages were all derived from this "mother language," or Bopp, who suggested that Sanskrit was merely the "elder sister," is of little consequence, for the question of the root language lost its importance (Foucault 1966/1970, 292). What mattered was Bopp's insistence that Sanskrit exceeded both Greek and Latin in structure and clarity. Hence, he argued that it was of the utmost significance (Müller 1861, 21–22). Sanskrit seemed to possess a dual privilege: it retained its status as a romantic language par excellence, for it opened the Western world to a knowledge of the sacred texts of the East; yet at the same time it played a privileged role in the new scientific discourse of comparative grammar. In relation to this, Schlegel's work was critical, and two aspects of his scholarship in particular would come to revolutionize philology and its ways of carrying out research. Indeed, it was on the basis of these two innovations that philology would come to represent itself as the science of language.

First, according to Max Müller, it was Schlegel who came forth with the propositions necessary to undermine the belief in hierarchical classes of languages predicated on age. In place of this, Schlegel suggested smaller language families that were aligned less by ancestry than by shared grammatical structures. Examining the languages of the world, Schlegel concluded by linking the significant European and classical languages together and then back to Sanskrit. Thus, while the terms "Indo-German" or

"Indo-European" language group were not his inventions, they were nonetheless an outcome of his work.[16]

Second, Schlegel developed the method of comparative grammar, which provided the theoretical basis for a detailed construction of language families and groups.[17] Comparative grammar offered, for the first time, a systematic means by which to trace language connections and privileges on the seemingly more scientific basis of syntactical structures. Schlegel's comparative grammar displaced the previous emphasis on the word. No longer would one inquire into the essential architecture of the word;[18] instead, one would focus on grammatical totality. The effect of this was significant for it broke the connection between language and human activity that had sustained the great philological homology between language and knowledge. With Schlegel's work, philology moved from this classical emphasis on reconciliation of the "word-thing split" to a more comparative frame where grammar and structure were central to all inquiries. Philology was no longer anchored to references in the Old Testament; it was no longer tied to grand homologies. In place of this, one discovers a more detailed, "rational," but esoteric and introspective study of language structures.

In this transformation one can see the beginnings of the disciplines, yet at the time, the importance of this shift was far from clear. The reasons for this opacity have to do with the dual register by which philology, like Sanskrit, valorized its privileged status. As Aarsleff (1982, 32) has noted, comparative philology had all the hallmarks of a new "model science," but it kept these behind a cloak of "spirituality." Comparative philology maintained the high-culture claim to be "opening the sacred books of the East" but now did so on the basis of rational scientific methods that enabled it to slide easily into a new world of rational disciplinary divisions. This shift to the more limited disciplinary mode was to have profound effects, not only in terms of the later discipline of linguistics, but also on the overarching field of Oriental studies.

"Linguistic finalism" would transform this once theologically inspired search for origins into a more limited but rational and scientific search for knowledge. Hence, the legitimacy of philology was no longer religiously based but dependent on the scientific claims it could make and the "form" of rational argumentation it followed. In terms of the latter, therefore, there were constant attempts by philologists to associate their discipline's methodology with those of the empirical sciences. Schlegel compared comparative philology with Georges Cuvier's comparative anatomy. "Comparative grammar," he wrote, "will give us entirely new information

on the genealogy of languages, in exactly the same way in which comparative anatomy has thrown light upon natural history" (quoted in Pedersen
1931, 19). The methodology for dissecting language, it seems, was the same
as that which ordered and dissected the human body. Methodologically,
the science of the living body and the science of the spoken word were
kindred spirits. For Müller, the science of geology was a more appropriate
analogy,[19] for one could compare rock strata in a quarry in the same way
philologists would compare language grammars. And just as one would
dig in a quarry and find ever more ancient layers, so too one could excavate language and discover its past. Yet this search was no longer stoked by
those old religious fires that dreamed of bringing to light the unity of
languages and peoples. By this time, even when philology looked back to
ancient languages, it also looked "inward" to their syntactical structures.
The one compensation in all this for the religiously inspired was that this
new positivistic approach would offer a more scientific means of translating the truth of Christ into other languages, making possible more Christian conversions. Hence, Müller's suggestion that the development of
comparative philology was a shift from the metaphor of Babel to that of
the Pentecost was not without a certain materiality!

Where Babel spoke of humanity recovered, the Pentecost spoke of hea-
thens converted. The metaphor of the Pentecost focused on religious sal-
vation, and comparative philology now had a new technical and scientific
means to advance this end. Thus, while the proselytizing and evangelical
aim of the Church was to save souls, it was, of necessity, built on a bedrock
of both colonial conquest and good translational skills. Little wonder that,
for Müller, this shift tied the new light of God into the very heart of this
new science. For him, philology would be the "technical" means by which
the light of Christendom would shine forth upon the heathen. Moreover,
it would give birth to a new positivistic social research program in which
"old words assumed a new meaning, old problems, a new interest, old
sciences a new purpose" (Müller 1861, 118). Through this new program all
peoples would become susceptible to "the highest mental culture" (118).

It is at this point, and with these words, that a crucial factor in the
development of Oriental studies begins to reveal itself. "Europe and its
other," that intellectual fulcrum generating Oriental studies, reveals its
Janus face in this Pentecostal claim and, in a very Schmittian way, even in
these early days, shows itself to be political. This desire to convert is the
very point at which "*faith* fights *errant faith*," and this, as Carl Schmitt so
clearly shows, is the most intense of all political moments (Meier 1998, 60).

As a religious quest, Europe and its other carries hidden within itself another potential translation: "friend and enemy."

It is this important religious element in the development of the science of comparative philology—a development that would give birth to both a politics and a field that would eventually, and in a secularized and much more overtly political form, take the name Asian studies—that one would miss if one were to read the account of the development of philology rendered by Foucault in *The Order of Things*. Strangely, for the author of *Power/Knowledge*, this element of the story and its implications are completely absent.

The Absent Orient of Michel Foucault

For Foucault, the key element in the episteme that was marked, in part, by the emergence of comparative philology was not the expansion and comparativism of the field, much less its political implications for the colonial world. What is important for him is the way that the advent of comparative philology announced a particular moment in Western reason when one could no longer speak of language being close to knowledge itself. Instead, as he puts it, a notion of reason came to prevail that would lead language to "fold in upon itself" and reduce it to a mere object of inquiry (Foucault 1966/1970, 296–297).[20] Henceforth, studies of language would speak only to the internal architecture of language, and though this was a demotion, this particular demotion had its compensations that would trail across an array of fields and leave a mark on the Western mind. One of these fields of compensation would speak to the heart and encourage a privileging of the creative language of literature. Another would speak to the head, leading to the table language of those who dreamed of scientific transparency. Still another would speak to a form of reason, the architecture of which was to be found in the syntactical structure of language itself. In all three cases, Foucault traces the shattering effect these "remnants" of the once powerful field of philology would have on the Western notion of reason as they splintered into other domains. There is, however, one splinter that his otherwise expansive account does not trace, and that is the emergence of Oriental studies as a discrete field. This, at first, may seem like Eurocentrism. After all, *The Order of Things* is organized around the appearance of "Man," and for Foucault, this appearance led to a dramatic rupture with classical forms of knowledge, of which the understandings of language were a central part (Rabinow 1989, 8). It was for this reason that language once again acquired an "enigmatic density" at this time. As we have already seen, such density around language was nothing new. What was significant in this new episteme was that this density emerged not because of the search for a primary word, but because of the ability of language study itself to create conditions for an epistemic *disruption* of that cosmology of the word. Indeed, it enabled the creation of a series of metalanguages through which the grammar of Western thought could be questioned. It was the appearance of "otherness" and "dissonance" that, Foucault argues, would come to orientate the critical accent of nineteenth-century thought.

From the grammar of words (Nietzsche) to the grammar of economic life (Marx) and, finally, to the grammar of those "unspoken phrases" that inhabit our unconscious and speak of our desires and dreams (Freud), Foucault's reading highlights the productive otherness of these "disruptive" discourses. Yet the question remains: What of the disruptive otherness of languages and cultures of the non-West? They may lack the single, famous proper name like *Marx, Nietzsche,* or *Freud* through which to summarize their project, but, given their disruptive effect on philology itself, surely they, too, are worthy of a proper place alongside these disruptive voices of European otherness? After all, part of their appeal to the nineteenth-century romantics was that their material otherness to the culture and logic of Western thought helped define the very notion of European selfhood. Given this, the exploration of the human condition (that is, the emergence of Man) must surely relate in some ways to the emergence of Oriental studies and help account for its once privileged role. As I have shown, studies of the Orient and its languages had, in the past and in part, been sutured into the theologically inspired quest for origin. And even after this theological quest for origin was no more, one could still find examples of romantic Oriental scholarship proffering the idea of an exotic yet profound Eastern knowledge that speaks to all of humanity. Oriental studies could still lay claim to a certain gravitas by keeping alive some of these pretensions.

Consider, for example, the fact that many of the romantic writings about the non-West appear, in hindsight, to have been as much a description of certain unconscious preoccupations and repressions about self— prior to the invention of these terms—as they were an exploration of non-Western societies. Could one not posit, for example, that much of the romantic literature discussing the journey of Eastern knowledge was, in part, an empirical metaphor and elucidation of what would now, in a very different "language," be described as the *fort-da* relation? Could one not also point to the endless mimetic appropriations of Eastern knowledge as one moves from Jules Michelet on individual intuition, Edgar Quinet on liberty, Adam Smith on universal sympathy, and, more explicitly, the physiocrats on good government?[21] This list of buried signs of significance is, in fact, endless, and if it is, as I have suggested, a key element in the formation of Western knowledge, then this Oriental splinter of philological discourse should have been of the utmost importance to Foucault. After all, the significance of this particular splinter seems to suggest that there could be no discussion of the emergence of Man within that domain of knowledge once known as philology without an understanding of the way philology engaged with a domain within its "womb" that spoke of cultures of difference.

The great philologist and Oriental scholar Eugène Burnouf offers an insight into the way this philological prestige and pretense lived on in Oriental studies in this 1823 description of translating a Sanskrit text: "It is more than India, gentlemen, it is a page from the origins of the world, from the primitive history of human species, that we shall attempt to decipher together" (quoted in Schwab 1986, 24). With such a strong romantic confirmation of the importance of this Oriental studies project, albeit one still anchored in origin, the absence of attention to this field in Foucault seems puzzling. Yet, strangely and, almost despite itself, buried within Burnouf's own romantic phrasing lies the answer.

Instead of producing a dissonant new discourse, Burnouf's "decipherment" confirmed the power of an existing one. The methods of textual translation he employed were now utterly dependent on the logic and reasoning of another "language game," namely, science. Here was a "logic" that, ten years hence and in the completely unrelated field of colonial engineering, could reverse Burnouf's high valuation of the East and go on to explain why West was best. It was a reversal summed up in the words of Prosper Enfantin: "Suez is the Centre of our life work. We shall carry out the act for which the world is waiting to proclaim that we are male!" (quoted in Abdel-Malek 1969, 189–198; cited in Bernal 1987, 269).

On the face of it, Enfantin's assertion of Western male sexuality and Burnouf's romantic quest for human origin may appear utterly unrelated. Yet what they shared was a belief in the language, logic, and power that came from different employments of the scientific method. It is this method that locates them both, as Müller puts it, in the "highest mental culture." Extraction, translation, mobility, and an ability to combine with and reconfigure other elements of an existing set of knowledges formed the methodological basis for both these disparate discourses. And just as scientifically based translational practices would render an exact knowledge of texts "from the origins of the world," so, too, the language of modern science, when applied to engineering works, would refashion the ground beneath our feet. The magnetic pull of science was beginning to draw a vast array of disciplines into its orbit. Some, as Foucault notes, would develop their own critical accents that would set them apart. Others, however, such as those that were more immediately and directly useful to the process of colonization, would be intellectually reduced, becoming mere foot soldiers of observation. Scientific method, therefore, not only reshaped the ground beneath our feet but also the mental landscape we inhabited. It was at this crucial juncture, a point at which this essay itself returns to its opening theme of science in action, that Oriental studies would be both born and cursed. In this subtle shift, which actually gave the field its name, Oriental studies would no longer command an alternative possibility of theoretical production but would instead be demoted to the rank of translator and supplier of observations valuable to the work of other (disciplinary) projects. Moreover, all this was taking place at around the time translation studies was reshaping its practices as a result of the magnetic pull of science. Indeed, these epistemic changes would pull even Burnouf's romantic sentiments into the logic of scientific reason and, from there, highlight the one remaining value Oriental studies had: relevance.

Transforming Translation

In classical times, what was essential in translation was not exactitude but expropriation to enrich one's own language. As Saint Jerome put it, "The translator considers thought content a prisoner which he transplants into his own language with the prerogative of a conqueror" (quoted in H. Friedrich 1992, 12–13). By the middle of the eighteenth century the revolution taking place in comparative philology changed this view.[22] The "original" text was no longer a prison but a laboratory, and the conqueror increasingly took on the guise of a scientist of language. While philology had abandoned studies of the word for studies that focused on the structure of language, translation studies rediscovered the importance of the word, albeit in a very different way. With word in hand, it demanded of itself the impossible: a word-for-word translation, or as near as one could get to that.[23] Whereas philology had abandoned the search for origin, translation, in a very different way, reinscribed origin in the privilege it accorded to the (original) text (Schulte and Biguenet 1992, 3). From the field of comparative philology, with its recently acquired concern for the internal grammars and structures of language, came a translational practice that similarly concerned itself with structure and detail. But the devil in this detail was a turning of the tables on theology's search for truth and transparency in origin. From this time on, translation studies looked forward to a time when the promise of a scientific knowledge matrix would fulfill its dream of transparency. Very quickly, however, it became apparent that good translation required more than a word-for-word account. Words required "contextualization," and it was Michel Bréal (in his "Les idées latentes" [1897], cited in T. Mitchell 1988, 141) who would state this succinctly: "It does not suffice at all, in order to give an account of a structure of a language, to analyze its grammar and to trace the words back to their etymological values. One must enter into the people's way of thinking and feeling."

It seems clear from this, as Timothy Mitchell intimates, that philology, in part at least, authorized the search not only for the nature of the human spirit but, in the case of knowledges that spoke of material states of being (such as Oriental studies), for a more modest, localized, and applied social research agenda. But why, one might wonder, would this field that required entering "into the people's way of thinking and feeling" approach this as a need for an applied, almost area studies social research agenda? This question is particularly apposite when one considers those other "splinters" of philological thought that were privileged because of their radically different and quite revolutionary notions of difference. These fields also would need to speak to the question of "the people's way of thinking and feeling," but they would do so not by reference to the surface appearance of things but by focusing on the buried processes of signification on which such surfaces were laid. It is at this point that we need to return to Foucault.

Foucault points out that the new "grammars" of Marx, Freud, and Nietzsche would build on the dissonance buried in Western knowledge of a certain otherness of economy, consciousness, and language. If it was indeed from within philology that such dissonance would grow, then religious methods cannot be ignored. This is because these new grammars would all, in their own unique ways, gain protean strength thanks to a long held but buried commitment in philology to what we might now call an early "philosophy of the dissonant sign." In classical times, nouns and verbs would be read beyond their literal meaning as signs through which one could trace the language and wonders of God.[24] It was just this attempt to reach beyond the manifest level of surface appearance and touch an inner symbolic meaning that would reemerge in a secular form and come to define these new grammars of dissent.

Freud's work, for example, would produce a dissonance that spoke directly to "the people's way of thinking and feeling" by attempting to unmask the meaning of the "unspoken phrase." In doing this, he would come to recognize the value of past symbolic, religious, and "fanciful" interpretations of dreams but would then pivot this question away from "dream content" operative at a manifest level toward the latent "thought content" that lay beneath the surface.[25] This approach required the disruption of the order of appearance of phenomena within the dream and led to an appreciation of compression and substitution as well as concealment. For Freud, such unconscious forms would often manifest themselves in the gesture, the utterance, or the slip of the tongue. They would hint at an unconscious, repressed thought that could be brought to the surface by his "talking cure." Where Freud would look at the internal grammar of the individual in his employment of otherness, Marx, if Slavoj Žižek (1989) is to be believed, offered an account of the collective unconscious of capitalism.[26] He would do this by pointing to the way social change was orchestrated in capitalism under the sign of the "natural laws of production." Such natural laws he would reveal as being little more than a form of repression that would enable exploitation to appear natural. But if the unconscious of these natural laws could be disinterred, they would be shown to be anything but natural (Marx 1976, 899). Even in linguistics, this type of analysis would eventually arise once the inward move of philology was halted by a recognition that language itself was a social phenomenon. Language research would return to social analysis with a recognition that language was a "social event," a "two-sided act," as V. N. Voloshinov (1930/1973a, 84, 94) puts it. Thus, far from being internal to itself, language was only explicable in terms of dialogue.

"Even an infant's cry," writes Voloshinov (1930/1973a, 87), "is 'oriented' towards the mother," and the growing recognition of this led away from the philological obsession with reviving "cadavers of written languages." As these "ancient monuments" of the "finished monologic utterance" gave way to a focus on lived verbal utterances (72), a second shift began to take place. In this post-Saussurian world, emphasis would be redirected to the multitude of ways in which dialogue would be inflected. Stylization, parody, *staz*, and dialogue were the devices employed by Mikhail Bakhtin when he set about to determine many of the verbal "postures," accents, and subtexts that could transform a remark into a sign of joyousness, anger, interrogation, and so on.[27] In other words, one begins to recognize that the "philosophy of language is the philosophy of the sign" (Voloshinov 1930/1973a, 3); herein lay the beginnings of Marxist semiotics.

Thus, in altogether different ways (words/signs, conscious/unconscious, economy/political economy), these types of latent analyses differed from manifest understandings of how one "must enter into the people's way of thinking and feeling."

To gain such entry, these dissonant discourses employed a kind of internal otherness to produce a "distanciation effect" with regard to prevailing knowledge forms, and it was this that created the otherness of which Foucault speaks. Yet, when it came to the very domain where otherness took on a lived material form (Oriental studies), the result was intellectual impoverishment brought on by an applied research agenda that operated almost entirely on a manifest level, one reinforced by a view of language itself as only a "tool." In this domain, "the people's way of thinking and feeling" was registered only by surface description and uncovered only at the level of applied, descriptive research using the skills acquired in applied language study.

It was this shift of focus away from questions about ontological and theological matters to those concerned with surface description that led to the demotion of Oriental studies from its once privileged place in philology. Moreover, it was this trajectory that would then form the contours along which area studies' "way of knowing" would eventually travel. The applied, descriptive quality of Asian area studies was, therefore, not simply an effect of cold war functionalism or a shift from the humanities to the social sciences, although, to be fair, these things would highlight and lay bare the politics behind the sign "Europe and its other" under which Asian area studies labored. In effect, however, the field had already been theoretically laid out long before it was named. As Oriental studies was demoted, the field opened itself to an area studies way of knowing. At the time, it looked like anything but a demotion.

By the late nineteenth century, the expansion and formalization of colonial governance had put Oriental studies knowledge in great demand. And although this would lead romantics like Schlegel to remark sarcastically that India, with the help of Oriental scholars, had become little more than "England's milch cow" (quoted in Schwab 1986, 88), such critiques were themselves, by this stage, little short of laughable. They mattered little in the face of a field that was both an urgent political necessity and could claim to employ the scientific method of the "highest mental culture." Besides, there was also the other undeniable fact that this utilitarian attitude produced the milk of colonial knowledge on which Oriental studies would feed and grow.[28]

One cannot deny that specific knowledge would be gained through such involvement with government, but one should not forget that the most valued form this knowledge would take was always one that could be interpolated into the machinery of colonial government. Here was a display of power/knowledge that, more than anything, demonstrated the "tamed" nature of what could, in theory at least, have been a disruptive domain of knowledge. Intoxicated by its proximity to colonial power and legitimized by its functional use value, Oriental studies, far from disturbing the grammar of colonial thinking, became utterly complicit with it. Far from "disturbing the words we speak" (Foucault 1966/1970, 298), it "translated" those disturbances into words that revealed the "truth" not only of India but, more important, of Western homogeneous, scientific reasoning. Yet, the more it reified Western reason as the organizing trope of its understanding of the non-Western world, the more it was forced to accept and employ the objective and rigorous language of scientific understanding that killed off the possibilities of expressing, even partly, the order of other cosmologies. The more such an understanding offered to governments and missionaries in terms of the functional knowledge value, the more the field split into "functional" subfields that spoke of specific country-based knowledges. As it did this, it further eroded its own status as an independent domain of knowledge that could speak to the essence of things. In heading down this path, Oriental studies not only squandered its potential to speak in its own tongue and produce dissonance within Western reason, but, in exchange for what intellectually, at least, were the meager privileges that would accrue from its status as colonial translator, it opened the door to its own demise at the hands of social sciences, for they would prove to be far more adept at speaking the objective language of science. At the time, however, this intellectual demise of Oriental studies appeared to contradict the facts.

Oriental studies emerged as a discrete domain at the very moment when the sciences themselves had begun to value the methodology of systematic observation and the so-called empirical style. By the nineteenth century, this methodology was increasingly finding a privileged reception in social inquiry, and the fact that Oriental studies dealt with "real places" and "real things" by employing applied techniques and translations made its empirical observations a model form of applied knowledge. Yet, in this claim to its own scientificity, Oriental studies would once again begin to falter.

By the turn of the nineteenth century, the way descriptive knowledge was viewed had changed dramatically. Earlier statistical analysis had been treated with immense skepticism in the nascent social sciences because of the problem of "like species,"[29] but by the beginning of the twentieth century, this was no longer the case. Francis Galton's work in anthropology, Francis Ysidro Edgeworth's in economics, and Karl Pearson's in the philosophy of science had begun to produce the type of statistical methodologies that were about to claim their own privileged status as the most objective approaches to questions of the social sciences. In effect, this quantitative methodology had already started to erode the more culturally based descriptive approaches at the heart of Oriental studies.[30] As these ideas spread into the social sciences, observational knowledge would no longer be the basis on which a model discipline would be built. Instead, such knowledge would be treated as little more than the raw data awaiting scientific systematization and quantification.

Wedded as it was to observational methods, Oriental studies was quickly becoming little more than a content provider for social scientific studies of other cultures. Long gone were the days when Oriental studies was an exalted domain from which one spoke to the essence of things, and squandered were the chances it had of achieving its potential as a site of disruption. Instead, the applied research programs of Oriental studies were increasingly dependent on the theories and scientific practices of other domains of Western knowledge. It was this trajectory that would simultaneously damn this domain intellectually and empower it politically. Thus, while Oriental studies was evacuated of any pretensions to theoretical critique, the one remaining compensation offered to this field lay in the claims it could now make to know "native" peoples and languages. Its one distinctive claim thus rested on its applied language training.

Curiously, then, this field that would speak directly to questions of material otherness and difference was never to be theoretically charged or privileged but was instead transformed into a mere domain of application and observation. Thus, while other protégés of philology would achieve exalted status and come to disturb the words we speak and the grammatical habits through which we think (Foucault), the applied nature of Oriental studies found itself increasingly reliant on the language and grammar of science to provide it with a translational key. Lashed firmly to this pole of Western scientific reason, the potentially radical, disruptive, and heterogeneous possibilities this field had to offer, if differently conceived, were brought meekly to heel as it became one more brick in the wall around the homogeneous world of reason. It was this style of thought that would offer Oriental studies its one remaining significant compensation: relevance. And this would go on to define Asian area studies.

Toward an Alternative Conclusion to Asian Studies

The renunciation by Oriental studies of grand universalizing claims and the birth of a new form of geographically specific knowledge about texts and society, which was later to take the name Asian studies, was brought on by neither a great revolutionary discovery nor a grand methodological shift in the field itself. Instead, the field was slowly transformed as it drew on the social sciences and began to produce work of definite utilitarian value to missionaries and colonial administrators. The increased productivity of translational practices, brought on through the use of new scientific techniques, also furthered this process and reinforced the awe with which scientific method was viewed. In the past, scarce textual evidence had been supplemented by individual imagination and creative fancy. With increased translation skills more material was rendered into Western languages and this, along with the high value now placed on observation, made imaginative leaps simply unimaginable. Instead of textual scarcity there was now abundance, and this, in turn, increased the tendency to specialize. Where once "the Orient" could be treated as a single object of scholarly inquiry, it was now far too big and complex for such simplicities. As I have already noted, specialized subdisciplines would emerge, and these would cluster around the languages studied. The resulting subfields —sinology, Egyptology, Indic studies, and so forth—reinforced an already existing trend to organize knowledge around country as well as culture, and this, in turn, furthered the functionality of these fields. Even within these subfields, the sheer density of knowledge that was emerging, coupled with the demand by government, business, and a range of other lobbies for this field to produce functional knowledge, meant that they were constantly being pulled into the orbit of various disciplines. These factors in turn reinforced the split between "real" as place of description covered by an area study and thought as scientific knowledge based in or on a discipline.

Somewhat later, and in the United States, these trends would finally express what had long been imminent. By forcing a move away from the humanities and highlighting utilitarian value above all else, what ended up being produced was what one scholar has termed a "North American way of knowing" (Rafael 1994, 91; see also Chakrabarty 1998). This would clear the field of its remaining romanticism and lead to a combination of language training and training in social science disciplinary skills. By the late 1920s the Library of Congress had begun to reorganize its collection into geographically specific domains,[31] and private organizations, such as the Carnegie Institute, were beginning to fund scholarly fieldwork that employed the new interdisciplinary social science methodologies in the study of specific non-Western societies. While the projects they funded and endorsed were still based on an examination of past great civilizations and therefore bore the hallmarks of Oriental studies, the methods being deployed betrayed the now almost complete dominance of the social sciences and offered "telltale signs" of things to come.[32] The arrival of area studies would not take long.

These trends would reach their apogee in the changed geopolitical climate that followed World War II, but they were already clearly imminent in Oriental studies. Thus, while Ruth Benedict's (1947) anthropological study of interned Japanese Americans, commissioned as part of the war effort against Japan, marked one of the first moments of this new field of applied area studies, it was in fact not a break but the culmination of a long trend. Yet it was also a template of things that followed. Here was a type of scholarship that was contemporary and country-based and, most important of all, had immediate policy dividends. Here was a type of scholarship that would inspire an entire generation of utilitarian cold war area studies scholars. By the late 1940s the applied models of the social sciences had begun to cast a shadow over the entire intellectual horizon. Increasingly, and much more explicitly than in the past, the new field of area studies would turn to the social sciences for explanations of global developments, for in these, it was hoped, a way would be found to counter the universalizing Marxist revolutionary accounts of development.[33] The politics of the field was now overt, and "friend and enemy" was more than a trope, it policed boundaries of scholarly acceptability. This part of the story of Asian area studies, when area studies becomes an overt weapon of the cold war, is well-known, as is the later "insurgency" (Barlow 1993) of left scholars attached to or associated with the Committee of Concerned Asian Scholars.[34] The overt politicization of this field is not what concerns me here. What does is the limited and limiting notion of what area studies can do intellectually. And that, I have argued, was a battle that was lost even before the invention of area studies knowledges.

With language as its only definable core—and, even here, the employment of language only as a domain to train in application—it is little wonder that the field now lacks any sense of its own intellectual identity.

Yet, as is clear from other domains, language offers a range of other, more intellectually exciting possibilities. To break the atheoretical cycle of area studies yet recognize its core therefore requires circling back to that moment of language dissonance that Foucault identified. It necessitates turning away from the temptation to regard itself only as a content provider for the disciplines and to take more seriously and develop theoretically the study of its core: language. This time, however, language study would not be undertaken purely to improve fluency or simply for application but to create a means of producing intellectual dissonance. It would become a means by which we could start to take cultural difference and the signs of such difference seriously. To do this, we need to return to those moments when philology gave birth to the language of dissent and realize that the moves that enabled Freud, Marx, and Nietzsche to speak in dissonance are historically and intellectually also a possibility for area studies.

To arrive back at that moment, to treat it not historically as the moment when Oriental studies began its slippage into area studies, but theoretically, as a moment of decision about which knowledge form this nascent domain should take, brings us back to the question of language theoretically. Here, the trajectory for the study of language is quite different from the training role it is currently ascribed. Here, it departs from these strictures to suggest a social semiotics that would begin to highlight the connotative possibilities inherent in language itself. Here is one way to unearth latent meaning and heterogeneous forms. It is a means of translating that can give voice to the murmurs of other cosmologies. Perhaps this way the Chinese dyke builders will have their day, not as part of the scientific world of incorporation but as a tale of otherness, difference, and dissent that lets us call into question the epistemic violence of scientific incorporation.

Notes

I would like to thank the Australian Research Council for funding this research and the Max Planck Institute for History in Göttingen, Germany, where I revised this piece during a month-long sabbatical.

1 I first took notice of this story when I heard it as an aside in a talk by a prominent historian of Chinese science, who was explaining the sophistication of Chinese dyke-making techniques. The story of ceremony was very much given as light relief, and when the account of the dykes was published, the story of the archers was omitted. It is still, however, very much in the consciousness of the people of Zhejiang. In a recent commentary on the topic, Ye Bingnan (1993, 23) retells the story of King Qian and the shooting of arrows. King Qian was head of a small state in the five dynasties period, which lasted from A.D. 825 to 932. Ye's commentary is as follows:

Concerning Qian's repairs of the seawalls to prevent calamities during the Yangtze River tide, there is a folk tale about "King Qian shooting the waves." The story of Qian comes to us from a portrayal in the "Record of the Shooting of the Tides," written by Qian's third-generation offspring, Sun Qian Weiyan. It is said of the early days of establishing the dyke that it took place in the eighth month, at a time of high tides and seasonal flooding. The raging tide and pounding swirl made it impossible to carry out construction work. Qian therefore ordered and led the deployment of soldiers to the site. From the hillsides down to the southern side of the mountain sturdy bamboo trees were made into three thousand arrows by woodworkers. These arrows were then adorned with the feathers of various birds and painted with a fiery red coloration, and newly fired metal was used to make the arrow tips. Five hundred soldiers who had the skill and strength to fire the crossbow were assembled at the banks of the Yangtze River and each archer was given six arrows. Each time there was a tidal rush, they would fire one arrow into the raging torrent. It was in this way that, after they had fired five times, they unexpectedly forced the tide to turn away from Hangzhou Bay and they made these eastern tides turn toward the western hills. It is said of these five hundred archers that they are all buried together at Pubing, an area between Houchaomen and Tongjiangmen. Above the ground in which they lay, a memorial was erected to them in a place called Tiezhuangpu. In Hangzhou's Jianggan district, even to this day, there are still two lane-ways bearing the names "the horizontal arrow lane-way" and the "vertical arrow lane-way." It is said that these names are related to the story of King Qian and the shooting of the tide.

2   For a very different take on a similar event, see Michel de Certeau's opening lines in *The Writing of History* (1988, xxv–xxvii). De Certeau begins this work by examining the etching by Jan van der Straet of Amerigo Vespucci's "discovery" of native Americans (they were not known before?) in the New World. It is with this encounter with the other that Certeau begins his examination of Western writing as historical practice.

3   T-O maps were popular in Christendom from about the seventh to ninth centuries until the mid-1300s. They were highly symbolic, being circular in shape and dividing the world into three parts to form a T, at whose center was the holy city of Jerusalem.

4   After its erection, the artists objected: "We come, writers, painters, sculptors, architects . . . in the name of French art and history that are both threatened, to protest against the erection in the very heart of our capital of the needless and monstrous Eiffel Tower" (Louis Chéronnet, cited in Buck-Morss 1991, 131). Guy de Maupassant, claims Roland Barthes (1982, 236), "often lunched at the restaurant in the tower, though he didn't much care for the food: '*It's the only place in Paris,*' he used to say, '*where I don't have to see it.*'" Despite these early artistic objections to the structural aesthetics of the tower, it was later hailed because it offered "the fundamental aesthetic experience of today's buildings" (Giedion 1926, 7, quoted in Benjamin 1983–84, 3). As Walter Benjamin elsewhere said, it was an "incomparable" monument to the "heroic age of technology" (quoted in Buck-Morss 1991, 130). Susan Buck-Morss notes that Benjamin believed that the artists, in attempting to defend themselves against the perceived threat of this new technology, missed the real danger, namely, the shop window, where the display of art was "in the service of the salesman" (134).

5   Indeed, according to Umberto Eco (1995, 209), one motive for the English search for a universal language key was that it would facilitate trade.

6   Little wonder that two of the most famous critics of rational choice theory from within

that logic, David Green and Ian Shapiro (1994), have pointed out that the only reason such modeling could be regarded as rigorous and universally applicable was because the models could never actually be falsified! All rational choice does, they claim, is reconfigure existing empirical knowledge into rational choice forms. For that reason, they conclude that rational choice theory has contributed "virtually nothing to the empirical study of politics" (195). For an excellent and succinct summary of the debate, see Brogan (1996).

7   Recent German scholarship on China challenges the philological roots of Chinese studies. For my argument, however, the veracity of this history is not the issue. Rather, I am interested in the effects of the belief in this past, irrespective of whether it is a post factum rationalization or not. For the controversial argument suggesting that German Chinese studies is not philological, see Leutner (2001). Thanks to Peter Mereker for guiding me through this.

8   Pierre Ryckmans (Simon Leys) (1983–84, 20), for example, has argued that "the sinological field is defined linguistically." More recently, Vicente L. Rafael (1994, 91) has defined the whole of area studies as "ensembles of knowledges and practices grounded on specific linguistic competencies and formulated within, as well as across, disciplinary boundaries."

9   In the case of Chinese studies, at least, this was reinforced by the *gaozhen* (or *K'ao-cheng*) approach to knowledge that emerged in the late Qing dynasty and stressed "facts" and philology. See Elman (1984).

10   Barthes's (1957/1972) famous example of denotative meaning—"Here's a black soldier saluting the French flag"—was deepened with a recognition of its "symbolic" connotative intent, which in this case suggested a mixture of colonialist nationalism and militarism. For an investigation of this linguistic link, see Coward and Ellis (1977).

11   Note, for instance, Luther's remark on Adam: "What an ocean of knowledge and wisdom there was in this one man!" (quoted in Aarsleff 1982, 281). For Locke, of course, such a "trick" was unavoidable, and my use of the term here is therefore ironic. Locke saw words as signs of ideas and language itself as a human invention. Words had no core that tied them back to objects any more than languages were divinely inspired. The whole idea of a search for an original universal language was, therefore, for Locke, a complete misunderstanding of the nature of words and language. For more details on Locke, see Aarsleff (1982, 42–83).

12   While some have regarded Enoch as "the scribe" and therefore become interested in the language in which he wrote, Augustine believed that Enoch, the seventh generation from Adam, was simply too ancient to be a reliable witness and that his book therefore could not be included in the ecclesiastical canon, for false things may have been inserted in it. I wish to thank Allen Kerkeslager (Department of Theology, St. Josephs University, Philadelphia) for his help in positioning Enoch in this debate. Perhaps it was because Aarsleff (1982, 33) was all too aware of the densely spiritual connection between questions relating to the origin of language and the representation of things that he was loathe to reduce things to a mere question of resemblance? Perhaps it was for this reason that he opted to employ the term Adamistic, which clearly carries more of a spiritual essence and which clearly takes one beyond resemblance. Louis Marin (1989, 4) similarly critiques the lack of the religious in that work.

13   Hebrew was central to this quest, as the early fathers of the Church attest. Saint Jerome, in one of his epistles to Damascus, wrote that "the whole of antiquity affirms that Hebrew, in

which the Old Testament was written, was the beginning of human speech" (quoted in H. Friedrich 1992, 12–13). Origen, in his eleventh homily on the Book of Numbers, expresses his belief that Hebrew, originally given by Adam, remained in that part of the world that was the chosen portion of God, rather than being left, like the rest of the world, to one of his angels. For further details and claims to this effect, see Müller (1861, 123).

14 Webb's words were as follows: "Scripture Teacheth, that the whole Earth was of one Language until the Conspiracy at Babel; History informs us that China was peopled, whilst the Earth was so of one Language, and before that Conspiracy. Scripture teacheth that the Judgment of Confusion of Tongues, fell upon those only that were at Babel; History informs, that the Chinois being fully settled before, were not there: And moreover that the same Language and Characters which long preceding that confusion they used, are in use with them at this very Day" (quoted in Kennedy 1965, 104).

15 So diverse was the philological community that even in 1804 the Manchester Philological Society was able to exclude from its membership anyone who spoke of Sanskrit or Indo-European languages and doubted the divine revelations. Moreover, it was not until 1866 that the Société de Linguistique of Paris stopped accepting communication on the question of a universal language (Eco 1995, 114–115).

16 See Müller (1861, 162) for the substantive point. It should be noted, however, that while Müller attributes the terms Indo-German and Indo-European to Schlegel (156–157), the former term is more readily identified with J. von Klaproth, and the latter is attributed to T. Young.

17 While Schlegel's work inspired the new comparativism, it was Francis Bopp who published the first detailed comparative text in 1816. See Müller (1861, 158).

18 Or, at the very least, when an emphasis on the word did return, as it would in V. N. Voloshinov's post-Saussurian "dialogical" approach, it would take Leibniz's idea of a "universal grammar" in a very different direction. No longer interested in etymological paths back to God, Voloshinov "demotes" the word to being merely the "purest," most universal and "neutral" of "signs" within any verbal process of communication. With a focus on the signification processes, rather than on the origin of words, Voloshinov (1930/1973a, 14) revalorizes the word but does so on a new basis: "The entire reality of the word is wholly absorbed in its function of being a sign," he stated, thereby offering what would become the beginnings of a Marxist semiology.

19 Müller (1864, 14) made his view on this point quite clear: "I believe there is no science from which we, the students of language, may learn more than from Geology. Now, in Geology, if we have once acquired a general knowledge of the successive strata that form the crust of the earth and of the faunas and floras present or absent in each, nothing is so instructive as the minute exploration of a quarry close at hand, of a cave or a mine, in order to see things with our own eyes, to handle them, and to learn how every pebble that we pick up points a lesson of the widest range. I believe the same is true of the science of language."

20 Foucault's (1970) reading of the effects of comparative philology is found in the chapter "Labor, Life, Language," and it is here that one will find the specific references to which I refer.

21 For signposts to these appropriations, see Schwab (1986) and Maverick (1946).

22 The history of translation is long and complex and varies from one country to another. Briefly, in English translation studies, at least two different positions prevailed. From the seventeenth century one notes the rise of "transparency" and fluency (or what

Lawrence Venuti labels "domestication") as considerations in translation. The other approach is much more literal, that is to say, it retains a certain textual fidelity that produced awkwardness and a certain foreignness in the text translated. For more details on this debate, see Venuti (1995).

23   One sees the contemporary effects of this translational method in the defense mounted by area studies against "alien" Western theory. Note, for instance, the argument proffered by Paul Cohen (1984, 196–197) for a China-centric approach:

[The] China-centred approach is intended to delineate an approach to recent Chinese history that strives to understand what is happening in that history in terms that are as free as possible of imported criteria of significance. . . . it will be countered, as long as the practitioners of China-centred historiography are Americans, no matter how hard we try to get "inside" Chinese history, we will still end up insinuating into this history vocabulary and concepts that are American. Outsiders can never really develop an insider perspective. . . . This is true—up to a point.

24   Even ostensibly secular readings of grammar, such as those offered by the Port-Royal logicians in the seventeenth century, when more closely scrutinized, turned out to be thoroughly imbued with Christian metaphoricity. As Marin (1989, 12–14) points out, the eucharistic model reveals "the profound coherence of the network of examples illustrating the semiotic theory of Port-Royal." Here is a theory of speech that "simultaneously" develops "a linguistic theology of the Eucharist."

25   While recognizing the limitations of past (largely biblical) interpretations of dreams, Freud was still quite clear about their value. In examining the dream books of old he stated that they should not be dismissed in their entirety, for they offer an example of "one of those not infrequent cases where ancient and stubbornly retained popular belief seems to have come nearer to the truth of the matter than the opinion of modern science" (1966, 191).

26   Žižek (1989, 11) goes so far as to suggest that there is a "fundamental homology between the interpretative procedure of Marx and Freud—more precisely, between their analysis of commodity and of dreams."

27   *Skaz* is a Russian expression with no English equivalent that is probably best described as "narration with marked speech-event features." See Titunik (1973, 191 n. 19). Here, of course, I am merely rehearsing the "dialogistic" thinking of Mikhail Bakhtin and repeating the point about the utterance he makes most forcefully in Bakhtin (Baxtin 1971, 196–198). It should be noted that this point also plays a key role in that classic Bahktin text on language, enigmatically authored by either a close follower or by Bakhtin himself under the alter ego identity of V. N. Voloshinov (1973a). See especially part 2, chapters 2 and 3, of the Voloshinov text.

28   Who could forget, after all, that the first Western school for the study of Sanskrit was opened by the British East India Company in Hailsbury College in 1805, or that Warren Hastings's plan of 1772 for better governance in Bengal ended up turning on the teaching of Sanskrit as a means to establish a pure "Hindu law." For further details on this, see Cohn (1985).

29   Note Stephen Stigler's (1986, 95) words on the problem of like species in statistical analysis: "Even as late as 1869 it was necessary for the economist William Stanley Jevons to defend his employment of statistics against the charges that he was wrong to combine prices of several very different commodities into one index in a study of variation in the value of gold."

30 On this importance of science as a "trope," see Latour (1993, 18, 35). On the rather slow spread of the statistical method to the social sciences, see Stigler (1986, 265–266).

31 In 1928 the Chinese-language books in the Library of Congress were the first holdings to be gathered together and housed in the newly constituted Division of Chinese Literature, and this would be the model used to reorganize all other Asian-language holdings. The Japanese collection would be rearranged sometime after 1930, and in 1938 the Indian collection would begin to be housed in a separate section that became, after 1942, the Indic Studies section of the library's Asian Division. See Library of Congress (2000, 13, 32, 46). Thanks to Mi Chu of the Library of Congress for pointing out to me this process of library rearrangement.

32 Dipesh Chakrabarty notes that the first such program undertaken under the auspices of the Social Science Research Council was a study of Mayan culture, which brought together archaeologists, ethnologists, historians, geographers, biologists, nutritionists, medical research workers, and other types of specialists (Chakrabarty 1998, citing Stewart 1950, xi).

33 For examples of this in relation to China, see Barlow (1993).

34 So one finds that in the postwar era in Chinese studies (like many other non-Western areas), the struggle was said to have taken place between the modernization paradigm and a more revolutionary outlook. For a critique of what in some respects foreshadows Cohen's work arguing for a China-centric approach, see R. Myers and Metzer (1980). For a critique that argues for the need for greater (not lesser) theoretical rigor, see C. Johnson (1982); yet even here, while theoretical rigor is said to be needed to sharpen our focus, what is meant by theory is little more than stronger reading glasses for the social translator.

ECONOMICS

Economists and the Economy in the Twentieth Century

TIMOTHY MITCHELL

W hat is the relation between economic knowledge and the main object of that knowledge, the economy? Most answers to this question would agree that the nature of the relationship changes as economists develop new tools of understanding and new methods of explanation. Most answers would also assume, however, that economic knowledge, despite these changes, always refers to substantially the same thing. The history of economics is taken to be the history of the development of different kinds of expert knowledge about an object, the economy, whose forms may change but whose underlying substance remains the same.

This essay offers a different answer to the question. It makes the following arguments. First, the economy became the object of economic knowledge only quite recently. Not until the 1930s did economists begin to write about an object called the economy, and only by the middle of the century was the term as it is understood today in general use. Second, "economy" was not just a new word for an existing sphere or underlying substance; its arrival marked the emergence of novel forms of sociotechnical practice that formed and performed the economy as a new object of professional knowledge and political practice. Earlier economists and political economists wrote about worlds in which the economy had not yet come about. Third, economics participated in making the economy, with the help of other forms of social theory, as well as statistics, policymaking, and other kinds of specialist and nonspecialist social practice. Fourth, many of the practices that gave rise to the economy involved processes of representation, whether in the form of new kinds of enumeration, image making, performance, or calculation. When economics produced accounts of these processes, it was making representations of representations. This had important consequences for the relationship between economic knowledge and its object.

Most thinking about the relationship between economics and the economy continues to reflect the influence of Karl Polanyi (1944; Polanyi, Arensberg, and Pearson 1957). Polanyi's well-known argument was that the economy emerged as an institutional sphere separate from the rest of society in the nineteenth century. Before this moment of separation, the economy was absorbed or embedded in wider social relations. It follows, he argued, that the formal rules of classical, Ricardian economics relate only to a particular historical period, when market exchanges ceased to be a minor aspect of broader social relations and became an apparently self-regulating system to which other social spheres were subordinated. Moreover, he argued, classical political economy helped to achieve this separation of the market system from society, in particular by formulating ways of treating land, labor, and money as though they were merely commodities, a fiction that was essential to the formation of the economy as its own institutional sphere.

More recent scholarship has elaborated different aspects of this view from a variety of perspectives. Tribe (1978) showed the absence of the modern concept of the economy among political economists of the seventeenth and eighteenth centuries, agreeing that the idea emerges only at the turn of the nineteenth century. Foucault (1991) identified the new conception of "government" that characterized the large-scale management of populations in the eighteenth and nineteenth centuries and associated these practices with the emergence of the economy as a new object of political management. Meurat (1988), N. Rose (1999; P. Miller and Rose 1990), and others (Hindess 1998; see also Buck-Morss 1995) have extended Foucault's analysis, relating changes in the methods of governmental power to changing conceptions of the economy in the nineteenth and twentieth centuries.

The consensus that the economy became a distinct object of intellectual knowledge and government practice in the late eighteenth or nineteenth century overlooks a surprising fact: no political economist of that period refers to an object called "the economy." In the sense of the term we now take for granted, referring to the self-contained structure or totality of relations of production, distribution, and consumption of goods and services in a given geographic space, the idea of the economy emerged more than a century later, in the 1930s and 1940s. Both in academic writing and in popular expression, this meaning of the term came into common use only during the years around World War II.

From the works of Thomas Mun and William Petty in the seventeenth century to Adam Smith in the late eighteenth, political economy was not concerned with the structure of production or exchange in an economy. In *The Wealth of Nations*, Adam Smith (1776/1950) never once refers to a structure or whole of this sort. When he uses the term economy, the word carries the older meaning of frugality or the prudent use of resources: "Capital has been silently and gradually accumulated by the private frugality and good conduct of individuals. . . . It is the highest impertinence and presumption . . . in kings and ministers, to pretend to watch over the oeconomy of private people" (327–328). The object of political economy was the proper husbanding and circulation of goods and the proper role of the sovereign in managing this circulation. Tribe (1978, 80–109) suggests that an earlier tradition of writing on the economy or management of the large household or estate was extended to discussions of the management of the state, imagined as the household of the sovereign. The term economy came to refer to this prudent administration or government of the community's affairs, the same practices of administering a population and territory examined in the essay on "Governmentality" by Foucault (1991). Political economy referred to the economy, or government, of the polity, not to the politics of an economy.

The political economists of the nineteenth century abandoned this image of the administration of the household or estate, but did not replace it with the modern idea of the economy. Their object of analysis was not a self-contained sphere, imagined as a machine whose internal mechanisms and exchanges separate it from other social processes. It was an organic world of human settlement, agriculture, and the movement of populations, goods, and wealth. Ricardo's "Essay on Profits" of 1815 (1951), a formative text of nineteenth-century political economy, presents not a model of an economy but a narrative of the cycle of corn production, beginning with "the first settling of a country rich in fertile land," and examining the relationship between increasing population, corn production, and profit, until "the natural limit to population" is reached (10–15). The term "population" here, as in the *Essay on the Principle of Population* of Thomas Malthus (1803), refers not to the number of inhabitants but to the process of peopling a place. The dynamic of the analysis is the cycle of population and cultivation. Its spatial image is not the space of the economy but the geography of land settlement and the difference between countryside and town. (German "central place theory" was the contemporaneous expression of this geographic model of circulation and population in arithmetical form.) These, rather than an abstract economy, construct the specific time and space of the analysis.

The phrase "political economy" continued to refer to the management or government of a polity. This meaning is especially clear in the work of Friedrich List, whose *National System of Political Economy* (1841/1856) is sometimes singled out as a precocious study of "the national economy" in its twentieth-century sense. List contrasted "the financial economy of the state" (which referred "to the collection, to the use, and the administration of the material means of a government") with "the economy of the people" (which referred to "the institutions, the regulations, the laws, and the circumstances which govern the economical conditions of the citizens"). Thus, economy referred to the forms of administration, regulation, law, and social circumstance that defined the processes known as government (281).

When the political economy of the nineteenth century was displaced by the marginalist revolution that began in the 1870s and was consolidated by the turn of the century, the possibility of conceiving of the economy in the twentieth-century sense of the term was pushed further back. The object of analysis was made up of forces, conceived as individual utilities, that were assumed to be in balance. The site of this mechanical equilibrium was "the market." This term no longer referred to the social marketplace of Ricardo or Marx, conceptualized in relation to the city, to agriculture, and to the factory, but to a utopic space, formulated geometrically, by the axes of a chart, as the two-dimensional plane on which numerical utilities could meet and balance one another (Walras 1874/1952). As a neutral, planar surface, the market of neoclassical economics had no depth, no dynamic structure, no forces of its own, no "macro" dimension that could be described apart from the individual utilities that moved across it. It was an inert, unmoving space.

As recently as the 1920s, the second edition of *Palgrave's Dictionary of Political Economy* (Palgrave 1925–26) contained no separate entry for or definition of the term economy. It used the word only to mean "the principle of seeking to attain, or the method of attaining, a desired end with the least possible expenditure of means" (678). In 1932 (1935), Lionel Robbins's classic *Essay on the Nature and Significance of Economic Science* described "The Subject-Matter of Economics" (chapter 1) as "human behaviour conceived as a relationship between ends and means" (21) and never employed the term economy in its novel mid-twentieth-century sense.

The emergence of the idea of the economy in the interwar period could be traced in a number of different disciplines. In anthropology, Malinowski (1922) argued that moneyless communities of the Trobriand Islands could be described as having an economy. Karl Polanyi (1944) was able to draw on Malinowski's work to distinguish between societies in which "market economy" was embedded in other social relations and those in which it emerged as a separate sphere. In projecting the term economy onto a period a century before the word was used in this sense, Polanyi can be read as an important figure in the creation of the concept of the economy in the 1940s.

   In sociology, one could trace the influence of Talcott Parsons and show in particular how he mistranslated critical passages from Weber's (1968) *Economy and Society*. The translation defined the term "economy" not as Weber glossed it ("autocephalous economic action," meaning action "concerned with the satisfaction of a desire for 'utilities' "), but as "an autocephalous *system* of economic action" (Weber 1972, 31; Weber 1947, 158, emphasis added). Inserting the word "system" made it seem that Weber was talking about the new conception of the economy as a self-contained structure or totality. The mistranslation was only partially repaired when Roth and Wittich (1968) incorporated Parsons's translation into the complete English edition of *Economy and Society*. They rephrased the earlier translation: "An 'economy' is autocephalous economic action" (63). The word "an" is not found in the original German and makes no sense in English. Other German sociologists, for example, Georg Simmel, were mistranslated in the same way, to make their work fit the new structure of U.S. social science (see T. Mitchell 2002, 80–81). The same thing happened when Léon Walras's classic work in equilibrium theory, *Eléménts d'Economie Politique Pure* (1874), was translated into English for the American Economic Association in 1954. The phrase "the economy" was inserted into the English version at various points, usually as a deliberate substitution for the term "society" (*société*) in the original.

   In the discipline of economics, the easiest place to trace the appearance of the idea that the economy exists as a general structure of economic relations is in the publication of John Maynard Keynes's *General Theory of Employment, Interest and Money* (1936). Although tending to employ phrases like "economic society" and "the economic system as a whole" where today one would simply say "the economy," *The General Theory* conventionally marks the origin of what would come to be called macro-economics.

The significance of Keynes is easy to exaggerate, however. There were several rival efforts in the same period to arrive at a scientific representation of the newly conceived totality. Keynes himself was critical of what was arguably a more important development of the 1930s: the birth of econometrics, or the attempt to create a mathematical representation of the entire economic process as a self-contained and dynamic mechanism. The first econometric model claiming to represent an entire economy was published in 1937, the year after as *The General Theory*, by Jan Tinbergen, who was later to share the first Nobel Prize in economics for this work. Three years later, working for the League of Nations, Tinbergen produced the first large-scale model of the U.S. economy (M. Morgan 1990, 101–130): "We may start from the proposition that every change in economic life has a number of proximate causes. These proximate causes themselves have their own proximate causes which in turn are indirect 'deeper' causes with respect to the first mentioned change, and so on. Thus a network of causal relations can be laid out connecting up all the successive changes occurring in an economic community" (Tinbergen 1937, 8, cited in M. Morgan 1990, 103).

As in *The General Theory*, phrases like "economic life" and "economic community" express the new idea of the network of relations that would come to be termed the economy. Keynes ridiculed the new econometric work of scholars like Tinbergen, describing the attempt to mathematicize the entire economy as "hocus." Schumpeter (1933, 12) came to the defense of econometrics in the first issue of the new journal *Econometrica* on the grounds that mathematical rigor would enable economists to speak with more authority to politicians.

One way to understand the birth of the idea of the economy is as the attempt to include in the picture of the economic process other forces besides the "energy" of individual utility (Mirowski 1989). It was quite clear by the 1920s and 1930s (indeed, long before then) that fluctuations of prices in the market were far too erratic to be explained simply by reference to changing utilities. It was necessary to theorize other kinds of energies or forces at work, subjecting what would otherwise be a stable equilibrium to random shocks. These energies would have to be conceived as "external" to the market, for the market itself was by definition composed only of individual energies. Because they were external, they would impact the market as a whole. These impacts would cause the market as a whole to move, setting up reverberations or oscillations that were distinct

from the individual movements caused by the energy of particular utilities. The market could no longer be pictured as merely an inert, planar
space, defined as the site of a static equilibrium; it would have to be
somehow imagined as a dynamic system. The name that emerged for this
energized totality was "the economy."

Previous efforts to imagine the impact of external shocks affecting the
market as a whole took the form of the study of business cycles. But before
the 1930s, business cycle theory was a relatively minor, sometimes ridiculed, field. And it was not clear how to imagine these cycles within the
framework of neoclassical economics. Wesley Clair Mitchell (1927, 2)
warned that business cycles are a "synthetic product of the imagination."

The transformation in economic thinking was understood at the time
not in terms of the birth of the idea of the economy but as a shift from a
static conception of economic processes to a dynamic one. (Even to those
looking back after World War II, for example, Schumpeter in his *History of
Economic Analysis* (1954), it was this rather than Keynesianism that appeared as the major development of the interwar period.) However many
elements could be manipulated in equilibrium models of the market,
these represented discrete movements within what was as a whole a sta-
tionary apparatus. What if the apparatus as a whole could be thought to
move? What if, as the Norwegian economist Ragnar Frisch (1933, 171)
asked, "certain exterior impulses hit the economic mechanism and thereby initiate more or less regular oscillations"? Frisch developed a complex
mechanical analogy to illustrate this, consisting of a small pipe attached to
a pendulum suspended beneath a bowl of water, the pipe ending in a valve
whose operation depended on the direction of the pendulum's swing
(203–204).

However, to conceive of the kinds of external forces that would produce
a dynamic impulse affecting the entire economic machinery required two
related conceptual shifts. First, a clear distinction had to be elaborated
between what Frisch called "the intrinsic structure" of the mechanism and
its exterior. Second, this intrinsic structure could no longer be imagined as
a single market, or even a series of interconnected markets, with a limited
number of buyers, sellers, and commodities. As a dynamic totality, it was
now thought of as "the whole economic system taken in its entirety"
(Frisch 1933, 172). The reworking of mechanical images in the 1930s to
imagine the possibility of an external force creating an impulse that reverberates through and sets up oscillations within a completely closed system
marks the birth of the idea of the economy. What was new in this idea was
not the treatment of economic processes as to some extent distinct from

other kinds of processes in society. Rather, it was the notion that these processes form a singular and self-contained totality whose internal mechanisms and balances were subject to external shocks or manipulations, such external impulses creating reverberations throughout the internal machine.

To follow the further development of these ideas through the 1940s and 1950s lies outside the scope of this essay. There were major developments during World War II, as Mirowski (2002), M. Bernstein (2001), and others have shown, including systems analysis, input-output analysis, and game theory, all of which shaped the way the economy was conceived, measured, and managed in the postwar period. Instead, I want to ask about the significance of the birth of the idea of the economy for answering the question with which I began, concerning the relation between economics and its object of study. To explore this question requires making connections between the intellectual developments I have sketched and other technical and political transformations.

The economy was formed as a new object in the context of broader developments. Tinbergen developed his first econometric model in response to a Dutch government request for policies to combat the depression (M. Morgan 1990, 102). Keynesian theory was also a response to the experience of mass unemployment and depression and to the emergence of fascist, Soviet, New Deal, and other general economic programs that addressed not just individual human behavior but the interaction of aggregate and structural factors such as employment, investment, and money supply. Also important was the emergence after World War I of welfare and development programs for European colonies (Keynes's first job was in the Revenue, Statistics and Commerce Department of the India Office) in response to the growing threats to colonial rule.

These broader events were not just the context for the emergence of a new conception of the economy. The possibility of making the economy in the mid-twentieth century arose out of these events, but economics was itself involved in the reconfiguring of social and technical worlds that gave rise to the economy. I look at three aspects of this reconfiguration: new forms of circulation of money, the weakening of European empires and other forms of imperial control and the creation of "national economies," and the rise of large corporations whose novel powers of management and marketing relied on new technologies for the manufacture and distribution of representations.

The interwar period saw a significant alteration in the forms of circulation of money in countries such as Britain and the United States. The most dramatic change was in the increase in the use of money for everyday transactions, in particular paper money. Before World War I, Keynes (1913) remarked on how seldom people in Britain used token or paper money for financial transactions. He could think of only two purposes for which he himself regularly used money: to purchase railway tickets and to pay his domestic servants. Most everyday transactions were settled by running an account or writing a check. In the United States, federal bank notes had been introduced by the National Currency Act of 1863, but their supply was limited. Their use remained unpopular and they competed with a range of other regional bank notes and local scrips (Zelizer 1997). Again, local accounts and personal checks were by far the most common ways to settle transactions. During the war, the situation began to change, with the rapid increase in the printing of money and the relaxing and later abandoning of the gold standard in most countries. The creation of the U.S. Federal Reserve in 1913 and similar reforms in other countries led to a standardization of bank notes and wide and rapid acceptance of the use of paper money.

The transformation in the use and circulation of money can illustrate how economic knowledge helped to form its new object. In the first place, economists developed new theories of money, entering into the political battles over questions of currency reform, the gold standard, and government control of exchange rates and money supply. Keynes's first published work, *Indian Currency and Finance* (1913), was a practical contribution to this politics and was followed by the publication of *A Treatise on Money* (1930). In the United States, the conflict between Irving Fisher's quantity theory of money and the "real bills" doctrine of J. Laurence Laughlin and his students shaped the creation of the Federal Reserve system (Mehrling 2002). The conceptions and calculative technologies provided by economists were built into the new financial institutions. In other words, economists developed practical tools for measuring and managing the value of money that became part of the novel day-to-day machinery of monetary circulation that was soon to be recognized as "the economy."

The next step was to begin to see this new mechanism of money circulation as a system in its own right, rather than just another "market." Following the publication of *A Treatise on Money* (1930), Keynes made a decisive break with the ideas of his predecessors at Cambridge, Marshall and Pigou, as well as the work of Fisher and Frisch. Earlier theorists, he argued, had treated money as simply a neutral signifier of value and thus saw no essential difference between a system of exchange using money and a barter system. In the earliest surviving drafts of *The General Theory*, which date from 1932 to 1933, and in fragments of his Cambridge lecture notes from the same period, he discusses the differences between the "real-exchange economy" or "neutral economy" of classical economic theory, and the "money economy" of the real world of the present (Keynes 1971–89, 13: 396–412, 420–21; 29: 54–55; Skidelsky 1992). These notes represent his first use of the concept of the economy in its contemporary sense.

Keynes's breakthrough was to conceive of the new totality not as an aggregation of markets in different commodities, but as the circulation of money. The economy was the sum of all the moments at which money changed hands.

A further step in the making of this economy was to construct mechanisms for measuring all the instances of spending and receiving money within a geographic space. These mechanisms were the new national income accounts. Before the interwar period, attempts to calculate national wealth or "national dividend" had come up against a series of insuperable obstacles. There was the problem of counting the "same" goods or money twice. For example, commodities sold at wholesale could not be counted again, it was thought, when sold at retail; income earned as a professional salary should not be included in national wealth a second time when paid as wages to servants. And, as Marshall (1920, 523) pointed out, there was the problem of accounting for all the waste that was incurred in the production of wealth—not only the depreciation of tools and machinery, but also the exhaustion of the country's natural resources.

After World War I, the Dawes Committee, set up to estimate Germany's "capacity to pay" economic reparations, discovered the lack of not just reliable data concerning national income but a manageable conception of what one was trying to count. In both Germany and the United States there were extensive interwar efforts to remedy this problem (Tooze 1998). It took two decades to solve it. The solution was not to count things more accurately, but to reconceive the object being counted. The goal was no longer to count the nation's wealth or dividend, but rather its aggregate "national income": the sum of every instance of money changing hands. Each such instance represented income to the recipient, however productive or unproductive the activity and regardless of the waste incurred. The work of Keynes again played a critical role. He not only helped imagine the new object being counted, he and his students worked closely with the Treasury in London to design the methods of estimating national income.

In the United States, Simon Kuznets of the National Bureau of Economic Research systematized the new methods. In 1942 the U.S. Department of Commerce began publishing national economic data, and in his 1944 budget speech President Roosevelt introduced the idea of "gross national product" (Bell 1973/1976, 331–332). Kuznets warned that "a national total facilitates the ascription of independent significance to that vague entity called the national economy" (1941, 1: xxvi). The warning was of no use. The subsequent elaboration of the GNP of each economy made it possible to represent the size, structure, and growth of this new totality. The making of the economy provided a new, everyday political language in which the nation-state could speak of itself and imagine its existence as something natural, spatially bounded, and subject to political management.

The example of national currencies and national statistical measures leads to a second general point about the role of economics in formatting the economy. The emergent national economy was dependent on a "nationalization" of political and administrative power—the emergence of large-scale, technoscientific governmental practices based on the vastly expanded administrative machinery of post-1930s national governments. It also contributed to the making of these nationalized machineries of government, in which economics superseded law as the technical language of administrative power (Lowi 1992).

For orthodox, pre-Keynesian economics, the sphere of economic behavior was the individual market. This was the abstraction in terms of which the relations between costs, utilities, and prices were to be analyzed. When Keynes's *General Theory* replaced this abstraction, which had no geographic or political definition, with the "economic system as a whole," it was a system defined by a set of geopolitical boundaries. The system was represented in terms of a series of aggregates (production, employment, investment, and consumption) and synthetic averages (interest rate, price level, real wage, and so on), whose referent was the geographic space of the nation-state (Radice 1984, 121). This "national" framing of the economy was not theorized, as Radice points out, but introduced as a commonsense construct providing the boundaries within which the new averages and aggregates could be measured. Subsequently, the division of economics into the separate fields of macro- and microeconomics inscribed this commonsensical reference to the nation-state in the structure of the discipline, where it remained unnoticed. Thinking of the national economy as simply the macro level provided a substitute for a theoretical analysis of its geopolitical construction. In place of a study of the institutional forms of the state, economics reproduced this institutional structure within the structure of the discipline.

The reorganization of economics as the study of an object defined by the borders of the nation-state paralleled a similar, if less successful, transformation in the other U.S. social sciences (T. Mitchell 2003). In earlier decades, what distinguished the different disciplines of U.S. social science were the different kinds of social questions they addressed. Economists were concerned with prices, markets, and business cycles; political scientists with public law, legislatures, and the behavior of parties and voters; and sociologists with the social problems arising from industrialization and the growth of cities. In a process beginning in the 1930s and completed by the 1950s, the social sciences transformed themselves into a kind of area studies. Each invented an object that marked the exclusive territory of the discipline and defined its boundary with others. The clearest example of this was provided by the construction of the economy in economics, but political science tried to do something similar, first by reworking the old idea of the state, and then in the late 1940s and 1950s by abandoning the state in favor of the more inclusive and scientistic idea of "the political system" (T. Mitchell 1999; Lowi 1992). In sociology, there was a corresponding shift from the study of discrete social problems and processes to the analysis of society as a whole, or, in the more elaborate Parsonian formulation, the social system. The change in anthropology gathered momentum in the same period, with Franz Boas, Ruth Benedict, Clyde Kluckhohn, A. L. Kroeber, and others reorienting the discipline in the United States around a new definition of the term "culture," meaning the whole way of life of a particular country or people.

The forming of the economy in terms of the nation-state was related to the recasting of the international order. The dissolution of the European and Japanese empires before and after World War II destroyed an older framing of political power in terms of position in an imperial order. Here, too, the economy provided a new way of constructing geopolitical space. Previously, it made little sense to talk of, say, the British economy, so long as Britain's economic realm was thought to include India and its other colonies. More generally, a world that was pictured as consisting, outside Europe, of a series of extensive but discontinuous European and other empires could not easily be imagined to contain a large number of separate economies, each economy coinciding with a self-contained geographic space and consisting of the totality of economic relations within that space.

The collapse of empire and the growing hegemony of the United States created a new order, consolidated first by the League of Nations and then by the UN, the World Bank, and the International Monetary Fund, in which the world was rendered in the form of separate nation-states, with each state marking the boundary of a distinct economy. Again, the new macroeconomics took these imagined objects as its untheorized referents: international trade was measured in terms of aggregates (imports and exports of goods and capital) and averages (terms of trade, exchange rates) that were defined in terms of the transactions between national economies (Radice 1984, 121). Economic expertise, institutionalized in the World Bank, the IMF, and other new agencies, helped construct the new global political order through the publication of statistics and the proliferation of political programs defining as their object these separate economies.

The framing of the Keynesian national economy was part of a program to limit and reduce the operation of market competition through increased management of finance, trade, migration, and, above all, the prevention of a global market in labor. It can thus be seen as a successor to the colonial order, an earlier and much older system of limiting market forces via monopoly, managed trade, the control of labor, and political repression, which began to collapse in the interwar period. Seen in this light, the making of "the economy" should be connected with a parallel development that also sought to frame politicoeconomic relations to exclude the operation of market competition: the development of the large corporation, including the multinational corporation.

The modern corporation provides a third sphere in which to consider the imbrication of economic knowledge in the construction of its new object. In the first place, corporations provided the bodies that helped to populate the space of the economy. The market of neoclassical economics was simple enough in conception to be populated only by individual buyers and sellers. The economy was a more complex object; its activities could not be measured and modeled simply as the actions of individuals. Instead, the new national statistical accounts divided the economy into three sectors: households, corporations, and the state. The purchasing, sales, employment, and other records of corporations provided regular sources of data for the compiling of national statistics. At the same time, corporations produced their own demand for statistical knowledge about markets, consumption, personal income, and so on. They also demanded general economic knowledge about the state of the economy and became significant consumers of the output of new econometric models attempting to forecast future changes in the economy as a whole. So the tools of statistical and econometric calculation developed in academic economics became incorporated into the policymaking and management practices of the corporate world.

Schumpeter (1933, 5) once argued that economists had more justification than natural scientists for using mathematical models to describe the world they studied. This was because the economic world, unlike the natural world, was actually constructed of numerical phenomena: prices, measures of quantity, interest rates, and so on. He saw this as an argument for the further development of quantitative and formal methods of economic analysis. This affinity between the methods of economics and the makeup of the world it studied was certainly a strength, but it was a strength that had further consequences. It made it relatively easy for economic knowledge to become involved in the everyday making of the objects of economic analysis (Callon 1998). As a result, there could never be any simple divide between the models and representations developed by academic economics and the world it claimed to represent.

The transformations I have been discussing created in the twentieth century a political and material world densely imbued with the expertise, calculative techniques, and conceptual machinery of modern economics. The so-called material world of governments, corporations, consumers, and objects of consumption was arranged, managed, formatted, and run with the help of economic expertise. The readiness with which it seemed that this world could be manipulated and modeled by economics reflected not simply that it was a naturally "quantitative" world, as Schumpeter suggested. It reflected this imbrication of the concepts and calculations of economic science in the world it was studying.

At the same time, as it seemed to become more quantitative and countable, however, the world that economics studies was also becoming more elusive and less calculable. This can be seen as a further consequence of the same transformations that made possible the emergence of the economy. A further aspect of the development of large-scale corporations, for example, was the rise of corporate advertising and branding (Stole 2001). In the United States, the new oligopolies formed in a wave of corporate mergers and acquisitions in the early part of the century sought new ways to avoid price competition. The large firms that now dominated many areas of production were large enough to survive price wars, so the only effect of lowering prices was to reduce the revenue shared by all. The establishing of brand identities and their promotion through corporate advertising provided a solution, giving firms a technique for holding or increasing market share without cutting prices. Advertising could not work simply by providing the consumer with information, as most everyday products were essentially similar to one another. It had to create a brand identity, associated with certain qualities, emotions, or lifestyles. Thus, the economy that was made in the interwar period was what Callon, Méadel, and Rabehari-soa (2002) call "the economy of qualities." It was an economy formed more and more out of sociotechnical processes concerned with the man-ufacture of images and the management of representations.

A related transformation was the rise of services and other economic activities concerned exclusively with products that were difficult to enu-merate, quantify, and assess the value of: forms of information, entertain-ment, expertise, and imagery. Asking why "economists have not been very successful in explaining what has happened to the economy" in recent decades, Zvi Griliches (1994), in an address as president of the American Economic Association, argued that whereas in the 1950s about half the overall economy was measurable, by 1990 the proportion had fallen to below one-third. In most sectors of the economy—construction, trade, services, and government and other public institutions—there were "no real output measures." Even in the "measurable" sectors, the accelerating rate of product development and the spread of price discounting, neither of which was properly captured in statistics, made picturing the size and growth of the economy less and less reliable (13). A few years earlier, Robert Eisner (1989, 2) argued in his own presidential address to the AEA that measures of the major macroeconomic variables—income, output, employment, prices, productivity, consumption, savings, investment, cap-ital formation, wealth, debt, and deficits—were so unreliable that he and his fellow economists "have literally not known what we are talking about."

In other words, the possibility of representing the economy as the object of economic knowledge rested on the proliferation of sociotechnical pro-cesses of representation. It was the spread of a world of representational practice that made it possible to attempt the social scientific representa-tion of that world. The economy, the new object of economics, was con-structed out of not only numerical quantifications but an entire process of "qualification," branding, product development, information production, and image making that formed both the possibility of the modern econ-omy and the increasing impossibility of its representation.

Karl Polanyi argued that although the economy emerged as a distinct institutional sphere only in the nineteenth century (a date we have moved forward to the twentieth century), nevertheless earlier societies always possessed an economy. This was not the formal, institutionalized economy of modern market-based societies and modern economics. It was the actual or "substantive" economy, whose elements were embedded or ab-

sorbed in a diversity of social practices. Whereas the modern, disembedded economy can be identified by following the movement of a series of
interconnected calculations, the premodern economy must be traced by
identifying the material objects that satisfy people's needs and following
their movement to see what patterns of use, exchange, and reciprocity
emerge (K. Polanyi et al. 1957, 241–242, 248–250; Humphries 1969, 166–
167).

Polanyi's attempt to universalize the concept of the economy has been
followed by almost all subsequent discussions of the relationship between
economics and the economy. Economies have always existed, it is assumed, and the role of economics has been to represent this object, or, in
the opinion of its critics, to misrepresent it. This assumption has hidden
from view the more complicated relationship between economic knowledge and its object. That object is not a fixed space of exchanges or set of
functions existing independently of the ways in which they are calculated,
represented, projected, and enumerated. It is not an object, therefore, that
always exists, becoming disembedded from other spheres and functions in
the modern period. The economy was made in the twentieth century, and
not by its disembedding. It was embedded in the expertise and calculations of twentieth-century economics.

The possibility of representing this calculative world as an economy
rested not only on new powers of calculation but also on the embedding of
calculative practice in the world. The world itself was formed more and
more of calculation, and also of other kinds of representation, imagery,
and effect. Its representational quality made it possible to count things and
make them count as the economy. But the ease with which representations
could be multiplied, modified, and transformed also rendered this world
of calculation increasingly incalculable.

How Positivism Made a Pact with the Postwar
Social Sciences in the United States

PHILIP MIROWSKI

ack in the 1970s, when I was a graduate student in economics, "positivism" was considered a term of opprobrium among both economists and philosophers of science. No one would admit to ever having been an adherent of the doctrine, although no one could manage to be very clear about what it encompassed, either. Sometimes, hostility to positivism was conflated with opposition to scientism as well, although if the former was vague in outlines, the latter was positively opaque. Now that, in the new century, we are experiencing a strange revival of fondness for the original logical positivists,[1] perhaps the time has arrived to revisit the relationship between positivism and the social sciences and, as George Steinmetz (introduction, this volume) puts it, "explore the intimacies between positivism and the disciplines in different times and places."

I wish to take a position diametrically opposed to that of Lawson (this volume): I think it can be demonstrated that positivism and the rise to dominance of the neoclassical orthodoxy in economics in the United States were so intimately linked as to be scandalous, particularly if we acknowledge their common descent from the wartime innovation of Operations Research (OR). I have made the case for the first leg of the OR saga, that of neoclassical economics (Mirowski 2002); in the interests of concision I will not recapitulate that argument here. In this essay I document the other leg of the argument: that once logical positivism came to the United States, it was co-opted to serve as an apologetics for a whole range of social theories growing out of OR, and, more importantly, to foster a new definition of "science" that would then inform and reinforce the transformation of the academic social sciences growing out of their wartime experiences. One reason I differ so starkly from Lawson is that this turns out to be concertedly a *U.S.* story, at least for the first three postwar decades; a British perspective would inevitably miss it, precisely because OR did not assume the same format and topics in Britain. Furthermore, British positivism diverged fairly dramatically from its U.S. counterpart, because it was to the United States that the key representatives of the Viennese Circle emigrated; the Brits got Wittgenstein and Freddie Ayer instead. Another source of our disagreement is that I view the positivist-economist axis not as an abstract proposition in epistemology or ontology, but as a historical fact. Only when that is adequately acknowledged can we begin to explore the subsequent legacy of positivism for the evolution of contemporary economics (or politics or psychology or . . .).

The rise of positivism in the United States is above all a political story, one in which a cadre of socialist-inclined individuals escaped from Nazi persecution only to become cheerleaders for their adopted homeland, innovating a new rationale for the success of its policies. Because they were philosophers of science, they came up with a portrayal of science that "explained" what had gone awry in the homelands of their youth. In a nutshell, their European counterparts had forsaken their base camps on the "icy slopes of logic" for the treacherous valleys of metaphysics and superstition, and this had corrupted what had previously been the font of all social progress. If legitimate science, which transcended all social determination, had been left to its own devices, and then if the rabble had pledged their troth to the scientifically trained rather than to failed artists and religious enthusiasts, then the conflagration that had swallowed up Europe would have been avoided.[2] The grand irony of this story is that, just as science funding and management was being transferred from the corporate sector to the military to an unprecedented degree in their adopted homeland, the positivists were singing the praises of a science that was self-contained and unsullied by social considerations. And to top it off, they resorted to the terminology and formalisms of the social theory most concertedly individualist and asocial in its construction, namely, neoclassical decision theory.

The coexistence of this bizarre conviction that science at its best was somehow asocial, both in its internal operation and in its external relations with the culture in which it was situated, juxtaposed with the demonstrable fact that very specific policies concerning the viability of particular social structures of science were being deployed in its day-to-day defense, constitutes the primary topic of the present paper. Philosophers are perhaps fed up with sociologists chiming in with the mantra, Science is social; I concede that there is no need for further repetition of that rallying cry at this late date. Rather, I am concerned to explore how it was that science came to be portrayed by philosophers as asocial and autarkic and value-free in the United States in the middle of the twentieth century. It so happens that this narrative is intimately intertwined with two other strands of discourse, ones that track attitudes toward the health of "democracy" in the United States and ones that describe the alliances between pragmatism and logical positivism and respective brands of social theory. Of necessity, this must be a historical inquiry, and thus we find that a few historians have cleared a path for exploration of this issue.[3] But I prefer this to be regarded as an exercise in the social epistemology of the relationship of science to society. I argue that certain configurations of science organization, in conjunction with certain widely accepted images of society, have given rise to very specific orthodoxies in the philosophy of science *as well as* orthodoxies in social science; these represent the scientific dimensions of social knowledge.

There have been (at least) three distinct positions regarding the relationship of science to society dominant in the U.S. philosophy profession in the twentieth century. For the purposes of exposition in the schematization in Table 1, I identify each with a representative agent: John Dewey, Hans Reichenbach, and Philip Kitcher. However, due to space constraints, I restrict my examination to the first two protagonists. This personalization of categories undoubtedly constitutes a misrepresentation of communally shared beliefs in their respective eras, but that should be regarded merely as a provisional point of departure in what will eventually become a larger research project. Characterization of the pragmatists or the positivists, even if restricted to the United States, requires extensive differentiation of the relevant players. Consequently, the dominant philosophical stance of the time should not be directly attributed to the actual charismatic protagonists named Dewey, Reichenbach, and Kitcher; rather, they should be first characterizations of a set of working beliefs related to the actual social structures of science dominant in those epochs. In particular, I seek to relate their philosophical pronouncements to the types of environments in which scientific research was being prosecuted, the types of social theories widely prevalent in their eras, and the conundrum of the role of the philosopher in those respective regimes. The variables that I touch on in this account are summarized in Table 1.

The correlation of regimes of science organization with contrasting philosophical accounts of the relationship of science to society is intended to raise some troubling questions: Just how effectively have philosophers been able to train their analytical skills on the complex of problems called

Table 1. Three Regimes and Their Philosophies

Time period	WWI–1940	1940–80	1980–present
Science organization managers:	Foundations' program officers	Cold War military officers	Global privatization corporate officers
Prime location:	Corporate lab	Research universities	Industry hybrids
Philosophical orthodoxy:	Pragmatism	Logical empiricism	Social epistemology
Exemplary philosopher:	John Dewey	Hans Reichenbach	Philip Kitcher
Social theory:	Institutionalism Historicism	Decision theory Operations Research	Game theory/ Neoclassical economics
Science exists for:	Communal welfare	Unimpeachable truth	Valuable information
Society is:	A democratic nation	A rational individual multiplied	A marketplace of ideas
Fundamental challenge:	National inferiority	Military dominance	Industrial control
The enemy:	Ignorance	Error	Inefficiency

The concept of regimes of science organization in the United States is discussed at some length in Mirowski and Sent (2002) and Mirowski (2003).

"social dimensions of science"? Were structural obstacles hampering their comprehension of the interplay of such vexing binaries as the connection of science to democracy, the mutual conditioning of science and the economy, the contrast of the natural to the social, the impact of educational formats on the flourishing of science, and the impact of science on the constitution of communal aspirations of its clients? Finally, what do these distinctions imply for the self-understanding of the structure and conduct of the postwar U.S. social sciences?

Dewey's Philosophy for the Masses

The notion of a complete separation of science from the social environment is a fallacy which encourages irresponsibility on the part of scientists regarding the social consequences of their work.—John Dewey, *Logic, the Theory of Inquiry*

[For most people,] science is a mystery in the hands of initiates who have become adepts in virtue of following ritualistic ceremonies from which the profane are excluded.—John Dewey, *The Public and Its Problems*

Our contemporaries may not generally regard John Dewey as a philosopher of science in good standing; nevertheless, that was perhaps the most important facet of his reputation in the first three decades of the twentieth century. Dewey was not only the best-known pragmatist philosopher of his era, but he was also a public intellectual, seeking to make philosophy speak to the most insistent and pressing problems of the general public. Lewis Mumford (1926) perceptively summed up his crusade as opposition to leisure-class notions of thinking, struggling to replace them with flexible, nondogmatic, and democratic modes of thought. In this quest, his characterization of science played a pivotal role. In the early twentieth century, it was a trite commonplace to assert that science had liberated humanity from earlier metaphysical, primarily theological, fetters; what made Dewey distinct from run-of-the-mill science idolaters was that he realized that contemporary practices of science had rendered any such emancipatory promise not only feeble but deeply implausible, and that if left unchecked, the corruption of this particular ideal would spread to other, even more important cultural values.

To understand Dewey's reasoning, it is important to first appreciate that science as pursued in the pre-Depression United States was a very different phenomenon from what we now conceive of as the conventional process and settings of scientific research.[4] Very little support for scientific research was provided by government funds a century ago, and most colleges were not set up to promote scientific research. U.S. higher education was largely patterned on the liberal education model, providing a generalist moral curriculum to a small proportion of the population not oriented toward vocational training. Indeed, most individuals who sought advanced academic training in the natural sciences had to go abroad, primarily to the German universities, then deemed the best in the world. Outside of a handful of universities, most scientific research in the United States was funded by and prosecuted under the auspices of large corporations. Behemoths such as General Electric, duPont, American Telephone and Telegraph, and Eastman Kodak employed the vast majority of scientifically trained personnel and even supported a few Nobel Prize winners. The motives for this configuration of privatized science had more to do with the fin de siècle merger wave, antitrust policies, and the need for routine in-house testing capabilities in the newer science-based industries than with far-sighted innovation policies or benevolent intentions toward the general welfare. Even the funding of the minuscule sphere of academic research into science was conducted on terms dictated by the industrial behemoths. The vast wealth amassed by families such as the Carnegies and the Rockefellers was partially diverted into eponymous foundations to give back something to the nation that had made them wealthy. Although the entire raison d'être of the foundations was to fund research that was *not* dictated by the exigencies of the pursuit of profit, these nominally eleemosynary institutions were still run by men whose backgrounds were in corporate bureaucracies, and therefore the very criteria of research funding did not escape the stamp of corporate imperative. For instance, a few favored private (not state-sponsored) universities were encouraged to nurture the role of academic entrepreneur, mimicking the captains of industry who had provided their seed capital. Grants became patterned on the business instrument of contracts rather than the previous template of handouts for poor relief. Application forms, progress reports, bureaucratic peer evaluation, and the other trappings of the hierarchical corporation were inserted into research protocols.[5]

The corporate sway over science bore many other consequences for public attitudes toward science and scientists' attitudes toward the public. For instance, we now tend to forget that the first formal initiative aimed at shaping the "public understanding of science" dates from the 1920s, with the Scripps Newspaper Service instituting its Science Service in 1921 (Tobey 1971, 67). The fact that the bulk of scientifically trained personnel were employed by corporations also was a major conditioning factor behind the cultural fascination with the newly professionalized engineers as a putatively progressive political force in the 1920s. In the popular press, scientific theories were being persistently dragooned into service to justify various forms of elitism, from Social Darwinism to technocracy to rehashes of the variational principles found in mechanics as grand theories of natural efficiency. The ambitions of many scientists/engineers to assume credit for the progress of the United States provoked a reaction in the form of questioning the baleful influence of scientists on their social surroundings.[6] The supposed meritocratic character of science was often parlayed into antiegalitarian precepts and corporate boosterism; for instance, Robert Millikan told a Chicago audience in 1919, "It is probable that the total possibilities of improvement of conditions through distribution are very limited, while possibilities of improvement through increases of production are incalculable" (quoted in Tobey 1971, 182–183).

This pervasive corporate character of early-twentieth-century U.S. science was the looming backdrop to Dewey's distress over the relationship of science to society. Science as then practiced constituted a problem because of the way it had been imperfectly integrated into the social fabric. As he wrote, "The concept that natural science somehow sets a limit to freedom, subjecting men to fixed necessities, is not an intrinsic product of science . . . [but] a reflex of the social conditions under which science is applied so as to reach only a pecuniary function" (1984, 105). Dewey suspected that the bureaucratic/industrial location of the scientist was a prime reason for the encapsulation of the scientific method in the cult of the expert, erecting an artificial barrier between science and society. He bemoaned the phenomenon that "the idea of experts is substituted for that of philosophers, since philosophy has become something of a joke, while the . . . expert in operation is rendered familiar and congenial by the rise of the physical sciences and by the conduct of industry" (1927, 205). Philosophers bore some of the responsibility for this sorry state of affairs, because "the philosopher's idea of a complete separation of the mind and the body is realized in thousands of industrial workers" (1984, 104). How one thought about the process of thinking was shaped by the social structures that enabled the activity of thought. As he wrote in *Experience and Nature*:

> The ulterior problem of thought is to make thought prevail in experience, not just the results of thought by imposing them upon others, but the active process of thinking. The ultimate contradiction in the classic and genteel tradition is that while it made thought universal and necessary and the culminating good of nature, it was content to leave its distribution among men a thing of accident, dependent upon birth, economic and civil status. Consistent as well as humane thought will be aware of the hateful irony of a philosophy which is indifferent to the conditions that determine the occurrence of reason while it asserts the ultimacy and universality of reason. (1981, 99)

In retrospect, we can appreciate that Dewey was casting about for a role for the philosopher in the Jazz Age U.S. system of science. His alternative to the prevailing cult of the expert was to imagine a different sort of science, a science dedicated to the promotion of communal intelligence, a generic experimental method that would be made available to all members of the community as a part of their birthright. Pragmatic knowledge of nature would shade imperceptibly into useful knowledge concerning regularities of communal behavior. To counter the corporatist and elitist connotations of science rife in his era, Dewey made a conceptual move that reverberates down through the remainder of this narrative. Through-

out his later career, Dewey concertedly and repeatedly blurred the definitions of "democracy" and "science" prevalent in his lifetime, so that he
could conflate the two and provide a counterweight to the forces dragging
science away from its liberal and liberationist potential. As he insisted,
"Democracy is not an alternative to other principles of associated life. It is
the idea of community life itself" (1927, 148.) And from the obverse side,
he saw himself "raising the question of what science can do in making a
different sort of world and society. Such a science would be the opposite
pole to science conceived merely as a means to special industrial ends"
(1984, 107).

The yoking together of science and democracy was not such an obvious
winning combination in the early twentieth-century context; it had yet to
attain its subsequent unassailable U.S. status commensurate with Mom
and apple pie. Indeed, Dewey's book *The Public and Its Problems* (1927)
was a response to an intellectual current that framed the duo as incompatible in structure and content.[7] A common form of naturalism was regularly being used for nativist, racist, antiegalitarian, and conservative ends.
But perhaps more disturbing, the spread of empiricist protocols to the
newly established academic social sciences was producing observations
that suggested conventional understandings of democracy were a sham.
Political scientists were demonstrating that the U.S. government was not
at all run by the people for the commonweal, but by a small handful of
insiders for their own power and enrichment. Legal realists were documenting that judicial decisions were neither impartial nor logical, but the
product of powerful interests. Psychologists were demonstrating that the
voters were largely irrational and easily swayed by those who controlled
the corporate media, particularly newspapers and the new-fangled radio.
The sum total of this research portrayed a populace so easily manipulated
and exploited that an expanded franchise and enhanced participation in
the political process was widely regarded as dangerous, if not foolhardy;
the democratic election of fascist parties in Europe only reinforced that
impression. Not only was science perceived as intrinsically undemocratic;
science when applied to society was uncovering the dark side of democracy. Perhaps there were some stones better left unturned.

Another Jazz Age trend that is often forgotten today is the existence of a
fair degree of academic opposition to the idea that there was or could be a
generic science that would apply equally to Nature and Society. High-
profile figures such as Frank Knight in economics and Pitrim Sorokin in
sociology were arguing that the natural sciences (especially physics) provided misleading paradigms for theory in the social sciences, and were

citing German philosophical theses that nothing like the laws of physics could be discovered when the subject was society. A general inclination toward evolutionary arguments was being deployed as explanations for why there were no absolutes in human experience and to argue in favor of the essential plasticity of human nature. But this opened the door to the cynical manipulation of the masses by experts. The major opponents to this relativist threat in social science were theological, and in particular Catholic, academics who sought to reassert the centrality of values through reimposition of theological absolutes (Purcell 1973, ch. 10). These were not the sort of people Dewey could see himself forging alliances with, and therefore he was driven to find a third way to relegitimize science and democracy.

Dewey's pathway out of the impasse was to insist that science would cease to undermine liberal democracy and that the corporate sway over science would be progressively diminished *if and only if* we came to regard science and democracy as inseparable parts of the same communal activity; that is, (1) the practice of democracy would come to resemble science at its best, which was procedurally nondogmatic and experimental; and (2) more science would be reorganized and conducted in the communal democratic interest. It will prove important for us to get the subtleties of Dewey's equation of science and democracy correct, because it would very rapidly become corrupted into something very different in World War II, especially under the auspices of Robert Merton and Michael Polanyi and James Conant, something that Dewey personally would have regarded as pernicious, and something that is sometimes mistakenly attributed to him. In World War II, under the imperatives of wartime mobilization of science, the *separate, autarkic, and self-governing* scientific community began to be held up as the icon of what a democratic community could aspire to be—in the guise of an ideal "republic of science." In this construction, scientists did lay claim to an esoteric expertise in generic rationality inaccessible to (or at least rare for) the common layperson. Dewey could never have been a proponent of this position, for a number of reasons but primarily because the corporate organization of science then dominant could never have been plausibly portrayed as self-governing in that era; nor, for that matter, could scientific rationality plausibly have been pictured as politically free from corporate imperatives. The separate constitution of the scientific community as a social formation was not yet a conceptual possibility. That could become conceivable only after the war.

Dewey's reconciliation of science and democracy did not come as a bolt from the blue, but was built up from resources available to him in the 1920s. Philosophy of science was just one component of theories of the social in that era, and not something notionally apart or distinct from them. Economics and psychology were other key components of the conflationist scheme. In Dewey's case, he left numerous clues that he had made an implicit pact with the institutionalist school of economics and the "habit" school of social psychology, both very active traditions in the contemporary U.S. context.[8] His position bore a number of striking resemblances in particular with the writings of the institutionalist Thorstein Veblen, one of the very few authors whom he regularly cites (1984, 102; Westbrook 1991, 310). The pediment of their shared themes was that metaphysics operated in the past to reinforce existing class relationships in society; hence, Dewey united in opposition with Veblen to "leisure-class thinking," first described in the *Theory of the Leisure Class* (1899/1965). Another was that the "individual" self is constantly under reconstruction in modern society, and therefore the older "individualist" orientation of both epistemology and social science stood as a major obstacle to the constitution of his ideal science. Dewey's *Individualism Old and New* is primarily one long argument against the classical economic elevation of the "natural" individual as the basis for understanding society: "The chief obstacle to the creation of a type of individual . . . in whom sociability is one with cooperation in all regular human associations is the persistence of that feature of the earlier individualism which defines industry and commerce by ideas of private pecuniary profit" (1984, 84). For Dewey, it was not that the average citizen was woefully irrational; rather, it was the received portrait of rationality that had led the social scientists astray. In Dewey's system, this implied the rejection of classical utilitarianism, and consequently, of neoclassical economics: "[Dewey rejects] . . . the idea that there is something inherently 'natural' and answerable to 'natural law' in the working of economic forces, in contrast with the man-made artificiality of political institutions. The idea of a natural individual in his isolation possessed of fully-fledged wants . . . and of a ready-made faculty of foresight and prudent calculation is as much a fiction in psychology as the picture of the individual in possession of antecedent political rights is in politics" (102).

Veblen famously asked, "Why is Economics Not an Evolutionary Science?" (1919). Dewey wanted to equate an evolutionary approach with what he considered to be the "experimental method." Yet this did not mean mimicking the actual quotidian procedures of the physical scientists, as he repeatedly insisted: "When we say that thinking and beliefs should be experimental, not absolutistic, we have then in mind a certain logic of method, not, primarily, the carrying on of experimentation like that of laboratories" (1927, 202). "What purports to be experiment in the social field is very different from experiment in natural science" (1939, 65).

Thus, by seeking to equate "good science" with democracy, Dewey was definitely not appealing to any theories of natural science to underpin theories of democracy: he was no friend of any social physics. His version of pragmatism led him to deflect attention from the ends and content of science and toward the means through which science was purportedly conducted. Thus, he leaned heavily on the institutionalist rejection of natural law theories of the nature of humanity in order to prevent misunderstanding of what he intended by a scientific democracy. His commitments to certain particular social theories were substantively more fervent than have been noticed by later commentators. This is significant, because incipient revolutions in social theory would have direct implications for the plausibility of his philosophical theses for his later audiences.

Even writers deeply sympathetic to Dewey's project have been forced to admit that his matchmaking activities between science and democracy subsequently proved practically barren, a most unhappy prognosis for a pragmatist philosopher. Long passages of clotted prose never led to any practical political programs. "He appeared to have given little thought to the problems and possibilities of participatory government. . . . Dewey had surprisingly little to say about democratic citizenship" (Westbrook, 1991, 317). Politics, one of his trademark concerns, ended up a lingering embarrassment, rather like a cynical guest at a patriotic gathering. As he wrote, "It is not the business of political philosophy and science to determine what the state in general should or must be" (1927, 34). More germane to our present concerns, he also made no suggestions as to how scientists could be unshackled from their lab benches in major corporations, much less the imperative of the profit motive; there was no serious consideration of how science was to be paid for at all. One got the impression that those questions would be in the nature of details to be worked out in the distant future, when, believe it or not, the captains of industry would grow bored and would relinquish their ownership of machine production to socialized entities "so that they may devote their energies to affairs which involve more novelty, variation and opportunities for gain" (61). And yet, Dewey also seemed to argue that the United States had the best chance of realizing his vague ideal of democracy as science, raising the bar for human excellence relative to the older, richer, but metaphysically lumbered cultures of Europe, producing a moral and intellectual advance in the career of mankind as a whole. This pie-in-the-sky aspect of Dewey's thought illustrates the fact that his popularity was frequently more directly attributable to his quest for a non-Marxian lowest common denominator of politics and economics that could attract the allegiance of the broadest array of U.S. left-leaning intellectuals (Purcell 1973, 202) than to any specific reform agenda.[9]

Yet, however toothless and nonspecific his reform program turned out to be in practice, it nonetheless proved to be untenable from World War II onward; furthermore, it unintentionally provided the major resource for certain more pointed and virulent doctrines on the social relations of science developed in the United States in the postwar period. In a subsequent degradation of his program for the conflation of science and democracy, university-accredited scientists were said to conduct their activities in an ideal democracy, namely, Merton's "norms" of universalism, communism, disinterestedness, and organized skepticism. No longer was democracy-in-the-making deemed a legitimate aspiration for the scientific community at large; instead, it became ossified as the esoteric virtue of the adept within the cloistered monastery of the newly reengineered U.S. research university. Rationality was increasingly deployed as a logical abstraction, the dogmatic preserve of the expert. These cloistered elect were explicitly absolved of all responsibility for the state of the larger society and its political aspirations. Indeed, this is what Conant and Weaver (Weaver 1945) meant by their championing of Free Science. And, in a twisted non sequitur, because the United States was putatively a democracy, it naturally acceded to the position of premier bastion of legitimate science, in comparison with a decadent and totalitarian Europe. Dewey's pragmatic stress on means over ends became transmuted into the elevation of pure science over application; his critique of corporate science became twisted into a denial of any relevance of economic support to the conduct of science; his advocacy of a pragmatic logic of inquiry became the reification of a language of science of almost mystical powers, namely, formal logic and mathematical axiomatization (Reichenbach 1938, 49).

I am not claiming that Robert Merton or anyone else intended this rout. Rather, in World War II and after, the social organization of science had been reengineered from the ground up, as had the universities and, to a lesser extent, the government. The science-industry partnership so inveighed against by Dewey was being replaced with a science-military partnership: Science had become betrothed to the State, but not in any way Dewey had imagined. Further, philosophers had learned in the interim a different way to make themselves useful. The world that had been the reference point of Dewey's philosophy no longer existed, so it was a fore-gone conclusion that Dewey's account of the social relations of science could no longer resonate with either the scientists themselves, a newer generation of philosophers, or with the broader public.

Reichenbach's Philosophy for the Operations Researcher

No human being is completely rational, i.e., makes decisions strictly according to the bal-ance of probabilities and valuations. The decision may depend on emotional factors, which vary from moment to moment, such as an "itch to fight," or inversely, an indolence to the challenge of reason. If a decision is made not by one person but by a body of persons, such as a government, there are further random factors to be envisaged. . . . the tiredness or sickness of leaders; the inertia of bureaucracy; the pleading of voices of people frightened by the horrors of war, constitute factors which may deter from a decision for war. All these factors are random factors; their effects are unpredictable and may extend in a positive or negative direction.—Hans Reichenbach, "Rational Construction of the Decision for War"

The philosopher James Robert Brown has written, "One of the travesties of current science studies debates is the branding of the positivists as political reactionaries. . . . Dealing with political issues meant as much or more to Neurath, Carnap, Frank and Hahn as coming to grips with sci-ence for its own sake" (2001, 54). There is no doubt that politics mattered for the logical empiricist movement, but the rather imprecise character-izations of the actual history exemplified by comments such as the above are yet another symptom of the weaknesses of contemporary philosophers in their quest to pronounce upon the "social dimensions of science." In this particular instance, the choice of relevant representatives of the posi-tivist movement is more than a little misleading: with the exception of Carnap, none played much of a role in the professionalization of academic philosophy of science in the U.S. context.[10] There is also the unfortunate tendency to think that, just because someone has self-identified as some species of socialist, that immediately absolves him or her from any accusa-tions of reactionary political activity.[11] For the reasons I outline below, it will prove rather too hasty to hew to the conviction that "logical positiv-ism was a casualty of the cold war, not one of its villains" (Reisch 2002, 391).

The predominant fact about U.S. science at midcentury was the as-sumption of its funding and organization by the military during World War II, establishing a novel regime of science management that lasted well into the 1980s.[12] As one can readily appreciate, this opened up a Pandora's box of problems for the relationship of science to society in general and

democracy in particular, problems that the various constituencies identified in this narrative were anxious to address. Scientists recruited to the
war effort were quick to realize that the newfound largesse came freighted
with dangers and responsibilities. One response in Britain was the social
planning of science movement of Patrick Blackett and J. D. Bernal, which
provoked a hostile response by Michael Polanyi, Friedrich von Hayek, and
others (McGuckin 1984). The latter conceived of their crusade as broadly
antipositivist, in that Otto Neurath was a prime target of their disdain
(Uebel 2000a). This dispute was closely related to another, which also
tended to draw on Viennese intellectual resources, namely, the "socialist
calculation controversy," of which Otto Neurath was again a major pro-
tagonist. Although some modern philosophers are sometimes quick to
point to Neurath as someone attuned to our fin de siècle conundrums, it
should be remembered that he bore little relevance for those weathering
the sea change in science regimes in the postwar United States. Denuncia-
tions of ambitions for the planning of science for social ends, such as those
mooted by Neurath, were the stock in trade of Vannevar Bush, James
Conant, and Warren Weaver; but ironically, these were the primary protagonists in the wartime mobilization of science in the United States, the
very people assigning the research tasks and cutting the checks. Indeed,
when the first refugees from the Vienna Circle such as Carnap and Reichenbach were seeking to find their footing in their newfound home, it was
Weaver to whom they first turned for support.[13]

　While public figures such as John Dewey had been talking about the
social planning of science in a vague way before the war, the prospect of
government direction of scientific research had abruptly become a much
more tangible prospect in the United States with the advent of the MIT
Radiation Lab, the Manhattan Project, and a host of lesser mobilizations.
The programs of science mobilization in Soviet Russia and Nazi Germany
also had to be somehow distinguished from what was going on in the
United States, if only to soothe anxieties about the global corruption of
science and maintenance of the real source of U.S. exceptionalism. It was
the very palpability of a model for socialist planning provided by military
mobilization, an important theme in Neurath's writings (Cartwright et al.
1996, 14–18), that called forth a response to the perceived dangers of the
reorganization of the social relations of science then in progress. And then,
we must never forget, after 1945 there lurked the vexed issue of the relationship of a democracy to the production and use of the Bomb. Philosophers were a little slow off the mark to respond to these controversies, but
they soon took their cue from some natural and social scientists who had

to come to rapid accommodation with the gales of change buffeting them from all sides.

It was these wartime-induced anxieties that prompted the first real appearance of the conceptual innovation of a free-floating "scientific community" that purportedly subsisted autonomously from the larger culture in which it was situated. Some scholars have argued that such a notion was not seriously entertained prior to the writings of Michael Polanyi (S. Jacobs 2002); others credit Merton. This, as I hinted in the previous section, was the key innovation that utterly transformed the terms of debate concerning the relationship of science to society. Yet the watershed was not simply conceptual; it was anchored in unprecedented innovations of social identities for scientists in wartime. When scientists were recruited into the military during World War II, they were very much concerned to differentiate themselves from the mass of conscripted manpower, but also to exercise a fair amount of discretion in the deployment of their expertise. What began as scientists serving as glorified troubleshooters for the creation and deployment of new weapons systems such as radar and the atomic bomb was transformed by the scientists themselves into a never before permitted institutional adjunct to the military, namely, as cadres of experts in a generic scientific method whose remit was to assist in the generation of rational strategy and tactics for battle. These scientists were frequently contemptuous of tradition and the conventional military doctrine that they encountered and sought to replace these with what they regarded as empirical methods. In practice, much of this methodological innovation consisted in the imposition of physical models, especially those adapted from thermodynamics and mechanics, on abstract agglomerations of men and machines. Because the quantum physics and nuclear cross-sections so bound up with the radar and atomic weapons that occupied their attention were so dependent on stochastic formalisms, facility with probability theory tended to be a hallmark of their models. This "profession," which did not even exist before World War II, grew rapidly during the war and came to be known in the United States as Operations Research, or OR.

Although it is impossible to adequately summarize the scope and content of OR in the space of this paper, it is important to appreciate that OR was a practical response to the problems and paradoxes of the military planning and organization of science in midcentury.[14] Physicists such as Patrick Blackett, Philip Morse, George Gamow, and Ivan Getting and mathematicians such as John von Neumann and Richard Bellman and their comrades wanted to enjoy the military largesse but maintain a fair amount of latitude in evading direct control by the military. Indeed, they believed that they were far smarter than your average lieutenant colonel and should be allowed to run things as they saw fit; in effect, they wanted to exist simultaneously *within* but *apart from* the military chain of command. They wanted to be paid by the military but not really be in the military; as physicists, they wanted to do social research for the military but not become confused with social scientists; they wanted to tell others what to do, but not be held responsible for the commands given. After the war, they wanted to return to their university posts without having to relinquish their lucrative military ties. To be granted these extraordinary dispensations, they had to innovate new roles that embodied this delicate amalgam of engagement and aloofness. The construct of the operations researcher was the professional device that fostered the reconciliation of these conflicting demands; significantly for our present concerns, it also became the empirical template for the idea of a free-floating scientific community, distinguished by its possession of a special expertise rooted in a generic scientific method, subsisting with a fair degree of autonomy within but apart from a larger social community. Operations Research was the anvil on which the postwar relationship between scientists and the U.S. state was hammered out; once successful, the blade was then turned to carve out a new model of society that could be amenable to the rapprochement of science and the military. Operations Research provided much of the metallic durability and intellectual firepower for postwar U.S. social sciences like decision theory, organization theory, management theory, and neoclassical economics; but it also provided the framework for cold war philosophy of science.

I do not intend this thesis to be regarded as trafficking in vague influences and murky insinuations about science tainted by military dollars. I am pointing out that the professionalization of U.S. philosophy of science in the immediate postwar era grew directly out of the soil of or; that major figures of the logical empiricist movement in the United States served their country in dual capacities as operations researchers; that the editors of the flagship journal *Philosophy of Science* in the critical transition period, C. West Churchman (editor, 1951–59) and Richard Rudner (editor, 1960–75), were better known as operations researchers; and that philosophers of science were employed at major OR research centers such as RAND (a fact discussed below). Much of the content of so-called analytical philosophy in that period, ranging from its disdainful attitude toward surrounding disciplines (not to mention its own history) to its preferred mathematical formalisms, is easily recognizable in its family resemblance to the contemporary subsets of OR known as decision theory and formal computational logic. The fascination with physics as the first science among equals reprised the historical fact that OR was first instituted by physicists for the protection and promotion of physics; the presumption that one could proceed to formalize the behavior of rational empirical man innocent of any familiarity with or acknowledgment of the social sciences that supposedly were already concerned with empirical humanity was also an echo of the credo of the operations researcher.[15] The conviction that prior practitioners simply did not sufficiently appreciate "the facts" was the complaint most frequently launched by operations researchers against their military patrons. The roots of postwar U.S. philosophy of science in OR is the smoking gun that critics of the thesis (Hudelson and Evans 2003) that the cold war shaped the philosophy profession have been insisting did not exist.

Rather than try to document these generalizations for an entire generation, I offer a brief account of a representative figure of this movement, Hans Reichenbach. Reichenbach's career began in Stuttgart and then the Berlin Circle for empirical philosophy, where he garnered a reputation as a socialist radical. Indeed, a certain political intolerance makes its appearance in his earliest writings: "Socialism not only teaches us a new form of society, but also shows us the way to reach it. It starts from the idea that we cannot sit and wait until mankind as a whole undergoes a rational awakening and introduces socialism of its own free will, as the rational form of society; instead we must exploit the economic development of present-day society in such a way that socialism will be forcibly introduced rather sooner" (1978, vol. 1, 149).

The rise of the National Socialists and the Race Laws of 1933 forced him out of Berlin and into exile in Turkey for five years, after which he managed to get an appointment at UCLA in 1938. Reichenbach's tribulations did not end there, for he had to suffer the indignity of house arrest as an "enemy alien" during a portion of World War II. Nevertheless, he did ultimately flourish in southern California until his death in 1953. Along with Rudolf Carnap's appointment at the University of Chicago in 1936 and Herbert Feigl's move to Iowa in 1931, his professorship was conceded to be one of the pivotal outposts for the promulgation of logical positivism on the U.S. landscape (Giere 1996).

Reichenbach's positivism, as is well-known, began with detailed examinations of recent theoretical developments in physics for the purpose of drawing out epistemological lessons. While he sought to derive anti-Kantian morals from the theory of relativity and uncover anomalies for standard ideas of causality from contemporary interpretations of quantum mechanics, he also was an advocate of some larger themes that bore relevance for the "defense" of science against those he deemed its detractors. For instance, he thought that one task of the philosophy of science was to provide criteria for the distinction between propositions that might be deemed conventional and those that were incorrigibly empirical in the language of physics. In *Experience and Prediction* (1938), he divided knowledge into those propositions that were governed by the ideal of truth, which were the province of logic, and those that were motivated by "volitional resolutions," which he called conventions. Conventions often masqueraded as logical statements, but in fact were nothing more than bald "decisions," in Reichenbach's lexicon. Decisions were neither true nor false, but nevertheless the philosopher could offer advice concerning their efficacy by, among other things, pointing out whether they were consistent with one another (9–13). Those familiar with decision theory in OR will recognize their discipline in embryo here in 1930s logical positivism.[16]

Whereas one might characterize the program of the left wing of logical positivism as an attempt to integrate scientists more closely with each other and with society, Reichenbach early on (even before his emigration to the United States) conceived of the program as more aloof; for instance, he did not subscribe to Neurath's unity of science movement:

The word Unity of science does not at all express what we want. It is unfortunate enough that this term has been used for the Encyclopaedia, but it should by no means be used for the journal. . . . The unity of science is not our program, but a special thesis maintained by some among us, or even by all of us if the term is sufficiently widely interpreted. As a program it would mean: calling all men of science together to cooperate for their special purposes, for instance summoning the biologists to use physical measurements, or the physicists to consider the physics of the human body. Now such a program though perhaps desirable is certainly out of our intentions and out of our reach. If *we* invite men of science to cooperate this is always in the special purpose to discuss the foundations of knowledge. Thus what characterizes our program is the study of the foundation of knowledge, and not the cooperation of all men of science; the latter will always be nothing but a means to our purpose, and we even would not hesitate to declare that sometimes the analysis of the foundations is better made by specialists than by the scientists themselves.[17]

Reichenbach never passed up an opportunity to vent his distaste for traditional wisdom, which he associated with the conventional character of certain epistemological precepts, and he was unapologetic about his contempt for history. Another task he undertook was the demonstration of the "fact" that physics had managed to solve the problem of induction, largely by means of formal models of statistical inference.[18] Perusal of his later popular works, such as *The Rise of Scientific Philosophy* (1951), shows that these projects melded imperceptibly into a defense of science as having stood stalwart and incorruptible, arrayed against Marxism (e.g., 1951, 71–72) and fascism—not such an unusual conviction for one who had endured the types of persecution he had suffered. It is noteworthy that the way Reichenbach went about this project was to posit the existence of a formal logic not readily accessible to the general public, conceived as a "language" that served to inoculate the scientific elect against the irrationality that plagued many nations in the 1930s and 1940s. Science, he maintained, was situated beyond dispute by the layperson, and the only people who could really appreciate this immunity were those who had taken the trouble to have immersed themselves in the technicalities of physics and mathematical logic: "Technicalities, not dialectic, is the instrument of modern philosophy" (1978, 253). This was also the program of Carnap, the other major émigré representative of logical positivism in the United States: "It is the task of logic and mathematics within the total system of knowledge to supply the forms of concepts, statements and inference, forms which are then applicable everywhere, hence also to nonlogical knowledge" (1963a, 12).

The retreat to technicalities did not altogether banish any consideration of older themes of the relationship of science to democracy, those troublesome holdovers from the earlier pragmatist tradition. In *Rise*, Reichenbach portrays the scientist as governed by an algorithmic logic and, by contrast, the general populace as governed by "volitions," which he then proceeded to equate with "preferences."[19] Although he does not make much of it, this move signals his implicit endorsement of the type of social theory that starts with given individual preferences of convenient properties, such as that found in neoclassical economics.[20] Logic is subject to codification by the philosopher, but "it is therefore irrelevant where volitions come from, and we do not ask . . . whether we are conditioned to our volitions by the milieu in which we grew up" (1951, 282). We are then informed that "moral directives . . . express volitional decisions on the part of the speaker" (291), and from this he concludes, "Science tells us what is, but not what should be."

Curiously, the first time democracy is mentioned by Reichenbach is with respect to the precept that "everybody is entitled to set up his own

moral imperatives and demand that everyone else follow these imperatives" (1951, 295), which constitutes his working definition of democracy.
Conflict is to be expected among the laity, because all they do is blindly try
to thrust their inexplicable and incompatible desires and volitions upon
one another. Scientists qua scientists managed to avoid all that (and corruption by fascists, etc.) by conforming to the dictates of a logic of empirical evidence, and therefore were located in a space situated outside of the
democratic sphere. Note well that science is *not* portrayed as an arena for
the democratic hashing out of workable ethics and values, because science
is not conceived as a part of society at all. As Reichenbach put it bluntly,
"Science is its own master and recognizes no authority beyond its confines" (214). Dewey had effectively been banished. But by then, so had any
encompassing notion of democracy.

In his famous essay in the Schlipp volume on Dewey's philosophy,
Reichenbach was not afraid to upbraid Dewey directly for not maintaining adequate separation of science from society. Although, as to be expected, Reichenbach berated Dewey for his lack of "technique" ("Philosophic analysis of modern science cannot be achieved without a profound
study of mathematical methods" [1989, 191]), it is important to observe
that he also backhandedly acknowledged that a major source of their
difference came in how they approached the social implications of their
respective philosophies. In a most dubious rhetorical move, Reichenbach
tried to make it appear that he, and not Dewey, was the standard-bearer of
a solid intellectual basis for the advocacy of socialism: "There are ethical
systems which for instance consider the idea that private property is sacro-
sanct as a demonstrable truth in the same sense it is demonstrable that
private property is destructible by fire. It is the danger of pragmatism that
its theory of reality is made to order for ethical theories of this type,
although the pragmatists themselves may not intend these implications"
(1989, 180).

The Popperians were among the first to flag this sort of argumentation
as illegitimately stacking the deck against democracy and free inquiry. For
them, "Democracy requires a view of rationality that permits dissent, and
inductive logic forbids it" (Agassi 1995, 158). The situation was even more
indefensible once one realized that the positivists could never really settle
on the unique inductive formalism that supposedly governed the scientists' activities; in that situation, the positivists had failed in providing
anything approaching a logical criterion that would demarcate the scientist from any other political actor. "Although [the positivists] have not
found the right inductive rule,[21] they know that it should justify estab-

lished scientific opinion, and so they demand that everyone follow this still-not-known rule of induction and endorse received scientific opinion under pain of being branded irrational" (158).

The other place where Reichenbach drove home his separation of science from society was in his infamous distinction between a context of discovery and a context of justification, which first appeared in his *Experience and Prediction* (1938, 6–7). He wrote there that "epistemology is only occupied in constructing the context of justification," but curiously enough for a topic relegated to the category of the descriptive tasks of epistemology, the philosopher would recover not the actual social modes of argumentation and reason, but rather a "rational reconstruction" of what should have been said according to the canons of the philosopher. Not only was a wedge being driven between philosophy and sociology, but another was driven between the actual prosecution of science and its supposed logical structure (381). As has frequently been noted, it was a convenient immunization stratagem for the logical positivists to prevent their theory of the scientific method from ever being falsified with data from the history of actual scientific inquiry: "All this is a *logical* reconstruction. It was never intended to be an account of the origin and development of scientific theories" (Feigl 1969, 17). But it was also much more than that. In *The Rise of Scientific Philosophy*, Reichenbach tied adherence to the distinction to the very legitimacy of a logic of inductive inference. There he admits that induction could never help the scientist find a new theory (a point made much more cogently by the pragmatist C. S. Peirce), but could only be used to evaluate it after the fact: "The act of discovery escapes logical analysis. . . . But it is not the logician's task to account for scientific discoveries . . . logic is concerned only with the context of justification" (1951, 231). Developments categorized as falling within the context of discovery were placed on the same epistemic plane as volitions: one did not ask where they came from. This policy of "don't ask, don't tell" proved extremely awkward for his philosophical system, for it threatened to situate a major component of what everyone else thought of as science, namely, its capacity to generate novel explanations of phenomena, stranded outside of the cloistered ideal community of scientists and leave it mired in the irrational bog of "society." Nevertheless, it would prove indispensable for his *political* program. It was almost as though the later Reichenbach was so driven to erect impermeable floodgates between science and society that he was willing to risk the interior of his citadel to provide shelter for the diminished scientific status quo containing a few reputable physicists and hardly anyone else. Insofar as any of the *Geistes-*

wissenschaften sought similar scientific status, they too built their own impregnable proud tower, situated beyond profane time and space.

Perhaps it commits the Whig fallacy, but it now seems a bit difficult to understand why anyone would find this version of positivism compelling on its face.[22] The answer tendered in this paper is that the explanation must be sought in the pact that postwar U.S. philosophy of science made with Operations Research. Put bluntly, it was no accident that so very much of Reichenbach's later philosophy resembled the attitudes and content characteristic of postwar OR, because for a short while, they were actually one and the same. The idolization of physics, the contempt for tradition, the insistence on a generic scientific method based on logic and probability and indifferently portable to any subject or discipline, the crusading stance of rooting out error that besets the masses, the role of the philosopher as a consultant therapist for decision theory, the postulation of a closed corporate priesthood who possessed sole control of these esoteric methods, the suggestion that the problem of induction had been dissolved by statistical algorithms, the conflation of mathematical prowess with intellectual virtue, and the assertion that the advice provided was pitched somewhere beyond ethics or morality—all were hallmarks of U.S. OR. Operations Research had begun as a negotiation to create a separate social identity for scientists operating in a semiautonomous capacity in the military; postwar logical positivism ended up as an ideology of science in general, a virtual community separate and autonomous from the social system as a whole.

The symbiotic pact between OR and logical positivist philosophy of science would not have flourished if it did not take root in fertile ground. There were a number of circumstances specific to the postwar U.S. context that were propitious for the graft. The first and most important was the shift in science funding and management from industry dominance to military dominance. The various protocols worked out during World War II—that scientists would conduct research under contracts that were issued by the military but managed through their universities, that they would be subject to indirect controls through security clearances and classification of secrets, that downstream development would be the province of the military science managers, that bureaucratic evaluation would be deployed through peer review, that grant overheads could buy off the principal investigator's academic obligations to his or her home institution—all militated in favor of treating the scientist as though he or she were a member of a community apart from the general run of intellectual life. This reification of a separate and unequal science reflected a cold war truth in a manner it never could have done under the previous industrial regime of science organization. The notion of the scientist as sequestered in an ivory tower was encouraged by the military, especially once a few of the elect physicists had suffered crises of conscience about "knowing sin" after the dropping of the bomb. The notion that scientists somehow were members of a commonwealth apart from society became smoothly integrated with the oft-intoned refrain that they could not be held responsible for how their discoveries in "pure science" were put to use by "others." Of course, the very plausibility of the notion of a free-floating pure science detached from its prospective utility and retrospective funding was itself the product of a fair amount of legal and economic construction initiated by the military.[23]

The relationship of military-organized science to democracy was perhaps the issue most fraught with controversy in the immediate postwar period. The military and the Operations Researchers shared a jaundiced view of democracy when it came to their profession of prosecuting wars, and the suppression of democratic debate over the use of the bomb was viewed by many in the political classes as a betrayal of fundamental principles which the bomb was conceived nominally to protect. Dewey's blind faith in democracy, therefore, had to be revised in the cold war era. OR theorists responded to the call and went to work describing various ways in which democratic decision procedures were irrational when it came to such momentous choices.[24] The most famous of these doctrines produced at RAND was the Arrow Impossibility Theorem, based directly on the assumptions of neoclassical economic theory: "If we exclude the possibility of interpersonal comparisons of utility, then the only methods of passing from individual tastes to social preferences which will be satisfactory . . . are either imposed or dictatorial . . . the doctrine of voters' sovereignty is incompatible with that of collective rationality" (Arrow 1951, 59–60). The upshot of this claim was that market expression of citizens' preferences was a faithful and dependable representation of their desires, whereas standard majority voting procedures were not. This was an extremely felicitous cold war doctrine from the military viewpoint, because it suggested that the military was legitimately defending the welfare of the citizenry by allowing them free choice in their purchases while simultaneously conducting national defense without the need for their explicit political acquiescence. This "double truth" doctrine had its exact parallel in Reichenbach's separation between science and society: scientists were furthering the welfare of the citizenry by allowing them free choice in the products of their endeavors in the marketplace while conducting their fundamental research without the need for prior accommodation or any explicit political acquiescence.[25] Democratic procedures were best kept well clear of such activities.

The cold war also constituted a watershed in the history of U.S. social sciences. The earlier orthodoxies of institutionalist economics and habit psychology had suffered precipitous declines during the war and after (Yonay 1998; Mirowski 2002). Hence, Dewey's program to "naturalize" philosophical inquiry, insofar as it bore its commitments to these particular social science doctrines on its sleeve, was increasingly seen as backing the wrong horse. Not only would European émigrés find these commitments utterly unintelligible, but indigenous philosophers would also be aware of more concertedly scientific trends in economics and psychology (often jump-started in the United States by other European émigrés). Psychology grew more behaviorist and individualistic under wartime exigencies, and neoclassical economics rose to dominance in this period. The gambling metaphor was suffused throughout postwar psychology (W. Goldstein and Hogarth 1997, 10), and, as Reichenbach himself put it, "The scientist resembles a gambler more than a prophet" (1951, 248). It is again no accident that both these movements in economics and psychology were themselves linked to OR, especially beholden to it for their trademark mathematical models and statistical protocols; any philosophy willing to posit the motivations of the larger public as volitions/preferences and the rationality of the scientist as algorithmic optimization would find that its doctrines would resonate with a new postwar cross-disciplinary orthodoxy of the sciences of man. Thus, OR reshaped both the social sciences and the philosophy of science in the United States. Philosophy as the logical ratiocination of the isolated individual, cocooned with his or her identical twins in research universities away from the temptations of the crass world of the public, was born.

The exact character of the role of the market in OR and logical positivism was also rooted in the politics of the immediate postwar era. How could the logical positivists have been such pliant cold warriors when they identified themselves as socialists? Here is where left/right distinctions should not be taken for granted as dictating political affiliations, but need to be translated into the specific spatiotemporal context. The fact of the matter was that in the 1950s, the OR profession was itself a veritable hotbed of self-identified socialists, both in Britain and in the United States. The reason for this incongruous fact was that they were staffed by people who regarded themselves as applying scientific methods of command, planning, and control to improve the efficiency of social action undertaken by groups such as armies and governments. It should be remembered that the military constituted the largest planned economy in any Western nation, and that the safest way to ward off perilous accusations of being soft on communism and un-American (a heightened concern for those having recently emigrated) was to sport a military clearance. A certain type of non-Marxian socialist found the broad church of OR a most congenial shelter from the storms of the McCarthy era; Reichenbach fit right in.[26] An American socialist (who was also a European refugee?) in the cold war would have enthusiastically embraced the notion that science existed in a world apart from the world he or she was forced to live in.

Hans Reichenbach did not just resemble an Operations Researcher in the immediate postwar period; he *became* an Operations Researcher. As his student Norman Dalkey (himself a RAND employee) informs us (in Reichenbach 1978, 51), Reichenbach signed on as a consultant at RAND in 1948, that is, very soon after it broke away from Douglas Aircraft and reconstituted itself as a free-standing nonprofit corporation.[27] So what would a logical positivist philosopher be doing in a military think tank dedicated to "thinking the unthinkable" about nuclear war? The clarification begins with comments by another Operations Researcher who came to RAND in 1951, Albert Wohlstetter:

> I had known some of the first people who were on the RAND staff because they were also mathematical logicians: J. C. C. McKinsey, and Olaf Helmer, and also M. A. Girschick. . . . [They told me about] one of the most important contributions to metamathematics by Alfred Tarski, which had never been published, which showed that it was possible to get a decision method, an *Entscheidungsverfahren*, for a rather large and rich section of classical geometry, corresponding to high school geometry. . . . Well, that was very interesting to mathematicians. I was surprised, however, to find that RAND, this organization that worked for the Air Force, was publishing a research memorandum by Tarski which presented this result, because it didn't seem to me [back then] to have much directly to do with strategic bombing or anything of that sort. . . . we just ran into Abe Girschick, Olaf Helmer and Chen McKinsey on the street, and they were overjoyed to see us. Mathematical logic was a very, very small world. There were only a little over a dozen mathematical logicians before the war in the US, and two jobs in mathematical logic. For the rest, you had to teach calculus, as Chen McKinsey did, or philosophy or something of that sort.[28]

Prior to the cold war, career options in mathematical logic and formalist philosophy of science were minuscule to nonexistent, as this comment acknowledges. When OR units at RAND, Stanford, and elsewhere began to hire mathematical logicians at "unprecedentedly remunerative" rates (Quine 1985, 217) with military funding, this fostered the basis for the professionalization of these disciplines in the postwar United States. During the war many logicians had worked on cryptography, command and control, and the development of the electronic computer, so they were predisposed to become integrated into the burgeoning world of the defense intellectual after the war. For these reasons, RAND stood out as the locus of the densest concentration of mathematical logicians in the United States in the 1950s. Furthermore, RAND was predisposed to hire a particular type of formalist philosopher: as another RAND consultant, Willard von Orman Quine put it, "young philosophers of the Carnap persuasion" (217). RAND did not employ this specialized class of philosophers because they were especially interested in the "elimination of metaphysics through the logical analysis of formal language" or anything else of that sort, but because the logical positivist program could readily be subordinated to the objectives of the Operations Researchers, as enumerated above.

The fact that the logical empiricist program in the United States owed its good fortune to OR has not previously been the subject of much commentary, at least in part because the linkage has been suppressed by the participants themselves. We must remember that a precondition of joining the defense establishment was a willingness to submit to its stringent requirements concerning classification, secrecy, and the "double truth" doctrine. In my experience, the vitas and bibliographies of the figures in question omit their military papers; their archives have been sanitized of most of their military records; their collected works have blank pages. In their retrospective accounts, if they mention their ties at all, they tend to treat them as "boondoggles" (Quine 1985, 217), "diversions" (Donald Davidson in L. Hahn 1999, 32), and other trivial pursuits. Even figures who are a bit more open about their RAND experience, like Nicholas Rescher (1997a, ch. 8), are still noticeably reticent about discussing exactly what it was they did under those auspices. The RAND archives themselves, long after the Fall of the Wall, are still effectively closed to many outside researchers. The dense web of interconnections that tied the fledgling OR community to the following important figures in postwar philosophy of science still awaits its historian: Olaf Helmer, Carl Hempel, Paul Oppenheim, Alfred Tarski, Willard Quine, John Kemeny, J. C. C. McKinsey, Patrick Suppes, Donald Davidson, Nicholas Rescher, Paul Kecksemeti,

Fred Bales, Leonard Savage, and Rudolf Carnap (Reisch 2003, ch. 17). The ability of Reichenbach to get his students (such as Dalkey and Abraham Kaplan) jobs at RAND is a subject that will bear scrutiny. However, we can give some idea of the shape that influence took in the work of Hans Reichenbach.

Norman Dalkey (in Reichenbach 1978, 52) informs us that Reichenbach wrote at least three papers for RAND while a consultant there. Two of them, both dated 1949, were "General Form of the Probability for War" (RAND D-515) and "Rational Reconstruction of the Decision for War" (RAND D-539). The objectives of these papers, consonant with the general orientation of OR at that time, was "based on a rational reconstruction of Russia's doctrines, [to] supply the mathematical form of the probability that Russia will go to war" (RAND D-539, 23). While one rather doubts that any U.S. war planner ever even entertained Reichenbach's master equations 35 and 36, much less found them useful, their significance from our present perspective is the extent to which they resemble his formalization of the inductive problems of the scientist and the way they draw a distinction between the "scientific" approach to war and the less-than-rational "political" approach presumed to hold sway over other sorts of social formations. Reichenbach starts out by distinguishing between an empiricist approach (i.e., actual intelligence gathering) and a "rational reconstruction" of the decision to go to war, "imagining ourselves in the enemy's place," which was the nature of his own exercise. His free flight of imagination is disciplined by the postulation of a "valuation function" resembling the utility function of neoclassical economics and his own volitional preferences, as well as construction of a formal model of inductive inference. While the decision to go to war sounds a whole lot like the decision whether or not evidence confirms a scientific theory in his account, the problem with understanding the enemy (as Reichenbach conceives it) is that he or she is susceptible to all sorts of irrational motivations (see the epigraph heading this section). Reichenbach's solution is to treat these irrational elements as random and adjust the model with a parameter κ to allow for the "degree of rationality" of the enemy (RAND D-539, 13). He then discusses the possibility of the empirical estimation of κ, but worries that it is observationally indistinguishable from another variable he calls "the scale of decision ratings"; to thwart the threatening underdetermination problem, he then posits a "coordinative definition," a theme borrowed from his earlier work on the philosophy of space and time.

Reichenbach's paper helps reveal the ways OR did not give rise to the philosophy of logical positivism, but it most certainly transformed it in the U.S. context as a prelude to launching it as the characteristically professionalized philosophy of science that came to dominate the U.S. landscape. Many of the representative themes are present there: the sharp separation between scientific rationality and social structures (as if the Russians did not have their own Operations Researchers!), the suspicion of democracy, the contempt for history and cultural considerations, the conflation of social groups with individual agency, the confusion of statistical inference with scientific method, the portrayal of science as algorithmic, the veiled endorsement of Western economics through recourse to a behaviorist decision theory, the posturing concerning agnosticism about values, the underestimation of the difficulties of empiricism (especially with regard to the underdetermination of theory by evidence), the conflation of mathematical logic with human rationality, the absence of any actual empirical evidence, the psychological metaphor of gambling, and the claim to esoteric expertise. Some holdouts from the previous pragmatist school may not have wanted to subscribe to much of this, but then they had less and less to say about it, as they were left out in the cold by the postwar reorganization of academic science by the military.

The Past, and a Bit of the Future

The historian of science Peter Galison (1996) has argued that the logical positivist movement was depoliticized when it crossed the ocean from Vienna to Chicago (and beyond). I argue that this notion is insufficient, and perhaps a little misleading, once one actually widens one's perspective to include the social sciences. Logical empiricism, as well as neoclassical economics and political theory, were revised by their encounter with Operations Research, and the result was a whole new tool kit and orientation for all concerned. Positivism did become central to the self-image and identity of the U.S. social sciences, in part because some key theoretical terms like "democracy" and "rationality" had become endowed with new meanings. Although I have declined to do so here, it can be argued that this process continues down to the present day as we bid farewell to the cold war regime of science and welcome in the regime of globalized privatization, as suggested earlier.

One relatively safe prediction is that the social sciences will continue to be recruited to help jointly redefine both science and society in the interests of fostering the impression that contemporary organization of inquiry is (once again) exquisitely tuned to produce the best of all possible worlds. If this involves exhuming a few selected logical positivists and tarting them up with a fashionable makeover, then so be it: it won't be the first time that the paymasters of science had to pay a visit to the undertaker.

Notes

This paper is based on a paper that appeared in *Studies in the History and Philosophy of Science 30*. It is part of a much larger project on the joint constitution of the social and natural sciences in the United States, and has benefited from my extensive discussions with Tom Uebel, Don Howard, and Wade Hands. I would also like to thank George Steinmetz, Sonia Amadae, Andres Rius, and the participants of the Science, Technology, Society and the State Seminar at the University of Chicago. Please direct all correspondence to Philip Mirowski, 400 Decio Hall, University of Notre Dame, Notre Dame, Indiana, 46556.

1   For present purposes, I define the original logical positivists as Otto Neurath, Rudolf Carnap, and Hans Reichenbach. For the recent revival, see, for instance, Cartwright et al. (1996); Reisch (2002, 2003); Richardson (2002); Gimbel (2003); Uebel (2004).

2   Neurath explicitly argued, "It is politically important to support activities which emphasize empirical and pragmatic philosophies, since Fascism and Communism depend essentially on metaphysical doctrines" (in Reisch 2003, ch. 15).

3   Here I would especially mention Hollinger (1996), Purcell (1973), and Westbrook (1991) as having provided important clues.

4   Descriptions of early-twentieth-century science are taken from Reingold (1991), Shinn (2003), McGrath (2002), and sources cited in Mirowski and Sent (2002). The failures of early-twentieth-century attempts to garner government support for science are recounted in Tobey (1971).

5   The corporate character of early foundations and their effect on scientific research in the early twentieth century is discussed in Kohler (1991).

6   See, for instance, Clarence Ayres (1927, 275): "Scientists frequently argue that apart from making science one's profession, the chief advantage to be obtained from the study of science is the scientific mind: freedom from dogma, hospitality to unexpected truth, the experimental attitude. . . . Theoretically, all may gain these insights. But actually, only a few of us have ever done so. Theoretically, we might become a scientific people; but we have not, and are not likely to, except in the sense in which we are now a Christian people." In a curious incident in 1936, Franklin Delano Roosevelt wrote a letter to *Science* in which he suggested that scientists and engineers were not doing enough to help society "absorb the shocks of the impact of science" (in McGrath 2002, 50).

7   This case has been made with great insight by Purcell (1973) and Westbrook (1991).

8   On the history of institutionalist economics, consult Mirowski (1988), Rutherford (1994), Yonay (1998). On habit psychology, see Camic (1986), Dalton (2002), Westbrook (1991, 286–293), Ayres (1927, ch. 22). His periodic discussions at Columbia with another of the leading institutionalist figures, Wesley Clair Mitchell, is documented in Mitchell (1969, 2: 450).

9   This may have some relevance for Richard Rorty's quest to revive Dewey for the modern reader. Rorty distances himself from Dewey's "habit of announcing a bold new

positive program when all he offers, and all he needs to offer, is criticism of the tradition" (quoted in Cahn 1977, 56). A very interesting exercise that situates Rorty in his social context, as I have attempted to do here for Dewey, is N. Gross (2003).

10 On this point, see Howard (2003a). Ron Giere has reminded us, "The European origins of logical empiricism are not intellectually continuous with its later development in North America. . . . It is with this fact that any future history of logical empiricism in North America must begin" (1996, 336).

11 That appears to be the thrust of comments such as the following: "A socialist and an internationalist, Carnap nevertheless lived through situations which demanded defense, retreat, self-criticism, stubborn decency, maximal intelligence about minimal possibilities. . . . In his passionate way, he was a man of the resistance" (R. Cohen 1971, xlii). Carnap's ambivalence toward democracy has only begun to be noticed: see Notturno (1999). Some evidence comes from the Unity of Science Collection, Regenstein Library, University of Chicago (henceforth USUC), Box 1 folder 4, Carnap to Neurath letter, dated 6/24/42: "I am looking forward to your article 'int. Planning f. Freedom.' In your letter, you put the alternative as: muddling vs. democracy; and then of course we all prefer the second. The question is, whether democracy is actually incompatible with efficient planning and regulation."

12 This is a well-established fact in the history of U.S. science, such that we should not need to document it here. See, for instance, Kevles (1995), Kragz (1999, ch. 20), Michael Dennis in Krige and Pestre (1997). The following three paragraphs are a summary of an extensive case made in Mirowski (2002, ch. 4).

13 See the letters between Weaver and Charles Morris in USUC, Box 2, folder 18. Carnap was always a little naïve about where his money was coming from and why. See the passage from the letter cited above in n. 12: "I shall be free from teaching duties for one year from now on, with the help of the Rockef. Found., for continuing my work in semantics. Is it not remarkable that even in times like these, purely theoretical research is encouraged and supported?"

14 There is no good history of OR that can be recommended to the general reader. Existing histories are summarized in Mirowski (2002, ch. 4). Kirby (2000) is a guide to the alternative trajectories of OR in the British and U.S. contexts.

15 Has anyone ever noticed that the Library of Congress call numbers that categorize the philosophy of science in U.S. libraries also designate books in OR of a postwar vintage? Clues are quite abundant if one just permits oneself to perceive them.

16 On pp. 27–31 of Experience and Prediction (Reichenbach 1938) one will also discover the "physical symbol systems hypothesis" of early artificial intelligence avant la lettre, itself soon to spring forth from its origins in OR.

17 Reichenbach to Charles Morris, 12/1/37, USUC, Box 2, folder 15.

18 Reichenbach's version of inductive causality underlies much of modern U.S. time-series econometric logic: see, for instance, Hoover (2003).

19 Here I differ from an interpretation in Richardson (2001, 2002) that portrays Reichenbach as arguing for an ineliminable role for volitions in science. It is true that Reichenbach thought they would never be altogether banished in practice, in the same sense he expected that sociology of science could never be banished in principle; but the role of the philosopher was to partition them off from the true account of the operation of rational science. One observes this in the RAND paper quoted at the beginning of this section. The effect was to ratify the scientist/layperson divide.

20   He was undoubtedly familiar with this school, as he had attempted when younger to try to mathematize economics in conjunction with his friend Carl Landauer. On this, see Reichenbach (1978, 29).

21   Many positivists were admitting this by the late 1960s. Witness Herbert Feigl: "The so-called problem of induction . . . cannot be solved either by the logical or the statistical concept of probability" (1969, 11). By the 1970s, it was clear that the positivists had completely misrepresented a monolithic character of probability theory; see Fine (1973).

22   As Ron Giere asks, "How did a naturalistic pragmatism incorporating an empirical theory of inquiry get replaced by a philosophy that regarded induction as a formal relationship between evidence and hypothesis?" (1996, 347).

23   This case has lately been made by Asner (2002), who describes many of the legal, accountancy, and economic devices invented to give some solidity to the category "pure science."

24   The complex interplay of attitudes toward democracy, OR, and decision theory in this period are covered at length in Amadae (2003); pp. 128–132 especially explain how decision theory was a negation and repudiation of Dewey's conception of science and democracy.

25   Here Reichenbach's autonomy of the scientist dovetails very nicely with the "linear model" of research and development popularized by Vannevar Bush in the same era.

26   Although I do not explore the issue here, this fact helps clear up the noxious fog that has surrounded Alan Sokal's quest to "save" the U.S. left from the postmodern left and its tendency to see scientists as co-opted by the right. The specifically U.S. politics of the science wars has been thoroughly misconstrued by Europeans generally and is left opaque by commentators such as J. Brown (2001) and Kitcher (2000).

27   The history of RAND has recently attracted the interest of a number of historians, even though access to their archives is still severely restricted to outside researchers. Some good sources are Hounshell (1997), M. Collins (1998), Jardini (1996), Hughes and Hughes (2000), Amadae (2003), and Mirowski (2002, ch. 4).

28   Albert Wohlstetter interview with Martin Collins, 7/27/87, pp. 1, 2, RAND Oral History Project, transcript from National Air and Space Museum, Washington, D.C. Wohlstetter studied with Tarski as an undergraduate at CCNY and did graduate work in logic and philosophy of science at Columbia. He was one of the earliest American enthusiasts for the positivist unity of science movement (Reisch 2003, ch. 3). He later was infamous as one of the hawkish operations researchers that defined RAND's systems analyses of nuclear war.

The Political Unconscious of Social and Cultural History, or, Confessions of a Former Quantitative Historian

WILLIAM H. SEWELL JR.

This paper straddles the boundary between scholarly essay and personal reflection. My topic is the strange career of social history in the U.S. history profession over the past forty years or so, that is, since I began graduate school at Berkeley in 1962. These four decades correspond rather neatly to an entire developmental parabola of the research program that was commonly called the "new social history"—from its meteoric rise in the 1960s and 1970s to its surprisingly rapid displacement by a "new cultural history" in the 1980s and 1990s. The new social history is of particular interest in the context of this book because its triumph marked the high point of a particular form of social scientific positivism in the history profession. Likewise, the recent eclipse of social history by cultural history has also meant the marginalization of a positivist program in the discipline.

In this essay, I do not attempt to survey the research accomplishments of social or cultural history but concentrate instead on the epistemological and methodological presuppositions that underlay these two types of historical research. I pay especially close attention to the relationship between epistemology and politics, a relationship that, in the case of social and cultural history, has been complicated, paradoxical, and at times even perverse. I do all of this from the perspective of my own experience in the field. I wish to make it clear from the outset that I write as a fully engaged participant in the history I am chronicling and that my critiques should be read, at least in the first instance, as a form of self-criticism.

My mode of political interpretation is a form of Marxist criticism. I try to indicate how changes in the social and political forms of world capitalist development have—for the most part unconsciously—affected the politics of social and cultural history. Although my title invokes Fredric Jameson (1981), my approach to the recent intellectual history of social and cultural history actually has more in common with the work of Raymond Williams (1973, 1977). Like Williams, I am attempting to trace the emergence and expression in discourse—but in historical writing rather than in literature—of "structures of feeling" that arise from writers' experiences of fundamental transformations in the social relations of capitalism. Finally, as will surely be evident to readers of this book, I have been much influenced by George Steinmetz's recent work (this volume, forthcoming a; Steinmetz and Chae 2002) connecting the postwar epistemological history of U.S. sociology to the rise and fall of Fordism as a mode of macroeconomic and macrosocial regulation. My interpretation of developments in the history profession is in many respects a variation on Steinmetz's theme.

My reflections are inevitably influenced by the peculiarities of my own experience. Three of these should probably be noted immediately. The first is that I work in French history. American historians of France have naturally been influenced by the example of the powerful and prestigious Annales School, which led the way internationally both in social history from the 1930s through the 1960s and in the turn to cultural history in the 1970s. This tended to give historians of France a sense of being in the historiographical avant garde and meant that the gravitational pull of political history, which outside France often remained the specialty of the vast numerical majority of historians, was particularly weak. The history of the past forty years might look significantly different to an American historian of Germany, the United States, Britain, or India.

The second peculiarity is that I was actually raised a positivist. My father was an eminent sociologist whose life project was to make his discipline more fully "scientific." He was instrumental in building the University of Wisconsin's powerful and notoriously positivist sociology department and in obtaining a place for sociology at the federal feeding trough, especially at the National Institutes of Mental Health and the National Science Foundation (Sewell Sr. 1988). I began my career as a historian fully equipped with a positivist vision of science that I had learned at my father's knee. My first published paper, which dates from my graduate student days, was an attempt to explicate Marc Bloch's use of comparative history according to a positivist notion of hypothesis testing (Sewell 1967), and I undertook a dissertation that involved a massive effort of quantitative research (Sewell 1971). It seems clear that I was more deeply imbued with positivist views than were most of my social historian contemporaries.

A third peculiarity of my experience is that it has been far less bounded by history departments than is the norm. Even in graduate school, my training was cross-disciplinary: my major concentration was in the inter-disciplinary field of economic history, and I completed significant course work in economics and did a minor field in sociological theory. Moreover, in only ten of the thirty-five years since I gained my first academic post has my appointment been exclusively in a history department. In addition to unalloyed history department appointments (at the University of Chicago from 1968 to 1975 and the University of Arizona from 1980 to 1983) I had a five-year interdisciplinary social science appointment (in the School of Social Science at the Institute for Advanced Study from 1975 to 1980) and have had joint appointments in sociology and history for seven years (the University of Arizona from 1983 to 1985 and the University of Michigan from 1985 to 1990) and in political science and history for thirteen (at the University of Chicago from 1990 to the present). This unusually inter-disciplinary professional experience means that I have, in effect, engaged in a good deal of participant observation of the theoretical, methodological, and rhetorical practices of several social science fields.[1] This has certainly made me far more aware than most historians of the wide range and the "culturally constructed" character of disciplinary epistemic practices, and it surely is at least partly responsible for the emergence in my work of a much stronger interest in theory than is generally characteristic of historians. (Of course, this last point could also be read the other way around; perhaps it was my interest in theory that led to my unusually interdisciplinary career.)

Despite these idiosyncrasies, I do not think that my methodological views or my styles of historical research have been radically different from those of the mainstream of my generation of social historians. I began as a committed new social historian and made considerable use of quantitative data in my early work; subsequently, I moved increasingly toward work with a cultural bent. This trajectory, as I argue later, was actually quite common in my age cohort. Meanwhile, my political views and experiences have been almost embarrassingly typical of historians of my generation. Like many of my contemporaries, I was involved in a whole range of "sixties" political and cultural movements: the civil rights movement, the movement against the Vietnam War, the university revolts (in my case, the Berkeley Free Speech Movement), and the counterculture. My active participation in politics slackened in the 1970s, as a result of both the declining vitality of the various movements[2] and changes in my personal and professional life: the demands of increased family responsibilities, of holding down a teaching job, and of producing publications as to attain tenure. But I remained politically on the left and eventually became one of the "tenured radicals" who were so vehemently bemoaned by right-wing commentators during the Reagan and George H. W. Bush presidencies (Kimball 1990) and who are, indeed, very plentiful on the faculties of major universities, in history departments as elsewhere.

Social History

Eric Hobsbawm, writing about social history in 1971, noted "the remarkably flourishing state of the field," concluding, "It is a good moment to be a social historian" (43). It certainly was a good moment for the large cohort of historians who, like me, had entered graduate school in the 1960s, chosen to write dissertations on social historical topics, and secured good academic jobs in the rapidly expanding U.S. university system with an ease that now seems almost obscene. Most of this rising generation of social historians was largely self-taught. We sought out dissertation advisors who were sympathetic to the kind of work we wanted to do, but found few who could give us detailed methodological guidance. We educated ourselves in method and theory largely by taking courses in sociology, political science, or economics. There were a handful of older scholars, in U.S. universities and abroad, whose work served as crucial models for our research, but most of us knew them by their books rather than as teachers. I was most influenced by three books published in 1963 and 1964, precisely when I was developing a dissertation topic: E. P. Thompson's *The Making of the English Working Class* (1963), Charles Tilly's *The Vendée* (1964), and Stephan Thernstrom's *Poverty and Progress* (1964). But even most of the elder statesmen of the new social history were still quite young in their careers when the 1960s ended. It was the entry into the profession of my cohort of social historians, and the outpouring of our articles and monographs over the course of the 1970s, that secured the ascent of social history in the United States. By the mid-1970s, the new social history had achieved a strong institutional presence and was quickly moving toward hegemony in the profession.[3] Dozens of social history monographs were flowing from the university presses; articles on social history flooded not only the specialized social history journals but also such general journals as the *American Historical Review* and the *Journal of Modern History*, and social historians were getting tenure and moving rapidly up the ranks in all the major departments.

The rise of social history not only represented the arrival of a new generation of historians; it also effected a profound and lasting intellectual transformation, something like a paradigm shift, in the field of history. Social history represented a change in subject matter, in methods, and in intellectual style. One of its most significant and lasting achievements was a vast enlargement of the scope of historical study. This enlargement was twofold. First, social history studied categories of people who had previously been ignored by historical scholarship. Rather than political leaders and great intellectuals, who had been the prime subjects of previous scholarship, social historians tended to work on the obscure and downtrodden: servants, workers, criminals, women, slaves, shopkeepers, peasants, and children. This interest in the forgotten millions of ordinary people was, clearly, consonant with the populist tendencies of 1960s political activism. Second, rather than concentrating on politics narrowly defined, social history attempted to capture the whole range of ordinary people's life experiences: work, child rearing, disease, recreation, deviant behavior, kinship, popular religion, sociability, procreation, consumption. Social history thus not only studied new categories of people but asked new questions about them. And to answer new questions about new categories of people, it used new forms of evidence. All sorts of records previously thought not to contain information relevant to historical research suddenly became goldmines of documentation. Old census manuscripts, tax registers, wills, advice books, inventories of estates, popular songs, city directories, statutes of mutual aid societies, building permits, records of marriages, baptisms, and deaths: all these and many other kinds of documents yielded evidence about the social structures, institutions, and life experiences of millions of ordinary people.

These new forms of documentation were also subjected to new methods of analysis. A characteristic mark of the new social history was the systematic use of quantitative methods. The kinds of people social historians studied were often illiterate, and even those who could read and write rarely left papers that revealed much about their lives. But such people came into contact with public authorities when they paid taxes or tithes; when they were drafted; when they registered births, marriages, and deaths; when they got counted by the census or were arrested by the police. It was largely by aggregating the rather thin and stereotypic information contained in the records of such encounters between ordinary people and public authorities that social historians were able to reconstruct the patterns of these otherwise anonymous lives. Quantification as a method of analysis was thus intimately linked to social history's radical expansion in subject matter.

It was from the social sciences that historians borrowed the quantitative methods they applied to these novel data sources. But the borrowing involved far more than a simple transportation of a set of methods: along with the methods came a distinctive theoretical and epistemological outlook. The borrowing of methods was but one aspect of a self-conscious modeling of ourselves and our work on the social sciences. Because we tended to regard what we called "traditional narrative history" as atheoretical and intellectually bankrupt, the neighboring social science fields of sociology, political science, economics, demography, and geography looked very attractive. These fields, of course, themselves had passed through a major transformation in the postwar years. As George Steinmetz's contribution to this volume details for the case of sociology, positivism and quantification triumphed in these fields in the 1950s and 1960s, greatly assisted by massive federal spending on social science research. By the 1960s, these quantitatively inclined social sciences were high in prestige in the academy and seemed far more methodologically rigorous and theoretically sophisticated than history. Not surprisingly, their positivist and objectivist stance was carried over into the new social history.

These various changes introduced by social history were mutually reinforcing: they made up a fairly coherent package, constructing a distinct epistemic object for social history. The new social historians' "social" was above all of what we (following our social scientist friends) called "social structure." Social structures were objective and transpersonal patterns or forces of which actors were at best incompletely aware and that tightly constrained their actions and thoughts. These social structures—occupational distributions, business cycles, demographic patterns, inheritance systems, hierarchies of wealth, urban settlement patterns, systems of land tenure, and the like—left palpable traces in historical records, especially in the quantifiable records that supplied what we called hard data. We thought of social structures as essentially autonomous from political or intellectual history. Indeed, we often argued that they formed the underlying conditions for, even the determinants of, the political and intellectual developments that historians had previously taken as primary. The distinction between the hard data of quantitative history and the soft or impressionistic data of political and intellectual history subtly implied an underlying ontological distinction between a determining social structure and a determined politics and culture. In short, the rise of social history entailed a redefinition of the primary object of historical knowledge, from politics and ideas to anonymous social structures, as well as the discovery of new means of gaining knowledge about this object.

The new social history paradigm I have just outlined is, of course, an ideal type. Not every social historian adhered equally to all aspects of this epistemic package. Those strongly influenced by demography or economics, for instance, tended to be particularly enthusiastic about quantitative methods and hard data, while those who worked on rebellions and social movements tended to combine quantitative data with verbal accounts culled from archives, memoirs, and newspapers. But for all the internal differences among social historians, we tended to adopt a common front in our struggles for recognition in the field, arguing for the necessity of interdisciplinary borrowing, for the recognition of quantitative methods as part of the historian's tool kit, for the expansion of history's subject matter beyond politics and great ideas, and for recognizing the historical importance of ordinary people's experiences. These arguments were, it seems to me, largely successful; social history did succeed in significantly redefining the object of historical knowledge. I would even say that social history briefly became hegemonic in the field. Although social historians never accounted for a numerical majority, they were hegemonic in the sense that they managed to define the terms of historiographical debate, so that, for example, political and intellectual historians themselves began to ask more social historical questions and to experiment with the new methods.[4] By the mid-1970s, social history was generally recognized, even by those skeptical of its claims or methods, as the cutting edge of historical research.

The relationship of this research program to the political commitments and sentiments of the rising generation of social historians was complicated, in part because the social historians' political commitments were themselves far from simple. As I have already intimated, quantitative techniques were quite consonant with the strong populist impulses of 1960s radicalism because they made it possible to carry out detailed studies of classes or categories of the population who were poorly represented in the sources used by more traditional historians. Quantification, in other words, was one important way of pursuing the populist goal of "history from the bottom up." But social historians' politics could also make their embrace of positivist social science significantly ambivalent. It is important to remember that the politics of the 1960s was by no means limited to an upsurge of populism; 1960s politics also featured a powerful revulsion against the bureaucratic conformity that student radicals saw as characteristic of contemporary U.S. society. Especially in its countercultural moment, 1960s radicalism must be seen as a rejection of the corporate political and cultural synthesis of "big government, big business, big labor" that became dominant in the 1950s and 1960s, what has since come to be called Fordism.[5] The term Fordism designates the mode of macrosocial and macroeconomic regulation that underwrote the long postwar economic boom, which stretched from the late 1940s to the early 1970s. The Fordist package combined mass production technologies, relatively high wage levels, stable systems of collective bargaining, Keynesian management of aggregate demand, full employment strategies, welfare state institutions, and highly bureaucratized forms of both public and private management (Aglietta 1979; A. Amin 1994; Gramsci 1929–35/1971a; Harvey 1989; Jessop 1992; Lipietz 1987).

From the perspective of the hypercompetitive, predatory, and extraordinarily inegalitarian U.S. capitalism of the early twenty-first century, the Fordist mode of regulation may seem remarkably humane, a kind of quasi–social democratic "world we have lost." But from the point of view of young critics of the system in the 1960s, its benefits (for example, economic stability and steady productivity gains) were hardly noticed. They seemed givens of modernity itself, permanent and unproblematic acquisitions of an irreversible social progress. Meanwhile, the defects of Fordist capitalism, especially corporate conformity, bureaucratic monotony, repressive morality, and stultifying forms of mass culture, were highly visible and repugnant, at least to the youthful political intelligentsia who made up the student movement. The countercultural style of the 1960s movements—psychedelic music, consciousness-altering drugs, infatuation with "Eastern" meditative practices, outlandish clothing styles, sexual experimentation—was largely a revolt against the standardization associated with the Fordist mode of socioeconomic regulation. And while the leftist political movements and the counterculture were by no means one and the same, it was difficult to participate in the political movements of the era without also exploring and embracing some of the new possibilities offered by the counterculture.

I am convinced that this anti-Fordist strain in the politics of the 1960s endowed many social historians with at least a latent ambivalence about quantitative methods and the positivist philosophical assumptions that came in their baggage. It certainly did so in my case. It seemed undeniable to me that quantitative methods were useful, indeed essential, for overcoming the "elitism" of "traditional" history, for expanding the social range and subject matter of history so as to encompass the lives of the poor, the oppressed, and the marginalized. Yet we social historians were to some degree aware that in adopting quantitative methodology we were participating in the bureaucratic and reductive logic of big science, which was part and parcel of the system we wished to criticize. At least in my case, this awareness arose in part from contacts with leftist students in disciplines like political science and sociology who in the 1960s were themselves criticizing the blind spots in their fields' positivist methodologies. As Steinmetz (this volume, forthcoming a; Steinmetz and Chae 2002) has pointed out, these critiques were based on an implicitly anti-Fordist political project. In retrospect, I would say that we new social historians found ourselves in the objectively contradictory situation of using big science Fordist methods in pursuit of an at least partly anti-Fordist political agenda.

One sign of my own ambivalence and, I believe, that of many of my contemporaries was the extraordinary role played by the work of E. P. Thompson as an inspiration even for new social historians who, like me, had enthusiastically embraced the possibilities of quantitative history. Many of us admired Thompson's work greatly, even though he was profoundly hostile, almost allergic, to quantification, which he regarded as a violent abstraction from the textures of lived experience. His own work probed the thoughts, feelings, and experiences of the English poor, attempting, as he put it, to rescue them from "the enormous condescension of posterity" (1963, 13). In retrospect, I think that Thompson was so appealing in part because he made the victory of laissez-faire capitalism in early nineteenth-century England seem contingent rather than necessary and set forth the alternatives championed by working-class communities in such vivid detail. The sheer richness of Thompson's history of working-class experience—his convincing reconstructions of manifold distinct, vibrant, and rebellious forms of life in late-eighteenth- and early-nineteenth-century England—struck a responsive chord among young women and men who were attempting to find radical alternatives to the rather different Fordist capitalist culture that formed our own social world. Hence, it was common for new social historians to mix a little E. P. Thompson with their quantitative sociology, to add to their quantitative analyses whatever they could glean about the lived experiences of the poor.[6] Although our epistemological stances may ultimately have been incoherent, it seemed clear in practice that both quantitative and Thompsonian qualitative methods helped us toward the ultimate goal, which was to understand the lives of ordinary people in the past. In my own case, at least, the qualitative material on lived experience served as a kind of supplement to the quantitative core of my research. This was reflected in an epistemic metaphor I used in the introduction to my dissertation, where I described quantitative methods as providing a hard skeleton to which the flesh and blood of available qualita-

tive data might be attached (Sewell 1971, 17–18).[7] In short, although quantitative history seemed both exciting and politically compelling in the late
1960s, the moral ambivalence of our embrace of quantification and the
incoherency of our epistemological stances probably rendered us vulnerable to the cultural turn once it got under way.

The Cultural Turn

As early as 1971, the year I completed my doctoral dissertation, I was
beginning to feel frustrated by the limits of positivist quantitative history.
It seemed to me that although quantitative methodology had enabled us to
understand more and more about the structural constraints and social
forces that shaped people's lives, it offered no guidance for understanding
how people actually made sense of and grappled with these forces and
constraints. The persistent objectivism of the new social history's practicing epistemology, the mode of thinking that C. Wright Mills (1959) brilliantly dubbed "abstracted empiricism," virtually ruled out some of the
most interesting questions about the past: the questions about agency,
culture, and the textures of experience that had been at the heart of E. P.
Thompson's work. I do not know at what point such doubts began to
haunt other new social historians, but it is clear that my case was not
unique. It is remarkable that the turn to what in the course of the 1980s
came to be called cultural history was actually pioneered by some of the
same historians who had initially adhered to the new social history. In my
own field of French history, for example, I would cite Joan Scott and Lynn
Hunt as historians who, like me, moved from early work in a quantitative
mode to later work in cultural history.[8] Unlike the rise of the new social
history, which was effected above all by a generational succession, the rise
of the new cultural history was at least in part a transformation of historical practices within the 1960s generation. In retrospect, I see my switch
from social to cultural history as a belated working out of the anti-Fordist
dimension of my 1960s radicalism. And I strongly suspect that many
others were affected by the same underlying political motivations. But
before discussing the politicocultural dynamics of history's cultural turn,
let me say more about when and how the turn took place.

My own path out of the new social history's abstracted empiricism, one
that was followed by a number of others as well, was inspired by cultural
anthropology. What anthropology offered was a way of getting at meaningful human action. Of course, questions about the history of meaning
already had a significant place in the field of intellectual history. The beauty

of cultural anthropology was that it made possible the pursuit of such questions not only in the texts of great thinkers, but in the rituals, conventions, language, and everyday conduct of ordinary people. It made possible, one might say, a kind of intellectual history of precisely the poor, marginalized, oppressed, illiterate or semiliterate groups whose study was the bread and butter of social history. In this respect, then, social history's turn to anthropology was perfectly consistent with the field's frankly expansive ethos. Just as the use of quantitative methods enabled social historians to grasp the social, economic, or geographic structures that shaped the lives of the poor, the marginalized, and the oppressed, so the use of anthropological methods could enable us to grasp such people's cultural systems. Adopting anthropological methods was therefore a means of expanding or supplementing our conception of the social by adding cultural structures to the familiar social structures. Anthropology implied that cultural structures, rather than being reflections or products of underlying social structures, were in fact equal to them in ontological standing.

Thus, although the search for cultural structures was consonant with social history's expansive ethos, the turn to anthropology had some unsettling epistemological and ontological implications. This was because anthropology, or at least the kind of Geertzian "symbolic anthropology" that historians tended to pick up (Geertz 1973c), was fundamentally incompatible with the new social history's basically positivist epistemology and objectivist ontology. Unlike the new social history's presumption that social structures were analytically prior to social action, cultural anthropology implied that the social world was constituted by the interpretive practices of the actors who made it up. Hence, rather than scientists whose analysis of hard data revealed the structures of an objective social world, social historians who made the anthropological turn had to recast themselves as interpreters of the inevitably interpretive practices that produced intersubjective cultural patterns. Cultural anthropology seemed to imply that even social and economic structures, which appeared to be the concrete foundations or bony skeletons of social life, were themselves products of the interpretive work of human actors. In some respects, cultural anthropology was, of course, merely reiterating themes that new social historians had long since encountered in the work of E. P. Thompson. But Thompson's work itself embodied a tension between a strong emphasis on culture and a strong commitment to a historical materialist explanatory strategy, in which the development of capitalism was determining in the final analysis.[9] Even if he disdained quantitative methods, Thompson ultimately affirmed the primacy of social and economic structures. But

Geertz's cultural anthropology entirely lacked Thompson's familiar and comforting materialism. Moreover, it also had an explicitly philosophical edge, both ontological (see, e.g., Geertz 1973b) and epistemological (see, e.g., Geertz 1973d).

Making the cultural turn was therefore an exciting but also profoundly troubling step for an adept of the new social history. In my case, and I think in others' as well, taking this step amounted to a sort of conversion experience: a sudden and exhilarating reshaping of one's intellectual and moral world. In my case, the initial conversion took place at the University of Chicago between 1972 and 1974, largely under the influence of Bernard Cohn and Ronald Inden.[10] My anthropological turn was powerfully confirmed and deepened during the academic year of 1975–76 at the Institute for Advanced Study, when I took part in an extraordinary seminar on symbolic anthropology. This seminar, led by Clifford Geertz, included the anthropologists Victor Turner, Hildred Geertz, James Fernandez, David Sapir, Michelle and Renato Rosaldo, and Ellen and Keith Basso, the sociologist Orlando Patterson, and five historians: Robert Darnton, Thomas Kuhn, William Reddy, Ralph Giesey, and myself. The seminar gave rise to an intense discussion of the relationship between anthropology and history, one that spilled over into lunch table conversations and the Shelby Collum Davis seminar at Princeton University. This interaction between anthropologists and historians gave me a strong sense that my own interest in cultural anthropology was part of a larger convergence between the two disciplines. Anthropologists, it appeared, were as interested in historicizing their traditionally synchronic discipline as historians were interested in applying to history the anthropological notion of culture. (For astute accounts of relations between history and anthropology at this time, see Cohn 1980, 1981). Nevertheless, I can also testify that going over to anthropological methods and theories could attract considerable hostility from one's erstwhile new social history colleagues, especially in my subfield of labor history, where anything smacking of "idealism" was taken as evidence of political as well as intellectual apostasy.[11] But the anthropologists' vivid and persuasive ethnographies contained a double promise: first, that interpretive methods could uncover structures or systems of meaning no less real or far-reaching in their implications than the social structures uncovered by quantitative research and, second, that by doing so they could restore to history the dimension of meaningful human action that had been marginalized in the new social history. Anthropological history, in short, seemed a risky but also an irresistible intellectual adventure.

It was by no means impossible to combine quantitative with interpretive methods, but it did require something of a balancing act. Moreover, the intoxication and sense of discovery involved in these pioneering searches for past cultural systems made it hard for social historians to sustain in practice an integrated sociological-cum-anthropological research strategy. Instead, many of us threw ourselves wholeheartedly into the study of culture, leaving our data sets, graphs, and statistical tables behind. My own experience indicates how difficult it could be in practice to combine cultural and social history approaches. I initially discovered the possibilities of cultural anthropology at a time when I was attempting to turn my dissertation on the workers of Marseille into a book. But before I could complete the task, an anthropologically inspired essay that I initially presented to the Symbolic Anthropology Seminar burgeoned into a very different book (Sewell 1980), interrupting my work on Marseille for several years. When I returned to the Marseille project, I managed to publish only a highly statistical and utterly sociological first volume of what I had actually planned as a two-volume work (Sewell 1985). The second volume, which was precisely projected to combine cultural and statistical methods, never got written. The question of the relationship between changing social structures and the emergence of working-class radicalism, which had seemed so compelling in the 1960s and 1970s, had lost much of its interest for me by the mid-1980s.[12] By then, I had effectively ceased to be a social historian.

Not all social historians found their way into cultural history by way of anthropology. Another, probably more common, route was via literary studies, which itself had been transformed in the 1970s by the various poststructuralisms associated with the names of Derrida, Lacan, and Foucault. Precisely how social historians negotiated the cultural turn surely depended on local ecologies of knowledge. My appointments at Chicago and then at the Institute for Advanced Study in Princeton put me at two of the major crossroads of history and anthropology in the 1970s. Lynn Hunt and Joan Scott, two other social historians of France of my vintage who also made the cultural turn, did so primarily through local connections with literary scholars, although in quite different ways. Hunt explained in the preface to her transitional book *Politics, Culture, and Class in the French Revolution* (1984) that she had begun her research with "a different project in mind," but that her "original social history of Revolutionary politics turned increasingly into a cultural analysis." She attributed this in part to "the impact of my friends at Berkeley," but did not mention who these friends were (xi). I think, however, that we can get some insight into her social circles by noting that she served on the editorial board of the celebrated interdisciplinary journal *Representations* when it was launched in 1983, the year before she published *Politics, Culture, and Class.* A quick check of the disciplinary affiliations of the editorial board indicates seven English professors, two professors of French, three historians, one anthropologist, and one (very maverick) political scientist. This affiliation with the humanities is also reflected in the theoretical references in part 1 of Hunt's book (entitled "Poetics as Power"), which include citations to Jean Starobinski, Kenneth Burke, Susan Suleiman, Northrup Frye, Hayden White, Michel Foucault, Jacques Derrida, and E. H. Gombrich, along with the historians J. G. A. Pocock, Ernst Kantorowicz, Mona Ozouf, and François Furet. The only social scientists mentioned are Emile Durkheim and the ubiquitous Clifford Geertz.

Joan Scott made the cultural turn during a period when she was teaching at Brown University and serving as director of the Pembroke Center for Research on Women. In her introduction to *Gender and the Politics of History* (1988a), the book that contains her writings from this period, Scott notes that the essays grew out of conversations in the Center's seminar. There, surrounded by feminist "literary scholars," she tells us that she "was forced to take post-structuralist theory seriously and wrestle with its implications for a social historian" (1). The theoretical citations in Scott's volume bear out this provenance: the poststructuralist humanities scholars Michel Foucault, Teresa de Lauretis, Barbara Johnson, Jacques Derrida, Michel de Certeau, Donna Haraway, Martha Minow, Gayatri Chakravorty Spivak, Denise Riley, and Homi Bhabha, together with the Marxist critics T. J. Clark and Fredric Jameson, are joined by one historian (Roger Chartier), two sociologists (Nancy Chodorow and Pierre Bourdieu), two anthropologists (Clifford Geertz and Michelle Zimbalist Rosaldo), and one political theorist (Carole Pateman). While Scott's theoretical references, like Hunt's, are largely to scholars in the humanities, hers are overwhelmingly to poststructuralists, whereas Hunt's include such classical humanities authors as Burke, Frye, and Gombrich. Moreover, feminist theorists are very prominent among Scott's references, making up fully half of the total, by my count. By contrast, only one feminist (Susan Suleiman) appears among Hunt's references. These striking differences mirror a fundamental divergence in the humanities in the late 1970s and early 1980s, when both feminists and poststructuralists were engaged in intense epistemological challenges to traditional humanistic scholarship. As these references imply, Scott's work includes a poststructuralist epistemological critique of historical thought, one that Hunt and her coauthors disagreed with emphatically in their epistemologically middle-of-the-road *Telling the Truth about History* (Appleby, Hunt, and Jacobs 1994, 226–228). Clearly, very different kinds of literary theory could be imported into history, with very different results.

It is instructive that both Scott's and Hunt's theoretical references were quite different from those in the introduction to my transitional book, *Work and Revolution in France* (Sewell 1980). My cited theoretical sources were five anthropologists (Clifford Geertz, David Schneider, Victor Turner, Max Gluckman, and Marshall Sahlins), two philosophers (Michel Foucault and Jacques Rancière), and four historians (E. P. Thompson, Ronald Inden, and Eugene and Elizabeth Genovese). The difference in profiles between these citations and those of Hunt and Scott are clear: a much higher proportion of anthropologists, no literary critics or feminists, and (to my surprise) a higher proportion, across all disciplinary categories, of Marxist scholars (by my count, five of eleven, as opposed to two of eighteen for Scott and none among Hunt's fourteen).[13] This quick and dirty exercise in citation analysis indicates that seemingly parallel and roughly simultaneous paths through the cultural turn could vary significantly in their fine structures.

But at the same time, all three of these cases illustrate a major shift in the epistemological frontiers of history. If the new social history was largely defined by its borrowing of method and epistemology from the quantitatively inclined social sciences, the new cultural history that took shape in the 1980s was defined instead by a large-scale transplantation of method and epistemology from the humanities. Even the theoretical references of someone like me, who followed a relatively social scientific route through the cultural turn, included anthropologists and philosophers, but no sociologists, let alone economists. Indeed, the only work by a sociologist cited by any of us was Emile Durkheim's (1912/1995) *Elementary Forms of Religious Life* (by Hunt), a book claimed as a founding text by anthropologists as much as by sociologists. Moreover, even historians who made the cultural turn primarily through borrowings from the officially social science discipline of anthropology found themselves in an intellectual world increasingly defined by literary studies. Geertz's (1973a) essay on the Balinese cockfight, which was the anthropological work that influenced historians most widely (see Walters 1980), was famous for introducing into anthropology the notion of culture as a text. Geertz's models of text interpretation, to be sure, were primarily drawn from hermeneutics or new criticism. But many in the generation of anthropologists who came of age in the 1970s and 1980s (including some of Geertz's own students) were increasingly attracted to the poststructuralist forms of literary theory that

had gained dominance in departments of English, French, and comparative literature. The manifesto of anthropological poststructuralism, a collection significantly entitled *Writing Culture* (Clifford and Marcus 1986),
was published in 1986. From that time forward, anthropology itself was
less an exporter of theory to other disciplines than an importer of theory
from literary studies.[14]

When the frontier with the humanities was breached in the early 1980s,
much of the theory that flowed into history was poststructuralist. As the
connections with literature multiplied, Foucault, Derrida, and Lacan became names to conjure with in historical circles. The influence of Foucault
on historians has been particularly notable (see J. Goldstein 1994). I believe that this prominence stemmed in part from the obvious fact that,
unlike Derrida, Lacan, and their literary epigones, Foucault consistently
worked on historical topics. Moreover, he focused on marginalized groups
and on the links between discourse, power, and inequality, interests that
fit, but also challenged, social historians' preoccupation with history from
the bottom up (see especially Foucault 1979).[15] If the hermeneutical approach of Geertzian anthropology introduced at least a potential epistemological break between social and cultural history, the influx of poststructuralist theory did much to radicalize that break, making any attempt
to develop a combined sociocultural history ever more difficult.

Both the rapidity of the rise of cultural history in the 1980s and the
widening of the epistemological fissure dividing it from social history were
disproportionately fueled by developments in women's history, or gender
history, to use the term that many would now prefer. Women's history was
easily the most politically intense and intellectually creative field in historical studies during the 1980s.[16] Thanks largely to the organized efforts of
feminist historians during the 1970s, there was a remarkable influx of
women into history departments in the 1980s (remarkable, that is, by
comparison with previous decades). Women's history was, therefore, also
the most rapidly growing field in the disicpline. Through the 1970s, wom-
en's history looked much like other subfields of social history, focusing on
the familiar tasks of documenting the experiences of a previously ignored
category of the population and specifying the structural sources of wom-
en's particular social and economic burdens. But during the 1980s, wom-
en's historians, increasingly influenced by feminist philosophers and literary scholars (as in the bellwether case of Joan Scott discussed above),
began to explore the intrinsically radical epistemological consequences of
the modern feminist movement. Feminism had, after all, challenged one
of the supposedly most natural of social distinctions, the difference be-

tween male and female, arguing that its meaning was contingent and susceptible to fundamental redefinition. Hence the problem for historians, stated most influentially by Joan Scott (1988a), became not to document the distinct historical experiences of women, but to decipher the processes by which gender difference—indeed, sexual difference itself—has been established, maintained, and transformed. In this effort the resources provided by literary theory have proved tremendously valuable. This critical and deconstructive historical analysis of central cultural categories—sex and gender—has unquestionably helped to radicalize and energize cultural history as a whole. The influence is particularly clear in histories of race, sexuality, and colonialism. Work in these areas has sustained both the political radicalism and the conceptual innovation that has characterized gender history since the 1980s. (Some examples are Bederman 1995; L. Briggs 2002; Chauncy 1994; Holt 1995; Roediger 1991; Stoler 1995, 2002).

Social history, even quantitative social history, has certainly not disappeared. But its decline from hegemony in the history profession in the late 1970s to a position of intellectual marginality by the late 1980s was almost breathtakingly rapid. In part because many of the most promising social historians themselves took the cultural turn, the no longer *new* social history failed to put up much of a struggle against the rise of cultural history. Abetted by the burgeoning of a culturally inflected gender history and the influx of women into graduate programs and faculty positions, cultural history quickly became the major growth area in the profession, attracting the best students in the major centers of graduate training. The publication in 1989 of an influential collection entitled *The New Cultural History* (edited by Lynn Hunt) might be said to mark cultural history's claim to have usurped definitively the hegemonic position achieved by social history only a decade earlier.

Because I was a pioneer in the field of cultural history, one might expect me to be thrilled by its rise to intellectual hegemony. The speed and thoroughness of the triumph, after all, has been quite exhilarating. As recently as 1985, I was convinced that the remainder of my academic career would be dedicated to a long and exhausting fight for the recognition of culture's role in social life. That the positions I had to argue for tooth and nail in the early 1980s had become the accepted wisdom by 1990 was a delightful surprise. Nevertheless, I have increasingly come to worry that the triumph of cultural history over social history has perhaps been too easy, that social historical methodologies of considerable power have been abandoned without resistance and that important concepts, especially the

fundamental social historical notion of social structure, have been abandoned almost without argument. Cultural history, it seems to me, has
been largely spared the potentially bracing task of working out its relationship to the fundamental problems and techniques of social history; it has,
instead, been able to dismiss them more or less out of hand. The result, I
fear, is a form of history that, for all its impressive achievements and in
spite of its continuing vitality and political relevance, nevertheless finds
itself disarmed in the face of some of the most important questions posed
to us by the history of our own era. Here, indeed, is a vexing paradox:
during the very period when historians have gleefully cast aside the notion
of structural determination, the shape of our own social world has been
fundamentally transformed by changes in the structures of world capitalism in ways I attempt to spell out below. Given the political and intellectual challenges facing us at the beginning of the twenty-first century, I
think that history can jettison the conceptual and methodological heritage
of social history only at its peril.

But how and why have the achievements of social history been so
quickly abandoned? I noted that the cultural turn involved a rejection of
the naïve objectivism of social history, the notion that social structures
were ontologically prior to thought and action and that various forms of
hard data afforded privileged access to these structures. One of the key
arguments against these objectivist prejudices was to demonstrate that the
documents containing so-called hard data were themselves cultural products that required interpretation and critique. Once again, Joan Scott's
work is emblematic of a mode of thinking that I believe was widespread
during history's cultural turn. In an essay originally written in 1984[17] and
eventually incorporated into *Gender and the Politics of History* (1988c),
Scott subjected a statistical inquiry into work in mid-nineteenth-century
Paris to a brilliant political and cultural reading, treating statistical categories themselves as discourse rather than taking the numbers they produced
as objective data about social life. Her astute deconstruction of the categories employed in the inquiry demonstrated that this statistical text was
structured throughout by a particular politics of gender. Her critique of
normal positivist research procedures was devastating. She pointed out
that "historians searching for unimpeachable data" have taken the report
"at face value, incorporating its documentation without questioning its
categories and interpretations." Such a procedure is doubly faulty, she
argues, because it both "perpetuates a certain vision of the economy and
of statistical science as an essentially objective enterprise" and "makes the
historian an unwitting party to the politics of another age" (137). This does

not mean that Scott disputed the utility of statistical reports as historical sources. "Rather," she asserted, "I want to argue against a simple positivist use of them and for a fuller and more complicated conceptualization of the 'reality' they represent; for a reading of statistical reports that problematizes and contextualizes their categories and conclusions; for an end, in other words, to the separation of statistical reports from other kinds of historical texts" (115).

But there is another question that Scott did not pose: Once the inquiry's categories had been subjected to criticism and reinterpretation, could the data it reports be used in a *statistically* critical fashion, perhaps revealing patterns that are present in the data but obscured by the inquiry's procedures of classification and interpretation? Scott successfully read the inquiry culturally to get at the mental categories and political strategies of its authors. But might the information gathered in the text also be read against the grain statistically so as to reveal other characteristics of the world of work that the report was ostensibly about? Because I have never worked with the statistical text in question, I cannot know the answer to this question. It is possible that the data in this inquiry are presented in such utterly ideological categories that there is no way to use them to probe the lifeworld that they purportedly represent. But I think the fact that the question was not posed by Scott, who in her earlier work had carried out extremely sophisticated and critical quantitative analyses (especially Scott 1974), speaks volumes about the epistemic assumptions of history's cultural turn. If social history tended to privilege quantifiable data as uniquely objective, cultural history, at least in its poststructuralist modality, seemed to deny the possibility of access to any realities beyond the discursive structures present in the text.[18]

It was above all poststructuralism, especially in its Derridean form, that made the unreflective realism underlying social history's evidentiary practices seem utterly naïve. It has taught us that all of the texts and text analogues we use as evidence, like Scott's statistical inquiry, must be subjected to an acute critical reading and that much of what once passed for direct evidence of past realities might be better thought of as a textual reference to yet another level of textuality. The "undecidability" of texts and the potentially endless play of intertextuality have made cultural historians extremely reticent about referring to social structures, social forces, modes of production, or class relations as facts standing outside of textual logics. The pasts that cultural historians feel comfortable making claims about therefore tend to be the pasts of discourse, and above all of those forms of discourse readily available in textual form. This reticence about naming an extratextual social puts many of the questions and problematics that were central to the new social history beyond the pale of the new cultural history: questions, for example, of the distribution of wealth, the dynamics of economic development, changing patterns of landholding and employment, demographic structures, and patterns of geographic concentration and dispersion.

Meanwhile, I think that the understandable preference of cultural historians for symbolically rich artifacts, usually texts, has also tended over time to displace our gaze from the poor and powerless, who were the favorite subject of the new social history, to those more favored categories who were likely to commit their thoughts to paper and whose papers were more likely to be conserved. This drift away from the socially marginal has been compounded by poststructuralist epistemological doubts about the possibility of knowing or representing the thoughts of the poor. Thus, Jacques Rancière (1981) showed that nineteenth-century French worker poets and intellectuals, who had been taken (by himself and by me, among others; Faure and Rancière 1976; Sewell 1980) as expressing the worker's point of view, were themselves in flight from the labor they glorified in print, leaving the implications of their writings open to doubt. More radically, Gayatri Chakravorty Spivak (1988) intimated that, try as we might, we cannot induce the subalterns to speak. In European history, at least, there has been a clear trend from studies of workers and peasants in the 1960s and 1970s to studies of the bourgeoisie since the 1980s. Lest it seem that I am chiding others for abandoning the poor and downtrodden, let me cite my own trajectory, which began with a study of the working class of Marseille (Sewell 1971, 1974b, 1974c), then moved to what might be characterized as a study of literate artisans and their political and intellectual relations with the radical intelligentsia (Sewell 1980), and most recently to a highly textual study of the Abbé Sieyes, one of the leading constitutional theorists of the French Revolution (Sewell 1994).

But in spite of my own trajectory (or perhaps because of it), I worry that the emergence of the current form of purely cultural history is extremely inopportune, coming as it does in a period of fundamental transformation of capitalism on a world scale: of decreasing ability of states to control their own destinies, of growing income disparities in the United States and in many other areas of the world, of ubiquitous declines in state welfare provision, and of sharp demobilizations of labor and the left, all pushed forward powerfully by the ascendant discourses of economic neoliberalism. Somehow, at the very time when particularly powerful changes in social and economic structures are manifested ever more insistently in our daily lives, we cultural historians have ceased not only to grapple with such structures but even to admit their ontological reality. In the next section of this essay, I attempt to sharpen the problem facing historians by suggesting that history's cultural turn was itself causally intertwined with these very socioeconomic transformations over the past three decades. If we historians hope to participate in what I see as the great political and intellectual battle of the coming years, attempting to reclaim effective political and social agency from the juggernaut of world capitalism and the hegemony of so-called free market economics, I think we need to understand our own epistemological and political entanglements in world capitalism's recent social history.

Post-Fordism and the Cultural Turn

Surely anyone who has made the turn from social to cultural history, myself included, could devise an essentially "internalist" story about how the intellectual and philosophical advantages of cultural history led to its inevitable triumph over an intellectually inadequate social history. Indeed, above I have actually sketched out the rudiments of one such account from my point of view. But I think there are reasons to be wary of the adequacy of any purely internalist account. First, such accounts tend to imply that the social history paradigm was more or less intellectually exhausted. I do not think that this was really the case.[19] Plenty of significant problems from within the social history research program still remained to be solved in the 1980s, or, for that matter, remain to be solved today. Data sources certainly were not beginning to peter out. At the very time when historians were turning away from quantitative analysis, the development of personal computers was making such research far easier to do. By the 1990s, a single graduate student with an up-to-date laptop had vastly more computational resources at her or his disposal than I had in the 1970s with two or three research assistants and a sizable grant from the National Science Foundation. Moreover, excellent work in the new social history mode has continued to be done, but increasingly by historical sociologists rather than historians. In the years since historians essentially went out of the business of quantitative history, three brilliant quantitatively based studies in the new social history mode have been published in my own field of French revolutionary studies: Mark Traugott's (1985) work on the Parisian Revolution of 1848, Roger Gould's (1995) on the Paris Commune, and John Markoff's (1996) on peasants in the French Revolution. These books indicate that pathbreaking historical discoveries can still be made by means of quantitative analysis. Historians did not exhaust the possibilities of the new social history; rather, they have shunned it for reasons of a quite different order.

Second, any purely internalist explanation of the cultural turn in history ignores the fact that in the 1980s, at precisely the time of history's cultural turn, a very widespread rise of interest in culture, almost a culture mania, swept across a broad range of fields in the human sciences. In literary studies, the key move was to use the now dominant poststructuralist theoretical categories to analyze texts and text analogues previously regarded as outside the canon of literature: popular fiction, science writing, film, journalism, television, museums, advertising, hip-hop—in short, culture in general. The new transdisciplinary (some would say adisciplinary) field of cultural studies has grown explosively in English, U.S., and Australian universities over the past twenty years.[20] Even fields like sociology, political science, and psychology, whose dominant scientism long made them highly resistant to taking culture seriously, now have important subfields devoted to the study of culture. Indeed, culture has become a buzzword of U.S. popular discourse as well. It is hard to turn on television news or National Public Radio without hearing some commentator pontificate about the "business culture of Silicon Valley" or the "culture of the Senate." And political claims about the value of cultural particularity, especially with respect to issues of race and ethnicity, are ubiquitous. As much as we historians might like to think that we adopt new questions and methods because they are intrinsically intellectually superior, there is good reason to believe that in taking the cultural turn, we were actually being swept along by much larger social forces of some kind.

The Marxist commentators Fredric Jameson and David Harvey have developed arguments that I find extremely useful for getting at the nature of these social forces. During the 1980s, they argued that the artistic and intellectual mutations that had come to be known as postmodernism should be understood as responses to an immense and systemic shift in the form of world capitalism (Jameson 1991, 1998a; Harvey 1989). Writing in 1984, Jameson identified a postmodernist sensibility, characterized by depthlessness, spatial disorientation, the collapse of the boundary between high and popular culture, a loss of the sense of historicity, a waning of affect, and the rise of pastiche, which he discerned in painting, sculpture, literature, cinema, and architecture.[21] He argued that the postmodernists had rather precociously found ways of expressing in their art the "structures of feeling" generated by the emergent logic of "late capitalism," the origins of which he traced back into the 1960s.[22] Jameson's argument relied largely on parallels between the formal features of contemporary capitalism and postmodern art. David Harvey, writing a few years later, attempted to specify more concrete changes in political-economic structures, above all the myriad effects of capitalism's current round of "annihilation of space through time," that made a postmodernist aesthetic and philosophical outlook plausible. Although both Jameson and Harvey were concerned specifically to explain the emergence of the postmodernist sensibility, I believe that their arguments are also highly relevant to the broad cultural turn undertaken by historians and other scholars in the 1980s.

In the course of the 1970s, many observers would agree, the Fordist regime of macroeconomic regulation unraveled and was gradually replaced by a very different regime. Harvey identifies the new regime as "flexible accumulation" (1989, 141–188), but this is only one of a number of terms that have been suggested; indeed, many writers have simply designated the new economic regime with the uninformative moniker post-Fordism. The transition between regimes can most conveniently be dated to 1973, the year of the "oil shock," the collapse of the postwar Bretton Woods monetary regime, and the onset of stagflation, a combination of inflation and economic stagnation that proved impossible to remedy with the standard Keynesian tools. The contours of the new regime have taken some time to emerge, and it is a matter of some dispute whether the current form of macroeconomic governance of world capitalism has jelled into a regime with anything like the coherence of the Fordist regime it replaced (A. Amin 1994). Nevertheless, the broad differences between the emerging form of capitalism and its Fordist predecessor are clear and not very controversial. During the forty years I am covering in this essay, we have lived through an epochal transformation in the nature of the capitalist world economy.[23] I believe that this great transformation must be taken into account in explaining the history of historical thought in these years.

Harvey (1989) calls the form of capitalism that had emerged by the 1980s "flexible" to indicate its contrasts with some of the key features of the regime prevailing in the 1950s and 1960s, features that had become dysfunctional "rigidities" by the early 1970s. As against the highly bureaucratized and vertically integrated firms that dominated the economy during the postwar boom, firms turned in the long economic crisis of the 1970s to downsizing, outsourcing, subcontracting, and the increasing use of temporary employees and business consultants, moves that made them able to reply more nimbly to changes in demand, supply, and technology. The introduction of numerically programmed tools and computer-based design enabled firms to move from mass production to smaller-batch, more niche-oriented production. Consequently, the turnaround time of capital has been significantly shortened. In the consumer sector, design and advertising have become increasingly central to the production of goods, speeding up the "fashion cycle" that Fordist capitalism had already spread far beyond its original home in the garment industry. In the post-Fordist period, advertising and design have worked to diversify consumer tastes by creating and commercially exploiting a multitude of consumer lifestyles. This effective merging of design, advertising, and production has made any distinction between culture and the economy ever more difficult to sustain. Meanwhile, entertainment—film, cinema, sport, spectacle, and tourism—has become one of the dominant sectors of the economy.

Improvements in transportation and communications technologies, especially containerization, telecommunications, computers, and the Internet, have enabled corporations to become increasingly transnational in character. Transnational corporations have adopted radically new forms of spatial division of labor, increasingly locating production facilities in low-wage countries while design, management, and financial functions are scattered through rich countries like the United States, Japan, and those in Western Europe. Increased internationalization of markets for labor, capital, and commodities, along with the end of the Bretton Woods system of strictly pegged currencies, has also tremendously increased the opportunities for worldwide financial speculation. Meanwhile, new information technologies that make possible so-called real-time worldwide trading, together with the invention of new financial products, especially derivatives, have led to the explosion of financial markets and the subjection of producers everywhere to increasing domination by the short-term logic of futures markets. This hypertrophic financial industry has also become increasingly offshore, that is, beyond the possibility of effective control or regulation by the governments of even the richest and most powerful countries. Increasingly, it is the whims of the world market (that is, the offshore worldwide financial industry) that determine the fate of firms, industries, classes, regions, and the populations of entire countries, without much hope of effective intervention from the governments of individual nation-states. This entire transformation has, of course, been pushed forward by an immense discursive shift in dominant political ideologies, with economic neoliberalism, whether of the Thatcherite-Reaganite or Clintonite-Blairite variety, either sweeping social democratic discourses from the field or, as in Germany and France, turning social democracy into a defensive holding operation. Unlike the expansive Keynesian welfare state of the Fordist era, consequently, the post-Fordist states have been either unwilling or unable to regulate economic activities for the benefit of disadvantaged sectors of society. Contemporary states tend to limit themselves to positioning national or local capital for effective competition in the global market, for example, by means of selective deregulation, tax breaks, cutbacks on expensive welfare provisions, and limiting the power of labor movements.

These systemic changes in the mode of economic regulation have had profound effects on people's daily social experiences. I mention only a few examples:

(1) The sharply increased geographic mobility of capital and information has been accompanied over the past thirty years by a huge surge of migration on a world scale, especially from poor countries in Asia, Africa, the Middle East, and Latin America to Western Europe and the United States. This migration has occurred at both the bottom and the top of the social scale, involving, for example, both poor Mexicans and North Africans who find work in factories and in menial service occupations and highly educated Indian programmers and engineers. This has resulted in the emergence both of strikingly cosmopolitan urban textures in Western cities and of what Arjun Appadurai (1996b) has dubbed "global ethno-scapes," in which the boundaries of states and national communities no longer coincide, so that, for example, Hindu fundamentalist movements that rise to prominence in India rely for much of their financing on prosperous Indian communities in the United States.

(2) "Global cities," those great urban agglomerations that have emerged as particularly dense nodes of communication and control in the foot-loose world economy, have largely left manufacturing behind and increasingly compete among themselves on the basis of their cultural life-styles for the most lucrative financial and business service firms and the most talented managers and "information" specialists. Urban beautification, the development of arts districts and their associated bohemias, and such "high-culture" institutions as opera companies, symphony orchestras, theater, galleries, and museums have become marks of and means of producing and sustaining top-flight nodes in the contemporary world economy. It is, moreover, precisely these global cities that tend to have the highest levels, and greatest complexities, of transnational ethnic diversity.

(3) Organized labor, which had been an essential component of the Fordist regime, has lost power everywhere. In the United States, where labor unions were attacked frontally by Reaganite Republicans in the 1980s, they have suffered a devastating collapse in membership. Real wages of

workers have essentially stagnated for the past thirty years, while incomes of the very wealthy have ballooned. At all levels of the occupational hierarchy, people's sense of job security has declined, and the well-defined career ladder, which was characteristic of the Fordist corporation both for managers and for production workers, has been increasingly replaced by a kind of occupational picaresque. Frequent lateral movement between firms, bouts of temporary work, frequent retraining, episodes of self-employment, and career changes are becoming the norm, even for middle-class employees.[24]

(4) These experiential shifts have been intertwined with and enhanced by discursive shifts. Especially since the mid-1980s, commentators, pundits, editorialists, and scholars constantly inform us that we are living in a new world, that old economic paradigms have been superseded, that ours is an entrepreneurial age, that contemporary global flows of populations and ideas are unprecedented, and so forth. The bursting of the late 1990s "dot com" bubble has quieted the endless babble about the "new economy," which supposedly could create wealth without generating actual revenues. Nevertheless, hyperbolic claims about the novelty of our current condition remain common. (It is a sobering thought that this essay might itself be cited as an example.) In any case, the experiential effects of changes in economic and social relations have been magnified in the past two decades by discourses telling us that the new flexible relations are particularly significant, just as the discourse of the Fordist era previously magnified our sense of the solidity and standardization of socioeconomic relations. Hence, while it is surely true that careers have actually become increasingly unstable and entrepreneurial over the past few decades, careers during the Fordist era were less stable than we imagined and those in the current era are probably more stable than we imagine. The changes in what we experience are products both of changes in social relations and of changes in the cultural ethos through which we understand them.

I think Jameson and Harvey are right to argue that this epochal increase in the experienced volatility of social and economic forms since the 1970s has been a fundamental source of the postmodernist sensibility. But the rise of postmodernism was just one of a range of possible intellectual responses to this subtle yet pervasive transformation of our social world. It is certainly plausible that the shift from Fordism to flexible accumulation lies behind the great wave of academic cultural turns in the 1980s and 1990s. The experienced decline in the regularity and predictability of life has surely made social structures seem far less solid and determining, and the progressive relativization of "majority" cultures and the ever increasing role of information and aesthetics in economic production have surely made it plausible that our world might profitably be understood as culturally constituted.[25] Thus, the turn from social to cultural history would seem to be, at least in part, a response to the changing structure and textures of our life experience in the contemporary world. The volatilization of social relations over the past thirty years certainly did not determine in a rigid sense any specific changes in social thought. But it does seem to have made strong structural determinisms less plausible across the board and to have induced thinkers in a number of different intellectual locations and with a whole range of epistemological proclivities to turn toward more microlevel or actor-based forms of explanation. Thus, the widespread concern in social theory with the problem of agency or action, the development of social network methodology in sociology, the immense influence of Foucault's claims for the predominance of the "microphysics" of power over the formal trappings of state authority, the victory by the 1980s of microeconomics over macroeconomics, and the rise of rational choice theory in political science and philosophy—all of these extremely diverse movements of thought, no less than postmodernism and the various academic cultural turns, can be read as alternative responses to the experienced volatilization of social relations that has accompanied recent transformations of world capitalism. It is noteworthy that some of these intellectual movements—microeconomics, rational choice, and social network methodology—are highly mathematical and positivistic in character. Recent transformations in social and economic relations have had major effects on both sides of the positivist/antipositivist epistemological divide.[26]

In any case, I am convinced that my fellow social historians and I were, when making our various cultural turns, significantly influenced in our thinking by the subtle yet pervasive changes that were wrought in our lives by the emergence of new forms of capitalist social relations. I believe that our conscious model of the social order during the time that we undertook our cultural turns was the collapsing Fordist order, not the newly emerging order of globalized flexible accumulation. As 1960s rebels, we had thought of ourselves as rising up against the interlocking and claustrophobic system of social determinations that dominated the contemporary corporate United States. Most of us would probably have agreed with Jürgen Habermas that in contemporary society, the possibility of human freedom was progressively threatened by an "escalating scale of continually expanded technical control over nature and a continually refined administration of human beings and their relations to each other by means of social organization" (1973, 254). During the 1960s, both as political radicals and as participants in the counterculture, we enthusiastically attempted to deny, by our own willful actions, some of the oppressive determinisms of the corporate social order. And when, a few years or a decade later, we revolted against the positivist research strategies of social history and undertook studies of the cultural construction of the social world, I think we obscurely felt ourselves to be freeing historical scholarship (and, vicariously, freeing ourselves) from a mute social and economic determinism that was incapable of recognizing human creativity. I can testify that it certainly felt liberating.

But in retrospect, our efforts seem to have been politically out of phase with socioeconomic realities. Our attack on the latent Fordism of social history was launched only at the time when the Fordist system of social regulation was itself entering into a deep and fatal crisis. The intensity and radicalism of this attack was heightened by a cresting wave of academic feminism, based on a political movement that remained vital long after the other 1960s movements had subsided, and that had its own epistemic scores to settle with determinist thinking. Thus, cultural historians were kicking down the door of Fordist social determinisms at the moment when such determinisms, Habermas's systematic "administration of human beings and their relations to each other by means of social organization," were collapsing. In the far more anarchic social world that was emerging, relations between human beings were increasingly determined by market forces rather than by systematic administration, social organization of the Fordist sort was being restructured into networks of entrepreneurial actors, and economic production itself was increasingly becoming a play of signifiers (although decidedly not a free play). Thus, the explicit or latent oppositional politicocultural project of the 1960s intellectuals who undertook the cultural turn was not entirely appropriate to the context in which it was occurring.

There is, I think, nothing shameful about this admission. It was, after all, not until the late 1970s and the 1980s that even scholars who studied political economy began to argue that the economic troubles since 1973 betokened a major reshaping of capitalism rather than simply another iteration of the business cycle (Aglietta 1979; Boyer 1986; Gordon, Edwards, and Reich 1982; Jessop et al. 1988; Lash and Urry 1987; Lipietz 1987; Piore and Sabel 1984). Such global economic restructurings take place piecemeal and are difficult to grasp until the pieces have begun to articulate into a system of some sort. It is only to be expected that those of us who were not experts on contemporary political economy would continue to carry the old models around in our heads for some time. I believe I first began to realize that the very structure of the world economy might be undergoing radical transformations when I participated in discussions with John Urry and Bob Jessop in Ann Arbor in the late 1980s. Nor were the old models a bar to serious and politically responsible intellectual work. The late 1970s and 1980s was the era of feminism's most intellectually far-reaching breakthroughs. And Jürgen Habermas (1984) erected an entire, and justly influential, philosophical project during these same years based precisely on the Fordist assumption that the lifeworld was increasingly being colonized by the "system." Besides, Fordist social science was still alive and well in the 1970s and early 1980s even if the Fordist system of economic regulation was collapsing. Indeed, as Steinmetz has argued elsewhere in this volume, Fordist sociology seems still to be alive and well, if less dominating and self-confident than it once was. The critique of abstracted empiricism and the development of interpretive methods were intellectually and politically necessary and remain so today.

I want to make it absolutely clear that I remain a determined advocate of the cultural turn. But at the same time, I think it is essential to recognize that the cultural turn was also fueled, in ways we were essentially unaware of, by a secret affinity with an emergent logic of capitalist development. Cultural history's tendency to celebrate the plasticity of all social forms made good political sense as a critique of Fordist social determinisms, as well as of the entrenched social determinisms of gender and race. But its critical force in the context of a capitalist regime of flexible accumulation is far more ambiguous. Indeed, such a celebration indicates an unacknowledged and troubling complicity between the cultural turn and the emergence of contemporary flexible forms of capitalism. Cultural history's lack of interest in, indeed effective denial of, socioeconomic determinations seems to me potentially disabling in an era when such determinations are so evidently at work in the world, including in our own conceptualizations of historical process. Critical awareness of the potential complicities between contemporary forms of capitalism and a purely cultural history seems to me an essential condition of clearheaded and efficacious epistemological, methodological, and practical work in historical studies today.

Toward a Reconstitution of the Social

Precisely what the implications of such a critical awareness might amount to is, of course, a matter for discussion and debate. Here I want to argue for one implication: that we need to rethink our general abandonment of social history. As I stated above, cultural history generally displaced social history without much argument, largely because so many social historians, myself included, had themselves taken the cultural turn and therefore put up no intellectual resistance. Yet some of social history's virtues remain as important as ever. For example, social history's insistence on examining the experiences of ordinary people, its populist bias, seems highly relevant in the context of sharply rising economic and political inequality in the contemporary world. Our turn away from the poor and disadvantaged was, of course, overdetermined, a consequence at once of our growing historiographical preference for rich textual sources and of the disappointment consequent upon political defeats of popular movements with which we sympathized, for example, First World labor movements put on the defensive by the flight of production to the periphery and Third World peasant movements wiped out by the global marginalization of peasant agriculture. But shouldn't the continued worsening of inequality in the present spark our sympathies for and curiosity about the experiences of the dispossessed both in the present and in the past?

Likewise, social history's claim that quantitative methods were an indispensable addition to the historian's tool kit continues to make sense. This is true for the familiar reason that quantification gives us important and unique forms of access to the historical experiences of otherwise undocumented categories of people. But a focus on numerical evidence seems particularly relevant in a moment like the present, when the world is being rapidly transformed by seemingly anonymous and unplanned structural shifts that cannot be recognized, let alone explicated, without recourse to some serious counting. Examples are the rapid displacement of manufacturing by service industries in contemporary European and U.S. cities, a change that has transformed the nature of both the working class and elites, and the astounding rise of trading in monetary futures, which has made it possible for entire countries, like Indonesia in 1998 and Argentina in 2002, to be plunged into sudden poverty as a result of currency speculation in the metropoles of world capitalism. The undeniable importance of numerical assessments for grasping such fundamentally important processes in the present ought to make us wonder whether quantitative methods might not be important for grasping historical transformations in the past as well. Finally, social history always insisted that socioeconomic structures and processes mattered deeply. In the confusing and contradictory 1970s, it seemed possible to imagine that economic determinism was an illusion. But the past two decades have made it clear that we are all in the grip of a powerful reordering of world capitalism and that changes in economic forms and forces have had an immense impact on all aspects of contemporary life. This certainly doesn't mean that we should return to any crude notion of economic determinism; after all, the worldwide economic transformation itself was crucially shaped by discursive changes in economic and political ideologies and imaginaries. But it certainly should reanimate the question of the relation of both present and past lifeworlds to forms of production, exchange, and economic governance. For all these reasons, social history, in some form, seems as essential as ever.

There is reason to think that I am not alone in this opinion; as usual, my own changes of mind seem to be more or less in tune with the thinking of other historical scholars. Lynn Hunt, who seems to have a peculiar genius for sniffing out changes in the historians' Zeitgeist, recently edited, with Victoria Bonnell, a new stock-taking collection of essays entitled *Beyond the Cultural Turn: New Directions in the Study of Society and Culture.* Published exactly a decade after Hunt's collection on *The New Cultural History,* which celebrated historians' embrace of culture, *Beyond the Cultural Turn* is rather more ambivalent. Bonnell and Hunt point out in their introductory essay that the authors represented in the collection, who "have all been profoundly influenced by the cultural turn," nevertheless "refuse to accept the obliteration of the social that is implied by the most radical forms of culturalism or poststructuralism. The status or meaning of the social may be in question . . . but life without it has proved impossible" (Bonnell and Hunt 1999, 11). A similar shift seems to be signaled by a change in the human sciences' leading buzzword, from "postmodernism" in the late 1980s and early 1990s to "globalization" in the late 1990s and early 2000s. Both postmodernism and globalization may be impossibly vague terms, and they may often be pointing at more or less the same set of very heterogeneous phenomena. But the shift from a term with basically epistemological meanings to one with substantive historical meanings seems to me another manifestation of a latent desire for a return to a more social or socioeconomic interpretation of the contemporary predicament.

In any case, neither I nor others who share my views advocate a return to the social history of the 1970s. I have no desire to revive the new social history's uncritical objectivism, its presumptive preference for quantitative data, its default economic determinism, or its blindness to questions of meaning. I continue to believe, as I did in the 1970s, that the cultural turn is in itself an immensely positive intellectual development for historical studies. The pressing intellectual task facing us in the present, as I see it, is to regain a more robust sense of the social, but to do so on the epistemological terrain that has been opened up by the cultural turn. My task in this essay has been one of diagnosis, of probing and characterizing our current historiographic condition. The reconstructive task of developing a conception of the social more adequate to our times is a topic for another essay.[27]

Notes

I would like to thank Jan Goldstein, Dagmar Herzog, Lynn Hunt, Joan Scott, and George Steinmetz for comments on this essay. My research has been supported by a Fellowship from the Institute for Advanced Study and the National Endowment for the Humanities. This essay incorporates portions of an earlier essay of mine, "Whatever Happened to the 'Social' in Social History," which appeared in *Schools of Thought: Twenty-Five Years of Interpretive Social Science*, edited by Joan W. Scott and Deborah Keates, © Princeton University Press, 2001.

1   Another important disciplinary influence that does not show up in this enumeration of academic appointments is anthropology, which, as will become apparent later in this essay, affected me profoundly in the course of the 1970s.

2   Of course, the great exception to the decline of such movements was the feminist movement, which became more prominent and more militant in the 1970s than it had been in the 1960s. But in this case, I could be only a supporter and sympathizer, not a direct participant.

3   One clear sign of the rise of social history was the proliferation of social historical journals. *Comparative Studies in Society and History*, founded in 1958, was the only U.S. journal devoted to social history before 1960. The *Journal of Social History* and *Historical Methods Newsletter* (later *Historical Methods*) appeared in 1967, and in the early 1970s there was a new social history journal virtually every year. These included the *Journal of Interdisciplinary History* (1970), *International Labor and Working Class History* (1971), *Peasant Studies* (1972), *Journal of Urban History* (1974), *Social Science History* (1976), and *Journal of Family History* (1976).

4   For two influential early articles about what was often called "the social history of ideas," see Robert Darnton (1971a, 1971b).

5   For similar arguments dealing primarily with European social movements of this era, see Hirsch (1983) and Steinmetz (1994).

6   For three examples from my own field of nineteenth-century French labor history, see Bezucha (1974), Joan Scott (1974), and Sewell (1974b).

7   On reading Lawrence Stone's *Crisis of the Aristocracy* shortly after completing my dissertation, I found that he had used precisely the same metaphor in his introduction (1965, 3).

8   Joan Scott (1974) and L. Tilly and Scott (1978) were in the quantitative mode, but the essays collected in Joan Scott (1988a), all written in the course of the 1980s, focused on the history of linguistic construction of gender difference. Although Scott does not actually identify herself as a cultural historian (personal communication), I believe that most historians would see these essays as fitting within the genre of cultural history, broadly construed. Hunt (1978) was a fairly typical work of the new social history. Hunt

(1984) was a particularly clear example of the shift from social to cultural history, in that half of the book was quantitative social history and the other (far more influential) half cultural history. Unlike Scott, Hunt embraced, indeed promoted, the cultural history label; by the end of the decade, she had edited and written the introduction to the book that declared the triumph of "the new cultural history" (Hunt 1989).

9 For an argument that this was true even of *The Making of the English Working Class*, see Sewell (1990).

10 Cohn was a pioneer in historical anthropology; Inden, a historian, had been a student of Cohn's and was also, at that time, something of a disciple of the anthropologist David Schneider. See Cohn (1987b), Inden (1976), and Schneider (1968). The published evidence of my initial conversion is Sewell (1974a).

11 For a concise account of a hostile interchange that involved the anthropological turn, see Eley (1996, 197–198).

12 I did manage to publish one article on Marseille that, I believe, combined quantitative sociological and interpretive anthropological perspectives more or less seamlessly, thus carrying out more or less the sort of analysis I had intended to apply on a larger scale (Sewell 1988).

13 This latter categorization is admittedly slippery. Among my citations, I did not count Sahlins, who had left his Marxism behind when he wrote the book cited, but did count Rancière, whose cited work was Marxist but who later distanced himself from Marxism. I say that the prominence of Marxist references in my footnotes surprises me because I certainly did not regard myself as a Marxist at the time I was writing *Work and Revolution.*

14 To be fair, it should be noted that new imports of anthropology by literary scholars associated with "the new historicism" went some way toward righting the intellectual balance of payments between the disciplines (Veeser 1989).

15 It is probably no accident that Foucault was the only theorist other than Geertz to appear in the theoretical references of Hunt, Scott, and Sewell alike.

16 For a lucid brief account of the politics and epistemology of women's history from the 1960s through the 1980s, see Joan Scott (1991b).

17 Joan Scott indicates in a footnote (1988c, 113) that the paper was initially delivered as a public lecture in 1984.

18 I hope it is clear that far from singling out Joan Scott as an epistemological offender, I mean to commend her for stating outright what others were thinking but lacked either the forthrightness or the clarity to say in published form.

19 For a different opinion on this matter, see Bonnell and Hunt (1999, 7).

20 For a particularly stimulating discussion of cultural studies, see Readings (1996, 89–118).

21 This essay was incorporated as the first chapter of Jameson (1991).

22 Jameson borrowed the term "structures of feeling" from Raymond Williams (1977).

23 A particularly acute history of this transformation is R. Brenner (2002).

24 These changes have also affected the academic humanists and social scientists, who frequently spend several years on postdoctoral fellowships, adjunct positions, or replacement jobs before finally landing a tenure-track position; indeed, a rising portion remain in adjunct jobs for many years. For those who attain tenure, however, the involuntary form of the occupational picaresque ceases.

25 My argument here has been much influenced by George Steinmetz's work on the

epistemic effects of the transition from Fordism to post-Fordism, effects discernable in the targets and discourses of social movements as well as in academic discourses. See his essay in this volume (also 1994, forthcoming a; and Steinmetz and Chae 2002). On this approach to social movements, see also Hirsch (1983) and Mayer and Roth (1995).

26   I owe this point to the comments of Moishe Postone on an earlier version of this chapter.

27   For a very preliminary attempt, however, see Sewell (2001, 217–224).

Defining "Theory" in Postwar Political Science

EMILY HAUPTMANN

The outside constructs the inside and then hides this work of fabrication in an entity that appears to give birth to itself. Thus to inquire "What is political theory?" is to ask about its constitutive outside as well as its techniques of dissimulating this constitution.—Wendy Brown, "At the Edge"

W hat kinds of constructs are called "theories," and who is responsible for their creation? A history of the discipline of political science after World War II might be built around addressing these questions. A comprehensive study of the many "theorists" working in different subfields, however, would extend far beyond the boundaries of one essay. In this piece, therefore, I limit myself to considering how the traditional political theorist,[1] Sheldon Wolin, and the rational choice theorist, William Riker, each developed new approaches to theory in postwar political science. I focus on Wolin and Riker not to make each stand for the whole of traditional or rational choice theory, but because each, as scholars and teachers, had an unusually strong influence on shaping a particular approach to political theory. I argue that each constructed the meaning of his approach to theory in opposition to what each took to be the most potent threat to his project. I then assess the degree to which these foundational conceptions of theory continue to define what traditional political theorists and rational choice theorists today say they do. I conclude that in the case of traditional political theorists, some elements of the self-definition constructed in opposition to the postwar behavioral movement persist even though behavioralism itself is no longer an organized opponent. In the case of rational choice theorists, however, early oppositional constructions of their theoretical identity show distinct signs of giving way to an accommodating, inclusive identity in which a sharply defined conception of theory is no longer at a premium. I also show that although Riker in particular sometimes invoked positivism in his initial attempt at theoretical self-definition, positivism has lately receded in significance either as a way of thinking to be opposed (in the case of traditional political theorists) or as a justificatory underpinning (in the case of rational choice theorists).

The Construction of Empirical, Positive, and Traditional Political Theory: Differing Responses to the Same Source

By the early 1960s, there were at least three contending understandings of the meaning of theory in political science: the behavioralist, the rational choice, and the traditional. Distinct and antagonistic as these understandings were, some of their most influential proponents were trained by the same small group of professors at the same university at the same time: David Easton, the behavioral or empirical theorist; William Riker, the rational choice or positive political theorist; and Sheldon Wolin, the traditional or "epic" theorist, all wrote dissertations under the theorists Carl Friedrich (Riker and Wolin) or William Y. Elliott (Easton) at Harvard in the second half of the 1940s. All wrote dissertations on topics compatible with Harvard's "ideas and institutions" approach to political theory,[2] an approach that flourished in both Britain and the United States in the early part of the twentieth century (Adcock and Bevir 2003, 2–5). This approach has been characterized as one in which "political theory complemented political science in that it, firstly, introduced students to the concepts employed across the discipline, and secondly, provided them with a historical survey of political ideas framed in relation to the development of institutions" (4). It is against this approach that Easton, Riker, and Wolin all rebelled, each creating his own conception of political theory in opposition to what each saw as the inadequacies of the kind of theory in which he had been trained.

Although some retrospective accounts of midcentury political science take polemics about its decline or death as historical fact, the graduate program at Harvard in the 1940s was hardly atheoretical.[3] Despite his having announced the decline of political theory in a much-cited 1951 article, Easton notes that the intellectual climate at Harvard's government department in the late 1940s was favorable to, indeed even saturated by theory: "I quickly discovered that it mattered little what you studied at Harvard; in the end it all turned out to be theory, a standard joke among us graduate students. So it was really a misnomer at that time to say that you concentrated in anything else, because almost every instructor had pretensions of being a theorist. This was probably the single greatest virtue of the curriculum at the time. You could not graduate from the program without being sensitive to the importance of theory in political research" (Easton 1991, 198).[4] So, to what about his graduate training in theory did Easton react? And what did Riker and Wolin find wanting in it?

Easton makes it clear that he meant to learn about politics for practical reasons, for the sake of effecting political change. He found what little he knew about how the scientific study of politics was being undertaken at Chicago promising as a means to these ends, but was disappointed to find this approach disdained at Harvard. From his perspective, what was missing was a "concern for rigorous empirical inquiry" (1991, 198). According to his students, Riker turned away from both the "then-popular case-study approach" he had been taught at Harvard, as well as his "roots in a discipline of political science governed by normative conclusions" (Amadae and Bueno de Mesquita 1999, 272–273). Wolin (1992), however, characterized his Harvard training as that of a generalist ("the last stand of liberal education for graduate students"), not a political theorist. Although his dissertation on British constitutional thought from 1688 to 1776 was directed by Friedrich, Wolin recalls that his work on it was not closely supervised. Indeed, many of the figures Wolin remembers as most influential during his time at Harvard—Louis Hartz, Werner Jaeger, Crane Brinton, Henry Aiken, among others—were not members of the Department of Government.

That the approach of a small number of the same faculty could be found wanting on such strikingly different grounds reveals, I think, how important the construction of "the opposition" is to the development of new academic fields. The construction of oppositions between fields can be a fruitful but also a potentially misleading focal point in the recent history of political science. It is fruitful insofar as it helps us see the terms in which the creators of new fields write about what they do as one half of an oppositional dyad (e.g., Riker's "positive political theory" versus "normative political theory"; Wolin's "epic political theory" versus "scientific methodism"). But it can also be misleading, particularly if one takes the constructions of the opponent too literally. In the sections that follow, therefore, I offer close readings of how Wolin and Riker, two important early figures in the development of traditional or epic political theory and positive political theory, respectively, construct what they believe political theory ought to be in opposition to what they believe most inimical to it.

The Oppositional Construction of the Subfield
of Political Theory: Sheldon Wolin and
the Argument against Behavioralism

Most accounts of the development of political theory as a subfield from the 1950s on place the conflict between traditional political theory and behavioralism or empirical political theory at center stage.[5] Indeed, traditional political theorists in the 1950s and 1960s are often concerned with defining what they do in opposition to the work of behavioralists, and vice versa. But although most retrospective accounts of this conflict agree that it was ultimately a clash between two rival conceptions of how to theorize about politics, some of those involved in the conflict were not so sure: Was behavioralism a rival theoretical enterprise or an attack on the very idea of theory itself? In my discussion of how the current subfield of political theory was constructed in opposition to behavioralism, I focus on the 1960s work of Sheldon Wolin to show how this indecision about how to assess behavioralism was bound up with the way Wolin developed his conception of political theory. Following Wolin's thinking on this issue is, I believe, particularly fruitful because by the late 1960s, he became convinced that his conception of theory no longer had a home in political science and, as a consequence, he sought to form a separate department of political theory. Although this aspect of Wolin's career is not well-known, his published work from this period continues to be widely cited and used by political theorists today; *Politics and Vision* (1960), his book on the history of political thought, is soon to be reissued. What is more, as I argue below, some elements of the conception of political theory Wolin first articulated in the 1960s continue to structure the subfield of political theory today. Understanding how and in opposition to what Wolin developed that conception, therefore, seems crucial to understanding how theory is understood by political scientists today.

One of the best-known polemics in the conflict between traditional political theory and behavioralism is Wolin's 1969 essay, "Political Theory as a Vocation." In this piece, Wolin criticizes empirical political scientists for their devotion to what he calls "methodism" as well as their antipathy to the tradition and practice of epic political theory. The essay constructs an explicit image of the sort of theory those called to the vocation ought to pursue in deliberate contrast with what Wolin takes to be the dominant attitude of behavioral political scientists toward theories of politics. In a number of passages throughout the essay, Wolin comes close to suggesting that behavioralists are simply antitheoretical. For instance, he remarks that "American political scientists . . . have not only generally supported the traditional American diffidence towards theories, but they have elevated it to scientific status" (1063), that theory for the behavioralists has been closely allied with and even subordinated to methods (1065), and that behavioralists have "trivialized" theory by treating it as synonymous with hypotheses or techniques (1075–1076).[6] But he concludes the essay on a slightly different note, writing, "The basic thrust of contemporary political science is not antitheoretical so much as it is deflationary of theory" (1082). Behavioralists, Wolin concludes, seek to redefine political theory rather than to eschew it.[7]

In marked contrast to the behavioralist understanding of theory (whether antitheoretical or just "deflationary"), Wolin presents what he calls the "nature and role of epic political theorists" (1078). Political theory, he argues, should entail deep political commitments as well as "an appreciation of the historical dimension of politics" (1075, 1078, 1077).[8] Its attention to the past, however, informs the theorist's concern for the present and future, for "introducing new generations of students to the complexities of politics and to the efforts of theorists to confront its predicaments" and for "exploring the ways in which new theoretical vistas are opened" (1077). Perhaps most important, its scope is sweeping: "By an act of thought, the theorist seeks to reassemble the whole political world" (1078). Such exercises in theoretical imagination are provoked, Wolin argues, by "systematic derange[ments]" in the political world; they are undertaken out of a sense of public concern for a political world in crisis and are therefore "critical and, in the literal sense, radical" (1079–1080). It is ultimately both radical engagement with the political world and the ambition to recast its fundamental principles that distinguish the epic political theorist from the "scientific theorist." "Although each attempts to change men's views of the world, only the [epic theorist] attempts to change the world itself" (1080).

As I have argued elsewhere (Hauptmann 2004), the conflict over what political theory meant took an important turn around the time Wolin's essay appeared. Although there had been some fundamental critiques of behavioral political science by traditional political theorists before the late 1960s (see, e.g., Storing 1962), Wolin and others continued to sound hopeful about a broad consensus on how to study and theorize "political things" until the late 1960s (Schaar and Wolin 1963). But by the end of the 1960s, deep political disagreements about the Vietnam War intensified the already marked intellectual divergence between behavioralists and left-leaning traditional political theorists like Wolin. "Political Theory as a Vocation" both acknowledged the rift in the discipline and channeled the bitterness it inspired into forming a new conception of political theory.

Although his 1969 piece characterizes behavioralism as methodism that is at best "deflationary of theory," Wolin, along with other members of the theory faculty, cedes considerably more theoretical territory both to behavioralists and to rational choice theorists in a much less well-known proposal to establish a separate department of political theory at U.C. Berkeley in the late 1960s. The effort failed (largely because of the opposition of the chair of Political Science and the dean of Arts and Sciences; Wolin 1992), but the justification for the plan illuminates how those most closely associated with it (Wolin and John Schaar) conceived of political theory: both how they believed it ought to be done and how they saw others in the discipline developing it in different directions.

Called "Proposal for a Department of Political Theory," this unpublished document discusses how traditional political theorists' sense of what they do diverges from the new emphasis on quantitative methods and behavioral science in political science departments.[9] It is most frequently claimed that this new emphasis is not theoretical and is not incompatible with traditional political theory and that therefore one academic department cannot easily house both. Infrequently, however, the authors appear to change course and say that what they are confronting is instead a different (and incompatible) conception of theory: "The decision to concentrate on the scientific study of politics carries with it a different notion of theory" (6). They also criticize the department for frustrating their efforts to hire like-minded theorists, a move they maintain shows that "the Department wishes to develop one kind of theory and discourage another" (7). At this point, the authors do not spell out what the kind of theory they oppose entails, except to imply that it "emphasize[s] the centrality of quantitative and behavioral methods" (7).

The only portion of this document that provides any insight into what its authors took to be the substance of the opposing conceptions of theory is the draft of the graduate curriculum in political theory. In a discussion of the fields graduate students in the proposed program would have to develop, the authors list two major theory fields, one empirical field and an "outside theory field." To illustrate what they mean by the last term, they write, "We want each student to become competent in some form or mode of theory other than political theory. Some examples: philosophy of science, empirical political theory, philosophy of history, theory of economic development, game theory, etc." (3). On the basis of this document, it is hard to say whether Wolin et al. had decided that they were up against another conception of theory or an approach to the study of politics that was principally a- or antitheoretical.

Although this document is first and foremost an announcement of an intended secession, the authors do not always cast aspersions on the department they wish to leave. Sometimes, they portray their planned departure as a response to moves already made by the political science department to marginalize them. Setting their specific experience in the context of nationwide trends in the discipline, they write, "A concerted effort is under way to unify Political Science by instituting a common methodology which is to serve as the basis for undergraduate and graduate instruction. . . . The traditional field of Political Theory has been allowed to languish; or has been drastically redefined; or has been eliminated altogether" (1). But what is currently a hostile environment for political theorists can easily be transformed into an institutional climate congenial to all: "We believe that a separation of Political Theory will facilitate the Political Science Department in its efforts to establish a more uniform program of instruction and training. All of those who would join the new department have given a considerable part of their lifetimes to the Department of Political Science and would wish it well in the future; furthermore, they believe that a separation will result in easier and more fruitful relationships between Political Theory and Political Science" (1–2). But the obverse of this hopeful prediction is a warning: "At present, we are trying to carry on two very different enterprises in a single department; though both may be worthwhile, the result is bound to be continuing and debilitating conflict" (7).

At the time that Wolin was most directly concerned with articulating his conception of traditional or epic political theory, he seems to have been torn about how to characterize behavioral political science. Did the behavioralists have their own, rival conception of theory? Or were they simply uninterested in theory as such? To be sure, each of these types of opposition is threatening. But to members of departments of political science in the 1960s, it was understandably unclear what the fate of traditional political theory as a field might be. Would it be transformed into a conception of theory more congenial to the behavioral movement? Or would it be allowed to develop as those who identified with it primarily chose?

What the Conflict between Traditional Political Theory and Behavioralism Meant: Some Recent Assessments

The subfield of political theory in political science departments today is mostly made up of people who were trained by traditional political theorists rather than empirical or rational choice theorists. Based on this outcome alone, it might seem reasonable to conclude that when contemporary political scientists talk about theory, they are talking about the kind of work their colleagues in the subfield of political theory do. This, however, is often not the case. Theory currently has a variety of meanings in contemporary political science, many of which, like rational choice theory, have little connection to what most self-described political theorists do.

How ought one to understand this outcome in terms of the recent history of the discipline? More specifically, what has been the legacy of the conflict between traditional political theory and behavioralism? In what follows, I discuss several assessments of this conflict, with particular emphasis on what each says about how it has shaped recent conceptions of theory in political science. I also attend to how each assesses the importance of positivism to the substance of the conflict.

John Gunnell, in *The Descent of Political Theory* (1993), argues that the conflict between traditional political theory and behavioralism must be understood as a clash of different conceptions of theory. According to Gunnell, the claims of what was called traditional versus scientific theory defined the conflict among political scientists over the meaning of theory in the late 1950s and early 1960s. The meaning of scientific theory was, at this time, predominantly defined by behavioralists. To be sure, behavioralists had no singular conception of theory; still, Gunnell argues that Easton's conception of "general theory" was the dominant one: "Although a significant dimension of political science clung to the notion that empirical theories would arise from inductive efforts of empirical research and the formulation of narrow-gauge theory, the dominant vision, represented most paradigmatically by the work of Easton, was that these constructs—these 'models,' 'approaches,' 'orientations,' or 'strategies'—were, at least, prototypes of an emerging 'general theory' based on a single concept, as physics is based on 'mass' " (262). Gunnell also maintains that although the behavioralists often talked about their contributions to the discipline as new or revolutionary, their work was in many respects an extension of earlier social scientific projects (221, 229, 269; see also Gunnell 1992). In large part because Gunnell reads behavioralism as continuous with established trends in U.S. social science, he sees the way behavioralists

began to employ logical positivism in the early 1950s as a late and sometimes awkward attempt to spell out the epistemological foundations of
their approach (223–225, 269–270). For Gunnell, then, behavioralism was
undeniably theoretical but rather superficially positivistic.

Although he has relatively little to say about rational choice theory
(except that "attempts to define a theoretical core organized around formal theories of public choice" failed [1993, 267]), Gunnell reads the plurality of conceptions of theory in political science that ensued in the 1970s
as a result of the professionalization of the discipline, most particularly, of
traditional theorists' reluctance to "flee the institutional structure of political science" (268). In addition, behavioralists had no strong reasons to try
to push their critics outside the discipline; they had, Gunnell argues,
achieved "hegemony within the profession and the university . . . less by
the defeat of the émigré position than by its isolation" (260). Given their
dominance, they "could afford to be generous," especially as an attempt to
excise traditional theory from the discipline would mean "cast[ing] adrift
a significant portion of [the discipline's] membership" (267). With respect
to the disputes among traditional theorists, Gunnell also emphasizes how
these might have been driven by institutional motives: "Now . . . that much
of political theory was becoming something other than an appendage of
mainstream political science, there was a question of its internal identity
and who represented its authentic voice. This was a professional as well as
an intellectual and ideological matter" (260).

In sum, while Gunnell does not disregard the substantive, conceptual
differences between how members of different subfields in political science understood the meaning of theory, he sees whatever "pluralism"
might now obtain in the discipline as the result of pragmatic professional
and institutional motives rather than as a conscious endorsement of theoretical pluralism for epistemological reasons. What is more, on Gunnell's
view, this pluralism has taken its toll on political theory; not only has it
become "alienated" from the rest of the discipline of political science, but
it has also lost its connection with what Gunnell believes ought to be its
central political concerns (see also Gunnell 1986).

According to several other accounts, the conflict between traditional
political theory and behavioralism also took its toll on the newly distinct
and redefined subfield that came to be called simply political theory from
the 1970s on. One might think that those associated with political theory
would think its separation from a discipline whose aims and methods they
rejected a salutary outcome. Yet, some retrospective assessments of the
conflict emphasize how the battles that traditional political theorists

fought against behavioralism at least temporarily narrowed the ways political theory could be practiced. For instance, Richard Ashcraft (1983)
mocks traditional political theorists' construction of their enemy: "an
unholy triple alliance [of behavioralism, positivism, and historicism]
which [in the 1950s] threatened political theory with total extinction"
(515). Ashcraft's point is not just that the construction of the enemy was
overwrought, but also that despite their avowed opposition to positivism,
a number of traditional political theorists obliquely endorsed some central positivist tenets openly affirmed by behavioralists. For one, Ashcraft
argues (using examples all drawn from Wolin's work) that traditional
political theorists implicitly accepted the distinction behavioralists asserted between facts and values by claiming that discourse about values
was their unique prerogative: "In its preoccupation with combating positivism, which it frequently took to be synonymous with social science,
political theory wholly identified itself as a branch of moral philosophy,
apparently on the presumption that only the uncompromising assertion
of 'values' by individual theorists could counter a fact-minded empiricism" (519).[10] Second, Ashcraft contends that traditional political theorists, like the behavioralists, avoided examinations of ideology and the
sociology of knowledge. So perhaps the principal reason "behavioralism
. . . proved to be an elusive enemy" (515) for traditional political theorists
was that they exaggerated their differences while not attending to the
points on which they agreed.

    On Ashcraft's view, one casualty of the conflict between traditional
political theorists and behavioralists was a concern for the history of
political thought, as neither side in the conflict had any patience for understanding "the problem of meaning within a sociological context" (1983,
543). To do so would mean attending to how what are now considered the
great works of political theory were written as contributions to immediate
political conflicts or, more controversially, trying to discover what their
authors intended to say.[11] Though he takes it for granted that behavioralists failed to understand meaning this way, Ashcraft is more concerned to
show that traditional political theorists have also not done so and that this
omission amounts to a serious flaw in their work (547–548). What is more,
he argues that the conflict between traditional political theorists and behavioralists had the immediate effect of narrowing the ways political theory could be done, a consequence he believes had only just begun to wane
by the early 1980s.

    Similarly, Terence Ball (2001) reads the behavioral critique of traditional
theory as primarily an attack on the "ideas and institutions" approach to

the history of political thought that dominated political science in the early part of the twentieth century. He notes that behavioralists did not voice an antipathy toward theory as such, "but they *were* hostile or at least antipathetic to the history of political thought, for this reason: if political science is to be a science in the fashion of physics or any of the other natural sciences, then there is no legitimate place for the history of earlier theorising" (108). In answer to such views, a number of new defenders of what was now beginning to be called traditional political theory argued for the importance of recovering earlier conceptions of or approaches to politics. In the 1950s and early 1960s, Leo Strauss, Hannah Arendt, and Sheldon Wolin all argued for the study of the political past, but for the sake of understanding the ills of the present, an approach Ball regards as too sweeping in its claims about the modern world to be properly historical (114–119).[12] Ball therefore sees the conflict between these theorists and the behavioralists' conceptions of theory as a conflict primarily between "grand," "epic," or "architectonic" theory and "empirically testable 'middle range' theories" (118) rather than as a conflict about the importance of the history of political thought.[13]

In the way Ball summarizes the history of academic political theory, it appears that it is traditional theory that has been alive and well (although now speaking in a number of "discordant voices") from the 1970s on, whereas behavioralism (along with, one assumes, any conception of theory ungirding it) "had come a cropper," a demise Ball attributes both to the proponents of behavioralism's close ties to the Vietnam War effort and to the philosophical attacks on logical positivism "which had supplied the philosophical *bona fides* for behavioralism" (2001, 120).[14] But telling the story of theory in political science this way makes it seem as if political scientists en masse have ceded all of what they take to be the theoretical territory of the discipline to those who now belong to the theory subfield. If those who are the most direct heirs of the behavioralist movement no longer express theoretical ambitions, rational choice theorists most insistently do, the philosophical discrediting of logical positivism notwithstanding.

Recent Political Theory: Lingering Traces of Antibehavioralism

Their differences notwithstanding, all of these accounts agree that the conflict between traditional political theorists and behavioralists is a thing of the past. But even though this opposition is no longer an active conflict, some elements of the conception of theory that Wolin, among others, developed during the 1960s still structure how theory is understood by members of the subfield of political theory today. Perhaps the most important of these elements is Wolin's conceptualization of theorizing as a creative act of vision, a conceptualization he explicitly opposes to the "methodical" quality of the scientific study of politics in "Political Theory as a Vocation" (1969). This way of conceiving of theory already structures Wolin's still widely read history of political thought, *Politics and Vision* (1960). Theorizing, Wolin argues here, is primarily a creative act of the imagination that both focuses on what is wrong in the world as it is and, in response, presents "what we can call 'a corrected fullness' " (19). Indeed, Wolin traced the activity of theory back to a specific ancient Greek exercise of imaginative sight: "Originally, a 'theorist' (*theoros*) was a public emissary dispatched by his city to attend the religious festivals of other Greek cities. *Theoria* referred at first to a festive occasion, but gradually it acquired the connotation of a long journey undertaken to see (*theorein*) different lands and to observe their diverse institutions and values" (1968, 319).

This image of the political theorist as one who sees the political world from some intellectually constructed distance and who by virtue of that sight critically reimagines that world persists in contemporary political theory. For instance, in her contribution to the journal *Political Theory*'s 2002 issue devoted to the question, "What Is Political Theory?," Wendy Brown writes that because theory is an essentially imaginative exercise, it ought to be judged by what seem to be aesthetic criteria: "Theory is never 'accurate' or 'wrong'; it is only more or less illuminating, more or less provocative, more or less of an incitement to thought, imagination, desire, possibilities for renewal" (574). As was the case for Wolin, Brown also pointedly presents political theory as a nontechnical, nonmethodical creative activity.[15] Another essay in the same issue challenges the apolitical aloofness implicit in the image of the theorist as one who sees from a distance, but does so precisely because this image has been such a dominant one (Cavarero 2002).[16] But as much as this image of theory as a visionary, creative activity persists, it is no longer elaborated in primary contrast to scientific or empirical theorizing, as it explicitly was by Wolin in the 1960s. When Brown asks of contemporary political theory, "What does it imagine itself not to be, to be different from? What epistemological, stylistic, and ontological conceits denote its significant others, its scenes of alterity?" (2002, 556), she focuses on how political theorists today try to distinguish what they do from those in other disciplines, such as "art history, anthropology, rhetoric, geography and literature," who also "[think] about political matters theoretically" (561). To be sure, Brown prefaces her examination of these issues by saying that "consider[ing] the border between political theory and the discipline of political science, or political theory's particular and peculiar border with what has come to be denominated as formal theory" would also be a "site of a productive inquiry" (559). But by choosing to examine the particular "others" she does, Brown implicitly tells us which of these others she believes loom largest in the imagination of contemporary political theorists. The conclusion that political science matters considerably less to contemporary political theorists' construction of what it is they do than it did thirty years ago seems inescapable.[17]

Assessing the Relation between Rational Choice Theory and Positivism

Although they shared the behavioralists' ambition for developing a science of politics, rational choice theorists conceived of that science in markedly different terms. Already in the 1960s, rational choice theorists were charging some associated with behavioralism with basing their conceptions of political life on unexamined and unwarranted assumptions. For example, in 1965, Mancur Olson argued that behavioral social scientists had uncritically assumed that groups would reliably arise to further common interests without considering the many obstacles that often block successful "collective action" (16–22, 117–131). The quarrel over how to do the science of politics has continued in the discipline ever since. A recent well-known critique of rational choice theory, Donald Green and Ian Shapiro's *Pathologies of Rational Choice* (1994), presents the central empiricist charge: rational choice theorists do not provide enough empirical grounding for their work. In these two charges, we may discern at least the outlines of the disagreement between rational choice theorists and the more empirically minded heirs to the behavioral movement in political science. Though these approaches may look similar from the perspective of traditional political theory, to those who hold them they are importantly distinct.

As I discussed above, there are a number of affinities between behavioral political science and positivism. Even though positivism was not immediately invoked by those who made the behavioral revolution, others later took up elements of positivist thought to defend the behavioralist position in the discipline. For example, when Robert Dahl, a first-generation behavioralist, reflected on the success of the approach in 1961, he cited "six specific, interrelated, quite powerful stimuli" (1993, 250); positivism, however, was not among them. Dahl singles out "the influence of Max Weber and . . . European sociology" instead as one of the most important extradisciplinary stimuli to behavioralism (251). Although some behavioralists were interested in positivism as early as the 1950s, it was only in the late 1960s and early 1970s that positivism was invoked by some in the discipline to provide philosophical credentials for what had become the dominant practice of empirical behavioral political science (Gunnell 1993, 223–225, 269–270).[18]

The affinities between rational choice theory and positivism, however, are more elusive. Indeed, several of the contributors to this volume disagree about how to assess them. I therefore preface my own discussion of the affinities between rational choice theory as practiced in political science by considering how Tony Lawson (this volume), George Steinmetz (this volume, "Sociology"), and Margaret Somers (1998) have gauged the influence of positivism on rational choice theory. I then move on to consider how theory was conceived by one of the first rational choice theorists of politics and the degree to which this conception has been changed by contemporary rational choice theorists.

Although Lawson, Steinmetz, and Somers all believe rational choice theory (or its close relative, neoclassical economics) has some debt to positivism, they differ in their assessments of that debt. For Lawson, although mainstream economics is informed by Humean positivism, this influence is much less significant than the discipline's debt to deductivism and mathematical formalism (this volume). Somers (1998) agrees that a nonpositivist theoretical realism is primary in much of rational choice theory, but argues that some of these theorists affirm positivist claims that are glaringly inconsistent with their realist commitments. By contrast, Steinmetz develops his definition of "methodological positivism" in acknowledgment of the partial and often inconsistent ways that contemporary social scientists affirm positivist views (this volume, "Sociology"). It is quite possible, then, that Lawson would not wish to call rational choice theory positivist, whereas Somers would call it partially so and Steinmetz would deem it an example of methodological positivism.

As these differing judgments suggest, assessing emphasis seems central to the task of gauging the influence of positivism on rational choice theory. Thinking of the matter as a question of influence or overlap steers one away from asking baldly, Is rational choice positivistic or not? There are several reasons not to accept the terms dictated by this question. First, rational choice theory is hardly monolithic. Because it has been practiced in the social sciences for over forty years and has gained a large number of adherents, one would expect to find some disagreements about its epistemological underpinnings to arise among its practitioners. I discuss one such disagreement over the merits and plausibility of "rational choice history" or "analytic narratives" below. Second, I wish to attend to how some elements of positivism have been used by rational choice theorists to construct the identity of their field in opposition to their image of the core of how political science is practiced. I conclude that positivism seems to have been more important to early rational choice theorists as a source of rhetorical weaponry than as a set of deeply held commitments. This view seems best illustrated by the early rational choice theorist William Riker's creation and defense of what he called "positive political theory."

Riker and the Creation of Positive Political Theory

Although most rational choice theorists do not explicitly label their approach positivist or construct unambiguously positivist justifications of their views, there is one group of rational choice theorists that calls itself "positive political theorists." Initially coined by Riker, one of the most influential proponents and teachers of rational choice theory in the United States, the term positive political theory has stuck; it now names a section of the American Political Science Association that members may join. In the centennial edition (2003) of the association's directory of members, around 450 are listed as belonging to that section. What do those who describe themselves this way take the term "positive" to mean? And how closely is their understanding of it aligned with the complex of ideas we call positivism? In what is probably one of his earliest uses of the term, Riker in 1959 defined positive political theory as follows: "I describe the field in which I expect to be working . . . as 'formal, positive, political theory.' . . . By formal, I mean the expression of the theory in algebraic rather than verbal symbols. By positive, I mean the expression of descriptive rather than normative propositions" (cited in Amadae and Bueno de Mesquita 1999, 276).[19] This passage appears in Riker's application to Stanford's Center for Advanced Study in the Behavioral Sciences and marks the beginning of his redefinition of the meaning of theory. During his time at Stanford, Riker wrote most of *The Theory of Political Coalitions* (1962), a book that, according to his students, became "the manifesto for his freshly articulated positive political theory" (Amadae and Bueno de Mesquita 1999, 276).

Riker's 1959 construction of the term positive political theory echoes

Milton Friedman's more widely known term, "positive economics." Friedman (1953b) clearly and explicitly distinguishes "positive" economics from "normative" economics, on the strength of the distinction made by John Neville Keynes in 1891 (3). Friedman's confidence in the merits of positive economics stems principally from his belief that when people disagree about economic policy, their disagreements can usually be traced back to "different predictions about the economic consequences of taking action" (5). Such disagreements can be resolved by a powerful, positive science: some predictions of consequences can be shown to be wrong. (Friedman concedes, however, that this "judgment . . . is itself a 'positive' statement to be accepted or rejected on the basis of empirical evidence" [6].) When people disagree about normative matters, however, "men can only fight" (5). The power of positive science, therefore, depends on defining the boundaries of its subject matter broadly and its substance as tractable.

Riker sees the challenges facing positive political theory in similar terms. In his first and in some ways most sweeping characterization of positive political theory as the basis for a new political science, he emphasizes his belief that social scientific theory ought to be modeled on his conception of theory in the physical sciences, a conception that highlights the deductive and the axiomatic. Riker begins the body of *The Theory of Political Coalitions* by announcing that the physical sciences ought to serve as a model for the social sciences (1962, 3). He then summarizes what he takes to be the most significant obstacles to the social sciences "direct[ly] emulat[ing]" the physical sciences: the presence of "normative considerations" in human life; the greater complexity of human action as compared to the motion of things; and the absence of a "notion of causal determinism" in the social sciences (4–6). These obstacles, though formidable, do not preclude the development of a political science. Indeed, Riker cites the progress of economics and psychology toward the status of "genuine sciences" as well as what he sees as the newness of efforts in political science to move in the same direction (6). He then enjoins those interested in the development of political science "first [to] become students of scientific method" (7): "The essential feature of this method is the creation of a theoretical construct that is a somewhat simplified version of what the real world to be described is believed to be like. This simplified version or model is a set of axioms (more or less justifiable intuitively) from which nonobvious general sentences can be deduced" (7). In this presentation, method frames the creation of theory (or a model or a set of axioms), and it is from theories/models/sets of axioms that verifiable claims are deduced. The power of models, Riker says, lies in how they help us "overcom[e] the special obstacles that stand so firmly in the way of a science of politics" (8). Models can help us isolate and excise "normative features" and can "cut behavior up into more manageable units than are given in common speech," thereby simplifying the complex (8).

Riker's ambitions for formulating a science of politics are the obverse of his caustic critique of the early 1960s discipline's muddled methodology and its lack of a general theory. He characterizes the shortcomings of contemporary political science in the early 1960s as failures of method: "These traditional methods—i.e., history writing, the description of institutions, and legal analysis—have been thoroughly exploited in the last two generations and now it seems to many (including myself) that they can produce only wisdom and neither science nor knowledge" (1962, viii). He then relates how he thinks distinct groups within the discipline have responded to this conclusion. Some, he says, have simply accepted that the study of politics cannot be a science; others have turned to policy science. Still others have "adapted the methods and theories [including behaviorist theory] of [psychology, sociology, and economics] to the study of politics and hence have described their work as the study of political behavior" (viii–ix). The group to which Riker says he belongs "has diagnosed the failure of traditional political science as the result of gathering information about political events without a theory of politics and has therefore been eager to create specifically *political* theories of behavior to serve as a base for a future *political* science" (ix). He then goes on to say that his ambition in the book is to offer a general theory and that he hopes that even if his attempt proves "false or unusable, it will inspire others to join in the work of creating a new political theory for a new political science" (ix).

In presenting his general theory of politics, based primarily on Von Neumann and Morgenstern's theory of n-person games, Riker (1962, 12–13) attempts to vindicate the truth value of the "rationality condition" on which his theory is based against the claim that "very few, if any, people seek to maximize money or to win." He does so by citing empirical evidence that people are maximizers, that is, by showing that maximizing behavior is observable. His examples are drawn from the behavior of trustees in fiduciary relations, a set of relations he says are particularly relevant to people acting in economic or political life (24–28). In these settings, Riker argues, people are expected to maximize and are thought either incompetent or immoral if they do not. And given that political figures act as trustees for their constituents, he concludes, one has good reasons to expect that politicians will behave as maximizers.

The issue that Riker addresses here has been a vexed one in economics and in rational choice theory for some time. If the theory relies on a handful of axiomatic assumptions, how ought one to think about the status of the claims embedded in these assumptions? Are they claims about the world the theorist believes are true? Are they simplifications of an unmanageably large collection of true claims? Or are they claims the truthfulness of which it would simply be inappropriate to try to assess?

Most neoclassical economists and rational choice theorists opt for saying that their assumptions about the instrumentally rational maximizing behavior of agents are simplifications of a large collection of true claims about behavior, or that asking whether its assumptions are at least proximally true is simply an inappropriate standard by which to judge a theory. Milton Friedman's *Essays in Positive Economics* (1953b) is often cited as the locus classicus for the latter point; however, Friedman makes just as strong a case for the simplification view. In his initial discussion of the meaning of theory in positive science, he speaks of theories as both "languages" and "hypotheses." When he says that theory is in part a language, he explains that theory's "function is to serve as a filing system for organizing empirical material and facilitating our understanding of it" (7). By contrast, "Viewed as a body of substantive hypotheses, theory is to be judged by its predictive power for the class of phenomena which it is intended to 'explain'" (8). Theories are also judged by criteria Friedman admits "defy completely objective specification," such as "simplicity" and "fruitfulness" (10). In addition to their function as "filing systems," economic theories are also dependent on "empirical evidence" in two ways: "in constructing hypotheses and in testing their validity" (12). But in making this point, Friedman does not wish to endorse the view that sound hypotheses are all realistic (or based on realistic assumptions):

> A hypothesis is important if it "explains" much by little, that is, if it abstracts the common and crucial elements from the mass of complex and detailed circumstances surrounding the phenomena to be explained and permits valid predictions on the basis of them alone. . . . the relevant question to ask about the "assumptions" of a theory is not whether they are descriptively "realistic," for they never are, but whether they are sufficiently good approximations for the purpose in hand. And this question can be answered only by seeing whether the theory works, which means whether it yields sufficiently accurate predictions. (14–15)

In this passage, Friedman invokes in one breath what seem to be two different standards for judging a theory by the truth-value of its assumptions: he says both that assumptions are simplifications of myriad true claims and that caring about the descriptive accuracy of assumptions is simply an inappropriate standard of judgment.

Riker's initial construction of positive political theory resembles Friedman's positive economics in several ways. Like Friedman, Riker uses the adjective "positive" as the opposite of "normative." And like Friedman, Riker treats his conception of theorizing in the physical sciences as the standard to which theorizing in the social sciences should aspire. But unlike Friedman, Riker is not willing to treat one of the primary assumptions of his theory—that politicians are rational maximizers—as either a simplification or as a claim the descriptive accuracy of which is beside the point. Instead, in 1962, Riker takes some pains to try to vindicate the descriptive accuracy of the rationality of political actors. In his first extended statement of positive political theory, then, Riker embraces positivism not only by using the label positive to justify his rejection of other ways of studying politics. He also maintains that the power of his theory depends in part on whether its central assumption about human behavior in politics is empirically true, a position that recedes in his later work.

Over ten years later, Riker, along with his student Peter Ordeshook, published what was intended to serve as a textbook for advanced undergraduates and beginning graduate students, *An Introduction to Positive Political Theory* (1973). Here, positive political theory is defined somewhat differently: "As the adjective 'positive' indicates, [the emphasis of this book is] on theory of an axiomatic, deductive type" (xi). Indeed, in this book, the rationality assumption functions much more as an axiom in a realist view (Somers 1998) than as a claim about human behavior that can be empirically vindicated. Rationality is no longer primarily defined as observable maximizing behavior, but as the more amorphous "goal-directed" behavior (Riker and Ordeshook 1973, 10, 12–16), the goals of which may themselves sometimes be assumed (14). In this statement of positive political theory, Riker and Ordeshook take some pains to show that observable features of human behavior, such as error, confusion, and perversity, should not prejudice us against the rationality postulate. Such appearances are deceiving. To think human behavior is often perverse is to be "undu[ly] gullibl[e]" when people bewail their plans gone awry (21); most error arises not from the chaos and complexity of human desire but because of "misinformation and reasoned rejection of the cost of correction," deviations one can make allowances for in terms of the rationality postulate itself (31).

In both *The Theory of Political Coalitions* (1962) and *An Introduction to Positive Political Theory* (1973), positive political theory derives much of its meaning from its opposition to what appears at each moment to be its major rival for theoretical status in the discipline. In the late 1950s and early 1960s, that major rival is what Riker calls normative theory; by 1973, Riker and Ordeshook devote their energies to criticizing theory of an empirical, inductive type.[20] Indeed, they present behavioral theorists as their only opponents of note by citing their work in their suggestions for further reading and telling their readers that they may "find it instructive to compare our approach with the very different approach of recent writers in the behavioral tradition" (1973, 7). But they make no secret of their contempt for behavioral political science, deriding behavioralists for their excessive reliance on observation as well as their suspicion of the methodological individualism central to rational choice theory (10–12, 33–37). Riker and Ordeshook deliver their coup de grâce against any claims behavioralists might still make to being the theorists in political science by remarking, "At a recent professional meeting, there were many papers on 'empirical theory,' which phrase makes no more sense than, for example, 'incorporeal body'" (12, n. 4).

Recent Rational Choice Theory: The Diffuse Identity of the Hegemon

One of the more recent features of the forty-some years in which rational choice theory has been practiced in political science is the advent of approaches that rely less on formal modeling and more on historical research or case studies while still identifying themselves as rational choice or game theoretic. While the dominant conception of theory among rational choice theorists until recently has been a primarily deductivist one, that conception has been significantly modified by a group of rational choice social scientists who have tried to use rational choice to analyze long-term historicopolitical developments. *Analytic Narratives* (1998) by Robert Bates et al. provides a good sense of how rational choice theorists are reinventing themselves in U.S. social science today. Although it certainly has been criticized for diluting rational choice theory so much as to rob it of any distinctive analytic flavor (Elster 2000), several of the authors (Bates, Margaret Levi, and Barry Weingast) are prominent political scientists in large graduate programs (Harvard, University of Washington, and Stanford). Contested as their approach may be within the rational choice community itself, it is nevertheless unquestionably a powerful one.

The authors introduce the term that serves as the title to their book, "analytic narratives," by saying that it "captures our conviction that theory linked to data is more powerful than either data or theory alone" and that they believe their work is "problem driven, not theory driven" (1998, 3, 11). What is more, this is an avowedly interdisciplinary project, in which the authors say they mean to use "analytic tools" most commonly associated with economics and political science along with the "narrative form, which is more commonly employed in history" (10). Still, the authors insist, rational choice theory plays an important and constraining role in this project. Rational choice or game theory functions as the conceptual storehouse from which the authors "construct" a particular model or game "that provides the link between the prominent features of the narrative and its outcome" (14).

The ambitions of the *Analytic Narratives* project are grand. The authors mean to show that the criticisms of rational choice theory—that it offers little better than post hoc explanations and disregards empirical evidence —cannot be leveled against their work (231). Notably, one way they revise the theory of rational choice is by criticizing Riker's 1962 conception of what theory ought to mean. They disown Riker's ambition to formulate "a universal approach to the social sciences, capable of yielding general laws of political behavior," adding that they "consider Riker's claims to be based on an 'overconfident' and naive vision of the sciences" (11, n. 11). In introducing their own work, the authors flatly say that it does not "conform to Riker's vision of the role of theory. Although informed by deductive reasoning, the chapters themselves seek no universal laws of human behavior" (11).

How ought we to read this brief but unambiguous dismissal of Riker's "vision of the role of theory" by some of the most prominent contemporary practitioners of rational choice theory? Unquestionably, rational choice theory is more powerful in political science today than it was when Riker published his *Theory of Political Coalitions* in 1962; therefore, if there is a kind of modesty to the way Bates et al. conceive of rational choice theory, it is the kind of modesty characteristic of those whose preeminent power affords them the ability to reevaluate, revise, and "reconcile alternatives" (the last of which the authors say Levi's and Weingast's chapters explicitly attempt to do [17]). Indeed, the preeminent power of rational choice in political science also makes any oppositional statement of "what we are not" unnecessary.[21] The diffuseness of the theoretical identity of the *Analytic Narratives* project is, I believe, best read as a mark of the hegemony of rational choice in political science.

One mark of this diffuseness can be seen in how theory operates at two different levels in the way Bates et al. write about their joint project.

Sometimes, theory means rational choice or game theory generally, as when the authors write, "When we refer to theory, we refer to rational choice theory and, most often, to the theory of games" (1). At other times, theory means a particular explanation, as in the claim, "In constructing our theories, we were often driven to the discovery of new features of our data" (231). The latter meaning also seems to be what the authors have in mind when they address the question, *"How well does the theory stand up by comparison with other explanations?"* (17). Clearly, in this question, "theory" is being used as a synonym for "explanation." Bates et al. cannot mean that what they are "constructing" is rational choice theory itself, but rather the particular analytic narratives that derive from its basic assumptions. And it is, I believe, these particular games and models that the authors believe are "vulnerable" to "the empirical record" (16); surely it is not rational choice or game theory itself that is the theory the authors say they "find . . . being shaped by the case materials" (16). What is being revised and what is being held constant here is not easy to specify. The authors mean to show the interdisciplinary reach of analytic narratives rather than identify what they are not.

Jon Elster (2000), in his extended review of *Analytic Narratives*, offers what is in my judgment a minority view of rational choice theory as a clearly defined and distinctly limited theory of social and political action. Elster rejects the whole project presented in Bates et al., not just because he thinks these particular examples of it flawed but also, as he admits, because he thinks "deductive history will forever remain impossible" (694). Elster's most basic objection concerns the way Bates et al. assume the rationality of the actors they analyze. Without saying so explicitly, he takes the authors to task for making what he believes is an unrealistic assumption. Not only are most people not cognitively capable of instrumentally rational calculation on a regular basis, but human action is moved by both rational and nonrational factors. And because of nonrational factors, people are not generally "reward-maximizing," even though they are often "reward-sensitive" (692). Given that Elster thinks these things to be psychologically or cognitively true of people, he believes they present any social scientist who wishes to construct a formal model of human behavior with formidable and probably insurmountable obstacles (692).

Another way to put Elster's principal criticism of the project is to focus on his criticism of the authors' untenably broad use of formal analysis: "Because formal analysis has nothing to say about the motivation of agents, it cannot by itself yield robust predictions. Although it is extremely useful to know that the structure of material interests in a given case is that of a one-shot Prisoner's Dilemma, that fact does not by itself imply anything about what the agents will do. . . . Rational choice theory tells us what to look for, not what we will find" (695). Elster argues that many who deploy rational choice theory, however, fail to take these limitations into account. As a consequence, what gets produced "is a combination of just-so stories and functionalist explanation. One constructs a model in which the observed behavior of the agents maximizes their interests as suitably defined, and one assumes that the fit between behavior and interest explains the behavior"(693). Again, ignoring what can be learned about the intentions and beliefs of agents is the culprit here; it seems wrong or at the very least incomplete to Elster for rational choice theorists to deploy a rational choice explanation without "looking for evidence that the agents whose behavior they want to explain did in fact have the goals and beliefs they describe" (693). Of course, part of the way the authors of *Analytic Narratives* make their case for what they do is by stressing their immersion in the data or the case; Elster's criticism, however, is more specific. He complains that most of the authors (Levi and Bates excepted) have not paid attention to the right kind of evidence to the extent that they have not looked for evidence about the "intentions and beliefs" of the agents with whose behavior they are concerned (693).

I have discussed Elster's critique of *Analytic Narratives* because it illuminates the theoretical diffuseness of contemporary rational choice theory in another way. Though Elster makes a coherent case for the delimited and sharply defined rational choice analysis he advocates, much of the recent rational choice literature in the social sciences must seem incorrigibly fuzzy by his standards. This, as I have suggested, may be one of the most distinguishing marks of its success.

Conclusion

The epigraph I have chosen for this essay makes two principal points. The first, that "the outside constructs the inside," has been the focus of what I have said about Wolin's contribution to traditional political theory as well as Riker's to positive political theory. Both Wolin and Riker rely on characterizations of approaches they oppose to construct the identity of how each thinks political theory ought to be done. But the epigraph also makes the point that though "the outside constructs the inside," this work is later hidden, making the constructed entity "[appear] to give birth to itself." Each of the approaches to political theory I have been concerned with here may now appear to be self-generated, at least with respect to intradisciplinary conflicts. Taken out of the oppositional context in which it was made, the claim of traditional political theorists that they are engaged in a conversation that began in ancient Greece certainly appears to grant the field a rare sort of autonomy. And the close ties between rational choice theory and neoclassical economics may make it appear as if rational choice came into political science as an extradisciplinary import as opposed to having been developed in part by political scientists for intradisciplinary reasons. Paying close attention to the ways the creators of these new fields constructed their identities in opposition to other approaches gives us a more complete picture of postwar political science.

Although what I have called traditional political theory throughout most of this essay has now become simply "political theory," the number of groups that lay claim to theorizing some elements of politics in the discipline has proliferated. Of all of these, rational choice theorists have become one of the most powerful. Their current power in the discipline, however, is displayed by the expansion of rational choice theory into new disciplinary territories. The expanding reach of rational choice theory has been accompanied by a diffusion of its initially oppositional theoretical identity. By contrast, political theorists continue to articulate what they do in oppositional terms. But, as Wendy Brown (2002) suggests, much of the relevant "outside" for contemporary political theorists now lies outside the discipline of political science itself. Neither of these developments means that opposition is no longer a fruitful way of understanding how academic fields constitute themselves, but perhaps it is now less fruitful for capturing the current state of the discipline.

Notes

My thanks to Dan Aalbers for reading earlier drafts of this essay. Thanks also to Robert Adcock, Terry Ball, Susan Hoffmann, and George Steinmetz for directing me to many helpful references.

1　"Traditional" in this phrase should not be taken as the opposite of "innovative" or "revolutionary." Rather, the adjective "traditional" in the label "traditional political theorist" indicates an approach to political theory that emphasizes a tradition of theorizing about politics from ancient Greece up until the present. Although this label helps distinguish among different approaches to political theory in the 1950s and 1960s, people in the subfield of political theory today no longer use it of themselves.

2　Riker, who received his PhD in 1948, wrote on the Council of Industrial Organizations (Amadae and Bueno de Mesquita 1999, 272); Wolin (PhD 1949) wrote on "the history of British constitutional theory" (Adcock and Bevir 2003, 14); Easton (PhD 1947) wrote on the theory of the elite (Bang 1998; Gunnell 1993).

3 In addition to Easton (1951), two of the most well-known pieces discussing the decline of political theory are Berlin (1963/1979) and Laslett (1956).

4 Right before these remarks, Easton notes how hostile Harvard's government department was to empirical inquiry: "I intuitively missed [that concern for rigorous empirical inquiry] during the whole of my stay [at Harvard]. It is difficult today to appreciate fully how inimical the whole atmosphere in the Department of Government was, at least among many of the senior professors, to scientific method for the study of politics and society" (1991, 198).

5 For characterizations of what some of its adherents believed behavioralism meant, see Dahl (1993) and Eulau (1962).

6 The full passage on the last point reads as follows: "Where our contemporary way of talking has not obscured the drama and demands of theorizing, it has trivialized them. Theories are likened to appliances which are 'plugged into' political life and, since it is the nature of appliances to be under sentence of built-in obsolescence, 'theories are for burning,' leaving only a brief funereal glow which lights the way to 'more scientific theories and more efficient research procedures'" (Wolin 1969, 1075). The quoted passages here are from Apter (1965, x).

7 Although in this essay Wolin does not draw an explicit connection between the elements of behavioralism he condemns and positivism, he does do so elsewhere (Wolin 1968). Specifically, he focuses on the "naive positivist assumption that facts can be known accurately if only we could lay aside our prejudices and biases" as the source of the belief that "there can be some kind of purely empirical theory" (1968, 328). I believe this line of argument is somewhat muted in Wolin's work because it had already been articulated so forcefully by Leo Strauss and his students in Storing (1962). Schaar and Wolin (1963) criticized the Storing volume for exaggerating the evils of scientism and positivism and their influence on U.S. political science.

8 By contrast, behavioralists pointedly said they found the kind of historical study that had been required of students of political science up through the mid-twentieth century unproductive. For instance, Adcock and Bevir note that the behavioralists rejected historically rooted theorizing (characteristic of the Harvard "ideas and institutions" approach) as "historicist," favoring instead "positivist criteria for judging theoretical frameworks in accord with their understanding of natural science. Their leading criteria were universality, deductive structure, and instrumental utility for empirical research" (2003, 7).

9 In the form most familiar to those who belong to the subfield today, Wolin et al. call what they do simply "political theory." "Proposal for a Department of Political Theory," n.d., Box 10, folder 129, Reinhard Bendix Papers, German Intellectual Émigré Collection, M. E. Grenander Department of Special Collections and Archives, University Libraries, University at Albany, State University of New York. Internal references suggest that the proposal was written in the summer of 1967; no authors are listed. I thank Robert Adcock for providing me with a copy of this material.

10 The essay by Mihic, Engelmann, and Wingrove in this volume presents a more extended argument about how the apparent opposition between "fact-neutral" normative theory and empiricism conceals a deeper union between these approaches.

11 One of the best-known representatives of this approach to the study of political

thought is Quentin Skinner. See his "Meaning and Understanding in the History of Ideas" (1988).

12   Ball's standards for how to study the history of political thought are similar to those of Skinner (1988).

13   R. Bernstein (1976) credits the sociologist Merton with the term "middle range theory." By contrast, recall Easton's ambition for formulating what he calls a "general theory."

14   Although the "postbehavioral" period of political science was announced as early as the end of the 1960s, behavioralism was, as Dahl (1993) said, a movement. Its enduring influence on the discipline is exerted perhaps most powerfully by how research methods are understood and taught. Schwartz-Shea and Yanow (2002) argue that the research methods texts they surveyed placed "an exclusive emphasis on positivist epistemology" (477) and that they equate the use of "empirical methods" with what "behavioralist Americanists do" (476).

15   Brown was a graduate student of Wolin's at Princeton.

16   Cavarero focuses on how this image is used by Hannah Arendt, rather than Wolin. See my discussion of the affinities between Wolin's and Arendt's work (Hauptmann 2004).

17   In another contribution to the same issue of *Political Theory*, Ian Shapiro (2002) criticizes contemporary political theorists for their inward focus and lack of attention to the rest of the discipline. Shapiro reinforces his critique by labeling what political theorists do "normative political theory" and then criticizing these "normative" theorists for their inattention to what logically seems to be their other half: empirical theorists. This dyad, however, has been resisted by traditional political theorists for some time (Wolin 1968, 328). See also the critique presented by Mihic, Engelmann, and Wingrove in this volume.

18   For example, A. James Gregor (1969) argues for the "methodological unity of the sciences," which he summarizes by saying that those who hold this view "need claim no more than that all the sciences, in varying measure and proportion, employ the same formal as well as empirical techniques for truth accreditation" (1255). Throughout the article, Gregor cites and relies heavily on the work of positivists, including Hempel and Ayer.

19   But consider, by contrast, Jon Elster's (1986) definition of rational choice theory: "The theory of rational choice is, before it is anything else, a normative theory. It tells us what we ought to do in order to achieve our aims as well as possible. It does not tell us what our aims ought to be" (1).

20   Riker (1982) attacks the "populist" strains in the history of democratic theory. See also my discussion in Hauptmann (1996).

21   A similar reading of recent rational choice theory may be found in Mansbridge (1995).

Beware Trojan Horses Bearing Social Capital: How Privatization Turned Solidarity into a Bowling Team

MARGARET R. SOMERS

etting what is surely an all-time record, in less than a decade the concept of social capital has shot with meteoric speed through the epistemological fast track to become one of the reigning ideas in the social sciences.[1] Even in the rarified air of conceptual superstars, social capital stands out for a charismatic appeal seemingly unmatched in recent memory. Few ideas have ever been projected into such an array of protean forms, displayed such remarkable theoretical promiscuity, or been endowed with such seemingly unlimited powers and capacities for good. From East to West, North, and South, from postmodern capitalist hegemons to struggling postcolonial regimes, the global reach of its ascribed value and applicability is stunning. Society, economics, politics, medicine, anthropology, psychology, epidemiology, ethnicity, history, economic development, marriage, child raising, international relations, sexuality, institutionality, constitutionality, legality, community, education, race, gender, family, civic affairs, democracy, and global poverty—these are just a few of the arenas and concerns to which the social capital concept has been applied in the role of what the World Bank program on social capital calls "the missing link" in the effort to end poverty in the developing world (Grootaert 1997).[2] The breadth of its resonance is equally astonishing: from economists to public health scholars, from public intellectuals to peripatetic health care workers, from World Bank and IMF financiers to NGOs across the globe, from New England town meetings to local civic groups and, of course, community bowling leagues—everyone, it seems, has fallen in epistemic love with social capital.[3]

This is a phenomenon that puzzles. For one thing, the actual term social capital is not new, having been in circulation for almost three-quarters of a century since it first appeared in Hanifan (1920), followed several decades later by J. Jacobs (1961), then brought into economics and public policy by Loury (1977) and Coleman et al. (1966), into sociology by Bourdieu (1986), and finally becoming established as a foundational concept of rational choice theory again by Coleman (1988/2000, 1989) and Gary Becker (Becker and Nashat 1997; Becker and Murphy 2000). For another, that successful market societies are foundationally dependent on nonmarket, noncontractual, and nonstate social relations can be readily traced back to Aristotle, Adam Smith, Marx, Tocqueville, Durkheim, Weber, Malinowski, and Karl Polanyi, again to name only some of the most obvious. The implication that it is a *new* discovery, moreover, that cooperative and cohesive social practices and associations are critically important for successful democratic politics and socioeconomic prosperity would make any social historian truly apoplectic. Legal historians would be equally provoked by such a claim, even with only a minimal familiarity with the preambles, statutes, and rule books characteristic of medieval and early modern guilds, apprenticeship regulations, tramping associations, eighteenth-century rural-industrial artisanal credit unions, or nineteenth-century Friendly Societies.[4] And as for its being *news* that family ties and community networks produce economic and political value, indeed, that they are a primary locus of a culture's resources—well, one does not even want to imagine the bemused reaction of an anthropologist.

This, then, is the conundrum that needs to be engaged: How and why is it possible that the recent adoption of the term social capital has come to represent a new discovery and a new theorization of social knowledge that has long been in circulation? Even more significant, why does the term have such crowding-out power that it is quickly becoming the sole occupant of the conceptual space once occupied by a multitudinous population of competing, jostling, differing ways to characterize the value of social relations? Clearly, it appears to have become an object of our culture's political imaginary: onto it has been projected an idealized realization and long yearned-for solution to a multiplicity of problems. But if social capital has been anointed as the object of a remarkable collective cathexis, why and how and to what effects it has come to assume this position still needs to be answered.[5] What is the work social capital is performing? What need is it fulfilling? One does not have to be a sociologist of knowledge to sense that coming to grips with the significance and implications, the causes and consequences of such a rare conceptual and political phenomenon is a matter of great import. But first we must ask, Does it even matter? After all, it's only an idea.

The answer is yes, it matters. Indeed, we can only answer the previous explanatory questions by reference to the independent causal powers of the idea of social capital as well as of the larger ideational regime of market fundamentalism in which it is embedded. Social capital is not a term that emerged to reflect changes that were actually taking place in the social world. Rather, it is the idea of social capital that has pushed, prodded, and reconfigured our knowledge and understanding of that world, especially the question of what is the appropriate distribution of power among the spheres of market, state, and civil society. As an independent causal mechanism social capital has played a mighty part in delegitimating the previous institutionalist/Keynesian regime and converting our political culture to the now dominant one of market fundamentalism. Social capital—not simply the words, of course, but the wider project of market fundamentalism in which it is conceptually located—is ideationally embedded in our contemporary political knowledge culture.[6]

The argument is this: the ideational and political work of social capital is that of privatization, marketization, of antistatism and of transforming rights into duties. The rise of social capital is part and parcel of the larger narrative of privatization of the public sphere, the public sector, and, above all, civil society or the sphere of "the social." All told, the work of social capital is that of the marketization and moralization of no less than democratic practices and citizenship rights. As an alternative to the state it saves the market from its own excesses, externalities, and imperfections. The work of social capital is entirely voluntary and carried out by unpaid citizens and neighbors simply living their everyday lives in their communities and doing the expected duties of good citizenship in a democratic political culture. These are relationships not of society as a whole, but those ties specific to the social sector, a k a civil society, the voluntary nonprofit sector, or, even more commonly, simply the "community" and its "families" so celebrated by public figures from Jerry Fallwell to Britain's Tony Blair. On the face of it this is the same territory as the "third sphere" of citizenship and civil society, a participatory and democratic site independent of both market and state made familiar to us by the Eastern European social revolutions against tyrannical states (Giddens 1998). But in the guise of social capital, civil society has taken an almost unrecognizable form. No longer made up of the social in its politically democratic sense of civil society—the symbol of movements for democratic citizenship—it has now become a "social auxiliary" to the market. The terrain of citizenship has been reconstituted as a form of capital. And civil society—once the vibrant social site from which was launched the great revolutions for political rights of the late twentieth century, as well as an enduring normative ideal for democratic participatory equality—has thus been reconstituted into social capital.

In what follows I use the metaphor of a perfect storm to diagnose and account for the causal powers, effects, and consequences of the social capital phenomenon that took off in 1993. A perfect storm is not one but a collision of multiple storms. One of these storms was the publication of two works by Robert Putnam. *Making Democracy Work* (Putnam et al. 1993) produced the counterintuitive finding that neither institutional anticorruption reforms nor progressive social programs but the participation of civic groups such as choral societies and church associations best explains what makes democracy work in Tuscany. Marking Putnam's achievement as a crossover success from academia to the global public sphere, the *Economist* celebrated the book under the caption "Civic Lessons" (1993). A second publication appeared in the *American Prospect*, a journal of the liberal intelligentsia; in "The Prosperous Community: Social Capital and Public Life" (R. Putnam 1993), he admonished and foretold the dangers to the United States of a society that is increasingly "bowling alone," both a metaphor and a symbol of the fact that "every year over the last decade or two, millions more have withdrawn from the affairs of their communities" (R. Putnam 1995, 68). No less than the future of democracy, Putnam forewarned in what became a series of articles and books, hangs in the balance of whether or not the nation's solitary bowlers would once again become team players (R. Putnam 1993, 1995, 1996, 2000).

The second of social capital's catalyzing storms was itself the outcome of a collision of other dynamic historical processes: intellectual, epistemological, and scholarly, but also cultural, economic, sociological, religious, and political. The four forces that are of interest to my story were (1) neoliberals looking for solutions to market externalities and transaction costs; (2) neoconservatives advocating for a new site of moral restraint and cultural alternatives to the "handouts" of the welfare state and the "excesses" of democratic participation of the 1960s and 1970s; (3) sociologists, political scientists, rational choice theorists, and economists (many of whom doubled as public intellectuals) competing over how to best include social relationships in prevailing economic models; and (4) the World Bank's search for a "post-Washington consensus" in dealing with global poverty and economic development (under the influence of Joseph Stiglitz).[7]

Call these the multiple streams of social capital, each starting with different origins and under different conditions and each with different political aims, but then all cascading toward the same point where (to painfully mix metaphors), upon colliding with Putnam's emergence into the public sphere, they erupted into the perfect storm of social capital. But what is most significant is that despite their radically competing political goals and ideologies, these many social capital trajectories all had the same epistemological agenda, namely, to develop a new theory and vocabulary that would name, explain, and thus "make true" for political knowledge a new "autonomous" sphere of society fully independent of the power of the state. Variously called civil society, community, new social movements, or social capital, the goal of all these movements was to establish and normalize for political knowledge an autonomous site of "the social" (Arato and Cohen 1984; J. L Cohen 1985; Kitschelt 1993; Offe 1985). Only by making such a site an accepted element of political life could they, in effect, actually bring it into epistemic being. Whether they knew it or not at the beginning, they were all in search of what was to become "social capital."

The motivational logic was this: the falsely exhaustive dichotomy between state and market was not a product of the empirical world but of our conceptual landscape. Breaking apart the dichotomy to make room for a third sphere of the social was initially triggered by the practical politics of Solidarity and other social movements. But to effect a permanent change in the distribution of conceptual power and space required a contest of epistemological politics over what kind of social knowledge would be accepted as true and "normal science." With each social capital trajectory being driven forward by this same epistemological desideratum, their actual collision sparked an enormous "opportunity structure" to capture, fulfill, and control this opportunity for a new conceptual vocabulary. In the face of this epistemological possibility, social capital was there to seize the prize.

It is entirely arbitrary to register 1993 as the year of social capital's perfect storm; I do so merely to register the general time frame of social capital's takeoff. In 1993 social capital became something little remarked on in social theory: an epistemological public good.[8] Like all public goods, its resources became part of the "commons," available to all, exploitable by many. When social capital entered the public sphere and became available as an epistemological public good, its inherent powers were put into circulation. Those who perceived and appropriated these powers found themselves in possession of a remarkable kind of social, political, and economic knowledge. For unlike the usual public goods, epistemological ones have unique powers by virtue of their ontological abstraction: they are infinitely expansive and there is no limit to their capacity for appropriation. Social capital would prove to be the gift that keeps on giving.

In what follows, I have grouped the multiple social capital trajectories under two broad, interweaving causal narratives, one primarily intellectual and scholarly, the other political and event-driven. Combined, they make up a larger canvas of multiple intersecting needs and intellectual resources that demonstrates the processes and powers, the causes and effects of the epistemological politics driving the social capital concept.

The academic/intellectual story is that of the complex relationship between economics and sociology over control for the soul of the social.[9] Because sociology is the discipline that has contributed the most to bringing social capital under the rubric of normal science, this is by necessity a tale of what I believe to be epistemological self-deception. In the guise of a Trojan horse, neoliberal public intellectuals and a small group of determined economists seem to be offering an olive branch of respect to sociology and the other social sciences. After so many years of "sneering contempt" (Deirdre McCloskey 1994), economists appear to have finally accepted the social dimension of markets. But it is just that: appearance. Blinded by their own desire for recognition by economists, sociologists have taken appearance for reality. In so doing they have inadvertently colluded with the neoliberal project of appropriating, domesticating, transforming, and evacuating the social from political knowledge. While sociologists feel pride that the social capital concept has finally socialized the economic, through the Trojan horse of social capital it is the economists who are successfully privatizing and marketizing the social.

The political story is one of the relationships in the 1990s between neoliberal and neoconservative movements on the one side, and the democratic communitarian left in Europe and the United States on the other. This story takes us from the revolutionary democratic shipyards of the Polish Solidarity trade union movement in Gdansk, to the recent U.S. trend of substituting "faith-based organizations" for aid to the poor once provided by welfare, to the current nostalgia for the bowling leagues and neighborhood church groups of 1950s America. This is also a story of appropriation and domestication; powerful neoliberal and conservative public intellectuals of the 1980s and 1990s were drawn to the antistatist and anticommunist idea of civil society, a concept in large part put in recirculation in 1980s Eastern Europe by Poland's Solidarity, the GDR's New Forum, and Czechoslovakia's Charter 77 (to name the best-known), as well as the new social movements in Western liberal democracies. Advocates of the new civil society concept saw it as both a normative ideal and a sociological site for autonomous democratic practices and self-organization and activist citizen participation, with the goals of contributing to public deliberation in the public sphere and influencing public policy and the state.[10] Given its antistatist origins, conservatives first eagerly appropriated the idea of civil society. However, once they recognized it as a site peopled by trade unionists, new social movements, and participatory citizen-driven politics, they quickly turned to taming and transforming its unruliness. In a truly Pygmalion achievement, civil society became but a shadow of its former identity as it morphed into social capital. As social capital it is politically manageable, tamed, respectable, domesticated, and bustling with bowling leagues, church picnics, home schooling, family values, moral regulation, backyard barbeques, volunteer labor, and faith-based soup kitchens. For neoliberals, social capital answered a different need: it is an ideal nonmarket yet privatized solution to the "externalities" and the "imperfections" that emerged from the rage for marketization both at home and abroad.

These are, in brief, the dynamic narratives that produced the perfect storm of social capital. But before turning to my causal stories, let me put my own cards on the table by delineating social capital's immanent incoherencies and the fundamental threat it poses for "the soul of the social."

Social + Capital = The Evacuation of the Social

The social capital literature is riddled with competing definitions. Still, at the most general level, most would agree that social capital refers to the economic value produced by social relationships (Åberg 2003; Arrow 2000; Becker 1997, 2000; Bourdieu 1986; Coleman 1998/2000; Fukuyama 1995a; Grootaert and Van Bastelaer 2002; R. Putnam 1993, 1995, 2000). These relationships are said to generate streaming utility by creating and maintaining social and normative cohesion over time in durable networks and communities. This is productive work that either cannot or will not be performed by markets but on which capitalism depends for its lifeblood. Thus the World Bank's definition of social capital: "Social capital consists of a set of horizontal associations between people, consisting of social networks and associated norms that have an effect on community productivity and well-being. Social networks can increase productivity by reducing the costs of doing business. Social capital facilitates coordination and cooperation" (World Bank 2004; italics added).[11]

At the heart of social capital theory is the thesis that capitalism is driven by what Durkheim famously called the "non-contractualism of contract": trust, transactional reliability, and the norms and networks of noncontractual social relations. Absent these attributes that the market cannot provide, there could be no meaningful contracts and society would be nothing but an aggregate of multiple "spot" markets. Under these conditions, market societies simply would not endure.[12]

Harmless and unobjectionable, to be sure. Still, there are ontological, methodological, and epistemological reasons why pairing social and capital actually undermines the significance of the very social relations to which are attributed the production of value. Parsing social capital into its separate elements of social and capital demonstrates just how much is compromised in their coupling.

What Is Capital?

Standard economics defines capital as any kind of resource (physical or otherwise) capable of producing streaming utility-resources, that is, with economic value over time.[13] Capital is also something that must be owned —it cannot be a public good—and thus is also a form of property. But if capital must be property, the inverse cannot be true; obviously, the vast majority of one's possessions do not produce economic utility over time. This may be obvious in some cases: automobiles most famously lose value quickly. But is the difference always so evident? We take for granted that whether or not something counts as capital is empirically inherent in the object itself (even if the capital in question is "human capital," because even mental skills must be manifested in a credential or certificate of training). But is the important distinction between mere property and capital always so easy to determine by having empirical access to the object?

Consider the case of two apples I have brought home from the grocery store. Both are my property, but, as it happens, only one of them is going to be also a form of capital. But how to tell which is which? After all, they look virtually identical. The answer will not be found in the apples themselves. The status of capital is not inherent in the object. Rather, the distinction must be found in my mental state of intentionality. Here's why. I bought each apple for a different purpose: the one to eat, the other to core the seeds to start an apple orchard. Thus, I gobbled up apple number one, seeds and all; after all, it was my property. And, as planned, I gathered the seeds of apple number two and planted them in my apple-orchard-to-be. The two apples were identical when I unpacked the groceries and put them on the kitchen counter, but even before I ate the first one, only the second was capital. Why? Because of my intentional investment decision, which not only existed before I ate the one apple but in fact determined the different fates of the two apples.

There is nothing inherent in machines, or skills, or culture, or computers that makes them recognizable as capital rather than simply someone's property. This is because capital is not a thing; it is not an external entity but resides in the heads of individual agents.[14] It is a mental state: a decision-choice theoretic to invest, to defer gratification in the case of apples and money, rather than consume. The very same object can be capital or property; the only difference is the mental state of who/what is acting upon it. To look at those apples before they were eaten or planted does not allow any distinction between the two. For economists, the only thing that defines property is the mind of the capitalist.

What Is Social?

If we start from the assumption that what is social is that which pertains to society, the sociological method tells us that that which is social is by necessity relational. Whether according to Hegel, Marx, Tocqueville, Durkheim, Bourdieu, or Giddens, sociology's foundational a priori is the social as a social fact, what Durkheim (1938) defined as external to the mind, a mechanism of institutional constraint, irreducible to its individual agents. Subfields as far apart in sociology as contemporary network theory and the now defunct holistic Parsonianism share this same foundational premise that society exists outside the mind of any individual agent (though not necessarily of all agents taken together). Call it a social formation, a social structure, a society, even a society of two, as the Victorian novelists liked to do; however unstable in a poststructuralist age, the social is performatively relational. In Geertz's (1973) famous formulation, the social is irreducibly relational "all the way down."

Sociology, however, has never had exclusive rights to the study of society. As much as sociology has tried to hold it at bay, there is a competing approach that lays equal claim to the study of society even while resolutely rejecting the relationality of the social. This is the social theory of utilitarianism, today known as rational choice theory. Although not dubbed as such until Bentham in the nineteenth century, utilitarianism properly begins with Hobbes's utilitarian man and becomes a full-fledged social theory with Locke's invention of civil society, a fully self-regulating social entity that exists fully independently of the state and acts as a countervailing source of power and social organization (Somers 1995b, 1999, 2001). Locke's vision of society couldn't be less relational. It is built on a presocial "state of nature," peopled by ontologically isolated, separate individuals who, in their natural state, are constitutively autonomous vis-à-vis any and all others and any and all relational entities: "[W]e must consider what state all men are naturally in, and that it is a state of perfect freedom to order their actions and dispose of their possessions and persons as they see fit, within the bounds of the law of nature, without asking leave, or depending upon the will of any other man" (Locke 1690/1952, ch. 2, sec. 4, p. 4).

A less sociological approach to society would be hard to find. Yet this methodologically individualist view of the social steadily developed from Hobbes, through Locke, to Smith, Bentham, Mill, and Spencer. It was above all Malthus who, beginning from the individual utility-maximizing agent, was the first to fully realize the utilitarian project of theorizing society as if it were a market. And after seemingly sleeping from the mid-nineteenth to the mid-twentieth century, it again manifested itself, first in Homans's and Coleman's "social exchange" theory, then in today's thriving neoutilitarian rational choice theory.[15]

Utilitarianism's society couldn't be more different from that of sociology's. Yet the problem utilitarianism has always posed for sociology is that this naturalized ontological individualistic social theory is a theory of society nonetheless. It is its shared object of study in society, rather than in a common sociological method, that allowed utilitarianism to be a fully justified alternative approach to sociology. Clearly, one doesn't have to be a sociologist to study the social.

And Social + Capital = ?

Two fundamentally opposing approaches to the study of society, then: the sociological and the utilitarian. Only the sociological has a commitment to the constitutive and irreducible relationality of the social. To be sure, the relational approach of the social does not deny the individual a purposeful mental state; the difference is that the source of agency is not a natural but a social phenomenon. However it is spun, a social condition of purposefulness is ontologically and irreducibly at odds with utilitarianism's competing conception of the social in social capital. Causally derived from an aggregate of individual agential intentionalities and behaviors, utilitarianism's methodological individualism always trumps the idea of a macrosocial relational entity.

The marriage of social to capital thus poses the question of *which* view of the social is the one coupled with social capital? If we take the sociological perspective, the result is incoherence; it becomes social capital evacu-ated of its constitutive sociality. The incoherence results from trying to conjoin sociology's relational view of the social with the constitutively agential capital and its foundationalist methodological individualism. The effort to attach the social to the intentional agent turns both into some-thing else entirely. One cannot have it both ways: social capital cannot be both externally relational and internally agentially intentional. It simply doesn't hold. The great advantage its advocates gain from this incoher-ence, however, is that it gives social capital the kind of capaciousness that readily provides it with the *appearance* of relationality.

By contrast, the meaning of social capital is entirely coherent if we accept the utilitarian view of society as an aggregate of interacting individ-ual agents. When this version of the social is linked to capital, the two methodologically individualist terms become compatible. This turns the social aggregate into a utility-generating valuable economic asset. Like-wise, the social is transformed from a relational entity to an agent's prop-erty qua social capital. The most that capital can do is evacuate the social into the property of the individual intentional agent.

Access to social capital is premised on the concept that the individual agent treats a social network as a form of personal property, property that the agent has decided to convert into capital by choosing to invest in it rather than to immediately consume or exploit these connections. In so maximizing the utility function of the social network, the agent might find different ways to add value to one or more of the individuals in the network, say by preparing meals for a sick family member or providing useful financial advice. But these are merely the agent's instrumental choices in the expectation that at a later point in time these investments of time or money or friendship will produce far greater utility returns (i.e., prove far more useful financially, socially, culturally, etc.) for her or his individual gain and profit than they would have had she or he simply "used" the connections right off the bat. Social capital is not only an agent- and utility-driven Rolodex concept of social connections, one that the individual carries around in a backpack to access as she or he sees fit. It is the distorted product of the ontological and methodological postulates of utilitarianism, which treat relationships (that cannot be owned or privat-ized) as if they were market economies.

Both rational choice theory and modern economics define the funda-mental unit of social analysis as the intentionality, choice, and purposeful-ness of individual agents. But the postulate that all social and political analysis must be built on microfoundations has two overwhelming difficulties: one is the long-standing difficulty of the externalities that result from rational actions applied to public goods; the other is the problem of basing a theory of causal mechanisms on the unobservable quality of a mental state. Both of these problems stem from the postulate that the individual agent's mind, and consequent behavior, is the foundational a priori of social life. This has the effect of treating the social world as if it were a market. Perhaps it is precisely this incoherence and contradictory dynamics that endows social capital with its remarkable ideational power and its promiscuity.

The social approach to society is one with an infrastructure built on the practices and performances of social membership. Social membership is practice-driven, not agent-driven. It is not composed of trust, the foundational postulate of rational choice theory's approach to the social, because trust is a characteristic exhibited by individuals. *Relationships don't trust, agents do (or do not)*. Relationality makes the foundational unit of analysis the dyad, never individual mental states or an agent's investment decision-choices. The numerous voluntary associations that Skocpol (2003) and others have shown to be thickly distributed throughout much of U.S. history as well as the modern university faculty are examples of relational bodies driven by membership practices, not by trust (R. Collins 1979).

The Struggle for the Soul of the Social: Sociology and Economics

As social capital fills so many intellectual and political needs, it is no surprise that, as almost all the literature on the subject complains, there exists no single definition. Nonetheless, all seem to agree that social capital is, by virtue of the term capital, something that produces value; by virtue of the term social, it is value that is in some way generatively connected not to standard market value (as in mainstream neoclassical economic theory), nor to state-expenditure value (as in Keynesian theory), but to something distinctively social. In fact, it is neither Coleman, the rational choice theorist, nor Becker (1990), the self-designated "imperialist" economist, but Pierre Bourdieu, the sociologist, who should be credited with the first fully developed theory of social capital.

The Protean Shape of Social Capital: Pierre Bourdieu

In "The Forms of Capital" (1986), Bourdieu addresses the types of capital, cultural and symbolic, that he was already well-known for having made the central theoretical elements of his theory of class reproduction, especially in the educational system. To expand the theory, Bourdieu introduced the *fungibility* of capital: the argument that market value and economic power, while always produced by capital, are not necessarily produced by standard monetary or economic capital. Just as likely, it is the cultural or symbolic capital of prestige and power that is generating value.

In a paradoxical response to his own success with cultural and symbolic capital, Bourdieu feared that too much attention to discourse and culture threatened to efface the reality of actual market power. In an effort to navigate a delicate balance between economism and "culturalism," he thus added social to his other forms of capital. Although he was explicit that the concept of social capital was still distinct from economic capital, he used the idea to capture the real economic value produced by nonmarket social connections and relations. The family was his primary exemplar, but the social connections holding corporations together also demonstrated the value-laden resources produced by group membership cooperation and coordination: "Social capital is the aggregate of the actual or potential resources which are linked to possession of a durable network. . . . The volume of the social capital possessed by a given agent thus depends on the size of the network of connections he can effectively mobilize and the volume of the capital . . . possessed by a given agent, or even by the whole set of agents to whom he is connected" (Bourdieu 1986, 248–249).

This succinct definition reveals much about Bourdieu's place in the social capital genealogy. It also suggests much about his virtual disappearance from the current literature on the subject. Bourdieu's short-lived influence in the field of social capital is, on one level, straightforward: he simply didn't focus on or theorize about social capital at any great depth. Instead, he turned back to a deeper exploration of symbolic capital, on the one hand and, on the other, to a direct assault on the power of economic and financial capital in the hegemony of neoliberalism (Bourdieu 1998). Although the term plays a significant role in *Distinction* (1979/1984), he nonetheless never produced a body of social capital literature comparable to these other kinds of capital, and it is these for which he will be primarily remembered.

But there are other, more significant reasons for the "missing" influence of Bourdieu. Unlike any of the social capital theorists to follow, Bourdieu's interest in social capital, from the earliest books on, was to synthesize phenomenological and structural analysis. His Marxist roots spurred him to explain the reproduction of class power, and he found social capital useful for this purpose. At the same time, his commitment to phenomenology ensured that agential analysis would be as important as that of class structure. Bourdieu pioneered this mix of structure and agency as interrelated poles of a single theoretical approach. The conceptual apparatus he used to do so was his term *habitus*, where structure and agency are always in mutual play. In this Bourdieu radically differed from all the social capital theorists to follow, indeed from the very utilitarianism with which he has so often been wrongly associated.

To be fair, however, Bourdieu makes getting right his use of social capital not at all simple. In the above quotation, for example, where he uses some form of the term "possession" three times in a five-line statement, his social capital seems eminently compatible with utilitarianism. The possessor, moreover, is a "given agent," or a "whole set of agents," for whom the "volume" of social capital, and thus its potential value, is determined by the "size" of her or his network of connections. This begins to sound suspiciously like a "Rolodex theory" of social capital.

The problem arises from viewing social capital apart from Bourdieu's master concept of habitus. He integrates the two points beyond the straightforward ownership of social capital and instead theorizes that you are "owned," that is, possessed, by social capital as much as you own it. He differs from utilitarianism, according to Bourdieu himself, not just because he links actors and structures; it is also because he doesn't theorize agency and strategy in the utilitarian sense of utility maximization and intentional choice. Bourdieu's agents, rather, are *social actors* who both act and are acted upon. And their actions are as much driven by the unconscious and their habits of practices.

In the end, Bourdieu's social capital is a great distance from the dominant utilitarian and rational choice approach. And if he has been read by some as too economistic in his use of language, he certainly compensates by his numerous and explicit critiques of the very notion of agential ownership that he sometimes appears to be embracing (Bourdieu 1986). Does this explain why today's social capital theorists have mysteriously forgotten their debts to one of sociology's greatest thinkers of the twentieth century? It's hard to know. James Coleman himself said explicitly that his notion differed from Bourdieu's insofar as Bourdieu was on the side of the "underdog," Coleman's semiarticulate way of pointing to Bourdieu's Marxist and structuralist influence, without which no class can be called an underdog. At the end of the day, it is most commonly believed that Bourdieu's ideas were not incorporated more broadly because he did not separate his mainly structural analysis of inequality from his own political commitments. After all, the disappearance of Bourdieu's social capital followed directly in the wake of the rise to prominence of the complementary forces of Becker and Coleman.

Sociology and Social Capital

For most sociologists, social capital refers simply to the value inherent in the networks and/or norms (values) that shape the quality and quantity of a society's social interactions. With the qualifying terms "networks and norms" always paired, it appears that even in this minimalist definition there is an internal contradiction. A network is a structure of relationships irreducible to its individual components. Network theory, which has contributed mightily to the growth and appeal of social capital, is fundamentally relational, and much of its own growth is a product of its opposition to methodological individualisms of all stripes. From this perspective, social capital is not just an aggregate of the individuals and institutions that underpin a society, it is the relational glue that holds them together.

The sociological concept of norms, by contrast, is a social psychological and culturalist approach to social organization. Variably associated with the Parsonian "political culture" paradigm of the 1960s, modernization theory, and the quantitative study of "empirical democracy," the approach focuses on the psychological values that citizens hold with respect to a host of measures of political cultural attitudes toward political and socioeconomic life (Somers 1995a). Using a normative yardstick modeled exclusively on an idealized Anglo-U.S. political culture, only certain measures of political norms added up to a "healthy" society. These include belief in democratic pluralism (not democratic outcomes but procedural neutrality), in modern industrial capitalism and its ancillary technologies of progress (Fordism), in the transcendence of all forms of traditionalism (familialism, clientalism, and nationalism), and in "the end of ideology" and class conflict. In these empirical studies of democracy, it was the summation of these values that bore the entire burden of explaining whether societies were deemed healthy and modern or potentially totalitarian and authoritarian.

Like social capital theory more generally, this norm-centric approach diverts attention away from economic inequalities, unemployment, race and gender discrimination, and public sphere activities and toward aggregates of individual values—the social capital—held by social groups. The incompatibility of the network and norms–based version of social capital is hard to reconcile. The latter presupposes a methodological individualism not only at odds with network analysis; it is also one that brings it perilously close to economics.

The Economists

Although the giants of mainstream academic economics (e.g., Arrow 2000; Akerlof 1984; Solow 2000) have criticized social capital vigorously, there are those who find it eminently compatible with the discipline's foundational precepts. From what Glaeser, Laibson, and Sacerdote (2002) call the "economic approach," the sociological method violates the very logic of capital, namely, its methodological individualism. Accordingly, they develop a "model of optimal individual investment decisions" (F438) and explicitly oppose it to "group-based analyses, which emphasize institutions, norms, conventions, social preferences, and aggregate/group outcomes rather than the investment decisions of individual actors" (F438). Their definition of social capital equally rejects anything sociological, building instead on a modified version of human capital theory with its incentive-driven and agent-centric understanding of market optimality: "Social capital [is] a person's social characteristics—including social skills, charisma, and the size of his Rolodex—which enables him to reap market and non-market returns from interactions with others. As such, individual social capital might be seen as the social component of human capital" (F438).[16]

The economic approach thus simply expands Becker's (1975, 1976, 1993) original human capital theory to include skills oriented to other people; personal skills, educational achievement, and individual character attributes (e.g., work discipline) are made the main source of responsibility for the success or failure of optimal market outcomes.[17]

Information-Theoretic Economics

A different definition of social capital derives from the recent disciplinary "revolution" of information-theoretic economics associated primarily with Joseph Stiglitz (1989, 1994, 2000). Social capital, from this perspective, is composed of the nonmarket relationships that individuals bring to bear to cope with the inevitable risks of market imperfections associated with asymmetrical knowledge between contracting agents (Stiglitz 1989). Strictly speaking, the very virtues of the information-theoretic conception of social capital prevent it from being considered an exclusively economic approach. Like Becker's theories of how the economic can be extended to explain social behavior, Stiglitz's incorporation of social variables as en-dogenous to market behavior violates the "rules" of mainstream neoclassi-cism, with its strict boundaries between endogenous market preferences and exogenous social context. Both are more properly grouped with the rational choice/utilitarian approach in which social capital refers to the aggregate of social control behaviors that individuals use to address nega-tive market externalities, especially those associated with public goods (e.g., Coleman 1989). Positive market externalities, by extension, are also a product of social capital, in this case not merely aggregate sanctions but, most important, the value generated by strong principles of trust among individuals (Fukuyama 1995a; Gambetta 1987, 1988; Dasgupta and Seragel-din 1999; Pharr and Putnam 2000; Åberg 2003).

The Neoutilitarians: Economic "Imperialism" at Play in the Site of the Social

Despite their common interest in social capital, the information-theoretic economists differ substantially from the real revolutionaries of social capi-tal theory. These are a distinct interdisciplinary breed of social scientists-cum-economists, public intellectuals, and policy wonks one could also dub the rational choice neoutilitarians (the academic school). Coleman and Becker, sociologist and economist, respectively, have done more than any others to advance rational choice's utilitarian principle of analyzing all of society as if it were a market. At its analytic core neoutilitarianism is built squarely on the foundations of the neoclassical utility-maximizing rational actor. Where it differs from standard economics, however, is in the reach of analytic scope to which it applies these foundational principles, one that transgresses the firm boundaries between the economic and the social set by the neoclassical paradigm (Becker 1976, 1986, 1990, 1995, 1997, 2000).

In a radical challenge to that paradigm, rational choice utilitarians extend the postulate of utility-maximizing human action to the entire social and political universe. In so doing, they "violate" the exacting rules established by the discipline more than a century ago that mandate the proper scope of investigation to a strictly bounded definition of the eco-nomic. In going off the disciplinary reservation, however, the neoutilitari-ans are going forward to the past; their approach is no less than an explicit embrace of the eighteenth- and nineteenth-century epistemological re-gime of classical utilitarianism, the most capacious approach to society ever claimed by a single theoretical tradition. For them, the work of social capital is an imperial project (Becker 1990, 39).

Eighteenth- and nineteenth-century utilitarianism was not a single discipline but an entire moral philosophy. Ridiculous would have been the idea that they should limit their analyses to the boundaries of the "market." For the very hallmark of utilitarianism was its claim that the self-regulating laws of nature drive not only the market but also society as a whole. Society was to be treated as if it were a market (Bell 1981; Malthus 1803/1992; K. Polanyi 1944/2000).

It was not until the 1870s that utilitarianism was cut down to size by what we now recognize as neoclassical economics. Only then did the marginalist revolution for the first time establish strictly defined limits to the proper scope of economic analysis. A Rubicon was laid down between the outside, the noneconomic terrain of the sociological, historical, or anthropological others, and the inside, the terrain of the economy proper, where the operative principles of market equilibrium and the origins of utility-driven preferences are treated as given: "What most economists would classify as *non-economic problems* are precisely those problems *which are incapable of being analyzed with the marginalist paradigm*" (Heilbroner and Milberg 1995, 7, emphasis added).

The marginalist revolution was the symbolic catalyst for years of sociological exile in the "wilderness of exogeneity" and decades of sociological *ressentiment* toward economists. Exiled from the terrain of power, sociologists duly turned their attention to the social detritus, the "nuts and the sluts," the non-utility-maximizers. But a small faction was not ready to walk away without a fight for recognition and inclusion. Economic sociologists launched a long-suffering sociological guerrilla war from without, shooting missiles across the bow in the form of intellectually indignant theoretical assaults: What about the *social?* Where do preferences come from? What about embeddedness? and What about "the noncontractual basis of contracts"? the sociologists demanded to know. Such assaults were brushed off as so many flies by the powerfully situated elephant of modern economics, and insult was only added to injury with Friedman's (1953a) influential reinforcement of the outside/inside boundary regime as set forth in his classic article on positivist economics.[18]

But we should all know by now that the favorite play of the gods is to inflict the most perverse of all curses upon the yearners—namely, to give people exactly what they want. Thus, in the last third of the twentieth century a new breed of economist was born in Gary Becker, one dedicated to violating the marginalist rules of the game in favor of an entirely new set of rules. These mandated that economists pay *a lot* of attention to that social world outside the previously insulated sphere of the strictly economic. After first converting the sociological topics of education and skills into human capital theory, Becker quickly enlarged his scope of attention to everything social, from drugs to sex and marriage, and so "invented" social capital: "Social capital [is] crucial not only for understanding addictions... *but also for most other behavior in the modern world, and probably in the distant past as well*" (1996, 6, emphasis added). And lest anyone doubt the literalness of Becker's reference to "most other behavior," *Accounting for Tastes* (1996) reveals that no less than everything from jogging to government propaganda, with child abuse and deception falling somewhere in between, fit under Becker's rubric of issues to be explained by human and social capital, and utilitarianism more generally (see also Becker 1995, 1997).

This was a project Becker proudly called one of "economic imperialism" (Becker 1990, 39): "From a methodological viewpoint, the aim ... is to show how [what] is considered important in the sociological and anthropological literature can be usefully analyzed *when incorporated into the framework provided by economic theory*" (194). Once colonized by the imperial power, what had been recognizable as sociological variables (such as power and politics) and thus exogenous to the market were now reframed to be newly analyzed and made intelligible by treating them as if they were market variables. Becker's arguments for social capital's breathtakingly wide reach are mirrored by the spectrum of concerns for which scholars, politicians, public intellectuals, and institutions have found it beneficial. Thus, for example, the World Bank uses the social capital concept to demonstrate that social cohesion is critical for societies to prosper economically and for development to be sustainable (www.worldbank .org/poverty/scapital/whatsc.htm).[19]

Neoutilitarian social capital theory has thus cycled back through time to once again display the startling hubris of classical utilitarianism's long-rejected expansive reach. In addition to physical, natural, financial, and human capital, economists and rational choice theorists have coupled the social in an intimate embrace with capital. Whereas the prevailing neoclassical orthodoxy has long distained and dismissed the social, neoutilitarians recognize the far greater advantage in hijacking the sociological paradigm and commandeering it into an appendage to the market. For this, social capital is the perfect Trojan horse.

Social Capital, Sociology, and the Trojan Horse

Sociology is besotted with social capital. But why do we really believe that social capital truly represents something innovative and new? Of course not; anyone who's read Durkheim knows otherwise. Rather, it is because of the deeper meaning and the sociological accomplishment we attribute to the success of the social capital concept: the embrace of the social seems to embody the surrender by economists to the constitutive role of society, of social relations, of social networks. Society has at last been anointed with the status of a valued source of streaming utility; after so many years of exile in the wilderness of exogeneity, it appears that society has suddenly become the economists' great conceptual hero (even savior) in the task of absorbing, correcting, and negotiating market imperfections and externalities.

Social capital thus signals the consummation of a long-desired marriage between sociology and economics. Alas, this marriage has more the whiff of a romanticized desideratum than a real union between equals, for there is a glaring imbalance in the distribution of desire and power between two putative lovers. Whereas economists and utilitarians have a purely instrumental and, well, utilitarian relationship to their social partners, sociologists are breathtakingly, disproportionately, and recklessly infatuated. Social capital seems to have become a totem animating a bundle of deep-seated desires about the implications of its success: sociologists are convinced that its meteoric rise to fame both registers and valorizes the currency of the social. Indeed, in the headiest of moments, the success of the social capital concept makes it appear that economists now recognize market embeddedness, that the social has at last been invited into that privileged circle of market endogeneity, that it is now necessary for market efficiency, for sustained market-driven global economic growth, even for successful capitalist democratization projects. This appears to be the ultimate validation: economists are actually using the social capital concept in their own work. Sociologists have achieved their deepest desire of all: the triumph of recognition.

Social capital's very success belies all our fantasies. Nothing better illustrates the wrongheadedness of the infatuation than Homer's tale of the Trojan horse. Beguiled by the economists' gift of a Trojan horse appearing to bear a long overdue recognition of social relations, sociologists have embraced that which may well undermine our fundamental commitments. We believe that we have at last convinced the economists to "sociologize" the market model. In truth, social capital signals not the sociologizing of the market model but a marketizing and privatizing of the social. To continue this love affair with social capital threatens sociology's very identity: the irreducible relationality at the heart of the social.

Robert Putnam: The Promise and the Disappointment

I turn to the work of the political scientist, Clinton advisor, and CSPAN, *New York Times*, and *People* magazine celebrity Robert Putnam. While Bourdieu, Becker, and Coleman may have been the theoretical pioneers of the revival of the social capital concept, there is no question but that Putnam triggered its real takeoff to fame among the broad public of policy intellectuals. It was he who brought it into circulation as a solution to what he and others saw as long-standing empirical problems of modernizing development in southern Europe and the developing world, as well as for the "malaise" of civil society in the United States.

Robert Putnam first impressed the public intelligentsia and political classes with his now famous articles on "Bowling Alone" (1993, 1995, 1996), in which he argued that current ills in the United States were caused by a precipitous decline in the life of civil society, specifically, in the sharp drop in the character of associational life, in communal trust and neighborly cooperation, and in civic commitments more generally. But true academic stardom first came to Putnam with his adventure as "Tocqueville in Italy" in his 1993 *Making Democracy Work*, a comparative historical study of Italian regional governance coauthored with several Italian colleagues over the course of the previous twenty years. In this study Putnam's aim was to compare the causal significance of different variables in "making democracy work." His focus was on a series of nationwide institutional reforms that were aimed toward sustained modernizing development, greater governmental transparency, and increased democratic participation (thus the elimination of corruption, cronyism, and patronage). More than a decade after their implementation, the outcomes were puzzling: real developmental success and genuinely reformed local governance (measured by quantifying civic practices) were in evidence, but exclusively in the northern Italian regions, and not in the southern.

Using macroanalytic comparisons, Putnam tested several explanatory hypotheses. Because the institutional reforms were nationwide and regionally uniform, he could effectively rule out any causal role for the Italian state and its local political institutions in explaining the regional variations. More generally, Putnam interpreted the defeat of this hypothesis to exclude any influence of political power tout court. That led to his now famous, and controversial, finding: the success of the northern regions could be attributed almost exclusively to their singular four-hundred-year histories of deeply embedded horizontal ties and community associations characterized by attitudes of trust and normative reciprocity.

As the embodiment of social capital, it was these horizontal ties and norms of trust that served as the lifeblood of democratic civic practices. Thus, social capital became the analytic and theoretical foundation of a new social theory of democracy.[20]

Crossing the pond to the late-twentieth-century United States, Putnam turns to what he defines as a quarter-century of increasing malaise in U.S. civil society. Once again he concludes that it is social capital that explains this phenomenon, but in this case it is due to social capital's dramatic decline and virtual disappearance over the past several decades of U.S. history, most famously manifested in the decline of bowling league membership, church choirs, community barbeques, and other kinds of associational decay and community involvement. Among other empirical highlights, he finds that the number of Americans who attend public meetings on community or school issues dropped between 1973 and 1993 by more than a third (R. Putnam 1995, 68). Here Putnam gives a lengthier exposition on the nature and limits to what can justifiably fall under the rubric of social capital. Included are horizontal social ties in local communities driven by cultural values and attitudes of trust and reciprocity among "joiners": bowling leagues, neighborhood barbeques, church choirs, the Girl Scouts. Explicitly excluded, just as in Italy, is any causal role for the decline not just of social capital but also of such politically embedded programs as federally funded job training, entitlement rights, and community social programs, as well as participation in politics, political parties, and political citizenship institutions more generally, and, most alarming, of the power and membership strength of trade unions. Indeed, neither the exercise of power, nor even basic struggles over the institutions of rights and civil liberties, have any causal significance for Putnam's findings.

As many have noted, moreover, not all relational entities are positive and healthy phenomena. What others have called the "dark side of social capital" has all too often been exhibited in fascist youth associations and Nazi brown shirts, in today's skinheads, urban gangs, and populist and racist evangelical churches, among others (Portes 1998). Before any sanguine theories of social capital continue on their present tack, empirical work is necessary to determine the conditions lending themselves to this dark side of social capital. Indeed, it is increasingly clear that excluding the issues of power and politics from the concept of social capital is tantamount to eliminating half of the human record of history and society.

But Putnam goes even further. Not only are politics, power, and the condition of the public sphere missing in his explanation for the condition of U.S. society; so too is any attention to the dramatic restructurings of the economy and the market over the same period of time (e.g., the privatization of public goods and services, the radical restructuring of firms and corporate downsizing, newly restrictive labor market rules and regulations, the systematic weakening of trade union institutional power). "Bowling Alone" (1995; 2000), the canonical text for the theory and empirical application of social capital, has summarily dismissed as causal factors for the poverty of civil society sociology's usual suspects, most prominently the collapse of the welfare state and its social safety nets, the neoliberal restructuring and privatization of the economy, and a newly regressive tax system that has been systematically shifting the tax burden from wealth to work.

Note the curious definitional narrowing that Putnam's use of social capital exhibits. From Becker's promiscuous vision in which social capital encompasses virtually any generative nonmarket phenomena to Putnam's version, excluded are not only all the personal behaviors that so preoccupy Becker, but also the entire spectrum of those institutions of governance, rights, and power itself, without which civil society could not be sustained against the corrosive effects of unregulated market forces. Putnam makes these exclusions of power, politics, and rights not merely as empirical findings of this or that case but as the very essence of the theoretical work that social capital has been invented to do. The weakened condition of citizenship rights and political participation, a degraded public sphere, and the dictates of market forces have all been taken off the agenda in accounting for the recent problems in U.S. society. Instead, we are implored to go bowling.

Robert Putnam is a committed civic democrat in search of the foundations for social justice, for whom building a democratic egalitarian civic culture is a consuming passion. He is explicitly not an apologist for the neoliberal project. In this commitment, however, I believe the use of the social capital concept is misapplied and wrongheaded. The antistatism, antirights, and anti-institutionalism underlying his version of social capital are indefensible. Accepting social capital demands an embrace of market principles extended to the arenas of social life where utilitarian ethics can do nothing but corrode and sabotage democratic goals. To achieve the practices and institutions of trust, communication, and reciprocity that the social capital concept attempts to represent requires abandoning its constitutive postulates of localism, acquisition, individualism, the market model of efficiency, the fictitious commodification of people, and the radical autonomy from power and politics. Success with these revisions, however, would leave us not with an improved version of social capital; instead, it would return us to the primacy and the irreducibility of the social where, ideally, we started in the first place. And this would take us back to the conceptual site and the normative and political ideal of civil society.

From Civil Society to Social Capital

This story begins with the decade up to and including the fall of the Berlin Wall in 1989. Although most would agree that it was catalyzed by Solidarity trade union workers in the Gdansk shipyards of Poland, interpretations of the remarkable episode are multiple. For the left, the fall of the Wall was the accomplishment of a new civil society movement, a launching ground for self-organized bodies of political activists committed to autonomy from state coercion in tandem with increasing democratic participation (Arato 1981, 1993, 2000; J. L. Cohen 1985, 1999; J. L. Cohen and Arato 1992; Habermas 1990; Isaac 1996; Keane 1994; Kennedy 1991, 1994, 2002). For neoliberals and conservatives, however, it signaled what Fukuyama (1992) famously labeled "the end of history" in his best-selling book of the same title. *The End of History* was a story and a prediction about the outcome to the decades-long duel to the death between capitalism and communism that had dominated the globe for the previous half century. In Fukuyama's story the fall of the Wall represented the triumph of free market capitalism, a victory over and against the *etatism* loathed by neoliberals, conservatives, and progressive democrats alike.

In retrospect, while there was unambiguous mobilization for civil and political rights, it is not at all clear what alternative economic system the anticommunist movements had envisioned. For Fukuyama and his "end of history" protégés, however, there was absolute clarity. His was a conceptual and political landscape limited to a single Manichaean dichotomy: the free versus the unfree, good versus evil. The fall of one meant the absolute triumph of the other. This was the ultimate meaning of the end of history; with the end of communism there was only one possible future for the ex-communist world: a laissez-faire society. Never again would history allow capitalist nations to shift their centers of gravity from market to state, from freedom to tyranny, from a nation of personal responsibility to one of moral hazards. History had in effect stopped with the end of Eastern European and Soviet communism. Any talk of market rules and regulations would now be outside the realm of thinkable rational discourse. The end of history created a new political culture now ruled by what Soros

(1998, 2000) calls market fundamentalism and Stiglitz (1994, 1998, 2002, 2003) "the Washington consensus," but that is most commonly known as neoliberalism and/or neoconservatism.

The pronouncement that history had ended, however, was more normative and ideological than empirically sound. For while history had in fact witnessed the defeat of state tyranny with the end of communism, Fukuyama's concurrent prediction of the future had no empirical model to build on. Never in history had any societies undergone the transition from communism to capitalism. There were, of course, no how-to models of democratization for those societies that had had minimal, if any, institutional frameworks for administering the rule of law and mechanisms of democracy before becoming communist. The absence of such models of transition thus made the end of history's view of the future the triumph of pure *theory*—an abstract model-driven commitment to remake the world in the image of market fundamentalism, yet one that was not based on any existing successful transformation from a communist to a fully functioning market economy. To make matters worse, the "designer-capitalists" of the 1990s were so driven by antistatist ideology that they stubbornly refused even to draw lessons from what was the closest analogue to the contemporary situation: the Marshall Plan's stunning success at nation building in Germany and Japan in the immediate aftermath of World War II (Glasman 1998). Instead, it was financiers and bankers at the IMF and the World Bank who made the global decisions about how market-driven shock therapy would be applied throughout Eastern Europe and Russia, indeed toward much of the developing world.

As Karl Polanyi (1944/2001) so brilliantly demonstrated over half a century ago, however, there is only one problem with the marketization of everything: it is impossible to achieve without threatening to destroy the fabric of society. Nurturing markets as part of a healthy social order is something very different from the dream of *governance* by the self-regulating market mechanism, or what Polanyi called the "stark utopia" of a "market society." The rest of the story is thus as familiar as it would have been predictable to any student of economic sociology and history. Absent the complex, sometimes invisible rules in which successful markets are necessarily embedded, the neoliberal model of governance by self-regulating markets revealed its inherent weaknesses. It was not long before shock therapy gave way to social, political, and economic chaos. Profound international difficulties began in Thailand in July 1997, spread to Malaysia, Indonesia, and South Korea, and in 1998 to Russia and Brazil. As safety-net institutions that were once taken for granted began to disappear, the new ex-communist capitalist nations succumbed to currency crises and sky-rocketing poverty. Without any constitutional institutional foundations, it was not democracy but the mafia that took power in Russia. Soon there was a resurgence of pro-communist sentiment in parts of the ex-communist world (Holmes 1997; M. Kennedy 2002; Maier 1997; Soros 1998, 2000).

Internally, in the United States and the United Kingdom, neoliberals used the end of history thesis to facilitate dismantling the welfare state and privatizing the increasingly degraded public sphere. As both cause and consequence of a larger culture of commodification and marketized citizenship, these in turn became the fodder for crises of public goods, increasing poverty, and spiraling crime rates. The corporate need for greater market flexibility in the interest of economic growth turned out to have been a code for the dissolution of the New Deal and Great Society social contracts. Clearly, the utopian dream that the self-regulating market could be the governing mechanism of the future had yet to become the end of history. Market failures and externalities, excess volatility and transaction costs have proved to be the norm and not the exception for today's global economies (Stiglitz 1998, 2002).

At this point, market fundamentalism faced a crossroads: How to solve these problems of externalities and diminishing public goods while continuing to privatize? Perhaps shock therapy was not working in quite the way the end of history had predicted. But in a zero-sum world of state versus market, there are no gray zones; any hint of return to the Keynesianism that had for so long saved capitalism from its own excesses would have betrayed the ideals of the new personal responsibility and independence from the state so valorized by the neoconservatives. Of course, there were, and are, plenty of societies—all of Western Europe, for example—that had never succumbed to the either/or of market versus state but flourished successfully as social democracies. For the market fundamentalist project, however, even the most modest of welfare states meant no less than tyranny and unfreedom—even under the moniker of a mixed economy. In this context, how to address the market's problems without turning back to the state became an urgent question.

Initially, the solution was to cling even more fervently to market fundamentalism on the grounds that meddling politicians had prevented it from having had the opportunity to be fully implemented. So stubbornly did neoliberals cling to absolute belief in their model that even in those countries with successful economies the IMF started to withhold loans until there was a commitment to "economic restructuring" (e.g., Mc-Michael 1998; Miller 1997). This in turn led to a rejection of any evidence that threatened to disconfirm the model; the practice was to save the model at all costs while blaming "reality" for the failings of the new world of marketization. So it was with the failure of Long-Term Capital Management, the giant hedge fund that made multibillion-dollar bets based on the complex models of the Russian transition built by their analysts. In a stunning inversion of the mantra of modern epistemology—theory proposes, data disposes—Martin Gruber, Nomura Professor of Finance at NYU's Stern School, remarked, "A series of events occurred that were outside the norm. . . . These catastrophes happen. The fault isn't with the models" (Morgensen and Neinstein 1998, 1). When challenged by the limits of its propositions, in other words, it was not neoliberalism but *reality* that took the blows for the failure of the world to conform to "the [model's] norms."

It is not clear, however, how long reality was going to lie down and take the blame for the failures of a "virtual" unhistorical model of governance. In a repetition of much of the past two centuries, the either/or of market versus state was proving inadequate to the task of achieving its own goals. Then a deus ex machina appeared in the new vocabulary of social capital. Not only was it a concept that relied on methodological individualism, it was also one built on a foundational antistatism. But I get ahead of myself. To explain how neoliberalism found its way to social capital we have to return to the struggle against communism and the rediscovery of civil society.

Enter Civil Society

Civil society is that sphere of social organization made famous by its political revival in Eastern Europe and South America's anti-authoritarian insurgencies of the 1980s (Arato 1981; Barber 1996; Calhoun 1993; J. L. Cohen 1999; Cohen and Rogers 1995; Ehrenberg 1999; Foley and Edwards 1996; Geremek 1992). Civil society, however, is an "essentially contested concept." The Tocquevillean-inspired view of civil society as a third sphere between market and state has always been rivaled by that of classical liberalism's. While both approaches pose civil society in sharp opposition to the state, for liberalism the Manichaean dichotomy of public versus private overdetermines any gesture toward a genuine third sphere. In a bivalent conceptual landscape of only private and public, market and state, civil society can only be part of the private side of the Rubicon that divides public from private (Somers 1995b, 1999).[21]

Following Locke, who first invented the idea of civil society in the seventeenth century as a robust, self-sufficient social entity and counter-vailing source of political authority and property exchange from that of the state, late-twentieth-century market fundamentalists unambiguously identified civil society as the "cultural" dimension of the private sphere. Many conservatives were attracted to this cultural view of civil society as an alternative and antidote to what they characterized as the moral degeneration caused by years of dependence on the handouts of the public welfare state and the excesses of a rights-laden political culture (Huntington 1975; M. Crozier et al. 1975; Pharr and Putnam 2000). Their vision of civil society makes it a facilitator of the market and a cultural bulwark against any resurgence of the "nanny state" (and of the perversions of moral character and moral hazards it encouraged). It thus became important as both an empirical and a normative site of private personal responsibility and moral autonomy. As such, conservatives hoped that civil society would be a critical mechanism in the effort to shift responsibility for social problems away from the state and onto the shoulders of civil society's "little platoons" of family, church, and community (Berger and Neuhaus 1996; Fukuyama 1992, 1995a, 1995b).[22]

At first, civil society served these needs well. But it shortly became clear that the concept of civil society, like all essentially contested concepts, could not be owned by any single interpretation. For one thing, there was the testy little problem of origins. The Polish Solidarity movement that had contributed so much to the rebirth of the civil society idea was, after all, not one of Edmund Burke's traditional little platoons; it was, of all things, a trade union. And even if some of its leaders became avid free marketers and antistatist politicians, conservatives could not sit comfortably with its trade union roots and its rejection of the neoliberal and neoconservative social and economic projects.

With the success of the Eastern European revolutions against communism, moreover, civil society had increasingly become a rallying cry for the new social movements of the democratic and communitarian left. These civil society social movements, while they invoked their independence from the state, were no allies of the U.S. or even the British versions of neoliberalism (Dean 2004). To be sure, history had given good reasons to renounce statism, but creating a market-governed laissez-faire society was no more of an attraction. For the political left, civil society was not captive to the limits of a public/private dichotomy but instead challenged the hegemony of *both* the coercion of the communist and administrative states *and* the aggressive competition of the global marketplace (e.g., Arato 2000; J. L. Cohen and Arato 1992; J. Keane 1994; M. Kennedy 1991; Somers

1999, 2001). Gdansk, Solidarity, and the rediscovery of civil society had become clarion calls not merely for freedom from state coercion but also for the *nonmarket* values of solidarity, reciprocity, horizontal ties, participatory civic values, and social justice. There was one more problem with the civil society movements of the 1990s. While they rejected the coercive tyrannical communist states, they differed radically from the neoconservatives in that their political project was deeply motivated by the normative ideals of democratic participation in the state, popular *political* empowerment, and the empowerment of rights-oriented social movements (Rosenberg and Post 2002). While fully embracing the institutions of liberal democratic societies (these were no Marxist movements) in the model of the Gdansk-based Solidarity movement where it was most famously invoked, civil society thus signified both the empirical and the normative grounds for cultivating democratic associations of rights-claiming citizens staunchly committed to influencing state policies toward more egalitarian and social justice policies (Arato 1981, 2000; J. L. Cohen and Arato 1992).

From Civil Society to Social Capital

It is hard to know what direction the political and knowledge culture of civil society would have taken if social capital had not suddenly been made available as a public good. But it was, in large part thanks to the simultaneity of neoconservative, neoliberal, and left-oriented social movements, social capital streams with similar needs. Timing was everything. Just as these different social capital trajectories collided, Robert Putnam's success catapulted the concept of social capital into the political public sphere, where it became available as an epistemological public good, and put its inherent powers into circulation. Across the ideological spectrum, intellectuals moved quickly. Conservatives, strategically, after first capturing the civil society concept, then tamed it, reframed it, and renamed it. In a truly Pygmalion-like achievement, civil society—the once unruly and unpredictable nurturing ground for the goals, practices, and normative ideals of democratic citizenship—reappeared throughout the 1990s in public and academic discourse as social capital. Quickly appropriating it as social, political, and economic knowledge, neoliberals and neoconservatives alike were able to fully exploit its epistemological powers.

As a public good the capacity of social capital to solve political problems was vast. Above all, it provided an antistatist alternative to civil society. Social capital provided a new political language to explain, justify, and obfuscate the processes by now shifting the burdens of social risk and market externalities from market and state to the personal responsibility of individual families and communities. Quickly appropriating it as social, political, and economic knowledge, neoliberals and neoconservatives alike were able to fully exploit its epistemological powers. From the social rights of the New Deal and Great Society, to the commodified free agents of the 1980s and 1990s, the work of saving capitalism from its own excesses was to be done by the newly discovered gold mine of social capital. In what follows, I parse this work of social capital into four dimensions:

1. Social capital provides a nonstate solution to the externalities that the market is not able (or willing) to solve. Call this the function of saving capitalism from its own excesses.

2. Social capital shifts the expectations of citizenship from rights-claims to the obligations of duties.

3. Social capital provides a nonstate alternative to what conservatives defined as the entitlement-driven welfare state and the excesses of rights claims. Call this the cultural sphere of moral regulation, self-help, and personal responsibility, or the reconstitution of citizenship.

4. Finally, social capital provides a spatial equivalent to civil society. Community is the nonstate site in which the relationships of social capital are confined.

The site of community

Let us start with the last of the four. The great value of the term "civil society" is that it refers to a real *place* in the topography of social life. Social capital, by contrast, does not signify any particular domain; it is inherently placeless. To overcome this deficiency, social capital has been coupled with community, a concept with a long and noble place in the political land-scape.[23]

The well-known phrase "It takes a village to raise a child" expresses nicely the relationship between social capital and community. The words most often evoke the normative values of more relational and socially shared view of parenting practices than those of the standard individualis-tic view. Yet its emphasis on the village as the appropriate site of conscien-tious parenting is just as strongly a *negative* injunction against expecting public support from the state. That this collective self-help approach to child work takes place in a village explicitly signals that this responsibility is not free-floating and universal but contained in a particular local com-munity. Traditional communities are seen to encourage respect for hard work, self-sufficiency, the values of the market, and distain for the state. Instead of doing something macropolitical about inadequately funded public schools, for example, "It takes a *village* to raise a child" implicitly blames parents and the community: for their lack of personal responsibility in participating in school events, for their inadequate attention to the child's homework, perhaps even for not taking on the responsibility of home schooling—in short, for their insufficient exercise of social capital. The aphorism could easily be social capital's own clarion call as it at once celebrates the (private) community's burden of accountability for child rearing even while, sotto voce, it almost shouts "as opposed to the state and the public."

The first asset for social capital that the site of community provides is thus a negative one: it is that place that everybody knows is *not* the state. The valorization of community for being antistatist and, more generally, anti-entitlement cannot be overstated in the project of redistributing the risks of market society from the market and state to families and communities. In the words of one of its most influential craftsmen, Francis Fukuyama: "If society is not to become anarchic or otherwise ungovernable, then it must be capable of self-government at levels of organization below the State. Such a system depends ultimately not just on law but also on the self-restraint of individuals" (1995a, 357–358).

Fukuyama is one of the best-known U.S. conservatives. But here is the British Labour home secretary, Jack Straw, in his keynote speech to the 1998 Nexus Conference on "Mapping Out the Third Way." "Community and personal responsibility, which have so long been buried in the futile arguments between Left and Right, are at the centre of everything we do. . . . [Therefore] we are literally handing over a huge amount of power to individual citizens and local communities away from the central State" (1998, 18). Note his almost evangelical celebration of community for being *not* the state.

Community as the site of social capital is morally obligated to compensate for the loss of public support and social rights: to provide shelter for the unemployed, the unemployable, and the socially excluded.

From the culture of entitlement to the ethos of self-help
and personal responsibility
Once social capital becomes identified with the particular conceptual terrain of community, the question of social action arises. This is the third dimension of the work of social capital. For conservatives, the great deficiency of civil society was its politically oriented content; the practices of

civil society could not easily be dissociated from a radical democratic ethos, a strong emphasis on participatory citizenship rights, and activist commitments to influence political and state policy (Habermas 1990; Laarman 1995; Merkl and Weinberg 1993). The generative value of social capital is not only that it rejects the state as the locus of social action. It also rejects the state as the source of support, rights, and entitlements. The community is responsible for its own moral and economic viability. This was the driving force behind the successful bipartisan campaign to abolish Aid to Families with Dependent Children on the grounds that the welfare state had perverse effects on moral character, sexual behavior, and the work ethic. As the alternative to the social state, social capital does not cause the culture of dependency and the moral decay associated with welfare.

Social capital requires that people in their churches, their communities, their city councils, their voluntary associations, their Rotary clubs, their women's societies, and their bowling leagues assume local civic duties and personal responsibilities. Its values are those of self-help, moral autonomy, personal responsibility, and collective self-restraint. These evoke Burke's conservative dream of "little platoons" as the foundation of social order, as well as Durkheim's revelation that society survives through moral coercion and normative regulation. Thus, in contrast to the "dutiless rights" of "excessive" citizenship, social capital works through networks of moral control, moral behavioral norms for conduct and interaction, ethical imperatives of self-help and personal responsibility. Here is Amitai Etzioni, the founder of communitarianism and a passionate advocate for social justice: "For a society to be communitarian, much of the social conduct must be 'regulated' by reliance on the moral voice rather than the law, and the scope of the law itself must be limited largely to that which is supported by the moral voice" (1997, 139).

From rights to duties: reinventing citizenship

Perhaps the greatest distinction of all between civil society and social capital is that the duties associated with community activity are not complemented by an equally robust set of rights; thus we arrive at the second dimension of the work of social capital listed earlier. It was the putative *excess of rights* and unrestrained freedoms without the corresponding sense of duties, merit, and personal responsibility that was one of the major catalysts in the search for a site of social life untouched by the state's entitlements (Berger and Neuhaus 1975). Here is Jack Straw again:

The old Left . . . failed to argue against . . . an extension of individual freedom [as] a license to do almost anything, and that *the State existed as some sort of universal great provider, which made no moral judgments regardless of the merits of those who were dependent upon it. . . . it has made rights appear like ready-made consumer items which the state can dispense at will and often for which the "consumer" never need pay.* As the philosopher David Selbourne has written: "In its thrall, the citizen comes to be perceived and treated by the civic order (and its instruments, the state and government) not as a citizen but as a consumer, customer, and bundle of wants; and the citizen, perceiving himself in like fashion, *loses sense of his duties, as a citizen, to himself, his fellows, and the civic order, at worst without sense of honour or shame"* [Selbourne 1994, 70]. . . . This led on to *a culture of dutiless rights—where rights are exercised without due recognition being given to our mutual responsibilities towards each other.* (1998, 6, emphasis added)

Conservative enthusiasm for social capital and the traditional community is thus driven mightily by a shift from rights to duties. In depleting civil society of rights and loading it up with duties, the work of social capital in local communities becomes a peculiarly modern inverted antistatist version of *Leviathan.* Like the absolute political control exercised by the Hobbesian state, the source of social order and community sustenance must shift from the state to social capital and the community. But, just as in *Leviathan,* the Faustian bargain requires that in return for the secure moral values of honor and shame inherent in community regulation, *political rights must be abandoned at the entry.* Social capital insulates the community from the excessive entitlements of the "culture of dependency."

It is one thing, however, to be seduced by the safety of community to give up rights and expectations of the polity. It is something else altogether to define this shift from rights to duties, from the public sphere to the privatized community, "the *essential* act of citizenship." And yet, this is exactly what Britain's Jack Straw says: "In many ways the most important example of our approach is our commitment greatly to extend the idea and practice of volunteering—of people doing something for each other *rather than having the State doing it for them and so diminishing them.* We have described this voluntary activity as '*the essential act of citizenship*'" (1998, 16, cited in N. Rose 2000, 1404; emphasis added).

Social capital thus detaches the "essential act of citizenship" from the institutions of state and political community. Instead, in this reconstituted site of community, the essential acts of citizenship are those in which it is a duty to *donate* one's labor to the stock of social capital because *it is social capital that in turn provides value to the nation's markets.* This is the stuff of citizenship qua social capital—a radically antipolitical, anti-institutional, presocial, stateless and rightless kind of citizenship. Dutiful citizenship demands that we freely contribute our own labor to the project of market fundamentalism. Social capital's redesigned citizenship is driven by the duties of individuals to the market, not by the rights and obligations of public membership; by conditional desert based on merit rather than by human rights and the equality of status; by moral restraints and self-sacrifice rather than the irresponsible license of equitable redistribution (Berger and Neuhaus 1975; Fukuyama 1995a, 1995b; Selbourne 1994; Saegert and Thompson 2001).

If markets fail to solve poverty, environmental problems, persistent unemployment, and the risks of private insurance, there is now another option, not that of the state: a new site of self-help citizenship. In place of welfare, let family and kin "wealth transfers" do the job; they are more efficient anyway (see Durlauf 2002). In place of federally funded policing, let the neighborhood police paid by local taxes do the job. Better yet, let the neighborhood use its own rich reservoir of information capital to be the eyes and ears of social control. In place of environmental regulations, let the community's voluntary civic associations exercise their own normative sanctions against free-riding corporate neighbors. And in place of public school funding, let the PTAs, and especially home schooling, provide the moral and educational guidance so desperately needed by the children (Bowles and Gintis 2002; Orr 1999; N. Lin 2001; Saegert and Thompson 2001; Munch 2002).

Liberated from the "diminishment" of excessive rights and readmitted into the constraints and expectations of community, people are now made accountable through the moral approbation and sanctions—the "naming, blaming, and shaming"—that only friends, neighbors, and communities can inflict to effectively govern behavior.

Saving the market from its externalities and excesses
Trust, self-sacrifice, volunteerism, social control, reciprocal information sharing, indeed, bowling leagues—this is the stuff of social capital (Åberg 2003; R. Putnam 2000, 2002; R. Putnam et al. 1993; J. Coleman 1988/2000): a bundle of voluntary, self-help, nonmarket social practices and non-market values and practices that add up to a fountain of previously un-tapped economic value. Recall that the turn to social capital on the part of

the neoutilitarians was not motivated by assumptions of perfect market equilibrium. Rather, it was their recognition of the market's inevitable limits, externalities, and imperfections that drove them to transgress into sociological fields beyond the traditional bounds of market analysis. Social capital provides a solution to the externalities that the market is not able (or willing) to solve. Call this the function of saving capitalism from its own excesses. The first item on my list of the work of social capital is therefore that of a collective citizen performing the duties of modern citizenship, mopping up the nasty messes generated by neoliberalism's own privatizing reforms. By absorbing the market's costs, social capital paradoxically adds value to the market's stream of utility functions. This is what makes it social *capital*.

Saving the market from its own excesses and limits, it is social capital that is now responsible for coping with unemployment, underemployment, loss of benefits, and low wage jobs—and all without asking the market to pay. Social capital turns citizenship into a form of capital that adds value to the wealth of the nation while preserving property rights and competitive markets. By protecting markets from government interference, social capital turns citizenship into capitalism's savior.

In sum, in our increasingly post-Marshallian world, true citizens take personal responsibility for their own welfare by investing in people and exploiting their friends, neighbors, relatives, fellow church-goers, and, of course, their bowling teams. In the paradoxical new message of a privatized citizenship, the social has been evacuated by an aggregate of purely instrumental connections "owned" by each individual. In this Orwellian world, exercising citizenship requires activating one's own personal stock of social capital by demanding support from others. Here is Jack Straw again: "It [community] asserts our mutual responsibility, our belief in a common purpose. And it also asserts that there is no such 'thing' as society; not in the way in which Mrs. Thatcher claimed, but because society is not a 'thing' external to our experiences and responsibilities. It is us, all of us" (1998, 17, cited in N. Rose 2000, 1395).

Alternative Knowledge

Whether in the hands of social scientists or self-styled imperialist economists, social capital is constituted by choice, duty, responsibility, cooperation, moral and religious values, voluntary labor, and absolute trust in the market—*but devoid of rights*. This sheds light on one of the most consistent absences from the social capital literature, namely, *trade unions*. Yet (in their ideal typical form), one could hardly think of a better normative and empirical exemplar for the kind of associational networks that the social capital concept wants to invoke. To garner the benefits of, say, a successful labor contract, a working person submits to the rules of membership, regardless of whether these rules appeal or are convenient. The rules demand accountability, from which follow the obligations not of access and ownership but of belonging and membership. And from these foundational membership practices flow the capacity to bargain for and act on their hard-won rights to collective power and influence. These in turn require involvement of the state, not its degradation and privatization. Clearly, the social capital concept appears not to be compatible with the irreducibly public and rule-driven infrastructures at the heart of effective trade unions.

Poland's Solidarity, the union of Gdansk ship workers that first came to the world's notice in the early 1980s, exemplifies the empowerment generated by membership's rule-driven practices. Solidarity membership was based on sanctions and obligations, risks, and sacrifices. Yet the union both catalyzed and provided leadership in the struggle against communism. Such extraordinary power was only possible because the workers displayed an overwhelming commitment to act first and foremost as members of a membership-driven entity. Solidarity's demonstration of how to win democratic rights is an example of the difference between social capital's individual choices–driven agency and the kind of agency characteristic of a membership-driven relational network. The union's membership practices were built on repositories of knowledge, skills, and rules that resided in the capacity of the social network to exercise associational power over the preferences and choices, even the "human capital," of individual agents. To be sure, individuals have choices within this relational entity, but they are framed within the rights and the obligations to participate in the union's rule-driven attachments. These are the choices of "voice" in an entity over which no one has ownership rights, and they are the rights of "exit"—knowing that to exit is to lose the inclusionary powers of membership.[24] These make relational networks and the attachments they embody not forms of capital but mechanisms of social belonging, mechanisms necessary to sustain the robust associational bodies that are required for social movements to be effective in their struggles for democratic freedoms. The kind of relationships, in other words, that enabled Solidarity to bring down a tyrannical state.

More generally, the history of market societies suggests that meaningful citizenship practices and durable relationships that are robust, relationally sturdy, reciprocally empowered, and characterized by high degrees of trust depend on deep links to public spheres, the national state, and the rule of law. Democratic practices and social cooperation alike both require a legal apparatus deeply embedded enough into the fabric of everyday life that the law will become constitutive to the infrastructure of membership rules, practices, expectations, and sanctioned obligations (Skocpol 2000, 2003; Somers 1993, 1994). This in turn provides the foundations for a relational body peopled by members, not users or owners. The paradox is that although these are the very conditions that are essential to the survival of the kinds of social relationships that the idea of social capital is meant to capture, they are precisely those that its advocates exclude. The relational networks that the social capital concept wants to evoke cannot be isolated from their social and political environments. Indeed, it is access and linkage to the rules of law and the institutions of state that determines the very strength and durability of those networks. Even the World Bank now recognizes "that the capacity of various social groups to act in their interest depends crucially on the support (or lack thereof) that they receive from the state as well as the private sector. Similarly, the state depends on social stability and widespread popular support. In short, economic and social development thrives when representatives of the state, the corporate sector, and civil society create forums in and through which they can identify and pursue common goals" (World Bank 2004).

Political institutions are the mechanisms that actually allow democratic claims to be practiced by rights-bearing people. Without these institutional expressions of legal embeddedness, middle- and working-class communities would quickly dissolve into competition, unemployment, and despair—precisely the social conditions that, in the context of modern market dynamics, would lead to the dissolution of strong social relations and social supports. In short, it would destroy social capital.

A Militant Antipositivism in Positivist Guise

Notwithstanding Becker's (1990, 30) and others' goal of colonizing the "rest" of the social sciences with "economic imperialism," coupling the social with capital is well intentioned. Because it ascribes value to non-market relationships, many see it as a way to civilize and humanize the otherwise brittle meanness of market forces. But even the most prestigious economists express serious qualms. Kenneth Arrow (2000) argues that the term social capital should be abandoned as the social relations to which it refers aren't actually a type of capital. Instead, he suggests we focus on studying alternative forms of social interactions. Robert Solow (1990, 2000) concurs, suggesting that the theory suffers from confusion about what constitutes capital, thus canceling out the well-meaning intentions to valorize social relations (see also Akerlof). It is time to follow suit.

One way to do so is to conclude by pointing to the politics of knowledge exhibited by the social capital stories—movements that demonstrate just how intimate is that link between what Foucault (1977a, 1995) calls the power/knowledge connection. This takes us into the territory of this volume's emphasis on the role of positivism and its epistemological others in the construction of knowledge, onto the terrain where knowledge and power are so deeply entwined. The social capital phenomenon entails three kinds of knowledge postulates, each of which has worked to reinforce social capital's ideational role in shifting the study of the social from sociology to economics, and in shifting economic responsibility from the social state onto the shoulders of individuals and their communities. The first knowledge postulate is ontological. The social sciences were born in a stream of history driven forward by two centuries of struggle for the triumph of political liberalism—a struggle for natural individual rights not only against the perceived chronic threat of coercion from the state, but also from the perceived tyranny of "feudal" social relationships. Political liberalism, however, came attached to its inseparable twin of economic liberalism, and many believed it was this—the natural freedoms of pre-political society, of property exhange, and of the market—that provided for political freedom. As part of the liberal imagination, the social sciences came to life with an intractable ontological conflict: Would "society" be a public entity and the site of social and political organization? Or would it be reduced to the antistatist site of natural liberties and the privatized freedom of market relations?

Today's triumph of social capital over civil society and the state tells us that for the time being the conflict has been resolved in the direction of freedom as privatization. Pairing social with capital thus destroys the very social it aims to valorize. It embodies a theory of the value of nonmarket practices that is built on the foundations of market theory. Its default ontology is utilitarian, its social is fully privatized, and its antistatism drives its privatization. The second postulate is social naturalism. That which is natural is that which has its own laws and regularities. Social naturalism extends the axiomatic laws of nature to society. The naturalist roots of utilitarianism's view of society as a prepolitical and presocial site endow it with lawlike regularities modeled on the self-regulating natural laws of the market. This in turn gives it the patina of a positivist science, one that lends itself to testable hypotheses. But ascribing the laws of nature to a sphere of social organization does not make it amenable to scientific analysis. Rather, it is a political epistemological strategy designed to justify market freedom from political interference. Social naturalism in this case leads directly to privatization.

Finally, there is an epistemological postulate at work in the social capital phenomenon. Neoclassical economics, neoliberalism, and rational choice theory all define capital as the result of a decision to invest. This decision-choice (to defer gratification) requires an intentional and rational mental state, yet intentions and rational thinking are unobservable processes without the evidential status demanded by positivist methodology. Absent epistemological access, unobservables must become theoretical constructs derived from the logic of realist thought experiments. But if the capital in social capital is a theoretical entity, its causal properties can never be fully confirmed or disconfirmed, cannot even be candidates for truth or false-hood. Its validity instead is entirely dependent on the logic of theoretical realism—a militantly antipositivist epistemology that mocks positivism for its naïve empiricist belief in the "illusion" of the empirical (see Somers 1998). Real causal mechanisms that operate unobservably at a deeper level of reality than the superficiality of actual appearance.

But here is the problem: If the capital in social capital is defined only by the logic of imputed causal mechanisms, when it rejoins the social half of the couplet, social capital's claim to science and positivism is radically undercut. The primacy of epistemologically inaccessible intentional states of mind leaves only *power* as the sole arbiter of what counts as knowledge. Social capital cannot be both scientifically positivist and dependent on militant antipositivism, cannot be based on both an ontological individualism and a commitment to the social without becoming an incoherent and unstable conceptual entity.

Conclusion

Where Solidarity once shined brightly in our political imaginations the Trojan horse of social capital now prevails. With its polysemic and protean language of social capital and community, social capital theorists have also been able to capture the spirit of civil society and democratic citizenship. Social capital now actually inhabits some of the greatest symbols of participatory democratic ideals. By appropriating the language of civil society, but domesticating and evacuating its political and egalitarian dimensions, social capital has turned the social against its natural constituents.

Clearly, the appeal of the social capital concept for the neoliberals and conservatives is in its indictment of public sector investment. It vindicates antistatism by blaming "civic decline" on the usual sociological suspects of the welfare state and its ancillary social supports. Most conveniently, it explains the intractability of market failures and externalities not by neoliberalism's starvation of the public sector and policies of privatization and structural readjustment, but by inadequate quantities of social capital. The message is that it is our fault—yours and mine—for our "excessive" commitment to greater democratization of the polity, for our lapsed bowling league memberships, for our neglect of neighborhood barbeques, for our insufficient faith-based volunteer services. Along with the privatization of citizenship has come the privatization of responsibility—and we are shamed by our loss of moral fortitude.

In its glorious heyday of the Gdansk-based Solidarity movement, civil society was the nurturing ground for democratic associations of rights-claiming citizens. More than a decade after the fact, it has been hijacked and misshaped into social capital, an antistatist appendage for the "compassionate" side of market society. Militant antistatism, completely understandable in the case of Eastern Europe's repressed trade unions and social movements fighting heroically against state tyranny, cannot be justified in the case of social capital. The exclusion of power, rights claims, and market responsibility from the social capital agenda is not a heroic act, but it is a clever one. Responding to the seductive siren of community, a stunning array of intellectuals, social justice advocates, and well-meaning communitarian proponents of the Third Way are being caught in the web of the privatization of citizenship through the allure of social capital and the ever-receding utopia of community. Dazed by the golden glitter of the Trojan horse, we have been dazzled by the social in social capital to collude with a tragicomedy of social science—one in which social capital is bereft of the social, and Solidarity's vision of civil society has been turned into a neighborhood bowling league. Social capital is bad for sociology as a discipline, and as a social project. And above all, it is very bad for democracy.

Notes

I would like to thank George Steinmetz, Fred Block, Mabel Berezin, Frank Dobbin, Hans Baker, and Mark Traugott for their helpful comments on earlier drafts of this essay. Versions of it were presented as keynote addresses at the Society for the Advancement of Socio-economics (SASE), Amsterdam, July 2001, and the Inaugural Chair's Session of the Comparative Historical Sociology Section, American Sociological Association meetings, August 2002. While working on this essay I received generous support for research and writing from fellowships in the Program in Agrarian Studies, Yale University (2000–2001) and the Center for Critical Analysis of Contemporary Culture, Rutgers University (2003–2004). I would like to especially acknowledge the support and inspiration I received from Jim Scott and Linda Bosniak, the directors for the two fellowship programs, respectively.

1   Following the lead of Steinmetz's introduction to this volume, I limit my scope of vision to the dominant social science paradigm in the United States today.

2   See the World Bank Web site on Social Capital: http://www.worldbank.org/poverty/scapital/whatsc.htm.

3   "It is difficult to think of an academic notion that has entered the common vocabulary of social discourse more quickly than the idea of social capital" (Dasgupta and Serageldin 2000, x) For a random sampling of the recent social capital literature, see Adler and Kwon (1999), Baron et al. (2000), Arrow (2000), Becker (1996), Becker and Murphy (2000), Body-Gendrot and Gittell (2003), Bowles (1999), Bowles and Gintis (1992), Dasgupta and Serageldin (1999), Edwards, Foley, and Diani (2001), Evans (1996), Fine (2001), Fukuyama (1995a, 1995b), Gambetta (1998), Glaeser, Laibson, and Sacerdote (2002), Grootaert (1997), Grootaert and Van Bastelaer (2002), Krishna (2002), Lesser (2000), Lin (2001), McLean and Schultz et al. (2002), Munch (2002), Orr (1999), Portes (1998), Putnam (1993, 1995, 1996, 2000, 2002), Putnam et al. (1993) Stewart-Weeks and Richardson (1998), Warren (1999), Taylor and Leonard (2002), Straw (1998), R. Rose (2000), Robalino (2000) Rotberg and Brucker (2001), Saegert et al. (2001).

4   Just as this essay was going to press Ogilvie's corroborative article appeared in the *American Historical Review* (2004).

5   In psychoanalytic terms, one would almost have to call it a *fetish*, although I prefer *totem* as a more Durkheimian approach to the way that inanimate objects, even social categories, can take on the characteristics of collective desiderata.

6   This concept of ideational embeddedness is developed at length in Somers and Block (forthcoming).

7   The World Bank's adoption of the social capital concept deserves its own story to even begin to do justice to the quantity and innovative quality of this work. See the World Bank Web site: http://www.worldbank.org/poverty/scapital/whatsc.htm.

8   My insistence on social capital as an *epistemological* public good distinguishes me from Coleman, for whom it is the functional *effects* of social capital's *actual* social relations (of family, community, etc.) that makes it what he called a collective good (Coleman 1988/2000, 317).

9   See Somers (forthcoming).

10 Although the civil society concept was equally a phenomenon of South American anti-authoritarian politics in the 1980s, I leave that aside in this essay. On the history and rediscovery of civil society, see, among many sources, Alexander (1993), Arato (1981, 2000), Barber (1996), Calhoun (1993), J. L. Cohen and Arato (1992), J. L. Cohen (1999), Edwards and Foley (1998), Edwards, Foley, and Diani (2001), Ehrenberg (1999), Foley and Edwards (1996), Geremek (1992), Giddens (1998), J. A. Hall (1995), J. Keane (1988, 1998), M. D. Kennedy (1991, 2002), Rosenberg and Post (2002), Seligman (1992), Somers (1995a, 1995b, 1999), Taylor (1990), Walzer (1991), and Wolfe (1989).

11 To be fair, the paragraph following this reads: "Social capital also has an important 'downside': communities, groups, or networks which are isolated, parochial, or work-

ing at cross-purposes to society's collective interests (e.g. drug cartels, corruption rackets) can actually hinder economic and social development" (World Bank 2004).

12   See Block (1990) for a discussion of spot markets versus contracts. There is also an enormous literature on the role of trust in social capital; see especially Fukuyama (1995a), Gambetta (1988), Warren (1999).

13   A Marxist or even an institutionalist definition of capital would be very different. A coherent Marxist perspective could not take on board the notion of social capital in the first place because Marxism and institutionalism *begin* from the premise that capital is constitutively social in the *first* place (see, e.g., Block 1990; Fine 2001). For Marxism, the term social capital is thus redundant. For social capital to make sense, capital would have to first be depleted of its social nature only to be a feeble conception of social, now conceived as the aggregate of individual actions, choice, and decision-theoretics.

14   By external I include the educational skills of human capital. They do not count capital if they're simply knocking about in your brain while watching television, not being put to any productive use. Only the intention to invest them endows them with the status of human capital.

15   Between editions, Randall Collins's widely used *Three Sociological Traditions* (1985) became *Four Sociological Traditions* (1997) with the addition of utilitarianism.

16   I have long thought of social capital theory as a Rolodex approach to social relations and social action, but always in irony, playfulness, and even parody. Reality—without a trace of irony—now imitates the art of caricature: "We assume that individual social capital includes both intrinsic abilities . . . and the results of social capital investments [e.g., a large Rolodex]" (F438).

17   See Bowles and Gintis (2002) for a brilliant critique of the "economic approach."

18   The image of elephants brushing off flies in reference to the contempt economists have long held toward their sociological challenges was given to me by Robert Solow (personal communication, 1990).

19   There is a vast literature on social capital and development. See especially Evans (1996), Fine (2001), McMichael (1998), and Woolcock (1998).

20   Among the universe of "Putnamian" literature on his Italian research, especially important are Levi (1996) and Tarrow (1996).

21   Hegel, of course, reversed Locke and reinstated a triadic conception of social organization. But paradoxically, this did not create civil society as the sphere of citizenship but as the site of the market tout court. For the most important contemporary treatise on civil society in general and Hegel's understanding of it in particular, see J. Cohen and Arato (1992).

22   For a sampling of the relevant neoconservative literature, see also Demuth and Kristol (1995); Gershon (1996a, 1996 b); Habermas (1989); Nicholson (1989); Kristol (1995).

23   "Concerns about social capital thus represent a return to classical sociological preoccupations with community as the foundation of social solidarity and social cohesion" (Gamarnikow and Green 1999, 111). See also Bowles (1999) and N. Rose (1999, 2000).

24   On exit and voice, see Hirschman (1970).

Scientific Authority and the Transition to Post-Fordism: The Plausibility of Positivism in U.S. Sociology since 1945

GEORGE STEINMETZ

From the Cold War to the "Science Wars" in U.S. Sociology

Exoticize the domestic.—Pierre Bourdieu, *Homo Academicus*

It has become manifest that in each age there is a system of science which rests upon a set of assumptions, usually implicit and seldom questioned by the scientists of the time.—Robert Merton, "On Sociological Theories of the Middle Range"

According to accounts in the mass media and the academic press, the social sciences have experienced a sharp increase in epistemological uncertainty in recent years. Various writers have described or decried moves toward relativism, philosophical conventionalism, and skepticism about truth and science itself, including social science (see especially Sokal and Bricmont 1998).[1] Historians went through a linguistic or cultural turn starting in the 1980s, accompanied by a distancing from the more social-scientific models and methods that had characterized their disciplines in the 1960s and 1970s (Sewell, this volume; Bonnell and Hunt 1999). Among the various social sciences, cultural anthropology has seemed especially prone to doubts about the possibility of choosing rationally among competing theories and interpretations. Historians and cultural anthropologists often reject the ideal of explanation tout court.[2] Cultural anthropologists have expressed increasing skepticism about the possibility of understanding other cultures—the very goal that defined their field in earlier decades. To critics, these trends threaten the tenuous and only recently attained scientific status of these endeavors.

What about sociology? Viewed from the outside, it is tempting to see U.S. sociology as being similarly engulfed by skeptical waves of epistemic self-reflexivity. A *New York Times* report on the annual meetings of the

American Sociological Association in 2000 was written in much the same tone as reviews of Modern Language Association meetings during the 1990s, suggesting a discipline engulfed by political correctness that had lost touch with its scholarly calling.[3] A glance at the sociology section of any local bookstore similarly suggests that this discipline is a hotbed of social constructionism and allied forms of nonpositivism. Many first-year graduate students in sociology arrive with strong political agendas and commitments to standpoint epistemology. They clearly expect sociology to be friendly terrain.

It is slightly startling, then, to realize that the leading journals and departments in U.S. sociology have remained almost pristinely aloof from these battles that are supposed to be roiling them. Epistemological questioning and self-reflexivity are still rare in the pages of the main sociology journals in the United States, suggesting a discipline that is secure in its scientific identity and assumptions. In the leading journals and in the curricula of the leading departments, explicitly nonpositivist positions are only tentatively articulated, with the exception of a few subfields such as the sociology of science and culture and ethnic and minority studies. U.S. sociology still seems to be operating according to a basically positivist framework, perhaps a crypto-positivist one, if I can use that term without any conspiratorial connotations. This diagnosis is especially accurate if we define positivism in terms of the tradition running from Locke and Hume in the seventeenth and eighteenth centuries to John Stuart Mill, Ernst Mach, and Karl Pearson in the nineteenth, through the logical positivists and their sociological acolytes in the twentieth century (e.g., Lundberg 1939a, 1939b, 1955; Blalock 1964, 1969; Hanushek and Jackson 1977; and even Arthur Stinchcombe 1968 in his earlier phase). Positivist philosophers like Carl Hempel (1948/1965, 1966) and Karl Popper (a positivist malgré lui; see 1934/1992, 1976b; Adorno 1969/1976) were read by sociologists, and sometimes addressed them directly (e.g., Popper 1957/1991; Neurath 1931/1973; Nagel 1961/1979, ch. 13).[4]

It has been impossible for mainstream sociology to completely ignore the long-term decline of positivism as a vital position in philosophy or the more contemporary epistemological upheaval in the human sciences. There have been repeated intellectual insurgencies and challenges since the late 1960s against the version of positivism that became dominant in sociology after World War II. One effect of these successive, overlapping, and partially cumulative waves of criticism was that the term positivism itself (and allied terms such as empiricism, discussed below) took on overwhelmingly negative and pejorative connotations. Mainstream sociology has mounted three kinds of response to these critics in recent decades. First, many sociologists have continued to work in the same way as before but have simply renamed their positions or ceased to describe their own work in epistemological terms at all. A second response has been to update sociological positivism in ways recommended by Carnap and the logical positivists after 1939 (see the introduction to this volume and H. Putnam 2002), integrating theoretical and unobservable constructs into a covering law framework. This involved the elaboration of universal social laws linking theoretical constructs to empirical events. A third response has been to separate the antipositivist critics' substantive topics of research from their epistemological challenges and to formulate positivist approaches to the new topics. Finally, some sociologists have taken the criticisms seriously and re-examined their positions.[5]

Because the first response is the most typical, positivist positions have become much more difficult to track since 1945. This differs from the situation in the 1930s, when positivism was openly defended and vigorously debated in U.S. sociology. Yet, even where the explicit label is disavowed or partial amendments are made to the basic position, it is still possible to characterize much of the field today as fundamentally positivist. This framework has remained dominant despite the antipositivist wave of the late 1960s and early 1970s, even if it is no longer "doxic." A new situation has arisen in the past decade, however, in which positivism is again forced to defend itself openly as a kind of disciplinary *orthodoxy* rather than simply being taken for granted as the way things are done (doxa).[6]

The initial paradox driving this essay is thus the depth of the positivist unconscious in U.S. sociology and the fact that this discipline has been penetrated to a lesser extent by antipositivist and postpositivist positions than some of the other human sciences.[7] To understand U.S. sociology's rather tenacious positivism, I argue, we need to reconstruct the earlier epistemological conflicts in the discipline and their resolutions, especially since the middle of the twentieth century. The period 1945–1965 was a foundational moment whose effects continue to be felt, even as many of the social conditions that originally supported the triumph of positivism in sociology have fallen away.

The first section of the paper offers a brief working definition of *methodological positivism*,[8] the specific cluster of ontological, epistemological, and methodological assumptions that has prevailed in U.S. sociology for the past half century. Drawing on discussions in the critical realist philosophy of science, I define this position as a combination of an empiricist ontology, a positivist epistemology, and a scientistic version of naturalism. The reason for initially defining this conglomerate object in such abstract terms is that it allows me to identify positivist positions even where writers eschew the self-description. It also permits me to distinguish different sorts of breaks with the earlier orthodoxy. It should be noted, however, that this is not an "ideal type" definition but one that attempts to extract the essential elements of a scientific formation from the writings and practices of sociologists.

The core of the paper is the second part, which proposes a historical sociology of the consolidation of positivist dominance in U.S. sociology during the cold war, roughly 1945 to 1989, with a focus on the first two decades. I argue that this success resulted from a contingent conjuncture of events and social structures located both in the discipline and beyond it. Although I do not ignore the role of the university and scientific fields and the flows of private and public funding, my focus is one that has been ignored in the existing work on the history of sociology: the impact of large-scale social structural processes and cultural discourses on sociologists' sense of the plausibility of different ways of thinking about the social. A useful framework for making sense of patterns of macrosocial and discursive change and their implications for perceptions of social ontology and epistemology is *regulation theory*.[9] Methodological positivism's picture of the social resonated in various ways with the Fordist mode of societal regulation, which also crystallized in the two decades after the war. While various Marxists have thematized for a general correspondence between positivist epistemology and capitalism (Lukács 1922/1968a) or late capitalism (Adorno 1969/1976), I am arguing for a much tighter and more historically specific fit between Fordism and the specific features of the version of methodological positivism that became dominant in sociology during the 1950s. Indeed, it is possible that the current post-Fordist mode of regulation, while thoroughly capitalist, favors *postpositivist* over positivist forms of social epistemology, a hypothesis that I explore in the conclusion.

My account also attends briefly to the growth of state funding for social research, which gave backing to the positivist wing that already existed in U.S. sociology before the war. The circulation of key actors between government agencies and sociology departments was critical in underwriting the ascendance of methodological positivism at this time (S. Turner and Turner 1990). A final factor contributing to the consolidation of positivist orthodoxy was the emotional-political landscape of the middle decades of the century, which brought certain critiques of normal positive science into disagreeable association with fascism and communism.[10]

The main outcome of the postwar conjuncture was the successful institutionalization of a system of some explicit, but most of them implicit, rules that guided the socialization of sociologists, the creation of knowledge, the channeling of resources, and the drawing of disciplinary boundaries. These rules were firmly consolidated despite scattered and quixotic resistance (e.g., Mills 1959).

In the last section of this essay I briefly discuss a series of challenges to methodological positivism that have emerged in sociology since the late 1960s, beginning with neo-Marxism and (second-wave) feminism, passing through the historical and cultural turns, and culminating in the current "epistemological" turn. This discussion parallels the section that precedes it in asking how field-specific and broader sociocultural conditions shaped the emergence and fate of these challengers to methodological positivism. Although none of these movements has succeeded yet in dislodging the central position of methodological positivism, I consider three possible future scenarios for sociology. In one, the current discontent with positivism will bundle together the intellectual resources generated by the earlier critical movements and spark a shift from quantity into quality. Another future would find nonpositivist approaches taking their place alongside methodologically positivist ones in an epistemically fragmented and pluralistic field. But this is unlikely to be a stable solution, as most fields tend to reconsolidate along an axis of dominant versus dominated poles. A third possibility is that the current epistemological turn will suffer the same fate as earlier moments of critique. Arguments that are incommensurate with methodological positivism will be ignored or ridiculed, or nonpositivists will be herded into a marginal subfield that has science itself as its specific object, creating a sort of quarantine zone for epistemological questions.

My own approach to historical reconstruction attempts to exemplify a methodological counterposition—a ridge riding, to use Alvin Gouldner's term—between the Scylla of positivism and the Charybdis of conventionalist constructivism. Key terms in this approach are *contingency* and *conjuncture*. This method, associated inter alia with contemporary critical realism, avoids idealism by embracing causal determinism and by refusing to equate "concept dependency" (defined below) with the view that society consists "entirely of concepts" (New 1998, 359).[11] It suggests that one can combine post-Kuhnian *epistemological relativism*, that is, the recognition that science is a thoroughly social and historical process, with *judg-mental rationalism* about theory choice.[12]

The Contours of Methodological Positivism
in Postwar U.S. Sociology

In this section I draw on the (mainly critical realist) philosophy of science for definitions of positivism, empiricism, and scientistic naturalism to provide a framework for analyzing the ongoing practices and method-ological statements of U.S. sociologists. Without a systematic framework for diagnosing the underlying ontological and epistemological assumptions of social research, any classification of the latter becomes descriptive and arbitrary. In addition to the more abstract literature on science, my working definition of methodological positivism is extracted from pro-grammatic and empirical work by sociologists, none of which can be analyzed in any detail here.[13]

Defining positivism in philosophical terms allows us to avoid using the term as an epithet. Positivism, as Sandra Harding emphasizes in her con-tribution to this volume, is a well-established position with a distin-guished tradition (Ayer 1959; Kolakowski 1966/1968; Giere and Richardson 1996). This legacy has special importance for sociology due to the role of Auguste Comte (1975) in coining not only the term positivism but also "sociology" itself (Halfpenny 1982; Scharff 1995). Yet self-identification as positivist has become exceedingly rare in sociology.[14] The more popular philosophical position in current sociology, at least for those who ex-plicitly embrace one, is some version of "constructivism" or "construc-tionism," even if, as Sergio Sismondo (1993, 1996) and Ian Hacking (1999) have shown, these terms are used to cover a vast array of often mutually exclusive viewpoints. Many constructivist views are coextensive with the widely accepted idea that human practices are not completely determined by biology or other physical causes. More typical than affiliation with constructivism or any other philosophical position, however, is simple avoidance of all philosophical terminology. The main source for the com-munication of positivist orthodoxy to sociology students for many years has therefore not been explicitly philosophical texts but instructions in statistics and methods construed as purely technical matter.[15] The wide-spread hostility to more general discussions, the reluctance to engage in them, is suggestive of their central importance (*pace* Foucault). A co-herent definition of positivism will allow us to identify the metaphysical assumptions underlying texts that present themselves as unconcerned

with such and to distinguish between sociologists' explicit "methodological" descriptions of their own positions and the assumptions implicitly
informing their research.[16]

Methodological positivism can mainly be defined as a cluster of specific
ontological and epistemological positions. This framework has also tended
historically to endorse specific research techniques, but it is by no means
limited to quantitative methods.[17] Methodological positivism contains first
of all a set of empiricist *ontological* assumptions about the nature of social
reality, objects, and causality. Closely articulated with these ontological
foundations but nonetheless distinct are properly positivist *epistemological*
precepts concerning the way social facts can be known.[18] The third component is a *scientistic-naturalist* belief in the identity of the social and natural
sciences. Scientism has important implications for ontology and epistemology and for methods and modes of presentation.

Empiricism can best be understood as a position within ontology according to which "there is no real difference between 'essence' and 'phenomenon' " (Kolakowski 1966/1968, 3). This results in a proscription on
theoretical, abstract, and unobservable objects or entities. Psychological
behaviorism, which claims that "we do not need to worry about what
actors think they are doing to explain their behaviour" (S. Smith 1996, 36),
is thus empiricist. Crucially, empiricism can be both realist and antirealist
about the objects it accepts into scientific statements. Indeed, much of the
confusion about the status of *critical* realism by those unfamiliar with it
results from a conflation of realism with *empirical* realism. Even Rudolf
Carnap, one of the central proponents of logical positivism, insisted, "I am
also a realist," so long as " 'realism' is understood as preference for the
reistic language" (which he defined as "language describing intersubjec-
tively *observable*, spatio-temporally localized things or events"; 1963b, 870,
my emphasis). As Collier (1994, 26) points out, empirical realism is simply
"realism about the concrete results of experience—an empirical realist
believes that chickens and blizzards and magnetic fields exist independently of the observer." Empirical realism is a label applied not just to
anyone who believes that concrete objects are real, however, but also to
"one who also *denies* the reality of *underlying* mechanisms, structures, etc.,
which don't appear in experience, but cause phenomena that do." Those
who accept the existence of such underlying and determining structures,
objects, or mechanisms are *depth realists*. Empiricism thus stands opposed
to depth realism, which begins from a vertically "stratified" picture of
reality. Such a vertical stratification allows for disjunctures between the
level of underlying causal structures and the level of observable phe-

nomena. Empiricism is therefore better described not as antirealist but as opposed to depth realism.

Positivism is a venerable position in epistemology that scientific explanations take the general form "if A then B," or more elaborate versions of these Humean "constant conjunctions." The logical positivists and their successors (Hempel, Popper) renamed these "covering laws." Once again, ontology and epistemology appear to imply one another almost inexorably. Just as empiricist ontology restricted the range of permissible knowledge statements, so positivist epistemology suggests that reality is ontologically structured as a closed system rather than an open one, as this alone would make constant conjunctions possible. If the cause (explanans) is uniform across all instances of a given explanandum, it can be either empirical, as in classical logical positivism, or theoretical, as in later versions of logical positivism and social science adaptions thereof (Ayer 1946; Blalock 1964, 19; Hanushek and Jackson 1977).

This is where the difference between generic depth realism and "transcendental" realism enters in, allowing us to specify the ontological limit conditions of positivist epistemology. The first limit condition is the openness of the system, in this case, the openness of the social system. How can we establish this openness? Bhaskar's (1986, 110) transcendental deduction of the ontological conditions of possibility of the natural science experiment points to the necessary existence of a "rainforestlike profusion" of causal mechanisms (a *horizontal* stratification); this suggests that a multiplicity of mechanisms will typically combine in conjunctural ways to produce empirical events (Collier, this volume). Of course, we cannot conduct true experiments in the social sciences both for the fundamental reason that it is impossible to bracket the effectivity of all causal mechanisms other than those of scientific interest and for the ethical-practical reason that it is indefensible to try to "rerun" the most significant events of human history, which are usually tragic. This means that the openness of the social cannot be *deduced* in the same way as in the natural sciences. But we do know that the level of the social is *emergent* from the biological and physical (Collier 1994, 107–118, 156–160). Regardless of what we do or do not know about the internal structuring of the social, then, it is safe to assume that the genesis of social events is at least as complex as the production of natural events. The sheer mass of evidence concerning social scientists' inability to predict world-historical events—most recently, the collapse of communism and the attacks of September 11, 2001—is also suggestive of social system openness. This failure to predict should not be read as a sign of these sciences' "immaturity," as they are perfectly capable of generating convincing conjunctural explanations of past events. Generic depth realism is compatible with ontologies of system closure, but transcendental or critical realism is not.

Sociology's methodological positivism has also embraced a strong version of scientific naturalism, that is, the claim that the social world can be studied in the same general manner as the natural world (Bhaskar 1979). *Scientism* is a more stringent variant of naturalism that "claims a complete unity" between the natural and social sciences (Bhaskar 1994, 89). The logical positivist thesis of the unity of the sciences (Carnap 1934; Hacking 1996) was taken literally by these sociologists.

Scientism has supplemental implications for ontology, epistemology, and methodology. Because quantification, experiment, and prediction are central to the natural sciences, it is assumed that these are also de rigeur for sociology. With regard to social ontology, scientism led sociologists to overlook the *concept, time*, and *space dependence* of social structures, as it held that natural causal structures were not variable across time, space, and interactional contexts.

Concept dependency means that social practices and structures are inextricably bound up with peoples' interpretations of the world and their own activities. The thesis of concept dependency, in other words, is opposed to the *dichotomy* of things (including material human practices) and words/ideas, even if it is willing to distinguish between the two analytically. This blending of things and words/ideas differentiates the natural from the human sciences and undermines any across-the-board scientism. With respect to this point at least there is agreement between the hermeneutic tradition (Dilthey 1910; Gadamer 1975) and poststructuralism (Laclau and Mouffe 1987) in the social sciences. One can recall Charles Taylor's (1979/1987) effective Saussurian image of the meaningful dimension of human practice and its material substrate as being as inseparable as two sides of a sheet of paper. Geertz's (1973d, 6–7) famous example of the indeterminate meaning of a rapid contraction of the eyelids makes a similar point. Without reconstructing the preinterpreted meaning of social practices, we literally will not be able to determine what kinds of practices they are, vitiating any attempt at social explanation, much less comparison.

The denial of concept dependency appears to receive support from the real world insofar as most natural phenomena are not concept-dependent in the same way as are human phenomena. Hacking (1995, 390; 1999) speaks of the *looping effects* of theoretical classifications on social realities, a "feedback mechanism" that distinguishes natural and human kinds. Natural objects are "intransitive," in Bhaskar's terms; or as Hacking puts it, quarks "do not form an *interactive kind*"; they "are not aware that they are quarks and are not altered simply by being classified as quarks" (1999, 32).

Sociology's scientism also led to an underestimation of the *relationality* of social structures, something always emphasized by critical realism, and of the time and space dependence of those structures. Methodological positivism's orientation toward general laws received its warrant from the apparent unchangeability of causal mechanisms in the natural world across time and space.[19] Natural scientists acknowledge that mechanisms like natural selection may not be valid across all time, of course, and physicists went even farther in the twentieth century (H. Putnam 1990c). But the idea that different places, cultures, or historical epochs might be organized differently, that modern European or U.S. analytic categories might not apply to the feudal past or to Chinese or African society, was anathema to mainstream methodological positivism.[20]

A further aspect of sociological scientism was its adherence to the fact/ value dichotomy (discussed by Mihic, Engelmann, and Wingrove in this volume). Value-freedom (*Wertfreiheit*) was enshrined in some of the earliest statements of sociology's mission (Weber 1949).[21] It was reasserted after World War II and in subsequent periods of epistemological-political unrest (e.g., Coleman 1992).[22]

Research methods in the narrower sense are selected and limited by these scientistic assumptions. The prominence of quantitative methods in the natural sciences led social scientists to privilege them, even though qualitative data and methods are also fully compatible with positivism and empiricism (e.g., Barton and Lazarsfeld 1956), just as quantitative data and methods are compatible with nonpositivist epistemologies (e.g., Bourdieu 1979/1984). Nor should it be assumed that quantitative methods are necessarily associated with empiricism. Hayek already endorsed quantification for depth-realist reasons, writing that "the main importance of [the] quantitative nature of most natural sciences is [not] their greater precision" but rather "substituting for the classification of events which our senses provide another based on relations established by systematic testing and experiment" (1942, 275). As mentioned in the introduction to this volume, contemporary statistical approaches allow for "latent" (theoretical-unobservable) constructs.

The full-fledged methodological positivist paradigm did, in fact, privilege quantification. But in sociology (as in political science, but perhaps not in economics, as Lawson argues here), the quantitative/mathematical rule has been easier to bend than the positivist commitment to covering laws. There has also been a continual return to the idea of experimentation in the social sciences, even though both critical realists and some philosophical positivists have rejected true experiments as ontologically impossible in these fields.

Methodological positivism in sociology has also privileged specific ways of representing social reality. Articles have been preferred to books; statistical and tabular forms to textual ones; analytic genres of writing to narrative or experimental forms; and written forms of inscription to visual ones. Authorial voice is disdained as subjective and the voiceless style felt to be more scientific. Multiple rather than single authorship is the norm (Hollinger 1996, 151, n. 64), providing a synecdoche of the "scientific community" of peers discussed by Michael Polanyi, Robert Merton, Thomas Kuhn, and others (see Mirowski, this volume).

In sum, methodological positivism combines positivism, empiricism, and scientism; the last encompasses the fact/value dichotomy, mimicry of hard science styles of presentation, a preference for quantification, and a belief in the concept, space, and time independence of social mechanisms. This cluster of premises has broadly defined the dominant position in U.S. sociology since the 1950s. But the specific combination of assumptions has varied across subperiod, subfield, setting, from one sociologist to the next, and even within individual texts.[23] The common denominator, the belief whose abandonment would signal a fundamental change in this formation, is the orientation to regularity determinism or covering laws. All of the other features may define methodological positivism's center of gravity, its modal type, but they are less essential.

What does this definition leave out? Some would argue that mainstream U.S. sociology in this period was unified as much by a specific understanding of its object domain, by adherence to a shared theoretical orientation, or by its orientation to a set of canonical texts. Yet methodological positivism was more significant for the practical unification of the sociological field. As Frisby and Sayer (1986) have argued, mainstream sociology has actually had a very weak conception of its supposed subject matter, society or the social. No general object of analysis united the discipline, despite the best efforts of the Parsonians and Marxists, who pursued parallel goals with respect to this issue. It is paradoxical that a field supposedly defined by the social has tended to adopt an atomized view of human life (Emirbayer 1997).

Nor was sociology integrated by adherence to any specific substantive theoretical paradigm. While Parsonianism may have unified many U.S. sociologists professionally and politically in the 1950s and early 1960s, it did not lend more than a superficial concurrence to their actual research and writing. There were as many dissenters as adherents to the supposedly all-powerful Parsons and even more who simply seemed oblivious. Kingsley Davis's 1959 presidential address to the American Sociological Association argued that structural-functional analysis was neither an agreed upon method nor a distinct theory but simply a "myth" or another name for explaining social phenomena socially (Davis 1960).[24] George Homans displaced Parsons in the sociology citation counts in the second half of the 1960s (Chriss 1995, 48–49). Of course, theoretical diversity is quite compatible with dominance by one or another specific theory. Epistemology and method were more fundamental than theory. Indeed, methodological positivism could be reconciled with theories ranging from Marx to Parsons.

A final alternative is to read the history of U.S. sociology in terms of canon formation. Prewar theorists like Sorokin (1928) and Parsons (1937/1968) actively excluded Marx and Engels from any claim to a place in sociology's canon.[25] Connell (1997) has argued that U.S. sociology was unified after 1945 by the creation of a canon that suppressed an earlier orientation toward the colonized and non-Western world, narrowing the discipline's vision to Eurocentric classics and metropolitan problems. One problem with this interpretation is that most sociologists after the war were little concerned with theoretical texts per se. Merton (1936/1968c) included exculpatory comments for his atheoretical colleagues, and Lazarsfeld (cited in Mills 1959, 60) juxtaposed the unspecialized, individual "social philosophers" who wrote books to the practical and scientific sociologists. Yet Connell (1997, 1511) is certainly correct in his claim that U.S. sociology became "centered on difference and disorder within the metropole" and turned away from problems of "global expansion and colonization," and that the construction of a European-theory-centered canon focused on problems of *European* modernity was related to this move. As I argue below, this narrowing of sociology's focus to Europe and the United States was related to the consolidation of methodological positivism, specifically to the division between the "nomothetic" social science disciplines and the "idiographic" fields of area studies.

Although few sociologists nowadays embrace the positivist label, many defend or rely on positions that closely match the definition of methodological positivism set out here.[26] This should not surprise us. As Jürgen Habermas (1969/1976, 1971) has noted, positivism was committed from Comte onward to avoiding all talk of epistemology and metaphysics and portraying itself as having transcended philosophy altogether. Deconstructionists have argued that the dominant pole in such binary oppositions (positivist versus nonpositivist) has the luxury of remaining un-marked. Methodological positivism became so prevalent in sociology dur-ing the 1950s and 1960s that it marginalized not only other positions but also philosophical discussion per se. C. Wright Mills's *The Sociological Imagination* (1959) is perhaps the only example of a direct and sustained critique of methodological positivism from within U.S. sociology during the 1950s (and even that book makes compromises with empiricism).

By speaking of the dominance of positivism I do not want to suggest that other approaches have been absent or unthinkable. The image I want to convey instead is closer to Bourdieu's notion of a "field" of diverse positions and viewpoints that is clearly "structured in dominance." As Bourdieu (1981, 260) argues, "A survey on power in the scientific field could perfectly well consist of . . . epistemological questions alone."[27] Certain ideological-methodological positions have more (field-specific) scientific capital than others. All players in the field recognize a common definition of scientific authority and competence, of distinguished and less distinguished positions, even if they develop a taste for their own domi-nated position within this hierarchy (see Bourdieu 1981, 1984/1988, 1985, 1986).[28] The resources that have allowed sociology to slowly begin thinking its way out of methodological positivism have often been literally foreign, emerging from other national contexts or disciplines. "Indigenous" sources for these arguments were also available, but the fact that these positions had been subordinated for so long lent them an air of lifelessness and defeat, leading critics to look for alternative backing elsewhere.[29]

U.S. Sociology's Postwar *Refondazione* (Refoundation) and the Consolidation of Methodological Positivist Orthodoxy

In the 1940s and 1950s . . . thanks to new techniques and the computer, the social sciences were perceived as becoming harder, that is, more like the hard sciences.—Charles Lindblom, "Political Science in the 1940s and 1950s"

A fruitful starting point for a sociology of sociology is thus the idea of the scientific field. A *settled* field is internally heterogeneous but at the same time biased toward a shared definition of distinction. The agreement by all actors on a certain definition of value is based on dynamics of mutual *recognition* (Steinmetz 2002). There is thus a basic, if tacit, level of agree-ment within settled fields. This consensus undergirds disagreements about taste, which are rooted in variations of individual and class/group habitus and capital. This means we should never expect absolute epistemological homogeneity within a scientific field. The presence of nonpositivist positions is fully compatible with positivist dominance (and vice versa).

Why do certain epistemological and theoretical preferences become entrenched within a given scientific field? This is similar to the question broached by Kuhn (1962/1970) in his famous intervention on scientific paradigms and scientific revolutions, except that Kuhn was more concerned with full-fledged theories than with more diffuse assumptions. The determinants of scientific doxa can be described heuristically as external or internal to the scientific field (or alternatively, as macroscopic versus microscopic). In explanations of the development of science, the adjective "external" has typically been used to refer to all those influences on science that are not intellectual (R. Hall 1963; Breslau 2003). "Internalist" historical analyses are those concerned with the correspondence between a scientific theory and its object, and that hold that "scientists themselves come gradually to perceive this trajectory over the course of history as they 'learn to learn' about the world" (Fuller 1993, 34). I draw the boundary between internal and external influences at a slightly different point, however, with the *inside* encompassing subfields, disciplines, universities, and research institutions, in addition to the storied point of contact between the scientist and his or her object. The *outside* then refers to all other sociocultural factors that influence science, including branches of the government concerned with science and private funding agencies, as well as macrosocial external factors like those associated with Fordism and post-Fordism.

In much of the recent sociology of science there has been a tendency to privilege what I am calling the internal level—the field of science itself and its immediate extensions—rather than its relations with its environment (but see Merton 1936/1968c; Gouldner 1965, 1970). Sociological research on science in the 1950s and early 1960s was strongly focused on the idea of the scientific community as "a kind of social and cultural system with its own powers of self-maintenance and self-regulation" (Shils 1954, cited in Hollinger 1996, 109). Although Kuhn may have been less convinced than earlier writers of the "judgmental rationality" of the choices of the scientific community, he still emphasized the latter as driving theory choice. Indeed, by breaking with the idea that theory choice is driven by correspondence with its object, Kuhn severed yet another link between scientific theory and science's outside. Sociologists have grown increasingly skeptical about the "gentlemanly" (or "communal") qualities of this "scientific community," but many of them continue to train their gaze on the internal features of science. They have emphasized competition among scientists (Ben-David 1960), patronage and gate keeping (Cole and Cole 1973, 1983), the enlisting of allies (Latour 1987),[30] personality conflicts (Abbott 1999), and the pressures of professional legitimation[31] in accounting for scientific behavior and change. Luhmann's (1989, ch. 12) theory, in which the border between autopoeitic science and its social environment becomes densely compacted and difficult to permeate except via indirect perturbation, is the apotheosis of this science-centered view of science.

How can internalist approaches explain fundamental agreement in scientific fields? One possibility, suggested by Camic (1995; Camic and Xie 1994), is that new sciences tend to emulate the currently most prestigious discipline. The problem is that other newcomer disciplines that emerged at the end of the nineteenth century, most notably anthropology, did not follow the same path as sociology (Stocking 2001a; Zimmerman 2001; Keane, this volume). Moreover, if we place sociology in a higher-order metafield of the sciences, it is not transhistorically obvious that sociologists would necessarily experience "physics envy" or "economics envy." In earlier periods, and in other national settings, philosophy, not physics (or economics), has figured as the queen of the disciplines. Camic's account thus throws us back on a historically and logically prior question: Why do fields differ in their selection of disciplinary "ego ideals"?

Bourdieu's approach seems to promise some level of generality with respect to these questions. For Bourdieu (1979/1984), the most distinguished positions in any given field will be the ones that exhibit the greatest "distance from necessity." In the arts this seems to point to more abstract or minimalist forms, or to a style of viewing that privileges form over content (but see Barthes 1980). In the field of sports (Wacquant 2000), distance from necessity accrues to bodily movements that are more artificial and are distinct from street gestures, or to games that are wasteful of time (sailing) and space (golf). But how could this line of reasoning account for the prestige of positivism in sociology? While *empiricism* is more concrete than depth realism, and thus in certain respects closer to "necessity," *positivism* can be seen as less concerned with the messy details of the individual case, which it subsumes under a general covering law. Quantification, as Hayek (1942, 275) suggested, can be described as a substitute for the cruder "classification of events which our senses provide." Although "distance from necessity" need not be defined in aesthetic terms, it is notable that sociological positivists spontaneously adhere to an aestheticizing language of "elegance" when describing statistical models or "parsimonious" explanations.

And so on. The problem with this Bourdieuian approach is its portmanteau and ad hoc quality. One could just as easily tell a story according to which nonpositivist approaches are *more* disdainful of necessity than positivist ones, and hence *more* distinguished. It could be emphasized that the parsimonious accounts preferred by positivism are actually *closer* to commonsense understandings of social causality. Bourdieu's theory is best equipped to account for the workings of consolidated, settled fields, but its analysis of the origins or substantive contents of any given "settlement" is less compelling. At best, it indicates what kinds of additional ideological framing are likely to be directed at practices and perceptions whose distinction is *already* being promoted. It points to the general kinds of arguments that will be mobilized by anyone trying to control a field. But Bourdieu cannot explain why certain definitions of distinction will be more successful than others.[32]

We are again thrown back on the problem: Why was positivism so successful in its bid for leadership and distinction after 1945? Obviously, economic (as well as political and social) capital can enhance the value of cultural capital. Research on the politics of the cold war and academia focuses on the role of the national security state in promoting and suppressing certain kinds of science and forging a military-academic complex (Leslie 1993; Robin 2001; Chomsky et al. 1997). Historians of postwar U.S. social science have often traced its scientist turn to the massive influx of resources offered by private foundations and government agencies to those who were willing to configure their work along the lines of the natural sciences (Gouldner 1970; Schwendinger and Schwendinger 1974; S. Turner and Turner 1990; Ross 1991; Ahmad 1991; Fisher 1993; Kleinman 1995). While this was undoubtedly crucial, there is still "a good bit of disagreement and uncertainty about just what effect the interests of federal and private patrons have on the intellectual shape of . . . science and scholarship" (Hollinger 1996, 142, n. 23).[33] One reason this account is obviously inadequate is that resources were already available during the prewar period, at least from private foundations, and still exist today. Yet the social science disciplines, including sociology, have varied across this period in their level of adherence to methodological positivism as well as theoretical fashions. Taken alone, funding cannot account for the waxing and waning of methodological positivism.[34]

The externalist theoretical approaches that I called "social-epochal" or "macrosocial" in the introduction to this volume offer an alternative, or at least a necessary supplement, to the currently popular approaches to the study of social science. Social-epochal approaches need not negate the existence and causal importance of intrascientific dynamics like competition, hierarchy, enlisting allies, and "trials of strength," but they shed light on the sources of the more widespread and often implicit ideas shared by all of the actors in a settled scientific field. Nor do such accounts have to ignore the role of class, but they are less interested in correlating particular class positions with specific ideologies.[35] Instead, they look at the production of more general ideological forms, the scientific aspects of the "cultural dominant" (Jameson 1984).

An early example of this approach is Lukács's analysis of reification as a universal condition besetting the minds of capitalists and workers alike, even if the latter have at least a chance of extricating themselves from it. Historians and sociologists have also dealt with "external" determinants of spontaneous scientific consensus. Following Max Weber, Merton (1936/ 1968b) traced the "enhanced cultivation of science" and the specific "attitudes of scientists to their work" in later seventeenth-century England to the ascetic ethic of Puritanism.[36] Foucault (1966/1970) traced the sources of writing in a wide array of classical scientific fields to a period-specific deep structure, which he called *episteme*. Shapin's (1994) study of the same period highlighted the role of the ideology of a community of *gentlemen* and of trust in the origins of natural science. Haraway (1989) ties the history of twentieth-century primatology to broader histories of capitalism, race, and gender. Ulrich Beck's (1986/1992; Beck, Giddens, and Lash 1994) theory of risk society and reflexive modernization takes a broadly similar analytic approach. Beck traces the new social risks largely to the runaway logics of contemporary capitalism, but he views their impact as more general than the older forms of exploitation and domination, which were stratified by social class. New types of risk, including pollution, nuclear proliferation, and heightened levels of competition and individualization, are spread across the entire social surface rather than being specific to any one group (Beck 1986/1992, 53; Heitmeyer 1992). Novel forms of anxious subjectivity and resistance arise in response. Beck's approach is relevant in the present context because he discusses the impact of "risk society" on scientific ideologies and practices. The expansion of science and its dangers encourages critique, demystification, and greater reflexivity with regard to expert practice and science.[37]

In another paper (Steinmetz 2004b), I show that most of the discursive and institutional building blocks for methodological positivism were already in place in U.S. sociology before 1940. As sociology began to constitute itself as an academic field in U.S. universities between the 1890s and the 1920s, there were two existing routes to disciplinization, one represented by the humanities and the other by the natural sciences. Many of the early founders of the field, including Giddings at Columbia and Albion Small at Chicago, embraced a scientific naturalism (Vidich 1985, ch. 8).[38] The Laura Spelman Rockefeller Foundation promoted a scientistic, policy-oriented approach in the 1920s and 1930s, making large grants to Chicago, Columbia, Harvard, Minnesota, North Carolina, and other universities and departments (Bulmer 1982; Fisher 1993; D. Ross 1991).[39] A recent historical study supports Donald Fischer's claim that the Rockefeller Foundation promoted a positivist form of social science, one that would appeal to business and the state, with an orientation toward practical applications and prediction (Ahmad 1991). Logical positivism was also dominant in Anglophone philosophy between 1930 and 1960. To the extent that sociologists attended to philosophical discussions at all—and they did so to a greater extent before 1945 than afterward—they tended to be channeled toward positivism.

Despite these favorable preconditions, methodological positivism did not dominate U.S. sociology departments during the 1920s and 1930s. Two explicit adherents of positivism observed in the pages of the *American Sociological Review* in 1939, "Sociology is at present divided in two conflicting schools. One believes that sociology must adopt principles and methods of the physical and biological sciences. The other maintains that sociology must use its own methods, since these are best adapted to its subject matter" (Levine and Dornblum 1939, 381).

The articles in the *American Journal of Sociology* and *American Sociological Review* (beginning in 1936) during the 1930s reveal a great epistemological and methodological diversity in comparison with subsequent decades. As Connell (1997) has remarked with respect to sociology in general before World War II, there was more interest in the colonized global periphery, although this was already tapering off in the 1930s. In a single year, 1939, the ASR included articles by a prominent antipositivist philosopher, Roy Wood Sellars (along with a response by an explicitly positivist sociologist, George Lundberg) and a historical analysis of "total war" by the German "émigré" sociologist Hans Speier, as well as essays on "Republican Turkey" and Brazil; the AJS carried a piece by Maurice Halbwachs on "Individual Consciousness and Collective Mind" and essays on Brazil and Hawaii (a quasi-colonial U.S. territory at this time). There were also examples in 1939 of inspired amateurism, reflecting sociology's lower degree of professionalization at this time, including C. Wright Mills's "Language, Logic, and Culture" (published while Mills was still an undergraduate at Texas). And in November 1939 the AJS published an entire special issue on psychoanalysis and sociology, which included essays by

A. L. Kroeber, Harold Laswell, Karen Horney, and Kenneth Burke (writing on "Freud and the Analysis of Poetry"), along with several medical doctors, psychiatrists, and, of course, sociologists. This collection suggests not only a lower level of anxiety about disciplinary boundaries than in subsequent periods (especially since the 1960s), but also an openness to the depth-realist theoretical concepts of psychoanalysis. As one of the contributors remarked, "Sociology is sufficiently mature to adopt the methods of contemporary psychological science," adding, "Among the latter, the phenomenon which Freud called the return of the repressed is of particular importance to sociology" (Zilboorg 1939, 341).[40] By the 1960s, however, the category of "the return of the repressed" was, to put it mildly, absent in most sociological analysis.

Leading sociologists rejected positivism during the 1930s, including Parsons and Howard P. Becker.[41] Parsons explicitly attacked "the positivistic-utilitarian tradition" at the beginning of The Structure of Social Action in 1937. Parsons's student, Robert Merton, wrote a series of influential historical and theoretical essays on the sociology of science and knowledge during the 1930s and 1940s that had little in common with the quasi-positivist doctrine of middle-range theory for which he became known in the postwar period (Steinmetz and Chae 2002). Influential figures in other fields, such as Friedrich von Hayek, warned against the danger of "scientism," which he defined as a "slavish imitation of the method and language of Science" and a "mechanical and uncritical application of habits of thought to fields different from those in which they have been formed" (1942, 268).

At the end of the 1930s, then, nonpositivists still had an important place in U.S. sociology, which was fragmented, polycentric, and methodologically unsettled (see S. Turner and Turner 1990, 75). Private foundation resources had not been sufficient to usher in an unalloyed triumph of positivism during the interwar period. Mounting anxieties around Nazism and Soviet communism were not yet focused on questions of epistemology and science.[42] Parsons opened his discussion of the positivist tradition in 1937 with the question "Why has it died"? and was less worried about empiricism than about a rising current of "irrationalism" that insisted that "sociology is an art" and threatened to abandon "scientific standards" altogether (1937/1949, 2: 774).

Soon after the war, however, the discipline of sociology experienced a dramatic turn toward methodological positivism. In the pages that follow, I want to reconstruct the external and intradisciplinary underpinnings of this installation of a new epistemological orthodoxy. In the spirit of the critique of positivism, my account of these developments is conjunctural and figurational. I have already dealt here and in the introduction with some of the intellectual raw materials for social science positivism, which can be traced back as far as Hume. I therefore emphasize the novel forces after the war, without meaning to suggest that the preexisting conditions did not play a crucial role as well.

The most important and all-encompassing of the new conditions after the war was the social formation that retrospectively has come to be known as Fordism. The Fordist security state relied to a greater extent than previous forms of governmentality on the skills of sociologists, and this entailed a greatly enhanced level of public funding for social research. By the 1950s and early 1960s, the intellectual, financial, and political forces that had existed before 1945 combined with the ideological effects of the newly consolidated Fordist mode of regulation to sweep methodological positivism to triumph. The heightened level of anxiety around totalitarian irrationalism also played a role in this rise to dominance, as did the field-internal dynamics that have been so central to recent writing on science.

The Resonance of Fordism with the
Positivist Vision of the Social

Regulation theory has described Fordism as an integral form of *societal-ization* (*Vergesellschaftung*),[43] that is, as a temporarily stabilized system for producing and reproducing (capitalist) society "despite and because of its conflictual and contradictory character" (Lipietz 1985, 109). Specifically, Fordism was geared toward maintaining a certain balance between capital accumulation and consumption. This emphasized a combination of mass production and consumption, which were associated with the system pioneered by Henry Ford; Ford's name therefore became associated with the more encompassing social form. Along with mass production and mass consumption of highly standardized products, Fordism also entailed some or all of the following elements: Keynesian-style policies aimed at smoothing economic cycles; welfare-statist programs that partially socialized the costs of reproducing labor power; collaborative relations between organized labor and management; mass culture offering homogeneous fare and tending to erode older distinctions between highbrow and lowbrow culture, converging in the middle; a family form emphasizing the male single breadwinner, at least as a sociocultural ideal; privatized single-family housing based on patterns of urbanization tending toward suburbanization (Graham and Marvin 2001); and a tendency for economic and social practices to be located within the "container" of the nation-state and evenly distributed across its surface (N. Brenner 1998; Peck and Tickell 1994). Each nationally specific "mode of growth" (Jessop 1989) emphasized some of the elements from this menu of Fordist practices and omitted others.[44]

Although Europeans often spoke of Fordism during the interwar period, they were usually referring to Henry Ford's system of high wages and assembly line production (e.g., Gottl-Ottlilienfeld 1924; Erfurth 1929). In his essay "Americanism and Fordism" (1929–35/1971a), however, Antonio Gramsci discerned the emergence of a full-fledged social system centered on the Taylorist and Fordist methods of production. Only in the 1950s was this "private sector" system articulated with systematic government policies. A full-fledged Fordist "mode of regulation" then began to crystallize in the United States, and somewhat later in Europe, culminating in the 1960s (see also Aglietta 1987; Boyer 1990; Lipietz 1987; Jessop 1990, 1999, 2003).

Regulation theory is concerned with the emergence, effects, and dissolution of modes of regulation such as Fordism and post-Fordism. The putative effect of a mode of regulation is to stabilize capitalist society, specifically, to provide the conditions for the accumulation of capital. But there are no guarantees that any solution to a capitalist crisis will be the optimal one, or even that it will even necessarily emerge at all in a given period. The centerpiece of regulation theory is its emphasis on crisis and contingency. Unlike functionalism and traditional Marxism, regulation theory stresses the improbability, or unlikelihood, of successful social reproduction (Demirović 2003, 46) as a result of the crisis-ridden, entropic dynamism of capitalist society. Elements of modes of regulation emerge in an uncoordinated and often chaotic manner that is different in each period and site. Another specific difference from traditional Marxism is the assumption that regulatory modes are provisional and will inevitably fall apart.[45] Regulation theory is also antireductionist: even within its contingent logics, it does not privilege a single causal mechanism, economic or otherwise, in explaining the origins or the effects of a mode of regulation.[46] Given its rejection of covering laws and prediction, regulation theory is "condemned, nolens volens, to ex-post observation" (Raza and Brand 2003, 10), that is, to an analysis of the (distant and more recent) capitalist past. It is not surprising, therefore, that the regulationist analysis of Fordism has become more complex and compelling as the Fordist period recedes in history, while discussions of post-Fordism are still somewhat confused and tentative.

The various patterns grouped by regulation theory under the heading of Fordism helped to render positivist approaches to social explanation more plausible both to sociologists and to other people exposed and attentive to the new logics governing activity in the advanced capitalist world. By contrast, positivism had been a less plausible description of the meta-conditions of society in the context of the deeply unstable conditions of the interwar period. After the war, however, social reality appeared increasingly to fit the positivist expectation that social practices could be subsumed under covering laws, that is, fall into patterns that were the same everywhere and always. Social actors now seemed atomized, rational, and interchangeable, lacking any distinctive cultural peculiarities; social practice was more predictable and controllable. In sharp contrast to the crisis conditions of the interwar years, orderly postwar Fordist societalization resonated with positivist notions of repetition.

The effects of postwar Fordism on the enhanced plausibility of sociological positivism can be summarized under five broad categories:

Science and the Fordist state

The first is the greatly enhanced role of science (including social science) in the Fordist form of governmentality. The 1940s and 1950s were not the first period in which significant funds were offered to sociologists willing to reconfigure their work in the image of the natural sciences, but the postwar period saw an unprecedented influx of new resources from the state sector to universities and think tanks and in the guise of contract research.[47] In 1958, government at all levels contributed only about 27 percent of all social science funds, but by 1976 the rate was about 56 percent (Useem 1976; Alpert 1961). In 1966, the federal government spent $26,621,000 on "basic and applied sociological research" alone (McCartney 1971, 385). In addition to the U.S. state's cold war support for research on counterinsurgency, which channeled copious resources to social scientists (Robin 2001), the domestic Keynesian dimensions of the security state relied on social science to track the economy, regulate business cycles, survey the population, and bring social practices into line with the regularities of mass production and mass consumption (Hirsch 1980, 1983, 1988).

The National Science Foundation was only one of the many military and civilian government agencies that funded sociologists' research, but there are good reasons for placing it at the center of this story. The NSF, created in 1950, was the single largest source of funding for sociological research. It was also crucial because of its orientation toward "pure science," which made it more immediately relevant than think tank research for defining the level of scientific capital of each form of sociological activity. Leading figures recognized this conjuncture of politics and sciences in the immediate postwar period as a critical opportunity to enhance sociology's standing and put it on a more "scientific" footing. In a paper read before the American Sociological Association meetings in Cleveland in March 1946, Phil Hauser of the University of Chicago called attention to the spectacular increase in the prestige and political usefulness of science resulting from "the blinding flash of the atomic bomb" (379). Turning to the bills for NSF funding that were being debated in Congress, Hauser asked, "Are the social sciences ready?" Inclusion in the new funding opportunities, he argued, required that sociology "meet the requirements of good design of experiment." This also entailed the manufacture of "social laws" and predictions (382). Talcott Parsons wrote a paper two years later for the Social Science Research Council as "part of a political maneuver to place the social sciences in a posture to obtain federal funds," in which he "touted the contributions of empirical social science" and argued that "the same philosophical principles that guided the natural sciences were at the heart of the social sciences" (Klausner and Lidz 1986, vii).

Resources for positivistic forms of sociology were greatly enhanced by the expansion of the NSF mandate in 1954 to begin supporting the social sciences, along with the availability of funds from other agencies such as the National Institutes of Health (created in 1930), the National Institute of Mental Health (1946), and a thicket of think tanks funded by the military, greatly enhanced the resources for positivistic forms of sociology. A series of articles in the *American Sociological Review* between 1954 and 1957 by Harry Alpert (1954, 1955a, 1955b, 1957; see also Lundberg 1947), a sociologist working at the NSF, laid out the conditions under which sociologists would be eligible for NSF funding.[48] The first criterion was "the *criterion of science*, that is, the identification, within the social disciplines, of those areas characterized by the application of *the* methods and logic of science" (Alpert 1955b, 656, my emphasis). This criterion was specified in naturalist terms as implying the "convergence of the natural sciences and the social sciences." The debates since the late nineteenth century around the proper epistemological logic and research methods for sociology were thus swept summarily under the rug. Attention to the "national interest" constituted the third criterion for funding, suggesting at the very least that sociologists would be expected to draw predictive lessons from their research. To underscore the payoff awaiting those who were willing to translate their research into the required idiom, Alpert listed some of the projects already funded on a trial basis. All had adapted their approach to fit the frame-work either of the NSF's Biological and Medical Sciences Division or its Mathematical, Physical, and Engineering Sciences Division. This under-lined two possible forms of scientism that would be available to sociolo-gists in the decades to come, one characteristic of the "physics envy" period and another looking forward to the present-day infatuation with the life sciences. Many sociologists were ready to pursue Latour's "second principle" of "science in action," according to which scientists "speak in the name of new allies that they have shaped and enrolled" and "add these unexpected resources to tip the balance of force in their favor" (1987, 259). The subordinate status under which sociology entered this brave new world of federal funding was underscored by the overall tone of Alpert's essays: the "Foundation," he wrote, "*utilizes* sociology in the pursuit of its policy and operating responsibilities"—referring to surveys—and "to a very limited extent, it supports them financially" (1955b, 654). The article concluded with a barely veiled warning: "The social sciences . . . are here to stay, but their future growth and development"—that is, their access to government funding—would "depend largely on their capacity to prove themselves by their deeds" (660).

Edward Shils worried in 1948 that the still feeble efforts toward theoret-ical development in sociology were "in danger of being suffocated in the stampede for concrete results with immediate descriptive or manipulative value," adding that "the post-war financial prosperity of American sociol-ogy with the vast sums of money made available by governmental bodies, foundations, and private associations and firms makes this danger a very real one" (55).[49] Before 1930, only 1.3 percent of articles in the *AJS* acknowl-edged financial support from any outside source at all. Between 1945 and 1949, the percentage of articles in the *AJS, ASR,* and *Social Forces* acknowl-edging outside funding was 17.4, and by the 1960–64 period this figure had risen to 52.5 (McCartney 1971, 387–388). Sociologists were being offered unprecedented new resources and powerful allies.

The integration of sociology into the Fordist domestic and foreign policy scientific infrastructure seemed paradoxically to validate the claim that science was "value-free": social scientists could conceive of themselves as a separate and autarkic scientific community only after they had freed themselves from the prewar corporate organization of science, dominated by private funding (see Mirowski, this volume). As autonomous profes-sionals, social scientists were released from responsibility for the ways policymakers would use their research. State Fordism thus buttressed the value/fact dichotomy, a mainstay of methodological positivism. By the

1960s, social policies with historical origins in socialist, corporatist, or religious traditions were being implemented by "postideological" governments. Sociologists offered their morally neutral services to their clients at the center of the welfare state. By 1967, Lazarsfeld, Sewell, and Wilensky could discuss sociology's relationship to its environment as generally one of scientist and "client" (x).

Fordist economy
The second way Fordism contributed to positivism's plausibility was by dampening economic turbulence and crisis through fiscal policy and by lessening some of the economic upheavals in the individual life course through wage and welfare state policies. These developments, which especially affected the middle wage-earning classes (including sociologists), made it seem more conceivable that social practices did in fact repeat themselves in ways that could be represented with general covering laws, statistical models, replicable experiments, and reliable predictions. The steady improvement of the standard of living and the thickening of the welfare statist safety net lent credence to the idea of general social laws. Wage earners in general, including the better-paid sectors of the working class, were able for the first time in the history of capitalism to develop a horizon of stable expectations concerning their own future, enhanced by relatively generous protection against the risks of unemployment, sickness, and poverty in old age. The social ontology of the Fordist subject was aligned with *security*. The real wages of wage earners rose over the long run in tandem with increasing productivity (Demirović 2003, 47), rather than stagnating or declining regardless of the tendency of profits. Historical analysis became less significant for sociology once the world had become more "synchronic" and history had supposedly ended. Thus, Bernard Brodie of the Rand Corporation could write in 1949 of the need to "go beyond history" (474) through the application of economic models.

Culture and the Fordist ideoscape
A *culture* that was increasingly replicated across regions and social groups and classes began to make economic and developmental-modernization models seem more convincing, predicated as they were on a picture of universal, interchangeable subjectivity. Arjun Appadurai's (1996a) notion of an *ideoscape* suggests that ideologies will be understood differently, depending on one's position in social space (similar to a landscape that looks entirely different depending on the viewer's spatial location).[50] As noted above, some social scientists resisted the turn to methodological

positivism even during the 1950s; others were positioned to profit from the new perspective. But even those who initially resisted positivism were more likely to gravitate toward it, as it resonated increasingly with their experience of their own sociotechnical world. The increasingly depthless culture of Fordism (Hirsch and Roth 1986) seemed to substantiate the behaviorist-empiricist models. Social-psychological experiments in which conclusions about human behavior were drawn from research on undergraduates at U.S. colleges began to seem less far-fetched, at least to social scientists.[51] The positivist impetus to abandon all analysis of subjective meaning resonated with a wider culture that really did seem to have transcended ideology. The postwar U.S. postideological character was demonstrated in numerous sociological studies of voting and military life (Shils and Janowitz 1948; Lazarsfeld, Berelson, and Gaudet 1948/1968; Stouffer 1949; Berelson, Lazarsfeld, and McPhee 1954; Converse 1964) and reinforced by discussions of "the end of ideology" (Bell 1960). Interpretation of culture in the sense of a deep structure (Lévi-Strauss) and the concept of the unconscious were both to be avoided.[52]

Fordist geospace

The refusal of a role for hermeneutic or cultural interpretation in sociology was paired with a denial of the importance of *spatial* or geographic difference. Two aspects of Fordism's spatial regime were especially significant for social epistemology, encouraging an understanding of sociology as based on covering laws and universal mechanisms. First, the concentration of economic development and transactions on the scalar level of the nation-state encouraged social scientists to take this scale for granted as their unit of analysis. The containment of most social practices within the boundaries of the nation-state made it seem more obvious that these practices could be accurately described by general laws. By contrast, where practices are situated in multiple and shifting sites and confound simple dichotomies of the local and the national, the treatment of countries as necessarily commensurable and self-contained units of comparative analysis becomes much less convincing (Marcus 1995).

Fordism's relative homogenization of domestic space also underwrote the positivist disavowal of the spatial variability of causal mechanisms. This tendency to seek global laws of human behavior, to disavow cultural difference (Bhabha 1994a), was strictly opposed to the humanist and historical-hermeneutic emphasis on the unique and idiosyncratic. For behavioralists in the 1950s, including those wedded to a scientist version of psychoanalysis, there were no salient differences between the United

States and the rest of the world. It therefore made perfect sense for a University of Washington sociologist (Stuart Dodd) to carry out research for the Korean War effort of the Air Force on the effectiveness of air-dropped leaflets in rural towns in Washington State (Project Revere). Rural Washingtonians stood in for Korean peasants (see DeFleur and Larsen 1958; Robin 2001, 100). Modernization theory treated the poorer parts of the world simply as less developed versions of the United States and "foreign nationals as 'underdeveloped Americans,' " in the words of one anthropologist (E. Hall 1959, 13). Sometimes it was impossible to overlook the fact that culture and ideology were impeding "moderniza-tion," as in Vietnam. But the eventual telos for all nations was identical: a condition exemplified by the United States, located beyond ideology and culture, in which social practice was reducible to the actions of rational individuals pursuing wealth, status, and power (Pletsch 1981). As a leading sociological modernization theorist insisted, there "cannot be one social science for the study of one's own country and a different one for the study of other nations" (Inkeles 1951, 269). Identical models were applied to U.S. inner-city rioters, campus antiwar protesters, and Vietnamese peasants (e.g., Popkin 1979).[53]

Fordist imperialism

A final structural characteristic of this period that was relevant for the fate of methodological positivism in sociology was the emerging role of the United States as imperialist global hegemon. U.S. imperialism cannot be subsumed under Fordism, even if it was entwined with it; indeed, we are currently in the midst of a rearticulation of U.S. imperialism with post-Fordism (Steinmetz 2003b).[54] Two aspects of the cold war global config-uration tended to work *in favor* of positivism: the U.S. orientation toward an "imperialism of free trade," and the government emphasis on counter-insurgency research, spawned at that time by the rivalry with the Soviet Union.

U.S. imperial hegemony after World War II was oriented toward mak-ing the world into an open capitalist market. The United States increas-ingly backed an imperialist but anticolonial stance, recalling the post–World War I Wilsonian era but now backed by unprecedented military predominance. This reflected the shift in U.S. priorities toward anticom-munism and containment (Louis and Robinson 1993) and a preference for free trade as against the more protectionist style of relationships between colonies and their metropoles (Schmitt 1950/2003; Gallagher and Robin-son 1953; Bergesen and Schoenberg 1980). Because the United States generally eschewed direct colonization it was not compelled to enforce a direct racial "rule of difference" (Chatterjee 1993) in its peripheral dependencies, which were treated as ostensibly self-governing.[55] Unlike colonial powers, for whom assimilation "taken to its extreme meant, quite simply, the ending of colonialism" (Sartre 1956/2001, 46), U.S. imperialism was directed toward a convergence of peripheral polities, cultures, and economic models with the American way.[56] Without gainsaying the exploitative, manipulative, and punctually violent character of U.S. imperialism, we should not ignore the fact that the postwar United States had fewer opportunities than the more directly colonial powers to intrude racist views of "native" life directly into the global peripheries. Postcolonials were increasingly treated as a mass of interchangeable potential customers, as junior Americans in the making; social scientists were enlisted in promoting this transformation. The organization of core-periphery relations in the period from the 1880s to 1945 had encouraged the development of separate theories and even sciences for the colonized (anthropology) and the colonizer (sociology, political science, etc.). By contrast, the new U.S.-dominated postwar global regime reinforced the positivist program of using a single model to analyze both "other nations" and "one's own country."[57]

The pressure to develop a generalizing approach to the non-West also stemmed from national security interests. Faced suddenly with the problem of managing a world of former European colonies and the "presumed imperial ambitions of the Soviet Union" (Pletsch 1981, 568), a major substantive focus of social science research was counterinsurgency. As Robin (2001) shows, the Korean and Vietnam wars were both accompanied by rapid expansions of social science contract research. Lest one think this involved only social scientists outside the research universities we need only recall Project Camelot, which involved many of the most prestigious U.S. social scientists in the early 1960s. Project Camelot's stated objective, according to the official description issued in 1964 by the Office of the Director of the Special Operations Research Office, was to "determine the feasibility of developing a general social systems model which would make it possible to predict and influence politically significant aspects of social change in the developing nations" (Horowitz 1967, 47; see also Herman 1996, ch. 6). A book like Rostow's *The Stages of Economic Growth* explicitly drew lessons from U.S. economic development for "the men in Djakarta, Rangoon, New Delhi, and Karachi; the men in Tehran, Baghdad, and Cairo; the men south of the desert too, in Accra, Lagos, and Salisbury," as well as Mexico, China, and India (1960, 166, xii).

Other aspects of this new U.S.-dominated world order were corrosive of the positivist unity of science program. Once the periphery is regarded from the standpoint of *production* rather than trade it takes on a very different appearance. First of all, Fordism was just one of the many forms of societalization, and usually a minor one, in the world system's margins (Alnasseri 2003). The social complexity that resulted from the articulation of "modes of regulation" and "modes of production" in the peripheries seemed to defy generalizing social science laws. These real differences made the application of universal models to peripheral societies less compelling. The complex cultural hybridity in postcolonial sites made generalization even more difficult, whether one was analyzing resistance to development or the microlevel processes of converting labor power into labor.[58]

Generalizing approaches were also continually undercut by the pervasive "three worlds" model (Pletsch 1981), which was predicated on the division between the communist, advanced capitalist, and postcolonial parts of the world system. This map called attention to the instability of the third category, which was permanently susceptible to the lures of communism, generally considered to be an "ideological" system rather than a "rational-natural" one.[59] The Third World was associated in this scheme with "tradition, culture, religion, irrationality, underdevelopment, overpopulation, political chaos, and so on" (Pletsch 1981, 574; Steinmetz 1999).

Another barrier to the universalization of generalizing models was racism. A common response to the scientific difficulties of encompassing the periphery within general developmental schemas has been to fall back on older discourses of cultural essentialism. A team of social scientists sponsored by the Human Relations Research Office (an army-funded think tank) to study the Korean and Chinese POWs at Koje Island during the Korean War pointed to "unchanging behavioral traits of 'orientals'" (authoritarianism, adaptability, an orientation to short-range calculations and personal bargaining, etc.) as reasons for communist organizational success. These categories were derived from "material on Korean and Chinese culture contained in existing studies, so far as it is consistent with the data of the existing study," and especially from the work of Lucien Pye, "America's foremost orientalist of the period" (Meyers and Bradbury in Bradbury, Meyers, and Biderman 1968, 281, n. 115; Robin 2001, 149). Similarly, some social scientists insisted during the Vietnam War that the Vietnamese were "peoples of the past," unsuited for modernization, with "no example, tradition, training, or even psychological aptitude for such an achievement" (Kahn 1968, 340–341). This flew directly in the face of the universal picture of human behavior. Huntington's *Political Order in Changing Societies* (1968) broke with the generic story about modernization by arguing for cross-national differences in the adoption of selected parts of the modernity package, partly in an effort to justify U.S. support for "unmodern"—that is, undemocratic—client regimes. As became clear in subsequent publications, this was connected to an essentialist differentialism according to which Muslims and Africans are said to refuse modernity for inherent cultural reasons (Huntington 1996; Harrison and Huntington 2000; see also Lewis 2002).

The partial resistance of the Third World to regularity determinism thus marked a limit condition, even in the golden age of Fordism, to the reach of social science positivism. It is thus perhaps no coincidence that sociology turned away from the periphery, and also no coincidence that the discipline dedicated to studying the colonized world, anthropology, was constitutionally unable to become positivist and continued to emphasize relatively ungeneralizable research (Stocking 2001a, 317; Keane, this volume). Even some well-funded social scientists who set out with a generalizing take on the (post)colonial periphery experienced an epistemological change of heart. For some participants in the Camelot Project the mid-1960s marked a turning point at which they recognized the futility of the "search for universal laws of human behavior" (Robin 2001, 214, discussing testimony to that effect by Gabriel Almond, Kalman Silvert, and Jessie Bernard). Methodological critiques of modernization theory began to appear in the second half of the 1960s (e.g., Bendix 1967; D. Tripp 1973).

Similarly, postwar area studies represented a compromise formation and a site of struggle between "generalists" and "particularists." Area studies originated as an effort to adapt "first world social science to particularistic second and third world contexts" (Pletsch 1981, 582). Yet, at the end of the 1960s, the "largest proportion of area specialists [still came from] history, anthropology, language and literature, and the particularistic segments of political science" (Lambert 1973, 3). Area studies retained connections to the interpretive, linguistic, and humanistic approaches that had been so contemptuously forsaken by methodological positivism.

These idiosyncratic and linguistic approaches were necessarily preferable to the generalizing approaches (Dutton, this volume). Indeed, there was continuity in some respects between the "tradition versus modernity" distinction and the earlier and more explicitly racist Victorian approaches, from a period in which humanistic and scientific approaches were less polarized. Tradition was an undifferentiated category functioning only as a "before" to modernity in the new schemas, and in this respect it played a role similar to the "summational statements" about the Orient in older Orientalist discourse (Said 1978, 255) or the raciological generalizations of the eighteenth and nineteenth centuries (S. Gould 1996). Some writers have therefore been able to charge that modernization theory was simply a "cleaned up" and more respectable version of earlier languages of "primitivism" and social Darwinism (Mazrui 1968; Pletsch 1981, 575). The failure of essentialism to accurately perceive cultural difference is as unsatisfactory as the outright denial of difference. More recently, area studies has started to move beyond both the essentialist and the difference-denying approaches (Gaonkar 2001; Eisenstadt 2000). The reasons for this movement beyond methodological positivism are discussed in the concluding section of this paper. As in sociology, however, it is significant that the positivist dream of replacing place-names by the names of general "variables" has not disappeared even in area studies.[60]

Even as the U.S. emphasis on free trade imperialism pressed toward a universalizing form of positivism in the postwar period, other forces undercut the tendency to enfold the periphery into general laws. We should not attribute this resistance solely to the object itself, for this would seem to accept the self-description of the advanced capitalist core as having transcended culture and ideology. Sociological discourse on the non-West was multivocal even during the Fordist period, fluctuating between nomothetic approaches that embraced the periphery into a universal framework and essentialisms that attributed unique and timeless traits to the (post)colonial other. The survival of nonnomothetic perspectives was related to the complex internal organization of postcolonial social systems, the instability of their political boundaries, the competition between the United States and the Soviet Union, the persistence of colonial and Orientalist representations of the non-Western Other, and the relative autonomy of area studies from the more positivistic social science disciplines.

My aim in this section has been to trace some of the ways Fordism resonated with, and directly promoted, U.S. sociology's positivist epistemic unconscious starting in World War II. To claim that sociologists' spontaneous images and theories of the social were influenced by the wider social structures they inhabit does not mean that such images and ontologies directly *reflect* social reality. On the one hand, the Fordist mode of regulation was accompanied by a series of self-interpretations that guided the way it was experienced.[61] The main components of U.S. Fordism—stabilization through demand management, homogenization of consumer tastes, rising worker incomes pegged to productivity, collaborative labor unions, nation-state centrism—were constantly broadcast to the denizens of the Fordist metropolises as the American Way of Life. When positivists pointed out the connections between existing social patterns and their preferred manner of studying society, reality seemed to ratify their approach.

Totalitarianism and Social Science Positivism

A further element of U.S. culture that tended to strengthen the positivist position in the social sciences was the discussion of the role of science in the rise of Nazism and totalitarianism. This was related to global Fordism but not reducible to it. Writing in 1941 when the target of his reference could not be mistaken, Marcuse accused the sociological positivism derived from Comte of bearing "the seeds of a philosophic justification of authoritarianism" by repudiating metaphysics and thereby also "man's claim to alter and reorganize his social institutions in accordance with his rational will" (Marcuse 1941/1960, 342, 344; see also Bannister 1992). Horkheimer and Adorno's 1944 *Dialectic of Enlightenment* (1986) opened with a Heideggerian critique of the Enlightenment and moved from there through a series of dialectically unfolding steps to industrial capitalist modernity, anti-Semitism, and Nazism. This text was the fount of an entire field of interpretations of fascism and totalitarianism as products of (a distorted) scientific modernity starting in the 1960s, when the Frankfurt School was rediscovered (see Arato and Gebhart 1988), and somewhat later with post-structuralism. Hollinger recalls that the literary cohort that was attacked by C. P. Snow in 1959 for their supposed proximity to fascism "regrouped, and came out some years later . . . to attack science itself as crypto-fascist" (1996, 166, 171). Much of this was "under the cover" of postmodernism and Michel Foucault, who published the memorable and provocative phrase "Knowledge is not made for understanding; it is made for cutting" (1977b, 154).

In the context of the cold war competition with the Soviet Union and in the immediate aftermath of Nazism and the Holocaust, however, it was difficult for antifascists to criticize modern science. The prestige of science had increased so dramatically that such critiques seemed quixotic if not treasonable. The exponential expansion of think tanks and research contracts in this period is extremely relevant here. This military-intellectual matrix integrated a huge number of social scientists into a culture that connected the struggle against the totalitarian enemy with emulation of the natural sciences and disdain for humanistic and historical approaches. Discussions of the assault on science shifted from the Nazi to the Soviet example (e.g., M. Polanyi 1945). In a study of voting by Lazarsfeld et al. (1948/1968), for instance, the authors pointedly refused to blame capitalism or communication technology for extremist psychopathologies in modern society (Robin 2001, 63), insisting instead that a robust fabric of primary groups and opinion leaders filtered the commodified messages emanating from the mass media.

Antifascism was at least as strongly associated with positivist as with nonpositivist positions. As Hollinger remarks, the "faith that science and democracy are indissolubly bound up in a single cultural mode . . . was passionately reaffirmed in the late 1930s and early 1940s by enemies of the Third Reich" (1996, 81). The suggestion that it was precisely the *lack* of a modern scientific culture that had contributed to fascism retroactively cast suspicion on the entire nonpositivist tradition running from Hegel and the German Romantics to Marx, Dilthey, and the critical theorists of the interwar period. This narrative was doubly damaging because most of the antipositivist thinkers had arisen in a German-speaking context and could therefore be connected to German exceptionalism at least through guilt by association. According to a version of the exceptionalist theory popular at the time, Nazism had resulted mainly from irrationalist trends in the German philosophical tradition.[62]

After 1945, Americans began to associate Soviet oppression with hostility to science. Because the word "science" in this period was usually understood as a description of the natural sciences offered by the logical positivists, this only bolstered any opposition to antipositivist criticism. It took someone with the intellectual and moral stature of Adorno to reopen the debate with his 1957 essay on "Sociology and Empirical Research" and his 1962 critique of Popper, "Logic of the Social Sciences."[63] Of course, even then Popper responded by calling the Frankfurt School "irrationalist and intelligence-destroying" and putting it in the same camp as the "enemies of the open society" (1976b, 289, 300; 1962/1971). Being called an enemy of the open society for criticizing positivism would perhaps not get you fired or investigated by COINTELPRO or the Verfassungsschutz (Office for the Protection of the Constitution, or the West German equivalent of the FBI), but it still had a chilling effect. Moreover, none of this was translated into English until the mid-1970s.

The Long Reign of Methodological Positivism

One result of this overdetermined conjuncture after 1945 was the solid implantation of methodological positivism as doxa in the sociological discipline.[64] Despite differences of taste or viewpoint, most of the players in the field seem to have recognized common stakes and agreed on legitimate definitions of field-specific cultural capital. Reputational, social, and economic capital in sociology tended to accrue to more positivist/empiricist/scientistic positions. Fluency in positivist methodological positions began to function as a field-specific form of scientific prestige. Even those who disagreed with the positivist position tended to collude in its dominance; those who did not adjust to this new regime were rechanneled willy-nilly into less rigidly positivist disciplines or into poorly regarded sociology departments. Sociology became a well-structured field at last.

The concept of the scientific field implies that alternative positions are dominated but not necessarily unthinkable. The entrenchment of positivist orthodoxy should be understood as a multifaceted process of rearticulating categories and definitions, graduate curricula, and funding priorities, and of redefining standard models for journal articles. Of course, social theory has taught us that the repetitive "physical" engagement in a practice that one disapproves of, or with which one disagrees "internally," can still have profound effects on habitus (Bourdieu) or take the form of an "ideological interpellation" (Althusser). Or, in Orwell's (1936/1968) description of a colonial official: "He wears a mask, and his face grows to fit it."[65] These unperceived effects of physical training can be as lasting and thoroughgoing as a deliberate conversion experience or a conscious "paradigm shift." Indeed, nonpositivist positions began to seem unscientific, unprofessional, or nonsociological partly as result of such training.[66]

There may indeed have been little knowledge of epistemological alternatives among sociology PhDs who were socialized into the discipline during the 1950s and 1960s, until the critical movements emerged in the later 1960s. But there were dissonant voices even in the heart of the cold war period. A short list of sociological critics of methodological positivism would have to include C. Wright Mills, Hans Gerth, Howard P. Becker, Howard S. Becker, Reinhard Bendix, Alvin Gouldner, and Theodor Adorno (and starting in the early 1960s, Jürgen Habermas). All of these critics lost some of their scientific authority in relation to the purveyors of the new dominant paradigm. Critics of the sociological mainstream during the 1950s and 1960s like Mills and Gouldner attacked quantitative methods and Parsonian grand theory even while they seemed to endorse other features of methodological positivism.[67] Some opponents of methodological positivism were "excommunicated," others "converted," and still others criticized the mainstream while reproducing some of its central premises. The role of Parsons, who shifted from being a critic of positivism to promoting it, is best understood as that of an insider critic.[68] Indeed, the self-proclaimed positivist sociologist George A. Lundberg pointed in 1964 to "convergences in the theoretical positions of Parsons and S. C. Dodd" (of leaflet-dropping fame), whose systems were "hitherto assumed by many" to be "incompatible" (169–170).

Conclusion: Toward a Third *Positivismusstreit?*

I have argued that Fordism was a key ingredient in the processes that tipped the hand of constituencies long bent on making methodological positivism dominant in sociology. Fordism helped to forge a form of social science that was acultural, ahistorical, and individualist with respect to its basic units of analysis and oriented toward general laws, replication, prediction, and value-freedom. The Fordist security state drew heavily on social knowledge packaged in a positivist format and pumped massive amounts of money into research organized this way.

The period between 1945 and 1965 was a powerful foundational moment in sociology whose effects continue to be felt today. Graduate students in the leading departments are still required to take statistics courses but not to study textual interpretation. The NSF still tends to support mainly quantitative research in sociology. Methodological concepts such as scope conditions, path dependency, and interviewer effects seem to acknowledge problems with positivism, but they retain the idea of general laws, social processes that are not shaped by history, and interviews purged of subjectivity. Some sociological subfields are only now beginning to question the adequacy of modernization theory. Although there is no space to treat the intervening period between the 1960s and the present in any detail, I want to consider briefly the effects of two processes that might have been expected to have undermined the reigning methodological positivism since then. The first is a series of epistemological challenges to the discipline's positivist mainstream since the late 1960s. The second is the collapse of Fordism (which began almost as soon as it reached its fullest elaboration) and the ongoing transition to post-Fordism.

A wave of challenges to the positivist metaposition began to appear just a few years after it became enshrined as orthodoxy. One year after the publication of the book *The Uses of Sociology* (Lazarsfeld et al. 1967) an essay appeared entitled (ironically, of course) "Tuer les sociologues" (Kill the sociologists) by Daniel Cohn-Bendit and other sociology students at Nanterre, translated into English under the less bellicose title "Why Sociologists?" (Cohn-Bendit et al. 1969). Although hardly a theoretical tour de force, this essay signaled the onset of a long period of challenges to the positivist mainstream in sociology, some of them cumulative, many of them recuperated. In 1968 a caucus was formed within the American Sociological Association called the Sociology Liberation Movement. Gouldner's *Coming Crisis*, a frontal assault on positivism, was published in 1970, followed by a series of (self-)critical studies of the history of U.S. sociology.[69]

The challenges to methodological positivism in the late 1960s and 1970s can be seen as a sort of intellectual pendant to the broader rejection of Fordist homogenization by the first wave of "new social movements" in that same era. Just as the anti-Fordist new social movements criticized capitalism while simultaneously providing models for a resolution of its crisis (Mayer 1988; Mayer and Roth 1995), the intellectual challenges to positivism during the 1960s and 1970s rejected positivism while generating intellectual resources for repairing some of its intellectually tattered loose ends. A depth-realist positivism modeled on mechanistic Marxism became palatable to some sociologists and was workable as a unifying ground for a refurbished discipline.

A similar set of parallels can be drawn between external and intra-disciplinary movements in the 1970s and 1980s. The new social movements of these decades were now responding to the final unraveling of Fordism rather than the pathologies that accompanied its era of greatest glory;[70] by the same token, the turn to history within sociology in the 1970s echoed the disappearance of the Fordist standardization of time, space, and culture. The relative decline in social science funding at the end of the 1970s corresponded to a crisis of confidence in big science sociology. The new cultural studies/cultural sociology of the 1980s and 1990s can in turn be related to the emergence of post-Fordist, globalized regulation and a version of capitalism that was increasingly centered on culture and self-promoting ("entrepreneurial") forms of subjectivity. The current epistemological turn, finally, has emerged contemporaneously with the consolidation of post-Fordism, indexing the central role of science, technology, and information in that formation (along lines first sketched by Lyotard 1979/1984).[71]

As with the account of methodological positivism in the previous section, the emergence of these critical movements can be understood only against the overall macrosociological and historical context. Although the earliest critical movements in the 1960s contained fundamental critiques of the dominant mode of sociology, they were also in many ways defined by the Fordist conditions that had originally underwritten methodological positivism. The latest critical movements, by contrast, have come into existence in a post-Fordist environment. Unlike the earlier criticisms, they do not share social "conditions of birth" with most of their positivist opponents. Nor do post-Fordist social conditions resonate as strongly with positivism as the earlier mode of regulation. While the intradisciplinary conditions may still disproportionately reward positivism, this is less the case with the world beyond the academy.

In their most radical forms, neo-Marxist, feminist, historical, and cultural sociology were corrosive of the central ontological and epistemological premises of methodological positivism. Neo-Marxism and feminism attacked empiricist ontology, historical sociology provided tools for dismantling the positivist emphasis on invariant and time-independent laws, and the cultural turn reasserted the importance of concept dependence. The paradox is that each of these challenges began to be recuperated almost as soon as it appeared. As with the 1950s and 1960s there were, of course, many exceptions. But just as Craig Calhoun (1996) has argued that there was a domestication of historical sociology, the epistemological challenges of these other critical movements were largely defused. These movements tended to attack only a subset of the main tenets of positivism or to scale back their epistemic agendas and advocate instead for the study of previously ignored objects. Sociologists began to produce positivist studies of class and gender and to use history as little more than a means of increasing the number of data points (Sewell 1996). Another strategy of (self-)containment was to translate a critical movement into the promotion of a new "independent variable" that needed to be thrown into the analysis (as in the now shopworn "bringing x back in" trope; see Homans 1964). Culture was redefined as a delimited set of objects rather than an optic for understanding the reflexivity and concept dependency of social life in general. U.S. sociology has not, until recently, seen many signs of a genuine crisis at the fundamental level of its philosophical and methodological assumptions, despite the proliferation of ostensibly dissident theoretical approaches and labels.

If I am correct that social epistemologies are undergirded not just by intradisciplinary mechanisms and funding patterns but also by the ways macrocultural conditions reverberate or collide with them, one might expect the cultural and epistemological turns to have some staying power. Each resonates in important ways with the flexible and information-centered world of the post-Fordist "new economy." Alvin Gouldner's (1970) prediction three decades ago that U.S. sociology would move through a period of crisis characterized by the collapse of theoretical hegemony to a less positivist and more reflexive polycentrism might then turn out to be correct, if premature.[72]

The most recent dissenting movement in sociology is the turn to epistemology and science itself.[73] The contributions of the current epistemological challenge to the possible dismantling of positivism are twofold. First, it intervenes much more centrally in the fact-value debate than the earlier movements. Second, by clarifying the basic stakes at issue, this epistemological turn may make it possible to perceive the complementarity of the earlier challenges, to bundle their critical potentials, and to ward off efforts to lasso them back into a recharged positivist orthodoxy. Recall that methodological positivism itself represented a joining together of empiricist ontology, positivist epistemology, and scientism. The epistemological turn, by clarifying the basic stakes at issue, might make visible the complementarity of the Marxist/feminist, historical, and cultural turns. Given my critique of the notion of invariant patterns of social behavior, it would be perverse to try to predict what direction sociology will take. But one possible future, at least, is postpositivist.

A second scenario, however, acknowledges the deep and abiding implantation of methodological positivism in disciplinary institutions, patterns of socialization, and the habituses of individual sociologists, and its reinforcement by extra-academic social structures other than the mode of regulation. The state, private organizations, and even social movements continue to demand social knowledge packaged in positivist formats. The reasons for this preference are complex. It may be that there is a built-in affinity between projects of societal regulation per se and positivist knowledge formats. The impetus behind projects of "flexibilizing" capitalism does encompass criticisms of the positivist forms of knowledge that undergirded less flexible models of production. An entire array of critiques of the Fordist welfare-security state, some of which have been built into post-Fordism, proposed alternative forms of social knowledge and intervention. At the same time, post-Fordist policies of privatization, localization, and flexibilization are oriented toward logics of recommodifying labor power and redisciplining the poor. Economic flexibilization has involved first and foremost the imposition of a *uniform* neoliberal model on all places and situations. The concept of social capital, which is linked to neoliberal policies of privatization, has been applied in an "imperialist" way, running roughshod over disciplinary distinctions (Somers, this volume). Post-Fordist interventions thus seem to rely as much as Fordism did on decontextualized economic models of human subjectivity.[74]

As for politics, post-Fordism has not led to the complete elimination of state-organized forms of regulation or to "spontaneous" forms of societal-ization organized by "invisible hand" mechanisms—despite the barrage of discourse and policy since 1980 organized around "deregulation" (Prasad 2000). Instead, new forms of state regulation have emerged in a series of wrenching moves and in the wake of the "creative destruction" of earlier schemas. The state is still the most important center, the primus inter pares, for organizing projects of societal regulation. This has become even more evident since the beginning of the Bush administration's new impe-rialism and war on terrorism (Steinmetz 2003b).[75] This is not to ignore shifts in emphasis and scale since the 1980s, including the increasing im-portance of parastatal and nongovernmental centers as organizers of so-cial regulation.[76] But even in the current period, the state, considered at all of its scalar levels, is still the superordinate coordinator even for privately financed regulatory initiatives, and it continues to organize most of the familiar legal, infrastructural, and welfare-statist interventions. Indeed, during the 1990s, when the post-Fordist regime seemed to achieve a sort of consolidation, state funding for science again began to increase in the United States.[77] Of course it is still an open question whether this form of governance will rely to the same extent as its predecessor on positivist forms of social science.

Post-Fordist governance may continue to privilege positivistically pack-aged social science knowledge even as the global conditions of post-Ford-ism make methodological positivism less spontaneously convincing.[78] Pos-itivists are also able to reproduce themselves intellectually through the academic equivalent of artificial fertility, defying the "nature" of environ-ing social trends. Whether "society's nature" or the discipline's "second nature" will prevail is impossible to predict.

Notes

This chapter has benefited from generous comments from Julia Adams, Bruce Curtis, Harriet Friedmann, Julia Hell, Webb Keane, Ching Kwan Lee, Jeff Paige, Monica Prasad, Ian Robinson, Bill Sewell Jr., Dan Smail, Mayer Zald, and a seminar at the University of Toronto sponsored by the Canadian Centre for the Study of the U.S. and the Toronto editors of *Critical Sociology* and organized by Y. Michal Bodemann.

1 Conventionalism, as I use the term here, includes standpoint theory, constructivism and constructionism (Hacking 1999), and epistemological idealism. Strictly speaking, conventionalism is the doctrine that the success or failure of scientific theories in achieving acceptance is based on convention, that is, on considerations other than the correspondence between theory and its object. "Idealism" is the term for the view articulated most famously by Berkeley (1734/1998) that denies the existence (or the

accessibility to the observer, which has the same consequences) of an external reality existing "independently of our theoretical beliefs and concepts" (Keat and Urry 1975, 5; also see Bhaskar 1975/1997, who speaks of "conventionalist super-idealism").

2   Keane (this volume) suggests that cultural anthropology in the United States has been less beguiled by positivism than the other social science disciplines, even during the strong push for scientific respectability during the first two-thirds of the twentieth century (but see Wax 1997 for a different assessment). *Cultural* relativism, a normative stance that has characterized U.S. cultural anthropology throughout most of the twentieth century, should be distinguished from *epistemological* relativism, which critical realism accepts, and judgmental relativism, which it rejects (Bhaskar 1986; Collier, this volume).

3   See Walter Goodman, "Thinkers Who Would Be Doers See Social Injustice Wherever They Turn," *New York Times*, August 19, 2000. Recalling Richard Bernstein's reports on the MLA meetings in the 1990s, this one is exercised mainly by a suggested loss of objectivity. See Bernstein, "The Rising Hegemony of the Politically Correct," *New York Times*, October 28, 1990.

4   Lundberg (1955) in the 1950s is typical in disavowing the label positivist, which he had openly embraced before the war (1939a), and in characterizing his own viewpoint more neutrally as that of "natural science." Even during the 1950s positivism was not so secure as to be *doxic*, at least when it presented itself in overt philosophical and methodological terms. Nagel (1961/1979) also eschews the term positivism. But see Riemer (1953) for evidence that sociologists in the 1950s clearly recognized the philosophical basis of Lundberg's position.

5   An example of such rethinking is Arthur Stinchcombe, whose *Constructing Social Theories* (1968) was largely positivist but whose *Theoretical Methods in Social History* (1978) represented a completely different epistemological position (see also Stinchcombe 1991). Eclectic and complex, Stinchcombe's work has reflected and contributed to the critical theoretical movements (including historical sociology) that intervened in the decade between the two books, while also constituting a target for some of them.

6   See Bourdieu (1972/1977) for the use of the terms doxa and orthodoxy in this context.

7   Positivism as defined below is even more entrenched in economics, demography, political science, and psychology. Economics and demography were already established and accepted as *sciences* when sociology, anthropology, and political science were still facing what Camic (1995; Camic and Xie 1994; see also Breslau 2003) calls the "newcomers' dilemma" in the mid-twentieth century, the dilemma of proving themselves as science by emulating the established natural sciences while simultaneously differentiating themselves from each other. Political science is similar to sociology with respect to the conditions it faced in the mid-twentieth century and the path that it followed as a result. The different ways the critical challenges to positivism since the 1960s have played themselves out in political science seem to stem largely from the former discipline's different position vis-á-vis the imperial U.S. state. Sociology has been articulated with, and drawn financial support and personnel from, the lower-prestige branches of the welfare state (see below). Political science has been integrated into the more prestigious foreign policy branches, as revealed most recently by the "Straussian" influence on the U.S. government's imperialist interventions (Atlas 2003). The various social sciences have also differed with respect to the postundergraduate careers and policy-relevant academic departments with which they are associated. Here again,

sociology has been connected to fields with lower cultural capital, such as social work, while political science has become a feeder for law schools. None of these claims can be generalized to countries other than the United States, of course.

8   I have found only one example of related use of this term, in an essay by a symbolic interactionist (Littrell 1997).

9   In other work I have proposed regulation-theoretic accounts of the rise of social policy and the welfare state (Steinmetz 1993), new social movements (1994), and right-wing social movements (1997b; forthcoming a). See Jessop (1990, 1999) and Brand and Raza (2003) for detailed recent discussions of regulation theory.

10 Of course, logical positivism itself was associated with the left, as Sandra Harding (this volume) reminds us. Some of the key contributors to methodological positivism in postwar U.S. sociology were associated with the old left, including Phil Hauser and Leslie Kish. Alvin Gouldner was a left-wing sociologist who seems almost to have kept his epistemological criticisms under wraps until the McCarthyite cold war began to thaw in the 1960s (see Gouldner 1962, 1970). Only since the 1970s and 1980s has the "epistemological left" (Novick 1991) differentiated itself clearly and sharply from the political left.

11 On critical realism, see Bhaskar (1979, 1989, 1994, 1975/1997), Collier (1994), Steinmetz (1998), Steinmetz and Chae (2002).

12 In terms of evidence not discussed here, my own participation in three U.S. sociology departments (Wisconsin, Chicago, and Michigan) and my personal socialization into a natural science version of positivism are important. As with Sewell's paper (this volume), mine is thus a form of autocritique. During the heyday of methodological positivism (and still today, to a lesser extent), sociologists believed that it was more scientific to work on topics in which they had *less* personal involvement and investment. This premise stemmed from a scientistic emulation of the natural sciences, which were thought to have successfully separated knowledge from values. The primary source of social distortion in social research was construed as bias, located in researchers' minds. It was correct that the relationship between the researcher and his or her object of research was more complex in the social sciences than in the natural sciences, given the *recursive* relations between the two. Yet the rejection of "value-laden" science was applied unsystematically only to some stages of the scientific process and not others. Social scientists seem to have believed, for instance, that they could not be as objective about themselves or their own discipline as about other scientists and other disciplines. Yet few argued at this time that middle-class sociologists' class position might prevent them from writing objectively about the lower classes, or that metropolitan observers' associations with colonizing or imperial states could hinder their ability to generate dispassionate knowledge about colonized or postcolonial peoples.

13 In a separate article (Steinmetz forthcoming) and in a book in preparation, I provide more detailed readings of core texts from the golden age of methodological positivism and the more recent period.

14 There are a few sociologists who still openly defend and embrace positivism, including Jonathan Turner, Gerhard Lenski (1988), Guy Swanson (see Bryant 1992), and, in his most recent work, Arthur Stinchcombe (2002). Griswold (1990) lightheartedly defended a "provisional, provincial positivism." Abbott (1992a) proposed what he called a "narrative positivism," but he combines this positivism with interpretivism in an eclec-

tic mix (1990) and offers some of the most trenchant critiques of mainstream sociological statistical method (1988b, 1992b, this volume). A recent Belgian conference discussed plural positivisms in sociology (see Despy-Meyer and Devriese 1999, 95–143).

15   See, for example, Blalock (1964, 1969) and the other key texts from the 1960s and early 1970s cited by Gartrell and Gartrell (1996, 144); for a critique of Blalock, see R. Miller (1987, 240–241, n. 11). Lazarsfeld and Rosenberg (1955) still included a section in their methods text on the "philosophy of the social sciences"—one that was explicitly positivist (see especially the entry by Hans Zetterberg in Lazarsfeld and Rosenberg 1955, 533–554).

16   See, for example, R. Collins (1989, 129), who implicitly stakes out a nonpositivist, even critical realist, position that contradicts his explicit endorsement of positivism there. Collins's arguments in this essay generally line up with realism, even critical realism, and against positivism. Yet he makes only one reference to a realist philosopher (H. Putnam 1983) and none to writers like Peirce, Harré, Bhaskar, Hacking, Collier, or Miller.

17   See Layder (1988) for an interesting discussion of the interdependencies between specific epistemologies, theoretical discourses, and methods.

18   As I argued in the introduction to this volume, the relationship between ontology and epistemology should be viewed as a distinction, not a dichotomy.

19   To the extent that sociologists began talking about *scope conditions*, they were acknowledging time dependence, even if the very need to coin such a term reflected a baseline scientism.

20   This refusal of the time and space dependence of concepts is usually implicit, as in theories of economic change that apply the same concepts to the ancient or medieval world as to the capitalist present (Rostow 1960; G. Cohen 1978). In the most self-conscious statements of methodological positivism, however, it is explicit; one thinks of Popper's (1957/1991) critique of "historicism" or the statements of some of the modernization theorists, like Inkeles (1951), discussed in the next section. See also the quote by Becker (1996, 6), quoted by Somers in her contribution to this volume, about the applicability of the concept of social capital to "the distant past."

21   On the political conditions in Wilhelmine Germany that led to German sociologists' rapid convergence around the doctrine of value-freedom (*Wertfreiheit*), see Rammstedt (1988); see also Abel (1929); for a recent discussion of Weber's "positivism," see Hekman (1994).

22   See also "Campus Life: Scholars' Group, Accused of Bias, Divides Faculty," *New York Times*, October 21, 1990.

23   In another essay I track the epistemic multivocality, or wavering, in a recent methodological treatise that attempts to stake out a depth-realist positivism (Steinmetz 2004b; see Mahoney and Rueschemeyer 2002).

24   The fact that Davis goes on to equate causal analysis with "discovering relationships among *phenomena*" (my emphasis) suggests again that methodological positivism was at least as influential as functionalism during the supposed heyday of Parsonianism. There was also an effort to render Parsons's theory compatible with positivist research methods (see note 69 in this essay).

25   Sorokin (1928, 727n, 545, quoted in Merton 1936/1968a, 25–26) actually argued that Franklin Giddings was a "pioneer of . . . world sociology," while insisting that Marx added nothing new and that "what is original is far from scientific" in Marx.

26   H. Friedrich (1992) criticizes certain self-proclaimed antipositivist approaches for their "cryptopositivism." King et al.'s *Designing Social Inquiry* (1994) defends a contemporary empiricist/positivist position while eschewing the label (see Mihic et al., this volume; Steinmetz 1998).

27   Bourdieu clearly had mainstream U.S. sociology in mind, as it figured prominently at the beginning of the paragraph from which this quotation is taken.

28   "Distinction" is field-specific. One can hardly ignore the fact that positivism and scientism have been less than distinguished positions in other fields, for instance, the arts, since the early twentieth century. In philosophy, positivism has had no eminent defenders for decades. Although it seems obvious to some writers (e.g., Bhaskar 1989, ch. 4; Bourdieu 1981, 282) that positivism is the "spontaneous ideology" of the natural sciences, I am less certain that positivism will continue to be the most influential position in sociology (see the conclusion to the current essay).

29   Marxism, feminism, historical and cultural sociology, critical race theory, and the sociology of science—probably the main critical movements in U.S. sociology during the past thirty years—all had precursors in the discipline before the consolidation of methodological positivism.

30   Paradoxically, Latour's (1987, 1999) approach ends up looking internalist even though he rejects the dichotomies of human and nonhuman, society and nature, epistemology and ontology, words and things, and so on.

31   With respect to the discipline of sociology, Camic (1995; Camic and Xie 1994) has argued that early U.S. sociologists were motivated by the scientific "newcomers' dilemma" to emulate more established scientific disciplines. In his work on Parsons, Camic (1987, 426; 1989) stresses the immediate university field, that is, the "Harvard scene."

32   Bourdieu's view of science is conventionalist in its rejection of the view that epistemologies or theories gain prestige simply because they are more adequate to their object. This applies only to the social sciences, however, if only by default, because Bourdieu does not extend his theory to the natural sciences.

33   Hollinger's (1996, 125–128) own account of "Academic Culture at the University of Michigan" and at U.S. research universities more generally in the key 1945–62 period focuses on the quantum leap in government funding after 1945 and suggests that it had strong effects on the resultant culture of "academic entrepreneurship" and on the research products.

34   Robin's (2001, 220–225) excellent book, for instance, provides a careful account of the role of military think tanks in promoting U.S. social science behavioralism, but it does not account for the *crisis* of this framework from the mid-1960s on except as a seemingly natural response to its political and epistemological inadequacies.

35   At more concrete levels of practice, the overall fabric of commonsense or agreed-upon culture will, of course, give way to patterned differences, and these will be correlated with social class or other dimensions of social hierarchy.

36   Merton's widely cited and often revised and reprinted "Note on Science and Democracy" (1942) focuses on "communism" and disinterestedness as transhistorical features of the scientific field, suggesting again than his historicizing focus was more externalist than internalist (see also Hall 1963).

37   See also Habermas (1970) and, for an earlier sociological diagnosis of the "anti-science movement" and widespread "latent and active hostility to science," Merton (1938, 336).

38   Albion Small, the first professor of sociology in the United States and founder of the first U.S. sociology department and journal, the *American Journal of Sociology*, is a slightly more ambiguous case. Small studied in Germany and published a book on the German Cameralists (1909), a topical choice that signaled an interest in the less positivist pole of the nineteenth-century intellectual division in Germany between historical economics and the "Manchester School." But he also published a book on Adam Smith and modern sociology (1907), and was influenced by the Austrian social Darwinist Gustav Ratzenhofer, both of which align him with the mainstream of sociological scientism. On Small, see Dibble (1975); on Giddings, see Camic and Xie (1994); on both, see O'Connor (1942).

39   Between 1922 and 1929, Chicago received the most money from the Laura Spelman Rockefeller Memorial and the Social Science Research Council (which itself received a great deal of its money from the Rockefeller Foundation): $3.5 million in institutional grants, including direct staff support, along with the "lion's share of the fellowship money and a new social sciences building" (D. Ross 1991, 402).

40   Of course, the fact that seven of the eleven contributors were listed as MDs underscored the ongoing medicalization of U.S. psychoanalysis (discussed in the introduction to this volume), which played a role in transforming the field in a more scientistic direction.

41   Gouldner's *Coming Crisis of Western Sociology* (1970) labels Parsons a positivist. This evaluation is based on placing Parsons politically in a lineage running back to Comte, the discipline's original positivist. But Gouldner ignores the redefinitions of positivism that had occurred during the twentieth century (see C. Bryant 1989).

42   This is not to say that sociologists were not concerned with this problem before the war and the Holocaust. Already in 1938 Merton discussed the ways "hostility toward science" in Nazi Germany was threatening to "curtail scientific activity" (321–322; see Hollinger 1996, 83).

43   *Vergesellschaftung* is defined as the various "complex social processes in and through which specific institutional orders and their broader social preconditions are secured." One premise of this concept is that "the existence of 'society' cannot be taken for granted: it must be constituted and reproduced through more or less precarious social processes and practices which articulate diverse social relations to produce a 'society effect' " (Jessop 1990, 4–5).

44   The fact that Fordism was centered on the scalar level of the nation-state allows us to privilege this unit of analysis and comparison. That this cannot be taken for granted in the discussion of post-Fordist regulatory projects, which take place on a variety of different scales, is a commonplace in current discussions (see Brand and Raza 2003).

45   Some regulation theorists see this as a problem. Discussions of whether regulation theory's usefulness is limited to analysis of the Fordist epoch are often tinged with regret. This is perhaps not surprising, given that most regulation theorists are economists (in France) or political scientists (in Germany) rather than historians, and are therefore focused on the present. Indeed, one regulation theorist suggests that we should "forget regulation theory" if it were only of "historical interest" (Röttger 2003, 39; 2001).

46   Indeed, even though the earliest regulation-theoretic interventions were by economists, they underscored the reciprocally determining relations between economics and politics (Röttger 2003, 18–19). More recent work in this tradition has encompassed all sorts of social practices without privileging one or the other (see Jessop 1990).

47   For accounts of the growth of public funding for science and sociology, see Geiger (1993), Gieryn (1999, 65–114), Kleinman (1995), J. Wilson (1983), Klausner and Lidz (1986), Larsen (1992), Featherman and Vinovskis (2001). On the specific military connections of this research money, see Needell (1983), Robin (2001).

48   As Keat and Urry (1975, 91) point out, Alpert's PhD thesis (1939) was influential in making Durkheim palatable to positivist sociology in the United States by arguing that Durkheim "did not adhere to such a strong interpretation of the social as had often been claimed" and because his aim "was to build up, inductively, general laws of social life through the accumulation of statistical findings." *Suicide* was privileged over *The Elementary Forms* (1912/1955) or *Primitive Classification* (1903/1963).

49   Of course, Shils played both sides of the street epistemologically, collaborating with Janowitz on the Wehrmacht study (1948) that denied the importance of ideology, and even coining the infamous phrase "end of ideology" (1955).

50   I am using "culture" in the broadest possible sense (see my introduction to *State/Culture* 1999) and "ideoscape," following Appadurai (1996b, 36), to refer to "concatenations of images" that are "often directly political."

51   I should note again that many of my arguments here are based on personal experience as well as reading the literature. In this case, I can report on a social psychology experiment in which I participated as a research assistant, in which the responses to pornographic films shown to male college undergraduates taking introductory psychology were discussed as indicative of the general human response to pornography. See Linz, Donnerstein, and Penrod (1988), which refers to male college students as generic "subjects" throughout. In parallel, Mueller and Donnerstein (1983, 62) use female college students "enrolled in an introductory psychology course" as stand-ins for women in general.

52   According to the postwar Parsonian division of academic labor, anthropologists were to focus on "cultural" (post)colonial peoples while sociologists focused on "social" practices in the metropoles.

53   Robin (2001, 189–199) traces this shift to the desire by the "softer" social scientists at Rand to collaborate with the economists and physicists, but it is unclear why they would not have felt this urge much earlier. The reasons for this shift need not detain us here, however, as both behavioralism and rational choice represented alternative forms of (depth-realist) positivism.

54   The first generation of regulation theorists was relatively uninterested in geopolitics. Aglietta's (1987) treatment of the "U.S. experience" insisted that "it should never be forgotten . . . that the rise of the United States to world hegemony forms an integral part of the social transformations" of Fordism, but he then proceeds to bracket this global aspect entirely (32). Lipietz (1987) discusses only the economic aspects of "global Fordism." Some of the essays in Brand and Raza (2003) begin to correct this shortcoming with respect to *post*-Fordism, as do Hardt and Negri (2000; but see Steinmetz 2003b). The regulationist literature still has not specified the geopolitical dimensions of Fordism, even though Aglietta claimed to be constructing "a set of concepts as a precondition of such investigations."

55   Competition with the Soviet Union for the allegiance of the Third World was another major impetus for the United States to distance itself officially from overt racism in this period, for instance, by integrating its army units during the Korean War.

56   See Steinmetz (2003b) for a discussion of the distinction between imperialism and

colonialism with respect to current U.S. geopolitical strategy. There was, of course, a huge literature in the nineteenth century that constructed non-Western cultures as earlier stages of European civilization (Stocking 1987), which legitimated colonization while simultaneously suggesting a certain kinship with the colonized (Steinmetz 2003c). In most colonies, however (including British), the colonized were treated as ineradicably inferior, or as assimilable only in the very longue dureé.

57   U.S. anthropologists had always been different from European anthropologists, of course, because the U.S. colonial empire was small and short-lived and the exact status of North American indigenous peoples with respect to the category of colonialism was unclear.

58   The problematic character of this conversion of labor power into labor is a "structural" reason for the lesser impact of positivism on studies of the labor process, from Mayo (1933) to Willis (1977) and Burawoy (1979).

59   A better illustration of this cold war assumption than theoretical texts on the end of ideology is the discussion in John Le Carré's novel *The Spy Who Came in from the Cold* (1963/1991, 114) between the British agent Leamas and the East German lawyer and spymaster Fielder. When Fielder asks about the philosophical motives of the British spies, Leamas replies, "What do you mean, a philosophy?" adding, "We're not Marxists, we're nothing. Just people." Fielder asks, "What makes them do it then?" and Leamas insists again, "Perhaps they don't even know; don't even care."

60   This is based on discussions with the current and former directors of the International Institute at the University of Michigan, David William Cohen and Michael Kennedy, and with the current and former directors of the Social Science Research Council, Craig Calhoun and David Featherman.

61   Of course, this was not a regulation-theoretic guidebook; that would not be logically impossible, however. Indeed, one of the directions regulation theory has taken in recent years is to propose itself as a policy science for capitalist crisis management (Röttger 2003).

62   See Lukács (1954/1981), Stern (1961), Plessner (1959), and Mosse (1964). For discussion of this tradition, see Blackbourn and Eley (1985) and Steinmetz (1997a).

63   Both were reprinted in the 1969 *Positivismusstreit* collection, translated into English in 1976 (Adorno et al. 1976).

64   Abbott (1999, 9) argues that there was a split between a positivist mainstream led by Columbia and a "Europeanized" theoretical orientation associated with Parsons and Harvard in the postwar period. Hollinger (1996) contrasts both Columbia and Harvard with a more firmly positivist University of Michigan in the same period. I hypothesize instead that there was a division of labor between these (and other) sociology departments, but with all of them agreeing on the same deeper set of underlying premises. The fact that Lazarsfeld and Rosenberg (1955) addressed philosophy of science issues more directly than Festinger and Katz (1953), for instance (Hollinger 1996, 149, n. 53), does not indicate any epistemological disagreement between the two books, but rather simply a difference between a more and less explicit positivism.

65   See especially Althusser's comments on Pascal (1971b, 168, 169) and Pascal's *Penseés*, sections 3 and 4, especially ¶282.

66   The view of David Riesman (best known for his 1950 book *The Lonely Crowd*) as unscientific that crystallized in this period is confirmed more recently by Clark (1996), who calls Riesman a "journalist." This is just one of a large array of epithets used to

denigrate nonpositivists. Riesman was able to attract large-scale funding for his research in the early postwar period, however (Abbott 1999).

67 Mills rejected positivism and scientism but embraced empiricism; Gouldner's *The Coming Crisis of Western Sociology* (1970) also contained empiricist elements (Steinmetz and Chae 2002). Glaser and Strauss (1967, 3), whose book is often recalled as a deviation from mainstream orthodoxy, referred to behavioral data and described the "job of theory in sociology" as "enabling prediction" and social control.

68 Even in the 1930s Parsons wrote that the goal of any analytical science was the discovery of "analytical laws" that state "*a uniform mode of relationship between* the values of *two or more* analytical *elements*" (1937/1949, 622, my emphasis). And despite Parsons's emphasis on values or norms, he fell into an objectivist analysis of the subjective, as Camic (1989, 64–69) notes, reducing it to the single category of the means-ends schema. After the war, Parsons began building various bridges between his theory and empirical research by deriving testable hypotheses of the positivist variety. He even adopted the language of "variables," writing in 1953, "Our attempt is to take the value system as the independent variable . . ." (630). Parsons encouraged a disciplinary division of labor between theory and empiricist research.

His theories were not the most obvious choice for a positivistic sociology, however, even if one was convinced that they could be tested empirically. The almost complete disappearance of Parsons from sociological research and teaching after the 1960s, and his reemergence as a topic for specialists in theory during the 1980s, suggests that he was not, in fact, a crucial component part of the positivist *dispositif*. His continuing influence during the two decades after the war was due not to his compatibility with positivism, which was always questionable. As Chriss (1995, 48–49) argues, one of the reasons for the rising popularity of Homans in the second half of the 1960s and his displacement of Parsons in the citation counts by this time was that his microsociological approach was much more amenable to quantitative testing and experimental design (see also Klausner and Lidz 1986). Gouldner suggested that Parsons's theories, especially in their postwar "structural-functional" guise, could be read as an attempt to mend a social whole that had been fragmented by capitalist modernity. Parsonian theory, according to this reading, was attractive less for its match with positivism or any other guiding metaphysical commitments than for its fulfillment of an ideological function. A more likely reason for Parsons's attractiveness has to do with his contribution to a discipline lacking an object. His work after the war, beginning with *The Social System* (1951), allowed U.S. sociology to rediscover its lost object realm, the social, which has perennially been considered too metaphysical and European. Yet sociologists could not hope to compete with the economists without a proper object. But Parsons reinvented sociology's object just at the moment when positivism was imposing a ban on such abstractions. Positivist sociology won the battle for pseudo-scientific respectability, but discipline's familiar symptoms of dissipation, fragmentation, and triviality are in part long-term consequences of the absence of a proper concept of the social.

Parsons's student Robert Merton played a paradoxically central role in translating Parsonian grand theory into terms compatible with methodological positivism. Beginning in the late 1940s, Merton developed a "program for concentration on 'theories of the middle range,' " as Parsons summarized it (1937/1968, 1: ix). In a paper on "The Bearing of Sociological Theory on Empirical Research," Merton argued that there was "no logical reason" for generalizers like Parsons to be ranged against the "hardy band" of empirical researchers (1948/1968d, 139). Merton's extremely influential paper on "theories of the middle range" (1936/1968b, 46) suggested that broad theories could not be "effectively developed before a great mass of basic observations has been accumulated," thereby turning Parsons's earlier theoreticism on its head. Although Merton did insist that such middle-range theories were "more than . . . mere empirical generalization" (41), they were not necessarily theories of real causal mechanisms. By acknowledging that a given middle-range theory could be "consistent" with a wide range of divergent "broad theoretical orientations" (such as Marxism, functionalism, and behaviorism), Merton pushed his conception of middle-range theory very close to empiricism. Indeed, middle-range theories were summarized as "verifiable statements of relationships between specified *variables*" (52; emphasis added), and not as pictures or models of theoretical mechanisms that might or might not give rise to events at the level of the empirical. In scientistic-naturalist style, Merton asserted that the long-range goal of the social sciences was to become like the natural sciences, even if sociologists were not yet ready to "compare biceps with their bigger brothers" (47). As a scion of Parsons and tenured professor at the Columbia department in the period of its greatest glory, Merton's intervention gave a green light to sociologists who hoped to operationalize Parsons's apparently abstruse concepts, to convert them into empirical generalizations—and essentially to continue working as before.

69   One of the most interesting studies from this period is Schwendinger and Schwendinger (1974). See also Herpin (1973) and Ladner (1973). The years 1970, 1973, and 1976 were the high points for books on this topic until the end of the 1980s, when the new sociology and history of science began to bear fruit.

70   I am thinking about the ways the new social movements of the 1970s and 1980s represented, on the one hand, cries of despair and symptoms of the destruction, atomization, and fragmentation wrought by the dismantling of Fordist protections (the decline of labor unions and the welfare state) and on the other hand, models of a post-Fordist form of sociality (social movements organized around niche subcultures, multiculturalism, and identity politics). Whether or not one supported these movements there is little question that the collapse of Fordism was one of their conditions of emergence and existence.

71   I offer a more detailed account of these theoretical-epistemic turns in sociology, especially the historic turn, in Steinmetz (2004b).

72   Gouldner understood positivism in very different terms from those used here, focusing on political conservatism. But his book also criticized tendencies toward "methodological empiricism" (1970, 454), defined as a form of "value free, high science sociology that . . . serves to defocalize the ideological dimensions of decision-making" and that is "congenial . . . to an 'engineering' or managerial position, in which the client specifies the ends to be pursued while the sociologist provides the means" (104). Like Mills, he criticized the ideas of the sufficiency of technique (Gouldner 1973, 111) and becoming the king's advisor (see Mills 1959, 180; Gouldner 1970, 445).

73   I have found one reference to the "epistemological turn in feminist theory" (Hallberg 1989) and another to the "epistemic turn" used in the sense discussed here (Cerullo 1994).

74   See the comments of Jeffrey Sachs (in Harrison and Huntington 2000, 29–43), who tellingly rejects even the conservative version of culturalism peddled by this volume.

75   The Bush administration's approach to overseas imperialism does not necessarily imply a need for positivist social science along the lines of the 1950s and 1960s, however. In certain respects this new imperialism is much more open to what it would describe as a more flexible, rapid, and improvisational approach to military matters—consider the lack of planning for "nation-building" in Iraq after the 2003 war and the shortage of military manpower and resources. There is more than a superficial resemblance between the military's approach to war and post-Fordist "just in time production." By the same token, the Bush administration's defiance of established realist theories of international relations and its "faith-based" policies suggest a lack of interest in social science per se.

76   I include local and state governments in the internally variegated category of the state here; for further elaboration of this point, see Steinmetz (1993).

77   After a nadir during the Reagan years, federal funding again increased, albeit with new emphases. Whereas the NIH and NIMH were at the core earlier, the life sciences have become crucial, and sociology is again being encouraged to repackage itself along the lines of another set of natural sciences (witness the rise of interest in sociobiology in recent years). See "Before Leaving Health Agency, Shalala Offers a Little Advice on a Big Job," *New York Times*, January 16, 2001, 16. Even more recently, funding has again dipped.

78   The massive uptick of interest in rational choice theory in political science and parts of sociology in recent years cannot be explained by "economics envy," because that was always present. One possible explanation is that rational choice seems to put the agentic individual at its center, corresponding to the felt increase in demands on the individual to be self-promoting and self-reflexive, while simultaneously promising to allow behavior to be predicted.

PART TWO

*Alternatives to Positivism
in the Human Sciences*

Critical Realism

ANDREW COLLIER

Critical realism (of the sort inaugurated by Roy Bhaskar's work) is now mainly a movement of thought among social scientists, but it started in the philosophy of science, natural as well as social, as an attempt to give the sciences the philosophy they deserved. Not a philosophy that would legislate for them, but one that would take their work as its premise and ask what the world must be like for this work to be possible.

However, existing sciences, particularly social sciences, are not innocent of philosophy. Many of them have from their outset assumed some philosophical position about what a science should look like and tried to imitate it. Further, their practitioners have often forgotten their philosophical premises and become skeptical of methodology, thereby turning these premises into unchallengeable dogmas. So critical realism often has to engage in dispute with older philosophies of science, particularly positivism and, in the social sciences, hermeneutic theories.

I look first at these philosophies and how critical realism, using arguments drawn from the natural sciences, shows them to have mistaken premises. This leads to a discussion of how critical realism enables us to overcome certain dichotomies that have haunted social science as a result of inadequate philosophical premises; I then move on to discuss what is unique about critical realism. Finally, I look at some examples of how critical realism can be helpful to work in the human sciences, particularly with reference to psychoanalysis.

1

While opponents of positivism have been more vocal than positivists for some decades now (leading Raymond Williams to describe positivism as a swearword by which no one is swearing), it is nevertheless in some way the "classic" position in the philosophy of science, and though largely discarded by philosophers, it is still very influential in some social sciences, particularly economics. Positivism sets up a certain model of science as value-free, atomistic, discovering causal laws of a "constant conjunction" model (whenever A happens, B happens), and able to express its results mathematically. These are supposed to be the characteristics of the natural sciences that have made them so successful, and the assumption is that if the social sciences could only imitate them, they would achieve similar success. Those philosophers of social science who have rejected this model have usually accepted the positivistic account of the natural sciences but claimed that social realities must be studied in a totally different way, hermeneutically, on analogy with the interpretation of texts. This interpretation is seen as noncausal and often as tied to the views of the people being studied, so that, for instance, an anthropologist must use the concepts of the group studied, and an economist the concepts used in business.

Critical realism starts by attacking the shared assumption of these two views that natural science produces laws of the "every time A happens, B happens" type, the constant conjunction model. It is true, as the hermeneutic schools point out, that constant conjunctions do not occur in society, that economists and psychologists hunt them in vain. But it is also true that there are none in (most parts of) nature. A dog barking may cause a squirrel to run up a tree, but it is not the case that every time a dog barks, a squirrel runs up a tree; there may be no squirrels around, or the squirrel may be blasé about dogs. There is nothing that always follows a dog barking or always precedes a squirrel running up a tree. Indeed, there is only one area of nature in which there are regularities at all: astronomy. But here it is odd to say that the regularly succeeding events cause each other: sunset on the equinox does not cause dawn to occur twelve hours later.

In fact, there is only one sort of process in the whole of nature and society where causal laws manifest themselves as constant conjunctions: scientific experiments. In the laboratory, a definite quantity of heat is applied to a definite quantity of water under carefully controlled conditions, and it boils exactly five minutes later. In the kitchen, it is not so. Polly puts the kettle on, but Sukey takes it off again and the water never gets to boil.

Yet, for all the unlikeness of experiments to anything that happens outside the laboratory, they are meant to tell us what goes on in nature, not in the laboratory. And unless one is quite insanely skeptical about science, one will admit that they do. How does this come about? The critical realist answer is that what an experiment does is to isolate *one* mechanism of nature and test it in a closed system, that is, where other mechanisms that are not being tested will not affect the outcome. The same mechanism does operate in nature outside the laboratory, but there it operates alongside other mechanisms, and these conjointly bring about an outcome that the one mechanism in isolation would not have brought about. In a closed system, when one mechanism in isolation is stimulated in a certain way, it will give a predictable response. But in nature, knowledge of the mechanism, derived from experiment, will help us explain what happens, but not predict anything with any great certainty. Hence the fact that in all nonlaboratory sciences apart from astronomy, predictions can fail without throwing doubt on the validity of the science. This is so in meteorology and medicine as well as social sciences; evolutionary biology does not even try to predict, yet it has high explanatory power. The exception of astronomy need not puzzle us: it is because there are normally no natural mechanisms strong enough to deflect the courses of heavenly bodies, so they act as if they were in a closed system. The problem in the history of philosophy is that seventeenth- and eighteenth-century philosophers took astronomy to be the typical case instead of the exceptional one.

To sum up the argument from experiment: (1) an experiment consists in setting things up so that if one causal law holds, one outcome will occur, and if another causal law, another outcome; (2) if causal laws manifested themselves as constant conjunctions in the natural course of events, there would be no need for experiment; observation of regularities would be enough; (3) if there were no causal laws, experiments would not work; (4) so there must be a multiplicity of causal laws such that no one law determines what happens in the natural course of events, but causal laws can be isolated experimentally.

All this has the consequence that natural laws should be expressed not as constant conjunctions—whenever a dog barks, a squirrel runs up a tree—but as tendencies: dogs tend to bark at squirrels, squirrels tend to run up trees if dogs bark at them. This applies even to the most rigorous and basic laws of nature. Take the law of inertia: bodies tend to remain at rest or in uniform motion in a given direction. Expressed that way, it is true. But what about the constant conjunction formulation of this law: whenever a body is at rest it will remain at rest, and whenever it is in motion in a given direction it will go on moving in that direction. So much nonsense: try kicking a football some time. Nothing has ever behaved in that way.

Now, if this is all true, human sciences may be less unlike natural sciences than the hermeneuticists suppose, though nothing like the positivist model of natural science. Constant conjunctions do not occur: deflationary budgets are not always followed by deflation, sexually abused people do not always become sexual abusers, arms races are not always followed by war, although in all these cases there may be causal links that would explain the expected outcome if it did happen. But people and institutions and structures, like bodies and dogs and squirrels, have tendencies: the rate of capitalist profit tends to fall (Marx), a liquid capital market tends to make speculation dominate over enterprise (Keynes), anal characters tend to make a pile (Freud), or more informally, men tend to grow facial hair, university lecturers in the United Kingdom tend to vote Labour, English people tend to eat boiled vegetables.

Now, it might be thought that tendency statements are just statements about what usually happens. But for such a tendency to be scientifically significant, it must be grounded in some natural or social mechanism: it is the tendency that a certain kind of being has by virtue of its inner structure. Once this is established, we may be able to attribute tendencies even when they are not usually realized, as in the case of the law of inertia. So if Marx's arguments are correct, the tendency of the rate of profit to fall follows from the increasing organic composition of capital and operates even if profits are actually rising. But if Marx is right and yet profits are not falling, there must be some counteracting tendency in operation as well, so it is not pointless to say that the tendency is operating; it puts one on track of the counteracting tendency.

If social science is to imitate the success of natural sciences, then, it will not look for strict regularities but for tendencies. But these tendencies (contra the hermeneutic philosophers) are causal. They explain as well as interpret. But they don't explain in a way that excludes human intentions from the equation. Social structures and institutions have tendencies, but so do human agents, whose tendencies are based on their desires and beliefs. So the hermeneutic theorists are right to think that in studying a society we must first understand how the people of that society think about what they do. However, they are not right when they refuse to go beyond and possibly contradict this starting point. People can be wrong about the way they perceive their own society, and social science can correct them. Indeed one could argue that that is what social science is for: if society were transparent to its members, we would not need social science. As Marx put it: "Scientific truth is always paradox, if judged by everyday experience, which catches only the delusive appearance of things" (1968, 209). This can be seen even at the most empirical level of social science. Tom Burns mentions the conclusions of a survey of morale among soldiers in the U.S. army that were the opposite of what everyone would take for granted as obvious: "Poorly educated soldiers were more neurotic than those with higher education; Southerners showed no greater ability than Northerners to adjust to tropical climate; Negroes were more eager for promotion than whites; and so on" (Burns 1970, 72). It is even more noteworthy where explanations are concerned; the Marx quote earlier comes from a place in the text where he is explaining that exploitation occurs when everything is sold at its value. This is important because if social science can be valuable from the point of view of human liberation, as a long tradition from Marx to critical realism has maintained, this can be so only by virtue of its ability to disabuse us of socially induced illusions. It is necessary to stress this at the present time because some postmodernists claim exactly the opposite: that the appearance/reality distinction is elitist, and appearances are all. But appearances are often the means by which the oppressed are kept oppressed, and criticizing them is necessary to expose and fight oppression.

The idea that the appearance/reality distinction is elitist is presumably held because all can see the appearances, whereas only those who have done the necessary cognitive work to see through the appearances can see the reality. But unless the capacity to do that work is somehow restricted to a privileged class or group, that is not elitist. If one is called an elitist simply because one believes that about some issues the minority is right and the majority wrong, then the charge of elitism has lost all force; indeed, the only alternative to being an elitist becomes being a conformist.

Social science, then, can provide causal explanations and can surprise us. In these ways it is like natural science. But in another way it is quite unlike the most successful of the natural sciences: it has no experiments. Of course, there are procedures *called* experiments, but they do not do what, as we have seen, experiments in the natural sciences do, that is, set up closed systems in which a tendency can be isolated from other tendencies so that it manifests itself in constant conjunctions. I recently saw on the television a so-called scientific experiment to test features of power relations between people. A group of men (no women) was locked in a building and observed through CCTV. Initially, certain power relations were set up between them. There occurred a "revolution," and a commune was set up. Before it had time to prove itself one way or the other, a small group of the men set about planning a "coup" against the commune. The experiment was terminated just before the time set for the coup, and conclusions were drawn about human responses to power vacuums (highly antidemocratic conclusions, it may be said). But of course, the experiment proves nothing about what human beings tend to do outside the laboratory, for the situation was completely artificial. The men were removed from their families and friends, their jobs and normal leisure activities, even the common light of day. Now of course, all experiments are artificial, but in a good experiment the artifice *removes* the effects of irrelevant variables on the matter being tested. In this case, it does not remove but introduces such variables, just as putting animals in cages makes it impossible to study their natural behavior. Establishing closure in the study of animals involves carefully concealing the observer in a natural habitat, so that the fact of observation does not alter the outcome observed. The proper way of studying the effects of power changes and power vacuums on humans would be by studying human behavior in the wild, so to speak, that is, in the open system of history, for instance, the history of the French Revolution.

As we saw, closed systems, established by experiment, are the only place outside astronomy where we can make more or less certain predictions. In the social world, there is nowhere where we can make such predictions. Critical realists are therefore not worried about the absence of predictions in existing social sciences. It is not a result of immaturity or faulty method in those sciences. It is to be expected. And it does not rule out explanations.

Critical realism, then, provides a third way as an alternative to positivism and hermeneutics. It rejects their common assumptions about the nature of natural science. It agrees with positivism rather than hermeneutics in saying that social science is like natural science in being causal and counterphenomenal (that is, contradicting appearances). But it is like hermeneutics rather than positivism in that it studies concrete realities rather than trying to make experiments and in recognizing that this reduces the role of mathematics to a very small one in social science. Like hermeneutics, too, it stresses the importance of the fact that social reality includes ideas and intentions. And so, unlike either, it can recognize that human reasons for actions can be the causes of those actions (for positivism tends to ignore or explain away reasons, and hermeneutics tends to deny that they are causes). And if reasons are not causes, then thinking, discussion, acquiring information all become ineffectual in the social process, and any attempt to improve the social existence of human beings is in vain.

Shortly, I shall discuss another way in which critical realism offers a way out of a long-standing dichotomy in social science. But first I want to look at a feature of the central argument that we have considered: the argument about experiment. It took the form, What must the world be like for experiment to be possible? and answered, There must be mechanisms that are distinct enough to be isolated in experiment, but that also operate outside experimental situations, where they can't be tested because they operate alongside other mechanisms that codetermine events. If the mechanisms were not distinct enough to be isolated, we could not make experiments, and if they normally operated distinctly so that they produced constant conjunctions in the actual flow of events, we would not need experiments, only observation of nature.

This sort of argument (What must be so for x, which is actual, to be possible?) is called a retroductive argument (one subspecies of them, called transcendental arguments, was made famous by Kant).

In the philosophy of social science, we can apply a similar argument to discover what sort of being society must have. Suppose we ask how any human activity in society is possible, say, voting or cashing a check. There must in the first place be a democratic constitution or a banking system, respectively. And in the second place there must be a person with reasons for acting this way, which reasons cause the action. In other words, there have to be two distinct kinds of being: social institutions that preexist the agent and are independent of him or her, and an intentional agent whose action presupposes and makes use of those institutions but is not explained by them. In other words, social theories that say, There are no societies, only people, or on the other hand, People are nothing but aspects of society (methodological individualism and methodological holism, respectively), are both inadequate. Critical realists have generally agreed with Marx that society is neither an aggregate of individuals nor a collective, but the totality of relations between individuals. But more than this, critical realists argue that, although there can be no asocial people or societies without people (so that people and societies are mutually dependent for their being), people and societies nevertheless have very different sorts of being, are governed by different sorts of tendency, and should be studied by different and mutually independent sciences. Psychology cannot be reduced to sociology, nor sociology to psychology. But at the same time, people and societies are related in a number of ways, which together constitute what Roy Bhaskar calls the transformational model of social activity (TMSA). This view comprises the ideas (1) that society is entirely the effect of human actions; (2) that every human action presupposes society with its relations and institutions as a condition of its possibility;

and (3) that human intentional activity, in addition to producing (when successful) what is intended, reproduces society (usually unintentionally). Thus, workers intentionally do their job and take home their pay, thereby unintentionally reproducing the capitalist mode of production.

This view enables us to avoid both kinds of reductive theory: that which reduces human individuals to social effects, and that which reduces society to human individuals. It justifies the separate existence of the sociological sciences and the psychological sciences, as well as explaining the need for conjoint application of these two groups of sciences in order to study concrete conjunctures of human social existence. The TMSA, which is outlined by Bhaskar in *The Possibility of Naturalism* (1979/1998), is elaborated into a more detailed theory of social and individual being by Margaret Archer (1995; see the note on critical realist literature at the end of this essay) as the "morphogenetic approach."

So far, I have presented critical realism's contribution to the social sciences as a resolving of old dichotomies, thereby establishing the autonomy and mutual irreducibility of the various human sciences. To an extent, this aspect of critical realism can be seen as providing a middle way, which incorporates what is true in conflicting positions, though it does this partly by challenging their shared assumptions. I now come to two ways in which critical realism is unlike almost all other philosophies of social science and social being, at least to the extent that it is at one extreme of the spectrum of views on these two issues. I refer to its maximalist ontology and its case for arguing from facts to values.

2

The first thing to be observed about critical realism's ontology, its theory about what there is, is that it is very inclusive and, one might say, luxuriant. Most people are realists about material objects, and some say that nothing exists but material objects. Berkeley was not a realist about material objects, but he was a realist about minds and their ideas. Methodological individualists believe that human agents are real, but not social structures; structuralists have been suspected of making the opposite judgment. Some postmodernists seem to be realist about discourses, but not about anything else. Critical realists are realist about all these things. If the American philosopher Quine said that his minimalist ontology expressed a preference for desert landscapes, critical realism's maximalist ontology might be likened to a rainforest.

It is worth listing some of the things that critical realism regards as real and some other positions do not. In the first place, critical realism accepts "commonsense realism" so far as it goes; concrete objects—people and animals and planets and trees—are real and independent of our knowledge of them; they are not just our ideas or constituted by our discourse. Critical realism rejects the "epistemic fallacy," which collapses the question, What exists? into the question, What can be known? Second, critical realism argues that the sciences uncover underlying mechanisms that explain the course of events but that are not always manifest in the course of events. For things have powers by virtue of their inner structures, even if these powers are not exercised; for example, a motorcycle may be able to do 100 mph even if it never does. Or again, powers may be exercised yet not actualized in the sense of manifest in events; for example, gravity affects a bird in flight, even though the bird does not drop to the ground as gravity on its own would lead you to expect. Hence, it is not just exercised powers that are real, as some philosophers, for instance, Nietzsche, argue. Hidden mechanisms, unexercised powers, and unrealized possibilities are all real and can have effects. To take an example from the human world, the power of the military to seize the state from an elected government may constrain that government's policies, even though in a given country that power is never used.

Third, the fact that nature is an open system and experiments are necessary to establish closed systems shows that there is a *plurality* of mechanisms conjointly determining events; this plurality is reflected in the plurality of sciences. We cannot reduce everything in nature to physics. Not only physics but several social sciences are prone to the illusion that they can explain away the subject matter of the other sciences and make those sciences redundant. Critical realism defends the idea that reality is many-layered, and each level has its own kind of laws, irreducible to those of any other level.

Fourth—this is really a special instance of the third point, but an especially important one—human mental reality is not reducible to brain physiology. While there is a sense in which critical realism is materialist—Bhaskar calls it "synchronic emergent powers materialism" (Bhaskar 1979/1998, 97)—it is a very open-ended sense and does not preclude mental causation and, in particular, people's reasons for their actions being the cause of those actions, an essential feature of the TMSA.

Finally, there has been a long-standing tendency in both ancient and modern philosophy (though not in medieval and some recent philosophy) to think that all reality must be positive, that there cannot be real absences or negative facts. In Bhaskar's book *Dialectic* (1993), he argues that absences have effects, and what has effects must be real. This is easy to illustrate from the human world: bank overdrafts, negative equity, or Bob Dylan's wonderful song "Visions of Johanna," a song about a party the salient feature of which is that Johanna is not there. But some recent philosophers who accept that there are negative facts (Russell and Sartre, for instance) think that they are dependent on human minds. Bhaskar argues that there are negative existences in nature, too, for example, droughts. Certainly in social science, one can easily think of instances where absences have profound effects (the absence of a strong executive at certain points in the French Revolution, the absence of a working-class party in U.S. politics, the absence of an independent "civil society" in post-Stalinist Russia; for a critical discussion of this theory of absences, see my essay "On Real and Nominal Absences" in *After Postmodernism* [2001]).

To sum up, critical realism holds that a rainforestlike profusion of different kinds of reality exists: things, events, experiences, natural mechanisms, social structures, possibilities, absences, and so on. One kind of reality that I have not yet mentioned because it is the subject of the next discussion is values. But first I want to answer one objection I foresee from contemporary nonrealists.

Many nonrealists say that they do not deny that things exist independently of our knowledge of them, only that we can have knowledge of things existing independently of our knowledge. Presumably, they are not just asserting the tautology that all we have knowledge of is things we have knowledge of; to be contentful, the claim must be that we are somehow trapped inside our own knowledge. Critical realists would say that we are not, because what we don't have knowledge of now, we may acquire knowledge of later. If the nonrealist says "Yes, but when we have that new knowledge it will be part of our knowledge, so we really can never get outside our own knowledge," that is just a verbal trick. It is as if someone were to say "I can't move from here," and when he or she did move, said, "But where I am now is 'here,' so I haven't moved from here." In some English pubs, there are notices saying "Free beer tomorrow," the joke being that tomorrow the notice still says "Free beer tomorrow" and you never get your free beer. "Tomorrow never comes," but of course, the day referred to as "tomorrow" yesterday has come. Likewise, yesterday's unknown fact is today's known one and is as independent of our knowledge of it as it was yesterday.

This justifies another distinction made by critical realists: between the transitive and the intransitive objects of a science. At any given time, what a science is about will be specified within that science. This is its transitive object. But science is always transforming its transitive object in order to dig deeper into reality, to discover what had been there before but undiscovered. The fact that science does not stay still but progresses shows that it also has an intransitive object: that reality, independent of science and at any time partly undiscovered by it, which it seeks to make known to us.

Now we come to the second unique feature of critical realism: the theory of explanatory critiques as an account of how we can logically argue from facts to values, "is" to "ought," indicatives to imperatives, despite the long-standing prejudice, first formulated by Hume and sometimes known as Hume's law, that we cannot.

An explanatory critique is an explanation that criticizes what it explains, not *in addition to* but *by virtue of* the explanation. The starting point of explanatory critiques is that a social science can study both the ideas that prevail in a given society about the features of that society and those features themselves. So it may discover that the beliefs held in that society are false. Further, these beliefs may not be accidental. It may be that the social structure inevitably generates these false beliefs, and that they function to make that society run smoothly. The classic instance comes from Marx. According to Marx, capitalist society spontaneously generates the belief that wages are payment for labor. This belief encourages the workers to think that they are not being exploited, because "a fair exchange is no robbery." But the truth is, says Marx, wages are not payment for labor but for labor power. They cannot be payment for labor, because the worker does not have labor to sell, for labor requires means of labor, and these the worker does not have—the capitalist has them. So all the worker can sell is his or her power to labor, the price of which will always be lower than the value added to the product by the labor that results from the sale.

If Marx is right about all this, then capitalism produces, and benefits from its production of, false beliefs about wage labor. But false beliefs are a bad thing, and a system that produces them and relies on them is to that extent a bad system which, other things being equal, it would be better to abolish and replace by a system that did not produce or rely on false beliefs. Hence, we have got a value judgment and a practical prescription out of purely factual premises.

If someone objects, "The value judgment got in when you said 'False beliefs are a bad thing,'" we can reply that the maxim that one ought to believe what is true is not derived from any moral position, but from the nature of belief: it is a logical ought, not a moral one. The conclusion, however, is a moral ought.

If this argument is valid, then the supposed logical gulf between facts and values has been bridged. And once that has been done, other fact-to-value arguments can pass across the bridge. For instance, if humans need clean air (as can be shown by medical science), then, other things being equal, they ought to have clean air. Only the false belief that it is *logically* impossible to pass from fact to value could prevent someone from drawing this conclusion.

It should be noted that, although the proof that one can pass from facts to values is in striking contrast to the orthodox view of the matter, and in that sense has a highly radical conclusion, it is a moot point how radical it is in practice, for it is modified by the fact that the practical conclusions of these explanatory critiques are always "other things being equal." While it is also true that there are very few moral judgments that aren't "other things being equal," this does mean that it is possible to accept Marx's argument here—and indeed, the many stronger arguments that he gives against capitalism—while rejecting his political conclusions, because other things are not equal (for instance, because revolutions always go wrong). This is a political position that some critical realists hold, if I interpret them right, though there are also many Marxist critical realists.

The argument from facts to values suggests that critical realism could have as far-reaching implications for ethics as for the philosophy of science, but about what sort of ethics this would be there is no unanimity among critical realists. Bhaskar's statement that all ills can be seen as absences suggests one line of thought, followed up by me in my book *Being and Worth* (1999). In his own recent writings (*Dialectic* 1993 and *Plato Etcetera* 1994), he develops an alternative approach based on the idea that all human action commits the agent to universal human emancipation, on pain of performative contradiction.

Whatever the content of critical realist ethics, two things can be said about it:

(1) It will be a species of moral realism. Just as the fact that science progresses shows that it is a (more or less successful) attempt to discover the truth about the world, so the fact of moral progress (at certain times and places) shows that morality has an intransitive dimension: there is something there to be discovered.

(2) Morality and social science will not be mutually exclusive zones. Social science need not have moral premises in order to have moral conclusions, derived from its explanatory critiques. So the idea of social science as a necessary condition of human emancipation is potentially justified.

3

It would be a mistake to see critical realism as a magic key that has only to be applied in the particular social sciences to produce good theories. The relation of critical realist philosophy to the work of social scientists who use it is not one of *application* but one of *intervention*. It presupposes the ongoing work of social sciences but helps to avoid certain mistakes in that work, often mistakes imported from other philosophies. There is no one-one correlation between philosophical positions and theories in social sciences. There may be a number of mutually conflicting theories in a social science, all of which are compatible with critical realism. Hence, in choosing one social scientific theory to which critical realism can have a supportive role and with whose ideas it shows some striking convergences, I am only illustrating the possible uses of critical realism, not trying to prove one particular theory. Nevertheless, I choose a theory for which I have a high regard, namely, psychoanalysis.

In origin, psychoanalysis was not the application of a ready-made philosophical theory to its subject matter. By comparison with many inaugurators of social scientific theories, Freud was a philosophically "naïve subject." But not entirely: he admits his dependence on Spinoza, though this is surely more the subliminal influence of attitudes, rather than the appropriation of ready-made ideas. He attended Brentano's lectures, and his own notion of ideas or representations owes much to Brentano; yet his method and his results (the unconscious) are very unlike Brentano's views. The supposed similarities to Kant and Schopenhauer are, I think, entirely illusory. In short, Freud picked up whatever ideas he could use, some of them from philosophers, but there is no relation between psychoanalysis and any one philosophy in the way that behaviorism relates to positivism or marginalist economics to utilitarianism. That this is no bad thing is shown by the fate of Freud's theories among the philosophers. For both continental phenomenologists and structuralists and English-speaking analytical philosophers have been fascinated by Freud's ideas and have often tried to supply the lacking philosophical premises. But in so doing, they have often watered down the theory and blunted its most original features. For example, several on both sides of the Channel have objected to the idea of mental causation and have assimilated the unconscious to the murkier parts of consciousness (Alasdair MacIntyre and Paul Ricoeur, for example).

From the point of view of critical realism, it appears that Freud had in practice hit upon many of the features that a social science ought to have, where other psychological theories had been led astray by ready-made philosophical models of what a social science should look like. I now briefly discuss five areas of convergence between psychoanalysis and critical realism.

Depth Explanation

Positivist philosophy applied to psychology gives you behaviorism. I once heard a behaviorist psychology professor read a paper comparing behavior therapy to psychoanalysis as to their scientific status. He appealed to the distinction in medical science between nosologic and nosographic concepts. Nosographic concepts describe a symptom: fever, a cough, a stomach pain would be nosographic concepts. Nosologic concepts explain the symptoms by an underlying cause: meningitis, tuberculosis, or a duodenal ulcer would be nosologic concepts. The professor claimed that behavior therapy uses only nosographic concepts (for example, fear of spiders). Psychoanalysis, on the other hand, uses nosologic concepts (for example, an unresolved Oedipus complex). He claimed that this made behavior therapy more scientific. But critical realists would argue that the opposite is the case: every advanced medical discipline uses nosologic concepts, and this is an instance of a general feature of science as distinct from prescientific knowledge. If laws are tendencies of things, which can be overridden by other tendencies in the open system of the world, they *underlie* symptoms and behavior rather than being constituted by them. As we have seen, to attribute a tendency is not just to say what often happens; it is to claim that some thing or person or institution has that tendency by virtue of its nature. A tendency belongs to the structure of an individual, whether human or otherwise. So, while the question of whether psychoanalysis has the *right* nosologic concepts can be decided only by analytic practice, that it *has* nosologic concepts makes it at least a candidate for a science, whereas behavior therapy's restriction to the nosographic classes it with prescientific disciplines like Ptolemaic astronomy, which describe what happens but don't reach the underlying causes.

Counterphenomenality

If applied positivism conflicts with psychoanalysis in one way, applied hermeneutics conflicts with it in another. Hermeneutic social sciences have often tied themselves to the self-understanding of the people they study. If carried out consistently (which it admittedly rarely is), this would have the consequence that one could not distinguish what a person or a community believes itself to be and what it is. There could be no deceptive appearances. And as we have seen, this has the consequence that knowledge could never be liberating, for it is liberating in just that case in which it replaces an enslaving appearance, whether in society or an individual. Just as Marx argued that the self-image of a community could disguise its oppression from itself and thereby keep it oppressed, so Freud argued that a person's self-image could be a defense that served to limit that person's autonomy. Psychoanalysis *starts* from the consciousness of the analysand, but it does not *confirm* it; rather, it finds underlying tendencies that are not manifest on the surface. The account of human sciences given by critical realism notes and endorses precisely this practice of starting with people's self-understanding but digging deeper and often, in the end, contradicting it. As a realist method, it recognizes the existence of desires and images and beliefs, not just behavior; as a nonreductive method, it refuses to explain these away in physiological terms; but as a depth method, it refuses to take them at face value and is amenable to the idea that different unconscious desires, images, and beliefs may underlie them. For critical realism, it is part of the essence of a science, and also part of the essence of any kind of knowledge, that it can be liberating, that it can be counterphenomenal, able to contradict appearances. Psychoanalysis shares all these features.

Meanings and Causes

Positivism typically deals in causes without meanings, explanation without interpretation; hermeneutics deals in meanings without causes, interpretation without explanation. Critical realism holds that meanings can be causes, and interpretation can be a species of causal explanation. It is, I think, uncontentious that Freud treated interpretations as explanations, and hence meanings as causes. But he is often criticized for this "confusion." If critical realism is right, it is not a confusion. And critical realism had better be right, because little is left of psychoanalysis if the interpretation of a symptom does not explain the symptom. To show that the separation of meanings from causes (implicit, I think, in MacIntyre's and Ricoeur's critiques of psychoanalysis) would not just be a revision of psychoanalysis but a loss of some of its useful concepts, let us look at one such concept, invented by Ernest Jones and adopted by Freud, and now passed into common usage: rationalization.

By way of example: Paul gives Jenny some hurtful information. He says, quite sincerely, that he does it because she "has the right to know." Actually, Paul has a grudge against Jenny and does it to spite her. Both the belief that Jenny has the right to know and the desire to hurt Jenny belong to the realm of meanings. The former is the one that Paul sincerely believes is his reason. What does it mean to say that it is not the *real* reason, but a rationalization? Surely, that of the two reasons, the latter only was the *cause*. If meanings (and therefore reasons) were one kind of thing and causes were another and never the twain could meet, this account would not be open to us. Yet it is not only an instance of psychoanalytical explanation, but one that we constantly encounter in everyday life.

Analysis of the Concrete

Experimental science can isolate tendencies from other tendencies in a closed system and define and measure them. But the aim of science is to explain the world, which is an open system. Science has never completed its task till it uses its knowledge of distinct tendencies to analyze systems in which many tendencies cooperate and conflict. This should be the end even of the natural sciences. Only when they have passed from the abstractions known through closed systems to the concrete situations in which such abstractions operate can any science be *applied* with benefit. But in the human sciences we not only end, we also begin with the analysis of concrete situations, because there are no experiments. The human world, like the natural world, is a complex world made of many interacting tendencies, but whereas in the natural world the individual tendencies can sometimes be really abstracted from other tendencies in experiments, in the human world we can't do this. We can abstract them only in thought, by analysis. We cannot isolate them in reality and measure them. The consequences of this for the human sciences are best described by Marx; this justifies Lenin's claim that "the concrete analysis of the concrete situation is the heart of Marxism." Note the two sides to this: the concrete situation, not tendencies isolated from the situation; but the *analysis* of that situation, not treating it as an unanalyzable totality.

Let us turn to two quotes from Marx himself: "The concrete is concrete because it is the concentration of many determinations, hence unity of the diverse" (1973, 101). That is to say, any concrete situation is a complex of many tendencies, which can be distinguished by analysis, but which conjointly make up the real situation. "In the analysis of economic forms, neither microscopes nor chemical reagents are of assistance. The power of abstraction must replace both" (1976, 90). In other words, we cannot do experiments in the human sciences; instead, we must analyze the different elements that go into the making of the concrete situations that we study.

Positivism tends to treat only the abstract sciences as the real sciences and to elevate generalizations above detailed accounts of particular beings. Hermeneutics, on the other hand, tends to focus on particular beings but be suspicious of the analysis of them, the unraveling of different tendencies in them, seeing this as falsifying their holistic form. Critical realism agrees with Marx in directing us to the analysis of the concrete—of human beings or human societies.

Two things stick out about psychoanalysis: it is analytical, and it focuses on concrete human beings. Take the treatment of dreams, for instance. Psychoanalysis does not accept dream dictionaries: to know the meaning of a dream, we need to know the dreamer's personal associations. Hence its concreteness. Yet it does not take the dream at face value, but looks for latent content, displacement, condensation, secondary revision, and so on. Here is its commitment to analysis. In this respect—its double commitment to the concrete and to analysis—psychoanalysis ought not to be a fringe science, as it is often regarded, but a model for other human sciences to imitate.

Explanatory Critiques

Although, when discussing explanatory critiques, I used a socioeconomic example (the wage form), examples from individual psychology are not lacking. People may have false beliefs about themselves. Such a belief may not be accidental, but the result of some defense mechanism. It may function to maintain that defense mechanism. But to say all this is to criticize that defense mechanism and, other things being equal, to motivate the attempt to remove it. The discovery of the truth by the subject is an essential part of the process of overcoming the defense mechanism. Of course, other mechanisms such as transference and abreaction are involved in bringing this about. But insofar as psychoanalysis works by increasing self-awareness, it is, among other things, an explanatory critique.

This explains why psychoanalysis is both an objective exploratory discipline and a discipline with emancipatory aims, not in addition to, but by virtue of, its exploratory work. That critical realism recognizes an internal link between explanation in the human sciences and emancipation is one reason why Marxists have often been attracted to critical realism. But it is equally a point of contact between critical realism and psychoanalysis.

These five points show that the peculiarities of psychoanalysis are not, from a critical realism point of view, a sign of defective scientificity; they are just what we should expect of a good example of a human science. In the United Kingdom at least, the role of psychoanalysis in the medical profession has been restricted as a result of criticisms from philosophers of science (notably, Sir Karl Popper). One function of critical realism is to intervene in such debates to obviate some of these criticisms.

A Note on Critical Realist Literature

Critical realism of the sort discussed in this paper is a developing and branching body of theory, and it will be useful to put this development into perspective. Roy Bhaskar's own work has passed through a number of phases, and not all critical realists follow all of them.

First, it should be said that the term critical realism, as applied to the sort of thinking inaugurated by Bhaskar, arose by conflating the terms "transcendental realism" and "critical naturalism" and eliding the terms "transcendental" and "naturalism." It refers, therefore, to a double body of ideas: transcendental realism (transcendental in a Kantian sense) to refer to a philosophy of (mainly natural) science, and critical naturalism to refer to a theory of social science and social being. The founding works of these theories are Bhaskar's *A Realist Theory of Science* (1975/1997) and *The Possibility of Naturalism* (1979/1998), respectively. His *Scientific Realism and Human Emancipation* (1986) and *Philosophy and the Idea of Freedom* (1991; mainly a critique of Rorty), with his collection of essays *Reclaiming Reality* (1989), can be grouped with these books as texts of critical realism without further qualification. (It should be noted that there is an independent movement also called critical realism that draws on the work of C. S. Peirce and includes writers such as Ian Barbour. There is some convergence of ideas between the two movements, and some critical realists stand in both these traditions of thought.)

It is this critical realism "without further qualification" that I have for the most part been discussing here. My own book *Critical Realism* (1994) is an introduction to this phase of Bhaskar's work. He has since moved from this position, which aims to be philosophical underlaboring for the sciences and for the politics of human emancipation, to a more systematic and all-encompassing philosophy, which he calls dialectical critical realism in his books *Dialectic* (1993) and *Plato Etcetera* (1994). These books follow Hegel in difficulty as well as systematicity (*Scientific Realism and Human Emancipation* [1986] is also a forbidding text), but they have been quarried for ideas by a number of social scientists. Third, Bhaskar has taken what has been termed a transcendental turn (no longer in the Kantian sense) with his book *From East to West* (2000), which, in part by means of a fictional narrative, explores ideas from a number of (mainly religious) worldviews for their contribution to human emancipation. This has been followed by a new series of books, published in India and drawing on Indian religious and philosophical ideas, giving (if I may say so without oxymoron) a more immanent view of transcendence. The first of these, *Reflections on Meta-Reality* (2002), is his most accessible book since *The Possibility of Naturalism* (1979/1998).

The most substantial body of critical realist work in a particular social science is probably Margaret Archer's sociological trilogy *Culture and Agency* (1988), *Realist Social Theory: The Morphogenetic Approach* (1995), and *Being Human* (2000). For an intervention in economics, see also Tony Lawson's (1997) *Economics and Reality* and, continuing the debate, the collection *Critical Realism in Economics* edited by Steve Fleetwood (1999). For approaches to environmental issues using critical realist ideas, see Ted Benton's (1993) *Natural Relations*, Kate Soper's (1995) *What Is Nature?*, Peter Dickens's (1996) *Reconstructing Nature*, and Andrew Collier's (1999) *Being and Worth*. For the relation between critical realism and Marxism, see Andrew Collier's (1988) *Scientific Realism and Socialist Thought*, Sean Creaven's (2000) *Marxism and Realism*, Jonathan Joseph's (2002) *Hegemony: A Realist Analysis*, and the collection *Critical Realism and Marxism* edited by A. Brown, Fleetwood, and Roberts (2002). For critical realist interventions in the philosophy of religion, see the forthcoming book *Transcendence: Critical Realism and God* by Archer, Collier, and Porpora.

There are two series on critical realism published by Routledge, *Critical Realism: Interventions* and *Routledge Studies in Critical Realism*. Several of the books mentioned are published in these series (see references), as well as a large book of readings called *Critical Realism: Essential Readings* (Archer et al. 1998).

Negotiating with the Positivist Legacy: New Social Justice Movements and a Standpoint Politics of Method

SANDRA HARDING

Starting with the Industrial Revolution and Romanticism

Positivism became a worldview in the second half of the nineteenth and early decades of the twentieth century. A spreading wave of enthusiasm for the successes of the Industrial Revolution in the context of the prevailing romanticism enabled positivism to become a great social movement during this period (Abbagnano 1967, 414–415). Three tenets that emerged at its origins have persisted through the diverse intellectual and political eras of positivism's history. They now have become part of the folk wisdom of industrialized societies. These are belief in the high value of scientific knowledge over every other kind of knowledge, in the importance of good method in achieving scientific knowledge, and that such good method inevitably makes a necessary contribution to social progress (414).

These beliefs have come to define the boundaries of what can be intelligible philosophies of science. They also, therefore, define what can be intelligible principles of social organization in industrialized societies. That is, far from positivism's being only a problematic and anachronistic philosophy of science (let alone a preference for quantitative research methods, as some social scientists put the matter), it has come to shape not only research disciplines but also, through their products, our social institutions and their cultures and practices in the industrialized West and around the globe.

A continuing source of positivism's power is the dominant conceptual frameworks of natural and social science disciplines and the practices they legitimate.[1] Disciplines work up the messy and confusing phenomena of daily life, natural and social, into categories and patterns of causal relations between them that enable efficient administration and management of social relations, as Canadian sociologist Dorothy Smith writes of her discipline. Research disciplines are complicitous with the conceptual practices of power, in Smith's (1990) phrase. Thus, as positivist philosophy came to shape research disciplines, it became part of a distinctive Western historical social formation. A better way to put this point is that positivist philosophy of science and modern forms of social organization coconstituted each other. Both were shaped by their context of emerging liberal democracies and capitalist social relations and subsequent transformations in these institutions and practices.

New social justice movements, such as feminism, race- and ethnicity-based movements, postcolonialisms, and new forms of class-based movements, persistently identify positivist rules of social and natural sciences as organizing and legitimating the oppression, exploitation, and domination that these groups have experienced.[2] From the perspective of these movements, becoming a serious, effective postpositivist requires much harder work and more effective transformations of both research disciplines and social institutions than most philosophers, social theorists, and science theorists who adopt antipositivist stances have been willing to recognize.[3]

My argument here is that while contemporary neopositivism tries to recuperate these and related tenets and antipositivism to abandon them, standpoint methodologies negotiate with the positivist legacy by refashioning its central beliefs in the superiority of scientific knowledge, the adequacy of scientific methods, and the efficacy of such methods' contributions to social progress. For leading postmodern tendencies in antipositivist social science and philosophy, the "social situatedness" of what counts as science, good method, and progress has undermined the legitimacy of invoking these notions for directing social relations.[4] These antipositivist theorists seem to agree with their critics that the social situatedness of scientific knowledge requires a relativist epistemology,[5] that good method is not a reliable contributor to social progress, and that even the notion of social progress is irretrievably damaged by its participation in a legacy of class, race, gender, and imperialism exploitation which positivist assumptions purportedly have supported.

Yet standpoint methodology revitalizes these central positivist assumptions in ways useful for the new social justice movements. Standpoint theorists justify this commitment to negotiation with the positivist legacy by their insistence on accountability to the new social justice movements. These movements demand critical, realistic analyses of what the "social situation" of knowledge production is today: a type of analysis that is woefully lacking in both the neo- and antipositivist accounts, as well as in self-proclaimed postpositivisms (see Mirowski, forthcoming). Far from a naïve attempt to jump on the train of positivism when it has already left the station, as some have charged, this project promises more effective strategies for living in a postpositivist world than do either neo- or anti-positivisms. Antipositivisms, I am arguing, can be only weak postpositivisms that overtly reject what they still largely accept. It turns out that neo- and antipositivisms, these two movements that define their projects against each other, share more than they imagine. Let us begin by looking further at their commonalities.

Neopositivists and Anti-postpositivists: Shared Assumptions

By now the recognition that sciences are socially situated, that they are coconstituted with the particular historical social formations that origi-nate or sustain them, should not need justification. Since Kuhn's *The Structure of Scientific Revolutions* (1962/1970), sociologists, historians, eth-nographers, and philosophers have produced a huge outpouring of ac-counts describing how sciences have been fully engaged, intentionally or not, in the social, economic, political, and cultural struggles of their days. Consequently, not even the cognitive, technical cores of the natural sci-ences can reasonably be regarded as immune to historical influences.[6]

This rich body of research is demonized or ignored by neopositivists. They admit that, of course, scientific claims are always open to revision and thus it may be impossible to arrive at known scientific truths. More-over, different researchers inevitably bring distinctive social assumptions to research processes. Nevertheless, they claim, social elements, not to mention political values, are undesirable cognitive components of scien-tific inquiry and can be eliminated through methods that produce con-sensus within the scientific community. For all practical purposes, scien-tific claims that achieve a broad consensus within scientific communities may be treated as if they were in fact true. This response intentionally recoups assumptions and practices of positivism that were challenged by recognition of the integrity of moments in the history of modern Western sciences with their social and cultural eras, to borrow a phrase from Kuhn (1962/1970).

This is still the vastly prevailing view in the natural sciences, as well as the dominant one in economics, political science, international relations, psy-chology, large areas of sociology, and philosophy of science. The notion of positivism claimed by neopositivists is a broad one, far broader than post-Kuhnian science studies would countenance. The excessive broadness of the notion is part of what the antipositivists adopt of the neopositivist position. For these neopositivists, as for much of the public, including, to be sure, many critics of modern Western sciences and their philosophies, the term stands for the modern scientific worldview. The various schools of positivism over the past century and a half have themselves encouraged this broad meaning of the term through their claims that positivism alone presents the only accurate scientific worldview, that it is the one and only legitimate philosophy of science, and that it is a direct descendant of the philosophies of Francis Bacon and the British empiricists (Abbagnano 1967; Passmore 1967).

Antipositivists claim to have abandoned positivism. Mostly, they focus on one of the particular, often disciplinary-specific appearances of this philosophy, such as logical positivism in philosophy or the positivism of quantitative methodologists in sociology or of rational choice theorists in economics, political science, and international relations (see Mirowski, this volume). Yet their attempts to move past the positivist legacy appear to have had little effect on natural and social science research disciplines that had emphasized positivist methodologies, let alone on the policies and institutions of society that such disciplines service. One can't "just say no" to this legacy.

While these two movements share the excessively broad understanding of positivism as the scientific worldview, they also share excessively re-stricted notions of "real science," good method, and social progress that characterize the positivist legacy and that have been widely challenged by new social justice movements. The fact of this particular source of crit-icism suggests that one likely reason for the resistance of both groups to engaging in a productive way with positivism's legacy is that to do so would require them to start their thinking from the lives of the groups disempowered by industrialized societies and represented by such move-ments. They would have to start off thinking about science and society from the lives of those groups whose daily lives positivist-organized social institutions have been assigned to manage. They would have to grasp the actual links between cognitive frameworks and historically specific social conditions, namely, "the conceptual practices of power" (D. Smith 1990). They would have to grasp the social conditions of knowledge production in ways that challenge the self-image as socially and politically progressive of both their research disciplines and those social institutions that the research disciplines serve. They would have to value the epistemological standpoint of precisely those groups of "barbarians" that were meant to be silenced "outside the gate" of scientific processes by the insistence within scientific institutions on the importance of consensus in narrowly conceptualized scientific communities about what counts as real science, good method, and social progress. They would have to stop defining scientific, epistemic, and political standards against whatever they associate with the feminine and/or the primitive, as feminist and postcolonial critics have pointed out.

This preoccupation with either recuperating or abandoning positivist tendencies in the social (and natural) sciences tends to blind theorists to alternatives that do not neatly fit into the neopositivism versus antipositivism binary. It blinds them to what we could refer to as robust postpositivisms. Here I focus on one such, standpoint theory, and on its feminist versions in particular. These retain those three central positivist commitments, I am arguing, but refashion them to the needs of today's social justice research and political practices.

Two caveats. First, I must immediately acknowledge that the recommendation to negotiate with the positivist legacy may well seem peculiar and perhaps odious to possibly all other standpoint theorists, including feminists, as well as to others committed to social justice research. To be sure, a main focus of feminist standpoint theory has been to develop philosophies and methodologies of research that can function outside and against the powerful positivist ones that dominate in all of the natural sciences and most of the social sciences. Here is sociologist Patricia Hill Collins, a leading developer of standpoint epistemology and methodology, on why African American women researchers who are studying African American women are unlikely to find useful positivist approaches to research:

> Several requirements typify positivist methodological approaches. First, research methods generally require a distancing of the researcher from her or his "object" of study by defining the researcher as a "subject" with full human subjectivity and by objectifying the "object" of study. . . . A second requirement is the absence of emotion from the research process. . . . Third, ethics and values are deemed inappropriate in the research process, either as the reason for scientific inquiry or as part of the research process itself. . . . Finally, adversarial debates, whether written or oral, become the preferred method of ascertaining truth: the arguments that can withstand the greatest assault and survive intact become the strongest truths.

Such criteria ask African-American women to objectify ourselves, devalue our emotional life, displace our motivations for furthering knowledge about Black women, and confront in an adversarial relationship those with more social, economic, and professional power. It therefore seems unlikely that Black women would use a positivist epistemological stance in rearticulating a Black women's standpoint. (1991, 205–206)

I agree with Collins's assessment. It would be all too easy to read her here as what I am referring to as an antipositivist. Yet I think her position is far more effective than that, for she, like other standpoint theorists, in effect negotiates with the standpoint legacy in powerful ways. Thus, I am not proposing that standpoint theory is reasonably understood as a form of positivism, let alone that it should claim that label.

Yet I think it important to draw attention to the difference between standpoint philosophies and those favored by both neopositivists and the antipositivists who, it turns out, can achieve only a weak form of postpositivism. Standpoint claims often have been assimilated to either neo- or antipositivist positions, and such interpretations have been put forth by both their defenders and their critics. In distinguishing between neo- and antipositivists on the one hand and, on the other hand, feminist standpoint theory, we are forced to reconsider which elements of the positivist legacy it can be important to refashion for pro-democratic research projects in today's actual social relations of the production of knowledge. We are forced to think more deeply and rigorously about just what the social relations are in which today's knowledge projects are situated.

Second, I do not claim that standpoint methodologies represent the only contemporary philosophy of science to critically engage, to negotiate with the positivist legacy. There are other self-proclaimed postpositivisms that certainly do so. However, I do claim that the particular terms of standpoint negotiations are distinctive, illuminating, and more powerful than those of other postpositivisms. These theorists have figured out how to use oppressed, dominated, and exploited social positions to identify otherwise hidden realities of social life, as well as of modern Western sciences and their philosophies. In such projects they also identify and design sources of political empowerment for oppressed groups. Moreover, such empowerment is intended to bring not only relief from their own oppressions, but also more general pro-democratic social transformations (P. Collins 1991; Hartsock 1983/2003).

Though positivism's roots can indeed be traced to Francis Bacon and the British empiricists, we can surmise that its great energy as a social movement that was thrilled with the Industrial Revolution remains a hidden inspiration for neopositivists who would nostalgically recuperate its romantic theses in today's very different world of global political economies and their technologies. Yet, turning one's back on such thrills and their appeal is insufficient to dislodge positivist legacies in the conceptual frameworks of research disciplines or of the dominant social institutions that such disciplines help to organize and maintain.

Standpoint Theory:
A Political-Scientific Logic of Inquiry

Feminist standpoint theory has been creatively formulated in different disciplinary concerns and frameworks in ways that create notable controversies even among its developers and defenders, quite apart from the criticisms of any and all standpoint theories (Wylie 1992/2003). Consequently, it might seem foolhardy to try to articulate a general account of the claims and arguments of these writers.[7] However, several features that are consistent across these different articulations (or, at least, most of them) have been so widely misread that it seems worthwhile to review its "logic of inquiry." These misconstruals are not accidental; they are the consequence of trying to make standpoint theory a version of either a neopositivism or an antipositivism. I present here what I take to be a strong general form of the theory, that is, its most innovative and, to my mind, desirably controversial claims, fully aware that others would wish to characterize it differently.

In the 1970s and early 1980s, a handful of sociologists of knowledge, political philosophers, and philosophers of science began to address two projects. All of these were or had been active in the new social movements of the 1960s and then in the emerging women's movement and its new research fields in the 1970s. They turned to resources they found in the Marxian epistemological legacy of the "standpoint of the proletariat."

One project was to explain better than could the prevailing feminist empiricist accounts (which were shaped by positivist assumptions) the relations between knowledge and power that were becoming visible in the new feminist research in biology and the social sciences. The other project was to identify the kind of research that could itself be a form of feminist activism or, to put the point another way, to identify the epistemological and scientific resources that feminist political activism itself seemed to be generating. These theorists were gifted by the availability of an already lively post-Kuhnian social and cultural studies of science and technology. They were the first generation to have had the opportunity to engage with this work in their formative years in graduate school or shortly thereafter, though the sociologists tended to take up standpoint projects directly from post-Marxian writings in the sociology of knowledge.

We can skip over the prefeminist history of the rise and decline of Marxian standpoint epistemology and the importance of this history to the early feminist standpoint project.[8] We can enter this history with so-called second-wave feminism at the moments when first Dorothy Smith (1974/2003, 1987, 1990, 1999a) and then U.S. political scientist Nancy Hartsock (1983/2003, 1998) independently began to develop what remain the most influential versions of standpoint theory. In 1983 appeared also accounts by British sociologist of science Hilary Rose (1983/2003) and U.S. philosopher Alison Jaggar (1983/2003), followed by historian of science Donna Haraway (1991), sociologist of knowledge Patricia Hill Collins (1991/2003), and a host of others (see Sandra Harding 2003b). I restrict my account here mainly to the influential work of Smith and Hartsock.

Dorothy Smith argued that sociology makes fundamental assumptions about the differing natures and social roles of women and men, the nature of and relation between private and public spheres, and about what constitutes social deviance, poverty, and violence against women, models of rationality and agency. Yet such assumptions appear reasonable and universally valid only from the perspective of the characteristic activities of the "rulers" of our kinds of societies, namely, administrators and managers, who have primarily been men from advantaged classes, races, and ethnicities. The effects of women's everyday activities as mothers, wives, daughters, assistants, nurses, secretaries, cooks, teachers, factory workers, domestic workers, and office cleaners enable elite men to design and maintain their own activities in characteristic bourgeois and patriarchal ways. Thus, women's work provides the ongoing material conditions for men's worlds. Its invisibility to men makes it seem part of the natural order. Women's constant interactions and struggles with the vicissitudes of natural and social relations leave administrative- and managerial-class men free of obligation to maintain their own bodies or anyone else's, or the physical sites of anyone's daily activities, and thus to imagine their abstract labor as the only truly human labor.

Smith developed an analysis of the potential of a "standpoint of women" to serve as a powerful criticism of such "conceptual practices of power." She argued that her discipline, sociology, was complicitous with the "ruling" of society through its everyday research procedures of producing categories and patterns of causal relations between them through which daily life could be administered by dominant social institutions. Smith's standpoint was not only critical; it was also intended to provide a "method of research," as she referred to it, that could generate the empirical and theoretical resources for a "sociology for women."[9] This sociology was to be *for* women in the sense that its goal was to answer the kinds of questions about social relations that arose in women's lives. A sociology for women would make visible these daily lives and those of researchers; it would reveal the activities from the perspective of which the researcher's assumptions could appear reasonable. Research that "started off" from women's everyday lives, that took its questions and problematics from their lives—in households, workplaces, public life, and community activities—had the potential for being able to detect the sexist and androcentric social and political interests embedded in disciplinary conceptual frameworks that were claimed to be value-neutral and universally valid. Such conceptual frameworks were complicitous with the power of social institutions to oppress, exploit, and dominate women.

Although standpoint methods were to start from women's lives, they were not to end there; women's lives were shaped by decisions made elsewhere, namely, in the elite men's worlds of public institutions. Standpoint methods were to "study up," to critically examine the dominant culture, rather than to "study down," to focus exclusively on the oppressed, as conventional social science projects all too often did. Sociologists Smith and, later, Collins studied the discipline of sociology and its suspiciously close fit with the conceptual frameworks of public institutions, on the one hand, and with the way administrative and managerial men understood their worlds, on the other hand. Other theorists studied how their own disciplines participated in such social relations.

Thus, standpoint theory's target was from the beginning the abstract conceptual frameworks legitimated by the dominant philosophies of science in the disciplines that function mostly out of reach, beyond awareness, of the everyday observation and reasoning that they guide. Such frameworks delineate what is intelligible and what is not in any particular cultural discourse or way of life. Consequently, standpoint project findings could not be simply the reports of what women say or think, valuable as are women's voices to such projects, for women, like men, have to learn how to detect such frameworks in patterns of public policies, everyday beliefs, institutional practices and their meanings, and other aspects of social relations. A standpoint is an achievement requiring both science and political struggle, as Hartsock (1983/2003) would subsequently put this point.

Independently, U.S. political philosopher Nancy Hartsock (1983/2003) also returned to Marx and Engels to construct a feminist standpoint theory that, like Smith's standpoint of women, explained the scientific and political importance of a powerful critical focus on some of the most fundamental assumptions of her discipline. Moreover, she saw this approach, as did Smith, as a distinctive method of research that could advance the growth of knowledge through serving feminist ends. The title of her 1983 essay, calling for a "specifically feminist historical materialism," echoes the standard characterization of Marxist research method. She, too, focused on a discipline that was complicitous with the ways public institutions and their cultures and practices were organized. And she, too, focused on the kinds of women's daily activities that supposedly enabled men to "transcend their bodies," thus revealing aspects of hegemonic belief invisible from the prevailing conceptual frameworks.

Hartsock's standpoint theory was influential for the discipline of political science and for political philosophers in such other fields as philosophy. An important contribution of this work was her focus on the significance of engagement, of political struggle, to obtaining knowledge of the conceptual practices of power. It takes both science and politics to see the reality "behind," "beneath," or "from outside" the oppressors' institutionalized vision, she argued.[10] Thus, as noted, a standpoint is an achievement, not an ascription, as she insists. It must be struggled for against the apparent realities made natural and obvious by dominant institutions and their ideologies and against the ongoing political disempowerment of oppressed groups. Dominant groups cannot imagine that their assumptions are false: that slaves are fully human, that men are not the only, or perhaps even not the most desirable, model of the ideal human, or that non-Western cultures have developed sophisticated and competent scientific and technological systems. Nor do they imagine that their assumptions are self-interested or have unjust political consequences. In fact, it takes methods that meet stronger standards of objectivity—"strong objectivity"—to locate the practices of power that appear only in the apparently abstract, value-neutral conceptual frameworks favored by dominant social institutions and the many disciplines that service them.[11]

Standpoint projects use the distinctive ways a group is oppressed, exploited, or dominated to reveal the "mechanisms" by which elite groups maintain their dominance. White bourgeois women, poor Black women,

Central European Jews, Palestinians, homosexuals, Chicanos/as, Asian Americans—each such group (and each of its subgroups) is oppressed, exploited, and dominated in a distinctive way. Starting research from the daily actualities of each kind of such lives can reveal different ways oppression is organized and maintained and point to what will be effective political struggles for that group. To put my point here another way, the distinctive forms of political activism characteristic of each group can generate particular insights about the sources and means of their oppression and about ways to combat these. To be sure, politics and culture are often prison houses of knowledge, but they can also advance the growth of knowledge; they can be scientifically and epistemologically productive.

Other feminists worked up similar accounts, sometimes independently, in other cases stimulated by the work of Smith, Hartsock, and the other early feminist standpoint authors. Centered in their critical focus were positivist assumptions about the desirable and achievable neutrality of research, the ideal knower as autonomous, perfectly rational, and an individual, and the possibility in principle of complete and unified, singular, total accounts of nature and social relations. Thus, British sociologist of science Hilary Rose (1983/2003) positioned her independently developed standpoint account of an epistemology for the natural sciences as a critique of the conceptual framework not only of mainstream philosophies of science, but also of the prevailing radical science movement in which she had been working. She pointed out that the latter in effect conjoined forces with the sociobiology it otherwise criticized in the way that it left sex and gender relations outside its accounts of the social features of the sciences, and thus as part of nature. Patricia Hill Collins (1991) developed the notion of the Black feminist standpoint researcher as the "outsider within," drawing on the sociological resources she found in Dorothy Smith and such earlier sociologists of knowledge as Karl Mannheim (1936), Robert Merton (1972), and Georg Simmel (1921). Yet other feminist theorists in various disciplines and political projects developed standpoint accounts, always both positioned against and yet negotiating with positivism, Marxian accounts, and the relativist stances of various interpretive social science schools. They sometimes did so without using the specific language of standpoint theory.[12]

Thus, standpoint theory reemerged in feminist work from a particular Western theoretical trajectory as it overtly revived Marxian insights abandoned by recent Marxists, as Fredric Jameson (1988/2003), among others, has pointed out. It also positioned itself as an alternative both to the mainstream positivism of post–World War II Western industrialized countries and to the phenomenological and hermeneutical/ethnographic research projects in the social sciences concerned to reject the positivist legacy. And it emerged in the climate of early post-Kuhnian science and technology studies. Yet, I suggest, it also retained, and even strengthened for the contemporary context, central beliefs of the positivist legacy.

I shall not here review the many criticisms of standpoint approaches that have again and again been answered in the existing literature. Thus, I do not rehearse how it need not be essentialist, does not commit a damaging judgmental relativism, does not propose substituting political and ethical claims for scientific and epistemological ones, is not another kind of ethnography, has ongoing productive relations to projects of oppressed groups other than white women, and so forth (see Sandra Harding 2003b). Instead, I review its continuities and discontinuities with positivism.

I first review what has attracted feminists and members of other new social movements to standpoint theory. This may already be obvious, but I want specifically to ask why methodologists from these movements couldn't just follow the prevailing positivist rules of inquiry in the disciplines—positivism as it appeared to researchers in the 1970s. This was Collins's question quoted earlier, and I take it up in a more general way. Then I ask how standpoint theorists refashioned positivist valuations of specifically scientific knowledge, of standards for good method, and the belief that such scientific methods could contribute to social progress.

Standpoint Methodology versus Positivist Taboos and Lacunas

To be sure, valuable feminist research has been done fully within the prevailing disciplinary rules, as has research generated by other new social justice movements. Even under what are widely recognized as inappropriate constraints, social justice researchers have found ways to produce and justify information that identifies inadequate empirical and theoretical claims that are used to support injustices. Not everything such researchers need and want to do, however, can be fit into a positivist framework.

First of all, standpoint methods are designed to generate questions about the selection and conception of research problems in the first place, prior to the point when methodological controls specified by research designs come into play. Yet for positivism, extending methodological controls back to the beginning of the "context of discovery" would stifle scientific creativity. The whole point of insistence on a context of discovery of phenomena and the hypotheses likely to explain them versus a context of justification where hypotheses are tested was to designate only the latter as the proper domain of methodological controls. There was a brief moment in the 1950s when Norwood Russell Hanson (1958) attempted to develop a logic of discovery, but this project soon met overwhelming obstacles and was abandoned (Caws 1967).

Second, this leads standpoint projects to focus on the conceptual practices of disciplines that direct the production of kinds of information that dominant social institutions need to direct, maintain, and legitimate their oppressive rule. And it leads them to argue for what could be liberatory, pro-democratic disciplinary practices. Yet, for positivism, sciences are supposed to be transparent to the world, not contributors of historically specific social, economic, political, and cultural values and interests. Standpoint projects try to identify the causal relations between the natures and practices of knowledge-production cultures and the structures and practices of the social institutions that they serve. Is this an example of "academic navel-gazing," as some have charged? Not at all. It is designed to identify the specific cognitive resources that disciplines provide to ruling groups and, in contrast, could provide to pro-democratic groups. It turns out that the disciplines are not at all only ivy towers, disengaged from the world. They are not "merely academic," as my activist students, fearful of being co-opted by university practices, often protest.

Thus, third, standpoint theory accounts for the scientifically productive nature of political struggles for oppressed groups. Yet this is unintelligible in the positivist philosophy, which can conceptualize politics only as an external threat to scientific processes that, in principle, can and must be kept isolated from political biases. To be sure, politics often can obstruct the growth of scientific knowledge, but it also can be productive. Thus, this theory recommends on scientific and epistemological grounds the very kinds of struggles to which such groups are already committed for ethical and political reasons.

Fourth, such scientific and epistemic struggles empower exploited groups and thus help to bring them into historical agency. Of course, such groups already exist "in themselves," with shared features that make them objects of interest to positivist social scientists and policymakers. But standpoint projects help to constitute such groups as subjects of knowledge and history, as critically self-conscious groups "for themselves."[13] Thus, standpoint projects stand at one rather abstract but nevertheless important end of the continuum of participatory action research methodologies in the social sciences (R. McTaggart 1997). Yet the subject of knowledge for positivism, the speaker of scientific claims, is to be the abstract rational knower, not some particular socially and politically constituted group of claimants.

Fifth, standpoint projects seek realistic evaluations of the strengths and limitations of past epistemological, methodological, and philosophy of science projects. Oppressed and exploited groups cannot afford the luxury of romanticism about Western modern sciences characteristic of the dominant groups. They cannot afford the epistemological underdevelopment characteristic of positivist epistemologies and philosophies of science. But neither can they afford to romanticize "science bashing" or any other kind of complete rejection of sciences and their philosophies.[14] Positivism asserts that the only rational accounts of science are those that come from the scientific community itself and its philosophic wing. It tends to see the more realistic accounts produced by the social justice movements as caused by ignorance, the impetuousness and false thinking of political groups (mob rule), and individual psychological malfunctioning.

Finally, standpoint approaches insist on a kind of concrete accountability to the groups most in need of social progress, which was never so articulated in positivism, which was envisioned as serving only social progress in general, not in the diverse and sometimes conflicting particular, historically specific ways different groups need and yearn for it.

We must note here that standpoint thinking has never been the sole possession of social justice movements. Indeed, the dominant conceptual frameworks also marginalize antidemocratic groups that lost power in the transition to modernity and nostalgically yearn for a return to what they perceive to be their happier times. Neo-Nazis and American Patriots, religious, ethnic, and land-based fundamentalisms have generated some of the most disturbing politics of recent times and justified these actions with something much like standpoint claims (Castells 1997; Pels 1996/ 2003). What feminist standpoint projects do, like projects of other social justice movements, is to bring to visibility the relations between politics and the scientific production of knowledge and to argue that on scientific as well as moral grounds the latter should be shaped by social justice politics. That is, contemporary social justice movements would argue that the antidemocratic commitment of those other social movements damages their scientific projects as well as the ethical justifiability of their political ideals. The peoples represented by such movements have indeed also suffered at the hands of history and, in particular, modern industrial society. But their nostalgia for a return to a predemocratic past leaves them scientifically as well as ethnically disadvantaged relative to the new social justice movements.

So standpoint methodologies respond to needs of the new social justice movements that the positivist legacy could not satisfy. How do they in other ways strengthen that legacy, refashioning it for today's social relations of the production of knowledge?

Critically Remodeling the Positivist Legacy

We can see now how standpoint theory has retrieved and revised positivist commitments to scientific knowledge, good method in its production, and the ability of such good method to contribute to social progress. Let us review how these three agendas have been achieved.

First, feminists and other social justice movements need more accurate sciences of nature and social relations. Yet, because the object and practice of such sciences each are embedded in rich networks of economic, political, social, religious, and cultural features, such sciences must be expanded to include methods and concepts capable of grasping such hybrid objects and practices of study.[15] Thus, they need also "sciences of science," that is, critical social studies of science, to examine scientific practices. "Real science" in these accounts must be much more comprehensive than positivist philosophies could countenance. It must include the social sciences and their far better developed self-critical epistemological projects, empirical studies that focus on a mix of social and natural phenomena, such as environmental and medical sciences, and empirical knowledge systems of other cultures that, like modern Western sciences themselves, are embedded in culturally local systems of value and interest. And it must include the everyday practices that produce, develop, revise, and store empirical knowledge of peoples and the world around them.

Second and relatedly, such social justice movements need more capable research methods than the favored ones that have been unable to detect the way everyday exercises of power relations tend to shape the cognitive content of beliefs. One important standpoint strategy has been to extend the domain of method back to the context of discovery, to the beginning of the research process. Another has been to expand its resources to include critical social theory.

Finally, standpoint projects hold that oppressed peoples can improve their lives only when their strategies are directed by just the kinds of more accurate accounts of nature and social relations that standpoint methodology can direct. It cannot be that such progress will universally, unilinearly, or necessarily occur. Nevertheless, small and not so small progressive changes can occur in social relations increasingly directed through the production and management of information. In an information society, where scientific knowledge increases its ability to organize and maintain social institutions, the ability to grasp and direct such processes constitutes social progress for groups to whom such agency has been denied (Castells 1996–98/2000b). Improving access to critical conceptual resources for such groups constitutes social progress.

Thus, standpoint approaches seek a robust postpositivism with resources that can make a difference to groups around the globe interested in transforming in a pro-democratic direction a world of social injustice for which the positivist legacy continues to provide a conceptual framework and legitimacy. Standpoint methodologies negotiate with the positivist legacy by retaining three of its most powerful commitments but redefining them in effective pro-democratic ways for the realities of today's social production of scientific knowledge.

Links to Other Social Theory Projects

In conclusion, it is worth noting four additional reasons that feminist standpoint methodology is fruitful to consider in relation to a project of transforming the positivist legacy. These all have to do with dimensions of what constitutes the specifically social situation of knowledge production in today's world. Positivism tried to keep social elements as distant as possible from the cognitive content of scientific claims. Yet, once social elements are understood as productive of the growth of knowledge, not only as obstructive (as indeed they often are), then identifying the relevant dimensions of the social becomes an important topic for sciences, their principles, practices, and philosophies (Mirowski, this volume).

First, feminist standpoint methodologies have remained controversial since their origins, and the particular focus of such continuing controversy is valuable. Puzzling to critics is the peculiar way these approaches to research, both natural and social, stand solidly on three legs—with one foot in modern and one in postmodern philosophies of science and a third in the Marxian legacy of contemporary social justice movements. This has made them the target of misreadings and vigorous controversies for over two decades. Controversial, too, is that the resources of these three philosophies are simultaneously challenged and transformed by insights from feminist social movements of the past few decades. Moreover, during this period, the influence of feminist and other standpoint approaches to research has spread across social and natural science disciplines. The combination of such widespread use and continuing controversy is itself valuable, in my view, for it indicates the power of standpoint methodologies to stage important, if disturbing, polemics about knowledge and power after positivism's heyday (as Fredric Jameson argued about the feminist versions; Sandra Harding 2004).

Second, they provide a good example of what Gibbons et al. (1994) refer to as the emerging "transdisciplinary" model for the new production of scientific knowledge.[16] This kind of research model is transported from one discipline to another, directing distinctive kinds of research projects yet fully embedded in the local research context. Gibbons et al. make a strong case that this new kind of transdisciplinary model will increase social inequality; I am close to convinced they are right with respect to the examples, entirely from the natural sciences, on which they focus. Yet the opposite would seem to be the case for standpoint theory. What is different about standpoint theory as a transdisciplinary model of the production of scientific knowledge? This issue will have to be addressed elsewhere.[17]

Third, these methodologies fill a lacuna in urban sociologist Manuel Castells's influential analysis of "the information society," which seems to be taking over important operations and functions of industrial society. Castells does not address epistemological or philosophy of science issues at all in his extensive account.[18] Yet attention to such issues seems called for in light of the new kinds of organization of information production and maintenance that electronic media have enabled. The global economy, politics, and culture are being transformed through these media. The "social" of socially situated knowledge is becoming reorganized to the benefit of those who are in a position to design and effectively use these media. It seems to me that it is standpoint research methodology that is needed to assist in transforming "resistance identities" into what Castells terms "project identities," that is, into identities capable of providing resources for transforming the institutions of industrial society into institutions more useful not only for the particular oppressed and marginalized identity group that uses such a research method, but also for all such groups that industrial society oppressed and marginalized. Standpoint methodologies overtly link politics and knowledge in the ways required for the success of such transformative projects.

Finally, it is striking that political philosophers have paid so little attention to the politics of the production and uses of (science and) technology when "modern state-power is inseparable from modern science and technologies. . . . from its beginnings the modern state was indelibly shaped by those who claimed to possess systematic forms of knowledge that would advance the power of the state and place it on firmer foundations," as political theorist Sheldon S. Wolin notes (1996, 36; see also D. Smith 1999b). This mention of science and technology is the only one that appears in an entire collection of twenty essays by eminent political theorists who look at the effects of "difference" on conceptions and practices of democracy today (Benhabib 1996). Standpoint methodology is precisely focused on the effects of difference on the links between power and knowledge, both for dominant and for oppressed groups.

It is a project for another time and place to pursue further the interesting existing and potential interactions between standpoint methodologies and these explorations and accounts of the social situations in which the production of scientific knowledge occurs today. Yet, noting such possibilities suggests how diverse are the dimensions of the social that are at issue in negotiating with the positivist legacy.

Notes

1   To be sure, in some social sciences phenomenological and hermeneutical frameworks are widely used. Yet these, too, have been influenced by positivism. For example, insofar as they take an oppositional stance to positivist tenets, they replicate binaries central to positivism's power.

2   The concept of social justice has itself been criticized by such movements as promising too little to oppressed groups. So, too, have other familiar terms for the goals of liberal democratic movements such as "democracy," "liberation," and "emancipation." For some of these criticisms, see Benhabib (1996). I use "social justice" and "democratic" to refer to these new social movements nevertheless, setting aside the important issue of how pro-democratic political philosophies could best specify the ideal political "goods" that we should seek.

3   Antipositivists can be found among self-declared postpositivists in philosophy and science studies, as well as among theorists in other research fields and activists. However, other postpositivists in philosophy and science studies do try to negotiate with the positivist legacy, though in ways that appear inadequate from the perspective of standpoint feminisms, race- and ethnicity-based movements, and poor people's and postcolonial movements. The standpoint postpositivisms are distinctive, as I delineate below.

4   Haraway (1991/2003), who emphatically does not take the antipositivist stance described here, introduced the term "situated knowledge" in an essay that originated as a comment on Sandra Harding (1986).

5   Recollect that this was a widespread response to Thomas Kuhn's argument that moments in the history of modern Western science revealed an "integrity with their historic era" (1962/1970, 1; Lakatos and Musgrave 1970).

6   For samples of this work, including feminist and postcolonial science and technology studies, see Biagioli (1999), Bloor (1977), Haraway (1989), Sandra Harding (1986, 1998), Hess (1995), Keller (1985), Knorr-Cetina (1981), Latour and Woolgar (1979), Rouse (1987), Schuster and Yeo (1986), Shapin (1994), Shapin and Shaffer (1985).

7   Dorothy Smith (1997) points out that general accounts, such as mine, have obscured the way her work is part of ongoing conversations in sociology.

8   Lukács (1971); Marx (1844/1964, 1970). For illuminating accounts of this history, see Hartsock (1983/2003, 1998), Jaggar (1983/2003), and Jameson (1988/2003).

9   Smith and other theorists often describe standpoint approaches to research as a method of inquiry, though other theorists refer to it as a methodology in contrast to such techniques ("methods") as collecting and manipulating quantitative data, observation, archival research, and interviews, which are the focus in methods courses in the social sciences. Yet "method" does seem like an appropriate term for standpoint recommendations for a distinctive way to go about doing research. Standpoint approaches generate a kind of "logic of discovery" and thus enable the development of a philosophy of science that, in contrast to contemporary work in that field, is not restricted to epistemological questions. To put the issue another way, standpoint approaches expand the concerns of epistemology to the entire scientific process rather than restricting them to only the nature and adequacy of processes of justifying hypotheses. (Rouse 1996 develops this criticism of the excessive restriction to epistemological issues of analytic philosophy of science.) It is important to note also that standpoint "method" is not a subcategory of qualitative research alone (let alone of ethnography, as some critics and defenders have claimed). One can use quantitative techniques to develop and test claims that "start from women's lives."

10 Of course, one's understanding can never completely escape its historical moment— that was the positivist dream that standpoint approaches deny. All understanding is socially, historically located. The success of standpoint research requires only a small degree of freedom from the dominant understanding, not complete escape from it. It is the structural positions of oppressed groups that provide the possibility of degrees of freedom from prevailing hegemonic discourses.

11 The phrase is mine; see Sandra Harding (1992/2003a, 1998). It is hard to overstress the importance of keeping clear that a standpoint is an achievement. If this point is lost, and even some standpoint defenders sometimes lose it, "standpoint" seems like just another term for a perspective or viewpoint. Yet the standpoint claim that some kinds of political struggle can advance the growth of knowledge and create a consciousness of an oppressed group for itself, rather than only a group that appears as a sociological fact to others, is thereby made obscure when its technical use, which I retain here, is abandoned. This point is related to the disagreement over whether the theory is best articulated as about a feminist or a women's standpoint. Hartsock has opted for the former, and Dorothy Smith for the latter for reasons that I think have to do with distinctive disciplinary concerns, as Smith (1997) suggests.

12 See representative writings by some of these in Sandra Harding (2003b).

13 The title of P. Collins's 1991 book identifies this political goal of Black feminist standpoint projects. As indicated earlier, Hartsock (1983/2003) first developed this theme.

14 It is striking that the feminist theorists most accused of "science bashing," of rejecting objectivity and rationality, and of embracing a self-damaging relativism are precisely those who have articulated a "third way" between science romanticism and rejection, between objectivism and relativism. See, e.g., P. Gross and Levitt (1994), P. Gross, Levitt, and Lewis (1996), Walby (2001). See also A. Ross (1996).

15 Donna Haraway (1991/2003) and Bruno Latour (1993) have written of such hybrids.

16   Transdiscplinary research is different from multidisciplinary and interdisciplinary research.

17   I discuss problems with the Gibbons et al. study in my *Must Science Advance Inequality?*
(forthcoming).

18   This is just an observation, not a criticism; Castells's monumental study has already
provided a valuable overview of huge changes underway in the global "economy,
society, and culture," as the subtitle of the series promises.

ECONOMICS AND CRITICAL REALISM

A Perspective on Modern Economics

TONY LAWSON

odern economics as practiced in the academy stands to benefit from a greater takeup of explicit, systematic, and sustained ontological analysis than has been its custom. This is my contention. By ontology I mean study of the nature or basic structure of a domain of being. Here I am concerned with social ontology primarily. Clearly, the contention advanced rests on certain presuppositions. First and foremost, I hold that the state of modern economics is in some sense not all that it might be. Second, whatever the limitations I have in mind, an ontological turn promises to be a solution, or at least helpful. I do indeed hold to both these assessments. But a good deal of elaboration is required to convey both what I take to be the current state of modern economics and also what I am supposing an ontological turn is able to achieve. It is with these two issues that the current essay is primarily concerned.

I do, though, go further. This book is concerned with the influence of positivist ideas on the various disciplines, and with how, if at all, more recent approaches define themselves as responses to any such influence. I have sometimes been interpreted as viewing the mainstream project of modern economics as a version of positivism, or (more or less) equivalently, a form of empirical realism. This, though, is not a correct characterization of my position. So I welcome the opportunity provided here to contrast my own assessment of the modern mainstream with the positivistic interpretation in question and thereby to elaborate the sense, if any, in which my own position, in its rejection of the mainstream orientation, is usefully conceived as a response to positivistic influence.

The State of Modern Economics

Most observers of modern economics recognize that it is dominated by a mainstream tradition, and is so to a degree that is rather unusual. There is, though, remarkably little sustained discussion or analysis of (as opposed to a few quick assertions about) the nature of that mainstream project (even though practicing economists usually suggest that they know it when they see it). Before giving my own assessment of the nature of the mainstream project, let me briefly consider two more widely held alternatives to it.

A first conception, the one most noneconomist commentators give the impression of holding, views mainstream economics as a project concerned primarily with defending the workings of the current economic system. Numerous economists take this view too, of course. Kanth (1999) provides an excellent contribution that does so. According to Kanth, mainstream economics (which he sometimes refers to as neoclassical economics) is deliberately "rigged" to generate results that support the status quo: "To state the moral: *the entire enterprise of neo-classical economics is rigged to show that laissez-faire produces optimal outcomes,* but for the disruptive operation of the odd externality (a belated correction) here and there" (1999, 191–192, emphasis in the original).

How is this rigging said to be achieved? One component of the strategy is everywhere to stipulate that human beings are rational (meaning optimizing) atomistic individuals. A second is the construction of theoretical setups or models specified to ensure that (typically unique) optimal outcomes are attainable.

There are indeed many economists who adopt the individualist framework and assumption that individual behavior is optimal (in the sense of always deriving from optimizing decisions in conditions where optimal outcomes are to be had). Perhaps most do. But this is not yet enough to show that the overall economic system is itself optimal in any way. If the claim is that mainstream economists seek to defend the economic system per se, something more is required to guarantee this result. This, it is supposed, is achieved by the commonplace construction of an equilibrium framework, the latter being so specified that the actions of isolated optimizing individuals somehow (tend to) work to bring an equilibrium position about. Thus, Kanth, for example, refers to the "economic science of capitalism" as "simply *irrelevant* for being a fantasy world of an ideal rational capitalism where all motions are mutually equilibriating, in a Newtonian co-ordination of the elements" (1999, 194).

I think we need to accept a less conspiratorial or functionalist interpretation of what is going on. There is little doubt that some mainstream economists approach their subject in the manner that Kanth and others describe. But most do not. Even those who have spent their careers studying models of equilibrium do not draw the sorts of inferences that can be used to justify the economic system. Consider the conclusions of Frank Hahn, a major contributor to general equilibrium theory who has also been concerned to comment continually on the nature of the enterprise. In both his Jevons memorial lecture, entitled "In Praise of Economic Theory" (1985), and the introduction to his collection of essays, entitled *Equilibrium and Macroeconomics* (1984b), Hahn explicitly acknowledges that he everywhere adopts (1) an individualistic perspective, a requirement that explanations be couched solely in terms of individuals, and (2) some rationality axiom. But in referencing questions of economic order or equilibrium, Hahn further accepts *at most* (3) a commitment merely to the *study* of equilibrium states. Poignantly, Hahn believes equilibrium outcomes or states are rarely, if ever, manifest: "It cannot be denied that there is something scandalous in the spectacle of so many people refining the analyses of economic [equilibrium] states which they give no reason to suppose will ever, or have ever, come about. It probably is also dangerous. Equilibrium economics . . . is easily convertible into an apologia for existing economic arrangements and it is frequently so converted" (1970/1984a, 88–89). Further, there are groups of economists, seemingly acceptable to the mainstream, who, though adopting the individualist-rationalistic framework, seem determined from the outset to demonstrate the *weaknesses* of the current economic system. Those economists who are often described as "rational-choice Marxists" seem to be so inclined.

Equally to the point, if not more so, most economists who accept the individualist and rationalistic framework do not actually concern themselves with questions of equilibrium at all, or, more generally, do not focus on the workings of the economic system as a whole. Most such economists, rather, concern themselves with highly specific or partial analyses of some highly restricted sectors or forms of behavior. Moreover, to the extent that it is meaningful for the various results or theorems of these economists to be considered as a whole or in total, the only clear conclusion to be drawn from them is that they are mostly wildly inconsistent with each other.

Notoriously, even econometricians using identical, or almost identical, data sets are found to produce quite contrasting conclusions. The systematic result here, as the respected econometrician Edward Leamer observes, is that "hardly anyone takes anyone else's data analysis seriously" (1983, 37).

If we turn away from econometrics to the mostly nonempirical "economic theory" project and look beyond its general equilibrium program (which, in any case, has been in decline for some time now), there seems not even to be any agreement as to the project's purpose or direction. As one of its leading practitioners, Ariel Rubinstein, admits:

> The issue of interpreting economic theory is . . . the most serious problem now facing economic theorists. The feeling among many of us can be summarized as follows. Economic theory should deal with the real world. It is not a branch of abstract mathematics even though it utilises mathematical tools. Since it is about the real world, people expect the theory to prove useful in achieving practical goals. But economic theory has not delivered the goods. Predictions from economic theory are not nearly as accurate as those by the natural sciences, and the link between economic theory and practical problems . . . is tenuous at best. Economic theory lacks a consensus as to its purpose and interpretation. Again and again, we find ourselves asking the question "where does it lead?" (1995, 12)

Mainstream Economics as the Study of
Optimizing Individual Behavior

So what are we to make of this situation? How are we to understand the project of mainstream economics in a manner that make sense of this more complex situation? An obvious alternative hypothesis to examine in the light of the discussion so far, perhaps, is that if there is anything essential to the mainstream tradition of modern economics, it is merely a commitment to individualism, coupled with the axiom that individuals are everywhere rational (optimizing) in their behavior. Perhaps the mainstream just is so committed, but without any overall common purpose in terms of the sorts of substantive results that "should" be generated?

This is the second widespread interpretation of the mainstream endeavor, the main alternative to the view that the mainstream project is concerned to defend the workings of the economic system. It constitutes an assessment, indeed, that is likely the more dominant among modern heterodox critics of the mainstream within economics.

I think this characterization of the mainstream program *is* closer to the mark, but in the end it, too, is found not to be sustainable. There are numerous game theory contributions where rationality is no longer invoked, and seemingly not even meaningful. Mainstream economists are sometimes even prepared to assume that people everywhere follow fixed, highly simple rules whatever the context (see references in Lawson 1997, ch. 8). Moreover, some mainstream economists are prepared to abandon the individualist framework entirely if this will help make the economic theory framework more productive in some way. As the economic theorist Alan Kirman writes: "The problem [of mainstream theorizing to date] seems to be embodied in what is an essential feature of a centuries-long tradition in economics, that of treating individuals as acting independently of each other" (1989, 137). He adds: "If we are to progress further we may well be forced to theorise in terms of groups who have collectively coherent behaviour" (138). So it is not obvious that even assumptions of individualism and rationality are ultimately essential to the mainstream position.

And yet, economists everywhere acknowledge that there is a distinguishable and enduring tradition that constitutes the current mainstream, one against which heterodox groupings such as Austrians, feminist economists, institutionalists, (non-rational-choice) Marxists, post-Keynesians, social economists, and others consistently stand opposed. Commentators in these latter groups tend to pick out the clearly widespread attachment to individualism and the rationality axiom as driving the project. Yet, as the few issues considered above suggest, if we inquire more closely we see that these emphasized features are not after all essential to the mainstream framework.

So what, if anything, is essential? The key to answering this question comes, I believe, through remembering an insight of Alfred North Whitehead's: that the more fundamental components of a position are often those that are so taken for granted that there is little attempt to defend them:

> When you are criticising the philosophy of an epoch do not chiefly direct your attention to those intellectual positions which its exponents feel it necessary explicitly to defend. There will be some fundamental assumptions which adherents of all the variant systems within the epoch unconsciously presuppose. Such assumptions appear so obvious that people do not know what they are assuming because no other way of putting things has ever occurred to them. With these assumptions a certain limited number of types of philosophic systems are possible, and this group of systems constitutes the philosophy of the epoch. (1926, 61)

The Mathematicizing Inclination

Is there something so taken for granted in modern mainstream economics that it goes largely unquestioned? I think there is. This is just the mathematical (deductivist) framework that mainstream economists everywhere adopt. Perhaps it is not correct to say that the mathematical framework goes unrecognized. This could hardly be the case. But the mathematical framework is usually only briefly noted at best; it is considered so essential that worries about its usefulness, if they are raised at all, tend to be summarily dismissed rather than seriously addressed. It is because mathematicization is understood as being so obviously desirable, indeed, that the project is rarely defined in such terms. Serious work, it seems to be supposed, could never be otherwise.

Consider just the economists already mentioned. Rubinstein, we can already see, notes in passing that (mainstream) economic theory "utilises mathematical tools" without questioning the legitimacy of this. Kirman recognizes that the specific form of maths used in modern economics may be questionable, but finds it difficult to believe that some form of mathematics would not be appropriate: "The argument that the root of the problem. . . . [is] that we are confined by a mathematical strait jacket which allows us no escape, does not seem very persuasive. That the mathematical frameworks that we have used made the task of changing or at least modifying our paradigm hard, is undeniable but it is difficult to believe that had a clear well-formulated new approach been suggested then we would not have adopted the appropriate mathematical tools" (1989, 137). Leamer notes a "wide gap between econometric theory and econometric practice" but fails to resolve the noted inconsistencies, writing: "Nor do I foresee developments on the horizon that will make any mathematical theory of inference fully applicable. For better or for worse, real inference will remain a highly complicated, poorly understood phenomenon" (1978, vi). The idea that there may be relevant nonmathematical theories of inference is seemingly never contemplated.

Frank Hahn probably best epitomizes widespread sentiment when he declares of any suggestion that the usual heavy emphasis on the mathematics is so misplaced that it is "a view surely not worth discussing" (1985, 18). In fact, Hahn later counsels that we "avoid discussions of 'mathematics in economics' like the plague" (1992a; see also 1992b). Even Kanth notes the emphasis on mathematics, but without quite appreciating its essentiality:

The apparent rigour of mathematics was recruited avidly by neoclassicism to justify and defend its truistic, axiomatic, and almost infantile, theorems that deeply investigated but the surface gloss of economic life. Indeed, for the longest time, Marxists (in the U.S.) had to live in the academic dog-house for not being familiar with matrix algebra, until keen (if not always scrupulous) Marxist minds, with academic tenures at stake, realised the enormous (and inexpensive) potential of this tool for restating Marxian ideas in formalised language and instantly acquiring the gloss of high science, the latter-day pundits of repute here being Roemer in the U.S. and Morishima in England, who were of course soon emulated by a host of lesser lights to whom this switch in language alone promised hours of (well funded) computerised fun and games.

Of course, all the formalisms did not advance a critical understanding of the *organon* of Marxian system, and its many difficulties, one iota; but it did succeed in generating grudging respect for the Marxist by the even more facile and shallow savants of neo-classicism. (1999, 189)

The truth is modern mainstream economics just is the reliance on certain forms of mathematical (deductivist) method. This is an enduring feature of that project, and the only one. Mathematical formalism has not just been recruited; for the mainstream tradition it is its unquestioned, and seemingly unquestionable, essential core. Moreover, this is a feature not shared by heterodox traditions. Some heterodox economists do experiment with formalistic models, but there is not the insistence on formalism that pervades the mainstream. The latter insistence is clearly an essential and also a distinguishing feature of the modern mainstream project.

Consider some more observations on the mainstream emphasis on formalism. A likely worry of noneconomist observers is that descriptions or overviews by critics of modern mainstream economics are likely to be uncharitable caricatures. So let me first consider some more impressions of mainstream economists themselves.

Richard Lipsey, an author of a best-selling mainstream economic textbook, acknowledges: "To get an article published in most of today's top rank economic journals, you must provide a mathematical model, even if it adds nothing to your verbal analysis. I have been at seminars where the presenter was asked after a few minutes, 'Where is your model?' When he answered 'I have not got one as I do not need one, or cannot yet develop one, to consider my problem' the response was to turn off and figuratively, if not literally, to walk out" (Lipsey 2001, 184). William Baumol focuses on hurdles facing students in particular: "These days few specialised students are allowed to proceed without devoting a very considerable proportion of their time to the acquisition of mathematical tools, and they often come away feeling that any piece of writing they produce will automatically be rejected as unworthy if it is not liberally sprinkled with an array of algebraic symbols" (1992, 2). Roger Guesnerie focuses on research: "Mathematics now plays a controversial but decisive role in economic research. This is demonstrated, for example, by the recourse to formalisation in the discussion of economic theory, and increasingly, regardless of the field. Anyone with doubts has only to skim the latest issues of the journals that are considered, for better or worse, the most prestigious and are in any case the most influential in the academic world" (1997, 88). Just as tellingly, when William Thomson was recently invited by a leading mainstream journal to provide a piece entitled "The Young Person's Guide to Writing Economic Theory," the taken-for-granted meaning of "writing economic theory" is clear in this author's opening three sentences:

> Here are my recommendations for writing economic theory (and, to some extent, giving seminar presentations). My intended audience is young economists working on their dissertations or preparing first papers for submission to a professional journal.
>
> Although I discuss general issues of presentation, this essay is mainly concerned in its details with formal models. (1999, 157)

And consider, too, the overviews or assessments of Wassily Leontief, Milton Friedman, and Ronald Coase, all Nobel Memorial Prize winners in economics:

> Page after page of professional economic journals are filled with mathematical formulas leading the reader from sets of more or less plausible but entirely arbitrary assumptions to precisely stated but irrelevant theoretical conclusions. . . . Year after year economic theorists continue to produce scores of mathematical models and to explore in great detail their formal properties; and the econometricians fit algebraic functions of all possible shapes to essentially the same sets of data without being able to advance, in any perceptible way, a systematic understanding of the structure and the operations of a real economic system. (Leontief 1982, 104)

> Economics has become increasingly an arcane branch of mathematics rather than dealing with real economic problems. (Friedman 1999, 137)

Existing economics is a theoretical [meaning mathematical] system which floats in the air and which bears little relation to what happens in the real world. (Coase 1999, 2)

Of course, heterodox economists do often capture the situation best. Consider the very apt assessment of Diana Strassmann, the editor of *Feminist Economics*. Like other heterodox economists, Strassmann certainly does not reduce economics to mathematical formalism but notices that this is an essential feature of the mainstream:

To a mainstream economist, theory means model, and model means ideas expressed in mathematical form. In learning how to "think like an economist," students learn certain critical concepts and models, ideas which typically are taught initially through simple mathematical analyses. These models, students learn, are theory. In more advanced courses, economic theories are presented in more mathematically elaborate models. Mainstream economists believe proper models—good models—take a recognizable form: presentation in equations, with mathematically expressed definitions, assumptions, and theoretical developments clearly laid out. Students also learn how economists argue. They learn that the legitimate way to argue is with models and econometrically constructed forms of evidence. While students are also presented with verbal and geometric masterpieces produced in bygone eras, they quickly learn that novices who want jobs should emulate their current teachers rather than deceased luminaries.

Because all models are incomplete, students also learn that no model is perfect. Indeed, students learn that it is bad manners to engage in excessive questioning of simplifying assumptions. Claiming that a model is deficient is a minor feat—presumably anyone can do that. What is really valued is coming up with a better model, a better theory. And so, goes the accumulated wisdom of properly taught economists, those who criticize without coming up with better models are only pedestrian snipers. Major scientific triumphs call for a better theory with a better model in recognizable form. In this way economists learn their trade; it is how I learned mine.

Therefore, imagine my reaction when I heard feminists from other disciplines apply the term *theory* to ideas presented in verbal form, ideas not containing even the remotest potential for mathematical expression. "This is theory?" I asked. "Where's the math?" (1994, 154)

So the mainstream project of modern economics ought not to be characterized in terms either of substantive results (such as demonstrating the desirability of the current economic order) or in terms of basic units of analysis (rationalistic or optimizing individuals), but in its orientation to method. The mainstream project just is a commitment to investigating economic phenomena using mathematical forms of reasoning. This is the one feature that remains common to all contributions regarded as mainstream, and a feature not accepted by its heterodox critics.

Mainstream Economics as an Explanatory Endeavor

Notice that the reference in the paragraph above to investigating economic phenomena is necessary here. Or at least it is essential that I acknowledge that mainstream contributors do also concern themselves with social categories. Mainstream economists do not usually deal abstractly just with the properties of (mathematical) operators and elements of sets, but concern themselves with variables labeled *consumption, income,* and so forth.[1] Although some, like Debreu (1959), profess attachment to the Bourbaki ideal of a framework free of any interpretation, this ideal seems never to be realized in its entirety. It does serve the function of loosening up the project from the goal of achieving immediate contact with reality. But practitioners of modern economics appear never to abandon all concern with social categories or the hope of illuminating social reality sooner or later. Ultimately, the aim, it seems, is to render aspects of the social world intelligible. There is a sense, then, in which the project always remains in essence an explanatory endeavor.

The point to emphasize here, though, is that this project's conception, or mode, of explanation is necessarily one that facilitates the widespread usage of mathematical formalism, including formalistic modeling. That mode of explanation called into play is *deductivism.*

Deductivism

By deductivism I mean a type of explanation in which regularities of the form "whenever event *x*, then event *y*" (or stochastic near equivalents) are a necessary condition. Such regularities are held to persist and are often treated, in effect, as laws, allowing the deductive generation of consequences, or predictions, when accompanied with the specification of initial conditions. Systems in which such regularities occur are said to be *closed.*[2] Of course, a closure is not restricted to cases of correlations between just two events or variables; there can be as many of the latter as you like. Nor is a closed system avoided by assuming a nonlinear functional relationship or by pointing out, as in chaos theory or some such, that what happens may be extremely sensitive to initial conditions. If, given the exact same conditions, the same outcome does (or would) follow (or follows on average, etc., in a probabilistic formulation), the system is closed in the sense I am using the term.

Notice that it is the *structure* of explanation that fundamentally is at issue here. The possibility either that many of the entities that economists interpret as outcomes, including events or states of affairs, are fictitious, or that claimed correlations do not actually hold, does not undermine the thesis that deductivism is the explanatory mode of this project. In other words, by deductivism I just mean explanation requiring closed systems as an essential component; no commitment to the realisticness of any closures or regularities posited is presupposed.

Observe, too, that it does not make any difference whether an inductive or a priori deductive emphasis is taken. If mathematical methods of the sort economists mostly fall back on are to be employed, closures are required (or presupposed), whether they are sought after in observation reports or data or are purely invented. Deductivism is an explanatory form that posits or requires such closures (whether or not any are actually found). And deductivism, so understood, clearly encompasses the greater part of modern economics, including most of modern microeconomics, macroeconomics, and econometrics.[3]

Reorienting Economics

Against the background of a discipline dominated by a project that insists everywhere on the wielding of mathematical formalism I urge an ontological turn, and argue in particular for the set of (ontological) insights systematized as (or within the project of) critical realism (see Archer et al. 1998). Why?

First of all, urging a turn of any kind presupposes that there is something wrong with the way things stand. That there is something amiss with the modern discipline is a contention sufficiently widely recognized by modern economists that it need not long detain us here. Indeed, we can rely on the acknowledgments of spokespeople of the mainstream tradition themselves. And, mindful again that a likely worry of some noneconomist observers is that critical assessments of mainstream achievements may be less than charitable caricatures, it seems strategically wise to do so.[4] On a slightly different point, I have seen it suggested that dominant economic theorists are happy with things as they stand, and that it is only heterodox economists or those marginalized within the discipline who worry about fit with reality. So it seems pertinent that I indicate that prominent or dominant mainstream economists regularly admit to being as exasperated about the current state of the discipline as the rest of us. In fact, it is sufficient if I concentrate on the assessments of those prominent spokes-people of the mainstream already introduced above. For the commen-taries that have been extracted reveal of the mainstream project not only that it is mathematical in nature but also that in performance, as an intellectual pursuit, it is something of a failure and a worry.

Thus, we have already seen passing admissions that, even though "eco-nomic theory should deal with the real world," as practiced, "economic theory lacks a consensus as to its purpose and interpretation. Again and again, we find ourselves asking the question 'where does it lead?' " (Rubin-stein 1995, 12); that "page after page of professional economic journals are filled with mathematical formulas leading the reader from sets of more or less plausible but entirely arbitrary assumptions to precisely stated but irrelevant theoretical conclusions" (Leontief 1982, 104); that "economics has become increasingly an arcane branch of mathematics rather than dealing with real economic problems" (Friedman 1999, 137); that "existing economics is a theoretical system which floats in the air and which bears little relation to what happens in the real world" (Coase 1999, 2).

Notice, too, that the problem is not just that the results of the project lack explanatory and predictive power and are widely regarded as irrele-vant. In addition, it is recognized that its theory and practice are highly inconsistent. For example, econometricians put huge resources into elab-orating the methods they take to be appropriate and justified, yet their practices diverge wildly from their own methodological strictures. Con-sider Leamer again:

> The opinion that econometric theory is largely irrelevant is held by an embarrassingly large share of the economics profession. The wide gap between econometric theory and econometric practice might be expected to cause professional tension. In fact, a calm equilibrium permeates our journals and our meetings. We comfortably divide ourselves into a celibate priesthood of statistical theorists, on the one hand, and a legion of inveterate sinner-data analysts, on the other. The priests are empowered to draw up lists of sins and are revered for

the special talents they display. Sinners are not expected to avoid sins; they need only confess their errors openly. (1978, vi)

Notice also that those who teach econometric theory and those who practice econometric modeling are usually the same individuals flitting between the noted incompatible activities:

> I began thinking about these problems when I was a graduate student in economics at the University of Michigan 1966–1970. At that time there was a very active group building an econometric model of the United States. As it happens, the econometric modelling was done in the basement of the building and the econometric theory courses were taught on the top floor (the third). I was perplexed by the fact that the same language was used in both places. Even more amazing was the transmogrification of particular individuals who wantonly sinned in the basement and metamorphosed into the highest of high priests as they ascended to the third floor. (vi)

Consider, too, the assessment of David Hendry, a second leading econometrician, remarking on Leamer's observations twelve years on: "At present there are peculiar gaps between theory and what people actually do: I think the sinners and preachers analogy in Leamer [1978] is the correct one here. The theoretical econometrician says one thing but as a practitioner does something different. I am trying to understand why economists do that, given that they know the theory, and they are obviously trying to solve practical problems" (Hendry, Leamer, and Poirier 1990, 179).

All in all, the discipline is replete with theory/practice inconsistencies, fares poorly by its own criteria, and lacks any clear idea as to where it is going. It is also full of anomalies that range over its various subprograms. Consider the observations of Richard Lipsey once again: "Anomalies, particularly those that cut across the sub-disciplines and that can be studied with various technical levels of sophistication, are tolerated on a scale that would be impossible in most natural sciences—and would be regarded as a scandal if they were" (2001, 173).

If a summary statement is required it is perhaps provided by Mark Blaug, a methodologically oriented economist, who has spent considerable resources throughout his career attempting to shore up the mainstream tradition. His current assessment runs as follows: "Modern economics is sick. Economics has increasingly become an intellectual game played for its own sake and not for its practical consequences for understanding the economic world. Economists have converted the subject into a sort of social mathematics in which analytical rigour is everything and practical relevance is nothing" (1997, 3).

Ontology

If the case for a reorientation of the discipline is indeed clear, why the call for an ontological turn specifically? Surely if I am supposing that ontology can help here I must be claiming too much for it. Maybe, but I think not. Let me indicate how I believe ontology can and cannot make a contribution.

One thing ontology cannot do is substitute for substantive economics (Lawson 1997, 326; 1999a, 14; 2003, 53–54, 61). Nor can it indicate how economists must proceed (see Lawson 2003, chs. 2 and 3). What it can do is guide or underlabor for the substantive process by indicating, among other things, dangers and contingencies for which researchers might sensibly be prepared. Let me briefly elaborate.

To see how ontology can make a difference it is important to consider two of the roles that can be accepted for it. First, we must recognize that specific methods and criteria of analysis are appropriate to the illumination of *some* kinds of objects and materials *but not others*. For the properties of material studied will always make a difference to how we can and cannot know it. This is not to suggest that there is a complete separation between any object of analysis and the analysis undertaken. It is, though, to accept that typically, the one is irreducible to the other. Marx once remarked that "in the analysis of economic forms neither microscopes nor chemical reagents are of assistance" (1974, 90). Here I am merely emphasizing the general situation for which Marx is indicating a special case.

One role for ontological inquiry, then, is to determine the (usually implicit) conceptions of the nature and structure of reality presupposed by the use of any specific set of research practices and procedures. Equivalently, ontology can identify conditions under which specific procedures are relevant and likely to bear fruit.

A second, equally fundamental role for ontology is the elaboration of as complete and encompassing as possible a conception of the broad nature and structure of (a relevant domain of) reality as appears feasible. The aim is to derive a general conception that seems to include all actual developments as special configurations. Put differently, a central objective is to provide a categorical grammar for expressing all the particular types of realization in specific contexts.

Now the (of course always fallible, situated, and practically conditioned) results achieved by ontology in each of these roles can be used in numerous ways. But of particular interest at this juncture is a recognition that the results achieved in these two roles can be used to especially good effect in combination. For if, by employing ontology in its second role, we can achieve a general framework, this can reveal the particularity of many scientific and practical ontologies revealed by employing ontology in its former role. In other words, applying ontology in both of the roles discussed allows us to compare the ontological presuppositions of specific methods with our best account of the nature of social reality. The application of ontological insight in this fashion can reveal in particular both the foolhardiness and the nonnecessity of universalizing any highly specific approach or stance a priori. Ontology, so fashioned, can identify the error of treating special cases as though they are universal or ubiquitous.

It is my assessment, elaborated at length elsewhere (e.g., Lawson 1997, 2003), that the problems of modern economics stem largely from its failure to match its methods to the nature of its subject matter. Indeed, modern economics provides a very clear example of a rather narrow way of doing research being unthinkingly universalized a priori, with unfortunate consequences. For it has been fairly easy to establish that the sorts of formalistic methods everywhere advocated by modern mainstream economists are in fact appropriate to at best a small subset of possible social configurations. This, I argue, is why the modern discipline of economics is in such disarray. The theories formulated by economists are necessarily restricted so as to conform to the worldview presupposed by their formalistic methods. Because this latter worldview is found not to typify human society, it is not surprising that mainstream theories are found to contribute very little to advancing understanding in most of the contexts for which they are constructed.

The argument is a long one, but it can be quickly summarized. Basically, the deductivist explanatory methods necessitated by the mainstream insistence on mathematical formalism require that formulations take the event regularity form. And the generation or construction of these regularities in turn requires of economists that they couch their analyses in terms of (1) isolated (2) atoms.

This metaphorical reference to atoms is not intended to convey anything about size. Rather, the reference is to items that exercise their own separate, independent, and invariable (and so predictable) effects (relative to, or as a function of, initial conditions).

Deductivist theorizing of the sort pursued in modern economics ultimately has to be couched in terms of such atoms just to ensure that, under given conditions x, the same (predictable or deducible) outcome y always follows. If any agent in the theory could do other than some given y in specific conditions x—either because the agent is intrinsically structured and can just act differently each time x occurs, or because the agent's action possibilities are affected by whatever else is going on—the individuals of the analysis cannot be said to be atomic, and deductive inference could never be guaranteed.

It is immediately clear, I think, that these latter conditions *need* not characterize the social realm. And the theory of social ontology that I think to be most sustainable, that which has been systematized as, or within, critical realism (see, e.g., Archer et al. 1998; Bhaskar 1975/1978, 1979; Collier 1994; Lawson 1997, 2003), gives reason to suppose that the noted conditions for closure may actually be rather rare in the social realm. Let me briefly indicate something of this ontological conception.

A Theory of Social Ontology

By social reality or the social realm I mean that domain of all phenomena whose existence depends at least in part on us. Thus, it includes items such as social relations, which depend on us entirely, but also others, such as technological objects, where I take technology to be that domain of phenomena with a material content but social form.

If social reality depends on transformative human agency, its state of being must be intrinsically dynamic or *processual*. Think of a language system. Its existence is a condition of our communicating via speech acts, and so on. Through the sum total of these speech acts the language system is continuously being reproduced and, under some of its aspects at least, transformed. A language system, then, is intrinsically dynamic, its mode of being is a process of transformation. It exists in a continual process of becoming. But this is ultimately true of all aspects of social reality, including many aspects of ourselves, such as our personal and social identities. The social world turns on human practice.

The social realm is also highly *internally related*. Aspects or items are said to be internally related when they are what they are, or can do what they do, in virtue of the relation to others in which they stand. Obvious examples are employer and employee, teacher and student, landlord/lady and tenant, and parent and offspring. In each case, you cannot have the one without the other.

In fact, in the social realm, it is found that it is social *positions* that are significantly internally related. It is the position I hold as a university lecturer that is internally related to the positions of students. Each year different individuals slot into the position of students and accept the obligations, privileges, and tasks determined by the relation. Ultimately, we all slot into a very large number of different and changing positions, each making a difference to what we can do. The social realm, then, is highly internally related or "organic."

The social realm is also found to be *structured* (it does not reduce to human practices and other actualities but includes underlying structures and processes of the sort just noted and [their] powers and tendencies). And the stuff of the social realm is found, in addition, to include *value* and *meaning* and to be *polyvalent* (e.g., absences are real), and so forth.

This broad perspective, as I say, is elaborated and defended at length elsewhere (see, e.g., Archer et al. 1998; Bhaskar 1975/1978, 1979; Collier 1994; Lawson 1997, 2003). But I doubt that, once reflected on, the conception is especially contentious. Nor, in its basic emphasis on organicism or internal relationality, is it especially novel. However, it should be clear that if the perspective defended is at all correct, it is prima facie quite conceivable that the atomistic and closure preconceptions of mainstream economics may not hold very often at all.

That said, I emphasize that the possibility of closures of the sort pursued by modern mainstream economists cannot be ruled out a priori. Certainly, there is nothing in the ontological conception sketched above that rules out entirely the possibility of regularities of events standing in causal sequence in the social realm (any more than it is possible a priori to stipulate that a fair coin tossed a thousand times will not show a thousand heads). But the conception sustained does render the practice of universalizing a priori the sorts of mathematical-deductivist methods economists wield somewhat risky if not foolhardy, requiring or presupposing, as it does, that social event regularities of the relevant sort are ubiquitous. And to the point, if the social ontology sketched above does not altogether rule out the possibility of social event regularities of the sort in question occurring here and there, it does provide a rather compelling explanation of the a posteriori rather generalized lack of (or at best limited) successes with mathematical-deductivist or closed-systems explanatory methods to date.

Actually, this ontological conception is more explanatorily powerful still. For not only does it explain the widespread continued explanatory failures of much of modern economics over the past fifty years or so, but it can account for both (1) the prima facie puzzling phenomenon that mainstream economists everywhere, in a manner quite unlike researchers in other disciplines, suppose that (acknowledged) fictionalizing is almost always *necessary* (typically with human beings portrayed as versions of isolated atoms), and (2) the types of conditions that prevail when mathematical methods in economics achieve such (limited) successes as are experienced. These, though, are not claims I can develop here (but see Lawson 2003, ch. 1).

I hope it is also clear that the contribution of ontology does not end with demonstrating the risk of universalizing special cases and the narrowness of those who insist that we all adopt but one sort of research practice. Not least it imparts directionality to social research. If social reality is shown to be open, structured, and dynamic, it follows that a reasonable thing to do is to develop or at least investigate the range of approaches seemingly appropriate to (whose ontological presuppositions match) such a reality. In developing this position elsewhere, I have stressed the insights of contrast explanation and feminist standpoint theorizing especially (see, e.g., Lawson 2003). But these are matters I leave aside here, and turn to address some questions that relate more directly to the theme of this book.

Positivism

Specifically, I turn to compare the interpretation of mainstream economics I am advancing with the yet further claim, one often found and germane to the scope of the current volume, that the mainstream project in modern economics is a form of, or is rooted in, positivism. To what extent does the latter assessment hold up? Or, to frame the question slightly differently, to what extent is it the case that, as some have supposed, I am interpreting the mainstream project of modern economics to be a form of positivism or empirical realism?

Much depends, of course, on what we mean by such terms. Positivism itself is a label seemingly mostly used by authors to signal some position, however vaguely formulated, to which they interpret their own position as standing opposed. I can but follow suit in adopting a negative orientation. But let me at least attempt to be clear about what I am here rejecting.

If there is a version of positivism whose *results* (as opposed to their mode of derivation) both prima facie claim some influence in economics and resemble features I am indeed associating with the mainstream project of modern economics, it is the form associated with Humean empiricism. Positivism, on this conception,[5] is first and foremost a theory of knowledge, its nature and limits. Specifically, it is a claim that knowledge takes the form of sense experience or impression. Hume encouraged this perspective with his attempted critique of any philosophical account of being, of ontology, with his denying the possibility of establishing the independent existence of things, specifically the operation of natural necessity.

But it is never possible to dissolve completely any conception of being, of the object of study. For any theory of knowledge must assume, even if only implicitly, that the nature of reality is such that it could be the object of knowledge of the required or specified sort. The Humean theory clearly presupposes an account of reality as consisting of the objects of experience or impression constituting atomistic events. In other words, an ontology is implicitly presupposed by Humean analysis, but restricted to events of, and so effectively constituted in, direct experience or perception.

If particular knowledge is of events sensed in experience, then any possibility of *general* (including scientific) knowledge must be of the constant patterns, if any, that such events reveal in space and over time. On this Humean view, clearly, these are the only forms of generalization conceivable. Such constant event patterns, that is, regularities of the form "whenever event *x*, then event *y*," of course, constitute the Humean or positive account of causal laws. If, moreover, such constant conjunctions are the only form of general, including scientific, knowledge that is possible, then, to the extent that successful science is acknowledged as pervasive, it follows that such constant event conjunctions must also be (thought to be) ubiquitous.

To repeat, any theory of knowledge presupposes an ontology, and, as noted, in the case of the version of positivism considered here, this comprises atomistic events and their (supposed ubiquitous) constant conjunctions. And it is precisely because (knowable) reality is essentially defined in positivism as that which is given in experience that some contributors to critical realism, including Bhaskar (1975/1978), have taken to referring to the perspective that arises as empirical realism. This explains the sometimes seemingly interchangeable references to positivism and empirical realism in some of the literature.

Any theory of knowledge also presupposes (in addition to an ontology) a social theory, that is, some account of human agency and institutions. For these must be of a form that enables knowledge of the specified type to be produced. Positivism, then, supports a conception of human agents as passive sensors of atomistic events and recorders of their constant conjunctions.

Further still, any theory of knowledge presupposes not only a theory of ontology and a social theory but also some philosophical method, some account of how its characteristic results are achieved. In positivism, because experience is effectively constitutive of the world (only what we experience exists), it is in consequence held to be certain. Science, then, is viewed as monistic, the accumulation of incorrigible facts. Even the reported constant event conjunctions are held to be perceivable via impression and, in consequence, constitute facts. A result, clearly, is that the incorrigibility of knowledge in positivism serves ultimately, if implicitly, to undermine the possibility of substantive scientific criticism. And the upshot is a conservative ideology that serves to rationalize contemporary orthodox practice, that is, the status quo, a perspective notoriously expressed in positivism itself precisely as a generalized denial of the usefulness of methodology/philosophy.

I think there is little doubt that very many of these positivistic results are widely in evidence in economics, specifically in mainstream contributions. In particular, the conception of science as the search for regularities of the form "whenever event (type) x, then event (type) y" can be seen to underpin most mainstream substantive positions; as I have already noted, it is the basis of all microeconomic, macroeconomic, and econometric modeling. Similarly, the specification of the human agent as the passive receptor of atomistic events goes relatively unchallenged. The events or states of affairs deemed relevant to behavior are interpreted usually as (price) "signals," and agents are assumed to respond uniformly, in typically optimizing fashion. Some variations on these themes can be found, but there appear to be none that undermines the basic conception of agents as automata with knowledge analyzed in a purely individualistic way. And modern mainstream economists are notoriously dismissive of methodology. Even Frank Hahn, one of the more reflective mainstream contributors, counsels young economists to "give no thought at all to methodology" (1992a; see also Hahn 1992b).

So, as I say, the sorts of results that an acceptance of the positivist perspective as interpreted here encourages are indeed rife in economics. In these circumstances, then, is it not reasonable to suppose that a widespread adherence to the version of positivism in question is the explanation? Moreover, is it not the case that this explanation is more or less identical to my own, and certainly no less explanatorily powerful?

Deductivism Rather Than Positivism

My contention, to the contrary, is that it is an adherence to deductivism, an orientation driven by the prior desire to construct mathematical models, *rather* than a commitment to positivist epistemology, that is the primary explanation of the orientation of modern economics. Why do I think this to be the superior explanation? Why even do I suppose the two positions are significantly different?

First of all, albeit most superficially, there is little if any evidence of economists acknowledging a commitment to positivism. At the same time, as I have already noted, the attachment to mathematics, though rarely explicitly defended, is regarded as being so obviously proper as to be beyond need of justification.

More significant, though, there are features of modern economic practice that are inconsistent with the positivist position but that sit easily with an attachment to formalistic-deductivist modeling. The first is that mainstream economists do not restrict themselves to considering phenomena that (to the extent that they are real at all) are open to direct experience. I acknowledge that human beings as represented by economic models *are* often interpreted as responding only to observable phenomena such as price signals, but economists themselves are more than happy to posit features that, to the extent that they exist at all, must be nonobservable. Utility, and processes of utility maximization, or equilibrium mechanisms are obvious examples, as indeed are aspects at least of (most) markets, economies, desires and preferences of others, and so forth.

Does this recognition challenge my earlier portrayal of mainstream theorizing as necessarily restricted to conceptions of closed atomistic setups? In practice, no. The reason for this is that the reliance on mathematical deductivist modeling constrains the manner in which non-directly perceivable features can be formulated.

Consider the notion of rationality as optimizing. Economists often discuss this as though it were a power or capacity. In this form, rationality is not open to direct experience. However, it is not enough that economists consider rationality only, or primarily, in this form. To generate mathematically tractable models this power of rationality must be assumed always to be reflected in actual *behavior*; rationality must always be exercised and actualized unimpeded, thus facilitating predictable outcomes. The central focus for economists here is *rational behavior*.

Of course, a further requirement is that economic situations are so constructed that a rational, meaning optimal, outcome always exists. In other words, human behavior must be so constrained that under given conditions x, the same predictable y always follows. Similarly, utility functions are constructed in such a way that they can be maximized, and so forth. The result has to be, and always is, a conception of some agency that in total is atomistic in the sense that under given conditions the same outcome necessarily follows, even if some component parts of the conception, though treated as known, are inherently unobservable.

Perhaps the point requires further emphasis. For it might be conjectured that mainstream economists are really concerned with real tendencies and state their results in the event regularity form merely as a sort of presentational device. Such a conjecture, though, simply does not receive support. The derivations of mathematical formulations, and the drawing of deductive arguments or predictions, are the primary goals, and the possibility of real insight is continually sacrificed to superficiality of specification in order to achieve this. This much is regularly admitted. In fact, such superficiality as is usually necessitated by the reliance on mathematical-deductivist method is not only *not* denied or masked by mainstream contributors but frequently is even hailed as a strength of the project in question. As Robert Lucas, another Nobel Memorial Prize winner in economics, rationalizes the situation: "To observe that economics is based on a superficial view of individual and social behaviour does not seem to me to be much of an insight. I think it is exactly this superficiality that gives economics much of the power that it has: its ability to predict human behaviour without knowing very much about the make up and lives of the people whose behaviour we are trying to understand" (1986, 425).

A major problem for this particular "justification" (and for the quasi-instrumentalist stance of Friedman [1953b] from which it derives; see Lawson 1997, 309–310) is that economists actually are not, and have never been, very good at predicting human behavior (i.e., at making relatively accurate predictions as opposed to producing countless rather inaccurate ones; see J. Kay 1995, 19).

A second feature of modern economics that does not fit with the positivist scenario is that many of the formulations, though taking the event regularity form, are couched in terms of categories that, though lying at the level of the actual, are not even real;[6] in so-called pure theory, economists concern themselves with constructs acknowledged as quite fictitious. These include assumptions of perfect foresight (or rational expectations), omniscience, people who live forever, two-commodity worlds, and so forth. Consider Frank Hahn once more: "When a mathematical economist assumes that there is a three good economy lasting two periods, or that agents are infinitely lived (perhaps because they value the utility of their descendants which they know!), everyone can see that we are not dealing with any actual economy. The assumptions are there to enable certain results to emerge and not because they are to be taken descriptively" (1994, 246). As Hahn states, the assumptions are typically not to be taken as descriptive but are adopted to enable certain results to emerge. By this Hahn means, of course, to enable such results to emerge by way of a mathematical modeling exercise.

Hahn is clear, though, that what we have here are not mere presentational devices or heuristics. Nor is the concern with really possible counterfactual scenarios. There is no point pretending that these mathematical models somehow enable us to understand real economies or have any bearing on policy issues. For example, according to Hahn, even if theorists were to be successful in determining "how far observed events are consistent with an economy which is in continuous Walrasian equilibrium . . . it would not be true that we understood the events. For we would not understand how continuous equilibrium is possible in a decentralised economy and we do not understand why a world with Trade Unions and monopolies behaves like a perfectly competitive one" (1985, 15; see also 1994, 240). And elsewhere Hahn reveals, albeit in a somewhat overly dramatic fashion, what he thinks of the practice of using mathematical models for drawing policy implications: "When policy conclusions are drawn from such models, it is time to reach for one's gun" (1982, 29).

Of course, if the sorts of features I am identifying as among the limitations of the mainstream project are clearly not caricatures but aspects of the project that its practitioners themselves emphasize, and often even embrace, they do encourage us to question the point of it all. At least, this is the case regarding the nonempirical "theoretical division." As we saw earlier, mainstream economists like Rubinstein are recently raising the same sorts of question themselves. The philosopher Alexander Rosenberg suggests an answer of sorts:

> Much of the mystery surrounding the actual development of economic theory—its shifts in formalism, its insulation from empirical assessment, its interest in proving purely formal, abstract possibilities, its unchanged character over a period of centuries, the controversies about its cognitive status—can be comprehended and properly appreciated if we give up the notion that economics any longer has the aims or makes the claims of an empirical science of human behaviour. Rather we should view it as a branch of mathematics, one

devoted to examining the formal properties of a set of assumptions about the transitivity of abstract relations: axioms that implicitly define a technical notion of "rationality," just as geometry examines the formal properties of abstract points and lines. This abstract term "rationality" may have far more potential interpretations than economists themselves realize, but rather less bearing on human behaviour and its consequences than we have unreasonably demanded economists reveal.

There are some important practical consequences of this answer to the question of what economics really is. If it is best viewed as more akin to a branch of mathematics on the intersection between pure axiomatization and applied geometry, then not only are several cognitive mysteries about economics solved, but more importantly our perspective on the bearing of economic theory must be fundamentally altered. For if this view is correct we cannot demand that it provide the reliable guide to the behaviour of economic agents and the performance of economies as a whole for which the formulation of public policy looks to economics. We should neither attach much confidence to predictions made on its basis nor condemn it severely when these predictions fail. For it can no more be relied on or faulted than Euclidean geometry should be in the context of astrophysics. (1983, 391–392)

Whatever the point or value of it, I think it is clear that the main driving force, the fundamental component of modern mainstream economics is this desire to address social phenomena using models that are mathematically tractable. My specific contention at this point is that in this endeavor the mainstream project, though in numerous ways resonating with positivist contributions, neither reduces to a form of empirical realism nor constitutes a straightforward application of positivist thinking.

Of course, resonance often serves as a mechanism by way of which support is achieved. So I do not deny all positivist influence. But support by this route is indirect and, in modern economics, rarely if ever explicitly noted. As I say, the one goal expressly acknowledged by mainstream economists, and indeed long cherished in branches of the discipline (see Lawson 2003, ch. 10), is simply the mathematicization of the study of social phenomena.

Final Comments

What might be said, finally, of the sort of reorientation of economics for which I am calling? Specifically, and once more mindful of the focus of the current volume, in what sense is it meaningful to interpret the orientation I urge and defend as a non- or antipositivist position?

Clearly, any contribution that defends a case for sustained ontological reasoning sits uneasily with positivism as conceptualized here. And the specific critical realist perspective briefly described above and elaborated and defended elsewhere (Archer et al. 1998; Bhaskar 1975/1978, 1979; Collier 1994; Lawson 1997, 2003) carries with it an explicit rejection of all the noted characteristic positivistic claims and results (experience defining knowable reality, generalities consisting only in constant conjunctions, human beings as passive sensors of atomistic facts, knowledge as the accumulation of incorrigible facts, methodology as inconsequential, etc.).

But in modern economics at least, the motivation for this realist project has not been to transcend the influence of positivist reasoning per se, but to undermine a methodological dogmatism that stems more from a somewhat different cultural naïveté. The primary problem of modern economics has long been, and remains, the composite belief that only one particular approach to analysis *need* be used and that it is transparent that this particular approach always *should* be used. Specifically, it is the view that any feature of social reality can be modeled mathematically, that mathematics is neutral or universal in this sense, and that only when phenomena are so modeled mathematically can their study be regarded as worthwhile, serious, or scientific.

It is in part because ontology can reveal such an apprehension to be false or at least highly questionable that it is at this point in time so urgently required. And it is because (or to the extent that) certain results of positivist reasoning constitute a subset of what passes as modern mainstream economics that, by casting doubt on the emphasis of the whole of the mainstream project, the positivistic subset is challenged as well. In this sense or manner at least, the project here supported, in its orientation to economics, can be regarded as an antipositivistic endeavor.

Notes

1   My own view, which I cannot elaborate here, is that mathematics is the science of operators. On this conception, although modern economics makes heavy use of the results of mathematics, in form it is at most a would-be branch of applied mathematics.

2   I am aware that across different literatures or disciplines (including mathematics), the category of closure is used to mean different things. Here, as I say (and elaborate at length in previous contributions; e.g., Lawson 2003), I take a closed system to be one in which event regularities of the noted kind occur.

3   I might also emphasize that this conception does not preclude a number of interpretations of how models are usually, or might best be, employed. Models may be viewed as alternatives to narratives or storytelling (about the world). This is (or was) Deirdre McCloskey's position (1990). Or storytelling may be treated as an essential aspect of the modeling process, as Mary Morgan maintains (e.g., 2001). Morgan's account perhaps best captures the practices of the majority. I certainly believe it gives the most charitable interpretation of what takes place. But if, with Morgan, we accept that there can be different stories told with a given model *structure* and allow that economists can be concerned to explore "the full range of features and outcomes compatible with the structure" (369–370), it nevertheless remains the case, as Morgan indeed recognizes, that "the structure constrains and shapes the stories that can be told with a model" (366). Specifically, it remains always the case that the "story is deductive because it uses the logic of the mathematics or materials of the model to answer the question" (370).

4   Actually informed external observers have noted the problems of the discipline themselves. Thus, the former British Minister Lord Howell assesses the state of modern economics as follows:

> The paradox of modern economics is that while the computers are churning out more and more figures, giving more and more spurious precision to economic pronouncements, the assumptions behind this fiesta of quantification are looking less and less safe. Economic model making was never easier to undertake and never more disconnected from reality.
>
> Somewhere along the way economics took a wrong turn. What has occurred, and what has been vastly accentuated by the information revolution and its impact, is that economists have drained economic analysis both out of philosophy and out of real life, and have produced an abstract monstrosity, a world of models and assumptions increasingly disconnected from everyday experience and from discernible patterns of human behaviour, whether at the individual or the institutional level.
>
> As a result, economists have not only failed to discern, explain or predict most of the ills which beset the world economy and society, but they have actively encouraged a deformity of perception amongst policy makers and communicators, which has led in turn to a deep public bewilderment and distrust of government authorities—and this at the very time when the need is greater than ever for a bond of trust between government and society.

This misleading "black box" view of the world purveyed by the economics profession (with heroic exceptions), at all levels from the most intimate micro workings of markets to the macro level of nation states and their jurisdictions, has been vastly reinforced by compliant statisticians who have brought a spurious precision and quantification to entities and concepts which may not in fact have any existence outside economic theory, or whose validity has been sapped away by the impact of information technology (2000, 203–204).

5   For a lengthier discussion of positivism from a historical perspective, a discussion that provides justification for the interpretation considered here, see Lawson (1997, 292–293).

6   By describing positivism as "lying at the level of the actual" but not being real, I refer to accepted-as-fictitious constructs treated not (or not primarily) as powers or possibilities but as actualities. For example, the assumption that people exercise perfect foresight is widely utilized in economics, even though it is equally widely acknowledged as a claim that is quite fictitious. In economic models, though, perfect foresight, if specified at all in the form of a potential, is treated as one that is always actualized. Human beings are assumed always to use their crystal balls.

The Idea of Outcome in U.S. Sociology

ANDREW ABBOTT

E arly in the movie *Saturday Night Fever* Tony Manero (John Travolta) asks his hardware store boss Mr. Fusco (Sam J. Copolla) for a pay advance with which to buy a pretty new shirt for Saturday night. Fusco refuses, saying Tony should plan for the future. "Fuck the future!" says Tony. "No, Tony, you can't fuck the future," says Mr. Fusco. "The future fucks you" (screenplay by Norman Wexler).

The issue between Tony and Fusco is the issue of now and later, of present and future, of moment and outcome. The plot of the movie, translated into simple economese, is that with the help of the marginally more rational Stephanie Mangano (Karen Gurney), Tony becomes a little less of a hyperbolic discounter; he starts to take the future a little more seriously.

But he does not choose Fusco's outcome. Later in the movie Fusco fires Tony over an irregular day off, but then rehires him, saying "You've got a future here. Look at Harold [he points], with me eighteen years, [points again] Mike, fifteen years." The camera pans in on Mike, presented as a colorless, becalmed middle-aged man, and then back to Tony's look of panic. That's not a future Tony wants. His ultimate choice is a more open, undefined future, which begins with moving to Manhattan and thinking of Stephanie not merely as a sexual event but also as a friend. At the movie's end he is still a young man in the middle.

The debate between Fusco and Tony captures something important about how we conceive of our research. In the last analysis, much of sociology is about the way things turn out. The typical dependent variable both today and for many years past is a result, an outcome, a Fusco-thing. In Frank Kermode's (1967) felicitous phrase, sociology has "the sense of an ending."

Economists, by contrast, often seem to write about things without ends. The balance of payments, unemployment, securities prices: these are things that fluctuate endlessly. There is no outcome, no result. Rather, there is an equilibrium level over the long run and various little perturbations around it in the short run.

That much of sociology is about ends rather than middles should not surprise us, because so much of sociology is about individuals: their social status, income, wealth, education, occupation, and so on, all the things Mr. Fusco has in mind. And unlike balances of payments and unemployment, individuals do not go on fluctuating forever. There is only one true outcome variable for individuals, and it has no variance.[1] In a way, that's what Tony is saying; as he puts it shortly after the first exchange quoted above, "Tonight's the future, and I'm planning for it." For him, beyond tonight is death, either the actual death of his foolish friend Bobby falling off the Verrazano Narrows Bridge or the living death of middle-aged Mike in the hardware store. Those of us with flatter discount curves know that death is usually not so soon. There are many human outcomes short term enough to resemble equilibriar variables like unemployment: driving habits, purchasing habits, dating styles, and so on. But the major foci of sociologists are not like that. They are bigger things, consequential outcomes like socioeconomic status, marriage duration, and education. And their consequence lies precisely in their irrevocability; we get only one or two chances.

In this paper I wish to analyze the concept of outcome. I begin by tracing the sociological concept of outcome, first as we find it in the midcentury corpus of one of sociology's founding methodologists, Paul Lazarsfeld, and then in some illustrative later work. I then introduce a contrast by considering concepts of outcome in economics. This leads into a further formalization of the problem of outcome, for which I invoke philosophical conceptions of time. From these I return to the original problem, laying out the dimensions of possible concepts of outcome in sociology.

Paul Lazarsfeld's Ideas of Outcome

I would like first to consider the notion of outcome in several important works of Paul Lazarsfeld. This reflection will introduce my broader inquiry into the way we think about processes and their results in social science.

I begin with Lazarsfeld's influential 1955 reader with Morris Rosenberg,

The Language of Social Research. In the introduction to the reader's section on "The Empirical Analysis of Action," Lazarsfeld and Rosenberg state that they are concerned with "actions many people perform repeatedly and under somewhat comparable circumstances." They go on to give examples: "Social reformers want to keep people from committing crimes; advertisers want to know how people can be made to buy their products; occupational counselors study how people choose their jobs. . . . Whatever the purpose all these studies have one central topic in common: What are the factors which account for the choices which people make among a specified number of alternatives?" (387). In the main, these are not irrevocable outcomes. Crime and occupation were well-known to be modifiable choices, often recurring throughout the life course. Purchase of goods was even more repetitive. These seem like repeated, equilibriar events, not final outcomes in any strong sense.

A more detailed exposition occurs in the much reprinted paper "The Analysis of Consumer Action" (Kornhauser and Lazarsfeld 1935/1955), which lays out Lazarsfeld's analysis of purchase, for him the very prototype of human activity. An individual, Lazarsfeld argues, is subject to many influences. The process of purchase begins when one of these turns him into "a new person," one with "a favorable feeling toward Y make of car or a belief that X dentifrice will protect his teeth." After some weeks, "This changed person hears a friend comment enthusiastically about the product." This creates yet another person, who now "yields to a leisurely thought-encouraging situation, where he deliberates about the new car or the dentifrice and definitely decides to buy." He then buys, but only when he finds himself "in a situation containing the precipitating influence to induce the purchase" (397).[2]

Lazarsfeld underscores the order of events, insisting on a strongly ordered list of experiences that culminates in purchase. Later in the paper he lists all the phenomena on this line in the case of "the simple matter of soap-buying." First, there are three things that lie "far back on the time-line":

a) Why the consumer buys soap at all.
b) Why she likes soap of a particular color, odor, hardness, etc.
c) Why she believes all soaps are equally good.

And then seven things "somewhat nearer the purchase and more concrete":

d) Why she buys soap of the X-type and price.
e) Why she buys X-soap specifically.

f) Why she buys one cake instead of several.

g) Why she buys at this particular time.

h) Why she buys at this particular place.

i) Why she buys as she does now (this month or this year) as contrasted with other months or years.

j) Why she buys (i.e., why this kind of person rather than others).

(Kornhauser and Lazarsfeld 1935/1955, 398)

Outcome here is a simple action: buying soap. There is some hint of soap consumption as a stable, oft-repeated phenomenon; that's the implicit grounding of the question "Why does she buy as she does now?" But for the most part, the focus is on the final act of purchase: the analysis follows what I have elsewhere called "the ancestors' plot" (Abbott 2001b, 144, 291), in which analysis means seeking all the (causal) ancestors of a particular event. Product choice is an outcome that lies at the current end of a long, backward-proliferating net of causes. Its own consequences are not considered, nor is it embedded as one small part of some larger web of events. Only those parts of the larger web are relevant that affect this choice to buy.

The model implicit in this early paper, an ancestors' plot leading to an "end," might be expected to undergird Lazarsfeld's later studies of voting.[3] Yet the reader of *Voting* (Berelson, Lazarsfeld, and McPhee 1954) will be astonished to discover that the authors almost nowhere discuss the outcome of the election they studied, even though the 1948 election was and is by universal consent an extraordinary one. We can see this disattention encapsulated in the celebrated sixteenfold table (SFT) with which the authors seek to untangle the relationship between saliency of class issues and attitudes toward Truman. The SFT is essentially a transition matrix for a standard fourfold crosstab of these two dichotomous variables; the four cells of the original table are each measured at two time points for all individuals, which allows estimation of transition probabilities from each of the four combination states to all the others. Lazarsfeld expected such SFTS to solve the riddle of causality. But what most strikes the modern reader about this particular SFT (265) is that if we treat it as the transition matrix of a regular Markov chain and square it until it converges, it predicts a solid swing to Truman that is not at all apparent in either the before or the after marginals, both of which have Truman's favorable rating at 54 percent, a stability of which the authors make much. By contrast, the actual limiting value is 68 percent, which indicates precisely the Truman swing that happened in fact. Thus, the SFT seems to a current reader like a secret weapon for predicting electoral outcome.

But what motivates Lazarsfeld is not this unsuspected implication about electoral outcome, but the hope that reflecting about particular transitions in this matrix can decide whether salience of class issues drove the image of Truman or the other way around. So the book disattends to the "big outcome" and focuses its attention on the local shifting around, the process. Indeed, its major theme is that the relative stability of aggregate election figures over time conceals a good deal of wavering and change, and that this wavering turns out to be quite concentrated in a small part of the voting population. To be sure, this in turn means that a relatively small group of voters determines the "big" outcome of the election by means of the "little" outcomes of their processes of decision. But even despite this turn toward a more "outcome-based" view of the election, the conclusions of the book emphasize the system's enormous long-run stability, arguing (e.g., 315) that today's "long-term precommitted voters" on each side derive from the controversies of another era, and hence, "The vote is a kind of 'moving average' of reactions to the political past" (316). It is the millions of minor motions, the little processes of action and change and aging, that produce the aggregate stability. At the same time, however, it is clear that Lazarsfeld believed that there were causally dominant factors (e.g., salience of class issues) that somehow played a more important part in those processes than did other factors. These causal forces somehow pervaded the recurring, endless processes that fascinated him. In that sense, his disattention to outcome took him in the same direction that other sociological methodologists were going (toward causality), but along a quite different ontological path.

The Berelson and Lazarsfeld approach to elections differs considerably from that of their great competitors in the election study game, the Michigan group led by Angus Campbell, Warren Miller, and Philip Converse at the Institute for Survey Research (ISR). In their monumental *The American Voter* (Campbell et al. 1960/1980), reporting detailed comparisons of the 1952 and 1956 elections, the Campbell group set forth a "funnel of causality" model for voting. The funnel model looks very much like the Kornhauser-Lazarsfeld purchase model, with the vote taking the place of purchase.

The funnel shape is a logical product of the explanatory task chosen. Most of the complex events in the funnel occur as a result of multiple prior causes. Each such event is, in its turn, responsible for multiple effects as well, but our focus of interest narrows as we approach the dependent behavior. We progressively eliminate those effects that do not continue to have relevance for the political act (Campbell et al. 1960/1980, 24).

Thus, although they are aware of "other effects"—the other grand-children of the vote's causal grandparents—Campbell et al. explicitly set them aside as irrelevant. Nor do they seriously consider the election as a mere moment in the ongoing political life of the nation. Eveything funnels into a particular moment of supreme importance, a particular election day, a final outcome.[4]

Moreover, the funnel model embeds itself not in the real social process but in what we might call "causal time." For despite the notion of a funnel channeling voters toward particular votes, the Michigan group did only one set of interviews before the election, whereas the Berelson-Lazarsfeld Elmira team had done four. In the thinking of the Michigan school, there was no real-time progress of individuals through the various moments of the campaign to the vote, but rather a causal structure starting with "big background factors" that set the stage, within which "smaller factors" then made minor adjustments.[5]

The Michigan group's vision of causality seems very familiar because it became quite dominant in U.S. quantitative research more generally. It focuses on one particular outcome, in this case, the vote. It arrays causes by the proximity of their impact on that outcome, explicitly separating the immediate from the distant both in social time and social space. The pattern of separating "demographic effects" or, as they were often called, "controls," from immediate causes and from "larger," conceptually relevant but contextual causes became standard in generations of U.S. sociology.

The contrast between the Lazarsfeld and the ISR approaches emphasizes Lazarsfeld's ambiguity on the outcome issue. Although his work drifted at times toward a "funnel of causality" approach, he retained a fascination for turnover and process in themselves, a fascination for the mere flow of variables through time. Much more than the ISR group, Lazarsfeld saw an election as one sample in an ongoing sequence of samples that makes up the political life of the nation, and even that one sample as contaminated by long-gone issues and questions: "The people vote in the same election, but not all of them vote on it" (Berelson et al. 1954, 316). To be sure, the Michiganders also saw this problem. Indeed, *The American Voter* was an attempt to move beyond the narrowly attitudinal conception of elections used by the first ISR report on the 1952 election, *The Voter Decides* (Campbell, Gurin, and Miller 1954). But the "move beyond" was made by envisioning a broader causal structure, not by moving toward a study of attribute transition in real time.

Let me turn now to a third major Lazarsfeld work, *Personal Influence* (Katz and Lazarsfeld 1955).[6] *Personal Influence* is really two books under one cover. The first is a theoretical book on the possible structure of personal influence, based on a review of existing research in public opinion and various adjacent and relevant fields. The second is a study of the structure of personal influence in four issue areas (shopping, films, fashion, and public affairs) among eight hundred women in Decatur, Illinois. It is the second book that interests me here, for it continues the processual line of argument present in *Voting*.

Put simply, there is no outcome whatsoever in *Personal Influence*. There is nothing like the election: no concern whatever with which appliance got bought, which movie was watched, which hairdo chosen, or which political view espoused. There is simply the flow of influence itself: the network and nothing but the network. Katz and Lazarsfeld are quite explicit in positioning their argument against the emerging Michigan survey tradition: "No longer can mass media research be content with a random sample of disconnected individuals as respondents. Respondents must be studied within the context of the group or groups to which they belong or which they have 'in mind'—thus which may influence them—in their formation of opinions, attitudes, or decisions" (1955, 131).

The book thus focuses on flow itself. In retrospect, of course, this gives it what now seems an excessively equilibriar feel, in which it is taken for granted that there is a structure through which influence flows, and it is not expected that that structure will be recursive in any fashion—either self-activating, as networks would become in the social movements literature, or self-perpetuating, as they would be in the interlocking directorate literature. In *Personal Influence*, networks have no particular outcome. They are simply there, the medium through which social life flows.

In a sense, then, *Personal Influence* carries to its natural extreme the view of outcome implicit in *Voting*. Society is viewed as a more or less steady state process, throwing off the multitudes of inconsequential outcomes discussed in the Lazarsfeld and Rosenberg reader. There is no grand narrative, no smiling Harry Truman holding up the *Chicago Daily Tribune* with its "Dewey Defeats Truman" headline. Rather, the book is almost completely descriptive. There are a few causal arguments, but in the main *Personal Influence*, like much of market research since, is largely a descriptive exercise.[7]

We see, then, that in much of Lazarsfeld's work, there is a tendency to ignore final outcome or to treat it as something of little importance. Lazarsfeld saw outcome as something waving now this way, now that, a repeated and endless cycling around some value that never reached a decisive result. By contrast, in *The American Voter* we have an analysis with clear outcomes, a type of analysis that has become paradigmatic in modern sociology.

Beyond Lazarsfeldian Outcome

The same division has characterized sociology since, although most of the discipline has followed the final outcome paradigm. It is useful to examine some later examples that illustrate various outcome conceptions.

Consider Blau and Duncan's justly celebrated *American Occupational Structure* (1967). This book is the very paradigm of outcome-based study. Prestige of respondent's occupation in 1962 is the final point. To be sure, a variety of elegant models focus in on this variable; we are far from the simple funnel of causality. But like *The American Voter, The American Occupational Structure* comes to a sharp and final outcome. A stratification narrative is assumed in each life and is realized in the analysis by a path model, the same for every respondent. By contrast, when Berelson et al. mentioned path models in *Voting*, they were seen as models for long-term stabilities (and that was indeed the use to which they were generally put in economics). That is, they weren't models of ends, but of middles.[8] But in Blau and Duncan they become metaphors for simple narrative; the funnel of causes was fashioned into the formal arrows of path analysis, shooting in toward the bull's-eye of occupation in 1962.

It might seem that such a concept of outcome at a point is confined to quantitative work, for it is a logical concomitant of a regression-based methodological framework. Yet the same view can easily be observed in the revolutions and social movements literatures, both known for their strong reliance on comparative and historical materials.

For example, Skocpol's classic book on social revolutions opens with two ringing questions: "How then are social revolutions to be explained? Where are we to turn for fruitful modes of analyzing their causes and differences?" (1979, 5). Skocpol organizes her argument around Mill's methods of agreement and difference, comparing successful and unsuccessful social revolutions and their various qualities. The French, Russian, and Chinese revolutions preoccupy the book because they are successful revolutions; they made "fundamental and enduring structural transformations" (161). But the major outcome of interest, certainly in terms of the later literature, was not so much these transformations (that is, the further consequences of revolution) as the success (or failure) of the revolution itself. When, the book asks, do revolutions succeed?

Skocpol's book is, of course, filled with thoughtful historical argument and processual thinking. But its conception of outcome is closer to out-come-at-a-point than to Lazarsfeldian endless process. For example, the Chinese revolution is a success for Skocpol—an outcome, a finished thing —even though as of today it does not seem to have effected the permanent transformation we thought it had. The major outcome for Skocpol, as for those who followed her, was the turning point of successful revolution itself.

We see the same approach in work on social movements more generally. Much work on social movements in the 1970s reacted to Gamson's (1975) attempt to discern the bases of successful movement outcome. Yet the outcome-based social movements literature eventually produced a much more elaborated story of social movement formation and development by interpolating into the story of social movements such matters as political opportunity, authorities' response, and movement framing (see the essays in McAdam, McCarthy, and Zald 1996). This kind of elaboration of a conception originally rooted in simple outcomes has occurred throughout sociology. The equivalent literature on stress evolved from a simple account of "what leads to stress" in the 1960s and 1970s to a more complex account of coping, social support, and the like in the 1980s (see Abbott 1990). Yet in both literatures, an implicit focus on final outcome (social movement success in the one case, stress in the other) remained in later literature, even though the complexities inherent in real social systems had led to an examination of the intermediate outcomes or stages. In the social movements literature, for example, the focus moved from successful final result to intermediate "successes" such as increase of movement member-ship, securing of financial resources, and professionalization of movement personnel. These were still seen as outcomes, but were now embedded as steps in a longer process moving toward a final result. There was thus a move from outcome-at-a-point toward a more flowing conception of intermediate, contingent outcomes. Yet it remains true that every concept of social movment inevitably involves a whiff of teleology; movements are still conceived to be trying to go somewhere, and in some sense to stop when they get there.

Outcome-based conceptions remain strongest, however, in the empiri-cal mainstream. The issue of the *American Sociological Review* current as of this writing (April 2002), provides some useful final examples. With respect to ideas of outcome, the simplest is the paper of Portes, Haller, and Guarnizo (2002) on immigrant entrepreneurs. The outcome is whether or not the respondent is an immigrant entrepreneur at a particular moment.[9] There are independent variables of varying "time horizons" (Abbott

2001b, ch. 1), from enduring things like sex and ancestry through slowly varying things like human capital to more rapidly varying things like current social networks. Noticing the time horizon of the independent variables is important because, as we shall see, the temporal extent of the outcome variable, the dependent variable, is one of the central issues in concepts of outcome. Having independent variables with varying time horizons but an outcome variable at a point is essentially the traditional funnel model or ancestors' plot.

Like the Portes et al. paper, the Walder (2002) paper on household income in rural China is a simple prediction of outcome-at-a-point, in this case, the outcome for a household, because the concept of individual income is not viable in such a setting. The independent variables are in two sets (this is a hierarchical linear model), some pertaining to the household, some to the village. Both sets include variables of varying time horizons. The inclusion of two levels of social entities—in this case, household and village—is an important one, for it raises the possibility of different outcome conceptions for the two levels, an issue that pervades the remaining papers. (Here, however, Walder is concerned only with the "lower" [household] level, and only with its outcome at a single point.)

The paper by Logan, Alba, and Zhang (2002) on immigrant enclaves also predicts an individual outcome-at-a-point: living in an ethnic neighborhood. As usual, the independent variables have varying time horizons: relatively long-term things like education, era of migration, and quality of English, as well as short-term ones like employment status, household income, and rental status. But while residence in an ethnic enclave is measured at a point, the authors are very much concerned to infer from their results something about trajectories of individual residence. For their major concern is ultimately not the individual behavior analogous to Portes et al.'s "being an entrepreneur," but rather the "function" of immigrant ethnic communities: whether they are permanent ethnic neighborhoods or mere enclaves that new immigrants pass through on their way to assimilation. This is a "larger" outcome, the status of a certain kind of community, and this larger community might have some autonomous (i.e., emergent) structure, in which the behavior of individuals might have a part but not a determining part. In that sense, the article really does concern separable outcomes at two levels of social reality.

Papers by Hout and Fischer (2002) and Brooks (2002) are both explicitly concerned with just such a higher-level outcome. But because the data are national surveys, these authors are not concerned with an outcome for something we commonly understand to be a real social entity possessing an autonomous internal social organization (e.g., a community). Rather, both focus on trends in national attitudes measured by repeated national probability surveys. Thus, on the one hand, the temporal sequence of events at the aggregate or emergent level is explicitly measured, whereas it was merely implicit in the Logan et al. article, but on the other hand, the aggregate-level events lack the emergent cohesion of Logan et al.'s communities.

Hout and Fischer are concerned with a startling rise after 1991 in persons claiming no religious affiliation. The data are from the GSS (General Social Survey), which means that the trend arises from a random sample, different in every year, taken over a thirty-year period. The outcome of interest is the trend, that is, the direction taken by an aggregate sum of individual behaviors. But the individual outcomes predicted by the equations are outcomes not over time, but at a point. The equation models the religious status (some or none) of each individual at the moment he or she is sampled. Thus, the paper implicitly takes two views of outcome over time, predicting individual outcomes-at-a-moment to understand an aggregate-outcome-over-time. More or less the same structuring of outcomes appears in Brooks's analysis of the increased concern about family decline. In neither paper is there any notion that the aggregate has some kind of emergent status. The aggregate trend has consequences—both papers are clearly animated by a concern for the political consequences of aggregate change—but it does not have any internal historical structure in itself. It is not a proper cultural entity.

The one paper in this group whose view of outcome is overtly processual is that of Paxton (2002). The unit of analysis here is the country. At the heart of the model (a reciprocal causation model) are two properties of these countries: level of democracy (an interval measure) and level of associational life (here measured by numbers of international nongovernmental organizations with an office in the country). Each dependent variable is hypothesized to determine the lagged values both of itself and of the other. There are the usual exogenous variables in addition to these two endogenous ones: energy use, world system status, school enrollment rates, ethnic homogeneity, and so on. There are four time points and hence three change equations are estimated.

What makes this design different is that, at least implicitly, the model takes a Markovian view of process; where a case goes next is a function of where it is now. From classical Markov theory, we know that such a design has a "final outcome" only in two cases. Final outcome can occur because the process has an "absorption state (or states)," which once entered cannot be left. Or, if the stage-to-stage parameters never change, the process will have a final outcome in that the percentages of cases in the varying states will become stable. If neither of these two conditions holds, the (implicit) process will simply wander around according to the varying transition rules. (The article seems to indicate, although it does not directly test, that the stage-to-stage parameters are constant.)

In such a design, then, we don't really have an outcome. We have, rather, in the Lazarsfeldian sense, a process continuously generating new results. The theoretical framing of the article is of course implicitly about democracy as a terminal, absorbing state. But the analysis does not in fact address that absorption, instead thinking about each disaggregated step toward it in the traditional outcome-at-a-point framework. (Just so did Lazarsfeld miss the transition-matrix character of his sixteenfold table.) With respect to long-term outcome, rather than thinking about ultimate democratization (the implicit theoretical core of the paper), one could by contrast think about the percentage of time spent in a democratized state. Particularly if the parameters of the process change steadily, there is no reason to expect convergence, and the percentage of time spent by various cases in various democratic or nondemocratic states could be of far more interest than their ultimate status at a given point.[10]

It is useful at this point to pull together the various theoretical distinctions made among conceptions of outcome so far. The analysis of Lazarsfeld produced a contrast between imagining the social process to be a continuous, more or less equilibriar sequence of interim results and imagining the social process to be a discontinuous sequence of final results. In literature since, it is common to move from the latter view toward the former by interpolating interim "final" results, but still to avoid the fully continuous concept of a social process with only interim outcomes. Note that the contrast between equilibrium outcome and irrevocable outcome is similar to that between short-term outcome and long-term outcome, but not quite identical. We usually think equilibrium processes entail short-term change within long-run stability, whereas irrevocable outcomes entail long-run changes that emerge from short-run instability. But there is a long and a short run for both types of outcome.

Mixed up in these distinctions is another, that of the social and the individual. Several of the papers just examined conceive of changing final outcomes at the individual level that produce progresses of interim outcomes at the social level. Whether or not the social-level phenomenon is considered emergent, its outcome characteristics need not be the same as those of the individual processes coeval with it. It is easy to conflate the two levels.

Finally, recall that what I have called equilibriar outcomes are global equilibria established by myriad individual transactions, things like the particular unemployment episodes and voter transitions mentioned earlier. But these kinds of minor local outcomes are not incompatible with long-run change. In between final point-outcomes and equilibriar outcomes lies a kind of outcome of which I have said little, but that is in fact implicit in several of the pieces just analyzed. This is what I call "trend outcome." A trend conception of outcome is common in sociology for variables like housing inequality and returns to education, for which the analyst doesn't expect a final outcome or an equilibrium, but something in between, a steady movement in some direction. Both the Hout and Fischer and the Brooks papers just examined are organized around the idea of trend as outcome.

Much of sociology today is concerned with trend outcomes, typically trends in inequality measures. Analysts usually don't worry much about a final outcome for variables like housing inequality or occupational segregation, but neither do they expect stable equilibria over time. As the late Bruce Mayhew (1990) found out from the uncomprehending reception of his "baseline models for human inequality," most sociologists think persistent inequality and even the halting of trends toward equality are things-to-be-explained. Trend outcomes are centrally important in sociology today, with its strong meliorist emphasis.

In summary, we seem to have three broad conceptions of thinking about outcome: equilibriar or process outcome, trend outcome, and point outcome. We consider these at the individual or social level, and sometimes both. We examine them over varying periods from short to medium to long term.

Discounting and Decision

Although there are some internal differences, sociology's modal tradition studies final point-outcomes, the results of an examined process at its end. We can discover another important quality of this view of outcome by comparing it to conceptions of outcome in economics. Economists (particularly microeconomists) also evaluate trajectories of value from a single point in time. But for them, this is not the moment of final outcome but that of decision. And unlike outcome, decision concerns not the past but the future; economists look ahead to potential rewards, not back to sunk costs. They use discounting to pull uncertain future results back into the present, where decisions are made. Note that this is precisely the reverse of the sociological ancestors' plot, which looks back at the causes funneling into a final result. Economists focus not on the end of a period, but on its beginning; they study not the origins of an outcome, but the descendants of a decision.

Economists accomplish this forward-looking trick by discounting potential future results and weighting them by their probability. The idea of discounting rests on the notion that, all other things being equal, it is better to have a given amount now than at some moment in the future. There are two chief philosophical justifications for this belief. The first is that money in hand now can be invested to grow in the time between now and that future moment. Although this is a justification for discounting now the value of resources in the future, it in fact judges the worth of an investment trajectory on the basis of its future outcome; the reason for wanting to invest now is to be better off later. To that extent, discounting is still concerned with a final point-outcome. This investment justification for discounting naturally entails the view that we should discount using a negative exponential function because of the implicit connection between discounting and investment at continuously compounded interest.[11]

By contrast, the second major justification for discounting is precisely that uncertainties between the present and any future moment may reduce the value of future rewards. Our tastes may change, our health or even life be lost, a hundred contingencies may intervene before a future reward is enjoyed. Hence, that future reward is worth less to us at present than a certain reward of equivalent value that we can enjoy immediately. Note the assumption, in each of the two major justifications of discounting, that the decider is a finite individual rather than a social structure with a temporal duration of many human lifetimes. As we have already seen, social and individual outcome can be completely decoupled.

Both of these justifications of discounting are in fact more empirical than philosophical. That present resources can be invested to yield future profits (in some finite time) is an empirical fact of most modern economies most of the time, although of course it has not been true for long stretches of history and for large portions of many societies. Similarly, it is an overwhelming empirical fact of the present age, established by endless psychological experimentation, that randomly chosen humans prefer rewards now rather than later. However, there are serious problems with both these empirical justifications. In the first case, standard negative exponential discounting fails as a justification because it presupposes continuous reinvestment of revenues, which is often impossible either in practice or in principle. Somewhat more problematic, the psychological evidence is strong that the negative exponential model predicts human time preferences rather badly. Rather than being exponential, individual time preferences are generally hyperbolic, with more rapid value loss than the exponential early in the future and slower value loss later. To be sure, the exponential can be motivated as a limiting form of one general type of hyperbola (Loewenstein and Prelec 1992), but even so, substantial irregularities in intertemporal choice remain unaccounted for.[12]

The discounting approach to outcome is well illustrated by cost-effectiveness analysis of health outcomes, recently standardized in the monumental text by Gold et al. (1996). Rooted in 1960s business-school-based decision theory (e.g., Raiffa 1968), this literature began with applications to clinical decision making (Lusted 1968; Weinstein and Feinberg 1980) and later moved into the allocation of scarce medical resources. By the mid-1970s it had converged on the concept of quality-adjusted life years (QALYs, in the standard abbreviation). QALYs rest on a formal estimation procedure that begins with ratings of the health-related quality of life (HRQL) for various disease states. (There has been an enormous philosophical debate over the proper way to do this; see Fitzpatrick 1996; Nord 1999, ch. 2). The appropriate HRQL is then attached to each year in any given illness/treatment trajectory and the total QALYs are calculated over the trajectory. In standard decision analysis style, the various possible trajectories make up a sequential tree of decisions, events, and contingencies (each with an associated probability), with QALYs attached as the final leaves on the branches. Cost-effectiveness analysis consists of back-calculating along each tree branch from the QALY leaves to the original trunk, weighting QALYs by their likelihood given the sequential probabilities of the eventualities leading to them. Decision then proceeds by dividing the incremental cost of one intervention (more generally, one branch or trajectory) over another (or over no intervention) by the incremental QALYs of that intervention (branch or trajectory) over the other (or no intervention).

At the outset, the health decision literature argued for discounting only of costs. There was doubt about discounting benefits, because it seemed worrisome "to assume that life years in the future are less valuable than life years today in any absolute utilitarian sense" (Weinstein and Fineberg 1980, 254). Discounting future benefits was eventually urged on pure measurement grounds, as dollars were the instrument of measurement in cost-effectiveness analysis and it was felt that anything measured in dollars must be discounted because dollars themselves are discounted. Today, the literature uniformly insists on discounting benefits as well as costs. Both are done at the same rate, which is at present typically 3 percent in U.S. studies and 5 percent elsewhere. A QALY now is worth more than a QALY ten years from now.[13]

The economic view of temporal trajectories thus differs considerably from the sociological one. The hegemonic view in sociology is to think of final outcome, the state of the trajectory at its end (in economic terms, the ordinate of utility at the end of the period). But economists do not think much about long-run results, reduced as they are by discounting. The economic approach sees trajectories from the present forward. Economics lives in the now.[14]

Note that the now moves with time in a way that final outcome does not. The now gets steadily later as time passes. Final outcome can't move quite as steadily; it is backed up against the ultimate outcome of decline and death. Thus, the economic framework for thinking about trajectories is not simply a matter of thinking about beginnings rather than endings. It also means thinking about trajectories in a more fundamentally dynamic manner.

This dynamism involves a philosophical difference in conceptions of temporality. In a famously controversial paper published in 1908, J. M. E. McTaggart noted that there were two fundamentally different ways of thinking about time, which he called the A series and the B series. The A series involves thinking about time in terms of past, present, and future: thinking in terms of tense. The B series involves thinking about time simply as a transitive order relation, governed by the concepts "earlier than" and "later than." This is thinking in terms of dates. Thus, we might say McTaggart wrote his paper ninety-four years ago or we might say McTaggart wrote in 1908. The first statement is indexical; we don't know what it means or whether it is true until we know when it was said. By contrast, the second statement is true no matter what.[15]

The two series are not connected logically; one brings them into alignment only empirically, with a statement of the form "2002 is now." But given that they are logically distinct, it is quite difficult to sustain a coherent philosophy of time, a fact that led McTaggart to insist on the unreality of time itself.[16] But this philosophical worry is of less interest than is McTaggart's original distinction. Perhaps differences among the various social scientific paradigms for appraising trajectories (i.e., paradigms for "outcome" broadly conceived) can be understood in terms of

McTaggart's different concepts of temporality: one tensed and emphasizing the passage of events from future into present into past, the other simply relative, emphasizing mere duration.

It is evident that microeconomics is a thoroughly A series enterprise. It concerns the now, a tensed moment in which the future is guessable but uncertain and the past known but unimportant. The now, this particular moment, is important because it is the present, in which we live. However, the present immediately becomes past. This was indeed the ground on which McTaggart found the A series incoherent. It assigned a property to events that changes, even though the events themselves do not change. (Whereas, as McTaggart [1993, 26] points out, the death of Queen Anne was the death of Queen Anne at the beginning of time and will be so at the end; its futureness has simply changed into pastness.)

By contrast, standard outcome sociology is more or less a B series enterprise. One reason sociological outcome seems worrying is that most of the outcomes we study are not really endings at all but arbitrary ends selected for some not very well understood reason. In Blau and Duncan, for example, why 1962? Why not 1960? 1963? The year 1962 is not a consequential moment, merely an arbitrary one. It simply happens to be the righthand end of the period investigated.[17] Men in Blau and Duncan's sample ranged from 20 to 64 years of age, and their fathers had been born as early as 1835 and as late as 1919 (Blau and Duncan 1967, 83). In dynamic, A series terms, 1962 came at widely differing points in these men's lives. Yet all followed the same "narrative of variables"—from father's education and father's occupation to son's education and first job, to son's job in 1962.

Outcome sociology thus has a strong B series character. It envisions a time line and slides a window of investigation along the line, cutting out a segment for investigation. Beginnings and endings are largely arbitrary, and separate time segments are surprisingly comparable (think again of Skocpol's three great revolutions—French, Russian, and Chinese—scaled into common, comparable trajectories). What gives final outcome its extraordinary rhetorical force is that once the temporal window of investigation is slid into a particular place, the forceful structure of narrative is implicitly invoked for the period involved. By the mere act of firmly defining a period of investigation, the period's beginning becomes a "real" beginning, its end a "real" end, and so on.[18]

It is difficult to locate Lazarsfeld's process fascination in terms of the McTaggart series. On the one hand, in B series fashion, Lazarsfeld's process work sought to look at an extended time interval rather than to privilege a particular now. But on the other, in A series fashion, it aimed to retain the "openness" of each moment in that extended interval, to insist on the moment's contingency. Lazarsfeld attempted to put McTaggart's Humpty Dumpty back together again. Perhaps that is the task that faces us in developing a new sociological conception of outcome.

Existing and Possible Concepts of Outcome

With the concept of tensed and untensed temporality in hand, we can review comprehensively the distinctions about outcome developed so far. Such a review shows how we have chosen different kinds of outcome conceptions for different kinds of questions and forces us to ask how we might appraise outcomes differently. This is not an idle question, for, as I argue, our choices of outcome measurement are by no means innocent. Indeed, it is surprising that they cause so little conflict, given how value-laden they are. One immediately important consequence of this value-ladenness is that the universe of possible conceptions of outcome is only sparsely colonized by the social sciences. I shall therefore have occasion, in what follows, to refer often to normative or even literary models of outcome and outcome-based decisions.

The first set of distinctions has to do with the relation of outcome to the time interval studied. Imagine some raw measure of utility or well-being as a real-valued function defined continuously through some time interval. We can first distinguish between outcome at a particular instant in that interval (what I have been calling point outcome) and outcome that cannot be located to a particular point (outcome with finite duration). In the first case, outcome is simply the value of the well-being function at a point: the ordinate. In the second, outcome is an integral or other composite function of the curve over some finite time period on the other. (This time period can be any finite period up to the entire interval with which we are concerned.) Note that the move to a duration or period conception could arise either because we think that point outcome is in principle a bad concept or because we think point outcome cannot be directly measured, but only approximated by some kind of average over a finite time interval. We should, however, treat the latter motivation as producing a version of point outcome, rather than a true period outcome, because it arises merely out of measurement considerations, not conceptual ones.

I have so far presented two of the many possible versions of period outcome: equilibrium and trend. These are both patterns of expectations for processes—paradigmatic patterns—against which we measure results over time. Such paradigmatic conceptions of outcome are slightly more complicated than simple "over-time measures of outcome." The latter require only some formal concept of aggregation to become single-figure outcome measures. This aggregation, however, can take several different forms. Integration is the obvious one, and yields a single number that can be compared to other outcomes. But one might also think a good duration was one in which outcome did not fluctuate wildly, for example, in which case, the proper measure would be some autoregression parameter or range of variation. In such cases, we are beginning to think more paradigmatically about outcome. The measure we propose is less a simple value for comparison than a general criterion for the well-being function.

Conceptions like equilibrium and trend are fully paradigmatic. They are general patterns against which trajectories of outcomes are assessed, expectations used to decide whether a trajectory needs to be explained or not. This last is by far the most common use of trend conceptions outcome in sociology, as I noted earlier (i.e., "good trends" don't need to be explained, "bad" ones do).[19] The dual use of period outcomes (both as aggregated single-figure measures and as paradigms) differentiates them slightly from untensed point outcome, the final outcome of the sociologists, which is almost always treated as a simple value for comparison. But taken together, these various measures—final point outcome, equilibrium, trend, and the many other possible period measures (integration, range parameters, etc.)—constitute the basic repertoire of untensed outcome conceptions.

A second basic distinction is that between the social and the individual levels of outcome. At the beginning, my examples seemed to suggest that social-level variables are often associated with period conceptions and individual ones with point outcome. As the examples have shown, however, this is not true. Equilibrium outcome patterns are expected in individual lives, if only at short time intervals: purchase of goods, interaction habits, and so on. Conversely, revolution is an obvious point outcome conception at the social level. The crucial constraint here is that individuals do have finite life, and hence equilibriar outcomes for them are constrained to a certain temporal duration, which we typically think is shorter than the duration over which we measure the "more important" individual point outcomes such as marital duration and education. (These are, of course, more important precisely because they aren't equilibriar.)

Thus, all types of outcomes occur at both individual and social levels. For example, certain variables at both levels are nearly always conceived in trend terms. Education, for example, is always seen as an ordered outcome monotonically increasing over at least a substantial period of the life course, an outcome paradigm that one would think researchers, who, after all, supposedly double as classroom teachers, would have seen for the extraordinary assumption that it is; many a college senior knows less on departure than on arrival, at least net of maturational change. (And of course, we ourselves are all losing education, forgetting things, all the time, in addition to gaining education through study and maturation.) At the social level, economic growth has enjoyed, since the 1930s, similar status as a trend both normative and empirical for nearly everyone in the society. As Offe (1985) and many others have pointed out, however, there is no particular reason, normative or empirical, why the economy has to grow. The belief that it does and that it must, implicit in the notion that growth is the paradigm within which the economy must be understood, is an outcome ideology.

The third fundamental distinction here made among conceptions of outcome is the one we get from McTaggart: outcome conceptions can be tensed or untensed. Some outcome conceptions take an A series view of temporality: all that matters is the dynamic now; results at other times must somehow be referred to that now. Other outcome conceptions take a B series view: time is a simple line of dates, and therefore understanding outcome does not require knowing temporal location in some contingent or dynamic sense. Any moment can be an end, any moment can be a beginning; outcome is simply the state of affairs in some arbitrary time period or at some point.

To deepen the concept of tensed outcome, I want to distinguish between consummated and unconsummated outcome. By this distinction I mean the difference between outcome that we either are having or have had and outcome we have not yet had but merely expect. Consummated outcome includes all the welfare enjoyed up to or at a particular point. The typical sociological outcome measured at the end of a period is consummatory either in that it is itself a result being enjoyed (or suffered) or in that it confers immediate access to other consummatory rewards. Hence, in the status attainment story of Blau and Duncan, achieving high occupational status is taken as valuable both in itself and because it gives immediate access to things like money and power that are (presumably) goods in themselves. These outcomes are all immediately available.

But note that the Blau and Duncan outcome does not include past benefits. One of the striking things about nearly all the outcome conceptions considered here is their disregard of past well-being. Economists have no interest whatever in the past. Sociologists are interested only in its causal implications for the present. That it might live on in memory to be enjoyed at later moments seems uninteresting to all concerned. (But see Tversky and Griffin 2000, where past welfare serves as a comparison standard for present welfare.) Nor is there much interest in the way past utilities can be changed, by later redefinition, into disutilities (and vice versa), despite the obvious occurrence of such redefinition in divorce, for example (Vaughan 1987, 271). Indeed, this deadness of the past is to a certain extent enshrined in the two senses of the word "consummatory," which refers both to things that are realized and things that are over.[20]

This disattention to a supposedly dead past makes a stark contrast with the common focus on a (lively) future, whose as-yet-unconsummated outcomes are at the center of economic thinking. It is therefore useful to distinguish outcome conceptions as prospective, momentary, retrospective, or pantemporal conceptions, depending on whether they look forward, to the present, backward, or in all temporal directions. This distinction applies mainly to tensed conceptions of outcome, but, as we shall see, it can be useful in thinking about untensed ones as well.

Generally, we employ prospective conceptions of outcome when we are interested in doing something or accomplishing something. The microeconomic concept of outcome considered earlier is an example: a prospective, tensed outcome conception in which we guess the trajectory of future outcome in order to make decisions. To be sure, even under the theory of discounting, the aim is to come out better (in consummatory terms) in the end. But in the meantime, the idea is to imagine unconsummated outcome in order to make a decision.[21]

But we can also imagine an untensed version of prospective outcome, in which a future outcome is established absolutely at a moment. In the simplest case, this is the sociological conception of ascription, which we generally consider both normatively wrong and scientifically somewhat uninteresting. Note that the equivalent situation (fixation of outcome very early in a period) arises for extreme hyperbolic discounters (like Tony Manero at the beginning of *Saturday Night Fever*). Hyperbolic discounting characterizes an interval's utility using an integral (as does exponential discounting), but in this case, the discounting function is of the form $1/rt$, where t is time and r is a parameter. As r gets arbitrarily large, the value of the integral moves arbitrarily closer to a point outcome at time zero. Someone who is so extreme a hyperbolic discounter ascribes an enduring outcome to himself or herself at the outset of an interval because of an unwillingness to postpone any form of gratification.

But this kind of outcome conception—prospective, untensed point out-come—governs much more than Tony Manero and his blue shirt. The formal outcome theory of Calvinist theology was predestinarianism, which is formally the reverse of what we might call the "last judgment" outcome concept of the sociologists. Predestinarianism fixed the (ulti-mate) outcome of life at its beginning. Social systems that do this are in fact quite common. Some are familiar ascription systems; English aristo-crats long justified the rule of landed elites on the grounds that their financial preeminence (an outcome guaranteed prospectively at the out-set) freed them to think about the interests of the nation as a whole. Closer to our own time, educational systems like those of France and Japan stake much of life outcome on single examinations very early in one's career, again to some extent justifying themselves on arguments about freedom from careerist interests. Similar are concepts of term limits—for elective office, for scholarly fellowships, even for marriage. They fix an outcome in advance, aiming to undercut the play of interests.[22]

Most of these forward-looking outcome structures aim to do things. The tensed ones are an aid to decision; the untensed ones are a way of undercutting certain social disutilities. But they differ in that the tensed prospective outcome conceptions are not in themselves consummatory; they appraise future outcome but do not determine it. By contrast, the untensed forward-looking structures simply determine the limits of cer-tain consummations in the future. That is why I have labeled them pre-destination outcomes, by contrast to the last judgment outcomes that come at the end of untensed intervals.

So far we have four particular types of untensed conceptions of out-come, each of which we have seen at the social and individual level. We have the two point outcomes: predestination and last judgment. We have the two types of period outcome noted earlier: trend and equilibrium. All of these are general models for outcome, ways we have of imagining and measuring the nature of outcome. As I have noted throughout, last judg-ment is the outcome model undergirding most of sociology. Predestina-tion is widespread in society, but somewhat uninteresting sociologically because it fixes things ahead of time. (Sociologists are not usually inter-ested in things that always turn out the same, despite their considerable social importance.) I have also suggested, but by no means explored, the enormous variety of aggregative period incomes, integrals and so on, possible as nonparadigmatic or semiparadigmatic versions of outcome over time.

On the tensed side, I have devoted most of my attention to prospective tensed outcome (PTO), as exemplified by the classic discounted future of the economists. I now consider the other possibilities. There is, first, a truly "point" version of tensed outcome. In one sense, of course, tensed outcome is always conceived in terms of a single point, the now. The very words prospective and retrospective are indexicals; they lack meaning until we know prospective or retrospective with respect to what. But there are tensed conceptions of outcome that are purely instantaneous. The most familiar are philosophical. For example, in conceiving happiness, Aristotle (*Ethics*, bk. 1, ch. 10, 1100a, 10; 1101a, 20) explicitly rejects the idea of last judgment. Although condoling the sadness of Priam, whose happy life was finally overshadowed by Troy's demise, he mocks Solon's advice to Croesus that no man count himself happy until he be dead and beyond misfortune. That is, he mocks the idea that outcome is how one is doing at the moment of death, a truly final point outcome. Happiness, Aristotle tells us, comes from within. For happiness consists in "active exercise of our faculties in conformity with virtue" (1100b, 9–10). And "none of men's functions possess the quality of permanence so fully as activity in conformity with virtue" (1100b, 11–14). Only the most overwhelming of external misfortunes can challenge this, he thought. Thus, outcome is essentially a tensed constant unique to the individual, determined by who we have made ourselves to be, always produced in action in every now of our lives.[23]

It is not impossible to envision a social science concept of outcome of this kind. Csikszentmihalyi's (1990) celebrated theory of flow is essentially about a momentary type of experience that "is its own outcome." The flow experience is absolutely tensed, in that it presupposes the separation of a now from past and future. Unlike the PTO conception of the economists, however, flow does not bother looking beyond the now, either to past or future. It is a microstructure within the now that depends on a number of external and internal conditions. External conditions are completable tasks, ability to concentrate and to control actions, and immediate feedback. Internal conditions are effortless involvement, decrease of self-consciousness, and deformation of temporal sense (49). The deformation of temporal sense is what is important for us. It is a kind of expansion: "Hours pass by in minutes, and minutes can stretch out to seem like hours." The former judgment seems to come from the outside; when one is not in flow, it seems to have passed quickly. And the latter judgment is from the inside; when one is in flow, it seems to last and last.[24]

Flow is clearly an outcome state, and one of the momentary tensed kind we have just seen in Aristotle. But it is not immediately clear how one would use flow as an outcome measure, although there are some obvious possibilities. One could simply measure amount of time spent in flow, although this seems a problematic concept given the deformation of time sense involved. Moreover, this approach simply treats flow as yet another kind of utility, rather than as a specific form of outcome conception. It would fall under the class of untensed period outcome conceptions discussed above.

A more subtle way to operationalize flow as an outcome conception would be to treat it as a fractal, taking literally the idea that flow constitutes a way of expanding time. Think of time for the moment as a B series line segment of a certain length or duration. Now imagine that we expand that line by replacing the middle third of it by the two sides of the equilateral triangle of which that middle third is the base. The segment is now a trajectory with a deviation in the middle and is ⁴⁄₃ as long as it was before, although its horizontal extension remains the same. Now do the same to each of the four segments of which the trajectory is currently composed. The total length is now ¹⁶⁄₉ what it was to start with, although the horizontal extension remains exactly the same.

This construction, the Koch fractal, can of course be repeated endlessly. We can think of it as an analogy for the expansion of time in flow. Linear time remains the same, but lived experience becomes much more than it was to start with. (It will pass twice the original length at the next iteration and is, in fact, infinite if we keep going.) Now the Koch fractal does not "fill a second dimension," but the degree to which it does can be measured. This number, its fractal dimension, is 1.26. Other linear fractals of this type (sometimes called meanders [Lauwerier 1991]; a different type of fractal would be one with a different generating rule) will of course have a different fractal dimension. That is, although there is no linear way to measure the "time expansion" because it involves another dimension not directly measurable, there is a monotonic scale directly related to that expansion, and that monotonic scale could be used in principle to measure a degree to which one's version of flow added extra lived experience time to the fixed horizontal period of the line segment.

How would we specify what could be meant by "different types of fractal time expansion in flow"? Note that in a finite system, there are two different parameters to this kind of time expansion: first, the one-step expansion induced by the fractal generator, and second, the number of times that generator is (recursively) applied. The first could in principle be estimated directly from individuals' flow experience. The second would be more difficult, as it refers to the extent to which people take the "ordinary time" leading up to flow and expand it into a little flowlike middle part, rather like somebody who has a special set of rituals or exercises before a big sporting match and a special way of celebrating afterward (and who would then take the before and after segments of the preparatory ritual and expand them on a flow basis, etc.). But in principle, these two parameters of time expansion could be measured; the measures are no more fanciful than the time tradeoff and standard gamble methods used to estimate HQRLs in the health outcomes literature (see Torrance 1986 for a review). It thus seems that one can imagine an empirically grounded program of research in which outcome is conceived as an instantaneous, tensed phenomenon, of which each individual might have a characteristic version or type. This instantaneous aspect of outcome would have an enormous impact on "total experienced outcome over a lifetime," but would not be retrievable by simple survey measures of "quantity of outcome over time," as it is concealed in the way that individuals experience the utilities that come to them.[25]

This approach implies that flow as an outcome measure would be independent of social scales of valuation. It would not be a function of money, for example. Nothing about being rich makes flow more possible, with the possible exception of conferring freedom to control actions. Also, because of flow's focus on the now, it is not at all clear how to aggregate it over the life course as an outcome or how to use its presence, absence, or possibility as a crucial criterion of decision. In a way, this is a problem with any tensed form of outcome conception. Referring all to the now, they remake possibility perpetually, whether they are prospective or retrospective, momentary or pantemporal.

Perhaps the most intriguing form of tensed outcome is retrospective. We have models for thinking about future outcome and present outcome. But there is little in the diverse social science literatures on outcome that really helps us conceive of the impact of past events on present outcome. Obviously, one could begin by recalling that untensed period outcomes essentially involve past outcome in a simple way. That is, if one considers the simple integral of utility as viewed from late in a duration, it obviously takes into account past as well as present welfare. One could move beyond this, toward a tensed conception of past outcome, by insisting that pleasant memory is itself part of present reward. To be sure, memories fade, and one might as a first rough approximation assume that memories fade exponentially, which leads one to a kind of reverse discount symmetric with the prospective discounting that is at the heart of standard microeconomic conceptions of outcome. This is the most simple form of retrospective tensed outcome (RTO).[26]

It is common to make decisions on an RTO basis. Some people choose to have children because they look forward to changing diapers a year hence (on a PTO basis) and some because they see everyone else do it. But a not insubstantial number of people have children to avoid regretting, at some much later point in life, that they had not had children. This is an RTO decision, not a PTO one, because on standard prospective discounting rates, even quite massive regrets thirty years hence are of no substantial disutility today. But seen from the viewpoint of the end, with the diapers and wakeful nights successfully discounted (by selective memory, if by nothing else), this regret looms as a massive loss.

One difficulty with this kind of RTO measure, however, is that it does not take account of the ways past utility remains in question. Put more formally, it does not recognize the historicality of consummation. The most obvious example of this has already been mentioned: divorce. It is well-known that the process of divorce produces a variety of redefinitions of past events, inter alia of past consummatory outcome. Some of these are simple redefinitions of the "You know, I never really loved you" form, which suddenly eradicate the meaning (even the discounted meaning) of large bodies of past pleasure. Some are strategic; as Vaughan (1987, ch. 10) points out, these very redefinitions can be used as gambits and responses in the process of uncoupling itself. Others arise simply from the "placing into question" of all past interpretations, which have been protected by the secure, factitious quality of marriage.

But all of these mean that not only is the past discounted, it can be redefined. This can be a literal redefinition, as we have seen. But it is more commonly a redefinition by a later act, as a marriage becomes merely a "first marriage" when the second occurs or the brilliant early literary success becomes merely "a flash in the pan" when the second and third masterworks fail to appear. This indeed was at the heart of Aristotle's condolence for Priam, whose many, apparently fully consummated years of success were redefined as "pride before a fall" by the Greeks' wasting of proud Ilion. And it was this logic that led Solon to tell the fabulously wealthy Croesus not to count himself happy until dead (Plutarch n.d., 114).

A truly effective RTO outcome measure must take account of these redefinitions. In prospective discounting, the uncertainty of the future is held to increase montonically from the present. It is by no means clear that events in the past are systematically more susceptible to redefinition as we move further from them. Indeed, a long literature on "sedimentation" (Berger and Luckmann 1967) assumes that quite the reverse is true. Hence, we are unlikely to handle the problem of redefinition by a simple negative exponential discount, even though the latter might seem the best way to deal with the easier problem of the forgetting of pleasures. Such redefinition at the social level can work extraordinary transformations of past consummations good or bad, as Peter Novick's (1999) brilliant book on the Holocaust demonstrates. At the social level, with its much longer time horizons and more commonly equilibriar framework, the impact of such redefinition on present outcome is enormous.[27]

When we turn from RTO to the problem of pantemporal tensed outcome, we have reached what should be considered the ideal of possible outcome conceptions. That outcome conceptions should involve prospect, moment, and retrospect seems to me absolute. We are not momentary creatures, but have pasts and futures, as do our social institutions. All parts of time are relevant to outcome at both levels—not perhaps equally so, but the balance of them is itself something we should explore, not simply make assumptions about. As for tense, it is clear that tensed outcome is at root preferable to untensed outcome because, as Bergson (1899/1910), Shackle (1961), and dozens of others have argued, we live in a tensed world, not an untensed one. Action, deliberation, anicipation, and memory are all fundamentally tensed. Whether we think at the individual level of decision making (my implicit focus in these past few pages), or at the group level of "history moving forward," as in Lazarsfeld's studies of elections, we want our concepts to work in a tensed environment, because the people and social structures we study are always in that tensed environment. It may be that the move to untensed outcome is necessary because of the need to compare outcomes across agents, or because it is mathematically simpler and more tractable. But that should not blind us to its fundamental undesirability.

Conclusion

In this paper I have tried to lay out a conceptual machinery for thinking about the results of individual and social life. In the ideas of tensed and untensed outcome, of consummatory and nonconsummatory outcome, of retrospective, momentary, prospective, and pantemporal outcome, and in the various versions of untensed outcome here discussed, I have tried to provide terms for thinking about this complex and difficult issue.

I have borrowed concepts widely and ranged over quite disparate literatures because there was no other choice. For the problem is urgent: the question of outcome is not an idle one. The vast majority of sociological inquiry aims to evaluate the "causes" of "what happens," even though we usually lack a reflective concept of how to appraise what happens. More important, we often aim to figure out whether what happens to one kind of person is better than what happens to another kind of person. But every time we commit to a particular way of envisioning these results, we make profoundly value-laden decisions about what outcome is better by deciding how we are going to define outcome in the first place. In particular, as I have argued throughout, making decisions about how to think about the distribution of welfare over a trajectory—the life course of an individual or the history of a social formation—is a thoroughly value-based action. This is yet another way in which there can be no value-free sociology. It is only the existence of widely accepted, and quite unreflective, conventions about ways to envision outcome that shield us from this fact.

It may thus seem to make perfect sense that research about whether marriage is a good thing should rest on measures that emphasize how people end up after a spell of marriage rather than nonmarriage: living longer, being more satisfied with life and friends and children, and so on. But such an emphasis imperceptibly but inexorably pushes us toward insisting that the ideal aim of erotic and family arrangements is to end up at 60 in reasonable health, with a paid-up mortgage, happy children who went to the right colleges, and ahead of us the pleasant vista of our life-table-promised 21.4 years of golf and merlot. But why not cut a broad swath and flame out at 45? A little calculus shows that Faust's discount rate, the rate at which twenty-four years of bliss starting now is worth the same as eternal bliss starting in twenty-four years, is a miniscule 2.89 percent, less than the 3 percent discount normally used in health evaluation studies in the United States. Faust was a cautious conservative for insisting on twenty-four years before damnation! European health discounting would have accepted only fourteen.

The question of outcome is not simply another methodological difficulty. Most of sociology's outcome conceptions enforce on our data a view of life that is thoroughly and completely bourgeois; there is nothing objective about it. It is a conception organized around decency, circumspection, normality, and a certain kind of highly regulated aspiration. It is a conception that devalues strong experience and overvalues caution. It is a conception that enforces future calculation and disregards memory. It leaves us with nothing to regret, and, all too likely, nothing to remember.

To return to my opening example from *Saturday Night Fever*, the outcomes-based conception that has dominated sociology for decades seems to me a little Fusco-like. It has us standing in the hardware store, dutifully putting the paint up on the shelves, each in our allotted roles like colorless, middle-aged analysts. But Lazarsfeld, like Tony Manero, realized that the essence of life was not so much about where you ended up as it was a commitment to the getting there. If you recall the opening of *Saturday Night Fever*, you will remember that it consists of a five-minute closeup of John Travolta's feet, encased in high-heeled red imitation-crocodile boots, walking straight at the camera in heroic foreshortening: five minutes of walking, five minutes of tensed process, of past, present, and future. We don't care about the final point outcome: that Tony gets to the hardware store with the paint can. We want to watch him getting there: buying his slices of pizza, turning around to chase the beautiful girls who undulate past him, listening to the el overhead. It is the whole walk that is the outcome, and for us as sociologists, understanding that walk is a crucial matter, a matter, like the music Travolta walks to, of staying alive.

Notes

A shorter version of this paper was written at Peter Bearman's invitation for the Paul Lazarsfeld Centennial Conference held at Columbia University, 29 September 2001. I would like to thank not only that audience, but also audiences at Michigan, Oxford, and Northwestern for comments on this paper. I also thank David Meltzer, Ray Fitzpatrick, and Avner Offer for stimulating advice, Richard Saller for spatial support, and Erin York for research assistance. I should like to dedicate this paper, which makes much of the finitude of human life, to the memory of my friend and colleague Roger Gould.

> Thou wert the morning star among the living
> Ere thy fair light had fled—
> Now having died, thou art as Hesperus giving
> New splendor to the dead.

1   The standard response to this bleak statement is, of course, to study the variation in the time till that outcome arrives. See Keynes's famous epigraph from *A Tract on Monetary Reform*: "But this long run is a misleading guide to current affairs. In the long run we are all dead" (1923, 80).

2   This framework for action is surprisingly like the language Bergson uses to discuss choice, in which we have "not two tendencies, or even two directions, but a self which lives and develops by means of its very hesitations, until the free action drops from it like an over-ripe fruit" (1889/1910, 176). See the discussion of Bergson in Abbott (2001b, ch. 7).

3   Lazarsfeld was involved in two major voting studies: *The People's Choice* (Lazarsfeld and Gaudet 1948) and *Voting* (Berelson, Lazarsfeld, and McPhee 1954). I focus on the latter, which is the more fully developed.

4   By comparison, Lazarsfeld had been trying to think of the entire network of phenomena moving forward in real time, at least in the period before the election, rather than a particular funnel of causes focusing in on one outcome. As Lazarsfeld argued, an

election is itself only an interim sample in a long run of samples. The Michigan approach justified itself, of course, by pointing to the consequences of that interim result. Yet the funnel model was easily and commonly moved to situations where the consequences were by no means so great.

5 The book actually proceeds backward in causal time, from these proximate factors to the larger background ones. It begins with "immediate psychological influences on the voting act" (popular perceptions of national politics, political attitudes about candidates, and individual sense of political commitment and efficacy). It then seeks "the roots of [these] proximal attitudes in either of two directions, moving deeper in time past or outward from the political core of the funnel" (Campbell et al. 1960/1980, 118). (Here the authors consider the effects of and origins of party attachment, the effects of issues themselves and of issue aggregation by parties, and the consequences of electoral laws and systems.) Finally, it turns to the social and economic origins of all these "more general" political factors: group memberships and their effects, class and its effect, ses effects, regional and sectoral effects, and so on. It is a simple and instructive exercise to create a narrative that rearranges these causal priorities, making the enduring political beliefs of individuals into a background that shapes party behavior, which then determines political structures and, thereby, the structure of ses and group membership. Pressure of space keeps me from an extended analysis of the relation of causality and outcome in this paper.

6 The actual amount of Lazarsfeld in various of these books is unclear. Although he was always careful to provide acknowledgments (off the title page), substantial parts of *Voting* were originally drafted by John Dean and Edward Suchman. Other parts began as dissertations, and Berelson attributed substantial portions of the ideas in chapter 14 to Edward Shils. As for *Personal Influence*, the entire text appears to have been drafted in three sections by (respectively) David Gleicher, Peter Rossi, and Leo Srole (see Katz and Lazarsfeld 1955, xiii). Given this corporate mode of production, one is reluctant to attribute ideas directly to Lazarsfeld. But for my purposes, I assume him to be the presiding genius of this work and attribute ideas to him on that basis.

7 Katz and Lazarsfeld defined themselves not only by contrast with emerging survey research, but also by contrast with the mass/disorganization view of public opinion, in which the sudden expansion of media was seen to be creating a "global village." They traced this argument to Cooley's *Social Organization* (Katz and Lazarsfeld 1955, 16, n. 1) and thought Wirth and Blumer its current exponents. Oddly, then, Columbia sociologists of the empirical tradition were arguing for location and grounding of social facts against two Chicago writers normally associated with strong insistence on precisely that location and grounding (see Abbott 1999, ch. 7).

8 Interestingly, Berelson et al. (1954, 281) cite Tinbergen, an economist modeling business cycles, as their source. Tinbergen had reinvented path analysis in the 1930s, its actual invention by Wright in the early 1920s (like its use in Wright's father's work on tariffs) being already forgotten. See the references in Abbott (1998).

9 Technically, one of the values of the dependent variable has extent in time, because the criteria for "transnational entrepreneurship" include having traveled abroad twice in the past year and having the success of one's firm depend on foreign contacts. But the essential goal of the article remains predicting an individual outcome at a point.

10 The technically inclined will note that I have slipped into a discrete language for an article whose endogenous variables are continuous. This is not a problem at so high a

level of abstraction. Markov chains provide a useful formal way of thinking about the difference between "final outcomes" and "interim outcomes," both as facts and as frameworks for thinking about the world. In regular Markov chains, we envision interim outcomes. If the chain is irreducible, every state will be visited at some point, and indeed will be visited an infinite number of times, although the proportions of time spent in various states are of course determined by the transition probabilities and estimated by the row proportions of the multiplicative limit of the transition matrix. There are no final outcomes. In absorbing Markov chains, there is a final outcome or outcomes, and we are interested in the periods of time spent in various states before getting there. These will be a function partly of transitions between transient states (the interstate probabilities that would completely determine a regular chain), but also, to a critical degree, of the transition probabilities into the absorbing state or states. People who think about the world in terms of final outcome must focus on these, the probabilities of irrevocable change.

11 In these intoductory paragraphs on discounting I have relied somewhat on the extremely interesting book of Colin Price (1993).

12 Sources in this area are legion, going back to the celebrated prospect theory of Kahnemann and Tversky (1979). Probably the most comprehensive current writer on hyperbolic discounting is Ainslie (1992, 2001). Economists have considered a variety of interesting outcome problems, such as how current consumption decisions make the actor into a different person when he or she later enjoys the chosen utilities and what happens when actors are no longer around to enjoy chosen future (social) utilities or disutilities. A few economists have turned to the Lazarsfeld question of how to think about whole sequences of consumption. It should be no surprise that the preferred sequence is of gradual increase (Loewenstein and Prelec 1991, 1992).

13 For these rates, see Muennig (2002, 151). A 3 percent discount gives a net present value of about 75 percent at ten years and about 54 percent at twenty. A 5 percent discount gives 61 percent at ten years and 37 percent at twenty. Obviously, such discount rates ensure that governments are unwilling to invest much in long-term prevention of chronic diseases with late onset, a fact that has fed an intense political debate about fairness. For a discussion, see Tsuchiya (2000). QALYs have also been used for simple inequalities measures; see Gerdtham and Johannesson (2000). Another important empirical discounting literature is that on lifetime earnings. Here, too, early controversies about discounting seem to have settled into later conventions. Creedy's (1977) classic paper points out that variation in earnings profiles over the life cycle means that differing discounting rates can produce differing rank orders of occupations in terms of lifetime earnings. But later literature (e.g., Dolton, Makepeace, and Van der Klaauw 1989; Makepeace 1996; D. Johnson and Makepeace 1997) has usually assumed standard discounting. Nonetheless, in an extremely cautious review, Creedy (1990) warns that any extending of the accounting period for earnings beyond instantaneous measure raises nearly insurmountable estimation difficulties. Some work in this literature does not formally discount. For example, Bosworth et al. (2000), working with U.S. Social Security data, simply divide all wages by the average wage for the year, which standardizes for temporal change without discounting.

14 For a forthright exposition of the "nowness" of economics, see the early chapters of Shackle (1961). I should note that the sociological conception of outcome is implicitly like the Christian one. The sociological aim of life, at least the aim that is implicit in

books like Waite and Gallagher's (2000) *The Case for Marriage*, is to end up well. This is analogous to the Christian aim to end up well: to have lived righteously and to die ready to face a final tribunal that evaluates a whole life in order to send a soul to its eternally constant outcome. Properly speaking, this is the Protestant view (at least as experienced by believers; as Weber and many others have pointed out, most Protestant theology doesn't recognize a quantitative final judgment). Roman Catholicism, by contrast, focuses on dying in a "state of grace"; like the microeconomists, it focuses on the now, in this case, the now of death. I am grateful to Colm O'Muircheartaigh for pointing this out.

15 McTaggart's paper set the problematic of the anglophone philosophy of time for the entire twentieth century. The continental tradition ignored it, preferring the phenomenological approach of Husserl and Heidegger, which I have ignored here. The McTaggart argument was restated, almost word for word, by the English heterodox economist G. L. S. Shackle, who does not seem to have been aware of McTaggart. "With this extended time seen from the outside by an extratemporal observer [i.e., the B series] we must contrast the time in which things happen to, and are perceived in their actuality by, an intratemporal observer, a living person in his act of living" (Shackle 1961, 17). The distinction is also cognate with Bergson's time as duration (A series, in Bergson's view legitimate) versus time as extension (B series, in Bergson's view illegitimate).

16 The details of this argument need not concern us here. Basically, once he has separated the two series, McTaggart shows that the B series cannot be a notion of time because it has no account of temporal direction, while the A series involves us in assigning to a single fact a property (futureness, presentness, pastness) that changes in a regular manner that we cannot specify without assuming the consequent: that time exists. For a detailed modern exposition of the McTaggart position and its sequelae, see Mellor (1981).

17 Duncan would no doubt have answered that there was no reason for 1962 other than convenience; the coefficients would probably be the same for any particular outcome moment, to a large degree. To illustrate the rather arbitrary nature of sociology's time intervals, I have taken a sample from Sociological Abstracts of 1,846 articles on the sociology of work. (This sample was for a paper on skill, but the results would be the same no matter where we looked.) Of these, 66 involve some form of inclusive dates. Of the 66, 16 are specified in decades (1970s, etc.). Another 26 start with a decadal year (1940, 1950, etc.), and 21 (with some overlap) end with a decadal year. Thus, most of the papers involve decadal specifications. There is, of course, no nonarbitrary reason why periods of investigation should start and finish with decadal years.

18 The outcome concept characteristic of much sociology draws its structure from the literary conventions of narrative (see Abbott 2001b, chs. 2, 6). So we read in Aristotle:
Now a whole is that which has a beginning, middle, and end. A beginning is that which is not itself necessarily after anything else, and which has naturally something else after it; an end is that which is naturally after something itself, either as its necessary or usual consequent, and with nothing else after it; and a middle, that which is by nature after one thing and has also another after it. A well-constructed plot, therefore, cannot either begin or end at any point one likes; beginning and end in it must be of the forms just described. (*Poetics* 1450b, 26–33)
Moreover, Aristotle earlier says, "[In Narrative] the end is everywhere the chief thing" (1450a, 23), and "[Narrative] is an imitation of an action that is complete in itself" (1450b, 23–24). These passages identify the concept of narrative with the concept of

final outcome. The Lazarsfeld process position is that, *pace* Aristotle, there is in social reality no end "with nothing else after it," except death. Note that there is no body of sociological methodology based on beginnings. One can think about time series in the ARIMA (AutoRegressive Integrated Moving Average) format as being completely about middles, as one can think about the standard regression model as an ancestors' plot focused on ends. But there is surprisingly little thinking in terms of beginnings, even though the mathematics we call event history analysis began life as waiting-time-till-failure models in studies of industrial reliability, which are essentially beginning-focused models.

19 The obvious example here is mobility studies, which has spent decades trying to explain departures from an outcome state of "pure chance" mobility. Yet pure chance intergenerational mobility would have struck virtually all residents of the nineteenth-century United States or Europe as completely and totally bizarre. It was certainly not for them something they conceived to be the "natural" state of affairs.

20 Thus, sexual congress "consummates" a marriage in the sense of fully realizing it, but also "consummates" a part of the relationship (courtship) that is now finished. This duality is evident in what is arguably the word's most famous use. When Jesus dies on the cross, he says, "Consummatus est" (Vulg. John 29:30), famously translated in the Authorized Version as "It is finished," meaning that the immediate drama of the Crucifixion is over, but equally interpretible in Christian theology as "It is completed," meaning that God's plan for redemption through Christ's incarnation and death has been brought to fruition. The same dual sense is in the Greek original, which uses the verb *teleo*, meaning both to bring to maturity and to finish.

21 I have here unpacked two distinctions run together by Kahnemann and Tversky (see 2000, 15, on "decision value" versus "experience value"). See also, on future outcomes, Shackle (1961, 9): "It is hard to give a sufficiently arresting emphasis to the idea, and what is implied by it, that outcomes are figments and imaginations."

22 One might ask whether predestination really fits this model; are people predestined so that they are free of the cares of life and can simply show forth God's grace in the manner they choose? The answer is no. Calvin believed it impious to pose the question of why God should have chosen to predestine (Constantin Fasolt, personal communication, 2 August 2002). An example of marriage limitations that were effectively term limits can be found in the Oneida Community (see Foster 1984, ch. 3), but of course, there are also the familiar cultural images of "shipboard romance" and other such limited dalliances. As for limited scholarly fellowships, the Rockefeller Center at Bellagio is famous for its one-month limit and ten-year waiting time till a return visit. Probably the oldest continuous example of a term-limit structure is the British Parliament, whose requirement of an election every seventh year (if not before) dates from 1716. (It was three years in 1694–1716.)

23 The Book of Job makes the same argument. Job's "outcome" in terms of worldly matters is an arbitrary result of God's hands-off response to Satan's dare. But Job's outcome as a human being, which is his ultimate justification in the sight of God and indeed the cause thereby of his return to riches, lies in his never ceasing to address God even in his bitterest moments, a quality that, like Aristotle's virtue, "comes from within." Such momentary tensed outcome concepts are common. A similar sense that all of life is always at risk in any moment and that outcome always depends on an instantaneous virtue in the now is central to the Japanese samurai ethic.

24   An excellent example of flow is expert speculation with money. Many extremely wealthy people continue to amass wealth not because they can in any way use it for consummatory pleasure (although one could try to save their behavior for standard utility theory by assuming that their utility lies in beating the other guy). Rather, they do it simply to enjoy the flow of the doing. It was perhaps for this reason that Weber described capitalism, on the last pages of *The Protestant Ethic*, as degenerating into sport.

25   I have dodged the problem that flow is very much tensed and hence that flow's "time expansion" does not take place uniformly across any given duration but in some sense from left to right. This question would need to be addressed before flow could be used as an outcome measure.

26   The importance of memory in RTO suggests the reverse importance of anticipation in PTO, something that is ignored in the microeconomic version of PTO. The thing that is lost (see n. 19 above) when pleasure is consummated is the anticipation of pleasure, which ought to be recognized as having utility in and of itself, extended over the full period of anticipation. And the vaguest, most long-term anticipations are often the strongest and most sustaining. Just as memory should form the core of RTO, anticipation should not be ignored in PTO, as it currently is. The whole concept of midlife crisis is at root about the death of anticipation in consummation.

27   I lack the space here to even begin to touch the literature on collective memory and its individual-level equivalent, the literature on oral history. Both of these could have much to say to RTO conceptions of outcome.

Psychoanalysis and the Theory of the Subject

ANTHONY ELLIOTT

The most radical and thoroughgoing attempt to erase the subject," writes Anthony Giddens, "is found not in structuralism, or in Deleuze and Guattari's *Anti-Oedipe*, but in Mach's positivism" (1979, 44–45). Yet, if it is so that positivistic philosophies lack any account of the reflexive and affective dimensions of subjectivity, it is also the case that a strange positivistic haunting is to be found in those alternative theoretical traditions that have sought to promote a recovery of subject. This is perhaps nowhere more evident than in Freud's psychoanalysis, the topic of this essay. To say, as Freud did, that the unconscious does not think is not only to underscore the profoundly imaginary dimensions of subjectivity, but also to call into question the logical form and past achievements of the social sciences. Yet, in an ironic twist, Freud's invention of psychoanalytic methods is, in various respects, closely connected with a naturalistic standpoint in social philosophy and shares an assumption that the logical frameworks of the natural and social sciences are in key respects the same.

A central purpose of this essay is to explore the theory of psychical imagination, especially of fantasy, uncovered (and required) by Freud. A related purpose is to examine some of the mechanisms by which Freud displaces this location of the creative and self-instituting capacity of the unconscious imagination. In what follows, I explore Freud's attempt to locate the foundations of psychical life in terms of a specifically modernist tension between imagination and rationality; this tension pervades much of Freud's work. In particular, I focus on his foundational (though unfinished) text, the "Project for a Scientific Psychology."[1] My argument is that the continuing significance of Freud's work for contemporary theory rests precisely in its uncertainty over fantasy and the unconscious imagination, an uncertainty that shifts between the boundaries of inside and outside, anxiety and control, psychic flux and scientific authorization. The final sections of the essay consider the relation between imagination and specialized knowledge in the age of liquid modernity.

The Origins of Psychoanalysis

The "Project for a Scientific Psychology" of (Freud 1895/1966) is a text marked by Freud's desire for mastery, an attempt to subject the workings of mind to the laws of motion on the physiological basis of neurology. The psyche, in this proto-draft of psychoanalytic theory, is conceptualized as an "apparatus," one made up of various subsystems and mechanisms. The study of hysteria and of neurotic disorders led Freud to grant the psyche a neuromechanical logic of its own, a mode of action that receives, transforms, and discharges energetic excitations. Freud's aim is to understand the laws of psychical economy, to master them, to render them transparent. The opening declaration of the "Project" is indeed full of self-masterful zeal and scientific certainty: "The intention is to furnish a psychology that shall be a natural science: that is, to represent psychical processes as quantitatively determinate states of specifiable material particles, thus making those processes perspicuous and free from contradiction" (1895/1966, 295).

Freud theorizes his multisystemic "psychical apparatus" as interlocking agencies of excitation homologous to physical energy, hence the grounding of psychology in natural science. He argues for the development of a quantitative framework in order to grasp, and thus also to colonize, the nature of mental functioning, thus rendering the secrets of psychical energy "free from contradiction."

Yet, while the introduction of this quantitative viewpoint derives much of its impetus from modernist procedures of enframing, ordering, and mastery, the "Project" is also rich in speculative insight about the imaginary contours of the primitive libidinal substratum. Repression and defense, the libidinal drives with their competing forces of energy, ego organization, and memory: these ideas are all present and inform the account of mental life sketched in this text.

What is perhaps most immediately striking about the "Project" is the manner in which Freud argues that the psychical elaboration of sexuality is not to be found in some free-floating realm of images and scenes, but rather in the objective determinism of energy and forces. Freud conceptualizes the heart of the matter as the transformation of energy or quantity (abbreviated as Q) into perceptual and instinctual stimuli within a neuronic framework. The psychical apparatus is a complex network of neurons, a network that follows the general laws of motion. The dynamics of force, attraction, and defense, Freud argues, dominates the mental apparatus. Through a blending of the ideas of Hermann von Helmholtz and J. F. Herbart, neurophysiological concepts are brought to bear on the functioning of desire and pleasure.[2] Quantity dominates the psychical apparatus from start to finish in the "Project": it is conceptualized as an energetic current that fills or drains, charges or discharges neurons. The powerful intensities of energy thus function as the primary source of psychical excitations, what Freud describes as a "cathecting" of neurons.

If it is the motions of energy that bring a psychical movement or action about in the first place (through the charging or discharging of neurons), then the registration of experience, including the capacity to store memories, should vary according to the flow of quantity available at any particular moment. Yet Freud's account of energy as the primary motor power of psychic functioning rejects this possibility, and instead connects the nature of quantity to what he calls "neuronic inertia," or, more commonly, the "constancy principle." The principle of constancy means that the psychic apparatus tends to reduce its own accumulation of energy to zero, to divest itself of force and tension. "The mind," as Richard Wollheim writes of Freud's "Project," "tries to expel all energy as and when it enters the system" (1971, 45). The psyche, then, works to defuse the impact of energetic excitations, to maintain the existing level of quantity as low as possible; and insofar as Freud's thought grants the psyche a determining power at all at this stage of his thinking, which will become clear when we consider the relation between energy and its psychic registration, it can be said that the creative function of such differentiation is itself central to the mental constitution of human beings.

The elimination of energy from the psychic apparatus, however, turns out to be not so simple. Freud's conception of the energetic filling of neurons and of the principle of inertia (that is, the draining of such quantity charges) only goes so far to comprehend the manner in which the psyche receives stimulation from the outside world, as with the nature and function of perception. The difficulty that arises is that the psychical apparatus cannot escape from, it cannot eliminate the voracious energy of internal demands (such as the needs of hunger and the desires of sexuality) in the same manner. As a result of internal demand, which produces an accumulation of energy, the psychical apparatus, Freud says, "must learn to tolerate a store of quantity sufficient to meet the demands for specific action." In other words, the mind must be able to register feelings and thoughts in such a way as to bring together internal demand with the objective conditions of discharge. In this way, when the mind is stimulated by certain thoughts, feelings, and wishes, the self will be able to respond with an appropriate action, and not some random response. At such a level of analysis, this involves a meshing of psychical enjoyment with the lived immediacy of self-other relations. As Freud puts this: "At first, the human organism is incapable of bringing about the specific action [of satisfaction]. It takes place by *extraneous help*, when the attention of an experienced person is drawn to the child's state by discharge along the path of internal change. In this way this path of discharge acquires a secondary function of the highest importance, that of communication, and the initial helplessness of human beings is the *primal source* of all *moral motives*" (1895/1966, 318). Crucially, the question of energy and the path of its discharge is inseparable from the question of communication, the dynamics of intersubjectivity. Seen in this light, energy is at once anchored in and the guarantor of intersubjective space.

But what of discharge? The ultimate and central means in which this is now explored—the problem of energy and the internal world—is through the pressing of quantity into the mode of operation of the psychical itself. Freud separates the sensory neurons into two types: o-neurons and u-neurons. An exegesis of the differences between these two classes is something that has already been well accomplished in the psychoanalytic literature (see Sulloway 1979, ch. 4; Wollheim 1971, ch. 2). In general terms, the o-neurons receive stimulation from the outside world (as in perception), whereas the u-neurons receive stimulation from the internal world (such as the needs of hunger). In Wollheim's gloss, "The o-neurones are totally permeable, they offer no resistance to the flow of quantity through them, and, consequently, are totally unaffected by it, whereas u-neurones are to some degree or other impermeable, they offer some resistance to, and hence retain permanent traces of, quantity as it flows through them" (46). The psyche in this conception is not defined by whether or not energy is eliminated, but by the maintenance of a certain level of tension in order for discharge. And discharge, Wollheim writes, is understood by Freud as a process of psychic repetition: "If a given quantity recurrently follows one specific path through the u-system, then it is safe to assume that this is the path along which relief, for that quantity, is to be found" (48).

There remains, however, the need to discriminate between the relief of discharges as regards the primary and secondary functions of the psyche, once it is granted that there is an originary productive dynamism at this energetic level of human functioning. The category of tension in the "Project" is linked to a regulatory mechanism that Freud calls the "pleasure-unpleasure series." Simply put, Freud postulates an equivalence between the experience of unpleasure and a rise in tension, on the one hand, and the experience of pleasure and a decrease in tension, on the other. The psyche for Freud functions according to the avoidance of unpleasure; pleasure, as indicated, is understood in terms of the sensation of discharge. At this point, however, a modification to Freud's energetic model, in particular to the functioning of the secondary processes, necessarily imposes itself. To understand how the pleasure-unpleasure combination achieves registration within the psychical apparatus, Freud introduces the concept of consciousness, which is conceived as an inhibiting system of bound energy that functions at a constant level. Consciousness is conceptualized in the "Project" through the positing of a third class of neuron: w-neurons. What changes everything in the discussion of the psychic apparatus at this point is that, although consciousness and reality testing can be understood as determined by quantity, Freud insists that the flow of energy as such never enters the w-system of neurons. Instead, he speaks of a transformation from quantity to quality with the mediation of an "indication of reality." Subjective experience of the outer world requires an inhibition of libidinal energy; this is an inhibition that is central to the capacity to distinguish between a desire for an object and the object itself.

An inhibition of quantity thus takes place in the psychical translation from the primary to the secondary process. Freud asserts that, as quantity flows through the u-system and is influenced by the memory of pleasure or pain, paths of discharge will be sought that bring internal needs into line with reality testing. That is, the psyche can either seize on or defend against the power of wishes as intersecting with interpersonal relationships. Meanwhile, the ego enters directly into this task of discrimination, pressing back memory images of the wished-for object in the primary process, and pressing toward "indications of reality" that will permit for a specific action to be carried out in line with internal demands and external requirements. As Freud puts this: "Where, then, an ego exists, it is bound to inhibit primary psychical processes." This inhibiting function of the ego involves a shift from energy as free-flowing in the primary process to energy as bounded in the secondary process. This shift also informs Freud's view that the ego can assert its rule over unconscious conflict and division; this can be pictured as a kind of reclaiming of subjective control in the name of rationality.

If the capacity for discrimination between imagination and reality is what sustains reflexive selfhood, however, it is also implicated in the realm of pathological defense. The nub of the problem, as the "Project" continuously reminds us, is quantitative. For excessive quantity conflicts with these regulatory functions of the ego; excessive quantity outweighs the ego's activity of inhibiting; indeed, in an act of violent incorporation, excessive libidinal eruptions can fuse a memory image of a wished-for object with perception itself. In this case, memory will be confused with reality, as happens with the conversion of affective intensities in hysteria, displacements of energy in obsession, and so on. The eruption of excessive quantity lies at the root of emotional pain, leaving the subject overwhelmed and anxious; it also leaves its mark in the form of permanent memory traces. Such an overflowing of energy is damaging because its path of release is illusory: discharge is sought through hallucination, not reality.

Seen in this light, the quantitative focus in Freud's "Project" redramatizes the relationship between libidinal desire and reality testing, particularly in the characterization of memory (that is, the memory of an experience of pleasure-unpleasure) as a condition in which the sense of reality is constituted. "Unpleasure," Freud writes in a sentence that anticipates the *Weltanschauung* (worldview) of psychoanalysis, "remains the sole means of education." (There is a close tie, it should be noted, between the negativity Freud attributes to "unpleasure" and the development of notions such as "frustration" [Bion] and "lack" [Lacan] in post-Freudian theory.) It is this linking of unpleasure and reality, this crushing of the narcissistic self-unity of the psyche, where Freud locates autonomous subjectivity as the capacity of the mind to distinguish between imagination and memory, on the one hand, and indications of reality, through perception, on the other. The creative mastery of this discrimination not only underwrites our mental capacities for attention, understanding, and cognitive thought; it also leads to a critical distance from the disabling influence of primary process regression.

It will be apparent from the foregoing commentary that the psychical apparatus as detailed by Freud in the "Project" is fixed on a mechanical register, quantitative, deterministic, and operationalized by three types of neurons. Indeed, in a letter to his friend and mentor Wilhelm Fliess, Freud says of the "Project": "Everything seemed to mesh, the gear mechanism fitted together, one got the impression the thing now really was a machine that would shortly go by itself" (Freud 1985, 146). A mental machine whose mechanisms are to function free from distorting contradictions: the determinism, and its guiding fantasy of control, is particularly evident here. In this quantitative psychology of desire, the transition from physical tension to a properly psychical elaboration is one of excitations that enter into the interconnecting pathways imprinted in the neuronic framework. In many respects, Freud's unyielding search throughout the "Project" for the quantitative foundations of psychological behavior drew its animus from his deep faith in science, reason, and objective knowledge. With such a faith, he deployed a litany of mechanistic metaphors—"charges," "quantity," "apparatus," "system," and the like—in the search for a truly *scientific* psychology. Indeed, the "Project" is a text that maintains the hopes and ambitions of positivism throughout, modifying the logic in operation at every point in which psychical life resists classification, squeezing the heterogeneous flux of desire, with Freud's characteristic relentless determination, into the design of an established scientific worldview. Freud's deep conviction that the psychical dimensions of human experience are open to codification by science is itself subject to repetition throughout this text: with further modification or tinkering to the system, sure knowledge lies around the next corner. In fact, even in the *Outline of Psychoanalysis*, written during the last year of his life, Freud expresses the hope that the psychoanalytic contribution to knowledge may one day "exercise a direct influence, by means of particular chemical substances, on the amounts of energy and their distribution in the mental apparatus" (1938/1964, 182).

However, it is now time to assess the central tension in Freud's work, a tension that runs throughout the "Project," between rationality and knowledge, on the one hand, and imagination and fantasy on the other. This specifically modernist tension is inscribed in Freud's division of psychical functioning between reality, logic, and the pleasure-unpleasure series. A number of important problems arise at this point. What, exactly, is the relationship between imagination and reality? What is left of imagination after the subject perceives an "indication of reality"? How do energy quantities shape psychical qualities? And is this a process of translation or of mediation? Freud's answer to this dilemma, as we have seen, is that energy, as the lifeblood of imagination, marks, structures, and indeed invades in mental disturbance the functioning of the psyche:

> Wishful cathexis carried to the point of hallucination and a complete generation of unpleasure, involving a complete expenditure of defence, may be described as "primary psychical process." On the other hand, those processes which are only made possible by a good cathexis of the ego and which represent a moderation of the primary processes may be described as "psychical secondary processes." It will be seen that the sine qua non of the latter is a correct exploitation of

the indications of reality and that this is only possible when there is an inhibition on the part of the ego.—We have thus put forward a hypothesis to the effect that, during the process of wishing, inhibition on the part of the ego leads to a moderation of the cathexis of the object wished-for, which makes it possible for that object to be recognized as not being a real one.

The objectivistic consequence of this description is one that derives from Freud's formalistic separation of imagination and logic, a separation in which imagination is subordinate to reason. Freud stamps the ideology of the Enlightenment onto this mapping of the psyche by insisting that an indication of reality is constituted when thinking is divorced from the processes of imagination, an "inhibition of the process of wishing." However, there is nothing in this description that accounts for the transformation of psychical energies into ego inhibition and discrimination; this difficulty is all the more compounded by Freud's uncoupling of consciousness from imagination in this passage.[3] Note too, that there is nothing in this perspective that suggests why excessive energy should overwhelm the subject in such a manner as to produce permanent memory traces.

But Freud maintains throughout the "Project" that the question of subjective meaning is an economic or quantitative one. For Freud, the quantitative buildup of tension is the pure point of energetic origin in the constitution of psychic functioning. However, as Paul Ricoeur has argued, the relation posited between quantity and quality soon outstrips itself, taking Freud's deterministic hypothesis in the "Project" to the breaking point. In this respect, the question that arises is this: What brings quantity, or energy, *into relation with* quality, or psychic meaning? The difficulty of coming to grips with this question within the energetic framework posited in the "Project" can be demonstrated by considering the nature of fantasy and, for our purposes here, especially the founding of fantasy.

The construction of fantasy, as various traditions in psychoanalytic theory make clear, involves the child in perpetual image constructions of its world. Fantasies are constituted through a transcription of the tension of biological need into the representational "expression of wishes and passions," to invoke Isaacs's definition (1991, 96). This means that when a longed-for object (initially the maternal breast) is found to be missing (through, for example, the unavailability of the mother), the child hallucinates it in its absence. In doing so, the breast is represented, and actually experienced, in fantasy, even though the mother is not present in material reality.

Now, even from the points raised thus far, it will be clear that there are immense conceptual difficulties in fleshing out the structure of fantasy in terms of the quantitative model offered in Freud's "Project." What emerges most strongly, perhaps, is the impossibility of assigning some energetic origin to something, namely fantasy, that posits an object as both existing and nonexistent; the founding fantasy is in itself a kind of "playing" with the unavailability of the mother. This seems to suggest that, in making something out of nothing, in the creation of a mental image, the psyche is located in an imaginary function that exceeds anything suggested by the quantitative aspects of Freud's theory.

What is in question, in other words, is the whole concept of the representational dynamics of energy itself. The representational status accorded to the psyche in the "Project" is that of the registration of perceived reality, of the perceptual apparatus. Perceptual stimulation, in the charging of neurons, is at the root of the construction of psychic reality and fantasies. (This proposed intersecting of reality and imagination is further expanded in a letter to Fliess in which Freud comments that fantasy is "derived from things that have been heard but understood [only] subsequently," a formulation to which Freud adds that "all their material is, of course, genuine"; 1892–1899/1966, 247). In these proto-psychoanalytical formulations, fantasy is viewed by Freud as a reproduction of something already perceived, an integration of elements that have been pressed into the internal world from elsewhere, whether the outside world (that is, of "things heard") or the neuronic system itself (through the discharging of energy). Backing away from the glimpses of the creative and dynamic nature of the unconscious he had in his clinical work, it is as if, once he has discerned the problem of subjectivity, experience, and meaning, Freud is anxious to be done with it. Fantasy in this view is a derived, or secondary, phenomenon. Yet it is precisely in the realm of fantasy, in the fantasmatic creations of the unconscious imagination, that the psyche outstrips biological need as well as the imprint of external reality.

Problems of Interpretation

It is with the "Project for a Scientific Psychology" that Freud first maps the psychical world, a world of free and bound energy, hallucinatory wish-fulfillment and delayed thought, disruptive affect and amassed excitation. As regards the erotic powers of unconscious imagination, this account of the psyche is to provide a skeletal structure for Freud's subsequent theoretical formulations on repression and defense, on the drives, on the primary process mechanisms of condensation and displacement, and on the time-lessness of infantile wishes. The "Project" is thus Freud's response, as a first approximation, to the problem of the turmoil of primitive mental life on perception and thought. It is a model that offers an access route to the distinctive features of normal mental functioning, that is, the inhibition of the primary process in the separating out of hallucination and perception. This separating out, or reality testing, is what secures planned action or agency in the intersubjective world; imagining, perceiving, and reasoning is how the human subject gathers its bearings. But it is also a model that recognizes the seductive power of instant gratification and hallucinatory wish-fulfillment, the hallmarks of the unconscious. It is a model that encounters the uncompromising and distorting realm of repressed desire; this is a conceptual structure that trades with terrifying hallucinations and traumatic inhibitions (a trade informed by the pathogenic experiences of the hysterics Freud encountered in the fashioning of psychoanalytic treat-ment). The "Project" is therefore rooted at once in observed reality and theorization. It presents a path that leads from the physiological substrata of the mind, enters and travels through the troubled waters of uncon-scious affective life, and then returns to the conceptual shores of scientific certainty—or at least this would have been so had Freud completed the text.

However, within this framework it is actually impossible, as we have seen, to think about the productive work of the psyche, the creative inde-termination of imagination and thought. The profound tension here is that Freud's "Project" uncovers and brings to light the powers of imagina-tion (hallucinatory wish-fulfillment and ego inhibition frame the discon-tinuity of human subjectivity), while simultaneously denying the full force of desire in the name of science, rationality, and objectivity. Freud reaches toward the self-instituting capacity of unconscious imagination, yet, caught up in the established mastery of science, displaces this element in favor of the psyche as a black box of energetic inputs and outputs. This brings into focus the incompatibility, in the cultural, historical, and scien-tific context of Freud's world, between imagination and science, desire and objective knowledge. And yet, as the "Project" itself demonstrates, the subordinate place that the imagination occupies to reason refuses to be contained; desire comes to invade and outstrip the colonizing power as-cribed to rationality. The disruptiveness of the primary process in this text works in part, then, to derail the language of science, resisting the enfram-ing and classification to which it has been submitted.

It is for this reason, perhaps, that Freud will abandon the "Project," failing to request the return of the manuscript from Fliess (to whom it was dispatched for criticism) and also omitting any mention of it in his autobiographical writings. The "Project" can therefore be understood to function as a displaced text, a kind of founding act of repression in the constitution of psychoanalysis itself. From this point of view, it can be said that Freud banishes the "Project," a text scarred by the scientific worldview of the late nineteenth century, to respond more effectively to his discovery of the unconscious imagination. Indeed, this banishment functions as a powerful form of liberation for Freud. For it was precisely at this point of his career that Freud abandoned his seduction theory, the notion that every neurosis conceals a history of real sexual seduction and actual trauma, and replaced it with a more critical interpretation of the relation of psychic life to the outer world. Central to this shift in Freud's approach was a radical revaluation of the internal processing of external reality, especially of how individuals interpret, frame, and fantasize experience (including memories of sexual experiences in childhood). Retracting his seduction theory, Freud wrote to Fliess of his "certain insight that there are no indications of reality in the unconscious, so that one cannot distinguish between truth and fiction that has been cathected with affect" (quoted in Masson 1984, 264–265). But if the unconscious fantasy life of the individual is not merely a copy of objective reality, then this significantly increases the autonomy of the imagination in its dealings with the social world. As John Toews comments:

> The collapse of the seduction theory in the fall of 1897 was marked by a collapse of Freud's confidence in his ability to use evidence from his patients' fantasies in reconstructing the real history of event sequences ... but this collapse was transformed into a "triumph" by his recognition that fantasies might be read a different way, as signs of the unconscious intentions that produced them rather than as the forgotten events to which they referred. From this perspective the "embellishments" and "sublimations" of fantasy were not so much outworks to be demolished as obscure revelations of a different kind of truth, the truth of unconscious psychical activity. They were openings into a hidden world of "psychic reality" that was not passive and objective but active and subjective, a world of unconscious psychosexual desire. (1991, 513)

Once Freud granted fantasy an active and subjective dimension, therefore, the psychic realm no longer functioned as a mirror to objective reality. "Freud democratized genius by giving everyone a creative unconscious"

(Rieff 1961, 36), writes one commentator of this recasting of the process of psychic investment. But what emerges in Freud, throughout various formulations and explanations, is a conceptual recognition of the location of desire that outstrips even this "active" or "subjective" component of fantasy. This amounts to saying that Freud's uncovering of the creative unconscious is at once imperative and displaced, given that it is precisely this fantasmatic dimension of human experience that captures the impasse between the inside and the outside, between the troubles of the life of the mind and the troubles of the social world. It is central insofar as Freud takes unconscious fantasy as the stake of meaning, deconstructing the radical otherness of the sense-making process, all the way from moral prohibitions to psychological disturbance. Dreams, of course, provide Freud's key reference point here in the attempt to put desire in its proper place—not merely in the sense of explaining desire and its difficulty away, but of understanding the ambiguity and undecidability of wish-fulfillment in its encounter with the primary processes of condensation, displacement, and distortion. Seen from this angle, the attachment of meaning to experience can be traced to unconscious wishes and intentions, and this for Freud forms part of the detective work of psychoanalytical practice.

There is, however, another Freud, sometimes explicit, sometimes less so, on the limits of psychoanalytical interpretation. This is the Freud who questions the nature and limitations of scientific knowledge in Western culture, and, in particular, it is the Freud who locates a hidden world of unconscious impulses and fantasies as dislocating the scaffolding of psychoanalysis itself. This emphasis stresses that scientific knowledge, even in the sphere of psychoanalysis, cannot provide protection from anxiety as regards living with the turbulence of desire. It cannot protect from anxiety because of the matchings and misalliances of passion and knowledge, fantasy and rationality, which inevitably recur and which also mark the impossibility of limiting the space of psychoanalytic interpretation. That is to say, desire at once confers and exceeds meaning, locating the human subject at a point of Otherness that is both ecstatic and intolerable. Consider, for example, Freud's comments on the "blind spot" of dreams, a point that is always already beyond the control or mastery of any shared, intersubjective knowledge: "We become aware during the work of interpretation that . . . there is a tangle of dream-thoughts which cannot be unravelled and which moreover adds nothing to our knowledge of the content of the dream. This is the dream's navel, the spot where it reaches down into the unknown. The dream-thoughts to which we are led by interpretation have to, in an entirely universal manner, remain without any definite endings; they are bound to branch out in every direction into the intricate network of our world of thought" (1900/1953, vol. 5, 525). In other words, the creative unconscious (branching out in all directions of mind and world) is that which plays tricks with explanation and rationalism.

The domain of imagination, as I emphasized earlier, was never fully integrated with the core suppositions of psychoanalytic theory; it was left by Freud as a kind of splitting or rupture of the inside and the outside. The balance of this inside/outside dualism tipped in different directions throughout Freud's career, and I have previously connected these strands of thinking to a modernist and postmodernist Freud on the powers and limits of the human imagination (A. Elliott 2002, 17–18). Freud the modernist is forever attempting, implicitly or otherwise, to enframe and master the laws of psychic processes, to lock the radical otherness of unconscious experience within the determinable. From this angle, the inventor of psychoanalysis is in the last resort colonizing the realm of desire and pleasure in order to know it, to make subjectivity more manageable. The "seduction" of trauma, the "secret" of dreams, the "sway" of reality over the pleasure principle, the "phylogenesis" of Oedipal rivalry: psychoanalysis revolves around creating conceptualization, classification, and boundaries. And yet Freud's metapsychology also works against itself, acknowledging the limits of science in favor of fantasy and the imagination. Representation, symbolism, hallucination, fantasy, omnipotence of thought: Freud refuses the human subject an easy relation to itself or the outside world. Questioning the enlightened values of the scientific tradition, this is the Freud who speaks of the fantastic creations of the unconscious imagination, of the "dark continent" of feminine sexuality, of the uncanny in sexuality and in language, and of psychoanalytic interpretation as interminable.

Something similar goes on in contemporary psychoanalysis. The creative power of unconscious fantasy is at once embraced and denied in a range of psychoanalytic traditions, as if the split in Freud between knowledge and imagination is condemned to repeat itself. The key strands of psychoanalysis that attempt to understand something about the self-instituting dimensions of fantasy range from the libertarian Freudianism of Herbert Marcuse, through the Kleinian and post-Kleinian tradition (with its strong emphasis on creativity and the aesthetic process), and is now perhaps best represented in the French psychoanalytic feminist work of theorists such as Julia Kristeva and Luce Irigaray. Here there is the explicit attempt to think of fantasy as a realm of indetermination, as central to a certain state of human relatedness, a generative space in which the capacity for feeling and thought develops, a capacity which is the primary basis for the transformation of human relationships.

There is, however, another strand in post-Freudian psychoanalysis that has sought to reduce the space of radical imagination in subjectivity and the social process. Sometimes this has been quite explicitly addressed to the stakes of knowledge and self-mastery, especially in the U.S. school of ego psychology, which tends to sidestep questions of sexuality and desire to upgrade the powers of the ego along the normative paths of rationality and social adaptation. Sometimes it has also been done in more radical schools of psychoanalysis; Lacanian theory, for example, flirts with a structuralist advocacy of the colonizing role of language in the constitution of desire, a standpoint that arguably displaces many of Freud's core insights into the creative figurability of fantasy and sexuality. Whether expressed in the name of rationalism or structuralism, however, the underlying aim is the attempt to oppose knowledge and structure (as objective reality) to subjectivity and fantasy and to wipe out the creative, self-instituting realm of representation and passion in which subjectivity and history interweave.

Pushed to an extreme, this reintroduction of reality leads to a rigid externalization of psychical space, that is, back to Freud's seduction hypothesis that psychic process mirrors objective reality, pure and simple. Indeed, this is precisely the charge that Jeffrey Masson makes against Freud, challenging him on rejecting the actuality of seduction in favor of fantasy and the Oedipus complex, in his book *The Assault on Truth: Freud's Suppression of the Seduction Theory.* "By shifting the emphasis from an actual world of sadness, misery, and cruelty," writes Masson, "to an internal stage on which actors performed invented dramas for an invisible audience of their own creation, Freud began a trend away from the real world that . . . is at the root of the present-day sterility of psychoanalysis and psychiatry throughout the world" (1984, 144).[4] The act of fantasy or memory for Masson is instead one that recalls real experience and actual trauma; there is, as it were, a one-to-one correspondence between the trauma of abuse or seduction and mental disturbance. Yet it is exactly this point of correspondence, or, more accurately, the wish for a direct fit between mind and world, that reveals most forcefully the distorting element in Masson's discourse. Without in any way denying the devastating psychic and social consequences of child abuse and trauma, it seems to me that Masson's rejection of fantasy is made in the name of establishing certitude and transparency. It is as if he believes that subjectivity, once stripped of fantasy, can operate without ambiguity and ambivalence; a uniform, standardized communication can take place between self and society; and mental disturbance or illness can be seen as the result of similar or identical instances of actual trauma. Seen in this light, as Jeffrey Prager writes of the contemporary attack on Freud and psychoanalysis, "Masson [expresses] nostalgia for a pre- (or early) Freudian world . . . a world where things are precisely as they appear, always reflecting a hard, obdurate reality that can be easily and readily perceived. No interpreting self, no unconscious one. What happens happens, and there is no mystery as to how one processes, interprets, and gives meaning to those occurrences" (1994, 214).

The relation between imagination and rationality documented thus far has been primarily considered from a psychoanalytic perspective. We need, however, to consider the broader social, cultural, and political influences shaping the core features of the imaginary in the contemporary epoch. We also need to consider the impact of specialized, expert knowledge on the domain of imagination and of the pathologies this produces.

Psychoanalysis and Social Science

Perhaps the best way to approach the broader sociological implications of the foregoing argument is to consider the linkage between the origins of psychoanalysis and modernity. One prominent interpretation points to the erosion of authority and community in the light of the waning of tradition, custom, and habit. Such a viewpoint is perhaps best expressed in the writings of Philip Rieff (1966, 1979). Rieff argues that psychoanalytic theory and therapy becomes "culturally appropriate" with the shift from traditional "positive communities," which anchored belief systems and symbols in stable social networks of custom, family, and religion, to "negative communities," in which individuals create meaning in terms of their own personal experience. In premodern societies, when people were in pain or distress, they sought meaning from the sureties of cultural tradition, habit, and religion. Positive communities might thus be said to have created their own therapeutic order. Modernity, as a posttraditional order, offers no such guarantees as concerns personal doubts and anxieties. In conditions of modernity, self and society are in greater flux, and hence there is a turn inward toward private, emotional experience. "In the age of psychologizing," Rieff writes, "clarity about oneself supersedes devotion to an ideal as the model of right conduct" (56).

Psychoanalysis becomes of crucial cultural significance, according to Rieff, because it forms a central connecting point between dislocating outer experience and the creation of inner meaning. In Rieff's terms, psychoanalysis emerges at a point of cultural "deconversion," a time of breakdown in frameworks of meaning, of startling social transformations and dislocations. With this erosion of tradition and, most important, religious authority, Freud's search for meaning in dreams, wishes, desires, and fantasies was a radical counterassertion of human possibility and hope. In a world of dislocation, uncertainty, and change, psychoanalytic theory and therapy creates an openness to the multiplicity of modern experience, offering the possibility of meaning and well-being. As Rieff puts it, psychoanalysis offers the individual a chance "to keep going."

The analysis set out by Rieff is of considerable critical power in terms of grasping the ways the cultivation of self-understanding and intimacies of the self emerge against the backdrop of the dislocations and uncertainties of the modern social order. Indeed, in recent formulations of this dynamic, it is often argued that, in the posttraditional order of modernity, self-revision or -reflexivity is intrinsic to the constitution of self-identity and intersubjective social relations (Giddens 1991). In terms of the opening out of the personal sphere, psychoanalytic theory and therapy can be said to offer individuals a radical purchase on the dilemmas of living in the modern epoch. From such a standpoint, it can be said that the subject is split, but crucially this is a splitting open to self-understanding. There is little in this account, however, to question the way an awareness of the more productive elements of imagination, and of unconscious imagination in particular, should have become open to cultural transmission at this historical point. Rieff's analysis seems to imply a causal connection between the breakdown of tradition and the rise of psychoanalysis. But, why psychoanalysis? Why was this conceptual map created to represent people's experience of subjectivity, sexuality, and meaning? Is the turn inward, of which Rieff speaks, merely a matter of the weakening of cultural tradition?

Unquestionably, reflexiveness relating to intimacies of the self is a highly personal matter, and there is an enormous variety of psychological approaches and schools from which people might choose today. However, the core importance of therapy, psychoanalytic or otherwise, does not relate primarily to issues of personal choice. Rather, it relates to the self-awareness of human imagination and the structuring role of fantasy in personal and social life. Rieff is led to obscure the decisive role of psychical imagination in the domain of culture by privileging social transformation, practice, and ideology. Yet the actual practice of psychoanalysis or psychoanalytic therapy can surely only be brought into existence if the discoveries of Freud, as founding father, hold up and can withstand critical examination. All of which is to say that psychoanalysis comes to depend more and more on criteria that are internal to its own legitimation, that is, the recognition of the structuring role of fantasy.

In analyzing the rise of psychoanalysis and therapy in modern societies, Rieff is undoubtedly correct to stress the central role of rapid social change in the fracturing of human experience. In the midst of an ever expanding globalization of the social environment, tradition no longer supplies binding cultural prescriptions, and selfhood as such becomes intrinsically problematic. By means of psychoanalysis and therapy, people can find a new language for addressing, and thereby coming to terms with, private dilemmas. For Rieff, however, this correspondence between the loss of tradition and the rise of therapy appears culturally structured and fixed: psychoanalysis functions essentially as a substitute for traditional moral, political, and religious guidelines. Without severing its relation to social transformation, however, we should also see the emergence of psychoanalysis as part and parcel of the modernist attempt to embrace imagination, to uncover the contradiction and conflict of human passion. Understanding the development of the self in modern societies, particularly its problematization, should focus on the imaginary capacities for self-representation and self-construction through which individuals express and transform themselves. In this view, psychoanalysis is not simply a social fabrication, but a creation of imagination and fantasy as well. We can thus supplement Rieff's account by highlighting that psychoanalysis plays a crucial role in the modern epoch in uncovering the presence of psychic processes hidden from awareness. The virtue of such an approach is that it underscores the point that it is the creative power of the unconscious imagination that underpins this searching of our innermost hopes and dreads.

In political terms, however, there is more at stake here than just personal and cultural self-understanding. Not only does modernity promote an uncovering of reflexiveness as concerns human subjectivity and the radical imagination, but this reflexiveness is itself embedded in a discourse of science and expert knowledge. That is to say, reflexiveness does not exist in a vacuum; it is situated in psychological, cultural, and political networks. And it follows from this that such reflexiveness can also be drawn into, and indeed fuel, asymmetrical relations of power. This embedding of reflexiveness in asymmetrical relations of power is a central component of a discourse that I call the *psychologization of desire,* those institutionalized aspects of specialized knowledge in the sphere of human sexuality. Doctors, social workers, psychologists, psychiatrists, and indeed many psycho-analysts (when analysis is practiced reductively) trade in the isolation, classification, and consolidation of a cohesive code of sexual rules. In ideological terms, the driving force here is the quest for sure knowledge: it is thanks to expert psychological insight that the "right" or "wrong" approach can be applied to troubled relationships in the home, school, business, bureaucratic organizations, and government agencies. Psychological expertise offers reassurance against the insecurities of living. Psychological know-how is also regularly used to keep at bay personal and cultural ambivalence, as the problems of daily life are recast in a fixed, technical vocabulary.

Surprisingly, Rieff has little to say about this rationalization of psycho-analytic knowledge. He does, as was stressed earlier, credit psychoanalytic therapy with supplying new personal and cultural guidelines in the late modern age. With the opening out of the personal sphere, psychoanalysis and psychotherapy become less centered on normative issues of a cure and more and more a matter of self-actualization. Yet the prospects for self-actualization are deeply constrained, by factors both inside and outside psychoanalysis. Rieff acknowledges that the professionalization and rou-tinization of therapy has softened the critical edge of psychoanalysis and has produced a "boredom" in psychoanalytic societies. Yet he fails to consider that the independence of psychoanalysis, at the levels of theory and clinical practice, has often proved incompatible with the authority of specialized knowledge in the psychological professions. For this reason alone, much that is vital and alive in psychoanalysis has declined into dogmatism. These are issues I now wish to consider in some detail.

To comprehend this psychologization of desire, we have to move away from an exclusive concentration on the sociology of modern societies and look to the structuring of fantasy and power in the modern era. Consider, for example, the creation of psychoanalysis and its embedding in moder-nity's institutional dynamics. Freud, as we have seen, uncovered the con-nections between self-identity and unconscious sexuality in a revolution-ary way, revolutionary because it led men and women into a reflexive encounter with the condition of subjectivity as fractured, split, and am-bivalent. At the same time, he anchored psychoanalysis in a medical dis-course of science, the design of which, I have suggested, sought to effect a subordination of inner nature to human control, order, and mastery.

This preoccupation with desire as subordinate to the world of scientific knowledge and power has also taken place as regards the cultural, institu-tional development of psychoanalysis. Once more, it is fairly easy to trace out the interplay of anxiety and denial, insight and repression, which pervades the ideological function of psychoanalysis in modern societies. Against the backdrop of Freudian psychoanalysis, people seek to explore their deepest intrapsychic experiences and personal relationships, an exploration that is underwritten by the creativity of the unconscious imagination. The Freudian revolution is, in this sense, a revolution of the personal sphere, an opening out of the self to anxiety and ambivalence. This infiltration of Freudian psychoanalysis into the everyday social world, however, also brings it directly into contact with those institutional dimensions of specialized knowledge and power. In many instances, this contact has led to a deadening of psychoanalysis as an open-ended system of meaning and also to a routinization in the application of its theoretical and conceptual resources. A marked self-containment and fixation of Freudian concepts has taken place, as psychoanalysis has increasingly become a world unto itself. The reduction of psychoanalysis to a medical, mechanistic treatment of behavior pathologies, seen as a method for adapting the individual to an objective, knowable reality, became widespread in the psychoanalytic movement, especially in the United States. Indeed, many psychoanalysts still understand the aims of clinical technique in such terms. On the other hand, and especially in France, psychoanalysis has been pulled in a highly abstract direction. In France, psychoanalysis became increasingly divorced from its founding concern with representation, fantasy, and passion, and instead was projected into the academic discourse of philosophy, being read as a dislocation of theoretical knowledge itself. Sherry Turkle expresses well the differences between these cultural, institutional appropriations of psychoanalysis:

> In the story of what happened to psychoanalysis in the United States, the fact that the "American Freud" was nearly monopolized by physicians, a social group under the greatest possible pressure to emphasize the useful, took the general American preference for the pragmatic and raised it to a higher power. In France, the psychiatric resistance to psychoanalysis allowed it a long period of incubation in the world of artists and writers before a significant breakthrough into medicine, a pattern which reinforced the French tendency to take ideas and invest them with philosophical and ideological significance instead of turning them outward toward problem solving. (1992, 49)

These cultural differences, between "useful" and "abstract" appropriations of psychoanalysis at the institutional level, have more in common than is often supposed, or at least this is the case as concerns the issue of expert knowledge. For both U.S. and French appropriations of psychoanalysis, despite differences of content, express an overriding emphasis on control: in the case of U.S. psychoanalysis, control over behavioral adaptation; in the case of French psychoanalysis, control over the metatheorization of the life of the mind.

The process of psychologization that I am describing here is but a variant of, in Michel Foucault's terms, the power systems of an "apparatus of sexuality," one of the most unrelenting forms of domination and social control, as it transforms polymorphous sexualities into culturally routinized prohibitions and permissions pertaining to pleasure.[5] Foucault's provocative studies of the connections between discourse and sexuality capture well the sense of fixity prompted by the more normalizing forms of psychoanalysis detailed in the foregoing paragraphs. Preexisting types of sensual pleasure, says Foucault, become "sex" as the creation of discourses about it—such as medical texts, therapeutic books, and self-help manuals—bring about an ordering of "normal" and "pathological" sexual practices. The subject, according to Foucault, is not "sexed" in any meaningful sense prior to its constitution in a discourse through which it becomes a carrier of a natural or essential sex. As Foucault puts this: "The notion of 'sex' made it possible to group together, in an artificial unity, anatomical elements, biological functions, conducts, sensations, and pleasures, and it enabled one to make use of this fictitious unity as a causal principle, an omnipresent meaning: sex was thus able to function as a unique signifier and as a universal signified" (1981, 154). As such, sexuality has as its focus the manipulation of the body, a manipulation that disguises and extends the power relations that connect domination directly with the individual subject.

For Foucault, sex infiltrates and controls everyday pleasure because the self-awareness of the individual as a subject of sexuality is the result of a forgotten coercion and subordination to power/knowledge networks. The production of sex as a category is the end result of the mystifying organization of power/knowledge relations. As Foucault writes of this intrinsic link between sexuality and expert knowledge:

> In the family, parents and relatives became the chief agents of a deployment of sexuality which drew its outside support from doctors, educators, and later psychiatrists, and which began by competing with the relations of alliance but soon "psychologized" or "psychiatrized" the latter. Then these new personages made their appearance: the nervous woman, the frigid wife, the indifferent mother—or worse, the

mother beset by murderous obsessions—the impotent, sadistic, perverse husband, the hysterical or neurasthenic girl, the precocious and
already exhausted child, and the young homosexual who rejects marriage or neglects his wife . . . caught in the grip of this deployment of
sexuality which had invested it from without, contributing to its
solidification into its modern form, the family broadcast the long
complaint of its sexual suffering to doctors, educators, psychiatrists,
priests, and pastors, to all the "experts" that would listen. (1981, 110–
111)

This process of psychologization, though, is in some ways even more
alienating than Foucault's characterization suggests. For what is psychologized, and hence appropriated, by modern institutions is an awareness of
the creative, dynamic realm of unconscious fantasy itself. The self-instituting force of imagination is translated and experienced as part of the iron
grip of expert, psychological systems on knowledge. Desire has moved out
of the domain of the self and into the institutional realm of laws and
regulations; it is thus projected into something outside and Other.

In Foucault's terms, the issue of a translation from fantasy to the institution as such is perpetually deferred because the sexualized subject is always
the product of subjection to power: a "deployment of sexuality which had
invested it from without." Yet, what is it that frames this "without"? What
elements of fantasy, desire, and affect are invested in systems of knowledge
and power? How does the human subject experience expert systems as
colonizing knowledge affecting personal relationships? How is psychoanalysis experienced as a delivery system of expert knowledge on sexuality,
love, and intimacy? These questions, so important to an adequate understanding of the relations between self and society, touch on some of the
core issues relating to the self-understanding of imagination in the contemporary era. Of crucial importance in this respect is the uncovering and
denial of unconscious fantasy.

Sexuality, Fantasy, Modernity

Let us, then, rethink the relation between modernity and imagination in a
way that seeks to establish a psychopolitical link between the recognition
and denial of fantasy. A driving concern with the fantasy life of the individual, with feelings, passions, wishes, fears, and anxieties, as well as with
the question of the delimitation of the psychic, emerges as intrinsic to
modernity. This delimitation of the psychic is, in large part, an outcome of

the transformation from premodern to modern cultures, a transition that, as seen by Rieff, emerges out of a loss of community and a softening of the boundaries between the private and public spheres. With the breakdown of tradition and the dissolution of meaning, the self turns inward. Yet there is more to this delimitation than sociology alone. The turn toward the "inner life" of the subject, to psychic interiority, is itself attained through the activity of the unconscious imagination and can be understood as a creative rewriting of the historical trajectory of modernity. It is a rewriting of the social-historical process insofar as it facilitates thinking, at once personal and social, of the *contingency of self and society.* "Freud," writes Richard Rorty, "suggests that we need to return to the particular—to see particular present situations and options as similar to or different from particular past actions or events. He thinks that only if we catch hold of some crucial idiosyncratic contingencies in our past shall we be able to make something worthwhile of ourselves, to create present selves whom we can respect" (1989, 33). This uncovering of the particularity of unconscious fantasy and sexuality (analyzed by Freud in terms of energy, pleasure, anxiety, and repression) provides for self-knowledge of the constitutive role of human ambivalence and promotes an engagement with psychic and sexual life.

My analysis of Freud in the stream of modernity, however, has also shown that the instituting power of fantasy has been correspondingly neglected and repressed in theoretical discourse and as part of modern social activity. As regards theory, it has been argued that there is a fundamental tension in Freud's thought between the creative power attributed to unconscious fantasy on the one hand, and a desubjectifying tendency that displaces imagination to the confines of rationalism, objectivity, and scientificity, on the other. Freud's thinking about the psyche takes place on these two distinct axes, which results in the radical power of unconscious imagination being at once discovered and expropriated, uncovered and denied. So, too, the difficulties of ambivalence are sidestepped, or displaced, in whole sectors of contemporary culture. What I have called the psychologization of desire arises directly out of this repression of awareness of the profound fantasization of all personal and social life. In such instances, fantasy has lost its intrinsic connection with self-institution as a central focus for "experience" and instead is brought under the control of technical knowledge and rationalism. The connection to psychical imagination is lost in the sense that matters concerning fantasy, sexuality, and intimacy are projected, and experienced, as part of the orderly, rationally structured domain of psychological and psychoanalytic expertise. The problem may lie within (at the level of the psychic), but it is a condition from which escape is sought from without (at the level of the social).

As regards the psychologization of desire, one can agree with Foucault that the pathologization of sexuality is constituted and reproduced by the expansion of power/knowledge systems. Discourses of science, especially psychological expertise, produce subjects by manufacturing the conditions and operation of sexuality, of normalization via the differentiation of sexual practices. This is achieved through the material inscription of discourses into social procedures and regulations that frame sex and sexuality and that constitute the way people forge self-awareness of their place in the sexual field. Yet this process of manufacturing sexual identity is much more of a psychical drama than Foucault recognizes. The self is both subject to power systems, such as discourses of the person and sex, and is engaged in responses to such classificatory operations through imagining, fantasy, and in-depth reworkings of psychical organization. Unlike Foucault, then, I think that psychological repression is produced not only as the normalization of sexuality, but also as the sexualization of normalizing power. The trials of sexual prohibition are highly fantasized settings.

Paradoxically, this sexualization of normalization works to reinforce the principal dualisms of the modern era, such as the split between the psychological and the social, norm and anomaly, rationality and imagination, objectivity and fantasy. Certitude as a strategy of survival is central to the symptoms of modernity. Yet not only subjectivity is at stake here. The modernist aims of ordering and enframing, which destroy the alterity of self and society, penetrate theoretical knowledge and, crucially, psychoanalysis itself.

Notes

1   Freud's "Project for a Scientific Psychology," written in 1895, was first published in 1950 as "Aus der Anfängen der Psychanalyse." It was then translated into English by Ernst Kris in 1954 (Freud 195/1954). References to the text in this chapter, however, are to the *Standard Edition* (Freud 1895/1966).

2   For a brief discussion of the influence of Helmholtz and Herbart on Freud, see Ricoeur (1970, 72–73).

3   Ricoeur's (1970, 80) critique of the "Project" makes a good deal of this point, highlighting that Freud cannot give a mechanistic explanation of how the threat of unpleasure leads to a noncathexis of quantities stored in the ego.

4   Perhaps this is also the place to note that I accept Masson's point concerning the sterility of psychoanalytic therapy, or at least of its failings when practiced reductively. However, against Masson, I locate the reasons for this in the growing psychologization of culture and the transformation of psychoanalysis into an expert system of spe-

cialized knowledge. As such, the undoing of such psychologization involves grasping the constitutive role of fantasy in subjectivity, culture, and society; it requires a postmodern turning back of fantasy upon itself. Such an undoing would involve, contra Masson, more fantasy, not less, or at least more of a critical appreciation of the structuring role of fantasy in personal and cultural life. My view on this issue is set out in greater detail in the following sections of this essay.

5   See Foucault, *The History of Sexuality*, published in three volumes, of which volume 1, *An Introduction* (1981), is especially relevant to the concerns of this essay.

The Real and the Imaginary in Economic Methodology

DANIEL BRESLAU

riters on the methodology (in the sense of the logic of inquiry rather than simply the technical tools of the discipline) of economics often point out an irony of their field: economics possesses a philosophical and methodological discourse that is more extensive and specialized than any other social science, and most fields of natural science, yet economists are generally dismissive of methodological writing and its relevance for their work. Rules for methodological hygiene have been proposed at least since John Stuart Mill's writings for this science that has been defined by its orthodoxy of method. There was an argument in the second quarter of the twentieth century about what kinds of assumptions or axioms or propositions were or were not permissible under different criteria of falsifiability (Hutchison 1938). Later, the framework provided by Imre Lakatos provided ready-made criteria for distinguishing progressive from degenerate research programs (de Marchi and Blaug 1991). Philosophers of economics have believed that, armed with these criteria for proper method, they could seat themselves outside of economic discourse and pass judgment on what goes on inside. Like referees who can determine the winner without playing the game themselves, methodologists of the "appraisal" movement felt they could bring some order to the process of theory selection (Blaug 1980).

Demarcation criteria and rules for distinguishing healthy from pathological research programs have not delivered on this promise. In economics, they've run into the same difficulties and objections that they met earlier in the natural sciences. The most general and easily demonstrated of these is that the practice of science, including economics, simply does not need a parallel methodological discourse. As Gaston Bachelard (1984) and many since have pointed out, there is no room for an evaluative method-ological discourse parallel to a field's substantive discourse. Method cannot be prescribed a priori but is the outcome of the same process that deter-mines what is certified scientific truth. For practicing scientists the rela-tionship between method and validation is, and must be, the reverse of the relationship that concerns the methodologist. The latter cares about spec-ifying what method yields reliable or valid results; the former accepts as good method whatever procedures have produced compelling results. The practical demands of a scientific field impose a methodological discipline that does not correspond perfectly to any formal philosophical methodol-ogy, although it may be more exacting.

The irrelevance of methodology also applies to the Lakatosian appraisal movement, which sought to use the Methodology of Scientific Research Programs (MSRP) to distinguish progressive from degenerative research programs. A program was launched with a great deal of optimism, with the hope that application of Lakatosian criteria would both hold eco-nomic work to a high methodological standard and reserve an important role for methodologists and methodological inquiry in economics. While a number of fascinating "rational reconstructions" of economic work resulted, this project also demonstrated that methodological assessment cannot function as a metadiscourse. Methodologists cannot hope to be referees whose judgments are separate from economics discourse proper. The most sustained efforts to apply Lakatosian criteria to economic theo-ries quickly found that the appraisals are debatable in exactly the same terms as the theory itself. Lakatosian variables, such as excess empirical content, cannot be estimated independently of one's position on the sub-stance of the theory being appraised (Salanti 1991; Weintraub 1985).

Toward a Sociology of Methodological Discourse in Economics

As a sociologist, and not a practicing economist, I have an interest in methodological discourse beyond the question of its relevance for the practice of economics, beyond asking if methodology is something I need to take into account or if it can be safely ignored. I am interested in the question of what the methodological discourse on economics, positivist and postpositivist, represents as a social phenomenon. Despite its failure to be enshrined as a discourse regulative of economic practice itself, the methodological discussion goes on. It features debates that are no less heated and in which the participants have no less of a stake than those in theoretical controversies in economics proper.

I begin by examining two methodological debates, both of which are defined by the opposition between realist and antirealist views. I then sketch a sociological account of economic practice that emphasizes the implicit and contextual methodological stances of economists and how methodological discourse arises spontaneously. I suggest that the explicit methodologies, far from being irrelevant to economic practice, are social strategies to valorize the practices of those situated in different locations in the social structure of the field.

Realism versus Antirealism: A Leitmotif

As with methodological discourse in general, the literature on the method of economics is structured by a set of basic oppositions that are repeatedly resurrected and transformed (Abbott 2001a). One axis of disputation that spans the divide between twentieth-century positivism and contemporary postpositivism is that distinguishing realism from antirealism, the real from the imaginary in economic thought and practice. This leitmotif running through the past century is perhaps more central to economics than other areas, as the role of the imaginary is acknowledged and celebrated here more than in other disciplines. Methodologies of the imaginary are based on a distinction between the instruments of knowledge and the objects of knowledge. Concepts and theories are instruments that allow us to do things, such as organize our observations (positivism), make predictions (instrumentalism), and persuade others (rhetoric). Their correspondence or resemblance to their objects is unknown and irrelevant. Realist methodologies insist that whatever instrumental success a theory has is the result of its success in capturing or describing a reality that exists independently of our knowledge. The opposition between realism and antirealism has been the key axis of positivist methodological differences, as well as debates among methodologies that share their rejection of positivism. I turn next to two historical permutations of the realism/antirealism opposition.

The Assumptions Debate

The midcentury controversy about the epistemological status of assumptions illustrates some of the logic of these debates. Milton Friedman's famous 1953 article, "The Methodology of Positive Economics" (1953a), was for decades the most read and most taught discussion of proper economic method. Postpositivist methodologists point to it as the epitome of the rule-based, scientistic, and straitjacketing approach that they have superseded. But when it was originally published, Friedman's article was a controversial take on positivist orthodoxy and challenged the empiricist insistence on the observability of theoretical constructs (e.g., Hutchison 1938). Friedman provocatively flaunted the lack of realism in economic assumptions, elevating it to a methodological virtue. His immediate target was criticism of neoclassical economics in terms of the implausibility of its assumptions. Periodically, since at least the nineteenth century, orthodox economic theory as a whole has been accused of setting out from axioms that are prima facie untrue. Calling his recommendations *the* methodology of positive economics, Friedman insisted that the empirical adequacy of assumptions in no way constitutes a test of a theory. Predictive success or, more precisely, survival of empirical test by the predictions that the theory generates is the sole test of its validity. The question of whether an assumption regarding the principle of action under a particular set of conditions—the shape of a utility function, for instance—describes the real principle regulating economic choice is irrelevant. We care only whether individuals behave "as if" the assumptions were true. Friedman was quite comfortable with the idea that the most we can say about a theory that yields successful predictions is that reality proceeds "as if" the theory were true. For this reason, his positive economics has been called an instrumentalist method (Boland 1979). Questions of the correspondence of a theory and its assumptions with reality are simply not relevant because (1) only predictive success should determine theory retention, and (2) any theory, to be general, must be based on assumptions that are descriptively false.

Friedman's essay has sustained an industry of interpretation and critique. He claims to be offering not simply a rejoinder to foundational criticisms of economics, but a self-sufficient methodology. This claim has motivated laudable, though generally unsuccessful efforts to extract such a methodology from the essay (Mäki 2003). But those who reacted to Friedman were disturbed above all by the paradoxical lack of interest in a "descriptively true" theory, despite his use of the term "positive economics." Some of these critiques have gone beyond simply reasserting the relevance of the empirical validity of assumptions to challenge the consequences of the philosophical antirealism of Friedman's method (Blaug 1980, 106; Rotwein 1959). It seems that Friedman's method negates the goal of causal analysis, as the theoretical models are only tools for prediction and cannot be taken as describing causes of observed events. Such critics were not simply calling for what Uskali Mäki (1996) calls "realisticness," but for philosophical *realism*, insisting that theories should attempt to describe an unobserved reality that generates empirical observations.

Postpositivist Method

The demise of positivist, rule-based method and demarcation criteria that any field calling itself scientific had to adhere to took place in economics with the same time lag from philosophical discourse as is found in other social sciences. Though rejecting positivist method, and in some cases any demarcation criteria, methodology continues to offer itself as a regulative discourse for economic practice. And it continues to fail in this aspiration. It has also retained the opposition of realism and antirealism within the broader antipositivist consensus.

Economics as Literature

The leading antirealist formulation of postpositivism consists of a literary or rhetorical methodology, developed by Deirdre McCloskey and her associates (Klamer and Leonard 1994; McCloskey 1985, 1994; Weintraub 1991). These approaches begin by rejecting the positivist project of demarcating science from nonscience on the basis of a universal scientific method. Economists are engaged in a conversation in which their resources for persuading others are not essentially different from those used in literature or any rhetoric. Figures of speech, appeals to authority, and other devices that positivist orthodoxy officially excludes from scientific method figure largely in this view. In fact, it is through creative and skillful use of these literary devices that economists succeed in persuading. The positivist characterization of the economist as a model of moral restraint and submission to universal rules is replaced by that of the literary creator. Economists are essentially writers and conversationalists who deploy whatever literary device will help them make their point. Methodological inquiry, in this view, should be a branch of literary criticism.

The rhetorical approach, despite itself, therefore shares some general features of Milton Friedman's so-called instrumentalism. It is above all a methodology of freedom, which rejects as pedantic demands to be somehow true to reality in preparing one's models and arguments. The indifference to the descriptive realism of theoretical assumptions is paralleled in McCloskey's work by the poetic license that she would accord the economist. For Friedman the proof of the pudding lies in its success, or failure to be contradicted, in prediction, whereas for McCloskey it lies in the success of economic work in persuading an audience. Prediction is ruled out in principle by McCloskey and is replaced by success in persuasion by any number of means, including those, such as appeals to authority and aesthetic criteria, that Friedman's "positive" method excludes. If McCloskey has a methodology, it is a kind of rhetorical reformulation of Occam's razor: purge economics of all elements that are not minimally necessary to convince an audience.

The Poverty of Rhetoric

The treatment of economic method as rhetoric is an attractive approach in a field in which the gap between the terms of theoretical models and the observable features of economic reality is so wide. Theoretical arguments are self-consciously rhetorical, and metaphorical, when they ask us to direct our attention from the empirical economy to a quite clearly imaginary and radically simplified stand-in. But, while they have no doubt been correct in pointing out the ubiquity and necessity of rhetorical forms that positivist orthodoxy has excluded, the rhetorical analysts draw too absolute a distinction between figurative and literal speech. As Klamer and Leonard have written, "Because we cannot know literally the nature of the natural and social worlds, we resort to the figurative in characterizing" (1994, 39). According to this Kantianism that equates literal statements with knowledge of things-in-themselves, all language is inevitably cut off from its referent, and we can refer to things only by means of what they aren't. McCloskey, too, writes about metaphors as though they will remain metaphors.

But metaphor, and figurative language in general, is not the whole of economic, or scientific, or any discourse. It is a moment in a circulation that must always draw from and aim toward literal reference. Not literal reference to absolutely transcendent, unknowable things, but to the objects of science, partly known and partly hidden. Metaphors depend for their force on some nonfigurative connections; as pure language they would bring nothing with them. When economists first said "labor market," they deployed the literal sense of market to suggest that the meeting of job seekers and employers could be treated in the same way. But the metaphor, to the extent that it succeeds, ceases to be a metaphor and becomes a literal reference. Any economist knows that a labor market is a labor market, and not something else that we find it illuminating to treat as though it is a market.

Critical Realism

A leading realist counterpoint to the rhetoric of economics is critical realism. It shares with rhetorical analyses a concern with the inevitable context-bound nature of any science, and thus rejects positivism's insistence on a universal set of methodological rules. But critical realism, inspired by Roy Bhaskar's writings and extended to economic methodology in the work of Tony Lawson (1994, 1997), contains a stronger normative element than the more methodologically libertarian rhetorical approach. Rather than calling for universal rules of method, it tries to establish metaphysical criteria for evaluating economic method and, ultimately, the content of economic theories. For Lawson, the problem with positivism, and the dominant methodology in economics, lies in its method of deductivism. By deductivism, Lawson means the hypothetico-deductive method, which renders explanations and predictions by coupling descriptions of initial conditions with scientific "covering laws." These laws, in turn, are derived from observed event regularities of the form "if A then B," Hume's "constant conjunctions." As Lawson explicates in his contribution to this volume, it is not this mode of reasoning per se that cripples economic analysis, but the ontology that it presupposes, even implicitly. A dependence on laws consisting of event regularities presupposes a closed reality composed of atomistic events, externally related to one another in the form of invariant sequences of cause and effect. But Lawson points out that event regularities are generally nonexistent in observed social phenomena, and that the real regularities are not to be found in constant conjunctions of events, but in the "intransitive" and transcendent reality of generative structures, forces, and tendencies. Economics can reverse its failings as a science by abandoning an insistence on deductivism and adopting a method that is consistent with the metaphysics of a structured transcendent reality, forever distinct from our knowledge of it.

Lawson is correct in describing a great deal of orthodox economics as deductivist in terms of its style of reasoning and argumentation. The characterization is even more apt when he includes economic theory, arguing that the axioms of economics, such as maximization of utility and the shape of utility curves, and the assumptions required to specify a theory take the place of laws derived from observed constant conjunctions. But, although much work in economics is either couched in deductivist terms or can be reconstructed in those terms, this methodological orthodoxy does not imply the ontological commitments that Lawson attributes to it. There is no necessary connection between deductivist reasoning and laws derived from constant conjunctions of events. Despite the classic statements of hypothetico-deductivism (e.g., Hempel 1948/1965), the conditional theoretical elements used to deduce observed or predicted states from initial conditions need not be composed of constant conjunctions, but can be compatible with a range of ontological statuses. They can be, and out of necessity often are, derived from theoretical descriptions of an unobserved generative structure. They are informed by a deeper ontology than Lawson gives them credit for (Mäki 2001).[1] A parallel contention of Lawson's is that deductivism presupposes a closed system, of the kind that is artificially induced in a laboratory experiment or computer simulation and that is nonexistent in the social world. But this reading is possible only if one arbitrarily and a priori restricts the subject-predicate statements of deductivism to covering laws that describe constant event conjunctions. It is quite possible to construct deductivist explanations that rely on statements of tendencies and capacities of the kind that critical realists say theories should be made of. More important, it is possible to interpret much existing economic work as offering explanations of this type.

Even the officially sanctioned, explicitly stated methodologies of economics are not generally consistent with the empiricist version of hypothetico-deductivism. Friedman's well-known positive method requires that the assumptions of economic theories *do not* correspond to observed generalities, let alone constant conjunctions of events. Though Friedman interprets such "descriptively false" assumptions in antirealist terms, others have argued that they do not correspond to empirical observation precisely because they are intended to capture generative mechanisms (e.g., Sugden 2000). Efforts to base unobserved theoretical constructs on generalization from empirical observation, such as the "revealed preference" theory of utility, have been controversial and judged by many as failures (Mirowski 1989, 358–369; Wong 1978). Those insisting on an inductivist basis for economic laws have not been successful in ridding the discipline of reliance on underlying, generative entities, which are known only through their surface appearances.

The practice of economics demonstrates abundantly the compatibility of deductivist arguments with a realist ontology not altogether different from the one that Lawson proposes as the basis of an alternative method. The subdiscipline of macroeconomics, for instance, which is almost entirely couched in a deductivist style of argumentation, is at the same time an effort to describe the underlying causal structure that generates the fluctuations and correlations among indicators. The important work of Frisch in the 1930s on business cycles sought to describe mathematically the underlying causal relationships that produced the observed patterns of economic oscillations with regular periods but irregular intensity (M. Morgan 1990, 90–100). In his book on causality in macroeconomics, Kevin Hoover (2001) develops a realist description of work in this specialty. His central argument is that, to the extent that macroeconomics succeeds in establishing any causal relationships, this is not the result of induction from observed constant conjunctions, but from hypothesized causal structures that are not directly observable.

By defending economics from Lawson's accusation that it is characterized above all by deductivism and the ontological baggage that he associates with it, I do not mean to defend its substance. There are many reasons to object to economic theories and their laws, but because these laws do not have a fixed ontological status, we cannot fault them on global methodological or metaphysical grounds. Conversely, an a priori metaphysics should not be used as a test for allowable alternative versions of economics. The description of generative structures underlying and causing surface phenomena is universal to science, and perhaps to human knowledge and perception. An official economic methodology that discounts or, in Friedman's case, excludes this component leaves itself vulnerable to the realist critique of methodology. But this critique does not apply to the practice of economics in general.

Critical realism, therefore, does not point the way to an alternative to economics as currently practiced. The merits of alternatives, such as the one sketched by Lawson, are not grounded in a superior global ontology but must be demonstrated in their ability to pose and answer research questions. Like the rhetorical approach, critical realism describes a subset of economic practices. By abstracting the transcendental realist moment from scientific work, the moment in which investigation and rhetoric are oriented to the description of an underlying causal and explanatory structure, critical realism skips over all the intermediate steps and proposes an economics that deals immediately with the "real" causal structure. A real, *underlying* structure, however, can be established only if one starts from a metaphorical, rhetorical, and *overlaying* structure of conjecture. While the antirealism of orthodox positivism is routinely violated in its practice, it should be clear that a realism of underlying generative structures is impracticable without constantly drawing on its opposite. The underlying must begin with, and return to, the overlaid, and the real of realism must draw from and return to the imaginary. Nor can it dispense with event regularities, however local and conditional.

The Negotiation of Economic Truth

Realism and antirealism both seem to abstract one moment of the construction of economic reality and enshrine it as a standard for evaluating the entire enterprise. To understand the social genesis and the reasons for the repeated reincarnations of this opposition, it will help to show how these methodological positions emerge spontaneously in economic discourse. But first I need to provide an account of how economic practice actually proceeds. This discussion is based on my joint research with Yuval Yonay, consisting of extensive interviewing and participant observation with academic economists. The focus of our research was on economic theorists, mostly using mathematical models, without systematic quantitative research. This is the most prestigious and highly rewarded activity in economics, and these comments are cast at a level of generality that I believe applies to theoretical work in general.[2] Our work consisted of a small number of intensive case studies of what can be loosely referred to as research programs, allowing our informants to define how a particular program is bounded.

When observing the development of these research programs, we were impressed by a number of features. First, the work is thoroughly collective, to an extent that is invisible to studies that examine only research products, such as published papers, where attribution of individual authorship is reasserted. Second, it is impossible to identify a priori methodological rules guiding practice. The same economists may, in one situation, take great pains to demonstrate the empirical adequacy of the assumptions of their model, and in another context adopt an indifferent attitude, asking their audience to evaluate the model only in terms of its results. This was initially quite baffling when we viewed our subjects through sociological biases and found that the assumptions that were most patently false from our perspective often required no justification, whereas great effort went into establishing the empirical validity of assumptions that, to us, had much greater prima facie plausibility.

If preformed philosophical stances do not guide economic method, then what does? Bruno Latour (1999, 24–79), in a small study of soil scientists in the Amazon, suggests a way of characterizing scientific work that I have found very useful in approaching the world of economics. When trying to make sense of scientific practices, one very quickly confronts the limitations of the problem of knowledge formulated as the bridging of the gap between words and the world by establishing a correspondence. Science, not excepting economics, consists of elaborating and maintaining a chain of mediations between elements that are progressively less local, material, and particular and more universal, formal, and general. Nowhere do we encounter pure material reality or pure ideas, only the mediations, the links of imperfect and transforming reference.

The work of constructing and promoting an economic model takes the form of a negotiation of these mediations/transformations. Between progressively more complex, messy, and local observations, anecdotes, data, in one direction, and the progressively more abstract and mathematical, the persuasive force of a model depends on the strength of these links. The links connecting mathematical expressions to typified economic agents, to actual individuals, and to those connecting the setup of a model to its solution are all potentially in play in these negotiations. Many of these links, such as that between an equilibrating system and a market, or a maximizing agent with declining marginal utility for an economic actor, are quite established and most of the time needn't be renegotiated. But any economic argument seeks to establish new links between a recognized phenomenon and a particular mathematical representation. In more theoretical areas such as game theory, the link in question may be that between an already mathematicized model and a particular solution concept. It is a negotiation, literally, because the proposer of a model asks to be allowed the weaker links on the strength of the more secure ones. If a very general solution follows by necessity from a set of assumptions, then a problematic link between those assumptions and an economic phenomenon may be overlooked. The clarity and aesthetics of a solution, or its connection with already established results, may be enough to get the audience to forget that the assumptions exclude what may be important counterexamples.

Reception, acceptance, and citation of economic work do not proceed according to rules or fixed methodological criteria. The criteria are themselves in play as generality is traded for robustness, consistency for plausibility. The degree of abstractness, or distance from empirical observation, is itself negotiated, not fixed, even by convention. Economists do not start with a real-world phenomenon and abstract a model, nor do they generally work in the opposite direction, refining a pure abstraction until it makes contact with a recognizable situation. Rather, they work both ways, at once or alternately, the alignment between various levels of abstraction or specificity determined by what their audience will tolerate.

The methodological stances of economists therefore depend on, and vary with, the links that are the focus of their current negotiation. Usually, these methodologies are implicit in the negotiations. An economist putting forth a model that is eminently solvable and connects with established theories is implicitly taking one methodological stance, but will take quite another when in possession of a model that tightens the link between the mathematics and reality—which is to say, an incrementally less formal representation than the mathematical one—at the expense of generality or unequivocal solvability.

Although de facto methodological stances are contextually variable, they do not vary randomly. The division of labor in the discipline means that most economists will find themselves in a narrow region of the chain of mediations. The dominant economic theorists, those who work in general theory, deal almost exclusively with the articulation of the most generic mathematical models, whereas those in more applied areas are plagued by demands that they justify their assumptions and encompass real-world phenomena. There is a tendency, therefore, for dominant economic theorists to prefer a methodology that tolerates a lack of realism in assumptions and emphasizes generality and clarity, while those in the intellectual provinces of the discipline will favor a realist method, emphasizing close links between elements of analytical models and real-world phenomena.

Spontaneous Methodology

The realism/antirealism opposition is not an invention of the methodologists, but arises spontaneously in the discourse of economics proper. Based on observations of economists at work, in discussions, in seminars, and in their published work, one can find nearly every known methodological position exemplified. A self-conscious rhetoric of economics is employed in theoretical papers that call for a suspension of disbelief on the part of the reader. The reader is asked to go along for the ride and see where a model leads in terms of results and predictions. If economists were too quick to challenge the manifestly absurd assumptions of the model, the analysis would never get off the ground. When faced with harassment to make their assumptions more realistic, economists spontaneously voice something very much like the antirealism associated with Milton Friedman's view. This should not be surprising, as Friedman himself developed his arguments to counter those who attacked the basic assumptions of neoclassical theory as implausible.

In one case study investigated by Yuval Yonay (Yonay and Breslau 2004), two collaborators working on a model of monetary shocks spontaneously raise the same issues around which the "assumptions debate" revolved. One assumption of their model, that sellers price their goods in order to clear their entire inventory in each round of trading, raised eyebrows among certain readers. The authors expressed their irritation by arguing that totally abstract work does not raise such objections. They felt they were punished for making any links to economic reality when one element of their model seemed to be grossly unrealistic: many commodities retain their value over time, and losses of unsold inventories can be overcome in subsequent periods. In a model for studying the generation of monetary shocks with two islands, each with a single household that is simultaneously employee, producer, and bank, two economists added the assumption that unsold goods in one period are lost in the subsequent period. Among the elements of a totally fictitious economy, this assumption was singled out by others as unrealistic. In indignation, one of the authors complained, "The moment you add some element of a real-world structure, they complain that 'it is not like that in reality,' " and went on to praise those who do not ask whether it is realistic or not, only whether it can explain the data.

Just as economists are antirealists as they defend the implausibility of their models, they are just as apt to suddenly appeal to reality to justify an assumption. For instance, in a well-known paper on the formation of trade policy, Gene Grossman and Elhanan Helpman (1994) constructed a model with the usual utility-maximizing actors, both in industry and in government. The government wants to maximize its campaign contributions, and industries want to maximize the price of the goods they produce while keeping the prices of other goods as low as possible. The elements of the model are introduced with little supporting justification or defense of their realism. For a Friedmanian, of course, none is required. But, when it comes time to justify other features of the model, we find the following: "Although we recognize the absence of explicit political competition as a potential shortcoming of our approach, we believe that the available evidence for the United States supports our assumptions as a reasonable first approximation. In particular, political action committees (PAC's) gave more than three-quarters of their total contributions in the 1988 Congressional campaigns to incumbent candidates" (835).

Employing Friedman's methodology, such appeals to empirical evidence in justifying assumptions would be ruled superfluous. Only the predictive consequences of the model should have a role in judging its validity. By supplying evidence to support their choice of model, Grossman and Helpman are not only conceding that the realism of assumptions matters, but also that the model, despite its manifest unrealism, is meant to somehow capture features of the real world (Breslau and Yonay 1999). The coexistence of realist and antirealist procedures in the same piece of research by no means indicates methodological inconsistency or confusion, but is a product of the negotiation by which certain mediating links must be supplied while others can be omitted.

Practicing economists do not seem troubled by the contentious philosophical question of realism versus antirealism and feel no need to come down on one side or the other. Models at times are thought of as ways of "explaining the data" and nothing more, especially when the realism of their assumptions is questioned. But claims based on formal models frequently shade into the claim that the model describes the mechanism that actually generates an observed pattern. As Sugden (2000) points out, models are imaginary and constructed worlds, but are nonetheless intended to contain mechanisms that produce observed phenomena in the real world. Whether, in any instance, they are regarded as rhetorical flourishes—or alternately, as filing systems—or as generative causal structures depends on the status quo of the discourse.

Practicing economists therefore adopt methodological stances—even in a single piece of research—that, according to the methodological literature, would seem incompatible and confused. Economists are alternately realists, empiricists, rhetoricians, and instrumentalists. Their arguments for the epistemological status of their work, and the particular modalities they attach to any claims about the real world, are contextually bound and variable.

The Methodological Struggle

The foregoing sketch of the social negotiation of economic knowledge suggests a sociological account of the realist/antirealist divide. With respect to the mid-twentieth-century assumptions debate, we find that the realism of assumptions turns out to be a practical issue on which economists do not betray an a priori position. It is not methodological principles, but demands of a social context that compel economists to seek observational grounding for their assumptions or frees them from that requirement. Nor does this depend on the location of assumptions in the Lakatosian topography of the discipline, where elements of the hard core, the axioms of neoclassical economics, require less justification than elements of the more fluid periphery. While novel assumptions are apt to be accompanied by more empirical evidence, economists often introduce assumptions in the hope that there will be no call for such justification. Economists are alternately instrumentalists with no concern for the adequacy of their assumptions, and realists who must say why theirs is a reasonable simplification of reality, depending on the negotiation that takes place around their models. They are alternately rhetoricians who ask their audience to suspend disbelief, and realists who insist that their terms refer to real entities out there.

But our tentative model of these negotiations allows us to say more about the conditions under which realism of assumptions is going to be problematized and empirical backing demanded. When the generality of models is high, when the assumptions are mostly those that are sacred within the discipline and are very costly to challenge except in heterodox gatherings, and when the speaker is in a dominant position in the field, assumptions are less likely to be empirically justified than when these conditions do not obtain. These conditions are historically specific as well, so that assumptions that were received without reservation can be questioned as to their empirical adequacy at a later state of the field. Freedom from such questioning is therefore a privilege of holders of dominant positions.

Friedman's stance is an elaboration and explication of the professional ideology of dominant economic theorists. Placed in historical context, it makes an epistemological virtue of the freedom of theorists from pedantic demands that they justify their assumptions. According to our analysis, the lack of realism of Friedman's assumptions is a luxury not available to all economists. The immunity of assumptions from empirical test is not a universal methodological precept adhered to by every competent economist, but is variable, depending on the particular assumptions, to what end they are used, and on the identity and social position of those using them. By elaborating a methodology, Friedman turns this privilege of dominant economic theorists into a virtue, an exemplar of the legitimate way to do economics.

The more recent incarnation of the realist/antirealist debate can also be related to the division of labor in economics. As an implicit metaphysical stance, realism is not an a priori belief adopted by certain economists, but is a practical requirement that is sometimes forced on them. This is often a burden that weighs most heavily on less prestigious economists studying less prestigious topics. Those who work in the applied specializations in economics, who are bound to work at a lower level of abstraction and to be true to the specifics of their empirical domain, are likely to object to the detachment and lack of "realisticness" among the dominant economic theorists, while championing a methodology that begins with the real-world objects of study. Dominant economists succeed in escaping realism: they are less likely to be forced to present their work as descriptive of an underlying reality. Forced on dominated economists, realism tends to be used as their critical resource par excellence.

As for the rhetorical approach, if we understand the field of economics as a social structure, it is possible to see it as a strategic move not all that different from Friedman's antirealist methodology. The economic field is not a frictionless one in which all strategies are equally accessible to all participants. In a field that is structured in terms of possession of skills, reputations, and a network of social ties, access to literary devices is itself socially structured. For instance, to legitimately use particular methods, one must show signs of skills that can be acquired only through direct contact with those who are already competent in those techniques (H. Collins 1992). Like Friedman's, McCloskey's methodology enshrines the freedom of dominant economists, giving a positive modality to their privilege of working in a world of pure abstraction, in which the quality of their argument rather than the force of evidence is their key resource. Poetic license is unequally distributed in economics.

Rhetorical analyses, however, in assuming that the key to the persuasive power of economic texts is to be found in the literary techniques of the text itself, neglect the extratextual elements that both limit and enable the persuasive force of texts. Implicitly, the rhetorical context, the conversation, is conceived as homogeneous, in which rhetorical devices are costlessly available to all and have the same persuasive efficacy independent of who uses them. Rhetorical studies of economics displace the hard-nosed, disciplined positivist as the idealized economist, with the writer creatively manipulating symbolic means to induce a reaction, hopefully assent, in the reader. The domain of language is also conceived as cut off from the objects of economics, a self-contained world that can only refer to the economic world through metaphor. There is a degree of creative freedom from the constraints of economic particulars.

It is reasonable to speculate that this abstraction of the literary practices of economics from the social constraints of the discipline and from the constraints of less abstract and more particular and local objects, such as quantitative data, is a universalization of the situation of those who are relatively free from these constraints. There is a subset of economists whose practices do approach those of a writer, for whom extratextual elements are less salient and for whom the power of an internally consistent, compelling story of broad generality will outweigh the demands of linking that story securely to traces of the world. For theorists, for whom the tools of thought are the object of study, practice does consist largely of assembling a set of symbolic resources, which are relatively cut off from their referents.

Conclusions

These two postpositivist methodologies of economics, rhetoric and realism, begin with an absolute distinction between words and things, between the literary tools of economic analysis and the mute objects of economic study. Each builds a methodology by privileging one or the other of these mutually exclusive domains and by affirming their separateness. At the same time, each privileges specific moments in the work of economics, giving it priority or even having it stand for economics as a whole. Economics as rhetoric reduces economics to a literary practice, the creative manipulation of figurative language. It universalizes the perspective of those who, insulated from the work of systematic description and aggregation of empirical materials, are apt to see their work as a literary practice, storytelling, as theoretical economists sometimes describe their work. It makes a virtue of the freedom that economic theorists have from linking their models to unwieldy particulars. In an antipositivist mode, it nonetheless recapitulates the tone of Milton Friedman's famous methodological statement, which called for the freedom of economic theory from the pedantry of those who would force them to provide empirical validation of their assumptions. The methodology derived from critical realism is an outsider's method, a voice of the dominated in economics. Those who are relatively marginalized and who by necessity must work in an applied area, close to the particulars of their area, have an affinity with the kind of methodology Lawson offers, of abstracting carefully and provisionally from the patterns of routinized behavior. It makes a virtue of the existential situation of dominated practitioners in the economic field.

Recently, at the initiative of a group of French graduate students, a pent-up dissatisfaction with the dominance of neoclassical orthodoxy and mathematical models in the profession's discourse and pedagogy has taken the form of an international movement of "postautistic economics" (see *Post Autistic Economics Newsletter* 2000). Many of the leading repre-

468   Daniel Breslau

sentatives of the postpositivist methods discussed here have been active in this intellectual revolt, calling for methodological pluralism and a return to an agenda driven by real-world economic problems. Nothing in this essay should be read as questioning the value of this project, which I personally believe is thoroughly called for. But arguments I have advanced here suggest that methodology, in its philosophical sense, is not the appropriate battleground for encouraging a pluralistic economics that would be reengaged in the scientific understanding of social problems. Like logical positivism, the postpositivist methodological critiques discussed here try to transform problems of the "what" of science into questions of "how." If economics has failed to answer the questions that it has posed for itself and seems to be more predictable in yielding pro-market answers than it is predictive of any novel observation, it is its substance, not its method, that is at fault. Insistence on a realist ontology or a recognition of rhetoric can be made totally compatible with the existing agenda of economics. Mathematics per se is not the problem, but the mathematical form taken by current orthodoxy requires that one implicitly accept its core theoretical elements as a precondition for participating in the conversation. It is by bringing substantive alternatives into being and demonstrating their productivity in posing and answering questions where the orthodoxy has failed that the limitations of orthodox practices will become apparent.

Finally, I would like to put forth the hypothesis that the philosophical distinction, and sharp metaphysical divide, between words and things and between knowledge and reality, assumed and reinforced by the methodologies I have discussed, is itself the product of the division of labor of knowing. From the chain of mediations linking the progressively more local, material, and specific to the progressively more abstract and general, methodologists tend to abstract one or the other extreme as the more basic and valuable, and thereby reinforce the distinction itself. We are left with a set of false choices: between the surface of empirical observation and the deeper reality of generative structures, between unencumbered literary creativity and subservience to one's object of study. Both draw a sharp divide between language and the real world, subjects and objects, transitive and intransitive strata, epistemology and ontology.

Notes

I would like to acknowledge the helpful comments of Sergio Sismondo, Margaret Somers, and George Steinmetz on earlier versions of this essay, and Yuval Yonay for the fruitful collaboration on which portions of this essay are based.

1   In his contribution to this volume, Lawson recognizes that the elements of economic models refer often to unobserved generative principles. Though he calls these "capacities," he insists that they must "always be exercised and actualized unimpeded," and are thus mechanical causes, not the capacities of philosophical realism. I argue, on the contrary, that there is nothing about economic method that restricts one to either type of cause.

2   Despite the growth of nonmathematical and empirical areas such as experimental economics, behavioral economics, and empirical econometrics, the vast majority of articles in the most prestigious general economics journals, such as the *American Economic Review* and the *Journal of Political Economy*, are theoretical papers relying on mathematical models. The belief in an orthodoxy of economic method is sustained by both its methodological proponents, such as Hausman (1992), and Lawson (this volume).

Facts, Values, and "Real" Numbers

SOPHIA MIHIC, STEPHEN G. ENGELMANN,
AND ELIZABETH ROSE WINGROVE

The fact/value dichotomy, typically associated with positivism in the social sciences, has of late become rather enfeebled. Granted, it was never a wholly secure creation to begin with: retracing its history, from Hume through Mill, Comte, and Weber, one notices an almost constitutive tension between the logical proposition that *ought* and *is* are different orders of things and the actual practices of social scientific inquiry (see Root 1993). And now in the aftermath of the linguistic turn, as well as more recent genealogical and gender spins, any insistence on a clear distinction between facticity (the quality or condition of being a fact) and normativity (the quality or condition of being a value) appears to be increasingly untenable. Political science, however, has been slow to get the news, and despite the recurrent criticisms of disciplinary practitioners, the fact/value dichotomy enjoys a robust good health there. This essay offers a diagnosis of that robustness, finding in its persistence a key to how positivism is reproduced in political science. This persistence, we argue, is less a function of researchers' chosen and fiercely held ontological or epistemological commitments than of a division of labor that promotes the practice of what we call fact neutrality. Value neutrality, the presumption that normative commitments and/or assumptions can and should be set aside, or "bracketed," in the process of scientific analysis, finds its mirror image in fact neutrality, which presumes that data are ancillary to the main preoccupations of the analyst. From this perspective, what requires interrogation is not the discipline's false claim to a value-free science, but how its aspirations to science are sustained through a curious ability to bracket facts.

Fact neutrality is endemic to political theory, the subfield whose focus on texts and ideas situates it firmly on the "value" side of the dichotomy.[1] It also characterizes the subfield of political methodology, which, despite ongoing challenges from within its ranks, retains a numerical orientation: that facts can be represented quantitatively remains the unthought assumption in relation to which the validity and preferability of any particular method are gauged. And positive theory, which is less a subfield than an analytic approach to political actors as strategic choosers, is arguably a growth industry within the discipline precisely because it is veritably fact-free. In each of these cases, political analysis proceeds and even thrives at a critical distance from the stuff to be analyzed: someone else ascertains and collects data, while the work of the theorist or methodologist is to evaluate, employ, manipulate, or otherwise assess the facts presented. In what follows our aim is to examine how these practices serve to reproduce a hegemonic positivism: the division of labor between theorists, methodologists, and empirical researchers, we argue, both reflects and promotes a disciplinary situation in which the ontological and epistemological status of facts goes unmarked.

Important in this context is the fact that challenges to the unmarked status of fact are prevalent in political science, both across the different subfields[2] and throughout the discipline's postwar history. Typically characterized as "interpretivist," these challenges have often explicitly interrogated the logics of inference and the standards of replication, prediction, and generalizability that together validate the process and the results of properly scientific inquiry; they have also produced a body of empirical, historical, and theoretical work adhering to different logics and standards. At a general level, interpretive approaches share the presumption that properly political analyses entail telling the meaning of events, actions, norms, and other pertinent phenomena. While every political analyst endeavors to make data meaningful, from an interpretive perspective the acts of translation that comprise this endeavor must themselves remain open to inspection: because worldly stuff becomes data only within structures of intelligibility (linguistic grammars, cultural value systems, statistical compilations, or numerical equations), the hermeneutic investment represented by these structures is always analytically pertinent. Facticity, in other words, remains an explicit feature in interpretive political analysis, rather than its naturalized antecedent.

As we've suggested, an interpretivist perspective is not uncommon among disciplinary practitioners, informing both their critical position in methodological debates and the everyday routines through which they conduct normal and extraordinary political science. Our use of the term "hegemony" derives in part from this ill fit between practice and disciplinary norms. The alternatives to positivism exemplified in Rabinow and Sullivan's (1979/1987) *Interpretive Social Science* are reflected in the work of many political scientists; disciplinary historians speak confidently of a postbehavioralist and postempiricist era; and yet proper scientificity remains the axis around which consensus, debate, success, and marginalization revolve. By concentrating on the resiliency of the disciplinary norms rather than on the multiplicity of exceptions, we do not mean to ignore the fact of these paradoxes but to account for them by figuring out what they might mean.

Consider, for example, the aftermath of interpretivist challenges in political science that originated from within our own subfield, political theory, in the 1960s and early 1970s. Precipitated by readings of Hegel and Wittgenstein, critics' arguments targeted the use of language as a neutral instrument and thus its occlusion as a political force and form. The political theorists developing these critiques again underscored the fragility of the distinction between fact and value and between the subjects and objects of political inquiry. The subsequent challenge to positivistic assumptions and the attendant legitimation of ethnographic and historical approaches influenced researchers in a range of subfields who made rich use, theoretically and empirically, of the notion that language, thought, and world are mutually constitutive. But the more general disciplinary reaction was akin to a chastening: generations of inquirers have subsequently learned to pay lip service to the interpretive critique's caveats regarding the inevitability of evaluation. Thus, one often hears from political scientists the doxic repetition that, whatever the field of study, their own "biases" must be recognized and/or acknowledged. But such declarations miss the suggestion that the discovery of one's, let us, following Gadamer, say prejudices in language and practice might be the end of inquiry, or a demanding dimension of the process of inquiry, rather than an easy propaedeutic to it. Indeed, when the discipline missed this suggestion—when it institutionalized the interpretive critique as a caution about particular normative investments and research biases—it performed what we argue has become a routinized practice of fact neutrality: the displacement of questions of facticity from the world and its characteristics to the inquirer and his or her subjectivity. What emerged is a peculiarly subject-centered and individualist reading of the insight that, in Charles Taylor's (1985c) phrase, man is a self-interpreting animal.

A recent challenge in political science, launched simultaneously from multiple subfields in what the *New York Times* characterized as a "revolution," would seem to offer more timely data apropos the vigor of disciplinary hegemony (Eakin 2000). The revolution, spearheaded by the self-styled perestroika movement, has charged the discipline's national organization with nondemocratic practices and the organization's flagship journal, the *American Political Science Review*, with extending unwarranted privileges to those using quantitative and game theoretic approaches. For many movement supporters, these approaches are the beneficiaries of an imperialistic scientism that determines what counts as good as well as mainstream political science. Thus, the *Times* explained that the discipline was embroiled in a "feud" pitting "rigorous" quantitative against "traditional" qualitative researchers, also figured as "pronumber versus nonnumber folks."[3] The initiating broadside, an epistolary "manifesto" disseminated by e-mail in October 2000 and signed "Mr. Perestroika," named names of researchers who found the APSR irrelevant (e.g., James C. Scott, Benedict Anderson) and others (e.g., Theda Skocpol, Susanne Rudolph) whose intellectual contributions were being ignored in the race to publish "failed economists."[4] As this volume goes to press, the revolution's aftermath would seem to be shaping up nicely for perestroikans: in early 2003 the American Political Science Association launched a new journal, *Perspectives on Politics*, dedicated to publishing a wider array of research and which, in a counterhegemonic coup, took over the APSR's book review duties (see Hochschild 2003); Theda Skocpol became American Political Science Association president in 2002, to be followed by Susanne Rudolph in 2003; and the just completed 2004 APSA Council elections included a fledgling attempt to offer a competitive ballot.

But however tempting it is to read a direct challenge to a hegemonic positivism in the current uprising and its immediate outcomes, we worry that such a reading risks misrepresenting the constituencies on both sides, as well as the uprising's potential long-term consequences. Consider, for example, that the pro-perestroika camp includes comparativists who champion area studies in resistance to that subfield's drift toward large-n analyses; for many of these comparativists, privileged methodologies are less the issue than is the proper scope of their application. Furthermore, many political scientists whose work falls under the category of traditional qualitative research and who would presumably benefit from a more expansive publication policy on the part of the APSR are loath to cede the ground of scientificity to their quantitative colleagues. Even a quick glance at qualitative methodology texts (beginning with King, Keohane, and Verba's widely used 1994 *Designing Social Inquiry: Scientific Inference in Qualitative Research*) shows that "scientific rigor" informed by a numerical aesthetic is not limited to the realm of quantitative methods. In other words, "pronumber" and "nonnumber" folks regularly subject their work, and/or have their work subjected, to similar terms of scientificity.

Likewise, political theorists prominent in the debate often point to the narrow range of work that has appeared in the *APSR*'s theory pages; the journal misrepresents the scope of political theory, they insist, when it privileges traditional canonical exegesis and the Straussian sensibilities that often inform such work. But these calls for a wider representation of the subfield do not trouble the larger disciplinary division of labor that we argue is critical to the reproduction of positivism. On the contrary, the prevalent demands among political theorists for work that is more empirically relevant and timely risk obscuring the issue even further, by focusing the debate on the proper objects of political theoretical analysis rather than on how the subfield's very existence is underwritten by a foreclosure on what "empirical analysis" means or on how it can or should proceed. Indeed, the politics of representation that thread through the discipline's current uprising—in whose name, whose interest, whose vision or version of worldly engagement will publication and organizational governance decisions be made—can reproduce the hegemony we seek to anatomize; to the extent the debate remains framed in terms of the discipline's scientistic versus nonscientistic self-understanding, it threatens to reproduce an uncritical positivism that many (but not all) perestroikans identify as the major impediment to disciplinary diversity if not maturation.[5]

That scholars with a range of methodological commitments have found common cause in challenging the unrepresentativeness of the *APSR* and the national association is extremely significant. So, too, are the steps that have been taken in the aftermath of these challenges. But it is possible that these significant developments might leave intact the processes through which interpretive inquiry is disciplined: processes that sustain a fact/value dichotomy as our epistemological unconscious and fact neutrality as our unthought practice. In short, our worry is that the "methodological pluralism" being advocated throughout the discipline is susceptible to the fate of so many other pluralisms, namely, to reproduce the underlying structures that sustain a uniform core. In what follows we examine those underlying structures as they have taken shape in the three areas that arguably define "approach" for the discipline as a whole. We begin by examining the institutional reproduction of political theory, considering two recent essays that explicitly and critically address the distance between theoretical and empirical analysis, between the passionate clarity of normative commitments and the "messiness" of the factual world. Through symptomatic readings, we show how the disciplinary labor of the political theorist perpetuates the fact/value dichotomy, even or especially as he or she labors to reimagine the subfield.

In the second section we turn to political methodology. We suggest that here, too, the fact/value dichotomy continues to underwrite researchers' labor such that it titrates the strength of the subfield's ongoing debates; their capacity to affect larger disciplinary transformations is held in check by the extent to which the dichotomy continues to dictate targets and terms. In a final section, we consider positive theory. We suggest that its uncertain status as both quasi-subfield and generalizable approach—as both a discrete body of knowledge and expertise and an all-purpose analytic with no set object(s) of inquiry—represents the triumph of fact neutrality. Secured as both scientific (because of its mathematical-deductive method) and not hermeneutically naïve (because of its insistence on agents who choose), positive theory exploits the logical tensions and disciplinary division of labor organized by a fact/value dichotomy.

Theory

A sight, a spectacle. Obs. rare. Mental view, contemplation. Obs. A scheme or system of ideas or statements held as an explanation or account of a group of facts or phenomena; a hypothesis that has been confirmed or established by observation or experiment, and is propounded or accepted as accounting for the known facts; a statement of what are held to be the general laws, principles, or causes of something known or observed.—*Oxford English Dictionary*

Our contention is that political theory contributes to positivism's disciplinary hegemony by championing the normative dimensions of its own arguments against the natural science model. In *Schools of Thought: Twenty-Five Years of Interpretive Social Science*, one reads of "political philosophy, which has redefined the moral discourse of political science" (Apter 2001, 253), and of political theory, which participates in "the rethinking of moral inquiry underway in the American academy" (Elshtain 2001, 315). These statements are indicative of a de-emphasizing of the epistemic grounds on which a fact/value dichotomy was rejected, a de-emphasis that allows arguments about the production of knowledge to be recast as triumphs of moral theory. By favoring the normative highground, by refusing, as it were, to swing both ways, as is required by the recognition of the *mutual* constitution of fact and value, political theory serves to produce and protect a space in which the status of facts can be bracketed, much as proponents of the natural science model would have us bracket value. The point is not that normativity lacks import; to probe the constitution of social and political fact is to probe the constitution of value. But we are persuaded that a failure to appreciate precisely this point—that a normative orientation is always also an empirical one—constitutes the greatest risk to the subfield's relevance. The change in perspective signaled by our diagnosis of fact neutrality brings this point and this risk to the fore.

Central to the institutional reproduction of the subfield of political theory is what one of us has termed "the hegemony of normative theorizing": the near-consensus (and thus unthought) position that the business of political theory is to assert, defend, and/or critique alternative conceptions of the "good"—the just, authentic, liberal, free-of-resentment, democratic, emancipatory, feminist, etc.—political life (Mihic 1999). This emphasis overshadows the interpretive insight that such evaluations are constituted by the determination of fact. And, as already mentioned, the excessive concern with evaluation reinforces an excessive concern with the evaluator, with the self as moral and acting subject.

The reality that many political theorists do not do normative theory—do not, in other words, pursue evaluative analyses of politics and political life whose animating drive is prescription—is less salient than is the work the hegemonic position does in reproducing disciplinary divisions of labor. We might locate the origins of this division of labor in the so-called second behavioralist revolution and in a sort of settlement that was reached in the discipline: if the privileged mode of analysis was scientific and the privileged goal prediction, then political theory's claim to expertise and legitimacy would be the domain of nonscientific study.[6] It was an odd settlement: inasmuch as what counted as the legitimately nonscientific was the nonempirical, the authority of political theory appeared to hinge on its distance from the real world. Canonical interpretation, comprising textual exegesis, intellectual history, and rational reconstruction, became the central mode of analysis, while clarifying and adjudicating concepts, values, and texts became the key tasks. On this account, political theory could address historically contingent facts only from an evaluative perspective, and empirical analysis, including the determination of what is intelligible as a historically contingent fact, remained the purview of quantitative and other behavioralist researchers. The consequences of this institutionalization of the fact/value dichotomy are ongoing, even as the somewhat caricatured alignment sketched above has undergone profound changes.

In 1967 in "Neutrality in Political Science," Charles Taylor sketched another possible direction for political theory and the other subfields of the discipline: a path of "convergence" that implies mutual transformation. "In particular," he wrote, "my aim is to call into question the view that the findings of political science leave us, as it were, as free as before, that they do not go some way toward establishing particular sets of values and undermining others. If this view is shown to be mistaken, then we will have to recognize a convergence between science and normative theory in the field of politics" (1985b, 60–61).

Note Taylor's emphasis on findings. In this passage, he sketches an interpretive challenge to the fact/value and subject/object dichotomies that depends on a hermeneutic orientation confounded by the discipline's division of labor. His argument swings both ways in that it refuses value neutrality and what we have called fact neutrality. It is not simply that claims of fact are normatively constituted; the determination of fact also constitutes evaluation and delimits the evaluator. Taylor maintains that our views of the world, including what he calls the findings of political science, are nonneutral constitutive forces.

For Taylor, the classical formulation—Can you derive an ought from an is?—asks the wrong question. Rather than a relationship of derivation, he views facticity and normativity as mutually supporting grounds. You can't have one without the other in an explanatory or a normative account of politics; Taylor demonstrates this by analyzing a series of writers on class conflict. He contrasts, for example, Plato's position that class conflict can be eradicated with Aristotle's contention that it must be domesticated. This contrast is not a problem simply of moral theory. Aristotle doesn't think a world without class conflict can exist, and this claim about reality is inseparable from his normative position. On this view, the settlement between political theory and the rest of political science is impossible because there is no such thing as the simply nonempirical. In another example, contrasting Marxian thought and the work of S. M. Lipset, Taylor argues that differences between descriptive and explanatory frameworks are again key, because such frameworks "can be said to distribute the onus of argument in a certain way" (1985b, 90). If we rule out the possibility of transformation to a classless society, as Lipset does, "we are left with the choice between different kinds of class conflict: a violent kind which so divides society that it can only survive under some form of tyranny, or one which can reach accommodations in peace." What is significant is that "this choice, set out in these terms, virtually makes itself for us" (68–69). The language of violence and peaceful accommodation, which captures and conveys the facts of the situation, constitutes the field of evaluation and delimits the choices of the inquiring and evaluating subject. A serious engagement with the linguistic turn would have brought these sorts of inspections to the fore in political science. But because the fact/value dichotomy operates as a kind of disciplinary unconscious, the traditional division of labor persists and the dichotomy's effects pop up in some surprising places.

Consider, for example, Rogers Smith and Jean Bethke Elshtain, both prominent disciplinary practitioners who have participated in and benefited from interpretive interventions in the study of politics. One would expect their work to exhibit the convergence Taylor forecasted and presumed, and in many ways it does. Elshtain has throughout her career pioneered factually engaged, problem-driven political theory (see, e.g., Elshtain 1987). And in a recent article on "what's wrong with political science," Ian Shapiro (2002, 605–606) cites Rogers Smith's *Civic Ideals* as a model for critically reappraising "what is to be explained." In this book, Smith reevaluates Louis Hartz's *The Liberal Tradition* by calling into question its descriptive accuracy. Investigating constitutive intersections between fact and value to redefine a dominant explanatory framework, *Civic Ideals* is an example of the convergence Taylor prospected. But in recent essays by both Elshtain and Smith on the role of political theory as a subfield in political science, the fact/value dichotomy proves resilient.

Smith is a prominent member of the perestroika movement, and as a leading scholar of both American political thought and American political development, he is particularly well suited to the task of assessing and addressing disciplinary and subfield shortcomings. In "Reconnecting Political Theory to Empirical Inquiry, or, A Return to the Cave?" (2004) he offers a qualified endorsement of the current call for theory to become more relevant and timely (see also R. Smith 2002). For Smith, as for many others, this means theorists must delve into the "messiness of the real world," and they are to do this by connecting "more closely with empirical studies and concrete political problems" (2004, 66–67). He notes approvingly that this is already to some degree underway, and he lists as examples recent works by David Miller and Ian Shapiro that address justice in contemporary polities. But there is a problem, Smith observes, with this felicitous rapprochement between theorists and empirical researchers. As researchers, "we seek to achieve genuinely scientific knowledge about politics, that is to say, descriptions, explanations, and arguments that are as precisely stated, logically rigorous, well tested, and empirically accurate as possible." However, "when we move on to larger questions . . . our best science is inevitably 'softer' science. We have to stitch together roughly and prudentially the findings of various pertinent but distinctive specialized studies, filling the gaps with cruder sorts of data and assumptions, and linking them all together with even more disputable normative evaluations" (68).

In considering why the call for an empirically liaised theory is happening *now*, Smith recapitulates a widely accepted intellectual historical account of the discipline that highlights the rise and fall of "grand theory" (the exemplar is Rawls's *A Theory of Justice*) in relation to both external political events and internal debates about the sufficiency of behavioralist and economic, specifically rational choice, approaches. Echoing the claims made by a range of disciplinary historians, Smith observes that political upheavals "cried out for normative as well as empirical analysis," while the internal debates highlighted both behavioralism's failure to address such topics "very fully" and its "tacit normative bias toward the status quo" (2004, 72–73). To this explanation of grand theory's waxing and waning Smith adds his own insight, that the move toward abstraction manifests a certain "desperation" on the part of authors apropos the conflictual times in which they lived: precisely the contested character of worldly events suggested "that they could do more through abstract, relatively disengaged forms of political writing" (76–77). Smith concludes that the current call for more empirically focused work can be linked to "less visibly polarized" disciplinary and political worlds: "even in the context of a new sort of global war, there is . . . less sense than in the 1960s that dramatic transformations are possible in the near future" (80–81). Translated into the terms of our analysis, Smith's claim is that facts are less fraught now than they have been in the past.

Smith's apparent comfort with the assumption that some *we* out there agrees on the facts is itself indicative of fact neutrality, but from our perspective this is not the most telling feature of his analysis. Note that his account reproduces a common view of political theory as a subfield, according to which there is a real world toward which theorists are ambivalent and from which they can disengage. And neither engagement nor disengagement entails a rejection of the fact neutrality that is their disciplinary inheritance. In this and other respects, "A Return to the Cave?" is marked by the imperatives of the current disciplinary division of labor even if Smith's own work is not. We take this disjuncture to be more than a moment of odd or interesting amnesia; on the contrary, it is highly symptomatic of how self-reflective inquiry—(re)consideration of how disciplinary practitioners practice their craft—tends unavoidably to take shape through the hegemonic terms of political scientific intelligibility.

Consider on this score how Smith's treatment of empirical research in this essay performs the erasure of interpretivist challenges, even or especially as he refers to a "failure to capture the interpretive dimensions of human life." Not only does he rehearse the distress over imprecision in measurement, he points to critiques of behavioral and rational choice approaches that center on the former's failure to produce "scientific results" and the latter's "unduly reductionist" approach to political phenomena (2004, 72). These characterizations are not so much wrong as they are woefully incomplete. We have more to say about this below, but here we want to emphasize how dissension in the field is being framed in terms wholly compatible with a hegemonic positivism: first, because the framing deploys the anti-interpretive categories of verification ("rigor," "precision," "testing") as the sine qua non of empirical method; second, because it presumes—even as it does not "endorse" (86)—the categorical difference between empirical work, which describes, organizes, and explains political reality through fact gathering, and theoretical work, which evaluates that phenomenon by shuttling between theory and political reality so rendered. Once the issue about how best to gather and process facts has been settled, the theorist stands ready to receive them and to begin the practice of evaluation.

This stance highlights how even newly engagé political theory, such as is called for by Smith and other perestroikans, forecloses the possibility that facticity is itself a proper object of theoretical solicitude. The consequence of this reiteration of the fact/value dichotomy is a continuation of the identification between grand theories and systematized normativities, on the one hand, and scientific methodologies and a real world whose facts resist easy capture, on the other. Smith, like so many others, is especially concerned by empirical "messiness"; he characterizes the theorist's proper response to this mess as tolerance and realism concerning the limits on what can ever *really* be verified. In so doing he reinforces the notion that the sense-making strategies currently used to manage facticity, the rubrics that connect facts to one another, remain beyond the purview of theorists. When these rubrics go uninterrogated, their analytic and descriptive categories (e.g., resources, interests, attitudes) can only be accepted or rejected as approximating stylistics. That they are instead deeply invested hermeneutics of social and political relations, identities, and dispositions is no secret, certainly not to interpretive researchers or to most political theorists, Smith included. But, again, our concern is with how the disciplinary division of labor preserves this fact as an open secret rather than a spur to a more radical questioning. Because disciplinary practices interpellate theorists as specialists in normativity and empirical researchers as specialists in facticity, interpretive political science remains difficult, if not impossible, to recognize in discussions about methods and goals.

Whereas Smith's essay suggests that a convergence between political theory and the rest of political science means in essence that theorists should "get with the facts" and empirical researchers should "get with the values," Elshtain recognizes the epistemic dimensions of arguments against the fact/value dichotomy. In her contribution to *Schools of Thought: Twenty-Five Years of Interpretive Social Science*, she does so by emphasizing the import of description; but even in this more nuanced account of political theory as a subfield, the fact/value dichotomy as disciplinary unconscious persists and her recognition of the factical requisites of interpretation disappoints. Elshtain tells us that the subfield of political theory is "an unabashedly normative enterprise" and explains that political theory has been "defined" as a "story of contestations *within* political theory." With the canon as point of departure, theorists quibble over which texts are in (and which are out), and theorists argue about how to approach and interpret these texts. "But," she continues, "whatever their answers to textual questions or modes of interpretation, political theorists come together to engage in a contest of another sort, one that pits political theory against political science" (2001, 315). At this point, the fact/value dichotomy as disciplinary unconscious emerges with a vengeance.

In a footnote designed to qualify her portrait of the field, the division of labor between an *us* that does normative work and a *them* that does not is even more sharply drawn. "I would be loath to give the impression of a war unto death," Elshtain writes, "and certainly many political theorists and political scientists have maintained diplomatic relations throughout the years." One wonders how recognition of the mutual constitution of fact and value fits into the warring encampments she describes. "Few political theorists," the footnote continues, "disdain altogether empirical research; rather it is a particular epistemology that precludes so-called 'normative' questions that draws their fire. The discussion that follows is about this debate and should not be construed as an attack on empirical research *per se*" (2001, 327–328). Empirical research per se is posited here as an enterprise separate from political theory, and a primary orientation to the facts is posited as the purview not of the political theorist but of somebody else.

Elshtain concludes by presenting the work of Václav Havel and Jane Addams as exemplars and by arguing that political theory should take direction from them. Havel, countering what Elshtain terms "abstract systematicity," rejects ideology and "tries to demystify and diversify, to look at the messy, complex realities of *this* situation, here and now, as that which requires our attention and calls forth our very best and clearest attempts at thick description laden with moral notions" (2001, 322–324). With Smith, Elshtain sees the real world as a site of messiness that complicates thinking, but she does not draw a sharp distinction between fact and value at this point. Reality's complexities and complications are due to the mutual constitution of fact and value. "Stories," in Addams's work, "are intrinsic to her method of social diagnosis: this is, in an interesting way, a method that enabled her to combine empirical observation—telling the facts—with strenuous moral lessons" (324–325). Why does, or rather who would, this disappoint? From the perspective of Taylor's forecasted convergence, the shared ground of an explanatory framework and even the practice of political science are undermined. All researchers are stripped of their expertise, in that the complex realities of any present situation are in Elshtain's view self-evident. "Telling the facts" matters to the extent that the story strengthens and is thus subjugated to a moral lesson. With Havel and Addams as exemplars, Elshtain celebrates description, but as an aid to evaluation. The determination of fact is not pursued as itself a problem of inquiry or as a theoretical task, and strikingly, she no longer views theorists as specialists in normativity. "Such a revival of moral inquiry," on the model of Addams and Havel, "strips the political theorist herself of any privileged role in the discussion." How so? "One engages then as a citizen among citizens, a neighbor among neighbors, and a friend among friends" (326–327). Our view is that the academic study of politics is both much more and much less than citizenship, and that to collapse the distinction between them destroys the ability of each role to inform the other. But such musings take us into a different line of inquiry.

The significance of these passages, for our purposes, is that the disciplinary division of labor produced by (and productive of) a distinction between fact and value is openly (yet, surely, unwittingly) reinstantiated in an account of the debate that Elshtain presents as the demise of the distinction between fact and value. She is forwarding a description disallowed by the epistemic stance of the interpretive insights she champions. Tellingly, however, her description is an accurate account of the history of the subfields in political science. It accords with accounts of the settlement between political theory and the rest of political science noted above and endorsed by Smith. And this accordance, in combination with the refusal to follow through implications of the demise of the fact/value dichotomy in Elshtain's essay, demonstrates why a historical account alone is insufficient to the task of demonstrating political science's hegemonic positivism. That history is crucial to this end. But the whole story, which we do not attempt here, is legible at points where the history of disciplinary practice and the logics of theoretical formulations meet, sometimes complement, and at other times exceed each other.

Data

Plural of datum. A thing given or granted; something known or assumed as fact, and made the basis of reasoning or calculation; an assumption or premiss from which inferences are drawn.—*Oxford English Dictionary*

Political methodology is a subfield in political science concerned with how empirical data are crafted and analyzed. Historically, this concern has focused on quantification; thus, *methodology* has become virtually synonymous with statistical and other mathematical approaches, and *methodological rigor* calls to mind the standards of reliability associated with this work. More recently, the subfield has incorporated nonquantitative approaches, dubbed *qualitative* methods, into its scholarly repertoire. Of course, political science has always relied on nonquantitative methods, including oral history, participant-observer research, institutional ethnography, and textual analysis. And it would seem obvious that these modes of inquiry also involve skill, as well as their own standards of rigor. The subfield's historical inattention to these obviousnesses reflects its origins in the discipline's behavioralist settlement. Initially charged with training students in statistical analysis, political methodology has long retained its focus on research into how empirical inquiry might proceed, while leaving the question of what empirical knowledge might be or entail to philosophers of social science. This institutionalized gap between methodology and epistemology has helped to obscure what might otherwise be a more accurate picture of the range of extant research practices: the actuality of divergent approaches has been offset by the singularity of the methods subfield, while general questions about the interpretive sufficiency of *any* particular approach remain relegated to the contemplative realm of philosophy.

The fact neutrality that characterizes methodology follows from this division of labor: inasmuch as their expertise has consisted in the development of increasingly sophisticated tools for quantitative analyses, scholars in methodology rarely, if ever, have had cause to (re)consider the assumptions about facticity that underlie their research protocol. The incorporation of qualitative approaches—the ongoing efforts to specify, systematize, and refine the procedures and skills appropriate to nonquantitative analysis—would seem inevitably to upend this fact neutrality. Surely, the structures of intelligibility that render facts meaningful as such must be directly addressed when the imperatives of numerical representation no longer dominate methodologists' understanding of political analysis. But there are several reasons why this sure deduction might remain at odds with the facts. First is the oft-noted tendency, mentioned in our introduction, to assimilate qualitative methods to the standards and expectations of positivistic inquiry. These assimilating moves occur along several different dimensions: in articles and symposia newly sensitized to the needs of qualitative researchers (Adock and Collier 2001), in newly established institutes dedicated to the advancement of qualitative research,[7] and, as Peregrine Schwartz-Shea and Dvora Yanow (2002) have recently demonstrated, in newly revised methodology textbooks that guide graduate training. Along each of these dimensions, the subfield's organizing assumptions about hypothesis-driven data are being retooled to accommodate the research sensibilities of interpretive researchers.

Although many subfield critics take these retooling moves to be unabashedly imperialistic, there is also an awareness among qualitative researchers that their field never entirely rejected positivist assumptions. Ann Lin (1998), for example, has persuasively shown how qualitative work has always encompassed two traditions, one positivist and the other interpretive; the goal of the former is to tease out causal relationships, she argues, while the latter is oriented toward understanding causal mechanisms, or otherwise put, "explaining how particular variables interact." Lin insists that what ultimately distinguishes these orientations are "the questions one asks of the data" (163). Likewise, many quantitative methodologists express support for pluralizing their field, sometimes in terms that go beyond tepid tolerance. The language used is often one of shared goals and similar processes; however distinct the analytic postures of quantitative and qualitative researchers might appear to be, they argue, there is ample common ground on which researchers might come together and be reconciled.[8]

Our own skepticism about such pluralist gestures arises not because we doubt the sincerity of those who make them, but because we notice how these gestures can leave untouched an underlying assumption about facts as "given": what differently questioning researchers do with the data is at issue, rather than the status of data as such. So while there is often an acknowledgment that political facts are "fuzzy," "historically contingent," or even "socially constituted," the imperative to render data intelligible as "variables"—figures in relation to which determinations of change over time, synchronic case comparison, or even mechanism identification can be made—cuts short the attention paid to facticity. Here the imperative to explain curtails the imperative to describe, much as in political theory, where description is ceded to evaluation. The fuzziness, contingency, and constitution of political facts thus remain challenges to be overcome, through the continuous monitoring of potential "biases" and full "immersion" in the political lives and worlds one is attempting to explain. We do not doubt that such monitoring and data-gathering techniques regularly produce excellent work. What we question is whether the debate about method shaped within the subfield—in its language, grammar, in short, its structures of intelligibility—will dislodge the discipline's unthought certainty that meaningful political analysis happens *after* the facts have been gathered. Indeed, even an arguably growing appreciation for work offering "thick description" can serve to prop up the status quo, by adapting the disciplinary division of labor to recognize as a speciality the work of those who describe. With the hermeneutically inclined so labeled and accommodated, the regular business of political science can continue more or less unchanged.

This interpretation suggests that the scientizing tendencies in qualitative methodology represent less a positivist capture than a fuller interpellation of the qualitative researcher. Certainly the moves many nonquantitative researchers make to couch their approach and conclusions in positivist terms make disciplinary sense: scientizing one's work is a rational response to the presumption that such work must otherwise consist in opining or evaluation, which, in a world built on the fact/value dichotomy, remain the illegitimate and legitimate alternatives, respectively, to hypothesis-driven empirical work. Thus, whatever might be the impact of positivist evangelism in the subfield, the assimilation of qualitative methods to a hegemonic scientism has been bolstered by the very reasonable insistence that qualitative research is not normative analysis. That it would be taken as such follows from the grossly attentuated choice between analyzing facts *or* assessing values sustained by the discipline's historical division of labor.

To be sure, the misrecognition of qualitative work as essentially normative is to some extent the result of semantic slippage: *quality* is both the foil to *quantity* and an evaluative term in its own right. Beyond a slippery vocabulary, however, is the resilience with which "facts" and "values" serve as the discipline's covering terms for "the given" and "the indeterminate." Here we notice a different kind of slippage: between an identification of *what* researchers are analyzing and *how* they analyze. Consider, for example, how normal political science typically approaches the study of values. Inasmuch as researchers rely on behavioralist techniques such as surveys, they successfully circumvent the verification problem that distinguishes normative analysis; as individual responses are measured, aggregated, and cross-tabulated, methodological technique crafts data according to the facticity of people's attitudes. Now rendered as the facts of what people report they think and feel, values can be figured in the grammar of objective science: as variables establishing relations of covariance that subtend the possibility of causal and thus predictive claims. But when qualitative analyses lack these or analogous mechanisms through which the subjectively wrought and complexly constituted is rendered commensurable and thus verifiable, they call attention to the ongoing uncertainty of their "data." With this breach in fact neutrality comes doubt about whether or how the analysis remains properly *empirical*. And if it is not properly empirical, and one is reluctant simply to dismiss it as bad science, then the remaining option is evaluation. In this way, the ongoing presence of indeterminate facts always threatens to raise the specter of normativity, regardless of what the inquiry's objects or goals might be.

The specter is mostly benign. As we have argued, normativity has a designated sphere in the discipline's division of labor and thus analytic validity. But that sphere also constrains: even hard-nosed positivists readily concede that interpretive work—under the various labels of constructivist, postpositivist, postempiricist, and critical theoretical—has its place when the issue is evaluation. Qualitative researchers who understandably do not want their work to be read exclusively or even primarily in these terms have incentives for fighting the science wars. Thus, qualitative research, a category we see entrenched in the professional self-understanding of current graduate student cohorts, allows its practitioners to navigate between the Scylla of quantitative facticity and the Charybdis of unverifiable normativity, even as the category serves to preserve these fantastical options. Among the beacons held out to help empirical researchers across the fact/value divide is positive theory, whose growing status in political science coincides with the intensification of debates in political methodology. The body count in this rescue mission is unknown, and how that number might be ascertained is unclear. Our interest lies instead in the extent to which positive theory continues and advances the fact neutrality that the empirical/normative, quantitative/qualitative, and fact/value divides have sustained in the discipline. As already suggested, we believe these divides constitute the hegemonic position through which positivism is perpetually reborn in political science.

Positive

Formally laid down or imposed; arbitrarily or artificially instituted; proceeding from enactment or custom; conventional; opp. to *natural.* Explicitly laid down; expressed without qualification; admitting no question; stated, explicit, express, definite, precise; emphatic; objectively certain.—*Oxford English Dictionary*

William Riker, the commonly acknowledged founder of positive theory, engaged in a self-conscious attempt to make political science scientific over and against what he called "the movement toward phenomenology and hermeneutics and other efforts to turn political science into a belles-lettristic study" (Riker [1982] 1993, 346). In 1962, long before positive theory had consolidated within the discipline, he wrote the following: "Even political science . . . within which the obstacles of normative sentences and oversized events loom larger perhaps than in any other study, can take some hope from the fairly recent achievements of economics and psychology. Instead of abandoning the effort to create a science, students of behavior generally and political behavior in particular ought rather to examine the procedures of the physical sciences to abstract from them their techniques of success" (Riker 1962, 6–7).[9]

These techniques, according to Riker, center on the deduction of non-obvious, testable generalizations from a few necessarily unobservable premises. Because of positive theory's deductive approach, it, like political theory, is frequently recognized as only tangentially connected to empirical study; also like political theory, it is routinely criticized, and often ridiculed, on these grounds. Unlike political theory, positive theory has no aspirations to provide "normatively compelling answers to [important] politically relevant questions" (R. Smith 2004, 68). Indeed, positive theory is defined *against* the "obstacle" of normativity; its stated purpose is not to evaluate political facts but to explain them.

By figuring decision making as preference aggregation or, more complexly, as strategic moves in a game, positive theorists seek to explain politics with reference to how actors, acting rationally, are enabled and constrained to make some choices and not others. Theorists deploy formal, typically mathematical accounts of hypothetical preferences, actions, and outcomes, representing actions as preference-based choices in interaction with one another and outcomes as equilibrium states. The project is to derive, from common but limited axioms and diverse but specified assumptions, nontrivial generalizations about the dynamics of diverse political situations and processes. In the main, positive theorists challenge and refine one another's formalizations of political questions and produce new puzzles and solutions to puzzles generated by these formalizations. And in the main, positive theorists work alongside empirical researchers in a posture consistent with Riker's proposal: they tend to see their conclusions as capable of generating testable hypotheses that, if verified, will share the crucial virtue of being deductively and not only inductively supported.[10] It is this deductive support that confirms these generalizations as explanations; they are distinct from the "merely descriptive" achievements of even the richest naïvely empiricist work. But we should avoid the highly contestable move of characterizing a common self-understanding here. Like political theorists, positive theorists approach their work with a variety of assumptions about and descriptions of what it is they are doing. What interests us is their predominantly fact-neutral practice. Just as normative political theorists construct analytical frameworks with which to evaluate "the facts," positive political theorists construct analytical frameworks with which to explain them.

Positive theory's deductions can also be aimed at the utopian excesses of normative theorizing. Because "ought" implies "can," positive theory is not wedded to the "neutrality" of political science; Riker's most prominent book can be characterized as taking up Taylor's proposal to acknowledge and develop the "normative consequences" of disciplinary findings. In *Liberalism against Populism* (1982) Riker uses Kenneth Arrow's social choice insights into the complex and contradictory varieties of preference aggregation to argue the incoherence of the idea of popular sovereignty. Instead of moving back and forth between observation and principle, however, Riker derives his support for a chastened conception of democracy from the manipulation of formal assumptions. Like political theory, positive theory can question the fact/value dichotomy yet reproduce it by systematically bracketing fact in its attention to a putatively fact-neutral conceptual framework.

Positive theory is usually criticized on other grounds. The assumption of rationality that undergirds it has been subjected to extensive critique, as has the limited success of the field in producing results that are both nonobvious and empirically corroborated (see Sen 1977; Luke 1985; Green and Shapiro 1994). So, too, its chronic problems with endogeneity—the problem of variables that affect choices but remain undetected because they are internal to the game—have been regularly aired. We do not question the impact or some of the insights of these criticisms (arguably, Green and Shapiro's *Pathologies of Rational Choice Theory* is as routinely assigned in graduate programs as is King et al. 1994). But we want to suggest that they remain wide of the mark to the extent they remain trained either on positive theory's failure to deliver the scientific goods or on its reductive rendering of the decision-making process. Although it had its beginnings in logical empiricist attacks on extant political science, positive theory's practitioners now include mathematical idealists, scientific realists, and more or less philosophically inclined skeptics and pragmatists, whose differences matter less than the unity provided by a common formal vocabulary. Criticism that imputes common claims or goals for this vocabulary and its procedures is likely to hit some targets and miss others. Indeed, on an aggressively good faith reading of positive theory, its practitioners are not attempting to provide faithful representations of human processes or predictions of same. Their project is to perfect a heuristic that might provide insight into political systems. In fact, a substantial body of positive theory seems to be devoted to the task of figuring out how different institutional structures and rules affect the aggregation of given preferences. This is obviously of importance in understanding a range of political processes. And when the language of prediction is used in this work, as it frequently is, it is used in a strictly formal rather than existential sense (see, e.g., Austen-Smith and Banks 1999).

Of course, even an aggressively good faith reading must acknowledge the consequences of the inevitable slippage between heuristic and representation. On this score, we share the concerns of many in the discipline that positive theory evinces a powerful tendency to distort political action by reducing it to choice, and to otherwise delimit the field to that which can be figured in the vocabulary of neoclassical economics. Here we would make a tentative, but we think critical, distinction between rational choice/public choice on the one hand and game theory on the other: the latter does not necessarily posit an economic rationality that optimizes among commensurable goals. If this distinction holds, then the insights and representations of game theory are arguably far more strategic and thus political.[11] In fact, nonoptimizing and nonglobalizing game theory is radically political; it is willing to dispense with many of political theory's common comforts: with the view from nowhere, with the ideal of the judge, with the sovereign and/or introspective subject. Of course, positive theory often overreaches, and it remains vulnerable to criticisms of ahistoricity, decontextualization, and reductionism. But on this score, it is in what we can only consider good company: many systematic theoretical endeavors risk such criticism.[12] And surely, all powerful analytic frames share a tendency to seduce their adherents into selectively perceiving the world only through the lens those frames provide.

We offer this rapprochement to underscore that a critical assessment of positive theory hinges neither on that theory's factual corroboration nor on its normative suppositions. Whether or not the heuristic of rational gaming can reveal something interesting about any particular political situation remains an open question. And it is not our question. Indeed, the answer in any given case would depend in large part on an interpretive process that specifies and investigates when and why that situation, in particular, yields to rational gaming interpretation. The problem with indictments of the heuristic's normative and scientific shortcomings is that they leave a more basic problem untouched: that of its hermeneutic and that hermeneutic's relationship to the condition of fact neutrality.

Positive political science calls for positive theory because it calls for a heuristic that can give theoretical form to otherwise potentially shapeless and even meaningless results. Positive theory answers this call with an interpretive framework that leaves fact production unmolested and that satisfies empirical researchers' need to construct meaning while eschewing evaluation. It develops and refines its axioms and lives in a productive tension with independent empirical research: the former can lament and police the lack of deductive rigor in the latter, and the latter can report on the distance between its results and any hypotheses generated by the former.[13] Like normative theory, positive theory is an ongoing effect and cause of a disciplinary division of labor produced by positivism's fact/value dichotomy: both leave the problem of facticity to others. Given our own qualified acceptance of nonempirical work (perhaps itself a product of our disciplinary training and thus a curiosity to other social scientists), our remedy for fact neutrality does not require every political scientist to become an interpretive empirical researcher. More practical, and potentially more far-reaching, would be a sustained interrogation of the facticities on which the discipline currently relies,[14] and thus a general admission that we cannot blithely cross intradisciplinary boundaries unchanged.

But positive theory has succeeded, perhaps more than any other approach, in crossing intradisciplinary boundaries (relatively) unchanged. When sufficiently challenged in the conquest of a new frontier, its solution has tended to be to make the formerly exogenous endogenous. One area where this creates special difficulties, however, is the consideration of rhetoric. Game theory's hermeneutic, centered as it is on the points of view of strategic actors and their consideration of the points of view of others, opens up a huge space for the role of persuasion in the construction of belief: everything depends on players' assessments of conditions, possible choices, and outcomes, and the relations between them. Realizing this, positive theorists have made such assessments endogenous and, not surprisingly, have found it easier to contain their role in models of highly structured environments.[15] But how to rely on while blurring the distinction between rhetorical and other uses of language, and how to insulate, as far as possible, identities and preferences from changes in beliefs?

Some game-theoretical scholars are now trying to take the insights of interpretive political science very seriously, acknowledging their value in addressing the roles of symbols and rhetoric in the changing constitution of belief in states in transition. Thus, Bates, de Figueiredo, and Weingast (1998) address successful symbolic street protest in Zambia and the ethnification of politics in Yugoslavia, modeling them as actions and responses appropriate to high-stakes games of incomplete information. In a rigorous critique of this work, James Johnson (2002) notes its conceptual muddles, specifically the authors' inability to recognize that changes in beliefs can change the makeup of players and the bounds and possibilities of their games. We note additionally that the authors are sensitized to players as interpreters, but not to their own interpretive acts.[16] Here fact neutrality obscures the challenges involved in the "mere description" of political contexts, challenges that should be especially apparent in the study of states in crisis. Game theory's perspectivist intuitions incite at least minimal attention to rhetoric as strategic resource, but the challenges posed by rhetoric cannot be resolved within a hermeneutic that insists on the a priori preeminence of the strategic actor. Positive theorists are thus compelled by their assumptions to acknowledge while drastically containing the constitutive capacities of language—to turn away from the challenge of description so that endogeneity won't go "all the way down" and destabilize an analytical framework that must remain independent of a real world.

Positive theory's problems with rhetoric and facticity are on full display in Riker's posthumous *Strategy of Rhetoric* (1996). A formal and substantive study of the debates preceding adoption of the U.S. Constitution, *Strategy* emphasizes the role of rhetoric in forging winning electoral support for a Federalist program quite distant from the preferences of the median American voter of the time. The book is peculiar on many fronts—for example, the power attributed to rhetoric as a kind of underdefined linguistic technique begs questions about positive theory's own anti-rhetorical rhetoric[17]—but we wish here only to call attention to Riker's use of evidence. Although ostensibly interested in rhetoric and rhetorical force, Riker adopts a crude content analysis to test and confirm his formal derivations. Words are literally counted in order to assess the "weight" of historical statements (26–31). We don't suppose that he believed that the less concise statements were, the more important they were to their writers and speakers and the more convincing they were to their readers and listeners. We suppose instead that Riker was reflexively transmitting data—describing the real world that would either confirm or disconfirm the hypotheses he was bringing to it—and understanding his interpretive moves to be ones of classification and coding alone. Here Riker and his assistants were doing their own primary research, but doing it according to the protocols of others, because positive theory's concern is not with description but with how the facts bear on the separate conceptual universe of the theorist. It doesn't matter that these rhetorical data concern the very meaning being made of a developing political context. Considering the political imaginary of the conceptual universe of contemporary game theory—that this universe has expanded to recognize a plurality of differently shaped actors with histories and a plurality of perspectives, goals, and types of resources—its continuing insulation is crucial to keeping its complications from becoming more than analytical. In other words, positive theory's bracketing of the empirical allows it to sustain a world picture of fact that sits uncomfortably with its increasingly sophisticated strategic hermeneutic. Just as the priority of evaluation over description relies on and reproduces fact neutrality against political theorists' better judgment, so the priority of explanation over description goes against the better judgment of positive theorists.

As we have been at some pains to make clear, the ongoing effects of a fact/value dichotomy and of a methodological discourse that relies on it continue despite the fact that political scientists are doing interpretive work. Indeed, this approach characterizes the work of some prominent and highly visible political science scholars. We'd like to conclude by pointing to some of the institutional features of this disconnection between research practices and the disciplinary grammar through which they are made intelligible as such across subfield divides. As already suggested, the dominant methodological discourse serves in many ways to deflect or minimize challenges through the assimilating category of qualitative methods. More particularly, however, and as evidenced by the (re)alignments in response to Mr. Perestroika's broadside, it appears to be in the interests of both interpretive and other, more positivistic researchers to maintain an alliance to counter quantitative hegemony. In addition, many interpretive social scientists also do more "traditional" qualitative and quantitative work, which has often been key to establishing their reputations in the discipline. So the reality of intra-associational alliances and of individual practitioners' pluralistic practice both serve to dissipate what might otherwise be a sustained focus on the disciplining effects of positivism.

Interpretive scholars who remain committed to specifically disciplinary practices—for professional, personal, intellectual, or more diffuse institutional cultural reasons—often find ways to connect their work to mainstream political science, for example, by showing how interpretation of a context shows a division masked, a distinction not made, or who the relevant players in the game might be. Here interpretive work performs the role of corrective or even disruptor of existing categories, without inducing the need for a critical examination of dominant approaches. It should also be noted that a number of these scholars look outside the discipline for receptive audiences. Mr. Perestroika highlights their absence from the pages of the APSR. More telling, we believe, is their steady attrition from political science departments. Often wholly or jointly appointed in other social science departments, as well as in public policy and law schools, interpretive scholars find interdisciplinary havens with a more catholic approach to empirical and theoretical work. And though interdisciplinarity can serve as an important force in countering departmental decrepitude, this doesn't always work to the advantage of the less positivistically inclined (political science's warm embrace of economics being the obvious case in point).

In sum, political science promotes a hegemonic positivism despite the intentions and orientations of individual practitioners, and any attempt to measure, evaluate, or reform this condition must first do what the disciplinary unconscious of the field frustrates: it must interpret it. The analysis on offer in this essay has attempted such an interpretation by focusing on an internal division of labor that institutionalizes the gap between political theory and political science and that fosters a methodological debate constrained by this division. Our conclusions thus echo the claims made by Breslau and Steinmetz in their contributions to this volume: that the ideological, intellectual, and ultimately philosophical struts of positivism are deeply embedded in the everyday routines and larger organizational imperatives of disciplinary fields. Whether or how political science's predominant scientism is likely to change cannot then be determined simply by assessing the facts of how prevalent interpretive work is in the discipline or by assessing practitioners' expressed values apropos the worthiness of interpretive work. Any such determination must remain a prospective judgment, inseparable from the hermeneutic investments in both fact and value through which we endeavor to make sense of our field.

Notes

For extremely helpful discussions on the state of the discipline, we thank Don Herzog, Andreas Kalyvas, Audie Klotz, Ken Kollman, Mika Lavaque-Manty, Ann Lin, Scott E. Page, Amalia Pallares, Arlene Saxonhouse, and participants in the Workshop on Women of Color Studies in Political Science at Northeastern University, August 2002. For comments on a draft of this article we thank Julia Adams, Ann Davies, George Steinmetz, and Lisa Weeden.

1   For an account of political theory's (self-)positioning within the discipline as a whole, see Emily Hauptmann's contribution to this volume.

2   Although the number of subfields varies somewhat between institutions and professional organizations, the typical disciplinary configuration recognizes five: comparative politics, American politics, international relations (also world politics), political theory, and political methodology.

3   The article adds parenthetically that this terminology "could no doubt spur a protest of its own" (Eakin 2000).

4   The original epistolary manifesto can be accessed at, among other places, http://www .uoregon.edu/7Ermitchel/PS620/original_perestroika_email.htm–28k. A collection of perestroika documents and articles is maintained by the Post-Autistic Economics Network at http://www.paecon.net/.

5   See Daniel Breslau's parallel argument in this volume regarding the limitations of field-specific challenges to positivism in economics.

6   For variations on and modifications of this historical rendering, see Gunnell (1986), Farr (1988), and essays by Terrence Ball and John Gunnell in Farr and Seidelman (1993).

7   See, for example, the Consortium for Qualitative Research Methods, hosted by Arizona State University: http://web.polmeth.ufl.edu/research.html.

8   For an intriguing and interestingly symptomatic account of this common ground, see Kritzer (1996). See also the critical discussion in Steinmetz (forthcoming a) apropos efforts in sociology to shore up an (ultimately positivist) distinction between interpretation and explanation.

9   Riker's department-building at the University of Rochester was enormously successful, to the point where positive theory and its axioms have supplanted "empirical theory," a phrase widely used in the 1960s, throughout the discipline. For a sympathetic history of positive theory, see Amadae and Bueno de Mesquita (1999).

10   Our description glosses over important distinctions. It is an attempt to capture the basics of a common ground shared by a diverse group of practitioners: formal modelers, rational choice theorists, public choice theorists, and game theorists. Many of

these practitioners are not at all preoccupied in the way that Riker was by epistemology and ontology, and those who are might range from scientific realists to positivist skeptics in their understanding of their program. Compare, for example, McCubbins and Thies (1996) with Ferejohn and Satz (1994).

11   On the difference between economic and strategic rationality, see Engelmann (2003). See also O'Neill (1999). Aside from O'Neill, this distinction is not the one attended to by positive theorists themselves, who distinguish game theory (sometimes "noncooperative" game theory) only by its consideration of players' anticipations of one another's moves; see Austen-Smith and Banks (1999).

12   The more algorithmic applications of Marx and Freud spring to mind here.

13   This dynamic can best be seen in the literature on the U.S. Congress, where positive theory has enjoyed a high profile and stimulated empirical researchers to ask new questions. Empirical shortcomings have in turn stimulated positive theorists to dramatically revise their premises by, for example, rendering institutional structures endogenous to their models, seeing them anew as equilibrium solutions to games of incomplete information; see Shepsle and Weingast (1995).

14   Such an interrogation seems to be well underway in the subfield of international relations, particularly in what have come to be called "constructivist" challenges to orthodox approaches. But the constructivist label itself may augur a positivist transformation and assimilation of these challenges, at least in U.S. political science. See, for example, the concerns expressed in European critiques of Alexander Wendt's *Social Theory of International Politics* (1999) in a special issue of *Journal of International Relations and Development* (2001) devoted to this text.

15   Ferejohn and Satz (1994) note the irony that choice theory works best in situations where choices are highly limited.

16   We should also note that a shortcoming of this piece is its mapping of contrasting rational choice and interpretivist approaches onto distinct objects of study, for example, interests versus culture: "Interpretivists focus on the politics of culture" (Bates, de Figueiredo, and Weingast 1998, 223).

17   Throughout Riker's scientific and philosophical efforts (as opposed to his more strictly historical and more strictly formal work) there is a problem in coming to any terms with language. Thus, already in his philosophy articles of the late 1950s language is both everything (it defines the very realities of political actors and scientific investigators according to a radical nominalism) and nothing (its use is merely "subjective" in relation to the prior world that it sometimes veils); see Riker (1957, 1958).

On Your Marx:
From Cultural History to the History of Society

GEOFF ELEY

hen I was deciding to become a historian, there was not much interdisciplinarity haunting the corridors of history departments, it's fair to say, and still less in Britain than here in the United States. When I arrived in Balliol College, Oxford, in October 1967 as a humble boy from the provinces, coveting access to a new universe of knowledge, poised at the portals of scholarship and learning, I was crestfallen to discover that the first term of required course work consisted of Gibbon and Macaulay, Tocqueville, Burckhardt, and, last but not least, the Venerable Bede. Amid this chronically unimaginative Oxford pedagogy, which sought to dampen the ardor of youth in the cold shower of antiquated knowledge, the nadir was the Venerable Bede's *Ecclesiastical History of the English People*, composed in the early eighth century. I could not believe the inveterate and asinine archaism of this requirement. Actually, in Bede's chronicling of the Christianizing of England, the main relief came from the marauding exploits of Bede's nemesis, King Penda of Mercia, whom I always imagine as a ferociously bearded avenger of truly Pythonesque proportions, heroically defending England's last redoubt of vigorous paganism, rampaging and pillaging his way across the monastic landscape.

I mention this experience mainly to set the scene for 1968. Lying in wait to ambush the complacencies of the British history profession were a series of quite different historiographies. In fact, the historiographical scene was about to be dramatically opened up, and it's impossible to exaggerate just how truly exhilarating that turned out to be. In the English-speaking world there were three principal sources of innovation: first, the long-gestating influence of the group who became known as the

British Marxist historians, together with the broader coalitions of economic historians, labor historians, and social historians they helped to
build; second, the more immediate impact of the social sciences, which
from the late 1950s began challenging the thinking and practice of many
historians; and third, the inspiration offered by the Annales School in
France, whose key works became systematically translated during the
1970s.

This is where Sylvia Thrupp's role becomes so impressive. As Terry
McDonald remarked, a "penchant for interdisciplinary study" was not
exactly very fashionable among historians in the 1950s and early 1960s. But
in this period *Comparative Studies in Society and History*, the journal
Thrupp founded in Chicago in 1958 and brought to Michigan three years
later, was entirely notable for the genuine reciprocity it fostered between
historical thinking and various kinds of social science. This unforced
eclecticism, and the willingness to think comparatively across the disciplines, across fields, and across periods was the hallmark of Thrupp's
editorship of the journal and became the Michigan History Department's
signal virtue by the 1970s, a virtue of which subsequent generations of the
Department remain the grateful legatees.

This relationship between history and social science is one strand of the
larger story I'm interested in telling, which concerns history's ability to
deal with the big questions of how and why societies change or not. For
me, neither history's pleasures nor its critiques can be complete without
this larger ambition, without the possibility of making the world more
knowable in some overall or meaningful sense, part of which, as Marx
reminded us, is to make the world more changeable, if not by actually
changing the world necessarily, as these days that seems to be too much to
expect, then at least by showing how the world's changeability might be
imagined and thought.

In relation to that larger ambition, there have been two massive waves of
innovation since the 1960s, each drawing its momentum from exciting
and contentious interdisciplinary conversations. The first of these extended from the 1960s into the 1980s and involved the discovery of social
history; the second wave produced the "new cultural history" and crested
during the 1990s. Both those movements shared a relationship to the
political debates of their times, reflecting the desire for greater democratic
inclusiveness, through which hidden and suppressed histories could be
recognized and disempowered groups enter the profession. Although the
main emphases differed—new social historians stressed material life, class,
and society, while their culturalist successors refocused on meaning and

the forms of perception and understanding that people make and display —each wave brought a radical broadening of the historian's legitimate agenda. Over a thirty-year period, accordingly, the practices, subject matter, and composition of the profession have been dramatically pluralized.

But the movement out of social history into cultural history was not a simple progression. It entailed some losses. In embracing the contemporary skepticism about "grand narratives," for example, and in substituting microhistories of various kinds for the macrohistories of capitalism, state making, revolution, and large-scale transformations, many historians have also retreated from social explanation of the ambitious kind so inspiring in the 1970s. Indeed, that is the setting for what I want to talk about in this essay. In 1971, the Marxist historian Eric Hobsbawm published an enormously influential essay titled "From Social History to the History of Society," in which he argued that the real point of the new approaches was less the recognition of previously "hidden" or marginalized subjects than the possibilities for writing the history of society as a whole. This meant partly a commitment to generalization and theory, to trying to keep the whole picture in view, and partly a particular analytical approach aimed at understanding all problems in their social context. And, of course, in 1971 that tended to imply that social causes and explanations were also the primary ones.

Here is one of my key contentions: we don't have to reinstate the primacy of social explanation and a materialist model of social determination to take seriously the tasks of social significance or social analysis. Now that much of the heat and noise surrounding the new cultural history has started to die down, it's time to reclaim social history in the main sense advocated by Hobsbawm, which involves always relating our particular subjects to the bigger picture of society as a whole, whether we're social historians, political historians, cultural historians, or whatever. Hence the terms of my title. That is, we can preserve the gains of the new cultural history without having to abandon everything we learned as social historians. Speaking for myself, I was trained as *neither* a social historian *nor* a cultural historian, but that has never stopped me from learning how to be both. For me, this is more a matter of general standpoint than of which card-carrying professional identity you sign up for.

I'd like to make my case using three examples. I won't talk about them in any full or rounded way, but instead I use them for a series of snapshots of the past forty years. Edward Thompson's *Making of the English Working Class* was published in 1963 and remains one of the several genuinely Great Books of the big social history wave; Tim Mason's (1993, 1995) studies of

Nazism during the 1970s took the explanatory ambitions of social history to what I'd call the outer limits of their potential; Carolyn Steedman's *Landscape for a Good Woman*, published in 1987, represented the best edge of the emerging new cultural history. I end with a peroration for the 1990s and the present. These three moments, each separated by about a decade— the moments of Thompson, Mason, and Steedman—can be summarized in a word as *optimism, disappointment,* and *reflectiveness.* I'll leave open the question of how the mood of the present might best be described.

Edward Thompson: Optimism

E. P. Thompson wrote *The Making of the English Working Class* from outside the academic profession while teaching in adult education in Leeds. He was an active Communist until 1956, when he left to become a leading voice of the British New Left. He remained a public intellectual for the rest of his life, most vitally during the 1980s in the international peace movement. He created the Center for the Study of Social History at Warwick in 1965, the only time he held a regular university job, directing that Center until 1970, when he resigned. This combination of professional marginality and intellectual radicalism was essential to Thompson's aura.

I deal with Thompson briefly because he's the best-known of my three cases. His book inspired most of all by advancing such an eloquent counternarrative of British history against the official story of slow and peaceful parliamentary evolution. It also made a highly original argument about class formation. It was an antireductionist manifesto, attacking narrowly based economic history, overdeterministic Marxism, and static theories of class. Through Thompson's example, the move from labor's institutional study to social histories of working people gained enormous momentum. His later work then focused on the transformations of customary culture beneath the onslaught of a rapidly commercializing capitalism. In these ways, he transformed our perceptions of industrialization.

What would I like to capture in this first snapshot? I first read *The Making of the English Working Class* in the winter of 1968–69, when my attention was very far from the official classroom and its curriculum, that hollowed-out and desiccated learning of the Oxford History School, which produced mainly cynicism about the purposes of becoming a historian. Discovering Thompson's book helped me recover some belief that doing history might make a difference. It showed me that the national narrative was unstable and could be told oppositionally in some very different ways. I'll mention four aspects in particular:

—Thompson uncovered suppressed traditions of popular democracy. In his account, British society and its institutions were forged from conflict and the effects of injustice, violence, and exploitation. Democratic goods came only as a result of collective action, mass politics, and insurrectionary resistance against a corrupt and coercively secured political system.

—Thompson also reclaimed certain national cultural traditions for the left, notably, the romantic critique of industrialism and other utopian moments of cultural criticism of the nineteenth century, including the ideas of William Morris, to whom Thompson had devoted an earlier enormous book. Here his work converged with that of Raymond Williams, whose own first book, the hugely influential *Culture and Society*, had just been published.

—Thompson's book recovered the ambiguities and complexities of cultural history, most powerfully in its extraordinary reading of Methodism. It insisted on the legitimacy of popular culture, which the dominant ideology refused to acknowledge and which the left had also found it surprisingly hard to see. This is where Thompson's influence connected with the growth of cultural studies.

—Finally, by pioneering research on popular protest, customary culture, and the transformations brought by industrialization, Thompson opened out the understanding of politics. In that sense, *The Making* belongs with Hobsbawm's *Primitive Rebels* and George Rudé's *The Crowd in History*, two other key texts of the late 1950s and early 1960s.

All of this added up to a particular sensibility, which was also profoundly the sensibility of Sixty-eight. One of the vital things about Thompson was that he was a leading member of a left intellectual generation in Britain who had *not* sold out, but who continued to live truthfully within an ethics of commitment that seemed worth trying to emulate. He held a place for a certain kind of eloquent, troublemaking, disobedient, and creative disrespect for the rules and decorums that the hierarchies of power and prestige require us to perform.

Tim Mason: Disappointment

There were key limitations in Thompson's work, too, and during the 1970s it became subject to far-reaching critique. But rather than going into the criticisms, I'm going to fast-forward to my second snapshot, which concerns the work of the German historian Tim Mason.

The author of a brilliant series of essays and a massive volume on Nazism and the working class, Mason was the premier social historian of the Third Reich during the 1970s, whose influence was absolutely crucial for my generation of German historians. More than anyone else, Mason rendered Nazism vulnerable to social history, not by "normalizing" it into a subject like any other, but by showing as carefully as possible how Nazism remained subject to social determinations. He insisted on the class-political context of Nazism's emergence, its origins in the field of conflict defined by the German Revolution and the polarized political culture of the Weimar Republic.

Mason began from deep skepticism about the impact of Nazi ideology. Both underrepresented in the Nazis' ranks before 1933 and solid in their own allegiances, he claimed, German workers resisted the Nazi political message. Even after the labor movement's violent destruction, in fact, the regime ruled only within certain practical limits, frustrated by the workers' strong residual and defensive class consciousness. Indeed, the potential for class conflict remained structural and endemic, a permanent and irreducible feature of social life under capitalism, giving working-class culture an imperviousness against ideological persuasion, which neither Nazi repression nor propaganda offensives could ever completely sweep away.

Mason took pains to distinguish between the political *resistance* of the labor movement's illegal Communist and socialist undergrounds, which were isolated from wider support, and the slow reemergence of class conflict in industry, which he termed the workers' *opposition*. Coerced and deprived of their historic organizations, ordinary workers pragmatically accepted the Third Reich's material improvements, he argued, while still withholding their positive allegiance. But that opposition was essentially nonpolitical. It was a silent refusal of the regime's ideological message: "It manifested itself through spontaneous strikes, through the exercise of collective pressure on employers and Nazi organizations, through the most various acts of defiance against workplace rules and government decrees, through slowdowns in production, absenteeism, the taking of sick-leave, demonstrations of discontent, etc." (Mason 1981, 120).

Mason was directly inspired by Thompson's *Making of the English Working Class*. In analyzing Nazism, he took an underlying master category of "society" as his guide. While accepting the breadth of the Third Reich's social support, he saw the existence of society as an intact and separable domain, as a source of viable agency that, however limited and compromised, still allowed Nazism's impact to be contained. Society in that sense remained a damaged but recuperable resource. Even during the war, when militarist expansion and the racialist frenzy of genocide overwhelmed everything else, the integrity of the "social context," however battered and reduced, could still be analytically upheld. Indeed, Mason's grand ambition was to build a general analysis of Nazi rule from the ground up in that way, deriving both its driving force and its continuing constraints from the shape-shifting dynamics of class conflict and class relations.

Twenty years later, German historians have jettisoned this attempt to explore the subtle and submerged ways in which the autonomy of society was preserved. Instead, they concentrate on showing how, under the Third Reich, the social order was comprehensively remade. Different social groups may have kept some defenses against Nazism's explicit ideological message, but their behavior succumbed more insidiously to the spreading of racialized discourse across all the shelters and crevices of ordinary life. That hegemony of racial thinking—across social groups, in multiple sites of policymaking and knowledge production, in state and nonstate institutions, in academic and popular culture—has become the new orthodoxy for historians of Nazism, irrespective of the complexities of social differentiation in that older, 1970s sense.

In fact, the immunity against Nazi influences Mason ascribed to the working class has definitively gone. Whether colluding in the exploitation of coerced foreign labor during the war, or wearing the uniforms of the genocidal army on the eastern front, or generally enjoying the "good times" of the Nazi era from the mid-1930s to 1942, German workers could no more withdraw themselves from the consequences of Nazi rule than any other group, whether those consequences were structural (like the racialized labor market and its rewards), social (as in the new patterns of discriminatory sociality), or cultural (in the new public mores and their sanctions). Thus, the social historical starting points of the 1970s have dissolved: "Theories of fascism have been replaced by models of the racial state, in which biological rather than social categories are preeminent" (Nolan 1995, 132). As the main organizing category of Third Reich historiography, "class" is now trumped by "race."

In this sense, Mason's project, of writing a general class-based account of National Socialism's relationship to German society, failed. In the early 1980s, he came to doubt his ability to carry it to a conclusion. He also resigned his teaching position in Oxford and moved to Italy in 1984, turning instead to the study of Italian fascism. Although he continued publishing essays of great brilliance, he never finished his magnum opus on Nazism and the working class. In fact, in March 1990, worn down by a sense of personal, scholarly, and political difficulty, he killed himself, quite carefully and deliberately, in a hotel room in Rome.

Carolyn Steedman: Reflectiveness

For someone of my generation, coming from the milieu we both shared, it's impossible not to read Tim Mason's story as a tragic allegory of the ambitions and disappointments not only of the social history wave of the 1960s and 1970s, but also of the politics that were always centrally involved.

By the mid-1980s, the cutting edge of innovation was shifting away from social history to the so-called new cultural history in its various forms. One aspect was again the opening up of new subject matters social historians hadn't explored, such as the history of sexuality and histories of art and aesthetics, histories of popular culture, and histories of "strange" and exotic beliefs. Another aspect was a different kind of interdisciplinary borrowing: no longer from the "hard" social sciences, but from anthropology, literary theory, and linguistics instead. Most important of all, social explanation and social causality lost their hold on the imagination. Historians became ever more skeptical about the answers social analysis seemed able to deliver. "Materialist" explanations based primarily on the economy and social structure now seemed to oversimplify the complexities of human action. Previously attractive structuralisms now seemed "reductionist" or "reductive" in their logic and effects.

Instead, it became important to concentrate on meaning and the forms of perception people make and display. Above all, language required attention in this respect, because in trying to understand past actions historians have only the extremely partial and arbitrary descriptions that happen to have survived, forming a screen of representations between now and then. Those surviving documentary traces are really "texts" requiring interpretation. In other words, rather than being a social scientist collecting, counting, and measuring data and placing everything in its social context in order to explain it, the historian should become an anthropologist or ethnographer, a literary critic or a linguistic analyst.

Out of this came the so-called linguistic or cultural turn, which proved as influential as the turn to social history twenty years before. This was especially clear among new graduate students entering the profession, in the subjects and approaches that got them excited, in the kinds of dissertations they wanted to write. Angry battles raged around all of this during the 1990s, field by field, in the journals and conferences, and of course in relation to hiring decisions and the main directions history departments wanted to take.[1]

There are many ways of parsing this story, and my choice of Carolyn Steedman's book is again partly autobiographical: reading it was key for my own encounter with the intellectual shift I'm describing; its author also belongs to the same generation inspired by Thompson's *Making*, and its reflections on English childhoods are to a very great extent also my own story. But in other respects, of course, our stories are quite different. I was a boy, not a girl, and through that particular difference Steedman composes a kind of counter-counternarrative that works deliberately against Thompson's radical-democratic counternarrative in *The Making*, although in the end I think it destabilizes and reenables the latter rather than overturning it. Moreover, it's precisely because of its gendered standpoint that I choose Steedman's book, because by far the most effective challenge to the given materialisms of social history during the 1980s came from feminists.

Landscape for a Good Woman: A Story of Two Lives uses Steedman's own and her mother's stories to challenge some of our main scripts about modern British history. She ranges back and forth between different parts of the nineteenth and twentieth centuries, between historical works and types of fiction, between history and pyschoanalysis, between the personal and the political, and between individual subjectivity and the dominant available narratives of a culture, whether in historiography or politics, grand theory or cultural beliefs, psychoanalysis or feminism. For my purposes today, I highlight three features of this extraordinarily rich book:

—Its use of the personal voice was immensely liberating. This was partly its freedom of form, its refusal of linear narrative, because it moved back and forth between Steedman's personal history, the wide repertoire of historical knowledges needed to shape it, and the forms of grand theory and types of determinism that have fixed its given meanings into place. In method, Steedman assembles a case history in that sense, giving us what she calls "the bits and pieces from which psychological selfhood is made" (1987, 7). Her use of the personal voice also authorized reflectiveness at a time when my generation was experiencing the kind of disappointments that drove Tim Mason so tragically over the edge.

—Those disappointments were about the collapse of grand narratives, or rather, about the inability of existing grand narratives to capture either the directions of contemporary societal change or the diversity of past historical experience. Steedman told a story of working-class lives that didn't fit, that didn't belong in the available scripts of socialism, the post-war democracy of opportunity, and the solidarities of working-class culture, and that couldn't easily be reconciled with the given frameworks of social history and cultural studies. Her story was about a mother who didn't want to mother, a patriarchy without a patriarch, and forms of longing and desire, envy and exclusion falling outside the acceptable frames of class and gender consciousness. Even more, it was about historians' inability to develop a language for dealing with personal longings. It was about what she called "lives lived out on the borderlands . . . for which the central interpretive devices of the culture don't quite work" (5).

—At the same time, Steedman's book constantly engages the big picture. It refuses to dwell exclusively inside the minutiae of personal experience and individual lives. On the one hand, it focuses on those places where history and culture meet subjectivity to explore how such encounters are converted into a sense of the self. On the other hand, it shows the ability of the given social and cultural environment to consign some types of self-hood to the margins. In showing us "the fragmented and ambivalent nature of experience and self," Steedman's case study exposes "the precariousness of theory and class consciousness when it fails to incorporate the wants and needs of the individuals—especially the women—within it" (Chamberlain 1986, 43).

In the end, it's vital that Steedman addresses the insufficiencies and exclusions of a class-centered approach to social history without abandoning the standpoint of class altogether. Likewise, I chose her book as my exemplar of the turning to cultural history because it makes the cultural turn without waving "the social" goodbye. In concluding, therefore, I'd like to return to my starting point concerning the gains and losses the cultural turn has entailed.

Conclusion

In many ways, of course, all the types of social history established during the 1960s and 1970s continue in practice much as before, often in great profusion. What has disappeared, or at least gone into definite recession, is the earlier totalizing ambition, the goal of writing the history of whole societies in some integral and holistic way. What seems to have become extremely hard to maintain is the macrohistorical understanding of whole societies changing across time, guided by a confident knowledge of developmental or structural models drawn from the social sciences. "Society," as a confident materialist projection of social totality in that way, has become much harder to find, because the antireductionist pressure of contemporary social and cultural theory has de-authorized it. Originally, that antireductionist logic was very empowering. As the hold of the economy became loosened during the 1980s, and with it the determinative power of the social structure and its causal claims, the imaginative and epistemological space for other kinds of analysis grew. The rich multiplication of new cultural histories was the payoff.

But there were also costs. The founding inspiration for much of the social history of the 1960s was a series of grand debates, concerning the general crisis of the seventeenth century, the nature of revolutions, the connection between popular revolts and early modern state formation, the rise of absolutism, and more. For a while, this impetus carried over. In the 1970s, the Brenner debate and grand designs by Perry Anderson and Immanuel Wallerstein were all major Marxist contributions, while combinations of modernization theory and neo-Braudelian vision inspired other attempts at capturing the structural transition to the modern world, from Charles Tilly to Keith Thomas. But now, among social historians (though not among historical sociologists), this ambition has withered on the vine. Eric Hobsbawm remains a lone exception in this regard.

This is the first point of my conclusion: some confidence in the possibility of grasping society as a whole, of theorizing its bases of cohesion and instability, and of analyzing its forms of motion needs to be regained. My second point is: things change. In my lifetime as a historian, I've seen two huge reorientations of historical studies, as I've been trying to describe. I see absolutely no reason why the cultural turn should be the end of the story or the final chapter in some whiggish romance of ever-improving historiographical sophistication. Something else, I'm sure, is waiting in store. Third, politics matters, and it does so in a doubled sense. On the one hand, the impetus for both shocks of innovation, the social history wave and the new cultural history, came from broader political developments extending way beyond the academy per se. Again, I see no reason why such political impetus should not recur, especially given the extraordinarily momentous and dangerous political time we're in the process of entering. On the other hand, each of the superb historians I've discussed—Thompson, Mason, Steedman—spent a large part of their careers *outside* the university involved in one kind of public activity or another. History as a discipline originally found no place for Steedman, and she made her way back into the historical profession only two decades later by the force of the excellence of her work, eventually by a nice symmetry directing the very same Center for Social History that Thompson had originally founded at Warwick thirty years before.

So if *optimism, disappointment,* and *reflectiveness* were the main registers of the radical historian's sensibility between the 1960s and the 1990s, maybe *defiance* is now the appropriate response for our new contemporary moment. For more than a decade we've been encouraged to see ourselves at "the end of history," in a world describable only through neoliberalism's redeployed languages of "modernity," through the relentlessly totalizing pressure of market principles, and through a new set of brutally demonizing rhetorics about good and evil. But the effectiveness of grand narratives can't be contested by skepticism and "incredulity" alone, least of all when new or refurbished grand narratives are already on the rampage so powerfully reordering the globe. Grand narratives can't be contested by pretending they don't exist. That's why we need new "histories of society." In their respective times, both social history and the new cultural history were *insurgent forms of knowledge,* and the relevance of historical studies for the future will certainly require renewing an insurgent spirit again.

Note

1   For my earlier reflections on these histories, see Eley (1996, 193–243; 2000, 93–109).

Provincializing the Social Sciences

MICHAEL BURAWOY

orn in the nineteenth century of Occidental descent, the social sciences have sought to transcend history in three ways. They have hidden their Eurocentric origins behind universalistic knowledge claims; they have perpetuated and justified the original division of disciplines by naturalizing and eternalizing their distinctive objects (the capitalist triumvirate of economy, state, and society); and they have secured their scientific truth by defining their methodology (positivism) as context-free. These are the sweeping claims of the Gulbenkian Commission on the restructuring of the social sciences, *Opening the Social Sciences* (Wallerstein et al. 1996), which caused a flutter of interest when it appeared in 1996. Written by eminent academics from different disciplines and chaired by Immanuel Wallerstein, the Gulbenkian Commission's historic role was to draw attention to the imperial birthmarks of the social sciences.

Exposing the parochialism of the social sciences, however, is only the first step toward restructuring. On the basis of its reading of current trends in the social sciences—new meanings of science and the rise of multidisciplinarity—the Gulbenkian Commission proposed a comprehensive unification of all academic knowledge. I argue that Wallerstein and his fellow commissioners overlook the constellation of interests that embroil the social sciences and, therefore, misread the empirical trends. In other words, the Gulbenkian restructuring veers toward another abstract universalism, passing over the ongoing historical context of the social sciences, their conditions of production, and their broader societal effects. Instead of an Olympian *restructuring*, I propose to bring the social sciences down to earth by *provincializing* their universalism, their disciplinary divisions, and their methodology, grounding them in their particularity and their specific context of production and exposing their contradictory participation in the social, economic, and political worlds they seek to comprehend.[1] To provincialize is to burst the bubble of disinterested knowledge and to address the role of social science in supplying ideologies that justify market tyranny and state unilateralism.

Wallerstein's Totalizing Utopia

For Wallerstein,[2] the social sciences, born in sin, are now on the way to redemption. False universalism, anachronistic disciplinary divisions, and a narrow methodological positivism[3] are being superseded in a totalizing social science.

—Claims to universalism by Western social science have been challenged by particularisms rooted in a variety of anticolonial and postcolonial struggles abroad and by excluded groups (racial minorities, women, popular classes, etc.) at home. Wallerstein does not, however, seek to replace the old universalism with a series of particularisms but with a new *pluralistic universalism*, "on the analogy of the Indian pantheon, wherein a single god has many avatars" (Wallerstein et al. 1996, 59–60).

—The social sciences, and here Wallerstein mainly focuses on the nomothetic sciences of politics, economics, and sociology, are themselves based on an outmoded distinction between state, market, and civil society. The rise of multidisciplinarity—new programs and even new departments, new scholarly associations, new journals—is the harbinger of the *decomposition and transcendence of the tripartite division of the social sciences*. Professional organizations are the die-hard defenders and enforcers of the anachronistic separation (46–47).

—The methodological positivism that underpinned Newtonian science and provided the model for social science has been replaced. Positivism's search for laws, induced from an empirical and passive world, that predict the future with certainty has given way to a conception of complex systems whose futures are radically uncertain, as they try to grapple with a nature that is now thought of as active and creative. Such a new self-understanding of the natural sciences (associated with chemist Ilya Prigogine) converges with cultural studies, where poststructuralism has introduced radical skepticism toward all foundational knowledge. The terrain of this convergence will be a reunified social science. "It also now seems that the social sciences are no longer a poor relative somehow torn between the two polarized clans of the natural sciences and humanities; *rather they have become the locus of their potential reconciliation"* (69, emphasis added).

Wallerstein, therefore, is proposing the supersession of all contradictions in a grand synthesis, a seamless integration of all disciplinary knowledge that will be centered in a comprehensive social science.

In short, if knowledge production in the nineteenth century was limited by the cradle of its creation, now, finally, knowledge has broken the bonds of its determination, constituting itself as a unitary system that transcends history. The social sciences, in particular, can finally escape the stamp of the society they interpret. In an uncharacteristic move, Wallerstein casts aside the constraints of space and time to take up a radically utopian project. He suppresses the conditions of the production of knowledge, the interests behind the production and consumption of knowledge, and the relations of power that define terrains of knowledge production. Far from rejecting positivism, Wallerstein fulfills its dream by arriving at pure science emancipated from its roots in society, at a science outside the society it describes and in which it dwells. Positivism's ambition to unify the sciences is realized but extended to incorporate the humanities, too. Far from provincializing the social sciences, Wallerstein gestures to another unelaborated universalism.

Knowledge and Human Interests

Recognizing their origins does not remove the three sins. It requires re-situating universal knowledge claims, disciplinary divides, and context-free methodologies in the world that constitutes them, even as they constitute it. We approach false universalism, disciplinary divisions, and unreflective positivism by asking two simple but fundamental questions never broached in the Gulbenkian Report:

—*Knowledge for whom?* To put it most crudely, as social scientists, are we merely talking to ourselves or are we concerned with an audience beyond the academy? To be sure, the raw material for the social sciences comes from the society in which we are embedded, but should and can social science be given back to the world from which it was taken? Can we and should we transcend Bourdieu's hiatus between analytical and folk theory, between the logic of logic and the logic of practice? We have devoted much energy to interpreting the world, with all the problems of translation, but what about changing the world, translating back our interpretations?

—*Knowledge for what?* If we are concerned about the world beyond, then, as social scientists, are we consigned to work out solutions to problems given to us from without? Are we servants of power, seeking the best means for a given end? Or are we also engaged with questions about those goals themselves? Is it, to use Weber's language, our business to engage in questions of value rationality (value discussion) as well as instrumental rationality? Are the social sciences part of a wider "eclipse of reason," as Horkheimer put it, as they, too, suppress a reflexive concern with ends?

Posing these two questions generates the fourfold Table 2.[4] *Professional social science* is instrumental knowledge inasmuch as it is organized to solve puzzles in research programs defined by assumptions, bodies of theory, methods, questions, exemplars—all of which have to be taken as given if a research program is to expand. The research program arises and functions in an institutional context that shapes it, a context that includes the university, itself embedded in society. Wallerstein's restructuring of the social sciences dwells on this category of professional knowledge, reiterating the positivist concern with mirroring reality.

If professional knowledge grows within taken-for-granted disciplinary frameworks, it is *critical social science* that calls into question these frameworks, whether they be singular research programs or multiple research traditions. Here we may find dissident economists such as Joseph Stiglitz and Amartya Sen, or critical sociologists such as Robert Lynd, C. Wright Mills, and Alvin Gouldner, or, more recently, feminism and poststructuralism. Critical theory is the conscience of professional knowledge. It is reflexive knowledge not only because it interrogates the normative foundations of professional knowledge but also because it does so through open discussion. Wallerstein's assault on the disciplines comes under the rubric of critical social science, although it does not explore the normative dimension.

Critical social science supplies the normative dimension of *public social science*, which elaborates and calls into question values held in society through the stimulation of open public discussion, what Jürgen Habermas calls "communicative action." There are many forms of public social science, depending on the nature of the public and the mode of communication, but we can most easily distinguish between elite forms that are disseminated through the media, what I call *traditional* public social science, and grassroots public knowledge that is an unmediated dialogue between social scientists and their publics, what I call *organic* public social science. Here we find the social scientist in dialogue with communities of

Table 2. Types and Dimensions of Disciplinary Knowledge

	Academic Audience	Extra-academic Audience
Instrumental Knowledge	Professional	Policy
Reflexive Knowledge	Critical	Public

faith, neighborhood associations, labor movements, social justice movements, and so forth. It is too easy to focus only on the traditional forms of public social science, associated with such renowned figures as Kenneth Galbraith and Paul Krugman in economics and Pierre Bourdieu, Anthony Giddens, William Julius Wilson, David Riesman, and Robert Bellah in sociology. Traditional public social science should not eclipse the organic public social science that may be less visible but is more ubiquitous and effective. The organic anchors traditional public social science just as the latter can inspire, contextualize, and link up different grassroots engagements.

Finally, we must distinguish between public and *policy social science.* In both cases, the audience is extra-academic, but whereas the former generates discussion over ends as well as means, the latter focuses exclusively on the most effective means for a predetermined end, predetermined by some client who "employs" the social scientist or by a patron who defines a broader agenda for research. As compared to the professional social science with its *puzzles* defined by research programs, policy social science focuses on *problems* defined by policy agendas. As we shall see, depending on historical context, some disciplines (economics in the United States today) are more effective in the policy arena, whereas other disciplines are more effective in the public sphere (sociology in the United States today).

There are many qualifications to this fourfold scheme, not least that each type of knowledge is itself internally complex. Professional and policy knowledges have their reflexive moments just as critical and public knowledges have their instrumental dimensions. In the same way, professional and critical knowledges have an interface with extra-academic audiences; think of the semipopular magazines associations put out or the connection of critical knowledge to social movements that flow into the academy. Equally, policy and public knowledges have an interface with the academic world. Indeed, we may say that each of our four types can itself be further subdivided into public, professional, critical, and policy quadrants.

In addition, one has to distinguish between this division of social science labor on the one side, and the location and/or trajectory of social scientists through that division on the other. Thus, an aspiring sociology student might begin her career in the public sphere working for the labor movement. On burning out, she decides to develop her talents in new directions. She enrolls as a graduate student, an aspiring critical sociologist. Confronted with an elaborate obstacle race that excises all moral moment, she considers dropping out—but where to? Instead, she tries to come to terms with professionalism, perhaps even pursuing two tracks at once: an academic on the inside, an activist on the outside. More than likely she accepts, for the time being, the strictures of the academic career. If she wins a tenure-track job, then by the time tenure finally arrives (or doesn't) she may be burnt out again or she may have lost touch with the critical and public impulses that motivated her commitment in the first place. Or perhaps those impulses resurface and flourish as never before.

Immanuel Wallerstein himself offers us an instructive career. Very much the critical sociologist in the years of the Columbia student protests of the late 1960s, Wallerstein's critical sociology began a decade earlier with his 1959 dissertation on independence movements in Africa. He then began to question reigning development theory that explained Africa's failure to develop by reference to the values or character of the African people: their countries couldn't catch up because Africans were not modern. He turned this claim upside down, arguing that countries cannot develop in the twentieth century in the same way that Europe developed in the sixteenth and seventeenth because the world itself has changed. It was one thing to be an early riser creating the modern world system; it was another to develop in the periphery of an already-existing rapacious world capitalist economy.[5] Wallerstein's success quickly turned world system analysis into a recognized research program in professional sociology, albeit still in its critical quadrant. He attributed sociology's resistance to the full acceptance of world systems theory to the compartmentalization of the disciplines. World systems theory itself brought together history, economics, political science, anthropology, and sociology without specializing in any one of them. Because it lay across disciplines, it never sat comfortably in any one. The new research program did find homes in Binghamton and Paris, but it was always hampered by its interdisciplinary character. From here it was a short step to an open attack on the disciplines themselves, turning Wallerstein once more into a critical theorist, arguing that the disciplines were a creature of the past and of limited relevance to the modern world.

Having deployed my four knowledge categories to provincialize Wallerstein's career, I propose now to use them to provincialize the Gulbenkian

Report itself and to address its three bêtes noires: positivism, universalism, and the disciplinary divide.

Provincializing Positivism without Losing Science

No matter how positivism is defined, and we've been treated to many definitions in the foregoing essays, it necessarily entails the suppression of both questions: Knowledge for whom? and Knowledge for what? Pursuing these questions allows us to provincialize positivism and understand its place in social science. But let us first specify the meaning of the social sciences, distinguishing them from the humanities on the one side and the natural sciences on the other.

Dividing disciplinary knowledge into these four types—professional, policy, public, and critical—clarifies why the humanities and the natural sciences cannot be simply fused into a unified system of knowledge. The natural sciences are primarily focused on instrumental knowledge whose criteria of validity are internal to science: science that is externally applied to problems defined for the scientist. Reflexive knowledge, in the sense defined above of engagement with normative issues, is not integral to the natural sciences. It does happen that natural scientists engage in the production of critical and public knowledges, as we know from the history of physics and the atom bomb. More recently, scientists have become embroiled in social movements opposing the ever closer relationship between industry and the university in such areas as genetic engineering, and contesting the direction of research on moral grounds (K. Moore 1996; Schurman and Munroe 2004). Although natural scientists have become more concerned with the public dimension of their research, especially as the university increasingly comes under attack, it is not an essential part of their enterprise.

Very different are the humanities, whose knowledge is concentrated in the reflexive mode. Poets and painters are fundamentally dependent on the expert critic or the wider public for validation of their work. In separating the reflexive from the instrumental, critical knowledge in the humanities takes on a slightly different meaning, one that is more hermeneutically focused on the preservation of the integrity of art and literature in the face of degradation from without. Yet the academic is on shaky terrain because there are no purely internal criteria for the validity of knowledge, although the movement toward cultural studies and literary theory is surely a move toward academicization of knowledge.

The social sciences, on the other hand, are at the intersection of the humanities and natural sciences because they necessarily partake in both instrumental and reflexive knowledge. Here are research programs that are deeply embedded in value premises that need to be critically fleshed out and become the object of public debate. Indeed, I would argue that the vibrancy of a social science depends on the reciprocal influence of all four types of knowledge: professional, policy, public, and critical. The flourishing of each is dependent on the flourishing of all. Professional social science, in varying ways, depends on critical analysis of its foundations. On being sensitive to the movement of public issues and policy agendas, just as public social science depends on the accumulated bodies of professional knowledge and the legitimacy it offers, it depends on an infusion of values from critical knowledges and, often, the debate that policy interventions so often generate. Critical social science could not exist were there no professional knowledge to criticize, but it also benefits from the examination of the hidden assumptions of policy research and public debate. Although policy social science does not necessarily appreciate the sometimes vigorous criticism it receives, subjecting itself to such critique strengthens its autonomy with respect to its clients. It may use professional knowledge, but it should not dictate professional knowledge by virtue of its control over purse strings.

This balance among the four knowledges is often hard to maintain in the face of centrifugal forces. On the one hand, there is a tendency for academic knowledge to regress toward the esoteric; on the other hand, there is a tendency for extra-academic audiences to capture the social scientist, who then becomes a servant of power, often blowing back into and distorting professional knowledge. Equally, pandering to publics leads to faddishness or pop social science, just as critical knowledge that is accountable to a community of intellectuals may turn inward and become dogmatic. Professional knowledge suffers from the same regressive temptation, self-referentiality and insularity, especially when it sees itself as competing with other professional knowledge. As Andrew Abbott (1988a) has pointed out and as Breslau makes clear in his essay on economics, the more abstract the knowledge, the higher its status.

In arguing for the reciprocal interdependence of these four types of social science practice, I am not at all suggesting that they simply blur into each other. To the contrary, their interdependence depends on their *relative autonomy*. Like Sandra Harding in this volume, I believe that an effective public social science, far from being incompatible with science, depends on the best of science. In my view, however, such a science has to be postpositivist in that it has to recognize its own implication in the world it studies. It is a view of science that focuses on the growth of knowledge and prediction rather than on a positivist concern with correspondence to reality. Specifically, I see such professional bodies of knowledge developing through what Imre Lakatos (1978) calls scientific research programs, which have their own relatively autonomous logic, although one that is not impervious to external stimuli: autonomy without insulation. Scientific research programs are impelled forward through their engagement with internal contradictions but also with external anomalies.

From the standpoint of this division of social science labor, *positivism* becomes the self-misunderstanding of professional knowledge, that knowledge is and has to be autonomously produced, an autonomy without embeddedness. Under certain historical conditions, such as the ones Philip Mirowski outlines in his contribution, positivism becomes part of the professional habitus and is seen to be necessary for knowledge to grow. It is, to use the vocabulary of Bourdieu, the *illusio* of the professional field, the rules of the game to which we are so riveted and that thereby eclipse the conditions of their existence. As we shall see, the conditions of the positivist illusio are eroding, forcing the rules out into reflexive deliberation and creating pressures for their transformation.

Provincializing Universalism without Resorting to Particularism

If positivism is the method, universalism is the project: to develop knowledges that are true in all contexts, context-free knowledge. In recent decades such unreflexive universalism has received hammer blows from social movements. The women's movement has been at the forefront in exposing the masculinist assumptions of social science, demonstrating their rootedness in the conditions of men, conditions that women daily create, conditions that were for so long invisible to social science. Anticolonial movements have been no less effective in unmasking racial and ethnic assumptions of Western social science. Such unmasking has been the project of postcolonialism and the critiques of Orientalism. The struggle between universalism and particularism is none other than the struggle between an instrumental knowledge that can be applied by experts in all situations and a reflexive knowledge that reveals the arbitrary grounds on which professional knowledge rests. Critical social science directly engages the assumptions of universalizing theory, while public social science enters a dialogue with local knowledges, demonstrating the limits of all-purpose recipes.

Exploring this matter further, we see that the division of social science labor harbors not just the possibility of reciprocal interdependence, but also the reality of antagonistic interdependence. Professional social science is accountable to a community of peers, concerned to establish themselves in the hierarchy of disciplines, vested in the monopoly of inaccessible knowledge. Public social science is justified by its relevance and accessibility to given publics to which it is, at least partially, accountable. With the funds it brings, policy research all too easily imposes its own agenda on professional knowledge. Open debate about the value foundations of social science disrupts the scientific process that takes them as given. Stable containment of these antagonisms requires hierarchy, and hierarchies come in different forms: despotic and coercive or hegemonic and negotiated.

The compromise and unstable hierarchies among our four types of knowledge vary with context. In the United States, we are accustomed to professional social science being hegemonic; in Third World countries it can happen that public knowledge is hegemonic. In the Soviet Union, policy social science imposed itself on the profession, blotting out (manipulating or forcing underground) critical and public social science. In Scandinavia, policy social science is also important but not so exclusively as to be at the expense of the other types of knowledge. Critical knowledge is rarely hegemonic, but it nevertheless plays its role not least in authoritarian regimes, where it also often succumbs to annihilation. In short, the configuration of professional, policy, public, and critical social sciences varies from country to country and from one historical period to the next.

This in turn can give rise to an emergent global division of social science labor. With their enormous resources, built on a vast complex of higher education, advanced capitalist countries dominate professional social science, leaving a vacuum in poorer countries, split between opposition and attachment to that Western professional knowledge.[6] A global division of labor that concentrates professional knowledge in the North, a division promoted by the World Bank, threatens to destroy local synergies of the professional, the public, the critical, and the policy knowledges. Social science that parachutes in from the United States, dealing in abstractions that are irrelevant to local needs, breaks up the production of local knowledge and directs it into fruitless channels, resulting in a clash of Western "universalism" and local "particularism."

Thus, countries of the global South find it an uphill task to retain a disciplinary nexus of all four knowledges worked out on a national terrain. Although it is undoubtedly true that the United States dominates the production of professional knowledge, it is nevertheless a terrain on which alternative professional knowledges, true to national contexts, might develop, professional knowledges that might emerge from the critique of Western paradigms but also from local publics and policy concerns. Crossing borders, social scientists from the South can collaborate in knitting together their own emergent body of professional knowledge, reconfiguring dominant paradigms by building them up from below. Beyond the antagonism of universalism and particularism are the struggles on the terrain of a hegemonic social science, itself a very complex and contradictory unity, emanating from the West. Provincializing social science cannot mean a *reactive devolution* into scattered and defensive nativist particularisms, but the *reconfiguration* of the existing global division of social science labor. The social scientists of the global North, particularly in the United States, must first recognize just how powerful they are and that their universal knowledges are universal only because of that power.

Provincializing the Disciplines without Dissolving Them

Tracing the social sciences back to their idiosyncratic birth, Wallerstein claims that the divisions among them are arbitrary and therefore should be abolished. Certainly, there are blurrings, overlappings, and hybrids, but the underlying distinctions, I argue, do have their rationale, rooted as they are in the abiding division of capitalism into the three spheres: economy, state, and civil society. There is no perfect fit here, and some social sciences (e.g., anthropology, geography, and history) do not have a clear object, which can be to their critical advantage. In the final analysis, to provincialize the disciplines is to recognize their continuity in the abiding foundations in the societies that created them. Thus, to wish them away is to indulge in utopian fantasy.

We can appreciate the distinctiveness of the different social sciences with the same grid that counterposes type of knowledge (instrumental vs. reflexive) to audience (academic vs. extra-academic). Put crudely, economics is oriented toward the instrumental and sociology toward the reflexive, with political science in between. This balance is reflected in the organization of professional knowledge. Economics has an integrated, coherent, and overweening research program, buttressed by a relatively authoritarian and elite dominated profession with its own internal hierarchy, as Dan Breslau shows in this volume. In its imposition of a singular paradigm, one might liken the economics profession to the Communist Party, both in its internal organization and its imperial ambitions. The organization generates rare but distinguished dissidents; a Nobel Prize often helps! The internal coherence of economics makes it an effective policy instrument: policymakers know they will get a definitive answer to their questions whether they are right or wrong.

Very different is sociology, with its multiple research traditions, its canonical return to the founders. If economics is like the Communist Party, sociology looks more like anarchosyndicalism, with its forty-three sections, its multiple journals (some two hundred). Its range of research traditions, self-conscious about their value premises, makes sociology less effective in the policy world but more responsive to critical thought and multiple interests arising in the public arena. Political science lies between these two disciplines, with dominant internal disciplinary pressures to emulate economics, the so-called rational choice framework, which has generated its own, more reflexive opposition, the perestroika movement. As we can see in the essays here by William Sewell, Geoff Eley, and Webb Keane, history and anthropology, although deeply divided, are bent more toward the reflexive than the scientific pole—and indeed they are an effective bridge to the humanities—while human geography can look in many directions, not least the physical sciences.

But here I focus on the triumverate of economics, political science, and sociology. Their divergent configuration of knowledges (public, professional, critical, and policy) in part reflects their relation to their objects of knowledge. As Tim Mitchell argues in this volume, over the past century, but particularly the past half-century, economics has been amazingly successful in defining and thereby constituting its object: the economy as seen through the lens of the market. The close link between economics and its project of expanding the market is not a nineteenth-century anachronism but a devastating twenty-first-century reality. In the same way, political science has historically made its object the state and its project the consolidation of political order,[7] just as sociology's object of knowledge is society, or more specifically, civil society, and its project the expansion of the social. By civil society I mean the constellation of popular associations that grew up in Europe at the end of the nineteenth century: political parties, trade unions, voluntary organizations, mass education, newspapers. Civil society is a messy residual concept, which perhaps accounts for why sociology is such a sprawling, undisciplined discipline. Be that as it may, state, economy, and civil society set the terms for the interests of their respective social science.

Of course, disciplines are not homogeneous but contested fields. But they are fields nonetheless; that is, they do have projects that define the stakes, the struggles, the issues. As I mentioned above, there are dissidents in economics, but there are also organizations opposed to the mainstream, the Union of Radical Political Economics and the movement for postautistic economics, just as in political science there has been a long history of opposition from political theory, and much more recently from the perestroika movement. Sociology is slightly different in that the radical challenge of the 1970s was absorbed rather than repelled and the critical opposition today comes more from the "pure science" wing of the profession, hostile to "politicization." These internal divisions within disciplinary fields are defined by the structure of the field itself. They do not directly correspond to the constellation of interests in the wider society but to those interests refracted through the academic field.

What, then, is the significance of multidisciplinary programs in area studies, the interdisciplinary fields such as communication studies and administrative sciences, the cross-disciplinary programs that recognize excluded others (African American studies, ethnic studies, women's studies), and more generally the overlapping of disciplines? For Wallerstein, they mark the untenable character of the disciplines, whereas it might be equally argued they mark their tenacity. Here, too, the demarcation into policy, public, critical, and professional knowledges is pertinent. Thus, as Michael Dutton argues in this volume, the *multidisciplinary* area studies, funded by state interests in the international balance of power, have often been tied to policy research, turning them into an arm of the disciplines. The new *joint disciplinary* programs of women's studies, ethnic studies, and African American studies are tied to publics and as such have often had a fractious history in the university, hostile to such an unmediated public connection. Poststructuralist *transdisciplinary* tendencies infuse critical knowledge with challenges to disciplinary foundations.

Finally, at the boundaries of the disciplines themselves, there is often *cross-disciplinary* fertilizing, so that we do find economic sociology and political sociology borrowing ideas from economics and political science, but economic sociology examines the social bases of the market just as political sociology studies societal bases of or challenges to state power. That is to say, these subdisciplines may appear to be crossovers, but in practice they are firmly rooted in the project of a single discipline. Indeed, they bespeak the power and the interests of the disciplines, as do the deep schisms in joint disciplinary programs.

There is no doubt that alternative projects and challenges to the disciplines are as likely to come from these hybrid endeavors as from anywhere; still, they all depend on the existence of disciplines. Thus, to seek to turn the disciplines into a melting pot of disinterested knowledge ignores the real and contradictory interests, both within and beyond the university, to which divergent disciplinary projects are connected. If within the social sciences economics, with its powerful instrumental knowledge, is hegemonic, that hegemony is always under reconstruction as historical forces give more or less weight to reflexive knowledge, associated, for example, with sociology or anthropology. Internal rearticulation of the hegemonic system is one way to think of change; the elaboration of an alternative hegemony is another, but altogether more difficult way. To think about these alternatives one needs to return to the present world-historical conjuncture of the production and consumption of official knowledge.

The University against Market and State

The social sciences were born in the nineteenth century; today, they are an anachronism. That is Wallerstein's case for a singular but comprehensive social science. I argue differently, that the twenty-first century looks ever more like the stereotype of the nineteenth century, with its division between state, market, and society. The twentieth century, from which Wallerstein spoke, was the age of extremes, with its anomalous interpenetration of state, economy, and society assuming the despotic forms of communism and fascism or the more benign state regulation of social democracy. This is now at an end as states increasingly pursue their own terrifying political logics, whether behind a democratic façade or not, allowing markets to devastate the conditions of human existence in the name of freedom. We are searching, therefore, for a Polanyian backlash from society—local, national, regional, or global—that will protect humanity's interests in economic security and political freedom.

In this theater of clashing forces, where do the disciplines lie? I have argued that political science and economics as they are presently defined only buttress these tendencies, but sociology, along with cultural anthropology and human geography, are rooted in the resilience of civil society. Immediately one must add that civil society is not some oasis of resplendent harmony and fructifying solidarity. It has its own scattered hegemonies, racial exclusions, and class dominations, compounded by if not the direct result of invasions by state and economy. Reflecting these divisions, sociology, like the other disciplines, is itself a heavily fractured and contested field. Some tout civil society as the answer to society's problems, absorbing the devastation wrought by markets and state deregulation, while others see civil society as the source of demands to reassert state regulation of markets. Margaret Somers, in her essay, captures this contestation over the meaning of the "social" in her passionate defense of the concept of an active civil society against its colonization by economic notions of social capital. She forcefully raises the question of whether the market will be socialized or civil society marketized. Just as civil society is the carrier of the last best hope against the depredations of state and economy, so sociologists, despite their differences, do promote an emergent and convergent ethos, hostile to unregulated markets and unilateralist states. And in this, they can join hands across the world.

Indeed, it is this critical ethos that finds its expression in public sociology. Yet here is the paradox. At the very time when sociologists desire greater connection to various publics, those publics are under threat or in retreat. Indeed, it is often argued that there can be no public sociology because publics are disappearing, at least in the United States, or if they do exist they are receding from the sociological ethos. The very forces we oppose have the upper hand, systematically eroding the terrain on which public sociology might sprout. I would argue that the situation is not so bleak. There are still plenty of publics to work with. Some sociologists spend time with communities of faith, others with labor unions. Some operate at the neighborhood level, others at the municipal level; others attach themselves to state-level organizations and movements. As I travel the country to state associations of sociology I discover all manner of interesting projects directed at displaced workers, environmental groups, homelessness, prisoners, HIV-AIDS and needle exchange, and immigrant rights. Sociologists are indeed in the trenches of civil society.

Sociologists are also specialists in the fabrication of categories and identities, helping to turn private stigma into public action, especially in the field of public health. Sociologists partake in the constitution of publics: people with AIDS, cancer, obesity, and so on. Finally, if publics are indeed on the wane, if the public sphere is a desert, and here again I'm talking about the United States, all the more reason to constitute ourselves, following the lead of other professional associations such as the lawyers and the psychologists, as a public with a political role to play. More broadly, the university itself moves from being an actor motivated by self-preservation to one with a broader vision of its mission.

There is one public that is here to stay. As long as there are faculty there will be students, and by students I mean undergraduates. They are our first and most important public, the public whose constitution we all share. We can relate to them like traditional public sociologists relate to their publics, raining down truth from above as though pouring wine into empty vessels, or we can look on them as partners in a collaborative venture, a process of mutual enlightenment in which students learn to locate their own experience in its broader historical, national, and even global contexts. We teach people, as C. Wright Mills famously put it, to turn private troubles into public issues, to transcend their possessive individualism. That surely is what a critical social science has to offer students, although it is often a painful experience for both teacher and taught. Such an impetus coincides with a growing interest in service learning, which, when properly carried out, takes sociology beyond the classroom: students become ambassadors to wider publics, to what you might call secondary publics. We are in the business of educating the educators, even as we educate ourselves.

Once more we face a paradox. Precisely when we are thinking of extending the impact of our teaching to wider publics, the university itself is under siege (Kirp 2003; Bok 2003). Under financial pressure from declining public budgets, universities intensively compete for students, marketizing admissions as sales ventures, appealing to the crudest of interests. Those universities that can, increasingly turn to corporate financing of research that further erodes the civic moment of education. Others can sustain themselves only through the proletarianization of teaching, making civic education far beyond our capacities so that we end up reinforcing alienated self-understanding (C. Nelson 1997). At the same time that the state withdraws material support it has begun to encroach on academic freedom, beginning with greater surveillance over programs of global import. And now we are facing new movements to "diversify" the academy, movements to root out its critical dispositions.

Where do the disciplines, particularly the social sciences, line up here? Even as they oppose the colonization and commodification of university life, they supply the very ideologies that justify such encroachments: the disciplinary projects of political order and market expansion. Like the physicists who invented the atomic bomb, they know not what they are doing, as their own existence, not to mention the rest of humanity, is put at risk by the ideological bombs they themselves have manufactured.

As state and market encroach on the university we can no longer regard ourselves as outside history, projecting a universal knowledge from a nonexistent Archimedean place. This was the illusion of positivism that, as George Steinmetz points out in his essay on sociology, was a feature of Fordism, with the protection and security it extended to the university. We have been living in a fool's paradise. The siege of the public university, and indeed everything public, calls forth two responses. We can accept the terms of the conjuncture and compete for privatization, turning to distance learning, sweetheart deals with bioengineering corporations, marketizing admissions, and so forth, or we can appeal to the very publics we serve. As producers of knowledge and thus of ideology, we have a particular responsibility to produce a reflexive knowledge that, on the one hand, enters a critique of professional and policy knowledges for, among other things, imprisoning the imagination but that, on the other hand, forges relations with publics, generating dialogue that calls into question the directions of society. The more the university loses its autonomy and the more it is colonized by market and state, the more desperately it will need to engage with publics that share a similar fate.

Reflexivity is but the first and indispensable step in provincializing social science, making it aware of its power and particularity. We need to reconfigure rather than dissolve professional knowledge, so necessary to comprehend the terms of public engagement. Professional knowledge helps us reconnoiter the patterning of civil society and thus the possibilities of a public social science. As I have argued, this is the province of sociology in particular, but it cannot be confined to sociology. To elaborate a critical perspective sociology needs all the help it can get from the humanities as well as from dissidents in the more instrumental social sciences. From Geoff Eley and William Sewell we have a sense of historians turning back from esoteric apolitical cultural analysis to a social analysis from whence they came, just as Emily Hauptmann's focus on political theory suggests deep critical rumblings in political science. Following the lead of Amartya Sen and Joseph Stiglitz, Peter Evans (forthcoming) has charted out an institutional turn that would pay attention to local knowledge and deliberative democracy.

At the same time, the project of public social science cannot be confined to a national terrain. It increasingly calls for engagements with and even the constitution of transnational publics. As the self-defense of social science converges with the self-defense of society, nationally and globally, so our shared fate depends, in part, on the ascendance of reflexive knowledge, although never to the exclusion of its instrumental companion.

Notes

Thanks to Jayati Lal for stimulating the title of this paper, to Davydd Greenwood for intense e-mail engagement about its content, to George Steinmetz for encouraging me to do it and supplying critical commentary at the crucial moment, and to the public at the University of Illinois, Urbana-Champaign for their many and varied stimulations.

1   I am taking the idea of provincialization from Chakrabarty (2000) that Western social

science is both indispensable and inadequate for understanding colonial history. It is similar to Edward Said's (1993) "contrapuntal analysis," which seeks to elicit and display the historical particularities that constitute the putatively universal.

2   From now on, instead of referring to all the Gulbenkian commissioners, I simply refer to their chair, Immanuel Wallerstein. He has also published other collections of papers on the topic of the social sciences that lay out the same argument (Wallerstein 1991, 1999).

3   "Methodological positivism" is the term used by George Steinmetz in his essay "Sociology," in this volume.

4   This scheme does not arise from nowhere, but from the writings of Max Weber and Jürgen Habermas on the one side and Emile Durkheim and Pierre Bourdieu on the other. Some might even discover parallels with Talcott Parsons's famous AGIL four-function scheme, in which A stands for adaptation or the economy (professional sociology?), G stands for goal attainment (policy sociology?), I stands for integration (public sociology?), and L stands for latency or pattern maintenance (critical sociology?). The more direct source of inspiration is Habermas's conceptions of system and lifeworld, based on strategic and communicative action, respectively, which parallels my distinction between instrumental and reflexive knowledge-practices.

5   You might have thought this would have put the final nail in the coffin of modernization theory, but theories rise up to meet interests, and today we see modernization theory reincarnated as a "new institutionalism" that speaks of global isomorphism and convergence.

6   For a depressing analysis of the worldwide power of U.S. economics, see Marion Fourcade-Gourinchas (2003).

7   Although one might argue that in its attempt to imitate economics, political science has temporarily lost sight of its object. See Sophia Mihic, Stephen G. Engelmann, and Elizabeth Rose Wingrove in this volume and Timothy Mitchell (2003).

REFERENCES

Aarsleff, Hans. 1982. *From Locke to Saussure: Essays on the Study of Language and Intellectual History*. Minneapolis: University of Minnesota Press.

Abbagnano, Nicola. 1967. Positivism. In *The Encyclopedia of Philosophy*, edited by Paul Edwards, 5: 414–419. New York: Macmillan.

Abbott, Andrew. 1988a. *The System of Professions*. Chicago: University of Chicago Press.

——. 1988b. Transcending General Linear Reality. *Sociological Theory* 6, 2: 169–186.

——. 1990. Positivism and Interpretation in Sociology: Lessons for Sociologists from the History of Stress Research. *Sociological Forum* 5, 3: 435–458.

——. 1992a. From Causes to Events: Notes on Narrative Positivism. *Sociological Methods and Research* 20: 428–455.

——. 1992b. What Do Cases Do? Some Notes on Activity in Sociological Analysis. In *What Is a Case? Exploring the Foundations of Social Inquiry*, edited by Charles C. Ragin and Howard S. Becker, 53–82. Cambridge: Cambridge University Press.

——. 1998. The Causal Devolution. *Sociological Methods and Research* 27: 148–181.

——. 1999. *Department and Discipline*. Chicago: University of Chicago Press.

——. 2001a. *Chaos of Disciplines*. Chicago: University of Chicago Press.

——. 2001b. *Time Matters*. Chicago: University of Chicago Press.

Abdel-Malek, A. 1969. *Idéologie et renaissance nationale: L'Egypte moderne*. 2nd ed. Paris: Anthropos.

Abel, Theodore Fred. 1929. *Systematic Sociology in Germany: A Critical Analysis of Some Attempts to Establish Sociology as an Independent Science*. New York: Columbia University Press.

Åberg, Martin and Mikael Sandberg. 2003. *Social Capital and Democratisation: Roots of Trust in Post-Communist Poland and Ukraine*. Burlington, Vt.: Ashgate.

Abu-Lughod, Lila. 1991. Writing against Culture. In *Recapturing Anthropology: Working in the Present*, edited by Richard G. Fox, 137–162. Santa Fe, N.M.: School of American Research Press.

——. 1999. The Interpretation of Culture(s) after Television. In *The Fate of "Culture": Geertz and Beyond*, edited by Sherry B. Ortner, 110–135. Berkeley: University of California Press.

Adams, Julia, Elisabeth Clemens, and Ann Orloff, eds. Forthcoming. *The Making and Unmaking of Modernity: Politics and Processes for Historical Sociology.* Durham, N.C.: Duke University Press.

Adcock, Robert, and Mark Bevir. 2003. The Remaking of Political Theory. Unpublished manuscript.

Adler, P., and S. Kwon. 1999. Social Capital: The Good, the Bad and the Ugly. World Bank Social Capital Library. Papers in Progress.

Adock, Robert, and David Collier. 2001. Measurement Validity: A Shared Standard for Qualitative and Quantitative Research. *American Political Science Review* 95 (September): 529–547.

Adorno, Theodor W. [1969] 1976. Introduction to *The Positivist Dispute in German Sociology*, translated by Glyn Adey and David Frisby, 1–67. London: Heinemann.

Adorno, Theodor W., et al. 1976. *The Positivist Dispute in German Sociology*, translated by Glyn Adey and David Frisby. London: Heinemann.

Agassi, Joseph. 1995. Contemporary Philosophy of Science as Thinly Masked Antidemocratic Apologetics. In *Physics, Philosophy and the Scientific Community*, edited by K. Gavroglu et al., 153–170. Dordrecht: Kluwer.

Aglietta, Michel. 1979. *A Theory of Capitalist Regulation: The U.S. Experience.* London: New Left Books.

———. 1987. *A Theory of Capitalist Regulation: The U.S. Experience*, 2nd ed. London: Verso.

Ahearn, Laura M. 2001. Language and Agency. *Annual Review of Anthropology* 30: 109–137.

Ahmad, Salma. 1991. American Foundations and the Development of the Social Sciences between the Wars: Comment on the Debate between Martin Bulmer and Donald Fisher. *Sociology* 25 (August): 511–520.

Ainslie, George. 1992. *Picoeconomics: The Strategic Interaction of Successive Motivational States within the Person.* Cambridge: Cambridge University Press.

———. 2001. *Breakdown of Will.* Cambridge: Cambridge University Press.

Akerlof, George. 1984. *An Economic Theorist's Book of Tales.* Cambridge: Cambridge University Press.

———. 1990. George A. Akerlof. In *Sociology and Economics: Redefining Their Boundaries: Conversations with Economists and Sociologists*, edited by Richard Swedberg, 61–77. Princeton: Princeton University Press.

Alcoff, Linda. 1991. The Problem of Speaking for Others. *Cultural Critique* 20: 5–32.

Alexander, Jeffrey. 1993. The Return to Civil Society. *Contemporary Sociology* 22: 797–803.

Almond, Gabriel. 1988. Separate Tables: Schools and Sects in Political Science. *PS: Political Science and Politics* 21 (autumn): 828–842.

Alnasseri, Sabah. 2003. Ursprüngliche Akkumulation, Artikulation und Regulation: Aspekte einer globalen Theorie der Regulation. In *Fit für den Postfordismus? Theoretisch-politische Perspektiven des Regulationsansatzes*, edited by Ulrich Brand and Werner Raza, 131–157. Münster: Westfälisches Dampfboot.

Alpert, Harry. 1939. Émile Durkheim and His Sociology. PhD diss. Columbia University.

———. 1954. The National Science Foundation and Social Science Research. *American Sociological Review* 19 (April): 208–211.

———. 1955a. The Social Sciences and the National Science Foundation. *American Sociological Review* 20 (December): 653–661.

———. 1955b. The Social Sciences and the National Science Foundation. *Proceedings of the American Philosophical Society* 99 (October 15): 332–333.

——. 1957. The Social Science Research Program of the National Science Foundation. *American Sociological Review* 22 (October): 582–585.

——. 1961. The Funding of Social Science Research. In *Trends in Social Science*, edited by Donald P. Ray, 152–166. New York: Philosophical Library.

Althusser, Louis. 1971a. Freud and Lacan. In *Lenin and Philosophy*, 195–219. London: NLB.

——. 1971b. Ideology and Ideological State Apparatuses. In *Lenin and Philosophy*, 121–172. London: NLB.

——. 1971c. *Lenin and Philosophy and Other Essays*, translated by Ben Brewster. New York: Monthly Review Press.

——. 1977. *For Marx*. London: NLB.

Althusser, Louis, and Etienne Balibar. [1968] 1979. *Reading Capital*. London: Verso.

Amadae, S. M. 2003. *Rationalizing Capitalist Democracy: The Cold War Origins of Rational Choice Liberalism*. Chicago: University of Chicago Press.

Amadae, S. M., and Bruce Bueno de Mesquita. 1999. The Rochester School: The Origins of Positive Political Theory. *Annual Review of Political Science* 2: 269–295.

American Anthropological Association. 2002. *El Dorado Task Force Papers*. 2 volumes. 18 May. Available: http://www.aaanet.org/edtf.

Amin, Ash, ed. 1994. *Post-Fordism: A Reader*. Oxford: Blackwell.

Amin, Shahid. 1995. *Event, Metaphor, Memory: Chauri Chaura 1922–1992*. Berkeley: University of California Press.

Anderson, Amanda. 2000. The Temptations of Aggrandized Agency: Feminist Histories and the Horizon of Modernity. *Victorian Studies* 43, 1: 43–65.

Anderson, Benedict. 1983. *Imagined Communities: Reflections on the Origin and Spread of Nationalism*. London: Verso.

Anderson, Perry. 1980. *Arguments within English Marxism*. London: Verso.

Appadurai, Arjun. 1986. Theory in Anthropology: Center and Periphery. *Comparative Studies in Society and History* 28: 356–361.

——. 1988. Putting Hierarchy in Its Place. *Cultural Anthropology* 3: 36–49.

——. 1990. Disjuncture and Difference in the Global Cultural Economy. *Public Culture* 2: 1–24.

——. [1990] 1996a. Disjuncture and Difference in the Global Economy. In *Modernity at Large: Cultural Dimensions of Globalization*. Minneapolis: University of Minnesota Press.

——. 1996b. *Modernity at Large: Cultural Dimensions of Globalization*. Minneapolis: University of Minnesota Press.

Appleby, Joyce, Lynn Hunt, and Margaret Jacob. 1994. *Telling the Truth about History*. New York: Norton.

Apter, David. 1965. *The Politics of Modernization*. Chicago: University of Chicago Press.

——. 2001. Structure, Contingency, and Choice: A Comparison of Trends and Tendencies in Political Science. In *Schools of Thought: Twenty-Five Years of Interpretive Social Science*, edited by Joan W. Scott and Debra Keates, 252–287. Princeton: Princeton University Press.

Arato, Andrew. 1981. Civil Society Against the State: Poland 1980–81. *Telos* 47: 24.

——. 1993. Interpreting 1989. *Social Research* 60: 609–646.

——. 2000. *Civil Society, Constitution, and Legitimacy*. Lanham, Md.: Rowman and Littlefield.

Arato, Andrew, and J. L. Cohen. 1984. Social Movements, Civil Society, and the Problem of Sovereignty. *Praxis International* 4: 266–283.

Arato, Andrew, and Eike Gebhardt, eds. 1988. *The Essential Frankfurt School Reader.* New York: Continuum.

Archer, Margaret. 1988. *Culture and Agency.* Cambridge: Cambridge University Press.

———. 1995. *Realist Social Theory: The Morphogenetic Approach.* Cambridge: Cambridge University Press.

———. 2000. *Being Human: The Problem of Agency.* Cambridge: Cambridge University Press.

Archer, Margaret, Roy Bhaskar, Andrew Collier, Tony Lawson, and Alan Norrie, eds. 1998. *Critical Realism: Essential Readings.* London: Routledge.

Archer, Margaret, Andrew Collier, and Doug Porpora. Forthcoming. *Transcendence: Critical Realism and God.* London: Routledge.

Arendt, Hanna. 1958. *The Human Condition.* Chicago: University of Chicago Press.

Arrow, Kenneth. 1951. *Social Choice and Individual Values.* New York: Wiley.

———. 2000. Observations on Social Capital. In *Social Capital: A Multifaceted Perspective,* edited by P. Dasgupta and I. Serageldin. Washington, D.C.: World Bank.

Asad, Talal, ed. 1973. *Anthropology and the Colonial Encounter.* New York: Humanities Press.

———. 1993. *Genealogies of Religion: Discipline and Reasons of Power in Christianity and Islam.* Baltimore: Johns Hopkins University Press.

Ashcraft, Richard. 1983. One Step Backward, Two Steps Forward: Reflections upon Contemporary Political Theory. In *What Should Political Theory Be Now?*, edited by John S. Nelson, 515–548. Albany: State University of New York Press.

Ashley, Richard K. 1984. The Poverty of Neorealism. *International Organization* 38 (spring): 225–286.

Asner, Glen. 2002. Corporate Fad or Government Policy? The Linear Model, the Department of Defense, and the Golden Age of Industrial Research. Paper presented to the Nobel Symposium. November. Stockholm, Sweden.

Atlas, James. 2003. A Classicist's Legacy: New Empire Builders. *New York Times,* May 4, section 4, p. 1.

Austen-Smith, David, and Jeffrey S. Banks. 1999. *Positive Political Theory I: Collective Preference.* Ann Arbor: University of Michigan Press.

Axel, Brian Keith, ed. 2002. *From the Margins: Historical Anthropology and Its Futures.* Durham, N.C.: Duke University Press.

Ayer, A. J. 1946. *Language, Truth, and Logic.* New York: Dover.

———. 1959. *Logical Positivism.* New York: Free Press.

———. 1982. *Philosophy in the Twentieth Century.* London: Weidenfeld and Nicolson.

Ayres, C. E. 1927. *Science: The False Messiah.* Indianapolis: Bobs-Merrill.

Bachelard, Gaston. 1984. *The New Scientific Spirit.* Boston: Beacon Press.

Bakhtin, M. M. 1981. *The Dialogic Imagination: Four Essays.* Translated by Caryl Emerson and Michael Holquist. Austin: University of Texas.

———. 1986. *Speech Genres and Other Late Essays.* Translated by Vern W. McGee. Austin: University of Texas Press.

Baldwin, Peter. 1990. *The Politics of Social Solidarity: The Class Bases of the European Welfare State 1875–1975.* New York: Cambridge University Press.

Ball, Terence. 2001. Discordant Voices: American Histories of Political Thought. In *The History of Political Thought in National Context,* edited by Dario Castiglione and Iain Hampsher-Monk, 107–133. Cambridge: Cambridge University Press.

Bang, Henrik P. 1998. David Easton's Postmodern Images. *Political Theory* 26: 281–316.

Bannister, Robert C. 1992. Principle, Politics, Profession: American Sociologists and Fascism, 1930–1950. In *Sociology Responds to Fascism*, edited by Stephen Turner and Dirk Käsler, 172–213. London and New York: Routledge.

Barber, Benjamin. 1996. An American Civic Forum: Civil Society Between Market Individuals and the Political Community. *Social Philosophy and Policy* 13: 269–283.

Barlow, Tani E. 1993. Colonialism's Career in Postwar China Studies. *positions* 1: 224–267.

Baron, S., J. Field, and T. Schuller. 2000. *Social Capital: Critical Perspectives*. New York: Oxford University Press.

Barthes, Roland. [1957] 1972. *Mythologies*. Translated by Annette Lavers. New York: Hill and Wang.

——. 1980. *Camera Lucida: Reflections on Photography*. New York: Hill and Wang.

——. 1982. Eiffel Tower. In *A Barthes Reader*, edited by Susan Sontag. New York: Hill and Wang.

Barton, Allen H., and Paul F. Lazarsfeld. 1956. Some Functions of Qualitative Analysis in Social Research. *Bureau of Applied Social Research* 181. New York: Columbia University.

Bataille, Georges. 1979. The Psychological Structure of Fascism. *New German Critique*, no. 16: 64–87.

Bates, Robert H. 1996. Letter from the President: Area Studies and the Discipline. APSA–CP (newsletter of the APSA Organized Section in Comparative Politics) 7, 1: 1–2.

Bates, Robert H., Rui J. P. de Figueiredo Jr., and Barry R. Weingast. 1998. The Politics of Interpretation: Rationality, Culture, and Transition. *Politics and Society* 26 (June): 603–642.

Bates, Robert H., et al. 1998. *Analytic Narratives*. Princeton: Princeton University Press.

Bateson, Gregory. [1955] 1972. A Theory of Play and Fantasy. In *Steps to an Ecology of Mind*, 177–193. New York: Ballantine Books.

Bauman, Richard, and Joel Sherzer, eds. 1974. *Explorations in the Ethnography of Speaking*. London: Cambridge University Press.

Baumol, William J. 1992. Towards a Newer Economics: The Future Lies Ahead. In *The Future of Economics*, edited by John D. Hey, 1–8. Oxford: Blackwell Publishers.

Baxter, William H. 2002. Where Does the "Comparative Method" Come From? In *The Linguist's Linguist: A Collection of Papers in Honour of Alexis Manaster Ramer*, edited by Fabrice Cavoto, 1: 33–52. München: LINCOM.

Baxtin, Mixail [Mikhail Bakhtin]. 1971. Discourse Typology in Prose. In *Readings in Russian Poetics: Formalist and Structuralist Views*, compiled by Ladislav Matejka and Krystyna Pomorska, 1796–1798. Cambridge: MIT Press.

Beck, Ulrich. [1986] 1992. *Risk Society*. London: Sage.

Beck, Ulrich, Anthony Giddens, and Scott Lash. 1994. *Reflexive Modernization*. Stanford: Stanford University Press.

Becker, Gary S. 1975. Human Capital: A Theoretical and Empirical Analysis, with Special Reference to Education. New York: National Bureau of Economic Research, Columbia University Press.

——. 1976. *The Economic Approach to Human Behavior*. Chicago: University of Chicago Press.

——. 1986. *An Economic Analysis of the Family*. Dublin: Argus.

——. 1990. Gary S. Becker. In *Sociology and Economics: Redefining their Boundaries: Conversations with Economists and Sociologists*, edited by Richard Swedberg, 27–46. Princeton: Princeton University Press.

——. 1993. *Human Capital: A Theoretical and Empirical Analysis, with Special Reference to Education*, 3d ed. Chicago: University of Chicago Press.

——. 1996. *Accounting for Tastes*. Cambridge: Harvard University Press.

Becker, Gary S., R. Febrero, et al. 1995. *The Essence of Becker*. Stanford: Hoover Institution Press.

Becker, Gary S., and K. M. Murphy. 2000. *Social Economics: Market Behavior in a Social Environment*. Cambridge, Mass.: Belknap Press.

Becker, Gary S., and G. Nashat. 1997. The Economics of Life: From Baseball to Affirmative Action to Immigration, How Real-World Issues Affect Our Everyday Life. New York: McGraw-Hill.

Bederman, Gail. 1995. *Manliness and Civilization: A Cultural History of Gender and Race in the United States, 1880–1917*. Chicago: University of Chicago Press.

Bell, Daniel. 1960. *The End of Ideology: On the Exhaustion of Political Ideas in the Fifties*. Glencoe, Ill.: Free Press.

——. [1973] 1976. *The Coming of Post-Industrial Society: A Venture in Social Forecasting*. 2nd ed. New York: Basic Books.

——. 1981. Models and Reality in Economic Discourse. In *The Crisis in Economic Theory*, edited by Daniel Bell and Irving Kristol, 46–80. New York: Basic Books.

Ben-David, Joseph. 1960. Scientific Productivity and Academic Organization in Nineteenth-Century Medicine. *American Sociological Review* 25 (December): 828–843.

Bendix, Reinhard. 1967. Tradition and Modernity Reconsidered. *Comparative Studies in Society and History* 9 (April): 292–346.

Benedict, Ruth. 1947. *The Chrysanthemum and the Sword: Patterns of Japanese Culture*. London: Secker and Warburg.

Benhabib, Seyla, ed. 1996. *Democracy and Difference: Contesting the Boundaries of the Political*. Princeton: Princeton University Press.

Benjamin, Walter. 1983–84. N [Theoretics of Knowledge; Theory of Progress]. *Philosophical Forum* 15: 1–40.

Benton, Ted. 1993. *Natural Relations*. London: Verso.

Berelson, Bernard R., Paul F. Lazarsfeld, and William N. McPhee. 1954. *Voting: A Study of Opinion Formation in a Presidential Campaign*. Chicago: University of Chicago Press.

Berger, Peter L., and T. Luckmann. 1967. *The Social Construction of Reality: A Treatise in the Sociology of Knowledge*. New York: Doubleday.

Berger, Peter L. and Richard John Neuhaus. 1996. *To Empower People: From State to Civil Society*, 2nd ed., edited by Michael Novak. Washington, DC: AEI Press.

Bergesen, Albert, and Ronald Schoenberg. 1980. Long Waves of Colonial Expansion and Contraction. In *Studies of the Modern World-System*, edited by Albert Bergesen, 231–277. New York: Academic Press.

Bergson, Henri. [1889] 1910. *Time and Free Will: An Essay on the Immediate Data of Consciousness*. Translated by F. L. Pogson. London: Allen Unwin. (Originally published as *Essai sur les donnees immediates de la conscience*)

Berkeley, George. [1734] 1998. *A Treatise Concerning the Principles of Human Knowledge*. Oxford: Oxford University Press.

Berlin, Isaiah. [1963] 1979. Does Political Theory Still Exist? In *Concepts and Categories*, edited by H. Hardy, 143–172. Oxford: Penguin.

——. 1969. *Four Essays on Liberty*. New York: Oxford University Press.

Bernal, Martin. 1987. *The Fabrication of Ancient Greece, 1785–1985.* Vol. 1 of *Black Athena: The Afroasiatic Roots of Classical Civilization.* New Brunswick, N.J.: Rutgers University Press.

Bernstein, Michael A. 2001. *A Perilous Progress: Economics and Public Purpose in Twentieth-Century America.* Princeton: Princeton University Press.

Bernstein, Richard J. 1976. *The Restructuring of Social and Political Theory.* New York: Harcourt, Brace and Jovanovich.

——. 1983. *Beyond Objectivism and Relativism: Science, Hermeneutics, and Praxis.* Philadelphia: University of Pennsylvania Press.

Bezucha, Robert J. 1974. *The Lyon Uprising of 1834: Social and Political Conflict in the Early July Monarchy.* Cambridge: Harvard University Press.

Bhabha, Homi K. 1994a. Of Mimicry and Man: The Ambivalence of Colonial Discourse. In *The Location of Culture,* 85–92. London: Routledge.

——. 1994b. *The Location of Culture.* London: Routledge.

Bhaskar, Roy. [1975] 1978. *A Realist Theory of Science.* Hemel Hempstead, U.K.: Harvester Press.

——. [1975] 1997. *A Realist Theory of Science.* London: Verso.

——. 1979. *The Possibility of Naturalism: A Philosophical Critique of the Contemporary Human Sciences.* New York: Humanities Press.

——. [1979] 1998. *The Possibility of Naturalism.* London: Routledge.

——. 1986. *Scientific Realism and Human Emancipation.* London: Verso.

——. 1989. *Reclaiming Reality: A Critical Introduction to Contemporary Philosophy.* London: Verso.

——. 1991. *Philosophy and the Idea of Freedom.* Oxford: Blackwell.

——. 1993. *Dialectic: The Pulse of Freedom.* London: Verso.

——. 1994. *Plato Etcetera: The Problems of Philosophy and Their Resolution.* New York: Verso.

——. 2000. *From East to West.* London: Routledge.

——. 2002. *Reflections on Meta-Reality.* New Delhi: Sage.

Biagioli, Mario, ed. 1999. *The Science Studies Reader.* New York: Routledge.

Blackbourn, David, and Geoff Eley. 1985. *The Peculiarities of German History.* New York: Oxford University Press.

Blalock, Hubert M., Jr. 1964. *Causal Inferences in Nonexperimental Research.* Chapel Hill: University of North Carolina Press.

——. 1969. *Theory Construction: From Verbal to Mathematical Formulations.* Engelwood Cliffs, N.J.: Prentice-Hall.

Blau, Peter Michael and Otis Dudley Duncan. 1967. *The American Occupational Structure.* New York: Wiley.

Blaug, Mark. 1980. *The Methodology of Economics.* Cambridge: Cambridge University Press.

——. 1997. Ugly Currents in Modern Economics. *Options Politiques* (September): 3–8.

Block, Fred. 1990. *Postindustrial Possibilities: A Critique of Economic Discourse.* Berkeley: University of California Press.

Bloor, David. 1977. *Knowledge and Social Imagery.* London: Routledge and Kegan Paul.

Boas, Franz. 1887a. The Study of Geography. *Science* 9, 210 (February 11): 137–141.

——. 1887b. Museums of Ethnology and Their Classification. *Science* 9, 228 (June 17): 587–589.

——. [1887] 1940. The Study of Geography. In *Race, Language, and Culture,* 639–647. New York: Free Press.

——. 1910. Introduction. *Handbook of American Indian Languages*. Bulletin 40, Part 1. Bureau of American Ethnology. Washington, D.C.: Government Printing Office.

Bodmer, Fredrick. 1944. *The Loom of Language*. London: George Allen and Unwin.

Body-Gendrot, Sophie, and Marilyn Gittell. 2003. *Social Capital and Social Citizenship*. Lanham, Md.: Lexington Books.

Bok, Derek. 2003. *Universities in the Marketplace*. Princeton: Princeton University Press.

Boland, Lawrence A. 1979. A Critique of Friedman's Critics. *Journal of Economic Literature* 17, 2: 503–522.

Bonnell, Victoria, and Lynn Hunt, eds. 1999. *Beyond the Cultural Turn: New Directions in the Study of Society and Culture*. Berkeley: University of California Press.

Bosworth, B., G. Burtless, and E. Steuerle. 2000. Lifetime Earnings Patterns, the Distribution of Future Social Security Benefits, and the Impact of Pensions Reform. *Social Security Bulletin* 63, 4: 74–98.

Bourdieu, Pierre. [1972] 1977. *Outline of a Theory of Practice*. Translated by Richard Nice. Cambridge: Cambridge University Press.

——. [1979] 1984. *Distinction: A Social Critique of the Judgement of Taste*. Translated by Richard Nice. Cambridge: Harvard University Press.

——. 1981. The Specificity of the Scientific Field. In *French Sociology: Rupture and Renewal since 1968*, edited by Charles C. Lemert, 257–292. New York: Columbia University Press.

——. [1984] 1988. *Homo Academicus*. Stanford: Stanford University Press.

——. 1985. The Genesis of the Concepts of *Habitus* and Field. *Sociocriticism* 2, 2: 11–24.

——. 1986. The Forms of Capital. In *Handbook of Theory and Research for the Sociology of Education*, edited by J. G. Richardson, 241–260. New York: Greenwood Press.

——. 1988–89. Vive la crise! For Heterodoxy in Social Science. *Theory and Society* 17, 5: 773–787.

——. 1990. *The Logic of Practice*. Stanford: Stanford University Press.

——. 1998. *Acts of Resistance: Against the New Myths of Our Time*. Cambridge: Polity Press.

——. 2001. *Science de la science et réflexivité*. Paris: Éditions Raisons d'Agir.

Bowles, S. 1999. 'Social Capital' and Community Governance. *Focus* 20, 3: 6–10.

Bowles, S. and Herbert Gintis. 2002. Social Capital and Community Governance. *The Economic Journal* 112 (November): F418.

Boyer, Robert. 1986. *La théorie de la regulation: Une analyse critique*. Paris: La Découverte.

——. 1990. *The Regulation School: A Critical Introduction*. New York: Columbia University Press.

Bradbury, William, Samuel Meyers, and Albert Biderman. 1968. *Mass Behavior in Battle and Captivity*. Chicago: University of Chicago Press.

Brand, Ulrich, and Werner Raza, eds. 2003. *Fit für den Postfordismus? Theoretisch-politische Perspektiven des Regulationsansatzes*. Münster: Westfälisches Dampfboot.

Brenner, Neil. 1998. Between Fixity and Motion: Accumulation, Territorial Organization and the Historical Geography of Spatial Scales. *Environment and Planning D: Society and Space* 16: 459–481.

Brenner, Robert. 2002. *The Boom and the Bubble: The U.S. in the World Economy*. London: Verso.

Breslau, Daniel. 1998. *In Search of the Unequivocal: The Political Economy of Measurement in U.S. Labor Market Policy*. Westport, Conn.: Praeger.

——. 2003. Economics Invents the Economy: Mathematics, Statistics, and Models in the Work of Irving Fisher and Wesley Mitchell. *Theory and Society* 32: 379–411.

Breslau, Daniel, and Yuval P. Yonay. 1999. Beyond Metaphor: Mathematical Models in Economics as Empirical Research. *Science in Context* 12, 2: 317–332.

Briggs, Charles L. 1984. Learning How to Ask: Native Metacommunicative Competence and the Incompetence of Fieldworkers. *Language in Society* 13: 1–28.

Briggs, Laura. 2002. *Reproducing Empire: Race, Sex, Science and U. S. Imperialism in Puerto Rico.* Berkeley: University of California Press.

Brodie, Bernard. 1949. Strategy as a Science. *World Politics* 1 (July): 467–488.

Brogan, Joseph V. 1996. A Mirror of Enlightenment: Rational Choice Debates. *Review of Politics* 58: 793–806.

Brooks, C. 2002. Religious Influence and the Politics of Family Decline Concern. *American Sociological Review* 67: 191–211.

Brown, Andrew, Steve Fleetwood, and John Michael Roberts, eds. 2002. *Critical Realism and Marxism.* London: Routledge.

Brown, James Robert. 2001. *Who Rules in Science?* Cambridge: Harvard University Press.

Brown, Norman O. [1959] 1985. *Life against Death: The Psychoanalytical Meaning of History.* Middletown, Conn.: Wesleyan University Press.

Brown, Wendy. 2002. At the Edge. *Political Theory* 30: 556–576.

Bryant, Christopher. 1975. Positivism Reconsidered. *Sociological Review* 23 (May): 397–412.

———. 1985. *Positivism in Social Theory and Research.* New York: Macmillan.

———. 1989. Le positivisme instrumental dans la sociologie américaine. *Actes de la recherche,* June 18: 64–74.

Bryant, Joseph. 1992. Positivism Redivivus? A Critique of Recent Uncritical Proposals for Reforming Sociological Theory (and Related Foibles). *Canadian Journal of Sociology* 17 (winter): 29–53.

Buckley, Kerry W. 1989. *Mechanical Man: John Broadus Watson and the Beginnings of Behaviorism.* New York: Guilford Press.

Buck-Morss, Susan. 1991. *The Dialects of Seeing: Walter Benjamin and the Arcades Project.* Cambridge: MIT Press.

———. 1995. Envisioning Capital: Political Economy on Display. *Critical Inquiry* 21 (winter): 434–467.

Bulmer, Martin. 1982. Support for Sociology in the 1920s: The Laura Spelman Rockefeller Memorial and the Beginnings of Modern, Large-Scale, Sociological Research in the University. *American Sociologist* 17 (November): 185–192.

Burawoy, Michael. 1979. *Manufacturing Consent: Changes in the Labor Process under Monopoly Capitalism.* Chicago: University of Chicago Press.

———. 2004. Introduction to "Public Sociologies: A Symposium from Boston College, by Michael Burawoy, et al." *Social Problems* 15, 1: 103–140.

Burawoy, Michael, and János Lukács. 1992. *The Radiant Past: Ideology and Reality in Hungary's Road to Capitalism.* Chicago: University of Chicago Press.

Burns, Tom. 1970. Sociological Explanation. In *Sociological Theory and Philosophical Analysis: A Collection,* edited by Dorothy Emmet and Alasdair MacIntyre, 55–75. London, Macmillan.

Butler, Judith. 1997. *The Psychic Life of Power: Theories in Subjection.* Stanford: Stanford University Press.

Cahn, Steven, ed. 1977. *New Studies in the Philosophy of John Dewey.* Hanover, N.H.: University Presses of New England.

Calhoun, Craig. 1993. Civil Society and the Public Sphere. *Public Culture* 5: 269.

——. 1996. The Rise and Domestication of Historical Sociology. In *The Historic Turn in the Human Sciences*, edited by Terrence J. McDonald, 305–338. Ann Arbor: University of Michigan Press.

Callon, Michel. 1998. *The Laws of the Markets*. Oxford: Blackwell.

Callon, Michel, Cécile Méadel, and Vololona Rabeharisoa. 2002. The Economy of Qualities. *Economy and Society* 31, 2: 194–217.

Camic, Charles. 1986. The Matter of Habit. *American Journal of Sociology* 91: 1039–1087.

——. 1987. The Making of a Method: A Historical Reinterpretation of the Early Parsons. *American Sociological Review* 52 (August): 421–439.

——. 1989. *Structure* after 50 Years: The Anatomy of a Charter. *American Journal of Sociology* 95 (July): 38–107.

——. 1995. Three Departments in Search of a Discipline: Localism and Interdisciplinary Interaction in American Sociology, 1890–1940. *Social Research* 62, 1: 1003–1034.

Camic, Charles, and Yu Xie. 1994. The Statistical Turn in American Social Science: Columbia University, 1890 to 1915. *American Sociological Review* 59 (October): 773–805.

Campbell, Angus, P. E. Converse, W. E. Milller, and D. E. Stokes. [1960] 1980. *The American Voter*. Chicago: University of Chicago Press.

Campbell, Angus, G. Gurin, and W. E. Miller. 1954. *The Voter Decides*. Chicago: Row-Peterson.

Carnap, Rudolf. 1928. *Scheinprobleme in der Philosophie*. Berlin-Schlachtensee: Weltkreis-Verlag.

——. [1930–31] 1959. The Old and the New Logic. In *Logical Positivism*, edited by A. J. Ayer, 133–146. New York: Free Press.

——. 1934. *The Unity of Science*. London. Kegan Paul.

——. 1956. The Methodological Character of Theoretical Concepts. In *The Foundations of Science and the Concepts of Psychology and Psychoanalysis, Minnesota Center for Philosophy of Science*, vol. 1, edited by Herbert Feigl and Michael Scriven, 38–76. Minneapolis: University of Minnesota Press.

——. 1963a. Intellectual Autobiography. In *The Philosophy of Rudolf Carnap*, edited by Paul Arthur Schlipp, 1–84. La Salle, Ill.: Open Court Press.

——. 1963b. Replies and Systematic Expositions. In *The Philosophy of Rudolf Carnap*, edited by Paul Arthur Schlipp, 859–1013. La Salle, Ill.: Open Court.

——. 1966. *An Introduction to the Philosophy of Science*. New York: Basic Books.

Cartwright, Nancy, Jordi Cat, Lola Fleck, and Thomas Uebel. 1996. *Otto Neurath: Philosophy between Science and Politics*. Cambridge: Cambridge University Press.

Castells, Manuel. [1996] 2000a. *The Rise of Network Society*. 2nd ed. London: Blackwell.

——. 1996–98/2000b. *The Information Age: Economy, Society and Culture*. Vol. 1–3. Oxford: Blackwell.

——. 1997. *The Power of Identity*. Vol. 2 of *The Information Age: Economy, Society and Culture*. Oxford: Blackwell.

Caton, Steven. 1999. *Lawrence of Arabia: A Film's Anthropology*. Berkeley: University of California Press.

Cavarero, Adriana. 2002. Politicizing Theory. *Political Theory* 30: 506–532.

Caws, Peter. 1967. Scientific Method. In *The Encyclopedia of Philosophy*, edited by Paul Edwards. New York: Macmillan.

Cerullo, John J. 1994. The Epistemic Turn: Critical Sociology and the "Generation of '68." *International Journal of Politics, Culture, and Society* 8 (fall): 169–181.

Chagnon, Napoleon. 1968. *Yanomamö, the Fierce People.* New York: Holt, Rinehart, and Winston.

Chaiklin, Seth, and Jean Lave, eds. 1993. *Understanding Practice: Perspectives on Activity and Context.* Cambridge: Cambridge University Press.

Chakrabarty, Dipesh. 1998. Reconstructing Liberalism? Notes toward a Conversation between Area Studies and Diasporic Studies. *Public Culture* 10: 457–481.

———. 2000. *Provincializing Europe: Postcolonial Thought and Historical Difference.* Princeton: Princeton University Press.

Chamberlain, Mary. 1986. Days of Future Past. *New Socialist* (April): 43.

Chatterjee, Partha. 1993. *The Nation and Its Fragments.* Princeton: Princeton University Press.

Chauncey, George. 1994. *Gay New York: Gender, Urban Culture, and the Making of the Gay Male World.* New York: Basic Books.

Chomsky, Noam, et al. 1997. *The Cold War and the University.* New York: New Press.

Chriss, James J. 1995. Testing Gouldner's Coming Crisis Thesis: On the Waxing and Waning of Intellectual Influence. *Current Perspectives in Social Theory* 15: 3–61.

Clark, Terry Nichols. 1996. Paul Lazarsfeld and the Columbia Sociology Machine. Unpublished Paper. Originally presented at the Paul Lazarsfeld Conference. Paris, December 1994.

Clifford, James. 1983. On Ethnographic Authority. *Representations* 1 (spring): 118–146.

———. 1988. *The Predicament of Culture: Twentieth-Century Ethnography, Literature, and Art.* Cambridge: Harvard University Press.

Clifford, James, and George E. Marcus, eds. 1986. *Writing Culture: The Poetics and Politics of Ethnography.* Berkeley: University of California Press.

———. 1999. Interview with Ronald Coase. *Newsletter of the International Society for New Institutional Economics* 2, 1 (spring).

Coase, Ronald. 1999. Interview with Ronald Coase. *Newsletter of the International Society for New Institutional Economics* 2, 1 (spring): 1–8.

Cohen, David William. 1997. Understanding the Globalization of Scholarship. In *Planning and Management for a Changing Environment*, edited by Marvin Peteron et al., 548–562. San Francisco: Jossey-Bass.

Cohen, G. A. 1978. *Karl Marx's Theory of History: A Defence.* Princeton: Princeton University Press.

Cohen, J. L. 1985. Strategy or Identity: New Theoretical Paradigms and Contemporary Social Movements. *Social Research* 52: 663–716.

Cohen, Jean L. 1999. American Civil Society Talk. In *Society, Democracy, and Civic Renewal*, edited by Robert K. Fullinwider. Lanham, Md.: Rowman and Littlefield.

Cohen, J. L., and A. Arato. 1992. *Civil Society and Political Theory.* Cambridge: MIT Press.

Cohen, Joshua and Joel Rogers. 1995. *Associations and Democracy.* London: Verso.

Cohen, Paul. 1984. *Discovering History in China.* New York: Columbia University Press.

Cohen, Robert. 1971. Homage to Rudolf Carnap. In *PSA 1970: Boston Studies in the Philosophy of Science*, edited by Roger Buck and Robert Cohen. Dordrecht: Reidel.

Cohn, Bernard S. 1980. History and Anthropology: The State of Play. *Comparative Studies in Society and History* 22: 198–221.

———. [1980] 1987a. History and Anthropology: The State of Play. In *An Anthropologist among the Historians and Other Essays*, 18–49. Delhi: Oxford University Press.

———. 1981. Anthropology and History in the 1980s: Toward a Rapprochement. *Journal of Interdisciplinary History* 12, 2: 227–252.

——. 1985. The Command of Language and the Language of Command. In *Subaltern Studies IV: Writings on South Asian History and Society*, edited by Ranajit Guha, 276–329. Oxford: Oxford University Press.

——. 1987b. *An Anthropologist among the Historians and Other Essays*. Introduction by Ranajit Guha. Delhi: Oxford University Press.

Cohn-Bendit, Daniel Jean-Peirre Duteuil, Bertrand Gérard, and Bernard Granautier. 1969. Why Sociologists? In *Student Power*, edited by A. Cockburn and R. Blackburn, 373–378. Harmondsworth, U.K.: Penguin.

Cole, Jonathan R., and Stephen Cole. 1973. *Social Stratification in Science*. Chicago: University of Chicago Press.

Cole, Stephen. 1983. The Hierarchy of the Sciences? *American Journal of Sociology* 89 (July): 111–139.

Coleman, James S. [1988] 2000. Social Capital in the Creation of Human Capital. In *Knowledge and Social Capital*, edited by E. L. Lesser, 17–42. Woburn, Mass.: Butterworth-Heinemann.

——. 1989. *Foundations of Social Theory*. Cambridge: Harvard University Press.

——. 1992. The Power of Social Norms. In *Duke Dialogue: Faculty Newsletter* 3, 7: 1–8.

Coleman, James S., et al. 1966. *Report on Equality of Educational Opportunity*. Washington, D.C.: U.S. Government Printing Office.

Collier, Andrew. 1988. *Scientific Realism and Socialist Thought*. Hemel Hempstead, U.K.: Harvester.

——. 1994. *Critical Realism: An Introduction to Roy Bhaskar's Philosophy*. New York: Verso.

——. 1999. *Being and Worth*. London: Routledge.

Collier, Andrew. 2001. On Real and Nominal Absences. In *After Postmodernism: An Introduction to Critical Realism*, edited by José López and Garry Potter, 299–310. New York: Athlone.

Collins, H. M. 1992. *Changing Order: Replication and Induction in Scientific Practice*. Chicago: University of Chicago Press.

Collins, Martin. 1998. *Planning for Modern War: RAND and the Air Force, 1945–50*. PhD diss. University of Maryland.

Collins, Patricia Hill. 1991. *Black Feminist Thought: Knowledge, Consciousness, and the Politics of Empowerment*. New York: Routledge.

Collins, Randall. 1979. *The Credential Society: An Historical Sociology of Education and Stratification*. New York: Academic Press.

——. 1985. *Three Sociological Traditions*. New York: Oxford University Press.

——. 1989. Sociology: Proscience or Antiscience? *American Sociological Review* 54, 1: 124–139.

——. 1997. *Four Sociological Traditions*. New York: Oxford University Press.

Comaroff, Jean, and John Comaroff. 1992. Ethnography and the Historical Imagination. In *Ethnography and the Historical Imagination*, 3–48. Boulder, Colo.: Westview.

Comaroff, John. 1981–82. Dialectical Systems, History and Anthropology: Units of Study and Questions of Theory. *Journal of Southern African Studies* 8: 143–172.

Comte, Auguste. 1975. *Auguste Comte and Positivism: The Essential Writings*. Edited by Gertrud Lenzer. New York: Harper and Row.

Connell, R. W. 1997. Why Is Classical Theory Classical? *American Journal of Sociology* 102, 6: 1511–1557.

Converse, Philip. 1964. The Nature of Belief Systems in Mass Publics. In *Ideology and Discontent*, edited by David Apter, 206–261. New York: Free Press.

Coronil, Fernando. 1996. Beyond Occidentalism: Toward Nonimperial Geohistorical Categories. *Cultural Anthropology* 11, 1: 51–87.

——. 2001. Review of Tierney's *Darkness in El Dorado. Current Anthropology* 42 (April): 265–266.

Coronil, Fernando, Alan G. Fix, Peter Pels, Charles L. Briggs, Raymond Hames, Susan Lindee, and Alcida Rita Ramos. 2001. Forum on Anthropology in Public: Perspectives on Tierney's "Darkness in El Dorado." Public Discussion and Criticism. *Current Anthropology* 42, 2: 265–276.

Coward, Rosalind, and John Ellis. 1977. *Language and Materialism: Developments in Semiology and the Theory of the Subject.* London: RKP.

Crapanzano, Vincent. 2000. *Serving the Word: Literalism in America from the Pulpit to the Bench.* New York: New Press.

Creaven, Sean. 2000. *Marxism and Realism.* London: Routledge.

Creedy, J. 1977. The Distribution of Lifetime Earnings. *Oxford Economic Papers* 29: 412–429.

——. 1990. Lifetime Earnings and Inequality. *Economic Record* 67: 46–58.

Crozier, Michel, Samuel P. Huntington, and Joji Watanuki. 1975. *The Crisis of Democracy: Report on the Governability of Democracies to the Trilateral Commission.* New York: New York University Press.

Csikszentmihalyi, Mihaly. 1990. *Flow: The Psychology of Optimal Experience.* New York: Harper and Row.

Cumings, Bruce. 2002. Seeing Like an Area Specialist. In *Learning Places: Area Studies, Colonial, Cultural, Ethnic Studies, and Received Disciplines,* edited by Masao Miyoshi and Harry Harootunian. Durham, N.C.: Duke University Press.

Dahl, Robert. 1993. The Behavioral Approach in Political Science: An Epitaph for a Monument to a Successful Movement. In *Discipline and History: Political Science in the United States,* edited by James Farr and Raymond Seidelman, 249–265. Ann Arbor: University of Michigan Press. (Originally published 1961)

Dalton, Thomas. 2002. *Becoming John Dewey.* Bloomington: Indiana University Press.

D'Andrade, Roy G. 1995. *The Development of Cognitive Anthropology.* Cambridge: Cambridge University Press.

Daniel, E. Valentine. 1996. *Charred Lullabies: Chapters in an Anthropography of Violence.* Princeton: Princeton University Press.

Darnton, Robert. 1971a. In Search of the Enlightenment: Recent Attempts to Create a Social History of Ideas. *Journal of Modern History* 43: 113–132.

——. 1971b. Reading, Writing, and Publishing in Eighteenth Century France: A Case Study in the Sociology of Literature. *Daedalus* 100: 214–256.

Dasgupta, P., and I. Serageldin, eds. 1999. *Social Capital: A Multifaceted Perspective.* Washington, D.C.: World Bank.

Davidson, Donald. [1974] 1984. On the Very Idea of a Conceptual Scheme. In *Inquiries into Truth and Interpretation,* 183–198. Oxford: Oxford University Press.

Davis, Kingsley. 1960. The Myth of Functional Analysis as a Special Method in Sociology and Anthropology. *American Sociological Review* 36, 2: 321–326.

Dean, H. 2004. Popular Discourse and the Ethical Deficiency of "Third Way" Conceptions of Citizenship. *Citizenship Studies* 8, 1 (March): 65–82.

Debreu, Gerard. 1959. *The Theory of Value.* New York: Wiley.

de Certeau, Michel. 1984. *The Practice of Everyday Life.* Translated by Steven Rendall. Berkeley: University of California Press.

——. 1988. *The Writing of History.* Translated by Tom Conley. New York: Columbia University Press.

DeFleur, Melvin L., and Otto N. Larsen. 1958. *The Flow of Information: An Experiment in Mass Communication.* New York: Harper.

Deleuze, Gilles, and Félix Guattari. [1972] 1983. *Anti-Oedipus: Capitalism and Schizophrenia.* Minneapolis: University of Minnesota Press.

de Marchi, Neil, and Mark Blaug. 1991. *Appraising Economic Theories: Studies in the Methodology of Research Programs.* Brookfield, Vt.: Elgar.

Demirovi, Alex. 2003. Stroboskopischer Effekt und die Kontingenz der Geschichte: Gesellschaftstheoretische Rückfragen an die Regulationstheorie. In *Fit für den Postfordismus? Theoretisch-politische Perspektiven des Regulationsansatzes,* edited by Ulrich Brand and Werner Raza, 43–57. Münster: Westfälisches Dampfboot.

Demuth, Christopher and William Kristol, eds. 1995. *The Neoconservative Imagination: Essays in Honor of Irving Kristol.* Washington, D.C.: AEI Press.

Derrida, Jacques. [1972] 1982. Signature Event Context. In *Margins of Philosophy,* translated by Alan Bass, 307–330. Chicago: University of Chicago Press.

——. 1974. *Of Grammatology.* Translated by Gayatri Spivak. Baltimore: Johns Hopkins University Press.

——. 1995. *The Gift of Death.* Translated by David Wills. Chicago: University of Chicago Press.

Despy-Meyer, Andrée, and Didier Devriese, eds. 1999. *Positivismes: Philosophie, Sociologie, Histoire, Sciences.* Bruxelles: Brepols.

Dewey, John. 1927. *The Public and Its Problems.* New York: Holt.

——. 1939. *Freedom and Culture.* New York: Putnam.

——. [1925] 1981. *Experience and Nature. The Later Works, Vol. 1.* Carbondale: Southern Illinois University Press.

——. 1984. *The Later Works, Vol. 5.* Carbondale: Southern Illinois University Press.

——. 1985. *The Later Works, Vol. 12.* Carbondale: Southern Illinois University Press.

Dibble, Vernon K. 1975. *The Legacy of Albion Small.* Chicago: University of Chicago Press.

Dickens, Peter. 1996. *Reconstructing Nature.* London: Routledge.

Dilthey, Wilhelm. 1910. *Der Aufbau der geschichtlichen Welt in den Geisteswissenschaften.* Berlin: Verlag der Königlichen Akademie der Wissenschaften, in Commission bei Georg Reimer.

Dirks, Nicholas, ed. 1992. *Colonialism and Culture.* Ann Arbor: University of Michigan Press.

Dolton, P. J., G. H. Makepeace, and W. Van der Klaauw. 1989. Occupational Choice and Earnings Determination. *Oxford Economic Papers* 411: 573–594.

Donham, Donald L. 1999. *Marxist Modern: An Ethnographic History of the Ethiopian Revolution.* Berkeley: University of California Press.

Douglas, Mary. 1966. *Purity and Danger: An Analysis of the Concepts of Pollution and Taboo.* London: Routledge and Kegan Paul.

Dumont, Louis. [1966] 1970. *Homo Hierarchicus: The Caste System and Its Implications.* Translated by Mark Saintsbury. Chicago: University of Chicago Press.

Durkheim, Emile. [1912] 1995. *The Elementary Forms of Religious Life.* Translated by Karen E. Fields. New York: Basic Books.

Durkheim, Emile, and Marcel Mauss. [1903] 1963. *Primitive Classification.* Translated by Rodney Needham. Chicago: University of Chicago Press.

Durkheim, Emile. 1938. *The Rules of Sociological Method.* Chicago: University of Chicago Press.

Durlauf, S. N. 2002. On the Empirics of Social Capital. *The Economic Journal* 112, 483 (November): 459–479.

Dutton, Michael. 1998. *Streetlife China.* Cambridge: Cambridge University Press.

Eakin, Emily. 2000. Political Scientists Leading a Revolt, Not Studying One. *New York Times,* November 4, B11.

Easton, David. 1951. The Decline of Modern Political Theory. *Journal of Politics* 13: 36–58.

——. 1965. *A Framework for Political Analysis.* Englewood Cliffs, N.J.: Prentice-Hall.

——. 1991. Oral History. In *Political Science in America: Oral Histories of a Discipline,* edited by Michael A. Baer, Malcolm E. Jewell, and Lee Sigelman, 195–214. Lexington: University Press of Kentucky.

Eco, Umberto. 1995. *The Search for the Perfect Language.* Translated by James Fentress. Oxford: Blackwell.

Economist magazine. 1993. Civic Lessons: *Pro Bono Publico.* February 6: 94.

Edwards, Bob, and Michael W. Foley. 1997. Escape from Politics? Social Theory and the Social Capital Debate. *American Behavioral Scientist* 40: 550–561.

——. 1998. Civil Society and Social Capital Beyond Putnam. *American Behavioral Scientist* 42: 124–139.

Edwards, Bob, M. W. Foley, and M. Diani. eds. 2001. *Beyond Tocqueville: Civil Society and the Social Capital Debate in Comparative Perspective.* Hanover, N.H.: University Press of New England.

Ehrbar, Hans G. 2002. Critical Realist Arguments in Marx's *Capital.* In *Critical Realism and Marxism,* edited by Steve Fleetwood, Andrew Brown, and John Michael Roberts, 43–56. London: Routledge.

Ehrenberg, John. 1999. *Civil Society: The Critical History of an Idea.* New York: New York University Press.

Eisenstadt, S. N. 2000. Multiple Modernities. *Daedalus* 129 (winter): 1–29.

Eisner, Robert. 1989. Divergences of Measurement and Theory and Some Implications for Economic Policy. *American Economic Review* 79 (March): 1–13.

Eley, Geoff. [1980] 1991. *Reshaping the German Right: Radical Nationalism and Political Change after Bismarck.* Ann Arbor: University of Michigan Press.

——. 1996. Is All the World a Text? From Social History to the History of Society Two Decades Later. In *The Historic Turn in the Human Sciences,* edited by Terrence J. McDonald, 193–243. Ann Arbor: University of Michigan Press.

——. 2000. Between Social History and Cultural Studies: Interdisciplinarity and the Practice of the Historian at the End of the Twentieth Century. In *Historians and Social Values,* edited by Joep Leerssen and Ann Rigney, 93–109. Amsterdam: Amsterdam University Press.

——. 2002. *Forging Democracy: The History of the Left in Europe, 1850–2000.* Oxford: Oxford University Press.

Elliott, Anthony. 2000. *Freud 2000.* New York: Routledge.

——. 2002. *Psychoanalytic Theory: An Introduction.* Durham, N.C.: Duke University Press.

Elman, Benjamin A. 1984. *From Philosophy to Philology: Intellectual and Social Aspects of Change in Late Imperial China.* Cambridge: Council on East Asian Studies, Harvard University.

Elshtain, Jean Bethke. 1987. *Women and War*. Chicago: University of Chicago Press.

——. 2001. Political Theory and Moral Responsibility. In *Schools of Thought: Twenty-Five Years of Interpretive Social Science*, edited by Joan W. Scott and Debra Keates, 315–329. Princeton: Princeton University Press.

Elster, Jon, ed. 1986. *Rational Choice*. New York: New York University Press.

——. 1998. A Plea for Mechanisms. In *Social Mechanisms*, edited by Peter Hedström and Richard Swedborg, 45–73. Cambridge: Cambridge University Press.

——. 2000. Rational Choice History: A Case of Excessive Ambition. *American Political Science Review* 94: 685–695.

Ember, Melvin. 1988. The Human Relations Area Files: Past and Future. *Behavior Science Research* 22, 1–4: 97–104.

——. 2001. From the President: What Cross-Cultural Research Is Really Good For. HRAF *News* (spring/summer): 1.

Emirbayer, Mustafa. 1997. Manifesto for a Relational Sociology. *American Journal of Sociology* 103, 2 (September): 281–317.

Engelmann, Stephen G. 2003. *Imagining Interest in Political Thought: Origins of Economic Rationality*. Durham, N.C.: Duke University Press.

Erfurth, Hans. 1929. *Das Problem des Fordismus dargestellt vom Standpunkt der Privatwirtschaftslehre aus*. Altenburg: R. Hauenstein.

Esping-Andersen, Gosta. 1990. *The Three Worlds of Welfare Capitalism*. Cambridge: Polity Press.

Etzioni, A. 1997. *The New Golden Rule: Community and Morality in a Democratic Society*. London: Profile.

Eulau, Heinz. 1962. *The Behavioral Persuasion*. New York: Random House.

Evans, Peter. 1996. Government Action, Social Capital, and Development: Reviewing the Evidence on Synergy. *World Development* 24, 6: 1033–1037.

——. Forthcoming. Development as Institutional Change: The Pitfalls of Monocropping and Potentials of Deliberation. *Studies in Comparative International Development*.

Evans-Pritchard, E. E. [1961] 1962. Anthropology and History. In *Social Anthropology and Other Essays*, 172–191. New York: Free Press.

Fabian, Johannes. 1983. *Time and the Other: How Anthropology Makes Its Object*. New York: Columbia University Press.

Farr, James. 1988. Francis Lieber and the Interpretation of American Political Science. *American Political Science Review* 82 (March): 51–69.

Farr, James, and Raymond Seidelman, eds. 1993. *Discipline and History: Political Science in the United States*. Ann Arbor: University of Michigan Press.

Faure, Alain, and Jacques Rancière. 1976. *La parole ouvrière (1830–1840)*. Paris: Union Générale d'Éditions.

Fay, C. R. 1951. *Palace of Industry*. Cambridge: Cambridge University Press.

Feagin, Joe. 1999. Soul-Searching in Sociology: Is the Discipline in Crisis? *The Chronicle of Higher Education* 46, 8: B4–B6.

Featherman, David L., and Maris A. Vinovskis. 2001. Growth and Use of Social and Behavioral Science in the Federal Government since World War II. In *Social Science and Policy-Making: A Search for Relevance in the Twentieth Century*, edited by David L. Featherman and Maris A. Vinovskis, 40–82. Ann Arbor: University of Michigan Press.

Feigl, Herbert. 1969. The Origin and Spirit of Logical Positivism. In *The Legacy of Logical*

Positivism, edited by Peter Achenstein and Stephen Baker, 3–24. Baltimore: Johns Hopkins University Press.

Ferejohn, John, and Debra Satz. 1994. Rational Choice and Social Theory. *Journal of Philosophy* 91 (February): 71–87.

Festinger, Leon, and Daniel Katz, eds. 1953. *Research Methods in the Behavioral Sciences.* New York: Holt, Rinehart and Winston.

Fine, Terrence. 1973. *Theories of Probability.* New York: Academic Press.

Fine, Ben. 2001. *Social Capital versus Social Theory.* New York: Routledge.

Fisher, Donald. 1993. *Fundamental Development of the Social Sciences: Rockefeller Philanthropy and the United States Social Science Research Council.* Ann Arbor: University of Michigan Press.

Fitzpatrick, R. 1996. Alternative Approaches to the Assessment of Health-Related Quality of Life. In *Pursuit of the Quality of Life*, edited by A. Offer, 140–162. Oxford: Oxford University Press.

Fleetwood, Steve, ed. 1999. *Critical Realism in Economics: Development and Debate.* London: Routledge.

Flyvberg, Bent. 2001. *Making Social Sciences Matter: Why Social Inquiry Fails and How It Can Succeed Again.* Cambridge: Cambridge University Press.

Foley, Michael W., and Bob Edwards. 1996. The Paradox of Civil Society. *Journal of Democracy* 7: 38–52.

Forrester, John. 1997. *Dispatches from the Freud Wars: Psychoanalysis and Its Passions.* Cambridge: Harvard University Press.

Foster, Lawrence. 1984. *Religion and Sexuality.* Urbana: University of Illinois Press.

Foucault, Michel. [1966] 1970. *The Order of Things: An Archaeology of the Human Sciences.* London: Tavistock.

——. [1971] 1972. *The Archaeology of Knowledge and the Discourse on Language.* New York: Pantheon Books.

——. 1977a. *Discipline and Punish: The Birth of the Prison.* New York: Pantheon Books.

——. 1977b. Nietzsche, Genealogy, History. In *Language, Counter-Memory, Practice: Selected Essays and Interviews*, edited by Douglas F. Bouchard, 139–164. Ithaca, N.Y.: Cornell University Press.

——. 1979. *Discipline and Punish: The Birth of the Prison.* Translated by Alan Sherridan. New York: Vintage Books.

——. 1980. *The History of Sexuality: An Introduction.* New York: Vintage Books.

——. 1981. *The History of Sexuality: An Introduction.* Harmondsworth, U.K.: Penguin.

——. 1991. Governmentality. In *The Foucault Effect: Studies in Governmentality*, edited by Graham Burchell, Colin Gordon, and Peter Miller, 87–104. Hemel Hempstead, U.K.: Harvester Wheatsheaf.

——. 1994. Lacan, le "libérateur" de la psychanalyse. In *Dits et écrits 1854–1988*, vol. 4 (1980–1988), 204–205. Paris: Gallimard.

——. 1995. *Discipline and Punish: The Birth of the Prison.* New York: Vintage Books.

——. 2000. *Power: The Essential Works of Foucault 1954–1984, Volume 3.* Edited by James D. Faubion. New York: New Press.

Fourcade-Gourinchas, Marion. 2003. The Construction of a Global Profession: The Case of Economics. Unpublished manuscript. Department of Sociology, University of California, Berkeley.

Freitag, Michel. 2001. The Contemporary Social Sciences and the Problem of Normativity. *Thesis Eleven*, no. 65: 1–25.

Freud, Sigmund. [1892–1899] 1966. Extracts from the Fliess Papers. In *Standard Edition of the Complete Psychological Works of Sigmund Freud, Volume I*, translated and edited by James Strachey, 175–280. London: Hogarth Press.

——. [1895] 1966. Project for a Scientific Psychology. In *Standard Edition of the Complete Psychological Works of Sigmund Freud, Volume I*, translated and edited by James Strachey, 283–397. London: Hogarth Press.

——. [1900] 1953. The Interpretation of Dreams. In *Standard Edition of the Complete Psychological Works of Sigmund Freud, Volumes IV and V*, translated and edited by James Strachey. London: Hogarth Press.

——. [1924] 1961. The Resistances to Psycho-analysis. *Standard Edition of the Complete Psychological Works of Sigmund Freud, Volume XIX*, translated and edited by James Strachey, 213–224. London: Hogarth Press.

——. [1926] 1959. The Question of Lay Analysis. *Standard Edition of the Complete Psychological Works of Sigmund Freud, Volume XX*, translated and edited by James Strachey, 179–258. London: Hogarth Press.

——. [1938] 1964. An Outline of Psychoanalysis. *Standard Edition of the Complete Psychological Works of Sigmund Freud, Volume XXIII*, translated and edited by James Strachey, 141–207. London: Hogarth Press.

——. 1966. *The Basic Writings of Sigmund Freud*. Translated and edited by A. A. Brill. New York: Random House.

——. 1985. *The Complete Letters of Sigmund Freud to Wilhelm Fliess, 1887–1904*. Edited and translated by Jeffrey M. Masson. Cambridge, Mass.: Belknap Press.

Friedman, Milton. 1953a. The Methodology of Positive Economics. In *Essays in Positive Economics*, edited by Milton Friedman, 3–43. Chicago: University of Chicago Press.

——. 1953b. *Essays in Positive Economics*. Chicago: University of Chicago Press.

——. 1999. Conversation with Milton Friedman. In *Conversations with Leading Economists: Interpreting Modern Macroeconomics*, edited by B. Snowdon and H. Vane, 124–144. Cheltenham, U.K.: Edward Elgar.

Friedrich, Hugo. 1992. On the Art of Translation. In *Theories of Translation: An Anthology of Essays from Dryden to Derrida*, translated by Rainer Schulte and John Biguenet, 11–16. Chicago: University of Chicago Press.

Frisby, David, and Derek Sayer. 1986. *Society*. Chichester, U.K.: Ellis Horwood.

Frisch, Ragnar. 1933. Propagation Problems and Impulse Problems in Dynamic Economics. In *Economic Essays in Honour of Gustav Cassel*, 171–205. London: George Allen and Unwin.

Frosh, Stephen. 1999. Psychoanalysis, Science and "Truth." In *Freud 2000*, edited by Anthony Elliott, 13–37. New York: Routledge.

Fukuyama, Francis. 1992. *The End of History and the Last Man*. New York: Free Press.

——. 1995a. *Trust: Social Virtues and the Creation of Prosperity*. New York: Free Press.

——. 1995b. The Primacy of Culture. *Journal of Democracy* 6: 6.

Fuller, Steve. 1993. *Philosophy of Science and Its Discontents*. 2nd ed. New York: Guilford Press.

Gadamer, Hans-Georg. 1975. *Truth and Method*. New York: Seabury Press.

Galison, Peter. 1996. Constructing Modernism: The Cultural Location of *Aufbau*. In *Origins of Logical Positivism*, edited by Ronald Giere and Alan Richardson, 17–44. Minneapolis: University of Minnesota Press.

Gallagher, John, and Ronald Robinson. 1953. The Imperialism of Free Trade. *Economic History Review* 6, 1: 1–15.

Gamarknikoff, E. and A. Green. 1999. Social Capital and the Educated Citizen. *The School Field* 10, 3/4: 103–126.

Gambetta, Diego. 1987. *Were They Pushed or Did They Jump? Individual Decision Mechanisms in Education.* Cambridge: Cambridge University Press.

——. 1988. *Trust: Making and Breaking Cooperative Relations.* New York: Blackwell.

Gamson, William. A. 1975. *The Strategy of Social Protest.* Homewood, Ill.: Dorsey.

Gaonkar, Dilip Parameshwar, ed. 2001. *Alternative Modernities.* Durham, N.C.: Duke University Press.

Gartrell, C. David, and John W. Gartrell. 1996. Positivism in Sociological Practice: 1967–1990. *Canadian Journal of Sociology and Anthropology* 33 (May): 143–158.

Geertz, Clifford. 1973a. Deep Play: Notes on the Balinese Cockfight. In *The Interpretation of Cultures,* 412–453. New York: Basic Books.

——. 1973b. The Growth of Culture and the Evolution of Mind. In *The Interpretation of Cultures,* 55–83. New York: Basic Books.

——. 1973c. *The Interpretation of Cultures.* New York: Basic Books.

——. 1973d. Thick Description: Toward an Interpretive Theory of Culture. In *The Interpretation of Cultures,* 3–30. New York: Basic Books.

——. 1983. From the Native's Point of View: On the Nature of Anthropological Understanding. In *Local Knowledge: Further Essays in Interpretive Anthropology,* 55–70. New York: Basic Books.

——. 2001. Life among the Anthros. *New York Review of Books,* February 8: 18–22.

Geiger, Roger. 1993. *Research and Relevant Knowledge: American Research Universities since World War II.* New York: Oxford University Press.

Gerdtham, U-G., and M. Johannesson. 2000. Income-related Inequality in Life-Years and Quality-adjusted Life-Years. *Journal of Health Economics* 19, 6: 1007–1026.

Geremek, Bronislaw. 1992. Civil Society Then and Now. *Journal of Democracy* 3: 4.

Gershon, Mark. 1996a. *The Neoconservatism Vision.* New York: Madison Books.

——, ed. 1996b. *The Essential Neoconservative Reader.* Reading, Mass.: Addison Wesley.

Gibbons, Michael, et al. 1994. *The New Production of Knowledge: The Dynamics of Science and Research in Contemporary Societies.* London: Sage Publications.

Giddens, Anthony, ed. 1975. *Positivism and Sociology.* London: Heinemann.

——. 1979. *Central Problems in Social Theory.* London: Macmillan.

——. 1991. *Modernity and Self-Identity.* Cambridge: Polity.

——. 1998. *The Third Way: The Renewal of Social Democracy.* Cambridge: Polity Press.

Giedion, Sigfried. 1926. *Bauen in Frankreich: Eisen, Eisenbeton.* Leipzig: Klinkhardt and Biermann.

Giere, Ronald. 1996. From Wissenschaftliche Philosophie to Philosophy of Science. In *Origins of Logical Empiricism,* edited by Ronald Giere and Alan Richardson, 335–354. Minneapolis: University of Minnesota Press.

Giere, Ronald N., and Alan W. Richardson, eds. 1996. *Origins of Logical Empiricism.* Minneapolis: University of Minnesota Press.

Gieryn, Thomas F. 1999. *Cultural Boundaries of Science: Credibility on the Line.* Chicago: University of Chicago Press.

Gimbel, Steven. 2003. If I Had a Hammer: Why Logical Positivism Accounts for the Need for Gender and Cultural Studies. *Studies in Practical Philosophy,* 2, 2: 150–178.

Glaeser, E., Laibson, David, and Sacerdote, Bruce. 2002. The Economic Approach to Social Capital. *The Economic Journal* 112.

Glaser, Barney G., and Anselm L. Strauss. 1967. *The Discovery of Grounded Theory: Strategies for Qualitative Research.* New York: Aldine de Gruyter.

Glasman, Maurice. 1998. *Unnecessary Suffering.* London: Verso.

Goffman, Erving. 1974. *Frame Analysis: An Essay on the Organization of Experience.* Cambridge: Harvard University Press.

———. 1981. *Forms of Talk.* Philadelphia: University of Pennsylvania Press.

Gold, Marthe R., J. E. Siegel, L. B. Russell, and M. C. Weinstein. 1996. *Cost-effectiveness in Health and Medicine.* New York: Oxford University Press.

Goldstein, Jan, ed. 1994. *Foucault and the Writing of History.* Oxford: Blackwell.

Goldstein, W., and R. Hogarth, eds. 1997. *Research on Judgment and Decision Making.* New York: Cambridge University Press.

Gordon, David M., Richard Edwards, and Michael Reich. 1982. *Segmented Work, Divided Workers: The Historical Transformations of Labor in the United States.* Cambridge: Cambridge University Press.

Gottl-Ottlilienfeld, Friedrich von. 1924. *Fordismus?* Jena, Germany: G. Fischer.

Gould, Roger V. 1995. *Insurgent Identities: Class, Community, and Protest from 1848 to the Commune.* Chicago: University of Chicago Press.

Gould, Stephen Jay. 1996. *The Mismeasure of Man.* 2nd ed. New York: Norton.

Gouldner, Alvin W. 1962. Anti-Minotaur: The Myth of a Value-Free Sociology. *Social Problems* 9, 3: 199–213.

———. 1965. *Enter Plato.* New York: Basic Books.

———. 1970. *The Coming Crisis of Western Sociology.* London: Heinemann.

———. 1973. *For Sociology: Renewal and Critique in Sociology Today.* London: Allen Lane.

Graham, Stephen, and Simon Marvin. 2001. *Splintering Urbanism: Networked Infrastructures, Technological Mobilities, and the Urban Condition.* London: Routledge.

Gramsci, Antonio. [1929–35] 1971a. Americanism and Fordism. In *Selections from the Prison Notebooks of Antonio Gramsci.* Edited and translated by Quintin Hoare and Geoffrey Nowell Smith, 277–320. New York: International Publishers.

———. 1971b. *Selections from the Prison Notebooks of Antonio Gramsci.* Edited and Translated by Quinton Hoare and Geoffrey Nowell Smith. New York: International Publishers.

Green, Donald P., and Ian Shapiro. 1994. *Pathologies of Rational Choice Theory; A Critique of Applications in Political Science.* New Haven: Yale University Press.

Gregor, A. James. 1969. Gunnell on "Deductivism," the "Logic" of Science and Scientific Explanation: A Riposte. *American Political Science Review* 63: 1251–1258.

Griliches, Zvi. 1994. Productivity, R&D, and the Data Constraint. *American Economic Review* 14, 1: 1–23.

Griswold, Wendy. 1990. Provisional, Provincial Positivism: Reply to Denzin. *American Journal of Sociology* 95 (May): 1580–1583.

Grootaert, C. 1997. Social Capital: The Missing Link? World Bank Website on Social Capital: Available: www.worldbank.org/poverty/scapital/whatsc.htm.

Grootaert, C., and T. Van Bastelaer. 2002. *The Role of Social Capital in Development: An Empirical Assessment.* Cambridge: Cambridge University Press.

Gross, Neil. 2003. Richard Rorty's Pragmatism: A Case Study in the Sociology of Ideas. *Theory and Society* 32: 93–148.

Gross, Paul R., and Norman Levitt. 1994. *Higher Superstition: The Academic Left and Its Quarrels with Science.* Baltimore: Johns Hopkins University Press.

Gross, Paul R., Norman Levitt, and Martin W. Lewis, eds. 1996. The Flight from Science and Reason. *Annals of the New York Academy of Sciences 775*.

Grossman, Gene M., and Elhanan Helpman. 1994. Protection for Sale. *American Economic Review* 84, 4: 833–850.

Grünbaum, Adolph. 1984. *The Foundations of Psychoanalysis: A Philosophical Critique*. Berkeley: University of California Press.

Guesnerie, Roger. 1997. Modeling and Economic Theory: Evolution and Problems. In *Is Economics Becoming a Hard Science?*, edited by Antoine D. Autume and Jean Cartelier, 85–91. Cheltenham, U.K.: Edward Elgar.

Gunnell, John G. 1975. Philosophy, Science, and Political Inquiry. Morristown, N.J.: General Learning Press.

———. 1986. *Between Philosophy and Politics: The Alienation of Political Theory*. Amherst: University of Massachusetts Press.

———. 1992. Continuity and Innovation in the History of Political Science: The Case of Charles Merriam. *Journal of the History of the Behavioral Sciences* 28: 133–142.

———. 1993. *The Descent of Political Theory: The Genealogy of an American Vocation*. Chicago: University of Chicago Press.

———. 1995. Realizing Theory: The Philosophy of Science Revisited. *Journal of Politics* 57: 923–940.

Gupta, Akhil, and James Ferguson. [1992] 1997. Beyond "Culture": Space, Identity, and the Politics of Difference. In *Culture Power Place: Explorations in Critical Anthropology*, edited by Akhil Gupta and James Ferguson, 33–51. Durham, N.C.: Duke University Press.

Habermas, Jürgen. 1970. Technology and Science as "Ideology." In *Towards a Rational Society*. Translated by Jeremy J. Shapiro, 81–122. Boston: Beacon Press.

———. 1971. *Knowledge and Human Interests*. Translated by Jeremy J. Shapiro. Boston: Beacon Press.

———. 1973. *Theory and Practice*. Translated by John Viertel. Boston: Beacon Press.

———. 1976. A Positivistically Bisected Rationalism. In *The Positivist Dispute in German Sociology*, translated by Glyn Adey and David Frisby, 198–225. London: Heinemann. (German edition published 1969)

———. 1984. *The Theory of Communicative Action*. 2 vols. Translated by Thomas McCarthy. Boston: Beacon Press.

———. 1989. Neoconservative Cultural Criticism in the United States and West Germany. In *The New Conservatism*, edited and translated by Shierry Weber Nicholsen, 22–47. Cambridge: MIT Press.

———. 1990. What does Socialism Mean Today? The Revolutions of Recuperation and the Need for New Thinking. In *After the Fall: The Failure of Communism and the Future of Socialism*, edited by Robin Blackburn, 25. London: Verso.

Hacking, Ian. 1983. *Representing and Intervening: Introductory Topics in the Philosophy of Natural Science*. Cambridge: Cambridge University Press.

———. 1995. The Looping Effects of Human Kinds. In *Causal Cognition: A Multidisciplinary Debate*, edited by Dan Sperber, David Premack, and Ann J. Premack, 351–394. Oxford: Oxford University Press.

———. 1996. The Disunities of the Sciences. In *The Disunity of the Sciences: Boundaries, Contexts, and Power*, edited by Peter Galison and David J. Stump, 37–74. Stanford: Stanford University Press.

———. 1999. *The Social Construction of What?* Cambridge: Harvard University Press.

Hahn, Frank H. [1970] 1984a. Some Adjustment Problems. *Econometrica* 38 (January): 1–17. Reprinted in *Equilibrium and Macroeconomics* (Oxford: Basil Blackwell, 1984).

———. 1982. *Money and Inflation.* London: Basil Blackwell.

———. 1984b. *Equilibrium and Macroeconomics.* Oxford: Basil Blackwell.

———. 1985. In Praise of Economic Theory. In *The 1984 Jevons Memorial Fund Lecture.* London: University College.

———. 1992a. Reflections. *Royal Economics Society Newsletter* 77.

———. 1992b. Answer to Backhouse: Yes. *Royal Economics Society Newsletter* 78: 5.

———. 1994. An Intellectual Retrospect. *Banca Nazionale del Lavoro Quarterly Review* 58, 190: 245–258.

Hahn, Louis, ed. 1999. *The Philosophy of Donald Davidson.* Chicago: Open Court Press.

Hale, Nathan G. 1995. *The Rise and Crisis of Psychoanalysis in the United States: Freud and the Americans, 1917–1985.* New York: Oxford University Press.

———. 2001. New Heads for Freud's Hydra: Psychoanalysis in Los Angeles. *Journal for the History of the Behavioral Sciences* 37: 111–122.

Halfpenny, Peter. 1982. *Positivism and Sociology: Explaining Social Life.* London: George Allen and Unwin.

Hall, J. A., ed. 1995. *Civil Society: Theory, History, Comparison.* Cambridge: Polity Press.

Hall, Edward Twitchell. 1959. *The Silent Language.* Garden City, N.Y.: Doubleday.

Hall, Rupert A. 1963. Merton Revisited: Science and Society in the Seventeenth Century. *History of Science* 2: 1–16.

Hallberg, Margareta. 1989. Feminist Epistemology: An Impossible Project? *Radical Philosophy* 53: 3–7.

Hands, D. Wade. 2001. *Reflection without Rules: Economic Methodology and Contemporary Science Theory.* Cambridge: Cambridge University Press.

Hanifan, L. J. 1920. *The Community Center.* Boston: Silver Burdett.

Hanks, William F. 1996. *Language and Communicative Practices.* Boulder, Colo.: Westview Press.

Hanson, Norwood Russell. 1958. *Patterns of Discovery.* London: Cambridge University Press.

Hanushek, Erik A., and John E. Jackson. 1977. *Statistical Methods for Social Scientists.* New York: Academic Press.

Haraway, Donna. 1989. *Primate Visions: Gender, Race, and Nature in the World of Modern Science.* New York: Routledge.

———. [1991] 2003. Situated Knowledges: The Science Question in Feminism and the Privilege of Partial Perspectives. In *Simians, Cyborgs, and Women: The Reinvention of Nature,* 183–201. New York: Routledge. Reprinted in *The Feminist Standpoint Theory Reader: Intellectual and Political Controversies,* edited by Sandra Harding (New York: Routledge, 2003).

Harding, Sandra. 1986. *The Science Question in Feminism.* Ithaca, N.Y.: Cornell University Press.

———. 1991. *Whose Science? Whose Knowledge? Thinking from Women's Lives.* Ithaca, N.Y.: Cornell University Press.

———. [1992] 2003a. Rethinking Standpoint Epistemology: What Is "Strong Objectivity"? In *Feminist Epistemologies,* edited by Linda Alcoff and Elizabeth Potter. New York: Routledge. Excerpted in *The Feminist Standpoint Theory Reader: Intellectual and Political Controversies,* edited by Sandra Harding (New York: Routledge, 2003).

———. 1998. *Is Science Multicultural? Postcolonialisms, Feminisms, and Epistemologies*. Bloomington: Indiana University Press.

———. 1999. The Case for Strategic Realism: A Response to Lawson. *Feminist Economics* 5, 3: 127–133.

———, ed. 2003b. *The Feminist Standpoint Theory Reader: Intellectual and Political Controversies*. New York: Routledge.

———. 2004. A Socially Relevant Philosophy of Science? Resources from Standpoint Theory's Controversiality. *Hypatia* 19, 1, Special issue, *Feminist Science Studies*: 25–47.

———. Forthcoming. *Must Science Advance Inequality?* Edwardsville: University of Illinois Press.

Harding, Susan Friend. 1991. Representing Fundamentalism: The Problem of the Repugnant Cultural Other. *Social Research* 58, 2: 373–393.

———. 2000. *The Book of Jerry Falwell: Fundamentalist Language and Politics*. Princeton: Princeton University Press.

Hardt, Michael, and Antonio Negri. 2000. *Empire*. Cambridge: Harvard University Press.

Harris, Marvin. 1968. *The Rise of Anthropological Theory: A History of Theories of Culture*. New York: Thomas Y. Crowell.

Harrison, Lawrence E., and Samuel P. Huntington. 2000. *Culture Matters: How Values Shape Human Progress*. New York: Perseus Books.

Hartsock, Nancy. [1983] 2003. The Feminist Standpoint: Developing the Ground for a Specifically Feminist Historical Materialism. In *Discovering Reality: Feminist Perspectives on Epistemology, Metaphysics, Methodology, and Philosophy of Science*, edited by Sandra Harding and Merrill Hintikka, 283–310. 2nd ed. Dordrecht: Reidel/Kluwer. Reprinted in *The Feminist Standpoint Theory Reader: Intellectual and Political Controversies*, edited by Sandra Harding (New York: Routledge, 2003).

———. 1998. The Feminist Standpoint Revisited. In *The Feminist Standpoint Revisited and Other Essays*, 227–248. Boulder, Colo.: Westview Press.

Harvey, David. 1989. *The Condition of Postmodernity: An Enquiry into the Origins of Cultural Change*. New York: Basil Blackwell.

Hassard, John. 1993. *Sociology and Organization Theory: Positivism, Paradigms and Postmodernity*. Cambridge: Cambridge University Press.

Hauptmann, Emily. 1996. *Putting Choice before Democracy: A Critique of Rational Choice Theory*. Albany: State University of New York Press.

———. 2004. A Local History of "the Political." *Political Theory* 32: 34–60.

Hauser, Philip M. 1946. Are the Social Sciences Ready? *American Sociological Reviews* 11 (August): 379–384.

Hausman, Daniel. 1992. *The Inexact and Separate Science of Economics*. Cambridge: Cambridge University Press.

Hayek, F. A. von. 1942. Scientism and the Study of Society (Part 1). *Economica* 9 (August): 267–291.

Hebdige, Dick. 1979. *Subculture: The Meaning of Style*. London: Routledge.

Hedström, Peter, and Richard Swedberg, eds. 1998. *Social Mechanisms: An Analytical Approach to Social Theory*. Cambridge: Cambridge University Press.

Heilbroner, R. and W. Milberg. 1995. *The Crisis of Vision in Modern Economic Thought*. Cambridge: Cambridge University Press.

Heitmeyer, Wilhelm. 1992. *Die Bielefelder Rechtsextremismus-Studie*. Weinheim: Juventa.

Hekman, Susan. 1994. Max Weber and Post-Positivist Social Theory. In *The Barbarism of Reason: Max Weber and the Twilight of Enlightenment*, edited by Asher Horowitz and Terry Maley, 267–286. Toronto: University of Toronto Press.

Hempel, Carl Gustav. [1948] 1965. The Function of General Laws in History. In *Aspects of Scientific Explanation and Other Essays in the Philosophy of Science*, 231–243. New York: Free Press.

——. 1966. *Philosophy of Natural Science*. Engelwood Cliffs, N.J.: Prentice-Hall.

——. 1974. Reasons and Covering Laws in Historical Explanation. In *The Philosophy of History*, edited by Patrick Gardiner, 90–105. London: Oxford University Press.

Hempel, Carl Gustav, and Paul Oppenheim. 1945. A Definition of Degree of Confirmation. *Philosophy of Science* 12: 98–115.

——. 1948. *Studies in the Logic of Explanation*. Indianapolis: Bobbs-Merrill.

Hendry, David F., Edward E. Leamer, and Dale J. Poirier. 1990. The ET Dialogue: A Conversation on Econometric Methodology. *Econometric Theory* 6: 171–261.

Herman, Ellen. 1996. *The Romance of American Psychology: Political Culture in the Age of Experts*. Berkeley: University of California Press.

Herpin, Nicolas. 1973. *Les sociologues américains et le siècle*. Paris: PUF.

Herzfeld, Michael. 1997. *Cultural Intimacy: Social Poetics in the Nation-State*. New York: Routledge.

Herzog, Don. 1998. *Poisoning the Minds of the Lower Orders*. Princeton: Princeton University Press.

Hess, David J. 1995. *Science and Technology in a Multicultural World: The Cultural Politics of Facts and Artifacts*. New York: Columbia University Press.

Hexter, J. H. 1991. Carl Becker, Professor Novick, and Me; Or, Cheer Up, Professor N! *American Historical Review* 96, 3: 675–682.

Hill, Jane H. 1995. The Voices of Don Gabriel: Responsibility and Self in a Modern Mexicano Narrative. In *The Dialogic Emergence of Culture*, edited by Dennis Tedlock and Bruce Mannheim, 97–147. Urbana: University of Illinois Press.

Hill, Jane H., and Judith T. Irvine, eds. 1992. *Responsibility and Evidence in Oral Discourse*. Cambridge: Cambridge University Press.

Hindess, Barry. 1998. Neoliberalism and the National Economy. In *Governing Australia: Studies in Contemporary Rationalities of Government*, edited by Mitchell Dean, Barry Hindess, Geoffrey Brennan, and Francis G. Castles, 210–226. Cambridge: Cambridge University Press.

Hirsch, Joachim. 1980. *Der Sicherheitsstaat*. Frankfurt/Main: Europäische Verlagsanstalt.

——. 1983. The Fordist Security State and New Social Movements. *Kapitalistate* 10: 75–88.

——. 1988. The Crisis of Fordism, Transformations of the "Keynesian" Security State, and New Social Movements. In *Research in Social Movements, Conflicts and Change*, edited by Louis Kriesberg and Misztal Bronislaw, 43–55. Greenwich, Conn.: JAI Press.

Hirsch, Joachim, and Roland Roth. 1986. *Das neue Gesicht des Kapitalismus*. Hamburg: VSA-Verlag.

Hirschman, Albert. 1970. *Exit, Voice, and Loyalty: Responses to Decline in Firms, Organizations, and States*. Cambridge: Harvard University Press.

Hobsbawm, Eric J. 1971. From Social History to the History of Society. *Daedalus* 100: 20–45.

Hochschild, Jennifer. 2003. Introduction and Observations. *Perspectives on Politics* 1 (March): 1–4.

Hollinger, David A. 1996. *Science, Jews, and Secular Culture: Studies in Mid-Twentieth-Century American Intellectual History.* Princeton: Princeton University Press.

Holmes, Stephen. 1997. What Russia Teaches Us Now. *American Prospect* 33 (July–August): 30–40.

Holt, Thomas C. 1995. Marking: Race, Race-making, and the Writing of History. *American Historical Review* 100: 1–20.

Homans, George. 1964. Bringing Men Back In. *American Sociological Review* 29: 809–818.

Hoover, Kevin D. 2001. *Causality in Macroeconomics.* Cambridge: Cambridge University Press.

——. 2003. Nonstationary Time Series, Cointegration, and the Principle of Common Cause. *British Journal for the Philosophy of Science* 54: 527–551.

Horkheimer, Max. 1995. Traditional and Critical Theory. In *Critical Theory*, 188–243. New York: Continuum.

Horkheimer, Max, and Theodor Adorno. [1944] 1986. *The Dialectic of the Enlightenment.* New York: Continuum.

Horowitz, Irving Louis. 1967. *The Rise and Fall of Project Camelot: Studies in the Relationship between Social Science and Practical Politics.* Cambridge: MIT Press.

——. 1993. *The Decomposition of Sociology.* New York: Oxford University Press.

Hounshell, David. 1997. The Cold War, RAND and the Generalization of Knowledge. *Historical Studies in the Physical and Biological Sciences* 27: 237–267.

Hout, M., and C. S. Fischer. 2002. Why More Americans Have No Religious Preference. *American Sociological Review* 67: 165–190.

Howard, Don. 2003a. Two Left Turns Make a Right: On the Curious Political Career of North American Philosophy of Science at Mid-Century. In *Logical Empiricism in North America*, edited by Gary Hardcastle and Alan Richardson, 25–93. Minneapolis: University of Minnesota Press.

Howell, David. 2000. *The Edge of Now: New Questions for Democracy and the Network Age.* London: Macmillan.

Hudelson, Richard, and Robert Evans. 2003. McCarthyism and Philosophy in the United States. *Philosophy of the Social Sciences* 33: 242–260.

Hughes, Thomas, and Agatha Hughes, eds. 2000. *Systems, Experts and Computers.* Cambridge: MIT Press.

Hume, David [1739–40] 1969. *A Treatise of Human Nature.* London: Penguin.

——. [1748] 1975. *An Enquiry concerning Human Understanding.* Oxford: Clarendon Press.

Humphries, S. C. 1969. History, Economics, and Anthropology: The Work of Karl Polanyi. *History and Theory* 8, 2: 165–212.

Hunt, Lynn. 1978. *Revolution and Urban Politics in Provincial France: Troyes and Reims, 1786–1790.* Stanford: Stanford University Press.

——. 1984. *Politics, Culture, and Class in the French Revolution.* Berkeley: University of California Press.

——, ed. 1989. *The New Cultural History.* Berkeley: University of California Press.

Huntington, Samuel. 1968. *Political Order in Changing Societies.* New Haven: Yale University Press.

——. 1975. The Democratic Distemper. *The Public Interest* 41: 9–38.

——. 1996. *The Clash of Civilizations and the Remaking of World Order.* New York: Simon and Schuster.

Hutchison, Terence W. 1938. *The Significance and Basic Postulates of Economic Theory*. New York: A. M. Kelley.

Hymes, Dell H. 1972. *Reinventing Anthropology*. New York: Pantheon Books.

——. 1975. Breakthrough into Performance. In *Folklore: Performance and Communication*, edited by Dan Ben-Amos and Kenneth S. Goldstein, 11–74. The Hague: Mouton.

Inden, Ronald B. 1976. *Marriage and Rank in Bengali Culture: A History of Caste and Clan in Middle Period Bengal*. Berkeley: University of California Press.

Inkeles, Alex. 1951. Understanding a Foreign Society: A Sociologist's View. *World Politics* 3 (January): 269–280.

Irvine, Judith T. 1996. Shadow Conversations: The Indeterminacy of Participant Roles. In *Natural Histories of Discourse*, edited by Michael Silverstein and Greg Urban, 131–159. Chicago: University of Chicago Press.

Isaac, Jeffrey C. 1996. The Meanings of 1989. *Social Research* 63: 291–344.

Isaacs, Susan. 1991. The Nature and Function of Phantasy. In *The Freud-Klein Controversies 1941–45*, edited by P. King and R. Steiner, 264–321. London: Routledge.

Ivy, Marilyn. 1995. *Discourses of the Vanishing: Modernity, Phantasm, Japan*. Chicago: University of Chicago Press.

Jacobs, J. 1961. *The Death and Life of Great American Cities*. New York: Random House.

Jacobs, Struan. 2002. The Genesis of "Scientific Community." *Social Epistemology* 16: 157–168.

Jacobsen, Kurt. 2001. Political Scientists Have Turned Guerillas in an Attempt to Shake Off the Stranglehold of the Dogmatic, Unworldly Theory That Dominates Their Discipline. *The Guardian*, April 3.

Jacoby, Russell. 1983. *The Repression of Psychoanalysis: Otto Fenichel and the Political Freudians*. New York: Basic Books.

Jaggar, Alison. [1983] 2003. Feminist Epistemologies. In *Feminist Politics and Human Nature*, 351–394. Totowa, N.J.: Rowman and Allenheld. Excerpted in *The Feminist Standpoint Theory Reader: Intellectual and Political Controversies*, edited by Sandra Harding (New York: Routledge, 2003).

Jakobson, Roman. 1992. On Linguistic Aspects of Translation. In *Theories of Translation: An Anthology of Essays from Dryden to Derrida*, translated by Rainer Schulte and John Biguenet, 144–151. Chicago: University of Chicago Press.

Jameson, Fredric. 1981. *The Political Unconscious: Narrative and a Socially Symbolic Act*. Ithaca, N.Y.: Cornell University Press.

——. 1984. Postmodernism, Or, The Cultural Logic of Late Capitalism. *New Left Review* 146: 59–92.

——. [1988] 2003. "History and Class Consciousness" as an Unfinished Project. *Rethinking Marxism* 1, 1: 49–72. Excerpted and revised in *The Feminist Standpoint Theory Reader: Intellectual and Political Controversies*, edited by Sandra Harding (New York: Routledge, 2003).

——. 1991. *Postmodernism, or, The Cultural Logic of Late Capitalism*. Durham, N.C.: Duke University Press.

——. 1998a. *The Cultural Turn: Selected Writings on the Postmodern, 1983–1998*. London: Verso.

——. 1998b. Globalization as a Philosophic Issue. In *The Cultures of Globalization*, edited by Fredric Jameson and Masao Miyoshi, 54–77. Durham, N.C.: Duke University Press.

Jardini, David. 1996. Out of the Blue Yonder. PhD diss. Carnegie-Mellon University.

Jay, Martin. 1984. *Marxism and Totality: The Adventures of a Concept from Lukács to Habermas.* Berkeley: University of California Press.

Jessop, Bob. 1989. Conservative Regimes and the Transition to Post-Fordism: The Cases of Great Britain and West Germany. In *Capitalist Development and Crisis Theory: Accumulation, Regulation and Spatial Restructuring,* edited by M. Gottdiener and Nicos Komninos, 261–297. London: Macmillan.

———. 1990. Regulation Theories in Retrospect and Prospect. *Economy and Society* 19: 153–216.

———. 1992. Fordism and Post-Fordism: Critique and Reformulation. In *Pathways to Industrialism and Regional Development,* edited by Michael Storper and Allen J. Scott, 46–69. London: Routledge.

———. 1999. Narrating the Future of the National Economy and the National State: Remarks on Remapping Regulation and Reinventing Governance. In *State/Culture: State Formation after the Cultural Turn,* edited by George Steinmetz. Wilder House Series in Culture, Power, and History. Ithaca, N.Y.: Cornell University Press.

———. 2003. Postfordismus und wissenbasierte Ökonomie: Eine Reinterpretation des Regulationsansatzes. In *Fit für den Postfordismus? Theoretisch-polititsche Perspektiven des Regulationsansatzes,* edited by Ulrich Brand and Werner Raza, 89–111. Münster: Westfälisches Dampfboot.

Jessop, Bob, et al. 1988. *Thatcherism: A Story of Two Nations.* New York: Polity Press.

Johnson, Chalmers. 1982. What's Wrong with Chinese Political Studies. *Asian Survey* (October): 919–933.

Johnson, D. H., and G. H. Makepeace. 1997. Occupational Advantage in the Eighties. *Work, Employment, and Society* 11: 401–411.

Johnson, James. 2002. How Conceptual Problems Migrate: Rational Choice, Interpretation, and the Hazards of Pluralism. *Annual Review of Political Science* 5 (June): 223–248.

Jöreskog, Karl G., and Dag Sörbom. 1996. *Lisrel 8: User's Reference Guide.* Lincolnwood, Ill.: Scientific Software International.

Joseph, Jonathan. 2002. *Hegemony: A Realist Analysis.* London: Routledge.

Journal of International Relations and Development 2001. 4, 4.

Kagan, Robert. 2003. *Of Paradise and Power: America and Europe in the New World Order.* New York: Knopf.

Kahn, Herman. 1968. Toward a Program for Victory. In *Can We Win in Vietnam?,* edited by Frank E. Armbruster et al., 304–343. New York: Praeger.

Kahnemann, D., and A. Tversky. 1979. Prospect Theory. *Econometrica* 47: 263–291.

———. 2000. Choices, Values, and Frames. In *Choices, Values, and Frames,* edited by D. Kahnemann and A. Tversky, 1–16. New York: Russell Sage.

Kanth, Rajani. 1999. Against Eurocentred Epistemologies: A Critique of Science, Realism and Economics. In *Critical Realism in Economics: Development and Debate,* edited by Steven Fleetwood, 187–208. London: Routledge.

Katz, E., and P. F. Lazarsfeld. 1955. *Personal Influence.* New York: Free Press.

Kay, John. 1995. Cracks in the Crystal Ball. *Financial Times,* September 29.

Keane, John. 1988. *Democracy and Civil Society.* London: Verso.

———. 1994. Nations, Nationalism and Citizens in Europe. *International Social Science Journal* 46: 169–84.

———. 1998. *Civil Society: Old Images, New Visions.* Stanford: Stanford University Press.

Keane, Webb. 1995. The Spoken House: Text, Act, and Object in Eastern Indonesia. *American Ethnologist* 22, 1: 102–124.

——. 1996. Materialism, Missionaries, and Modern Subjects in Colonial Indonesia. In *Conversion to Modernities: The Globalization of Christianity*, edited by Peter van der Veer, 137–170. New York: Routledge.

——. 1997. *Signs of Recognition: Powers and Hazards of Representation in an Indonesian Society*. Berkeley: University of California Press.

——. 1998. Calvin in the Tropics: Objects and Subjects at the Religious Frontier. In *Border Fetishisms: Material Objects in Unstable Spaces*, edited by Patricia Spyer, 13–34. New York: Routledge.

——. 2002. Sincerity, "Modernity," and the Protestants. *Cultural Anthropology* 17, 1: 65–72.

Keat, Russell, and John Urry. 1975. *Social Theory as Science*. London: Routledge and Keagan Paul.

Keller, Evelyn Fox. 1985. *Reflections on Gender and Science*. New Haven: Yale University Press.

Kennedy, George A. 1965. The Selected Works of George A. Kennedy. New Haven: Yale University Press.

Kennedy, M. D. 1991. *Professionals, Power, and Solidarity in Poland: A Critical Sociology of Soviet-Type Society*. Cambridge: Cambridge University Press.

——. 1994. *Envisioning Eastern Europe: Postcommunist Cultural Studies*. Ann Arbor: University of Michigan Press.

——. 2002. *Cultural Formations of Postcommunism: Emancipation, Transition, Nation, and War*. Minneapolis: University of Minnesota Press.

Kermode, Frank. 1967. *The Sense of an Ending: Studies in the Theory of Fiction*. New York: Oxford University Press.

Kevles, Daniel. 1995. *The Physicists*. Cambridge: Harvard University Press.

Keynes, John Maynard. 1913. *Indian Currency and Finance*. London: Macmillan.

——. 1923. *A Tract on Monetary Reform*. London: Macmillan.

——. 1930. *A Treatise on Money*. London: Macmillan.

——. 1936. *The General Theory of Employment, Interest and Money*. London: Macmillan.

——. 1971–89. *The Collected Writings of John Maynard Keynes*. Edited by Donald Moggridge. 30 vols. London: Macmillan.

Keynes, John Neville. 1891. *The Scope and Method of Political Economy*. London: Macmillan.

Kimball, Roger. 1990. *Tenured Radicals: How Politics Has Corrupted Our Higher Education*. New York: Harper and Row.

King, Gary, Robert O. Keohane, and Sidney Verba. 1994. *Designing Social Inquiry: Scientific Inference in Qualitative Research*. Princeton: Princeton University Press.

Kirby, Maurice. 2000. Operations Research Trajectories: Anglo-American Experience, 1940–1990. *Operations Research* 48: 661–670.

Kirman, Alan. 1989. The Intrinsic Limits of Modern Economic Theory: The Emperor Has No Clothes. *Economic Journal* 99, 395: 126–139.

Kirp, David. 2003. *Shakespeare, Einstein, and the Bottom Line*. Cambridge: Harvard University Press.

Kirsch, Stuart. 2001. Lost Worlds: Environmental Disaster, "Culture Loss," and the Law. *Current Anthropology* 42, 2: 167–198.

Kitcher, Philip. 1993. *The Advancement of Science*. New York: Oxford University Press.

——. 2000. Reviving the Sociology of Science. *Philosophy of Science* 67 (Proceedings of the 1998 Philosophy of Science Association): S33–44.

Kitschelt, Herbert. 1993. Social Movements, Political Parties, and Democratic Theory. *The Annals of the American Academy of Political and Social Science* 528 (July): 13–29.

Klamer, Arjo, and Thomas C. Leonard. 1994. So What's an Economic Metaphor? In *Natural Images in Economic Thought: "Markets Read in Tooth and Claw,"* edited by Philip Mirowski, 20–51. Cambridge: Cambridge University Press.

Klausner, Samuel Z., and Victor D. Lidz, eds. 1986. *The Nationalization of the Social Sciences.* Philadelphia: University of Pennsylvania Press.

Kleinman, Daniel Lee. 1995. *Politics on the Endless Frontier: Postwar Research Policy in the United States.* Durham, N.C.: Duke University Press.

Kloppenberg, James T. 1989. Objectivity and Historicism: A Century of American Historical Writing. *American Historical Review* 94, 4: 1011–1030.

Knauft, Bruce. 1996. *Genealogies for the Present in Cultural Anthropology.* London: Routledge.

Knorr-Cetina, Karen. 1981. *The Manufacture of Knowledge.* New York: Pergamon.

——. 1991. Epistemic Cultures: Forms of Reason in Science. *History of Political Economy* 23: 105–122.

Kohler, Robert. 1991. *Partners in Science.* Chicago: University of Chicago Press.

Kolakowski, Leszek. [1966] 1968. *The Alienation of Reason: A History of Positivist Thought.* Garden City, N.Y.: Doubleday.

Kornhauser, A., and P. F. Lazarsfeld. [1935] 1955. The Analysis of Consumer Actions. In *The Language of Social Research*, edited by P. F. Lazarsfeld and M. Rosenberg, 392–404. Glencoe, Ill.: Free Press.

Kragh, Helge. 1999. *Quantum Generations.* Princeton: Princeton University Press.

Krige, John, and Dominique Pestre, eds. 1997. *Science in the Twentieth Century.* Amsterdam: Harwood.

Krishna, A. 2002. *Active Social Capital: Tracing the Roots of Development and Democracy.* New York: Columbia University Press.

Kristol, Irving. 1995. *Neoconservatism: The Autobiography of an Idea.* New York: Free Press.

Kritzer, Herbert. 1996. The Data Puzzle: The Nature of Interpretation in Quantitative Research. *American Journal of Political Science* 40 (February): 1–32.

Kroeber, Alfred Louis. 1915. Eighteen Professions. *American Anthropologist* 17, 2: 283–288.

——. 1917. The Superorganic. *American Anthropologist* 19: 163–213.

——, ed. 1953. *Anthropology Today: An Encyclopedic Inventory.* Chicago: University of Chicago Press.

Kuhn, Thomas. [1962] 1970. *The Structure of Scientific Revolutions.* 2nd ed. Chicago: University of Chicago Press.

——. 1977. Second Thoughts on Paradigms. In *The Structure of Scientific Theories*, edited by Frederick Suppe, 459–517. Urbana: University of Illinois Press.

Kuper, Adam. 1999. *Culture: The Anthropologists' Account.* Cambridge: Harvard University Press.

Kuznets, Simon. 1941. *National Income and Its Composition, 1919–1939.* Vol 1. New York: National Bureau of Economic Research.

Laarman, Peter. 1995. Religious Right Thrives in a Red-Hot Vacuum. *Dissent* 42: 389–392.

Laclau, Ernesto, and Chantal Mouffe. 1985. *Hegemony and Socialist Strategy: Towards a Radical Democratic Politics.* London: Verso.

——. 1987. Post-Marxism without Apologies. *New Left Review*, no. 166: 79–106.

Ladner, Joyce A. 1973. *The Death of White Sociology.* New York: Random House.

Lakatos, Imre. 1970. Falsification and the Methodology of Scientific Research Programmes. In *Criticism and the Growth of Knowledge*, edited by Imre Lakatos and Alan Musgrave, 91–95. Cambridge: Cambridge University Press.

——. 1978. *The Methodology of Scientific Research Programmes: Philosophical Papers Volume I.* Cambridge: Cambridge University Press.

Lakatos, Imre, and Alan Musgrave, eds. 1970. *Criticism and the Growth of Knowledge.* London: Cambridge University Press.

Lambert, Richard D. 1973. *Language and Area Studies Review.* Philadelphia: American Academy of Political and Social Science.

Larsen, Otto N. 1992. *Millstones and Milestones: Social Science at the National Science Foundation.* New Brunswick, N.J.: Transaction Publishers.

Lash, Scott, and John Urry. 1987. *The End of Organized Capitalism.* Cambridge: Polity Press.

Laslett, Peter. 1956. Introduction to *Politics, Philosophy and Society*, 1st series, edited by Peter Laslett. Oxford: Blackwell.

Laswell, Harold D., and Abraham Kaplan. 1950. *Power and Society: A Framework for Political Inquiry.* New Haven: Yale University Press.

Latour, Bruno. 1987. *Science in Action: How to Follow Scientists and Engineers through Society.* Cambridge: Harvard University Press.

——. 1993. *We Have Never Been Modern.* Translated by Catherine Porter. Cambridge: Harvard University Press.

——. 1999. *Pandora's Hope: Essays on the Reality of Science Studies.* Cambridge: Harvard University Press.

Latour, Bruno, and Steve Woolgar. 1979. *Laboratory Life: The Social Construction of Scientific Facts.* Beverly Hills, CA: Sage.

Lauwerier, H. 1991. *Fractals.* Princeton: Princeton University Press.

Law, John, and John Hassard, eds. 1999. *Actor Network Theory and After.* Oxford: Blackwell.

Lawson, Tony. 1994. A Realist Theory for Economics. In *New Directions in Economic Methodology*, edited by Roger E. Backhouse, 257–285. London: Routledge.

——. 1997. *Economics and Reality.* London: Routledge.

——. 1999a. Developments in Economics as Realist Social Theory. In *Critical Realism in Economics: Development and Debate*, edited by Steven Fleetwood, 3–20. London: Routledge.

——. 1999b. Feminism, Realism, and Universalism. *Feminist Economics* 5, 2: 25–59.

——. 2003. *Reorienting Economics.* London: Routledge.

Layder, Derek. 1988. The Relation of Theory and Method: Causal Relatedness, Historical Contingency, and Beyond. *Sociological Review* 36 (August): 441–463.

Lazarsfeld, Paul F., Bernard Berelson, and Hazel Gaudet. [1948] 1968. *The People's Choice: How the Voter Makes Up His Mind in a Presidential Campaign.* New York: Columbia University Press.

Lazarsfeld, Paul F., and Morris Rosenberg, eds. 1955. *The Language of Social Research.* Glencoe, Ill.: Free Press.

Lazarsfeld, Paul F., William H. Sewell, and Harold L. Wilensky, eds. 1967. *The Uses of Sociology.* New York: Basic Books.

Leach, E. R. [1959] 1961. Rethinking Anthropology (Malinowski Lecture). In *Rethinking Anthropology*, no. 22, 1–27. LSE Monographs on Social Anthropology. London: Athlone Press.

Leamer, Edward E. 1978. *Specification Searches: Ad hoc Inferences with Non-experimental Data.* New York: Wiley.

——. 1983. Lets take the Con out of Econometrics. *American Economic Review* 73, 1: 34–43.

Le Carré, John. [1963] 1991. *The Spy Who Came In from the Cold.* New York: Pocket Books.

Lee, Benjamin. 1997. *Talking Heads: Language, Metalanguage, and the Semiotics of Subjectivity.* Durham, N.C.: Duke University Press.

Lenin, Vladimir Il'ich. [1908] 1927. *Materialism and Empirio-Criticism.* London: M. Lawrence.

Lenski, Gerhard. 1988. Rethinking Macrosociological Theory. *American Sociological Review* 53 (April): 163–171.

Leontief, Wassily. 1982. Letter to the editor. *Science* 217: 104–107.

Leslie, Stuart. 1993. *The Cold War and American Science: The Military-Academic Complex at MIT and Stanford.* New York: Columbia University Press.

Lesser, Eric L. 2000. *Knowledge and Social Capital: Foundations and Applications.* Boston: Butterworth Heinemann.

Leutner, Mechrhild. 2001. Politik und Wissenschaft: Die Marginalisierung nicht-philologischer *Ansätze* und die Konstruktion der Sinologie als Philologie. *Berliner China-Hefte,* no. 20: 7–30.

Levi, Margaret. 1996. Social and Unsocial Capital. *Politics and Society* 24, 1: 45–55.

Levine, Saul M., and Arthur Dornblum. 1939. The Implications of Science as a Logical System. *American Sociological Review* 4 (June): 381–387.

Lévi-Strauss, Claude. [1962] 1968. *The Savage Mind.* Chicago: University of Chicago Press.

Lewis, Bernard. 2002. *What Went Wrong? The Clash between Islam and Modernity in the Middle East.* Oxford: Oxford University Press.

Library of Congress. 2000. *Library of Congress Asian Collections: An Illustrated Guide.* Washington, D.C.: Library of Congress.

Lieberson, Stanley. 1991. Small N's and Big Conclusions: An Examination of the Reasoning Based on a Small Number of Cases. *Social Forces* 70 (December): 307–320.

Lin, Ann Chih. 1998. Bridging Positivist and Interpretivist Approaches to Qualitative Methods. *Policy Studies Journal* 26 (March): 162–180.

Lin, N. 2001. *Social Capital: A Theory of Social Structure and Action.* Cambridge: Cambridge University Press.

Lindblom, Charles. 1997. Political Science in the 1940s and 1950s. *Daedalus* 126, 1: 225–252.

Linde, Charlotte. 1993. *Life Stories: The Creation of Coherence.* New York: Oxford University Press.

Linz, Daniel G., Edward Donnerstein, and Steven Penrod. 1988. Effects of Long-Term Exposure to Violent and Sexually Degrading Depictions of Women. *Journal of Personality and Social Psychology* 55, 5: 758–768.

Lipietz, Alain. 1985. Akkumulation, Krisen und Auswege aus der Krise: Einige methodische Überlegungen zum Begriff "Regulation." *PROKLA* 58: 109–137.

———. 1987. *Mirages and Miracles: The Crisis in Global Fordism.* Translated by David Macey. London: Verso.

Lipsey, Richard, G. 2001. Successes and Failures in the Transformation of Economics. *Journal of Economic Methodology* 8, 2 (June): 169–202.

List, Friedrich. [1841] 1856. *Das nationale System der politischen Oekonomie.* English translation, *National System of Political Economy.* Translated by G. A. Matile. Philadelphia: J. B. Lippincott, 1856.

Littrell, Boyd. 1997. Carl Couch and Pragmatism: Naturalism, Temporality and Authority. *Studies in Symbolic Interaction* 3 (Supplement): 3–20.

Liu, Lydia, ed. 1999. *Tokens of Exchange: The Problem of Translation in Global Circulation.* Durham, N.C.: Duke University Press.

——. Forthcoming. *The Clash of Empires: The Invention of China in Modern World Making.* Cambridge: Harvard University Press.

Lloyd, Christopher. 1986. *Explanation in Social History.* London: Blackwell.

Locke, John. [1690] 1952. *The Second Treatise of Government.* Edited by T. P. Peardon. New York: Bobbs-Merrill.

Loewenstein, G., and D. Prelec. 1991. Negative Time Preference. *American Economic Review* 81: 347–352.

——. 1992. Anomalies in Intertemporal Choice. In *Choices over Time,* edited by G. Loewenstein and J. Elster, 119–145. New York: Russell Sage.

Logan, J. R., R. D. Alba, and W. Zhang. 2002. Immigrant Enclaves and Ethnic Communities in New York and Los Angeles. *American Sociological Review* 67: 299–322.

Lopez, José, and Garry Potter, eds. 2001. *After Postmodernism: An Introduction to Critical Realism.* London: Athlone Press.

Louis, William Roger, and Ronald Robinson. 1993. The Imperialism of Decolonization. *Journal of Imperial and Commonwealth History* 22, 3: 462–511.

Loury, G. 1977. A Dynamic Theory of Racial Income Differences. In *Women, Minorities, and Employment Discrimination,* edited by Phyllis A. Wallace and Annette A. LaMond, 153–186. Lexington, Ky.: Lexington Books.

Lowi, Theodore J. 1992. The State in Political Science: How We Become What We Study. *American Political Science Review* 86 (March): 1–7.

Lowie, Robert H. 1920. *Primitive Society.* New York: Liveright.

Lucas, Robert E. 1986. Adaptive Behaviour Economic Theory. *Journal of Business* 59, 4, part 2: S401–S426.

Lucy, John A. 1993. *Reflexive Language: Reported Speech and Metapragmatics.* Cambridge: Cambridge University Press.

Luhmann, Niklas. 1989. *Ecological Communication.* Chicago: University of Chicago Press.

Lukács, Georg. [1922] 1968a. *History and Class Consciousness.* Cambridge: MIT Press.

——. [1954] 1981. *The Destruction of Reason.* Atlantic Highlands, N.J.: Humanities Press.

——. 1968b. Reification and the Consciousness of the Proletariat. In *History and Class Consciousness,* 83–222. Cambridge: MIT Press.

——. 1971. *History and Class Consciousness.* Cambridge: MIT Press.

Luke, Timothy W. 1985. Reason and Rationality in Rational Choice Theory. *Social Research* 52 (spring).

——. 1999. The Discipline as Disciplinary Normalization: Networks of Research. *New Political Science* 21, 3: 345–363.

Lundberg, G. A. 1939a. Contemporary Positivism in Sociology. *American Sociological Review* 4, 1: 42–55.

——. 1939b. *Foundations of Sociology.* New York: Macmillan.

——. 1947. The Senate Ponders Social Science. *Scientific Monthly* 64 (May): 397–411.

——. 1955. The Natural Science Trend in Sociology. *American Journal of Sociology* 61, 3: 191–202.

——. 1964. *Foundations of Sociology.* New York: Macmillan.

Lusted, L. B. 1968. *Introduction to Medical Decisionmaking.* Springfield, Ill.: C.C. Thomas.

Lyotard, Jean-François. [1979] 1984. *The Postmodern Condition: A Report on Knowledge.* Minneapolis: University of Minnesota Press.

Mahmood, Saba. 2001. Feminist Theory, Embodiment, and the Docile Agent: Some Reflections on the Egyptian Islamic Revival. *Cultural Anthropology* 16: 202–236.

Mahoney, James, and Dietrich Rueschemeyer. 2002. Comparative-Historical Analysis: Achievements and Agendas. In *Comparative-Historical Analysis in the Social Sciences*, edited by James Mahoney and Dietrich Rueschemeyer, 3–38. New York: Cambridge University Press.

Maier, Charles S. 1994. Democracy and Its Discontents. *Foreign Affairs* 73: 48–64.

——. 1997. *Dissolution: The Crisis of Communism and the End of East Germany*. Princeton: Princeton University Press.

Makepeace, G. H. 1996. Lifetime Earnings and the Training of Young Men in Britain. *Applied Economics* 28: 725–735.

Mäki, Uskali. 1996. Scientific Realism and Some Peculiarities of Economics. In *Realism and Anti-Realism in the Philosophy of Science*, edited by R. S. Cohen, R. Hilpinen, and Q. Renzong, 427–447. Dordrecht: Kluwer.

——. 2001. *The Economic Worldview: Studies in the Ontology of Economics*. Cambridge: Cambridge University Press.

——. 2003. "The Methodology of Positive Economics" (1953) Does Not Give Us *the* Methodology of Positive Economics. *Journal of Economic Methodology* 10, 4: 495–506.

Malinowski, Bronislaw. 1922. *Argonauts of the Western Pacific*. London: Routledge.

——. [1922] 1984. *Argonauts of the Western Pacific*. Prospect Heights, Ill.: Waveland Press.

Malthus, Thomas. 1803. *Essay on the Principle of Population*. London: T. Bensley.

——. [1803] 1992. *An Essay on the Principle of Population*. Edited by Donald Winch. Cambridge: Cambridge University Press.

Mandelbaum, Maurice. 1938. *The Problem of Historical Knowledge*. New York: Harper Torchbooks.

Mannheim, Karl. 1929. *Ideologie und Utopie*. Bonn: Verlag Friedrich Cohen.

——. 1936. *Ideology and Utopia: An Introduction to the Sociology of Knowledge*. New York: Harcourt and Brace.

Mansbridge, Jane. 1995. Rational Choice Gains by Losing. *Political Psychology* 16: 137–155.

Marcus, George. 1995. Ethnography in/of the World System: The Emergence of Multi-sited Ethnography. *Annual Review of Anthropology* 24: 95–115.

Marcus, George E., and Michael M. J. Fischer. 1986. *Anthropology as Cultural Critique: An Experimental Moment in the Human Sciences*. Chicago: University of Chicago Press.

Marcuse, Herbert. [1941] 1960. *Reason and Resolution: Hegel and the Rise of Social Theory*, 2nd ed. Boston: Beacon Press.

——. 1964. *One Dimensional Man: Studies in the Ideology of Advanced Industrial Society*. Boston: Beacon Press.

Marin, Louis. 1989. *Food for Thought*. Translated by Mette Hjort. Baltimore: Johns Hopkins University Press.

Markoff, John. 1996. *The Abolition of Feudalism: Peasants, Lords, and Legislators in the French Revolution*. University Park: Pennsylvania State University Press.

Marshall, Alfred. 1920. *Principles of Economics*. 8th ed. London: Macmillan.

Marx, Karl. [1844] 1964. *Economic and Philosophic Manuscripts of 1844*. Edited by Dirk Struik. New York: International Publishers.

——. 1968. *Selected Works in One Volume*. London: Lawrence and Wishart.

——. 1970. *The German Ideology*. Edited by C. J. Arthur. New York: International Publishers.

——. 1973. *Grundrisse*. Harmondsworth, U.K.: Penguin.

——. 1974. *Capital*. Vol. 1. Edited by Frederick Engels. London: Lawrence and Wishart.

——. 1976. *Capital*. Vol. 1. Harmondsworth, U.K.: Penguin.

Mason, Tim. 1981. The Workers' Opposition in Nazi Germany. *History Workshop Journal* 11 (spring): 120.

———. 1993. *Social Policy in the Third Reich: The Working Class in the "National Community."* Edited by Jane Caplan. Providence, R.I.: Berg.

———. 1995. *Nazism, Fascism and the Working Class.* Edited by Jane Caplan. New York: Cambridge University Press.

Masson, Jeffrey. 1984. *The Assault on Truth: Freud's Supression of the Seduction Theory.* New York: Farrar, Straus and Giroux.

Mauss, Marcel. [1935] 1979. Bodily Techniques. In *Sociology and Psychology: Essays by Marcel Mauss.* Translated by Ben Brewster, 95–123. London: Routledge and Kegan Paul.

Maverick, Lewis A. 1946. *China: A Model for Europe.* San Antonio, Tex.: Paul Anderson.

Mayer, Margit. 1988. The Changing Conditions for Local Politics in the Transition to Post-Fordism. Paper presented at the International Conference on Regulation Theory. Barcelona, Spain.

Mayer, Margit, and Roland Roth. 1995. New Social Movements and the Transformation to Post-Fordist Society. In *Cultural Politics and Social Movements,* edited by Barbara Epstein, Marcy Darnovsky, and Richard Flacks, 299–319. Philadelphia: Temple University Press.

Mayhew, B. 1990. *Researches in Structural Sociology.* Unpublished collection of previously published papers, compiled and edited by John Skvoretz. Department of Sociology, University of South Carolina.

Mayo, Elton. 1933. *The Human Problems of an Industrial Society.* New York: Macmillan.

Mazrui, Ali A. 1968. From Social Darwinism to Current Theories of Modernization: A Tradition of Analysis. *World Politics* 21 (October): 69–83.

McAdam, Doug, J. D. McCarthy, and M. N. Zald. 1996. *Comparative Perspectives on Social Movements.* Cambridge: Cambridge University Press.

McCartney, James L. 1971. The Financing of Sociological Research: Trends and Consequences. In *The Phenomenon of Sociology: A Reader in the Sociology of Sociology,* edited by Edward A. Tiryakian, 372–397. New York: Appleton-Century-Crofts.

McCloskey, Deirdre N. 1985. *The Rhetoric of Economics.* Madison: University of Wisconsin Press.

———. 1990. Storytelling in Economics. In *Economics and Hermeneutics,* edited by Don Lavoie, 61–75. London: Routledge.

———. 1994. *Knowledge and Persuasion in Economics.* Cambridge: Cambridge University Press.

McCloskey, Donald. 1985. *The Rhetoric of Economics.* Madison: University of Wisconsin Press.

McCubbins, Matthew D., and Michael F. Thies. 1996. Gourisei jissou shugi seiji riron no kiso [Rationality and the Foundations of Positive Political Theory]. Available: www.bol.ucla.edu/~thies/mcthiesRatch031.pdf.

McGrath, Patrick. 2002. *Scientists, Business and the State, 1890–1960.* Chapel Hill: University of North Carolina Press.

McGuckin, William. 1984. *Scientists, Society and the State.* Columbus: Ohio State University Press.

McLean, S. L., D. A. Schultz, et al. 2002. *Social Capital: Critical Perspectives on Community and "Bowling Alone."* New York: New York University Press.

McMichael, Philip. 1998. Development and Structural Adjustment. In *Virtualism: A New Political Economy,* edited by J. G. Carrier and D. Miller, 95–116. New York: Berg.

McTaggart, J. M. E. 1908. The Unreality of Time. *Mind* 17: 457–474.

———. 1993. The Unreality of Time. In *The Philosophy of Time*, edited by R. Le Poidevin and M. MacBeath, 23–34. Oxford: Oxford University Press.

McTaggart, Robin, ed. 1997. *Participatory Action Research: International Contexts and Consequences*. Albany: State University of New York Press.

Mead, George H. 1934. *Mind, Self, and Society from the Standpoint of a Social Behaviorist*. Chicago: University of Chicago Press.

Megill, Allan. 1989. Recounting the Past: "Description," Explanation, and Narrative in Historiography. *American Historical Review* 94, 3: 627–653.

———. 1991. Fragmentation and the Future of Historiography. *American Historical Review* 96, 3: 693–698.

———, ed. 1994. *Rethinking Objectivity*. Durham, N.C.: Duke University Press.

Mehrling, Perry. 2002. Economists and the Fed: Beginnings. *Journal of Economic Perspectives* 16 (fall): 207–218.

Meier, Heinrich. 1998. *The Lesson of Carl Schmitt: Four Chapters on the Distinction between Political Theology and Political Philosophy*. Translated by Marcus Brainard. Chicago: University of Chicago Press.

Mellor, D. H. 1981. *Real Time*. Cambridge: Cambridge University Press.

Merkl, Peter and Lenard Weinberg, eds. 1993. *Encounters with the Contemporary Radical Right*. Boulder, Colo.: Westview Press.

Merton, Robert K. [1936] 1968a. History and Systematics of Sociological Theory. In *Social Theory and Social Structure*, 1–38. New York: Free Press.

———. [1936] 1968b. On Sociological Theories of the Middle Range. In *Social Theory and Social Structure*, 39–72. New York: Free Press.

———. [1936] 1968c. Puritanism, Pietism, and Science. In *Social Theory and Social Structure*, 628–660. New York: Free Press.

———. 1938. Science and the Social Order. *Philosophy of Science* 5, 3: 321–337.

———. 1942. A Note on Science and Democracy. *Journal of Legal and Political Sociology* 1: 115–126.

———. [1948] 1968d. The Bearing of Sociological Theory on Empircal Research. In *Theory and Social Structure*, 139–171. New York: Free Press.

———. 1972. Insiders and Outsiders: A Chapter in the Sociology of Knowledge. *American Journal of Sociology* 78: 9–47.

Merton, Robert K., and Harriet A. Zuckerman. 1973. Age, Aging, and Age Structure in Science. In *The Sociology of Science*, edited by Robert K. Merton, 497–559. Chicago: University of Chicago Press.

Meurat, Denis. 1988. A Political Geneaology of Political Economy. *Economy and Society* 17, 2: 225–250.

Meyerson, Harold. 2003. Clash of Civilizations: In the Battle between America and Europe, We Better Hope That They Prevail. *American Prospect* (April): 30–32.

Mignolo, Walter D. 1993. Misunderstanding and Colonization: The Reconfiguration of Memory and Space. *South Atlantic Quarterly* 92: 209–260.

Mignolo, Walter D., and Freya Schiwy. 2003. Double Translation: Transculturation and the Colonial Difference. In *Translation and Ethnography: The Anthropological Challenge of Intercultural Understanding*, edited by Tullio Maranhao and Bernhard Streck, 3–29. Tucson: Arizona University Press.

Mihic, Sophia. 1999. Flirtations with Wissenschaft: Thinking Thinking and Thinking Politics in, and out of, the Work of Hannah Arendt. PhD diss. Johns Hopkins University.

Miller, Daniel. 1987. *Material Culture and Mass Consumption.* Oxford: Basil Blackwell.

———. 1997. *Capitalism: An Ethnographic Approach.* New York: Berg.

Miller, Peter, and Nikolas Rose. 1990. Governing Economic Life. *Economy and Society* 19, 1: 1–31.

Miller, Richard W. 1987. *Fact and Method: Explanation, Confirmation and Reality in the Natural and Social Sciences.* Princeton: Princeton University Press.

Mills, C. Wright. 1959. *The Sociological Imagination.* Oxford: Oxford University Press.

Mink, Louis O. 1987. *Historical Understanding.* Edited by Brian Fay, Eugene O. Golob, and Richard T. Vann. Ithaca, N.Y.: Cornell University Press.

Mirowski, Philip. 1988. *Against Mechanism.* Totowa, N.J.: Rowman and Littlefield.

———. 1989. *More Heat Than Light: Economics as Social Physics, Physics as Nature's Economics.* Cambridge: Cambridge University Press.

———. 1991. When Games Grow Deadly Serious: The Military Influence on Game Theory. *History of Political Economy* 23 (Annual supplement): 227–255.

———. 1996. The Economic Consequences of Philip Kitcher. *Social Epistemology* 10: 153–169.

———. 1998a. Confessions of an Aging Enfant Terrible. In *Passion and Craft: Economists at Work,* edited by Michael Szenberg, 213–226. Ann Arbor: University of Michigan Press.

———. 1998b. On Playing the Economics Trump Card in the Philosophy of Science: Why It Didn't Work for Michael Polanyi. *Philosophy of Science,* PSA 97 (Supplement to vol. 64): S127–S138.

———. 2002. *Machine Dreams: Economics Becomes a Cyborg Science.* Cambridge: Cambridge University Press.

———. 2003. The Commercialization of Science and the Future of the University in the 21st Century. Multimedia presentation. Available: www.nd.edu/~pmirowsk/lecture.

———. Forthcoming. The Scientific Dimensions of Social Knowledge and Their Distant Echoes in 20th Century American Philosophy of Science. *Studies in History and Philosophy of Science* 35, 2: 283–326.

Mirowski, Philip, and Esther-Mirjam Sent, eds. 2002. *Science Bought and Sold.* Chicago: University of Chicago Press.

Mitchell, Juliet, and Jacqueline Rose. 1982. *Feminine Sexuality: Jacques Lacan and the École freudienne.* New York: Norton.

Mitchell, Timothy. 1988. *Colonizing Egypt.* New York: Cambridge University Press.

———. 1990. Everyday Metaphors of Power. *Theory and Society* 19: 545–577.

———. 1999. Society, Economy, and the State Effect. In *State/Culture: State Formation after the Cultural Turn,* edited by George Steinmetz, 76–97. Wilder House Series in Culture, Power, and History. Ithaca, N.Y.: Cornell University Press.

———. 2002. *Rule of Experts: Egypt, Techno-Politics, Modernity.* Berkeley: University of California Press.

———. 2003. The Middle East in the Past and Future of Social Science. In *The Politics of Knowledge: Area Studies and the Disciplines,* edited by David Szanton. University of California Press/University of California International and Area Studies Digital Collection, vol. 3. Available: http://repositories.cdlib.org/uciaspubs/editedvolumes/3/3.

Mitchell, Wesley Clair. 1927. *Business Cycles: The Problem and Its Setting.* New York: National Bureau of Economic Research.

———. 1969. *Types of Economic Theory.* Vol. 2. New York: Kelley.

Miyazaki, Hirokazu. 2000. Faith and Its Fulfillment: Agency, Exchange, and the Fijian Aesthetics of Completion. *American Ethnologist* 27: 31–51.

Miyoshi, Masao, and Harry Harootunian, eds. 2002. *Learning Places: The Afterlives of Area Studies*. Durham, N.C.: Duke University Press.

Moi, Toril. [1988] 1999. Patriarchal Thought and the Drive for Knowledge. In *What Is a Woman? And Other Essays*, 348–368. Oxford: Oxford University Press.

Moore, Henrietta L. 1999. Anthropological Theory at the Turn of the Century. In *Anthropological Theory Today*, edited by Henrietta L. Moore, 1–23. Cambridge: Polity Press.

Moore, Kelly. 1996. Organizing Integrity: American Science and the Creation of Public Interest Organization, 1955–1975. *American Journal of Sociology* 101: 1592–1627.

Morgan, Lewis H. 1851. *League of the Ho-De'-No-Sau-Nee, Iroquois*. Rochester, N.Y.: Sage.

Morgan, Mary S. 1990. *The History of Econometric Ideas*. Cambridge: Cambridge University Press.

——. 2001. Models, Stories and the Economic World. *Journal of Economic Methodology* 8, 3: 361–384.

Morgenson, Gretchen, and Michael M. Weinstein. 1998. *New York Times*, November 14: 1–3.

Mosse, George L. 1964. *The Crisis of German Ideology; Intellectual Origins of the Third Reich*. New York: Grosset and Dunlap.

Mueller, Charles W., and Edward Donnerstein. 1983. Film-Induced Arousal and Aggressive Behavior. *Journal of Social Psychology* 119: 61–67.

Muennig, P. 2002. *Designing and Conducting Cost-Effectiveness Analyses in Medicine and Health Care*. San Francisco: Jossey-Bass.

Müller, Max. 1861. *Lectures on the Science of Language*. Vol. 1. London: Longman Green, Longman and Roberts.

——. 1864. *Lectures on the Science of Language*. Vol. 2. London: Longman Green, Longman and Roberts.

Mumford, Lewis. 1926. *The Golden Day*. New York: Boni and Liveright.

Munch, R. 2002. The Limits of the Self-organization of Civil Society: The American Debate on Multiculturalism, Public Spirit, and Social Capital from the Point of View of Modernization Theory. *Berliner Journal Fur Soziologie* 12, 4: 445ff.

Mungello, David E. 1985. *Curious Land: Jesuit Accommodation and the Origins of Sinology*. Stuttgart: Franz Steiner.

Murdock, George Peter. 1949. *Social Structure*. New York: Macmillan.

Murphy, Robert F. 1976. Introduction: A Quarter Century of American Anthropology. In *Selected Papers from the American Anthropologist 1946–1970*, edited by Robert F. Murphy, 1–22. Washington, D.C.: American Anthropological Association.

Myers, Fred R. 1988. Locating Ethnographic Practice: Romance, Reality, and Politics in the Outback. *American Ethnologist* 15: 609–624.

Myers, Ramon H., and Thomas A. Metzer. 1980. Sinological Shadows: The State of Modern China Studies in the U.S. *Australian Journal of Chinese Affairs*, no. 4: 1–34.

Nagel, Ernest. [1961] 1979. *The Structure of Scientific Explanation*. Indianapolis, Ind.: Hackett.

Nancy, Jean-Luc. 2000. *Being Singular Plural*. Stanford: Stanford University Press.

Needell, Allan A. 1983. "Truth Is Our Weapon": Project TROY, Political Warfare, and Government-Academic Relations in the National Security State. *Diplomatic History* 17 (summer): 399–420.

Needham, Rodney. 1962. *Structure and Sentiment: A Test Case in Social Anthropology*. Chicago: University of Chicago Press.

Nelson, Cary, ed. 1997. *Will Teach for Food*. Minneapolis: University of Minnesota Press.

Nelson, John S., Allan Megill, and Donald N. McCloskey, eds. 1987. *The Rhetoric of the Human Sciences*. Madison: University of Wisconsin Press.

Neurath, Otto. [1931] 1973. Empirical Sociology. In *Otto Neurath: Empiricism and Sociology*, edited by Marie Neurath and Robert S. Cohen, 319–421. Dordrecht: D. Reidel.

New, Caroline. 1998. Realism, Deconstruction and the Feminist Standpoint. *Journal for the Theory of Social Behaviour* 28, 4: 349–372.

Nicholson, Shierry Weber, ed. 1989. *The New Conservatism*. Cambridge: MIT Press.

Niranjana, Tejaswini. 1992. *Siting Translation*. Berkeley: University of California Press.

Nolan, Mary. 1995. Rationalization, Racism, and *Resistenz:* Recent Studies of Work and the Working Class in Nazi Germany. *International Labor and Working-Class History* 48 (fall): 132.

Nord, Erik. 1999. *Cost-Value Analysis in Health Care: Making Sense out of QALYs*. Cambridge: Cambridge University Press.

Notturno, Mark. 1999. Popper's Critique of Scientific Socialism. *Philosophy of the Social Sciences* 29, 1: 32–61.

Novick, Peter. 1988. *That Noble Dream: The "Objectivity Question" and the American Historical Profession*. Cambridge: Cambridge University Press.

———. 1991. My Correct Views of Everything. *American Historical Review* 96, 3: 699–703.

———. 1999. *The Holocaust in American Life*. Boston: Houghton Mifflin.

Oberndorf, Clarence Paul. 1953. *History of Psychoanalysis in America*. New York: Grune and Stratton.

Obeyesekere, Gananath. 1992. *The Apotheosis of Captain Cook: European Mythmaking in the Pacific*. Princeton: Princeton University Press.

Ochs, Elinor. 1979. Transcription as Theory. In *Developmental Pragmatics*, edited by E. Ochs and B. B. Schieffelin, 43–72. New York: Academic Press.

O'Connor, William Thomas. 1942. *Naturalism and the Pioneers of American Sociology*. Washington, D.C.: Catholic University of America Press.

Offe, C. 1985. Three Perspectives on the Problem of Unemployment. In *Disorganized Capitalism*, 80–100. Cambridge: MIT Press.

Ogilvie, Sheila. 2004. How Does Social Capital Affect Women? Guilds and Communities in Early Modern Germany. *American Historical Review* 109, 2 (April): 325–359.

Olender, Maurice. 1992. *The Languages of Paradise: Race, Religion, and Philology in the Nineteenth Century*. Translated by Arthur Goldhammer. Cambridge: Harvard University Press.

Olson, Mancur. 1965. *The Logic of Collective Action*. Cambridge: Harvard University Press.

O'Neill, Barry. 1999. *Honor, Symbols and War*. Ann Arbor: University of Michigan Press.

Orr, M. 1999. *Black Social Capital: The Politics of School Reform in Baltimore, 1986–1998*. Lawrence: University Press of Kansas.

Ortner, Sherry B. 1984. Theory in Anthropology Since the Sixties. *Comparative Studies in Society and History* 26: 126–166.

———. 1994. Theory in Anthropology Since the Sixties. In *Culture/Power/History: A Reader in Contemporary Social Theory*, edited by Nicholas B. Dirks, Geoff Eley, and Sherry B. Ortner, 372–411. Princeton: Princeton University Press.

———. 1995. Resistance and the Problem of Ethnographic Refusal. *Comparative Studies in Society and History* 37, 1: 173–193.

Orwell, George. [1936] 1968. Shooting an Elephant. In *The Collected Essays: Journalism and Letters*, 1: 234–242. Boston: Nonpareil Books.

Palgrave, Robert Harry Inglis, ed. 1925–26. *Palgrave's Dictionary of Political Economy*. 2nd ed. London: Macmillan.

Parsons, Talcott. [1937] 1949. *The Structure of Social Action.* 2 vols. New York: Free Press.
——. [1937] 1968. *The Structure of Social Action.* 2 vols. New York: Free Press.
——. 1951. *The Social System.* New York: Free Press.
——. 1953. Some Comments on the State of the General Theory of Action. *American Sociological Review* 18 (December): 618–631.
Passmore, John. 1967. Logical Positivism. In *The Encyclopedia of Philosophy,* vol. 5. Edited by Paul Edwards, 52–57. New York: Macmillan.
Patterson, Thomas Carl. 2002. *A Social History of Anthropology in the United States.* Oxford: Berg.
Paxton, P. 2002. Social Capital and Democracy. *American Sociological Review* 67: 254–277.
Peck, Jamie, and Adam Tickell. 1994. Searching for a New Institutional Fix: The *After-*Fordist Crisis and the Global-Local Disorder. In *Post-Fordism: A Reader,* edited by Ash Amin, 280–315. Oxford: Blackwell.
Pedersen, Holger. 1931. *The Discovery of Language.* Bloomington: Indiana University Press.
Peirce, Charles Sanders. 1955. *Philosophical Writings of Peirce.* Edited by Justus Buchler. New York: Dover.
Pels, Dick. [1996] 2003. Strange Standpoints: Or, How to Define the Situation for Situated Knowledge. *Telos,* no. 108: 65–91. Reprinted in *The Feminist Standpoint Theory Reader: Intellectual and Political Controversies,* edited by Sandra Harding (New York: Routledge, 2003).
Pharr, S. J., and R. D. Putnam. 2000. *Disaffected Democracies: What's Troubling the Trilateral Countries?* Princeton: Princeton University Press.
Pickering, Andrew, ed. 1992. *Science as Practice and Culture.* Chicago: University of Chicago Press.
Piore, Michael J., and Charles F. Sabel. 1984. *The Second Industrial Divide: Possibilities for Prosperity.* New York: Basic Books.
Plessner, Helmuth. 1959. *Die verspätete Nation: Über die politische Verführbarkeit bürgerlichen Geistes.* Stuttgart: W. Kohlhammer.
Pletsch, Carl. 1981. The Three Worlds, of the Division of Social Scientific Labor, circa 1950–1975. *Comparative Studies in Society and History* 23 (October): 565–590.
Plutarch. n.d. *Lives.* New York: Modern Library.
Pohlhaus, Gaile. 2002. Knowing Communities: An Investigation of Harding's Standpoint Epistemology. *Social Epistemology* 16, 3: 283–293.
Polanyi, Karl. 1944. *The Great Transformation.* New York: Rinehart and Company.
——. [1944] 2001. *The Great Transformation.* Edited by Fred Block. Boston: Beacon Press.
Polanyi, Karl, Conrad M. Arensberg, and Harry W. Pearson. 1957. *Trade and Market in the Early Empires: Economies in History and Theory.* Glencoe, Ill.: Free Press.
Polanyi, M. 1945. The Autonomy of Science. *60* 2: 141–150.
Poovey, Mary. 2001. The Model System of Contemporary Literary Criticism. *Critical Inquiry* 27, 3: 408–438.
Popkin, Samuel L. 1979. *The Rational Peasant: The Political Economy of Rural Society in Vietnam.* Berkeley: University of California Press.
Popper, Karl R. [1934] 1992. *The Logic of Scientific Discovery.* London: Routledge.
——. [1957] 1991. *The Poverty of Historicism.* London: Routledge.
——. [1962] 1971. *The Open Society and Its Enemies.* Princeton: Princeton University Press.
——. [1969] 1976a. The Logic of the Social Sciences. In *The Positivist Dispute in German Sociology.* Translated by Glyn Adey and David Frisby, 87–104. London: Heinemann.

——. 1976b. Reason or Revolution? In *The Positivist Dispute in German Sociology.* Translated by Glyn Adey and David Frisby, 288–300. London: Heinemann.

——. 1983. *Realism and the Aim of Science.* London: Routledge.

Porter, Theodore M. 2001. Economics and the History of Measurement. *History of Political Economy* 33 (Annual supplement): 4–22.

Portes, A. 1998. Social Capital: Its Origins and Applications in Modern Sociology. *Annual Review of Sociology* 24: 1–24.

Portes, A., W. J. Haller, and L. E. Guarnizo. 2002. Transnational Entrepreneurs. *American Sociological Review* 67: 278–298.

Povinelli, Elisabeth. 2001. Radical Worlds: The Anthropology of Incommensurability and Inconceivability. *Annual Review of Anthropology* 30: 319–334.

——. 2002. *The Cunning of Recognition.* Durham, N.C.: Duke University Press.

Prager, Jeffrey. 1994. On the Abuses of Freud: A Reply to Masson and Crews. *Contention* 4, 1 (fall): 211–219.

Prasad, Monica. 2000. *The Politics of Free Markets: The Rise of Neoliberal Economic Policy in Britain, France, and the United States.* PhD diss. University of Chicago.

Price, Colin. 1993. *Time, Discounting and Value.* Oxford: Blackwell.

Proposal for a Department of Political Theory. n.d. Box 10, Folder 129, Reinhard Bendix Papers. German Intellectual Émigré Collection. M. E. Grenander Department of Special Collections and Archives, University Libraries, University at Albany, State University of New York.

Przeworski, Adam. 1985. Material Interests, Class Compromise, and the State. In *Capitalism and Social Democracy*, 171–203. New York: Cambridge University Press.

Przeworski, Adam, and Henry Teune. 1970. *The Logic of Comparative Social Inquiry.* New York: Wiley-Interscience.

Purcell, Edward. 1973. *The Crisis of Democratic Theory: Scientific Naturalism and the Problem of Value.* Lexington: University of Kentucky Press.

Putnam, Hilary. 1975. The Meaning of "Meaning." In *Mind, Language and Reality: Philosophical Papers.* Vol. 2, 215–271. Cambridge: Cambridge University Press.

——. 1983. *Philosophical Papers.* Vol. 3, *Realism and Reason.* Cambridge: Cambridge University Press.

——. [1986] 1990a. Why Is a Philosopher? In *Realism with a Human Face*, edited by James Conant, 105–119. Cambridge: Harvard University Press.

——. 1990b. After Empiricism. In *Realism with a Human Face*, edited by James Conant, 43–53. Cambridge: Harvard University Press.

——. 1990c. Realism with a Human Face. In *Realism with a Human Face*, edited by James Conant, 3–29. Cambridge: Harvard University Press.

——. 2002. *The Collapse of the Fact/Value Dichotomy and Other Essays.* Cambridge: Harvard University Press.

Putnam, Robert D. 1993. The Prosperous Community: Social Capital and Public Life. *American Prospect* 4, 13: 35–42.

——. 1995. Bowling Alone: America's Declining Social Capital. *Journal of Democracy* 6, 1: 65–78.

——. 1996. The Strange Disappearance of Civic America. *American Prospect* 24: 34–48.

——. 2000. *Bowling Alone: The Collapse and Revival of American Community.* New York: Simon and Schuster.

———. 2002. *Democracies in Flux: The Evolution of Social Capital in Contemporary Society.* Oxford: Oxford University Press.

Putnam, Robert D., et al. 1993. *Making Democracy Work: Civic Traditions in Modern Italy.* Princeton: Princeton University Press.

Quine, W. V. O. 1969. *Ontological Relativity and Other Essays.* New York: Columbia University Press.

———. 1985. *Time of My Life.* Cambridge: MIT Press.

Rabinow, Paul. 1986. Representations Are Social Facts. In *Writing Culture: The Poetics and Politics of Ethnography,* edited by James Clifford and George E. Marcus, 234–261. Berkeley: University of California Press.

———. 1989. *French Modern.* Cambridge: MIT Press.

———. 1996. *Making PCR: The Story of Biotechnology.* Chicago: University of Chicago Press.

Rabinow, Paul, and William M. Sullivan, eds. [1979] 1987. *Interpretive Social Science: A Second Look.* Berkeley: University of California Press.

Radcliffe-Brown, A. R. 1952. *Structure and Function in Primitive Society.* London: Cohen and West.

Radice, Hugo. 1984. The National Economy: A Keynesian Myth? *Capital and Class* 22: 111–140.

Rafael, Vicente L. 1994. The Cultures of Area Studies in the United States. *Social Text,* no. 41: 91–112.

Raiffa, Howard. 1968. *Decision Analysis: Introductory Lectures on Choices under Uncertainty.* Reading, Mass.: Addison Wesley.

Rammstedt, Otthein. 1988. Wertfreiheit und die Konstitution der Soziologie in Deutschland. *Zeitschrift für Soziologie* 17, 4: 264–271.

Rancière, Jacques. 1981. *La nuit des prolétaires.* Paris: Fayard.

Rasch, William. 2003. Human Rights as Geopolitics. *Cultural Critique* 54: 120–147.

Raza, Werner, and Ulrich Brand. 2003. Einleitung: Der Regulationsansatz als Fordismus— oder Kapitalismustheorie? In *Fit für den Postfordismus? Theoretisch-politische Perspektiven des Regulationsansatzes,* ed. Ulrich Brand and Werner Raza, 7–16. Münster: Westfälisches Dampfboot.

Readings, Bill. 1996. *The University in Ruins.* Cambridge: Harvard University Press.

Reichenbach, Hans. 1938. *Experience and Prediction.* Chicago: University of Chicago Press.

———. 1951. *The Rise of Scientific Philosophy.* Berkeley: University of California Press.

———. 1978. *Selected Writings.* 2 Vols. Edited by M. Reichenbach and R. S. Cohen. Dordrecht: Reidel.

———. 1989. Dewey's Theory of Science. In *The Philosophy of John Dewey,* edited by Paul Schlipp and Lewis Hahn, 157–192. Chicago: Open Court Press.

Reidy, David A., Jr. 1992. Eastern Europe, Civil Society and the Real Revolution. *Praxis International* 12: 169.

Reingold, Nathan. 1991. *Science American Style.* New Brunswick, N.J.: Rutgers University Press.

Reisch, George. 2002. Review of McCumber. *Time in the Ditch: Philosophy of Science* 68: 389–392.

———. 2003. *On the Icy Slopes of Logic.* Unpublished manuscript. Available: http://pages .ripco.net/7Ereischg/coldwarbook/index.htm.

Rescher, Nicholas. 1997a. *Instructive Journey.* Lanham, Md.: University Presses of America.

Ricardo, David. [1815] 1951. An Essay on the Influence of a Low Price of Corn on the Profits of Stock. In *The Works and Correspondence of David Ricardo*. Vol 4., *Pamphlets and Papers, 1815–1823*, edited by Piero Sraffa, 9–41. Cambridge: Cambridge University Press.

Richardson, Alan W. 1996. Introduction: The Origins of Logical Empiricism. In *Origins of Logical Empiricism*, edited by Ronald N. Giere and Alan W. Richardson, 1–13. Minneapolis: University of Minnesota Press.

———. 2001. Science as Will and Representation. *PSA 98 Proceedings, Philosophy of Science* 67: S153–S162.

———. 2002. Engineering Philosophy of Science: American Pragmatism and Logical Empiricism in the 1930s. *PSA 99 Proceedings, Philosophy of Science* 69: S36–S47.

Ricoeur, Paul. 1970. *Freud and Philosophy: An Essay on Interpretation*. New Haven: Yale University Press.

———. 1971. The Model of the Text: Meaningful Action Considered as a Text. *Social Research* 38: 529–562.

Rieff, Philip. 1961. *Freud: The Mind of the Moralist*. New York: Harper and Row.

———. 1966. *The Triumph of the Therapeutic*. New York: Harper and Row.

———. 1979. *Freud: The Mind of the Moralist*. Chicago: University of Chicago Press.

Riemer, Svend. 1953. Empirical Training and Sociological Thought. *American Journal of Sociology* 59 (September): 107–112.

Riesman, David. 1950. *The Lonely Crowd: A Study of the Changing American Character*. New Haven: Yale University Press.

Riker, William H. 1957. Events and Situations. *Journal of Philosophy* 54 (January): 57–70.

———. 1958. Causes of Events. *Journal of Philosophy* 55 (March): 281–291.

———. 1962. *The Theory of Political Coalitions*. New Haven: Yale University Press.

———. 1982. *Liberalism against Populism: A Confrontation between the Theory of Democracy and the Theory of Social Choice*. San Francisco: W. H. Freeman.

———. [1982] 1993. The Two-Party System and Duverger's Law: An Essay on the History of Political Science. In *Discipline and History: Political Science in the United States*, 345–361. Ann Arbor: University of Michigan Press.

———. 1996. *The Strategy of Rhetoric: Campaigning for the American Constitution*. New Haven: Yale University Press.

Riker, William H., and Peter Ordeshook. 1973. *An Introduction to Positive Political Theory*. Englewood Cliffs, N.J.: Prentice-Hall.

Riles, Annelise. 2000. *The Network Inside Out*. Ann Arbor: University of Michigan Press.

Robalino, D. A., et al. 2000. Social Capital, Technology Diffusion, and Sustainable Growth in the Developing World. Santa Monica, Calif.: Rand.

Robbins, Lionel. [1932] 1935. *An Essay on the Nature and Significance of Economic Science*. 2nd ed. London: Macmillan.

Robin, Ron. 2001. *The Making of the Cold War Enemy: Culture and Politics in the Military-Intellectual Complex*. Princeton: Princeton University Press.

Roediger, David R. 1991. *The Wages of Whiteness: Race and the Making of the American Working Class*. London: Verso.

Roemer, John E. 1982. *A General Theory of Exploitation and Class*. Cambridge: Harvard University Press.

Rofel, Lisa. 1999. *Other Modernities: Gendered Yearnings in China after Socialism*. Berkeley: University of California Press.

Root, Michael. 1993. *Philosophy of Social Science*. Cambridge, Mass.: Blackwell.

Rorty, Richard M. 1979. *Philosophy and the Mirror of Nature.* Princeton: Princeton University Press.

——. 1989. *Contingency, Irony and Solidarity.* Cambridge: Cambridge University Press.

Rosaldo, Renato. 1989. After Objectivism. In *Culture and Truth: The Remaking of Social Analysis,* 46–67. Boston: Beacon Press.

Rose, Hilary. [1983] 2003. Hand, Brain, and Heart: A Feminist Epistemology for the Natural Sciences. *Signs* 9, 1: 73–90. Reprinted in *The Feminist Standpoint Theory Reader: Intellectual and Political Controversies,* edited by Sandra Harding (New York: Routledge, 2003).

Rose, Nikolas. 1999. *Powers of Freedom: Reframing Political Thought.* Cambridge: Cambridge University Press.

——. 2000. "Community, Citizenship, and the Third Way." *American Behavioral Scientist* 43, 9 (June–July): 1395–1411.

Rose, R. and University of Strathclyde. Centre for the Study of Public Policy. 2000. *How Much Does Social Capital Add to Individual Health?: A Survey Study of Russians.* Glasgow: Centre for the Study of Public Policy, University of Strathclyde.

Rosenberg, Alexander. 1983. If Economics Isn't Science, What Is It? *Philosophical Forum* 14: 296–314. Reprinted in *The Philosophy of Economics: An Anthology,* edited by D. M. Hausman, 376–394. 2nd ed. Cambridge: Cambridge University Press.

Rosenberg, N. L. and R. C. Post. 2002. *Civil Society and Government.* Princeton: Princeton University Press.

Ross, Andrew, ed. 1996. *Science Wars.* Durham, N.C.: Duke University Press.

Ross, Dorothy. 1991. *The Origins of American Social Science.* Cambridge: Cambridge University Press.

Rostow, W. W. 1960. *The Stages of Economic Growth: A Non-Communist Manifesto.* Cambridge: Cambridge University Press.

Rotberg, R. I. and G. A. Brucker. 2001. *Patterns of Social Capital: Stability and Change in Historical Perspective.* Cambridge: Cambridge University Press.

Roth, Guenther, and Claus Wittich, eds. 1968. *Economy and Society: An Outline of Interpretative Sociology.* New York: Bedminster Press.

Röttger, Bernd. 2001. New Economy—Old Theory: Die Regulationstheorie am Ende der Fahnenstage? *Blätter des iz3w,* no. 254: 38–41.

——. 2003. Verlassene Gräber und neue Pilger an der Grabesstätte. In *Fit für den Postfordismus? Theoretisch-politische Perspektiven des Regulationsansatzes,* edited by Ulrich Brand and Werner Raza, 18–42. Münster: Westfälisches Dampfboot.

Rotwein, Eugene. 1959. On "the Methodology of Positive Economics." *Quarterly Journal of Economics* 73, no. 4: 554–575.

Roudinesco, Elisabeth. 1990. *Jacques Lacan and Co.: A History of Psychoanalysis in France, 1925–1985.* Chicago: University of Chicago Press.

——. 2001. *Why Psychoanalysis?* New York: Columbia University Press.

Rouse, Joseph. 1987. *Knowledge and Power: Toward a Political Philosophy of Science.* Ithaca, N.Y.: Cornell University Press.

——. 1996. Feminism and the Social Construction of Scientific Knowledge. In *Feminism, Science and the Philosophy of Science,* edited by Lynn Hankinson Nelson and Jack Nelson, 195–215. Dordrecht: Kluwer.

Rubinstein, Ariel. 1995. John Nash: The Master of Economic Modeling. *Scandinavian Journal of Economics* 97, 1: 9–13.

Russell, Bertrand. [1945] 1972. *A History of Western Philosophy*. New York: Touchstone.

Rustin, Michael. 1991. *The Good Society and Inner World*. London: Verso.

——. 1999. Psychoanalysis: The Last Modernism? In *Psychoanalysis and Culture: A Kleinian Perspective*, 105–121. London: Duckworth.

Rutherford, Malcolm. 1994. *Institutions in Economics*. New York: Cambridge University Press.

Ryckmans, Pierre [Simon Leys]. 1983–84. Orientalism and Sinology. *ASAA Review* (Australian Asian Studies Association): 18–20.

Ryle, Gilbert. 1946. Knowing How and Knowing That. *Proceedings of the Aristotle Society* n.s. 46: 1–16.

Saegert, S., J. P. Thompson, et al. 2001. *Social Capital and Poor Communities*. New York: Russell Sage Foundation.

Sahlins, Marshall D. 1962. *Moala: Culture and Nature on a Fijian Island*. Ann Arbor: University of Michigan.

——. [1968] 1972. The Original Affluent Society. In *Stone Age Economics*, 1–39. Chicago: Aldine.

——. 1976. *The Use and Abuse of Biology: An Anthropological Critique of Sociobiology*. Ann Arbor: University of Michigan Press.

——. 1985. *Islands of History*. Chicago: University of Chicago Press.

——. [1988] 2000. Cosmologies of Capitalism: The Trans-Pacific Sector of "the World System." In *Culture in Practice: Selected Essays*, 415–469. New York: Zone Books.

——. 1995. *How "Natives" Think: About Captain Cook, for Example*. Chicago: University of Chicago Press.

Said, Edward W. 1978. *Orientalism*. New York: Vintage.

——. 1993. *Culture and Imperialism*. New York: Knopf.

Salanti, Andrea. 1991. Roy Weintraub's *Studies in Appraisal:* Lakatosian Consolations or Something Else? *Economics and Philosophy* 7, 1: 221–234.

Samuelson, Paul A. 1992. My Life Philosophy: Policy Credos and Working Ways. In *Eminent Economists: Their Life Philosophies*, edited by Michael Szenberg, 236–247. Cambridge: Cambridge University Press.

Sapir, Edward. [1925] 1949a. Sound Patterns in Language. In *Selected Writings of Edward Sapir in Language, Culture, and Personality*, edited by David G. Mandelbaum, 33–45. Berkeley: University of California Press.

——. [1927] 1949b. The Unconscious Patterning of Behavior in Society. In *Selected Writings of Edward Sapir in Language, Culture, and Personality*, edited by David G. Mandelbaum, 544–559. Berkeley: University of California Press.

Sartre, Jean-Paul. [1956] 2001. Colonialism Is a System. In *Colonialism and Neocolonialism*, 30–47. London: Routledge.

Saussure, Ferdinand de. 1959. *Course in General Linguistics*. Translated by Wade Baskin. London: Peter Owen.

Schaar, John H., and Sheldon S. Wolin. 1963. Essays on the Scientific Study of Politics: A Critique. *American Political Science Review* 57: 125–150.

Schabas, Margaret. 2002. Coming Together: History of Economics as History of Science. *History of Political Economics* 34 (Annual supplement): 208–225.

Scharff, Robert C. 1995. *Comte after Positivism*. Cambridge: Cambridge University Press.

Schlipp, Paul Arthur, ed. 1963. *The Philosophy of Rudolf Carnap*. La Salle, Ill.: Open Court Press.

Schmitt, Carl. 2003. *The Nomos of the Earth in the International Law of the* Jus Publicum Europaeum. Translated by G. L. Ulmen. New York: Telos Press.

Schneider, David M. 1965. Some Muddles in the Models: Or, How the System Really Works. In *The Relevance of Models for Social Anthropology*, 25–85. London: Tavistock.

———. 1968. *American Kinship: A Cultural Account.* Englewood Cliffs, N.J.: Prentice-Hall.

———. 1972. What Is Kinship All About? In *Kinship Studies in the Morgan Centennial Year*, edited by P. Raining, 32–63. Washington, D.C.: American Anthropological Association.

———. 1976. Notes toward a Theory of Culture. In *Meaning in Anthropology*, edited by Keith H. Basso and Henry A. Selby, 197–220. Albuquerque: University of New Mexico Press.

Schulte, Rainer, and John Biguenet, eds. 1992. *Theories of Translation: An Anthology of Essays from Dryden to Derrida.* Chicago: University of Chicago Press.

Schumpeter, Joseph. 1933. The Common Sense of Econometrics. *Econometrica* 1, 1 (January): 5–12.

———. 1954. *History of Economic Analysis.* New York: Oxford University Press.

Schurman, Rachel, and William Munroe. 2004. Intellectuals, Ideology, and Social Networks: The Process of Grievance Construction in the Anti-Genetic Engineering Movement. Unpublished manuscript, Department of Sociology, University of Illinois, Urbana-Champaign.

Schuster, John A., and Richard R. Yeo, eds. 1986. *The Politics and Rhetoric of Scientific Method: Historical Studies.* Dordrecht: Reidel.

Schutz, Alfred. [1932] 1967. *The Phenomenology of the Social World.* Translated by George Walsh and Frederick Lehnert. Evanston, Ill.: Northwestern University Press.

Schwab, Raymond. 1986. *The Oriental Renaissance: Europe's Rediscovery of India and the East, 1680–1880.* Translated by Gene Patterson-Black and Victor Reinking. New York: Columbia University Press.

Schwartz-Shea, Peregrine, and Dvora Yanow. 2002. "Reading" "Methods" "Texts": How Research Methods Texts Construct Political Science. *Political Research Quarterly* 55 (June): 457–486.

Schwendinger, Herman, and Julia R. Schwendinger. 1974. *The Sociologists of the Chair.* New York: Basic Books.

Scott, James C. 1990. *Domination and the Arts of Resistance: Hidden Transcripts.* New Haven: Yale University Press.

Scott, Joan W. 1974. *The Glassworkers of Carmaux: French Craftsmen and Political Action in a Nineteenth-Century City.* Cambridge: Harvard University Press.

———. 1988a. *Gender and the Politics of History.* New York: Columbia University Press.

———. 1988b. Gender: A Useful Category of Historical Analysis. In *Gender and the Politics of History*, 28–50. New York: Columbia University Press.

———. 1988c. A Statistical Representation of Work: *La Statistique de l'industrie à Paris, 1847–1848.* In *Gender and the Politics of History*, 113–138. New York: Columbia University Press.

———. 1991a. The Evidence of Experience. *Cultural Inquiry* 17: 773–797.

———. 1991b. Women's History. In *New Perspecives on Historical Writing*, edited by Peter Burke, 42–66. Cambridge: Polity Press.

Scull, Andrew. 1999. A Quarter Century of the History of Psychiatry. *Journal of the History of the Behavioral Sciences* 35, 3: 239–246.

Selbourne, David. 1994. *The Principle of Duty: An Essay on the Foundations of the Civic Order.* London: Abacus.

Seligman, Adam 1992. *The Idea of Civil Society*. Princeton: Princeton University Press.

Sellars, Roy Wood. 1939. Positivism in Contemporary Philosophic Thought. *American Sociological Review* 4 (February): 26–42.

Sen, Amartya K. 1977. Rational Fools: A Critique of the Behavioral Foundations of Economic Theory. *Philosophy and Public Affairs* 6 (summer): 317–344.

Sewell, William H. [Sr.] 1988. The Changing Institutional Structure of Sociology and My Career. In *Sociological Lives: Social Change and the Life Course*, vol. 2, edited by Matilda W. Riley, 119–143. Newbury Park, Calif.: Sage.

Sewell, William H., Jr. 1967. Marc Bloch and the Logic of Comparative History. *History and Theory* 6, 2: 208–218.

——. 1971. The Structure of the Working Class of Marseille in the Middle of the Nineteenth Century. PhD diss. University of California, Berkeley.

——. 1974a. Etat, Corps and Ordre: Some Notes on the Social Vocabulary of the French Old Regime. In *Sozialgeschichte Heute: Festschrift fur Hans Rosenberg zum 70 Geburtstag*, edited by H. U. Wehler, 49–68. Gottingen: Vandenhoek und Ruprecht.

——. 1974b. Social Change and the Rise of Working-Class Politics in Nineteenth Century Marseille. *Past and Present* 65: 75–109.

——. 1974c. The Working Class of Marseille under the Second Republic: Social Structure and Political Behavior. In *Workers in the Industrial Revolution*, edited by Peter Stearns and Daniel Walkowitz, 75–115. New Brunswick, N.J.: Transaction Books.

——. 1980. *Work and Revolution in France: The Language of Labor from the Old Regime to 1848*. Cambridge: Cambridge University Press.

——. 1985. *Structure and Mobility: The Men and Women of Marseille, 1820–1870*. Cambridge: Cambridge University Press.

——. 1988. Uneven Development, the Autonomy of Politics, and the Dockworkers of Twentieth-Century Marseille. *American Historical Review* 93: 604–637.

——. 1990. How Classes Are Made: Critical Reflections on E. P. Thompson's Theory of Class Formation. In *E. P. Thompson: Critical Debates*, edited by Harvey J. Kaye and Keith McClelland, 50–77. Oxford: Basil Blackwell.

——. 1994. *A Rhetoric of Bourgeois Revolution: The Abbé Sieyes and What Is the Third Estate?* Durham, N.C.: Duke University Press.

——. 1996. Three Temporalities: Toward an Eventful Sociology. In *The Historic Turn in the Human Sciences*, edited by Terrence J. McDonald, 245–280. Ann Arbor: University of Michigan Press.

——. 1999. Geertz, Cultural Systems, and History: From Synchrony to Transformation. In *The Fate of "Culture": Geertz and Beyond*, edited by Sherry B. Ortner, 35–55. Berkeley: University of California Press.

——. 2001. Whatever Happened to the "Social" in Social History? In *Schools of Thought: Twenty-Five Years of Interpretive Social Science*, edited by Joan W. Scott and Debra Keates, 209–226. Princeton: Princeton University Press.

Shackle, George L. S. 1961. *Decision, Order, and Time in Human Affairs*. Cambridge: Cambridge University Press.

Shankman, Paul. 1984. The Thick and the Thin: On the Interpretive Theoretical Paradigm of Clifford Geertz. *Current Anthropology* 25, 3: 261–279.

Shapin, Steven. 1994. *A Social History of Truth: Civility and Science in Seventeenth-Century England*. Chicago: University of Chicago Press.

———. 1995. Here and Everywhere: Sociology of Scientific Knowledge. *Annual Review of Sociology* 21: 289–321.

Shapin, Steven, and Simon Shaffer. 1985. *Leviathan and the Air Pump*. Princeton: Princeton University Press.

Shapiro, Ian. 1990. *Political Criticism*. Berkeley: University of California Press.

———. 2002. Problems, Methods, and Theories in the Study of Politics, or What's Wrong with Political Science and What to Do about It. *Political Theory* 30 (August): 596–619.

Shepsle, Kenneth, and Barry Weingast. 1995. *Positive Theories of Congressional Institutions*. Ann Arbor: University of Michigan Press.

Shils, Edward. 1948. *The Present State of American Sociology*. Glencoe, Ill.: Free Press.

———. 1954. The Scientific Community: Thoughts after Hamburg. *Bulletin of the Atomic Scientists* 10: 151–155.

———. 1955. The End of Ideology? *Encounter* 5: 52–58.

Shils, Edward, and Morris Janowitz. 1948. Cohesion and Disintegration in the Wehrmacht in World War II. *Public Opinion Quarterly* 12 (summer): 280–315.

Shinn, Terry. 2003. The Industry, Research and Education Nexus. In *Cambridge History of Science*, vol. 5, edited by Mary Jo Nye, 133–153. New York: Cambridge University Press.

Shryock, Andrew. 1997. *Nationalism and the Genealogical Imagination: Oral History and Textual Authority in Tribal Jordan*. Berkeley: University of California Press.

Silverstein, Michael, and Greg Urban, eds. 1996. *Natural Histories of Discourse*. Chicago: University of Chicago Press.

Simmel, Georg. 1921. The Sociological Significance of the "Stranger." In *Introduction to the Science of Sociology*, edited by Robert E. Park and Ernest W. Burgess, 322–327. Chicago: University of Chicago Press.

Sismondo, Sergio. 1993. Some Social Constructions. *Social Studies of Science* 23 (August): 515–553.

———. 1996. *Science without Myth*. Albany: State University of New York Press.

Skidelsky, Robert. 1992. *John Maynard Keynes*. Vol. 2, *The Economist as Saviour, 1920–1937*. London: Macmillan.

Skinner, Quentin. 1988. Meaning and Understanding in the History of Ideas. In *Meaning and Context*, edited by James Tully, 29–67. Cambridge: Cambridge University Press.

Skocpol, Theda. 1979. *States and Social Revolutions: A Comparative Analysis of France, Russia, and China*. Cambridge: Cambridge University Press.

———. 1984. Emerging Agendas and Recurrent Strategies in Historical Sociology. In *Vision and Method in Historical Sociology*, edited by Theda Skocpol, 356–391. Cambridge: Cambridge University Press.

———. 2003. *Diminished Democracy: From Membership to Management in American Civil Life*. Norman: University of Oklahoma Press.

Smail, Dan. 2000. Positivism and Medieval History. Paper presented at the annual meetings of the Social Science History Association. Pittsburgh, Pennsylvania.

Small, Albion. 1907. *Adam Smith and Modern Sociology: A Study in the Methodology of the Social Sciences*. Chicago: University of Chicago Press.

———. 1909. *The Cameralists: The Pioneers of German Social Polity*. Chicago: University of Chicago Press.

Smelser, Neil J. 1986. Die Beharrlichkeit des Positivismus in der amerikanischen Soziologie. *Kölner Zeitschrift für Soziologie und Sozialpsychologie* 38 (March): 133–150.

Smith, Adam. [1776] 1950. *An Enquiry into the Nature and Causes of the Wealth of Nations.* London: Methuen.

Smith, Dorothy. [1974] 2003. Women's Perspective as a Radical Critique of Sociology. In *Sociological Inquiry* 44: 1–13. Reprinted in *The Feminist Standpoint Theory Reader: Intellectual and Political Controversies,* edited by Sandra Harding (New York: Routledge, 2003).

——. 1987. *The Everyday World as Problematic: A Sociology for Women.* Boston: Northeastern University Press.

——. 1990. *The Conceptual Practices of Power: A Feminist Sociology of Knowledge.* Boston: Northeastern University Press.

——. 1997. Comment on Hekman's "Truth and Method: Feminist Standpoint Theory Revisited." *Signs* 22, 2: 392–398.

——. 1999a. *Writing the Social: Critique, Theory, and Investigations.* Toronto: University of Toronto Press.

——. 1999b. The Ruling Relations. . . . In *Writing the Social: Critique, Theory, and Investigations.* Toronto: University of Toronto Press.

Smith, Laurence D. 1986. *Behaviorism and Logical Positivism: A Reassessment of the Alliance.* Stanford: Stanford University Press.

Smith, Laurence D., and William R. Woodward. 1996. *B. F. Skinner and Behaviorism in American Culture.* Bethlehem, Pa.: Lehigh University Press.

Smith, Rogers M. 2004. Reconnecting Political Theory to Empirical Inquiry, or, A Return to the Cave? In *The Evolution of Political Knowledge: Theory and Inquiry in American Politics,* edited by Edward D. Mansfield and Richard Sisson, 60–88. Columbus: Ohio State University Press.

——. 2002. Putting the Substance Back in Political Science. *Chronicle of Higher Education* 48, 30 (April 5): B10. Smith, Steve. 1996. Positivism and Beyond. In *International Theory: Positivism and Beyond,* edited by Ken Booth, Steve Smith, and Marysia Zalewski, 11–44. Cambridge: Cambridge University Press.

Smith, Steve, Ken Booth, and Marysia Zalewski, eds. 1996. *International Theory: Positivism and Beyond.* Cambridge: Cambridge University Press.

Sokal, Alan, and Jean Bricmont. 1998. *Fashionable Nonsense: Postmodern Intellectuals' Abuse of Science.* New York: Picador.

Solow, Robert M. 1990. Robert M. Solow. In *Sociology and Economics: Redefining their Boundaries: Conversations with Economists and Sociologists,* edited by Richard Swedberg, 268–284. Princeton: Princeton University Press.

——. 2000. Notes on Social Capital and Economic Performance. In *Social Capital: A Multifaceted Perspective,* edited by P. Dasgupta and I. Serageldin. Washington, D.C.: World Bank.

Solow, Robert. 2001. L'économie entre empirisme et mathématisation. *Le monde,* January 3.

Somers, Margaret R. 1993. Citizenship and the Place of the Public Sphere: Law, Community, and Political Culture in the Transition to Democracy. *American Sociological Review* 58, 5: 587–620.

——. 1994. Rights, Relationality, and Membership: Rethinking the Making and Meaning of Citizenship. *Law and Social Inquiry* 19, 1: 1301–1350.

——. 1995a. What's Political or Cultural about the Political Culture Concept? Toward an Historical Sociology of Concept Formation. *Sociological Theory* 13, 2 (July): 113–144.

———. 1995b. Narrating and Naturalizing Civil Society and Citizenship Theory: The Place of Political Culture and the Public Sphere. *Sociological Theory* 13, 3 (November): 229–274.

———. 1996. What's Political or Cultural about Political Culture and the Public Sphere? Toward a Historical Sociology of Concept Formation. *Sociological Theory* 13 (July): 113–144.

———. 1998. "We're No Angels": Realism, Rational Choice, and Relationality in Social Science. *American Journal of Sociology* 104: 722–784.

———. 1999. The Privatization of Citizenship: How to Unthink a Knowledge Culture. In *Beyond the Cultural Turn: New Directions in the Study of Society and Culture*, edited by Victoria E. Bonnell and Lynn Hunt, 121–161. Berkeley: University of California Press.

———. 2001. Romancing the Market, Reviling the State: Historicizing Liberalism, Privatization, and the Competing Claims to Civil Society. In *Citizenship, Markets, and the State*, edited by Colin Crouch, Klaus Eder, and Damian Tambini, 23–48. New York: Oxford University Press.

———. Forthcoming. Citizenship Troubles: Genealogies of Struggle for the Soul of the Social. In *Remaking Modernity: Politics, and History in Sociology*, edited by Julia Adams, Elisabeth Clemens, and Ann Orloff. Durham, N.C.: Duke University Press.

Somers, Margaret R. and Fred Block. Forthcoming. From Poverty To Perversity: Malthus, Murray, and Market Fundamentalism. *American Sociological Review*.

Soper, Kate. 1995. *What Is Nature?* Oxford: Blackwell.

Sorokin, Pitrim. 1928. *Contemporary Sociology Theories.* New York: Harper and Bros.

Soros, George. 1998. *The Crisis of Global Capitalism.* New York: Public Affairs Press.

———. 2000. *Open Society: Reforming Global Capitalism.* New York: Public Affairs Press.

Sperber, Dan. 1996. *Explaining Culture: A Naturalistic Approach.* Oxford: Blackwell.

Spivak, Gayatri Chakravorty. 1988. Can the Subaltern Speak? In *Marxism and the Interpretation of Culture*, edited by Cary Nelson and Lawrence Grossberg, 271–313. Urbana: University of Illinois Press.

Sponsel, Leslie E., Fernando Coronil, Alan G. Fix, M. Susan Lindee, and Peter Pels. 2002. Discussion and Criticism: On Reflections on "Darkness in El Dorado." *Current Anthropology* 43, 1: 149–152.

Stam, Henderikus J. 1992. The Legacies of Operationalism and Positivism in Psychology: Introduction. *Theory and Psychology* 2, 3: 259–260.

Steedly, Mary Margaret. 1993. *Hanging without a Rope: Narrative Experience in Colonial and Postcolonial Karoland.* Princeton: Princeton University Press.

Steedman, Carolyn Kay. 1987. *Landscape for a Good Woman: A Story of Two Lives.* New Brunswick, N.J.: Rutgers University Press.

Steinmetz, George. 1992. Reflections on the Role of Social Narratives in Working-Class Formation: Narrative Theory in the Social Sciences. *Social Science History* 16 (fall): 489–516.

———. 1993. *Regulating the Social: The Welfare State and Local Politics in Imperial Germany.* Princeton: Princeton University Press.

———. 1994. Regulation Theory, Post-Marxism, and the New Social Movements. *Comparative Studies in Society and History* 36, 1: 176–212.

———. 1997a. German Exceptionalism and the Origins of Nazism: The Career of a Concept. In *Stalinism and Nazism: Dictatorships in Comparison*, edited by Ian Kershaw and Moshe Lewin, 251–284. Cambridge: Cambridge University Press.

———. 1997b. Social Class and the Reemergence of the Radical Right in Contemporary Germany. In *Reworking Class: Cultures and Institutions of Economic Stratification and Agency*, edited by John R. Hall, 335–368. Ithaca, N.Y.: Cornell University Press.

———. 1998. Critical Realism and Historical Sociology. *Comparative Studies in Society and History* 39, 4: 170–186.

———. 1999. Culture and the State. In *State/Culture: Historical Studies of the State in the Social Sciences*, ed. George Steinmetz, 1–49. Ithaca, N.Y.: Cornell University Press.

———. 2002. Precoloniality and Colonial Subjectivity: Ethnographic Discourse and Native Policy in German Overseas Imperialism, 1780s–1914. *Political Power and Social Theory* 15: 135–228.

———. 2003a. The Implications of Colonial and Postcolonial Studies for the Study of Europe. *European Studies Newsletter* 32, no. 3/4: 1–3.

———. 2003b. The State of Emergency and the Revival of American Imperialism: Toward an Authoritarian Post-Fordism. *Public Culture* 15, 2: 323–345.

———. 2003c. " 'The Devil's Handwriting': Precolonial Discourse, Ethnographic Acuity, and Cross-Identification in German Colonialism." *Comparative Studies in Society and History* 45, 1: 41–95.

———. 2004a. Odious Comparisons? Incommensurability, the Case Study, and "Small N's." *Sociological Theory* 22, 3: 371–400.

———. 2004b. The Epistemological Unconscious of U.S. Sociology and the Transition to Post-Fordism: The Case of Historical Sociology. In *Remaking Modernity: Politics, and History in Sociology*, edited by Julia Adams, Elisabeth Clemens, and Ann Orloff, 109–157. Durham, N.C.: Duke University Press.

———. Forthcoming. Rethinking the Domestication of a Discipline: American Sociology after World War II (1945–1965). In *History of Sociology in America: ASA Centennial Volume*, edited by Craig Calhoun. Washington, D.C.: American Sociological Association.

Steinmetz, George, and Ou-Byung Chae. 2002. Sociology in an Era of Fragmentation: From the Sociology of Knowledge to the Philosophy of Science, and Back Again. *Sociological Quarterly* 43: 111–137.

Stern, Fritz. 1961. *The Politics of Cultural Despair: A Study in the Rise of the Germanic Ideology.* Berkeley: University of California Press.

Stewart, Julian H. [1949] 1976. Cultural Causality and Law: A Trial Formulation of the Development of Early Civilizations. In *Selected Papers from the American Anthropologist*, edited by Robert F. Murphy, 56–82. Washington, D.C.: American Anthropological Association.

———. 1950. *Area Research: Theory and Practice.* New York: SSRC.

———. 1955. *Theory of Culture Change.* Urbana: University of Illinois Press.

Stewart-Weeks, M., C. Richardson, et al. 1998. *Social Capital Stories: How 12 Australian Households Live their Lives.* St. Leonards, N.S.W: Centre for Independent Studies.

Stigler, Stephen M. 1986. *The History of Statistics: Measurement of Uncertainty before 1900.* Cambridge, Mass.: Belknap Press.

Stiglitz, Joseph E. 1989. Markets, Market Failures and Development. *American Economic Review* 79, 2: 197–202.

———. 1994. *Whither Socialism?* Cambridge: MIT Press.

———. 1998. More Instruments and Broader Goals: Moving Toward the Post-Washington Consensus. The 1998 WIDER Annual Lecture, 7 January, Helsinki.

———. 2000. *Economics of the Public Sector.* 3rd ed. New York: Norton.

———. 2002. *Globalization and Its Discontents*. New York: Norton.

Stinchcombe, Arthur L. 1968. *Constructing Social Theories*. Chicago: University of Chicago Press.

———. 1978. *Theoretical Methods in Social History*. New York: Academic Press.

———. 1991. The Conditions of Fruitfulness of Theorizing about Mechanisms in Social Science. *Philosophy of the Social Sciences* 21 (September): 367–388.

———. 2002. Epistemology as an Optimizing Discipline. Paper presented at the Department of Sociology, University of Michigan, Ann Arbor.

Stocking, George W., Jr. 1968. *Race, Culture, and Evolution: Essays in the History of Anthropology*. New York: Free Press.

———. 1987. *Victorian Anthropology*. New York: Free Press.

———. 1992a. Ideas and Institutions in American Anthropology: Thoughts towards a History of the Interwar Years. In *The Ethnographer's Magic and Other Essays in the History of Anthropology*, 114–177. Madison: University of Wisconsin Press.

———. 1992b. Paradigmatic Traditions in the History of Anthropology. In *The Ethnographer's Magic and Other Essays in the History of Anthropology*, 342–361. Madison: University of Wisconsin Press.

———, ed. 1996. *Volksgeist as Method and Ethic: Essays on Boasian Ethnography and the German Anthropological Tradition*. Madison: University of Wisconsin Press.

———. 2001a. Delimiting Anthropology: Historical Reflections on a Boundless Discipline. In *Delimiting Anthropology*, 303–329. Madison: University of Wisconsin Press.

———. 2001b. *Delimiting Anthropology*. Madison: University of Wisconsin Press.

———. 2001c. Basic Assumptions of Boasian Anthropology. In *Delimiting Anthropology*, 24–48. Madison: University of Wisconsin Press.

Stole, Inger L. 2001. Advertising. In *Culture Works: The Political Economy of Culture*, edited by Richard Maxwell, 83–106. Minneapolis: University of Minnesota Press.

Stoler, Ann Laura. 1995. *Race and the Education of Desire: Foucault's History of Sexuality and the Colonial Order of Things*. Durham, N.C.: Duke University Press.

———. 2001. Tense and Tender Ties: The Politics of Comparison in North American History and (Post) Colonial Studies. *Journal of American History* 88 (December): 829–865.

———. 2002. *Carnal Knowledge and Imperial Power: Race and the Intimate in Colonial Rule*. Berkeley: University of California Press.

Stoler, Ann Laura, and Fred Cooper. 1997. Between Metropole and Colony: Rethinking a Research Agenda. In *Tensions of Empire*, edited by Frederick Cooper and Ann Laura Stoler, 1–56. Berkeley: University of California Press.

Stoler, Ann Laura, and Karen Strassler. 2000. Castings for the Colonial: Memory Work in "New Order" Java. *Comparative Studies in Society and History* 42, 1: 4–48.

Stone, Lawrence. 1965. *The Crisis of the Aristocracy, 1559–1641*. Oxford: Clarendon.

Storing, Herbert J., ed. 1962. *Essays on the Scientific Study of Politics*. New York: Holt, Rinehart and Winston.

Stouffer, Samuel A., et al. 1949. *The American Soldier*. 2 vols. Princeton: Princeton University Press.

Strassmann, Diana. 1994. Feminist Thought and Economics; Or, What do the Visigoths Know? *American Economic Review, Papers and Proceedings* 84, 2: 153–158.

Strauss, Leo. 1962. An Epilogue. In *Essays on the Scientific Study of Politics*, edited by Herbert J. Storing, 306–327. New York: Holt, Rinehart and Winston.

Straw, Jack. 1998. Building Social Cohesion, Order, and Inclusion in a Market Economy.

Paper presented to the Nexus Conference on Mapping Out the Third Way. Available: www .netnexus.org.

Sugden, Robert. 2000. Credible Worlds: The Status of Theoretical Models in Economics. *Journal of Economic Methodology* 7, 1: 1–31.

Sulloway, Frank J. 1979. *Freud: Biologist of the Mind.* New York: Basic Books.

Swedberg, Richard, ed. 1990. *Sociology and Economics: Redefining their Boundaries: Conversations with Economists and Sociologists.* Princeton: Princeton University Press.

Tarrow, S. 1996. Making Social Science Work Across Space and Time: A Critical Reflection on Robert Putnam's *Making Democracy Work. American Political Science Review* 90, 2: 389–397.

Taylor, Charles. [1979] 1987. Interpretation and the Sciences of Man. In *Interpretive Social Science: A Second Look,* edited by Paul Rabinow and William M. Sullivan, 33–81. Berkeley: University of California Press.

——. 1985a. The Person. In *The Category of the Person: Anthropology, Philosophy, History,* edited by Michael Carrithers, Steven Collins, and Steven Lukes, 257–281. Cambridge: Cambridge University Press.

——. 1985b. Neutrality in Political Science. In *Philosophy and the Human Sciences,* 58–90. Cambridge: Cambridge University Press.

——. 1985c. Self-Interpreting Animals. In *Human Agency and Language: Philosophical Papers 1,* 45–76. Cambridge: Cambridge University Press.

——. 1990. Modes of Civil Society. *Public Culture* 3: 95–118.

Taylor, M., and S. Leonard. 2002. *Embedded Enterprise and Social Capital: International Perspectives.* Aldershot: Ashgate.

Tedlock, Dennis, and Bruce Mannheim, eds. 1995. *The Dialogic Emergence of Culture.* Urbana: University of Illinois Press.

Thernstrom, Stephan. 1964. *Poverty and Progress: Social Mobility in a Nineteenth Century City.* Cambridge: Harvard University Press.

Thompson, Edward P. 1963. *The Making of the English Working Class.* London: Gollancz.

——. 1966. *The Making of the English Working Class.* New York: Vintage.

——. 1978. The Poverty of Theory. In *The Poverty of Theory and Other Essays,* 1–210. New York: Monthly Review Press.

Thomson, William L. 1999. The Young Person's Guide to Writing Economic Theory. *Journal of Economic Literature* 37: 157–183.

Tierny, Patrick. 2000. *Darkness in El Dorado: How Scientists and Journalists Devastated the Amazon.* New York: Norton.

Tilly, Charles. 1964. *The Vendée.* Cambridge: Harvard University Press.

Tilly, Louise A., and Joan W. Scott. 1978. *Women, Work, and Family.* New York: Holt, Rinehart and Winston.

Tinbergen, Jan. 1937. *An Econometric Approach to Business Cycle Problems.* Paris: Hermann.

Titunik, I. R. 1973. The Formal Method and the Sociological Method (M. M. Bakhtin, P. N. Medvedev, V. N. Voloshinov) in Russian Theory and Study of Literature. In *Marxism and the Philosophy of Language,* edited by V. N. Voloshinov, 175–200. Cambridge: Cambridge University Press.

Tobey, Ronald. 1971. *The American Ideology of National Science, 1919–30.* Pittsburgh, Pa.: University of Pittsburgh Press.

Toews, John. 1991. Historicizing Psychoanalysis: Freud in His Time and for Our Time. *Journal of Modern History* 63 (September): 504–545.

Tolman, C. W. 1992. *Positivism in Psychology.* Berlin: Springer Verlag.

Tooze, Adam. 1998. Imagining National Economies: National and International Economic Statistics, 1900–1950. In *Imagining Nations*, edited by Geoffrey Cubitt, 212–228. Manchester, U.K.: Manchester University Press.

Torrance, G. W. 1986. Measurement of Health State Utilities for Economic Appraisal. *Journal of Health Economics* 5: 1–30.

Traugott, Mark. 1985. *Armies of the Poor: Determinants of Working-Class Participation in the Parisian Insurrection of June 1848.* Princeton: Princeton University Press.

Tribe, Keith. 1978. *Land, Labour and Economic Discourse.* London: Routledge and Kegan Paul.

Trigg, Roger. 2001. *Understanding Social Science: A Philosophical Introduction to the Social Sciences.* Malden, Mass.: Blackwell.

Tripp, Dean C. 1973. Modernization Theory and the Comparative Study of Societies: A Critical Perspective. *Comparative Studies in Society and History* 15 (March): 199–226.

Trouillot, Michel-Rolph. 1991. Anthropology and the Savage Slot: The Poetics and Politics of Otherness. In *Recapturing Anthropology: Working in the Present*, edited by Richard Fox, 18–44. Santa Fe, N.M.: School of American Research Press.

Tsing, Anna Lowenhaupt. 1993. *In the Realm of the Diamond Queen: Marginality in an Out-of-the-Way Place.* Princeton: Princeton University Press.

Tsuchiya, A. 2000. QALYs and Ageism. *Health Economics* 9: 57–68.

Turkle, Sherry. 1992. *Psychoanalytic Politics.* London: Free Association.

Turner, Jonathan H. 1993. *Classical Sociological Theory: A Positivist's Perspective.* Chicago: Nelson-Hall.

Turner, Stephen Park, and Jonathan H. Turner. 1990. *The Impossible Science: An Institutional Analysis of American Sociology.* Newbury Park, Calif.: Sage.

Turner, Victor. 1967. *The Forest of Symbols: Aspects of Ndembu Ritual.* Ithaca, N.Y.: Cornell University Press.

Tversky, A., and D. Griffin. 2000. Endowment and Contrast Judgments. In *Choices, Values, and Frames*, edited by D. Kahnemann and A. Tversky, 702–725. New York: Russell Sage.

Uebel, Thomas. 2000a. Some Scientism, Some Historicism, Some Critics: Hayek's and Popper's Critiques Revisited. In *The Proper Ambition of Science*, edited by M. Stone and J. Wolff, 151–173. London: Routledge.

———. 2000b. Logical Empiricism and the Sociology of Knowledge: The Case of Neurath and Frank. *Philosophy of Science Proceedings* 67: S139–S150.

———. Forthcoming. Towards a Critical Political Philosophy of Science. *Studies in the History and Philosophy of Science.*

Ulmen, G. L. 2003. Translator's Introduction. In Carl Schmitt, *The Nomos of the Earth in the International Law of the* Jus Publicum Europaeum, 9–35. New York: Telos Press.

Ulrich, Preub. 1995. *Constitutional Revolution: The Link Between Constitutionalism and Progress.* Translated by Deborah Lucas Schneider. Atlantic Highlands, N.J.: Humanities Press.

Urban, Greg. 2001. *Metaculture: How Culture Moves through the World.* Minneapolis: University of Minnesota Press.

Useem, Michael. 1976. State Production of Social Knowledge: Patterns of Government Financing of Academic Social Research. *American Sociological Review* 41 (August): 613–629.

Van Dyke, Vernon. 1960. *Political Science: A Philosophical Analysis.* Stanford: Stanford University Press.

Vaughan, Diane. 1987. *Uncoupling: Turning Points in Intimate Relationship*. New York: Vintage.

Veblen, Thorstein. [1899] 1965. *The Theory of the Leisure Class, 1899*. New York: A. M. Kelley.

———. 1919. *The Place of Science in Modern Civilization*. New York: Huebsch.

Veeser, H. Aram, ed. 1989. *The New Historicism*. New York: Routledge.

Venuti, Lawrence. 1995. *The Translator's Invisibility: A History of Translation*. London: Routledge.

Vidich, Arthur. 1985. *American Sociology: Worldly Rejections of Religion and Their Directions*. New Haven: Yale University Press.

Voloshinov, V. N. [1930] 1973a. *Marxism and the Philosophy of Language*. Cambridge: Cambridge University Press.

———. [1930] 1973b. *Marxism and the Philosophy of Language*. Translated by Ladislav Matejka and I. R. Titunik. New York: Seminar Press.

Von Neumann, John, and Oskar Morgenstern. [1944] 1964. *Theory of Games and Economic Behavior*. New York: Wiley.

Wacquant, Loïc. 2000. *Corps et âme: Carnets ethnographiques d'un apprenti boxeur*. Marseilles: Comeau and Nadeau.

Waite, L. J., and M. Gallagher. 2000. *The Case for Marriage*. New York: Doubleday.

Walby, Sylvia. 2001. Against Epistemological Chasms: The Science Question in Feminism Revisited. *Signs: Journal of Women in Culture and Society* 26, 2: 485–510.

Walder, A. G. 2002. Markets and Income Inequality in Rural China. *American Sociological Review* 67: 231–253.

Walras, Léon. [1874] 1954. *Elements of Pure Economics, Or, The Theory of Social Wealth*. Translated by William Jaffé. Homewood, Ill.: Richard D. Irwin. Originally published as *Eléménts d'économie politique pur, ou, théorie de la richesse sociale*.

Wallerstein, Immanuel. 1991. *Unthinking Social Science*. New York: Polity Press.

———. 1999. *The End of the World as We Know It*. Minneapolis: University of Minnesota Press.

Wallerstein, Immanuel, et al. 1996. *Open the Social Sciences: Report of the Gulbenkian Commission on the Restructuring of the Social Sciences*. Stanford: Stanford University Press.

Walters, Ronald. 1980. Signs of the Times: Clifford Geertz and the Historians. *Social Research* 47: 537–553.

Walzer, Michael. 1991. The Idea of Civil Society. *Dissent* 38, 2: 293–304.

Warren, M. 1999. *Democracy and Trust*. Cambridge: Cambridge University Press.

Wax, Murray. 1997. On Negating Positivism: An Anthropological Dialectic. *American Anthropologist* 99 (March): 17–23.

Weaver, Warren. 1945. *Free Science*. Oxford: Society for Freedom in Science.

Webb, John. 1669. *An Historical Essay Endeavouring a Probability That the Language of the Empire of China Is the Primitive Language*. London: Printed for N. Brook.

Weber, Max. 1947. *The Theory of Economic and Social Organization*. Edited by Talcott Parsons. Translated by A. M. Henderson and Talcott Parsons. New York: Oxford University Press.

———. 1949. "Objectivity" in Social Science and Social Policy. In *The Methodology of the Social Sciences*, edited by Edward A. Shils and Henry A. Finch, 50–112. New York: Free Press.

———. 1968. *Economy and Society: An Outline of Interpretive Sociology*. Edited by Guenther Roth and Claus Wittich. Berkeley: University of California Press.

———. 1972. *Wirtschaft und Gesellschaft: Grundriss der Verstehenden Soziologie*. 2 vols. in 1. Tübingen: Mohr.

Weinstein, Milton C., and H. V. Fineberg. 1980. *Clinical Decision Analysis.* Philadelphia: Saunders.

Weintraub, E. Roy. 1985. *General Equilibrium Analysis: Studies in Appraisal.* New York: Cambridge University Press.

———. 1991. *Stabilizing Dynamics: Constructing Economic Knowledge.* Cambridge: Cambridge University Press.

———. 2002. *How Economics Became a Mathematical Science.* Durham, N.C.: Duke University Press.

Wendt, Alexander. 1999. *Social Theory and International Politics.* Cambridge: Cambridge University Press.

Westbrook, Robert. 1991. *John Dewey and American Democracy.* Ithaca, N.Y.: Cornell University Press.

White, Leslie. 1949. *The Science of Culture.* New York: Farrar, Straus.

Whitebook, Joel. 1999. Psychoanalysis and Democracy. *Dissent* 46, 2: 59–66.

Whitehead, Alfred North. 1925. *Science and the Modern World.* New York: Macmillan.

———. 1926. *Science and the Modern World.* Cambridge: Cambridge University Press.

Der Wiener Kreis. [1929] 1973. Wissenschaftliche Weltauffassung: Der Wiener Kreis [The Scientific Conception of the World: The Vienna Circle]. In *Otto Neurath: Empiricism and Sociology,* edited by Marie Neurath and Robert S. Cohen, 299–318. Dordrecht: D. Reidel.

Will, David. 1984. The Progeny of Positivism: The Maudsley School and Anti-Psychiatry. *British Journal of Psychotherapy* 1, 1: 50–67.

Williams, Raymond. 1973. *The Country and the City.* Oxford: Oxford University Press.

———. 1977. *Marxism and Literature.* Oxford: Oxford University Press.

———. 1983. *Keywords.* New York: Oxford University Press.

Willis, Paul. 1977. *Learning to Labor.* New York: Columbia University Press.

Wilson, Edward O. [1998] 1999. *Consilience: The Unity of Knowledge.* New York: Vintage Books.

Wilson, John T. 1983. *Academic Science, Higher Education, and the Federal Government, 1950–1983.* Chicago: University of Chicago Press.

Winch, Peter. 1958. *The Idea of a Social Science and Its Relation to Philosophy.* London: Routledge and Kegan Paul.

Wingrove, Elizabeth. 2000. *Rousseau's Republican Romance.* Princeton: Princeton University Press.

Wittgenstein, Ludwig. 1953. *Philosophical Investigations.* Translated by G. E. M. Anscombe. New York: Macmillan.

Wolf, Eric R. 1980. They Divide and Subdivide and Call It Anthropology. *New York Times,* November 30, Ideas and Trends section, E9.

———. 1982. *Europe and the People without History.* Berkeley: University of California Press.

———. 2001. *Pathways of Power: Building an Anthropology of the Modern World.* Berkeley: University of California Press.

Wolfe, Alan. 1989. *Whose Keeper? Social Science and Moral Obligation.* Berkeley: University of California Press.

Wolin, Sheldon S. 1960. *Politics and Vision: Continuity and Innovation in Western Political Thought.* Boston: Little, Brown.

———. 1968. Political Theory: Trends and Goals. In *International Encyclopedia of the Social Sciences,* vol. 12, 318–331. New York: Macmillan.

——. 1969. Political Theory as a Vocation. *American Political Science Review* 63: 1062–1082.

——. 1992. Interview by Nicholas Xenos, tape recording. In Whitethorn, California, 10–11 July 1992. American Political Science Association Oral History Archive, University of Kentucky Library, Lexington.

——. 1996. Fugitive Democracy. In *Democracy and Difference: Contesting the Boundaries of the Political,* edited by Seyla Benhabib, 31–45. Princeton: Princeton University Press.

Wollheim, Richard. 1971. *Freud.* London: Fontana.

Wong, Stanley. 1978. *The Foundations of Paul Samuelson's Revealed Preference Theory.* Boston: Routledge and Kegan Paul.

Woolcock, M. 1998. Social Capital and Economic Development: Toward a Theoretical Synthesis and Policy Framework. *Theory and Society* 27, 2: 151–208.

World Bank. 2004. What Is Social Capital? Website on Social Capital. Available: http://www.worldbank.org/poverty/scapital/whatsc.htm.

Wylie, Alison. [1992] 2003. Why Standpoint Matters. In *Science and Other Cultures: Issues in Philosophies of Science and Technology,* edited by Robert M. Figueroa and Sandra Harding, 26–48. New York: Routledge. Revised and reprinted in *The Feminist Standpoint Theory Reader: Intellectual and Political Controversies,* edited by Sandra Harding (New York: Routledge, 2003).

Ye Bingnan. 1993. *It Is Said That in Zhejiang: A Selection of Literary and Historical Documents from Zhejiang.* Vol. 54. Editorial Board of the Zhejiang Provincial Political Consultative Conference, literary and historical materials. Zhejiang: Zhejiang People's Publishing House.

Yonay, Yuval. 1998. *The Struggle over the Soul of Economics.* Princeton: Princeton University Press.

Yonay, Yuval P., and Daniel Breslau. 2004. Economic Theory and Reality: A Sociological Perspective on Induction and Inference in a Deductive Science. Unpublished manuscript.

Zald, Mayer N., and John D. McCarthy, eds. 1979. *The Dynamics of Social Movements: Resource Mobilization, Social Control, and Tactics.* Cambridge, Mass.: Winthrop Publishers.

Zaretsky, Eli. 2000. Charisma or Rationalization? Domesticity and Psychoanalysis in the United States in the 1950s. *Critical Inquiry* 26, 2: 328.

——. 2004. *Secrets of the Soul: A Social and Cultural History of Psychoanalysis.* New York: Alfred A. Knopf.

Zelizer, Viviana A. 1997. *The Social Meaning of Money: Pin Money, Paychecks, Poor Relief and Other Currencies.* Princeton: Princeton University Press.

Zilboorg, Gregory. 1939. Sociology and the Psychoanalytic Method. *American Journal of Sociology* 45 (November): 341–355.

Zimmerman, Andrew. 2001. *Anthropology and Humanism in Imperial Germany.* Chicago: University of Chicago Press.

Žižek, Slavoj. 1989. *The Sublime Object of Ideology.* London: Verso.

CONTRIBUTORS

Andrew Abbott is Gustavus F. and Ann M. Swift Distinguished Service Professor at the University of Chicago. Abbott has written several books on professions and disciplines and has done extensive work on temporality. He is currently completing a book on time and social structure.

Daniel Breslau is an Assistant Professor in the Center for Science and Technology Studies and the Department of Sociology at Virginia Tech. His research has dealt with the historical sociology of the social sciences and statistics and with general theoretical concerns in the sociology of science. He is the author of *In Search of the Unequivocal: The Political Economy of Measurement in U.S. Labor Market Policy* (Praeger, 1998). His current research examines the construction of mathematical objects in the international network of game theorists.

Michael Burawoy has spent most of his life thinking about how to translate fieldwork into theory; he is now embarked on trying to understand the reverse translation, from theory back into lived experience. He teaches sociology at the University of California, Berkeley.

Andrew Collier is Professor of Philosophy at the University of Southampton and has written books on critical realism and Marxism, including *Critical Realism: An Introduction to Roy Bhaskar's Philosophy* (Verso, 1994), *Being and Worth* (Routledge, 1999), and *Christianity and Marxism: A Philosophical Contribution to Their Reconciliation* (Routledge, 2001). He is the trustee of the Centre for Critical Realism in London.

Michael Dutton is Reader/Associate Professor of Political Science at the University of Melbourne, Australia. The author of *Policing and Punishment in China: From Patriarchy to "the People"* (Cambridge University Press, 1992) and *Streetlife China* (Cambridge University Press, 1998), he is a coeditor of the journal *Postcolonial Studies.*

Geoff Eley is the Sylvia L. Thrupp Collegiate Professor of Comparative History at the University of Michigan. He has published widely on matters of modern German and European history, nationalism, the relationship between history and theory, questions of interdisciplinarity, and general historiography. He recently published *Forging Democracy: The History of the Left in Europe, 1850–2000* (Oxford University Press, 2002).

Anthony Elliott is Professor of Sociology at the University of Kent at Canterbury. His recent books include *Social Theory and Psychoanalysis in Transition* (Free Association Books, 1999), *Concepts of the Self* (Polity Press, 2001), *Psychoanalytic Theory: An Introduction* (Duke University Press, 2002), and *New Directions in Social Theory* (Roman and Littlefield, 2003).

Stephen Engelmann studied political theory at Johns Hopkins University and is currently an Assistant Professor at the University of Illinois at Chicago. He is the author of *Origins of Economic Rationality: Imagining Interest in Political Thought* (Duke University Press, 2003), a treatment of economic rationality as political rationality from Lipsius through Bentham. His current research is on liberal government and British and U.S. critiques of social engineering.

Sandra Harding is a philosopher who teaches in the Graduate School of Education and Information Studies at the University of California at Los Angeles. She is the author of *The Science Question in Feminism* (Cornell University Press, 1986), *Whose Science? Whose Knowledge? Thinking from Women's Lives* (Cornell University Press, 1991), and *Is Science Multicultural? Postcolonialisms, Feminisms, and Epistemologies* (Indiana University Press, 1998), and is the coeditor of *Signs: Journal of Women in Culture and Society*.

Emily Hauptmann is Associate Professor of Political Science at Western Michigan University and the author of *Putting Choice before Democracy: A Critique of Rational Choice Theory* (State University of New York Press, 1996).

Webb Keane is an Associate Professor in the Department of Anthropology, University of Michigan (Ann Arbor). He has written extensively on language ideologies and practices, material culture, exchange and value, and religion. He is currently engaged in two projects based on research in Indonesia: a study of colonial missionaries, conversion, and the idea of modernity; and a historical semiotics of the national language and public culture.

Tony Lawson is Reader in Economics at the Faculty of Economics and Politics at the University of Cambridge. He sits on numerous editoral boards, including the *Cambridge Journal of Economics* and *Feminist Economics*, and is organiser of the Cambridge Workshop on Realism and Economics. The paper in the current volume draws on his research on realist social theory. The most sytematic presentations of his work are found in *Economics and Reality* (Routledge, 1997) and *Reorienting Economics* (Routledge, 2003).

Sophia Mihic is Assistant Professor of Political Science at Northeastern Illinois University in Chicago. A graduate of the University of Florida, she received her MA and PhD degrees from Johns Hopkins University and has been a fellow at the Illinois Program for Research in the Humanities in Urbana and at the Walt Whitman Center for the Culture and Politics of Democracy at Rutgers, The State University of New Jersey. She writes on the philosophy of inquiry in political science and the structural grounds of identity politics, and is completing a book titled *What Does the Debate over Physician-Assisted Suicide Teach Us? An Essay on Politics and Political Theory in a Society of Jobholders.*

Timothy Mitchell is Professor of Politics at New York University. His books include *Colonising Egypt* (Cambridge University Press, 1988), *Questions of Modernity* (University of Minnesota Press, 2000), and *Rule of Experts: Egypt, Techno-Politics, Modernity* (University of California Press, 2002).

Philip Mirowski is Professor of Economics at the University of Notre Dame. His is the author of *More Heat Than Light: Economics as Social Physics* (Cambridge University Press, 1989) and *Machine Dreams: Economics Becomes a Cyborg Science* (Cambridge

University Press, 2002) and coeditor with Esther-Mirjam Sent of *Science Bought and Sold: The New Economics of Science* (University of Chicago Press, 2001).

William H. Sewell Jr. is the Max Palevsky Professor of Political Science and History at the University of Chicago and the author of *Work and Revolution in France: The Language of Labor from the Old Regime to 1848* (Cambridge University Press, 1980) and *A Rhetoric of Bourgeois Revolution: The Abbé Sieyes and What Is the Third Estate?* (Duke University Press, 1994). He is currently working on a book on history and social theory.

Margaret R. Somers is Associate Professor of Sociology and History, University of Michigan, Ann Arbor, and specializes in comparative historical sociology and historical institutionalism, economic sociology, historical epistemology, and the sociology of ideas. She served as Chair (2001–2002) of the Section in Comparative Historical Sociology of the American Sociological Association. Somers's research focuses on comparative citizenship formation and rights, the historical epistemologies of neoliberalism and the market, rational choice theory, and social science studies. Her recent publications include " 'We're No Angels': Realism, Rational Choice, and Relationality" in *American Journal of Sociology* (1998) and "Romancing the Market, Reviling the State: Historicizing Liberalism, Privatization, and the Competing Claims to Civil Society" in *Citizenship, Markets, and the State* (Oxford University Press, 2001).

George Steinmetz is Professor of Sociology and German Studies at the University of Michigan and is the author of *Regulating the Social: The Welfare State and Local Politics in Imperial Germany* (Princeton University Press, 1993) and *Precoloniality: Ethnography and the German Colonial State in Qingdao, Samoa, and Southwest Africa* (Duke University Press, forthcoming) and editor of *State/Culture: State Formation after the Cultural Turn* (Cornell University Press, 1999). He is currently making a documentary film called *Living among Ruins: Detroit (USA) and Komsomolsk on Amur (Russia)* with Michael Chanan and Thomas Lahusen.

Elisabeth Rose Wingrove is Associate Professor of Political Science at the University of Michigan. She is the author of *Rousseau's Republican Romance* (Princeton University Press, 2000). Her current research combines contemporary social theory, literary theory, intellectual history, and canonical political theory in an exploration of eighteenth-century epistolary culture. She has also written on educational crises in advanced democracies and the uses and abuses of civil society as a political concept.

CITATION INDEX

George Steinmetz is Professor of Sociology and German Studies at the University of Michigan.

Library of Congress Cataloging-in-Publication Data
The politics of method in the human sciences : positivism and its epistemological others /
edited by George Steinmetz.
p. cm. — (Politics, history, and culture)
Includes bibliographical references and index.
ISBN 0-8223-3506-9 (cloth : alk. paper) — ISBN 0-8223-3518-2 (pbk. : alk. paper)
1. Social sciences—Methodology. 2. Positivism. I. Steinmetz, George, 1957– II. Series.
H61.P5875 2005
300′.1—dc22   2004022945